Support for asylum-seekers

a guide to legal and welfare rights

Sue Willman is a solicitor at Hammersmith and Fulham Community Law centre specialising in housing and community care law. She has developed an expertise in welfare law as it affects asylum-seekers, through her litigation, writing, training and policy development work.

Stephen Knafler is a barrister at 2 Garden Court, who formerly practised as a solicitor and transferred to the bar in 1993. He specialises in housing, community care and support for asylum-seekers and has acted in many of the leading cases in these areas. He is the general editor of *Community Care Law Reports*, author of *Remedies for Disrepair and other Building Defects* and co-author of *Repairs: Tenants' Rights (3rd edn)*.

Stephen Pierce is a partner at Pierce Glynn solicitors, specialists in housing, community care and social security law. He has written and lectured in these areas and is an editoral board member of the *Community Care Law Reports*.

The Legal Action Group is a national, independent charity which campaigns for equal access to justice for all members of society. Legal Action Group:

- provides support to the practice of lawyers and advisers
- inspires developments in that practice
- campaigns for improvements in the law and the administration of justice
- stimulates debate on how services should be delivered.

Support for asylum-seekers

a guide to legal and welfare rights

Sue Willman, Stephen Knafler and
Stephen Pierce

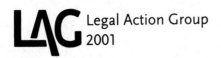
Legal Action Group
2001

This edition published in Great Britain 2001
by LAG Education and Service Trust Ltd
242 Pentonville Road
London
N1 9UN

British Library Cataloguing in Publication Data
A CIP catalogue record for this book is available from the British Library.

ISBN 1 903307 02 3

Typeset by RefineCatch Limited, Bungay, Suffolk
Printed in Great Britain by Bell & Bain Limited, Glasgow

Foreword

by Helen Bamber OBE, Director of the Medical Foundation for the
Care of Victims of Torture

In October 1997, the Medical Foundation for the Care of Victims of
Torture published a report entitled *Past Misery, Present Muddle*. It was
a council-by-council survey of the support being provided to asylum-
seekers under the National Assistance Act and the Children Act, one
year after the Asylum and Immigration Act 1996 had removed the
entitlement of in-country applicants to welfare benefits. Past misery,
present muddle. It is a title we could have used almost every year to
introduce our comments on the support provided to those survivors
of torture seeking asylum who are our clients. It remains as valid in
2001 as in any year before. Rereading the report today, I find many of
the comments we made are just as applicable as they were in 1997:

> Although the then Government claimed that genuine asylum-
> seekers would not suffer as a result of these measures, that was not
> the experience of over 100 Medical Foundation clients initially left
> destitute when their benefits were withdrawn. The removal of the
> means to provide the basics of life made it impossible to do any
> useful rehabilitation work with the clients affected. While we tried to
> protect our core work with torture victims, a particularly susceptible
> group of asylum-seekers, we had to use great effort and ingenuity to
> meet their essential needs.
>   The Medical Foundation still finds its work disrupted by the
> inadequacy and confusion surrounding provision . . . We still
> supplement what our clients are getting . . . with foodstuffs provided
> to us by the Red Cross and other agencies. Without this, our clients
> would be unable to benefit much from the medical and other
> therapeutic help we can offer. Often our first intervention with
> clients has to be to ensure that they are getting the basic subsistence to
> which they are entitled but which may be hard for them to get. Only
> then can we turn to the essential rehabilitation work of helping them
> to come to terms with their experience of torture.

The misery continues. The muddle has increased. The provisions
surrounding support for asylum-seekers have become increasingly
complex. Clients, organisations such as the Medical Foundation,
legal and other advisers, struggle to discern to what a client is

entitled, and how this entitlement can be claimed. Faced with the complex provisions of the Immigration and Asylum Act 1999, the mass of regulations, and all the different forms of guidance, circular and instructions, it can be difficult to know where to start.

We hope that this book will provide a guide through the muddle. Those to whom we already refer clients for help with support problems will welcome a reference work of this type. Perhaps even more importantly, by providing a guide, it may encourage others to tackle this seemingly impenetrable area of the law and to get involved in tackling the misery that our clients are experiencing.

Clients arriving in the UK have many preoccupations: the question of whether they will be given sanctuary, the difficulties of pursuing the asylum claim, together with their experiences of torture, violence, atrocity and exile. Their ability to claim their rights for themselves is limited not only by the complexity of the system, but by their poverty. They are provided with support for 'essential living needs'. But, as this book explains, 'essential living needs' are deemed not to include payment for travel or telephone calls. Many asylum-seekers are housed in areas where there is no one to whom they can turn, no one who speaks their language. There is no one to tell them whom can they trust, and they are too often frightened to go outside because of the hostility they face. Advisers who have not previously worked with asylum-seekers and refugees are daunted by the complexity of the provisions they will have to master in order to assist.

This book not only helps advisers to understand the law, but also points them toward how to change it. It is for advisers to use it to challenge both muddle and misery.

Acknowledgements

The authors are particularly grateful to Jerry Clore (Clore & Co solicitors), Deborah Gellner and Polly Glynn (Pierce Glynn solicitors), Hammersmith and Fulham Community Law Centre, Alison Harvey (Medical Foundation), Angela Jackman and Pip Salvador-Jones (Hackney Community Law Centre) and staff at LAG for their support and assistance.

We would also like to thank the following for information, ideas or comments: Kate Bell, Eileen Bye, Saimo Chahal (Bindman & Partners solicitors), Simon Cox (Doughty Street Chambers), Alison East (Fulham CAB), Nadine Finch (Two Garden Court Chambers), Neil Froom, Melanie Gonga (Hodge, Jones & Allen solicitors), Housing and Immigration Group, Immigration Law Practitioners' Association, Sue Lukes, Kate Markus, Pierre Makhlouf, NASS, Rebecca Owens, Bharti Patel and Caroline Welch (Refugee Council), Sheona York.

We have endeavoured to state the law as at 1 April 2001.

Sue Willman
Stephen Knafler
Stephen Pierce
June 2001

Contents

Table of cases

Table of statutes

Table of statutory instruments

Table of European legislation

European Convention on the Protection of Human
    Rights and Fundamental Freedoms 1951 *continued*

Table of international legislation

Decisions

Commission Decisions *continued*

Council Decisions

Social Security Commissioner's Decisions

Abbreviations

AIA 1996	Asylum and Immigration Act 1996
AIAA 1993	Asylum and Immigration Appeals Act 1993
Appeals Rules	Asylum Support (Appeals) Procedure Rules 2000 SI No 541
AS Regs	Asylum Support Regulations 2000 SI No 704
CA 1989	Children Act 1989
CESC	Council of Europe Social Charter (European Social Charter)
CSDPA 1970	Chronically Sick and Disabled Persons Act 1970
ECSMA	European Convention on Social and Medical Assistance
EEA Regs	Immigration (European Economic Area) Regulations 2000 SI No 2326
HA 1996	Housing Act 1996
HB Regs	Housing Benefit (General) Regulations 1987 SI No 1971
HRA 1998	Human Rights Act 1998
HSPHA 1968	Health Services and Public Health Act 1968
Human Rights Convention	European Convention for the Protection of Human Rights and Fundamental Freedoms
IA 1971, 1988	Immigration Act 1971, 1988
IAA 1969, 1999	Immigration and Asylum Act 1969, 1999
Interim Regs	Asylum Support (Interim Provisions) Regulations 1999 SI No 3056
IS Regs	Income Support General Regulations 1987 SI No 1967
LASSA 1970	Local Authority Social Services Act 1970
MHA 1983	Mental Health Act 1983
NAA 1948	National Assistance Act 1948
NHSA 1977	National Health Service Act 1977
NHSCCA 990	National Health Service and Community Care Act 1990

Refugee Convention	1951 United Nations Convention relating to the Status of Refugees and 1967 Protocol
SSCSDA Regs	Social Security and Child Support (Decisions and Appeals) Regulations 1999 SI No 991
SSIA Regs	Social Security (Immigration and Asylum) Consequential Amendments Regulations 2000 SI No 636
VOLO	Variation of Leave Order 1976 SI No 1572
ASU	Asylum Screening Unit
CLS	Community Legal Service
CTB	council tax benefit
DfEE	Department of Education and Employment
DMG	Decision-Makers' Guidance
DSS	Department for Social Security
ECO	entry clearance officer
EEA	European Economic Area
EHO	environmental health officer
ELR	exceptional leave to remain
FEFC	Further Education Funding Council
HB	housing benefit
HR	habitual residence
IAT	Immigration Appeal Tribunal
ICD	Integrated Casework Directorate
IND	Immigration and Nationality Directorate
IS	income support
JCWI	Joint Council for the Welfare of Immigrants
JSA	jobseeker's allowance
LGA	Local Government Association
LSC	Legal Services Commission
NASS	National Asylum Support Service
NINO	National Insurance number
PAQ	political asylum questionnaire
PFA	person from abroad
PSIC	person subject to immigration control
SAL	standard acknowledgement letter
SEF	statement of evidence form
UCP	urgent cases payment
UN	United Nations
UNHCR	United Nations High Commission for Refugees

Asylum and immigration law

For complete chapter contents, see overleaf

Introduction

1.1   Immigration law is the starting point for most decisions about an asylum-seeker's legal or welfare rights. This chapter aims to provide non-immigration specialists with a background in asylum and immigration law and practice to inform their advice about welfare law issues.[1]

1.2   The chapter begins with an outline of the legal framework and an explanation of common immigration law terms and concepts. It is then divided into three parts: the asylum process, decisions/remedies, and rights/duties during the process. The first part explains the meaning of 'asylum-seeker' and the different stages in an asylum claim, both at the port of entry and 'in-country'. In the second part, favourable and unfavourable decisions are considered, as are the 'date of determination' and the appeals process. Finally, the rights of the asylum-seeker pending a decision, and problems such as access to immigration advice and documentation are discussed.

1.3   Immigration documents referred to in this chapter are reproduced in the Appendices. Reference materials relied on by immigration practitioners include Butterworths' *Immigration Law Service*, a comprehensive looseleaf volume containing the legislative and policy materials, and *Macdonald's Immigration Law and Practice*. The Joint Council for the Welfare of Immigrants (JCWI) publishes accessible handbooks on immigration and asylum law.

The administration of asylum and immigration decisions

1.4   The Home Secretary is responsible for immigration policy and asylum decision-making through the Home Office's Immigration and Nationality Directorate (IND). The Immigration Directorate has formed an Integrated Casework Directorate (ICD) to improve co-ordination of decision-making. The IND is based at Croydon but has regional offices where decisions are also made.

1.5   The new National Asylum Support Service (NASS) is also part of the IND with offices in Croydon.[2]

---

1   The provision of immigration advice is an offence unless a person is registered, authorised or exempt under IAA 1999 Part V, see para 1.121.
2   See Appendix H for addresses.

Leave to enter and leave to remain

1.6 It is the Home Secretary, through the IND, who has the power under Immigration Act (IA) 1971 s4(1) to grant or refuse *leave to remain* in the UK. Immigration officers have the power to grant *leave to enter* the UK (IA 1971 s4(1)). The Immigration and Asylum Act (IAA) 1999 introduced the power for entry clearance officers (ECOs) based outside the UK to grant *leave to enter* the UK.[3]

1.7 The immigration rules[4] explain the relationship between the powers of the immigration service and the Home Office in asylum applications. Only the Home Secretary can decide asylum applications. An asylum application made to an immigration officer at the port should be referred to the IND for a decision.[5]

The immigration service

1.8 The immigration service employs immigration officers, who are appointed by the Home Secretary, at 'ports of entry' to the UK. These include Waterloo International railway station, airports such as Heathrow and Gatwick, and sea-ports such as Dover. The administrative provisions governing control of entry to the UK are found in IA 1971 Sch 2, which provides for immigration officers to detain and/or to give directions for removal to illegal entrants and people refused leave to enter. The powers of immigration officers were extended by IAA 1999 ss1 and 2.[6] If asylum-seekers claim asylum at the port, an immigration officer can either detain them or grant 'temporary admission'. The immigration officer must refer applicants to the IND for a decision on the asylum claim. In these 'port cases' if the IND decides to recognise an asylum-seeker as a refugee, or to grant exceptional leave to remain, it will advise the immigration service at the port of entry. An immigration officer will then formally grant leave to enter. If asylum is refused or an appeal dismissed, the immigration officer must reconsider the original application for leave to enter. If that is refused, the immigration officer may start removal proceedings.

---

3 See IA 1971 s3A introduced by IAA 1999 ss1 and 2, and the Immigration (Leave to Enter and Remain) Order 2000 SI No 1161. The statement of changes in immigration rules laid 28 July 2000 allows immigration officers to vary leave.
4 *Hansard*, HC 395 paras 328–333. See para 1.9 below.
5 *Hansard*, HC 395 para 328 introduced by AIAA 1993 s6.
6 See para 1.6 above.

The legal framework

1.9   The Immigration Act 1971 forms the framework of domestic immigration law. Section 3(2) gives the Home Secretary power to make 'rules' about when 'leave to enter or remain' in the UK is needed and when it will be granted by laying a 'statement of changes in immigration rules' before parliament. The current immigration rules are HC 395. They are amended by statements of changes, eg, Cmnd 4851 which came into force on 2 October 2000, amending the rules to take account of the Human Rights Act (HRA) 1998. The immigration rules are not a statutory instrument and are amended to accommodate legislative changes and political developments. In addition to the rules there are a number of extra-statutory 'concessions' which are matters of policy outside the immigration rules, eg, the 'long residence' concession provides for leave to enter or remain to be granted to those who have lived in the UK for 14 years continuously. The government had announced its intention to review existing concessions with a view to incorporating them into the rules. Only some of the concessions were included in the October 2000 changes.[7]

1.10   An asylum-seeker applies to be recognised as a refugee within the meaning of the 1951 United Nations Convention and 1967 Protocol relating to the Status of Refugees. An asylum-seeker (or other 'person subject to immigration control') may also claim that to return him or her to his/her country of origin would be a breach of article 3 or other articles of the European Convention for the Protection of Human Rights and Fundamental Freedoms ('Human Rights Convention'[8]). The Human Rights Convention is now incorporated into UK law by the HRA 1998. IAA 1999 s167 refers to the UN Convention as 'the Refugee Convention' and the European Convention as 'the Human Rights Convention' and so the same terms are used in this book.

1.11   In reaching a decision on an asylum claim, the IND should have regard to other international human rights instruments to which the UK is a party, as a matter of international law.[9] These include, in particular, the UN Convention against Torture and other Cruel,

---

7   Eg, the concession granting leave to enter or remain to unmarried partners of two years' standing is now part of the rules after the Statement of Changes in Immigration Rules, 2 October 2000 amended HC 395, para 295.
8   See Appendix A.
9   These instruments are not currently incorporated into domestic law or referred to in the immigration rules or IND instructions.

Inhuman or Degrading Treatment or Punishment 1984 and the International Covenant on Civil and Political Rights 1966.

1.12 The domestic law governing an asylum claim is derived from the Asylum and Immigration Appeals Act (AIAA) 1993, the Asylum and Immigration Act (AIA) 1996 and the IAA 1999. These statutes, referred to here as 'the Asylum Acts', are supplemented by the immigration rules, concessions, and internal IND policy. Most of this material is published on the Home Office's website.[10] The website publishes an IND 'country assessment' of each of the main asylum-producing countries. This should be treated as a relevant consideration when the Home Secretary decides an asylum claim.

1.13 The IAA 1999 amended the previous Asylum Acts and the IA 1971. The changes which are most relevant to those advising asylum-seekers about welfare provision include:

- the overhaul of asylum/immigration appeal rights (s10 and Part IV). Section 10 abolishes the rights of many overstayers to appeal against deportation (with some limited exceptions). Part IV governs appeals, including a new 'one-stop' appeal at which all arguments against removal and HRA points must be made. The procedure for asylum appeals and notices are contained in regulations.[11] They are relevant to cases where asylum support has been withdrawn after a decision to refuse asylum;
- the regulation of immigration advice so that it is an offence to give immigration advice without authorisation (Part V);
- the new support scheme for asylum-seekers (Part VI).

Immigration law concepts

'Subject to immigration control'

1.14 The IA 1971 distinguishes between people who have the 'right of abode' in the UK and those whose right to live, work and settle here is subject to regulation and control under the Act. A person who is subject to immigration control needs permission to enter the UK and

---

10 www.homeoffice.gov.uk/ind/hpg.htm.
11 Immigration and Asylum Appeals (Procedure) Rules 2000 SI No 2333, Immigration and Asylum Appeals (One-Stop Procedure) Regulations 2000 SI No 2244 and Immigration and Asylum Appeals (Notices) Regulations 2000 SI No 2246.

remain here. These permissions are known as 'leave to enter' and 'leave to remain'. The meaning of 'subject to immigration control' in the context of the IA 1971 is different from the definition of 'person subject to immigration control'(PSIC) in Part VI of the IAA 1999. Section 115(9) of the 1999 Act introduced a definition of PSIC for welfare purposes, excluding PSICs from social security benefits and other forms of assistance.

'Person from abroad'

1.15   The term 'person from abroad' (PFA) was previously used in social security law to refer to certain persons subject to immigration control as well as persons who were not subject to immigration control but who were not 'habitually resident' in the UK, such as British citizens who had recently arrived in the UK after living abroad. The IAA 1999 and Social Security (Immigration and Asylum) Consequential Amendments (SSIA) Regs[12] have amended various social security regulations to replace PFA with the new s115(9) definition[13] of 'person subject to immigration control'. The term PFA now applies only to those who have failed the habitual residence test.

1.16   British citizens under the British Nationality Act 1981, Commonwealth citizens with the right of abode, and citizens of the Republic of Ireland are not subject to immigration control under the IA 1971.

1.17   A citizen of a country within the European Economic Area (EEA) is not a PSIC for the purposes of welfare provision according to the s115(9) definition, and so is not excluded from social security benefits.

1.18   Immigration control of the citizens of the EEA[14] is derived from European law. The Treaty on European Union 1992 (the Maastricht Treaty) provides freedom of movement to an EEA national if s/he is a 'worker', self-employed, providing or receiving services. The

---

12   SI 2000 No 636. See Appendix A.
13   See para 2.28.
14   The EEA consists of the states which are contracting parties to the Economic Area Agreement, signed at Oporto on 2 May 1992. They are the countries of the European Union: Austria, Belgium, Denmark, Finland, France, Germany, Greece, Italy, Luxembourg, the Netherlands, the Republic of Ireland, Portugal, Spain, Sweden, and the UK, together with Iceland, Liechtenstein and Norway.

Immigration (EEA) Regulations 2000[15] (the EEA Regs) interpret the European law position, ie, that EEA nationals and their family members are entitled to remain in the UK provided they are here to exercise their EU Treaty rights. Certain EEA nationals should be regarded as having the right to remain in the UK without any restriction on the period for which they may remain.[16] Extended family members may fall within the regulations' definition of 'family member'. The EEA provisions are relevant to some asylum-seeker households. An asylum-seeker may have the right to live in the UK, and access to benefits and housing, if s/he is the family member of an EEA national, eg, if the asylum-seeker is married to a French citizen who is working in the UK.[17]

1.19   Everyone not mentioned in the above categories, is 'subject to immigration control', and so needs leave to enter or remain in the UK under the IA 1971 and immigration rules. The category includes other specified types of British citizen (eg, British Overseas citizens), Commonwealth citizens without the right of abode, and citizens of other non-EEA countries (who are known as 'aliens').

'Leave to enter or remain' and 'public funds'

1.20   The length of leave to enter or remain in the UK may be 'limited' or 'indefinite' (IA 1971 s3(1)(b)). Limited leave and indefinite leave are defined by IA 1971 s33. Where limited leave is granted, it may be subject to conditions:[18]

(i)   a condition restricting his employment or occupation in the United Kingdom;

(ii)   a condition requiring him to maintain and accommodate himself, and any dependants of his, without recourse to public funds; and

(iii)   a condition requiring him to register with the police.[19]

1.21   A breach of a condition may lead to an asylum-seeker being prosecuted or detained.

---

15 SI No 2326.
16 EEA Regs, reg 8.
17 See EEA Regs and para 2.28.
18 The Home Secretary has power to add to these conditions (IA 1971, inserted by IAA 1999 ss1 and 2).
19 IA 1971 ss3 and 4 and Immigration Rules, para 8.

Variation of leave

1.22   A person who has 'limited leave' or 'exceptional leave' can apply to the IND to vary it, before it expires. So a person with exceptional leave which is due to expire could apply for another period of exceptional leave or indefinite leave, as appropriate. The original leave then continues until 28 days after a decision has been made. Any entitlement to benefits would continue on the same basis. If leave is refused and an appeal is then entered, the leave will continue until the determination of the appeal.[19a] Local authorities and the Benefits Agency should accept (as evidence of immigration status) the original leave, combined with evidence that an application to vary has been made before the expiry of the original leave to enter or remain. The authority for this was previously the Immigration (Variation of Leave) Order 1976 (VOLO)[20] and is now IAA 1999 s3 amending IA 1971 s3B.[21]

Sponsorship and recourse to public funds

1.23   Leave to enter the UK may be granted subject to a condition or requirement that the person coming here will be able to maintain and accommodate him/herself 'without recourse to public funds'. In the case of elderly dependent relatives coming to live with relatives in the UK, for example, there is a requirement that a 'sponsor' will maintain and accommodate them.[22]

1.24   A sponsor of a person seeking leave to enter or remain in the UK may be asked 'to give an undertaking in writing to be responsible for that person's maintenance and accommodation for the period of any leave granted . . .'.[23] If such an undertaking has been signed (currently on form RON 112 or SET(F)), the dependant falls within the IAA 1999 s115 definition of PSIC, who is not entitled to benefits.[24]

1.25   Recourse to public funds means 'additional public funds' so the rule does not prevent the sponsor from claiming benefits for him/

19a IAA 1999 Sch 4 para 17.
20   SI No 1572.
21   See also the Immigration (Variation of Leave) (Amendment) Order 2000 SI No 2445.
22   HC 395 para 317(iv).
23   Ibid, para 35.
24   But see further para 2.34 (death of sponsor).

herself, provided that s/he is not claiming additional funds for the person s/he is sponsoring.[25]

1.26   'Public funds' are defined by para 6 of the Immigration Rules, as amended. They include attendance allowance, child benefit, council tax benefit, disability living allowance, housing benefit, income-based jobseeker's allowance, income support, invalid care allowance, severe disablement allowance, and housing as homeless or public housing (provided under Housing Act 1996 Parts VI and VII). Disabled person's and working families' tax credits, and social fund payments are likely to be added to the list.[26]

Common travel area

1.27   A person who is resident in or a citizen of the UK, the Channel Islands and the Isle of Man or the Republic of Ireland may travel freely within this area, which is defined by IA 1971 as the 'common travel area'. Anyone who is subject to immigration control, but passes through Ireland on the way to the UK, is still subject to immigration control at the UK border.

'Pre-entry' immigration control and 'visa nationals'

1.28   'Immigration control' is classified into 'pre-entry', 'on-entry' and 'after entry' control.

1.29   The IA 1971 categorises countries as 'visa national' or 'non-visa national' countries. The immigration rules list the countries that come within these categories.[27] A citizen of a visa national country needs to get a visa (which may be referred to as 'entry clearance') from a British ECO outside the UK, in order to enter the UK lawfully. A grant of 'entry clearance' may now include leave to enter.[28] The IAA 1999 empowers ECOs to grant leave to enter the UK, but since there is no 'asylum visa' it seems likely that the majority of asylum-seekers will continue to apply for asylum on or after arrival in the UK.

25 HC 395 para 6A.
26 An IND Policy Directorate letter of 5 December 2000 confirmed that social fund payments, disabled person's and working families' tax credits were not yet specified as public funds in the Immigration Rules but pointed out that overseas nationals were excluded from these benefits by IAA 1999 s115 except where a reciprocal agreement applied.
27 Appendix 1 of the Immigration Rules, which is periodically updated.
28 See IA 1971 s3A introduced by IAA 1999 s1 and Immigration (Leave to Enter and Remain) Order 2000 SI No 1161.

1.30   A citizen of a non-visa national country does not need to obtain a visa before entering the UK if the visit is for certain temporary purposes, such as for a holiday or to study. If s/he wishes to settle in the UK, eg, on grounds of marriage, a visa must be obtained. A visitor or student from a non-visa national country can apply for a visa before entry and may wish to do so if s/he thinks that there is a chance the immigration service will refuse entry. There is a right of appeal against refusal from within the UK if a visa has been obtained pre-entry. Anyone entering the UK without a visa, who is refused entry, has to leave the UK to exercise a right of appeal. There is no right of appeal for visitors from visa national countries who are refused entry except for family visitors, who can only exercise the right of appeal from outside the UK and must pay a fee to do so.[29]

Asylum-seekers, illegal entrants and overstayers

1.31   The Home Office treats some asylum-seekers as 'illegal entrants'. IA 1971 s33(1) defines 'illegal entrant' as:

> a person –
> (a) unlawfully entering or seeking to enter [the UK] in breach of a deportation order or the immigration laws; or
> (b) entering or seeking to enter by means which include deception by another person.

1.32   An asylum-seeker cannot usually obtain entry clearance from his/her country of origin to enter the UK as a refugee or asylum-seeker. An asylum-seeker in another country would be expected to claim asylum there unless it was not a 'safe third country'.

1.33   The term 'illegal entrant' is most commonly used to refer to people who come to the UK clandestinely, eg, hidden in a lorry. It may also be used to refer to asylum-seekers who have used forged documents or who misrepresented the purpose of their visit, eg, someone who entered the UK with a student visa and then claimed asylum. The Refugee Convention provides that receiving countries should not 'impose penalties' on refugees who enter illegally.[30]

1.34   Illegal entry, assisting illegal entry and 'harbouring an illegal entrant' are all offences under IA 1971 ss24 and 25.[31] The Immigration

---

29 IAA 1999 s60, Immigration Appeals (Family Visitor) (No 2) Regulations 2000 SI No 2446, as amended by Immigration Appeals (Family Visitor) (Amendment) Regulations 2001 SI No 52.
30 Article 31(1). See further para 1.46.
31 As amended by IAA 1999 ss28 and 29.

(Carriers Liability) Act 1987 introduced fines for airlines which transport people to the UK without a valid visa. IAA 1999 Part II extended this to lorries and ships.

1.35   The ability of an asylum-seeker to enter the UK legally has increasingly been restricted. The immigration rules' list of 'visa national' countries whose citizens need a visa to enter the UK includes most of the countries which are seen as generating asylum-seekers. Home Office airport liaison officers are stationed at strategic overseas airports to 'advise' airlines about prospective illegal entrants who are attempting to be passengers.[32] Document checks by airlines and other carriers mean that it is difficult for asylum-seekers to travel to the UK unless they enter clandestinely using an agent and/or obtain forged documents. As a result many obtain entry by using forged documents or otherwise enter illegally (eg, in container lorries).

1.36   An illegal entrant can be expelled from the UK after removal directions have been issued by an immigration officer (IA 1971 Sch 2). Directions should not be acted on if there is an outstanding claim under the Human Rights Act 1998 or an asylum claim[33] (or if those claims have been refused but there is an appeal or judicial review application to challenge the refusal).

1.37   An 'overstayer' is a person who originally had limited leave to enter or remain in the UK, but whose leave has expired. Before the IAA 1999 became law, the normal procedure for expelling an overstayer from the UK began when the Home Office served a notice of intention to make a deportation order under IA 1971 Sch 3, which allowed a right of appeal. Since 2 October 2000, overstayers have no right of appeal before removal except on asylum, human rights or discrimination grounds.[34] An illegal entrant or overstayer who is challenging removal must be served with a 'one-stop' notice to allow him/her to raise any grounds for remaining in the UK, including Human Rights Convention points, before removal.

---

32 See White Paper *Fairer, Faster and Firmer – A Modern Approach to Immigration and Asylum* July 1998, Cm 4018 Chapter 11.
33 IAA 1999 s10.
34 Ibid.

The asylum application – law and procedure

Meaning of 'asylum-seeker' and 'refugee'

1.38   A 'refugee' is 'a person who has a well-founded fear of persecution for reasons of race, religion, nationality, membership of a particular social group or political opinion and who is outside the country of his nationality or former habitual residence and is unable or, owing to such fear, is unwilling to avail himself of the protection of that country or return to it'.[35]

1.39   The UK is a signatory to the 1951 Refugee Convention, and to its 1967 Protocol. The approach to considering whether an asylum-seeker should be recognised as a refugee stems from the principle of non-return or 'non-refoulement'.[36] A 'refugee' cannot be lawfully returned to his/her country of origin except in very limited circumstances. The government is allowed to return the refugee to the country of origin where s/he has committed a serious crime and is a danger to the community, or presents a serious security risk.[37] Domestic law now incorporates Human Rights Convention obligations, prohibiting the removal or return of a refugee even in these circumstances, if s/he has a valid Human Rights Convention claim, usually under article 3.[38]

1.40   The immigration rules provide that an 'asylum applicant' is a person (of any age) who claims that it would be contrary to the UK's obligations under the Convention and Protocol for him/her to be removed from or required to leave the UK.[39] In very simple terms, an asylum-seeker needs to show that s/he is:

– in the UK;
– a refugee as defined by the Convention and Protocol; and
– 'refusing his application would result in his being required to go . . . in breach of the Convention and Protocol, to a country in which his life or freedom would be threatened on account of his

---

35   Refugee Convention art 1A(2).
36   Ibid, art 33(1).
37   Ibid, art 33(2).
38   See paras 1.10 and 1.48. Removal may be prohibited if it interferes with other Human Rights Convention rights such as the art 8 right to family life, but unlike art 3 claims, art 8 allows a balancing exercise. This book focuses on art 3 claims because they provide access to Part VI support, unlike a claim under the other Convention articles.
39   HC 395 para 328.

race, religion, nationality, political opinion or membership of a particular social group'.[40]

1.41   The definition of 'asylum-seeker' for the purposes of entitlement to asylum support is wider than the immigration law definition. Under IAA 1999 Part VI, for example, if the asylum-seeker has a dependent child, the applicant continues to be defined as 'an asylum-seeker' for support purposes for as long as they both remain in the UK and the child is under the age of 18 (IAA 1999 s94(5)).

1.42   The Refugee Convention is interpreted by case-law and by ICD instructions. Case-law makes reference to the UNHCR's *International Handbook on Procedures and Criteria for Determining Refugee Status 1988*. The Immigration Rules contain the separate procedure for claiming asylum, the factors which the ICD must consider in decision-making, and the appeals process. The IND should consider the facts of each application and grant asylum, ie, recognise the applicant as a refugee, if the Home Secretary is satisfied that the Convention criteria are met. If the Home Secretary considers the criteria are not met, but there are compelling reasons why an asylum-seeker should not be forced to return to the country of origin at that time, exceptional leave to remain (ELR) may be granted outside the Immigration Rules.

1.43   It is useful for those advising about support to be aware of the decision-making criteria because the asylum-seeker's actions in relation to a support claim may have an impact on the asylum claim. The Immigration Rules outline the factors which may lead to a refusal of an asylum claim:

> A failure without reasonable explanation to make a prompt and full disclosure of material factors, either orally or in writing, or otherwise to assist the Secretary of State to the full in establishing the facts of the case may lead to the refusal of an asylum application.[41]

1.44   IAA 1999 s20 provides that information held by contractors providing housing or support under the asylum/interim support scheme may be supplied to the Home Secretary 'for use for immigration purposes'. Supported asylum-seekers should be aware that theoretically this allows information provided to NASS to be used by the Home Office in relation to their asylum claim.

---

40 Ibid, para 334.
41 Ibid, para 340.

1.45   An asylum-seeker's credibility is central to the success or failure of his/her asylum claim. The actions which the Immigration Rules state may damage credibility include:

(a) delay in making a prompt asylum application unless the claim is based on events occurring after arrival in the UK,

(b) making false oral or written representations,

(c) destroying or disposing of documents relevant to the claim,

(d) undertaking activities which are inconsistent with previous beliefs and behaviour and which are intended to strengthen the asylum claim,

(e) making concurrent applications for asylum in or outside the UK.[42]

1.46   The above must be read in conjunction with article 31(1) of the Refugee Convention:

> The contracting states shall not impose penalties, on account of their illegal entry or presence, on refugees, who coming directly from a territory where their life or freedom was threatened in the sense of Article 1, enter or are present in a territory without authorisation, provided they present themselves without delay to the authorities and show good cause for their illegal entry or presence.

In *R v Uxbridge Magistrates' Court ex p Adimi*[43] the High Court decided that to convict an asylum-seeker for using false documents would be in breach of article 31.

1.47   In the context of social security law, *Adimi* was considered by a commissioner who was evaluating the meaning of 'on arrival'. He decided that to exclude from income support an asylum-seeker who applied for asylum shortly after entry in the UK could constitute 'a penalty' within the meaning of article 31(1).[44] The 'penalty' argument is relevant in other asylum support contexts.

Article 3 of the Human Rights Convention

1.48   An asylum-seeker who would suffer torture or inhuman or degrading treatment or punishment (within the meaning of article 3) if returned to his/her country of origin, should not be expelled from the

---

42   Ibid, para 341.
43   [2000] 3 WLR 434.
44   Commissioner's Decision CIS 4439/98.

UK.[45] This applies even if s/he does not meet the Refugee Convention criteria, as in cases where the applicant is likely to be tortured for a 'non-Convention' reason. An article 3 claim can be made concurrently with an ordinary asylum claim under the Refugee Convention, or at a later stage, eg, where asylum has been refused.[46]

1.49   In *D v UK*[47] the European Court of Human Rights held that it would be a breach of article 3 to return a person with AIDS (who was an illegal entrant with a conviction for drugs offences) to St Kitts because vital medical treatment was not available there and his removal would expose him to a real risk of dying in circumstances which would amount to inhuman treatment. If an article 3 claim is pending, whether at first decision stage or at appeal stage, the applicant for asylum support or interim support must be treated as an 'asylum-seeker' entitled to support for the purposes of IAA 1999 s94.

1.50   The IAA 1999 requires an asylum-seeker to raise any article 3 or other Human Rights Convention points at the earliest opportunity. This is usually when grounds of appeal are entered, no later than within ten working days of the 'one-stop notice' being served. There is provision for grounds to be served later than this if the applicant has 'reasonable excuse for the omission'.[48] The one-stop notice and appeal procedure is explained below at para 1.102.[49] Article 3 grounds may arise after the determination of the appeal, eg, if the appellant's health deteriorates dramatically or if conditions in the country of origin change suddenly. If an applicant is prevented from raising new article 3 grounds after the determination, this may violate the Human Rights Convention.

Unaccompanied minors

1.51   There is a special regime for asylum-seekers under 18 who come to the UK without a parent or guardian. The immigration rules state that a child who appears to be under 18 should be treated as a minor, unless there is documentary evidence to suggest s/he is 18 or over. Where there is a doubt, it is the (difficult) role of the Home Secretary to establish the age of a young adult. The immigration rules state that an 'unaccompanied minor' should not be interviewed about his/her

---

45 See para 8.14 for meaning of 'torture or inhuman or degrading treatment'.
46 But see para 1.123.
47 (1997) 24 EHRR 423.
48 IAA 1999 s76(3).
49 Ibid, ss74 and 75.

asylum claim unless s/he is of sufficient understanding and there is no practical alternative.[50] A responsible adult must be present at any interview including the screening unit interview. Minors should be referred to a social services department and should not be detained. The Home Office should refer asylum-seekers who claim to be minors to the Refugee Council's Children's Panel of Advisers for assistance. The Home Office 'will not seek to remove an unaccompanied minor unless it is possible to put in place acceptable reception and care arrangements in their country of origin'.

1.52   Unaccompanied minors are entitled to support and housing under the Children Act 1989, usually under s20. They are not eligible for IAA 1999 Part VI asylum support because they do not fall within the s94(1) definition of an asylum-seeker until they reach the age of 18. Although it is common practice to transfer unaccompanied minors to Part VI asylum support as soon as they are 18, it is arguable that local authorities retain a duty to them under the Children Act 1989 s24 duty to 'advise, assist and befriend' children who have been 'looked after' by social services.[51]

The procedure for claiming asylum

1.53   A person who claims that it would be contrary to the Refugee Convention for him/her to be removed from the UK is an 'asylum applicant'.[52] An asylum claim can be made either 'in-country' or at the port of entry but all applications are decided by the Home Office.

1.54   An asylum-seeker may present him/herself to the immigration officer at the port of entry while passing through immigration control at, eg, Heathrow airport. If the word 'refugee' or 'asylum' is not used, the asylum-seeker should at least have indicated a fear of returning home. This may be relevant at a later stage to demonstrate that asylum was claimed 'on arrival' for benefit purposes (in pre-3 April 2000 asylum claims). There are cases where an asylum applicant who is treated as 'in-country' by the Home Office for immigration purposes is an 'on-arrival' applicant entitled to benefit for social security law purposes.[53]

---

50 HC 395 para 352.
51 See further para 7.122.
52 HC 395 para 327.
53 If an asylum claim was made before 3 April 2000 and is not yet determined. See para 2.51.

1.55   Alternatively, an asylum claim can be made 'in-country' by an application in person to the Home Office (initially by post if it is too far to travel to London).

When is an asylum claim recorded?

1.56   Eligibility for support under the Asylum Support Regulations 2000[54] ('AS Regs') or Asylum Support (Interim Provisions) Regulations 1999[55] ('Interim Regs') starts when a claim for asylum under the Refugee Convention or a claim under article 3 has been recorded but not determined.[56] A claim is recorded when it is notified to the Home Office in person, or in writing if the applicant lives outside London.[57] A solicitor's letter notifying the IND of a claim under article 3 of the Human Rights Convention that it would be contrary to the UK's obligations under that Convention for the claimant to be removed from the UK should be sufficient evidence that the claimant is an 'asylum-seeker' for support purposes.[58]

1.57   Whether an asylum claim is on or after arrival, the following is a general guide to the stages in the procedure:[59]

–   fingerprinting;
–   screening interview (and issue of standard acknowledgement letter SAL1 or SAL2);
–   consideration of removal to 'a safe third country';
–   decision by immigration officer to grant temporary admission or detain (issue of form IS96);
–   issue of asylum questionnaire (SEF) and/or interview to establish details of claim;
–   referral of destitute asylum applicants to reception assistants for asylum support under IAA 1999 Part VI;
–   substantive interview of asylum-seeker;
–   Home Office decision to grant or refuse asylum;
–   removal directions;
–   appeal against refusal of asylum claim.

54 SI No 704.
55 SI No 3056.
56 IAA 1999 s94(1).
57 ICD open letter, Chris Hudson, 15 September 2000.
58 See chapter 3. As yet there is no court decision on the point.
59 The procedure has been subject to frequent policy changes. The usual procedure at the time of writing is set out. Advisers may encounter pilot schemes, special procedures and other variations.

Fingerprinting[60]

1.58   Fingerprints may be taken from an asylum-seeker and any dependants if an asylum claim is made.[61] Fingerprints may not be taken from
a child under 16 unless a parent, guardian or responsible adult is
present.[62] The police and immigration officers have a power to arrest
without a warrant anyone who claims asylum and refuses to supply
fingerprints. The fingerprints may be held on a computerised central
database and circulated to other EEA member states.[63] The fingerprints should usually be destroyed after ten years or within a month
of the grant of indefinite leave to remain but some could be held
permanently.[64] A refusal of fingerprinting could prejudice the asylum
claim. Fingerprinting takes place at ports or at the Asylum Screening
Unit (ASU) interview.

Screening interview

1.59   An asylum-seeker who applies for asylum on arrival at a port will
usually be briefly interviewed by an immigration officer to establish
his/her identity. This is known as a 'screening interview'. A standard acknowledgement letter is issued (SAL1). Where identity is not
established the SAL will state 'claims to be' in front of the asylum-
seeker's name. Questions will usually be asked to establish the
method of entry and details of the journey to the UK, to ascertain
whether there are grounds for removal of the asylum-seeker to a safe
third country. In-country applicants will be required to attend an
interview at an ASU (currently at Croydon, Leeds and Liverpool) with
any dependant who entered the UK with them, so as to establish
identity and method of entry. S/he should take any original documents showing identity, photographs and confirmation of an address
in the UK. The ASU records asylum claims, and issues SALs. If the
Home Office does not have time to carry out a screening interview at
the first visit (or if the application is made by post) the applicant will
receive an appointment letter to attend the ASU. If the asylum-seeker
does not give details of a legal representative who is acting for him/
her, the substantive interview may take place at this stage, subject to

60   IAA 1999 ss141–144. The Immigration (PACE Codes of Practice No 2 and
      Amendment) Direction 2000 governs the fingerprinting procedures.
61   IAA 1999 s141(1).
62   Ibid, s141(3).
63   See para 1.60 below.
64   IAA 1999 s143.

resources. The Legal Services Commission has agreed to finance legal representatives' attendance at interviews involving unaccompanied minors.

Removal to a 'safe third country'[65]

1.60 If an asylum applicant has travelled through a 'safe third country' s/he may be returned to that country without consideration of the asylum claim and will have very limited rights of appeal against the removal directions.[66] For port applicants, the decision is usually made at the port in the initial interview with the applicant. The decision is made by the Home Office in 'in-country' cases. The asylum-seeker can only apply for judicial review if the country is not one which is *deemed to be* safe, and if it can be shown that the country *is not* 'safe', eg, that it might return the applicant to his/her country of origin, or if s/he has close relatives living in the UK. The Dublin Convention 1990,[67] to which the UK is a signatory, is based on the principle that asylum applicants should have their claim considered in the first EU country that they reach. An EEA member state is automatically treated as a safe third country.[68]

1.61 An asylum-seeker may appeal on limited grounds in relation to a third country removal under IAA 1999 s11 or s12. If that appeal is unsuccessful, there may be a judicial review or appeal under IAA 1999 s65 on Human Rights Convention grounds.

Temporary admission and detention

A person liable to detention or detained under paragraph 16 above may, under written authority of an immigration officer, be temporarily admitted to the United Kingdom without being detained or be released from detention; but this shall not prejudice a later exercise of the power to detain him.[69]

1.62 When an asylum claim is made at the port, the immigration officer will consider whether to grant 'temporary admission', or whether to

---

65 Ibid, s11.
66 Ibid, s12(1).
67 The Convention determining the state responsible for examining applications for asylum lodged in one of the member states of the European Communities, signed in Dublin on 15 June 1990 (ratified by the UK and all member states).
68 IAA 1999 s12(1)(a).
69 IA 1971 Sch 2 para 21(1).

detain the applicant under IA 1971 Sch 2 para 16 pending a decision on the asylum claim. Detention should be a last resort, to be considered where there are doubts about the asylum applicant's identity or a fear that s/he may abscond. Guidelines[70] state that as a general principle asylum-seekers should not be detained and there is a presumption against detention. Detention appears to be used mostly in relation to single adult males and the male head of household, with some nationalities more commonly detained than others. Families can be detained at Oakington Detention Centre (see para 1.68 below). At the time of writing it was usual practice for immigration officers to grant asylum applicants temporary admission, documented by form IS96.

1.63   Temporary admission may include restrictions preventing the asylum-seeker from working, as well as requirements about where s/he must live and to report to a specified police station.[71] A breach of these conditions can lead to detention (and withdrawal of support). In order to be granted temporary admission, the asylum-seeker must usually provide an address in the UK.

1.64   The IAA 1999 provides for regulations (which must be laid before and approved by parliament) prohibiting asylum-seekers from living in certain parts of the UK as a condition of their temporary admission. Such regulations could also require asylum-seekers to live, eg, at accommodation provided under IAA 1999 s4 and prohibit them from leaving that accommodation at certain times or at all.

> (2B) The regulations[72] may, among other things, provide for the inclusion of provisions –
> (a) prohibiting residence in one or more particular areas;
> (b) requiring the person concerned to reside in accommodation provided under section 4 of the Immigration and Asylum Act 1999 and prohibiting him from being absent from that accommodation except in accordance with the restrictions imposed on him . . . [73]

1.65   When a person subject to immigration control applies for asylum 'in-country', there is a risk that the conditions of any current leave to enter or remain in the UK may be varied or the leave may be curtailed. Again, immigration officers usually grant temporary admission, but they can also detain under the IA 1971.

70 UNHCR's *Guidelines on applicable Criteria and Standards relating to the Detention of Asylum-seekers*, 1999.
71 IA 1971 Sch 2 para 21(2A).
72 No regulations have yet been laid before parliament.
73 IA 1971 Sch 2 para 21(2B) as amended by IAA 1999 Sch 14 para 62.

1.66   Asylum-seekers and their dependants may be held in detention centres such as Campsfield, or in ordinary prisons such as Holloway. Although the Home Office describes the regime in detention centres as less restrictive than a prison, detention centres have a different regime for monitoring and inspection. The IAA 1999 extended the use of detention of asylum-seekers, while improving controls by introducing routine bail hearings.[74] The bail provisions in Part III of the Act are more limited than bail for ordinary prisoners.

1.67   Temporary admission, which is evidenced by form IS96, is not the same as leave to enter. The Home Office has suggested that it is a form of 'licence' to be in the UK. Whether temporary admission amounts to 'lawful presence' in the UK affects the question of whether nationals of north African countries, Turkey, Poland, Cyprus and countries which have ratified the European Social Charter are eligible for benefits and housing.[75]

Oakington[76]

1.68   Some adults who apply for asylum at the port of entry are detained, with (or without) their families, including young children, at Oakington detention centre, a former military barracks in Cambridgeshire. When the IAA 1999 was debated, it was initially understood that Oakington was to be established under s4. This empowers the Home Secretary to provide for facilities for asylum-seekers with temporary admission or who are released from detention. The Home Office later stated that detention at Oakington would be under existing powers contained in the IA 1971. In law and practice, Oakington constitutes a detention centre although the Home Office still refers to it as a 'reception centre'.

1.69   Detention at Oakington is initially for a short period of about seven to ten days to enable an interview and an accelerated initial decision. Immigration advice is available at the site from the Immigration Advisory Service and the Refugee Legal Centre before and after the substantive interview. After a period of detention, the possible outcomes are:

– grant of refugee status or ELR;
– refusal of asylum;
– grant of temporary admission or transfer to another detention

74 IAA 1999 s44.
75 See chapter 2.
76 See para 4.47.

centre while the IND further considers the application (or while any appeal is pending).

1.70   If asylum is refused, the applicant may appeal, leave the UK voluntarily, or be removed from the UK. If the asylum-seeker is granted temporary admission pending a first asylum decision or appeal, s/he may apply for NASS support. Voluntary sector reception assistants are on site at Oakington to discuss appropriate support arrangements.

1.71   It is arguable that detention at Oakington is a 'penalty' which breaches article 31(1) of the Refugee Convention (see para 1.46 above) or that it constitutes 'inhuman and degrading treatment' which violates the HRA 1998 under article 3, and/or interferes with the article 8 right to family and private life, in conjunction with the anti-discrimination article 14, particularly where children are involved. There are also arguments that detention at Oakington falls outside the immigration service's existing powers to detain as set out in guidelines (see footnote 70).

Referral of asylum-seekers to reception assistants

1.72   Voluntary sector organisations are being funded by NASS to provide emergency accommodation for new asylum applicants while a claim for asylum support is being considered. The immigration officer at the port should refer an asylum applicant and any dependants who are in need of support to a voluntary sector reception assistant who acts as an agent for NASS and can arrange 'temporary support' under IAA 1999 s98.[77] A similar procedure applies to new in-country applicants who are destitute and homeless. The services of reception assistants are currently available only to newly arrived and newly presenting asylum-seekers. They do not extend to 'disbenefited' cases where the asylum-seeker has lost entitlement to social security benefits or housing as homeless after a negative asylum decision.[78]

1.73   Temporary support includes emergency accommodation pending a decision about eligibility for full asylum support. The reception assistants should assist asylum-seekers to obtain resources by putting them in touch with relatives or relevant services, helping them to complete an application for asylum support where necessary.[79]

77 See Appendix F for list of one-stop services where voluntary sector reception assistants are employed.
78 See further chapter 3.
79 See para 3.93 onwards.

1.74   Where an asylum-seeker has a disability or special need, NASS should also make a referral to social services. There is some dispute as to where the dividing line in providing for disabled asylum-seekers falls. The notes which form a Schedule to the AS Regs suggest that NASS will provide support to meet needs related to a disability. However, the Court of Appeal has held that the local authority is responsible for accommodating an asylum-seeker with community care needs.[80] The Court of Appeal has also confirmed that social services have a duty to carry out a community care assessment and assist in cases where the need for residential accommodation does not arise solely as a result of destitution, or where the applicant has other community care needs.[81]

Asylum questionnaires, interviews and 'non-compliance'

1.75   Usually an asylum-seeker who applies at a port will be called back to the port at a later date for an asylum interview. If no substantive interview is carried out initially, the immigration officer issues a 'statement of evidence form' (SEF) previously known as a 'self-completion questionnaire' or political asylum questionnaire (PAQ), which the applicant has to return within a short period, currently ten working days. In some ports the asylum-seeker may have a substantive interview on arrival or soon after arrival, depending on interpreting facilities. Ten days is a short period for an asylum applicant who has not had a substantive interview to get help to complete the SEF in English and return it with all supporting documents, particularly if s/he has been sent to an area where interpreters and immigration advisers are in short supply. The Home Office has discretion to extend the period.

1.76   An asylum-seeker who applies 'in-country' may be interviewed immediately or may be given or sent a SEF, which again must be completed and returned within a short period, currently ten working days.

1.77   It is Home Office practice to allow applicants to be accompanied at the substantive interview by a representative or friend. The interviewing officer should not refuse this but the representative would not usually be expected to intervene during the interview, except in extreme circumstances. The protocol is for the applicant or observer to wait until the end of the interview to inform the interviewing officer of any concerns and ask for a note to be made, eg, if the interview was not conducted properly or the interpreting was inadequate. The asylum applicant is entitled to a copy of the asylum interview record or

80 *Westminster CC v NASS* (2001) 4 CCLR 143. See para 8.57.
81 *R v Wandsworth LBC ex p O* (2000) 3 CCLR 237, CA. See further para 7.53.

notes. The immigration service sends interview notes or question-
naires completed at the port to the IND which makes the substantive
decision on the claim in the same way as for an 'in-country' applicant.

1.78   The government has stated that after the substantive interview the
asylum applicant has a limited period, currently seven days, to submit any further evidence.[82] In practice, no time is usually allowed if a
completed SEF has been returned.

1.79   In January 2001 the press reported that as many as 40 per cent of
asylum claims were being refused on the grounds of technical 'non-
compliance', ie, alleged failure to submit the SEF within the time
limit. In many of these cases the SEF has been submitted within the
time limit but the Home Office has not linked it to the correct file. In
other cases the applicant has been unable to comply because of other
difficulties such as language barriers. Non-compliance cases are currently the subject of considerable litigation and many such decisions
are overturned on appeal.

Favourable and unfavourable decisions

What is the 'date of determination' of the asylum claim?

1.80   The 'date of determination' is crucial to those advising about welfare
entitlements because the right to receive asylum or interim support
ends after a prescribed period beginning with the date of determination. The date also affects entitlement to social security benefits and
the time limits for an asylum appeal.[83] In simple terms, an asylum-
seeker remains an asylum-seeker, entitled to asylum or interim support under IAA 1999 Part VI until s/he receives a decision refusing a
grant of refugee status *with full reasons for the refusal*, or an appeal
decision. There is a different test of date of determination for asylum-
seekers who lose entitlement to social security benefits after a
negative asylum decision (see chapter 2).

1.81   For the purposes of support provided under Part VI of the IAA
1999, s94(3) states:

> (3) A claim for asylum is determined at the end of such period
> beginning –
>   (a)   on the day on which the Secretary of State notifies the
>   claimant of his decision on the claim, or

82   HC Written Answers cols 263–264, Barbara Roche MP, 16 March 2000.
83   See paras 1.100 and 2.93.

(b) if the claimant has appealed against the Secretary of State's decision, on the day on which the appeal is disposed of, as may be prescribed.

(4) An appeal is disposed of when it is no longer pending for the purposes of the Immigration Acts or the Special Immigration Appeals Commission Act 1997.

1.82   The prescribed period is 14 days beginning with the date of the notice for the purposes of support under both the AS Regs and the Interim Regs. The determination must be in writing and if it is posted either to the asylum-seeker or his/her representative, 'it is to be taken to have been received by the asylum-seeker on the second day after the day on which it was posted'.[84]

1.83   IAA 1999 s58 provides:

(5) For the purposes of the Immigration Acts, an appeal under this Part is to be treated as pending during the period beginning when notice of appeal is given and ending when the appeal is finally determined, withdrawn or abandoned.

(6) An appeal is not to be treated as finally determined while a further appeal may be brought.

The meaning of 'notice'

1.84   In cases where refugee status is not granted, the Home Office sends a letter (currently ICD 1029) which notifies the applicant that s/he does not qualify for asylum within the terms of the Refugee Convention, but which does not give reasons for the decision. Some local authorities have incorrectly treated this letter as a 'notice' that 'a claim for asylum is determined' within the meaning of IAA 1999 s94(3) and have stopped providing support after the pre-decision letter. The letter gives a date on which the application 'is recorded as determined'. The asylum-seeker will later receive a letter which gives reasons for the refusal of refugee status, and which may grant exceptional leave to remain. It is at this stage that an appeal may be entered against the refusal of asylum. The initial letter refusing refugee status is not a notice of the decision on the claim within the meaning of IAA 1999 s94 because it does not include reasons.[85] The Home Office has confirmed that the letter which informs the asylum-seeker 'that his claim for asylum has been recorded as determined and ... that he will

---

84 IAA 1999 s94(9).
85 By letter dated 14 July 2000, Hilary Tarrant, Asylum Group, IND to the Refugee Legal Centre.

receive a further letter from his port of entry relating to his immigration status in the United Kingdom does not mean that [he] is no longer an asylum-seeker for the purposes of Part VI of the Immigration and Asylum Act 1999 . . . The decision referred to in s94(3) is the substantive decision against which there may be a right of appeal . . . '.

1.85   The Immigration and Asylum Appeals (Notices) Regulations 2000[86] provide that the obligation to provide a written notice of a decision only applies where the decision is appealable. The notice is to include a statement of reasons for the decision or action to which it relates.[87] The ICD 1029 letter is therefore not a notice within the meaning of IAA 1999 s94(3) (see para 1.81 above) because it does not include a statement of reasons. The 14-day prescribed period (for support purposes only) starts when the applicant receives the letter containing reasons for the refusal and can enter an appeal.

Grant of asylum or other immigration status

1.86   An asylum-seeker who is granted ELR or refugee status may not receive accurate documents granting refugee or other immigration status until some time after 'the date of determination'. In such cases they may be eligible for community care help from local authorities (see chapter 7). Tactics for ensuring that social security benefits are processed as soon as possible are discussed in chapter 2.

Refugee status

1.87   Where an asylum applicant is recognised as a refugee under the Refugee Convention, s/he will receive a decision letter giving indefinite leave to enter or remain in the UK (ILR). The document is currently in form ICD 0725 (previously known as a GEN 23). The Refugee Convention provides for recognised refugees to have civil rights and duties such as rights to work or receive welfare provision on the same terms as UK nationals, eg, refugees qualify for student grants on the same terms as home students without the need to reside in the UK for a qualifying period.[88]

1.88   It would be incompatible with the grant of refugee status for the refugee to travel with his/her own national passport. S/he can

---

86   SI No 2246.
87   Reg 5.
88   See further para 1.117 below.

apply to the Home Office for a Refugee Convention travel document, which is an entitlement under the Refugee Convention.

1.89   If a refugee is receiving interim support or asylum support, the support will end after a period of 14 days from the date the determination is received (see para 1.80 above). The exception is where the Home Office appeals against an appeal decision, in which case support should continue.

1.90   Refugees can claim backdated social security benefits for the whole period from their claim for asylum until their grant of refugee status.[89] They only have 28 days from the date of the Home Office decision in which to make the claim for backdated income support, as well as housing benefit and council tax benefit if appropriate.[90] It is important to check the documents and advise an asylum-seeker who is granted refugee status to make a claim for backdated benefit within the 28 days, perhaps drafting a letter on his/her behalf.

Exceptional leave to remain

1.91   An asylum-seeker who is not recognised as a refugee under the Refugee Convention criteria may be granted exceptional leave to enter or remain in the UK (ELR) outside the immigration rules. ELR may be granted on compassionate grounds, where it would be difficult or dangerous for the asylum applicant to leave the UK and return to the country of origin and/or where it is impracticable to remove him/her. The IND states that ELR should be granted if removal to the country of origin would violate article 3 of the Human Rights Convention.

> Exceptional leave to enter or remain must be granted to asylum applicants if they fall under one of the following criteria: Where the 1951 UN Convention requirements are not met in the individual case but to return to the country of origin would result in the applicant being subjected to torture or other cruel, inhuman or degrading treatment . . . [91]

1.92   Where there is a grant of ELR following a refusal of refugee status, the asylum-seeker will be sent a letter with a stamp endorsing a period of leave. Port applicants may be given a document, which is stamped, or a letter without a stamp. ELR is currently for four years,

---

89   IAA 1999 s123.
90   See further para 2.96.
91   IND Asylum Directorate instructions on ELR, July 1998.

after which the immigration rules allow an application for ILR to be made. People with ELR whose national passports have expired can apply for a UK travel document (brown in colour), as opposed to a Refugee Convention travel document (blue), which is only granted to refugees.

1.93   People with ELR have leave to enter or remain in the UK so they are not 'persons subject to immigration control' excluded from benefits for the purposes of Part VI of the IAA 1999.[92] However, they are subject to immigration control for ordinary immigration law purposes, eg, ELR might be curtailed if they return to the UK after a visit to their home country. Anyone with ELR is entitled to work or receive social security benefits, housing and community care help on the same basis as a refugee. S/he is entitled to income support and housing benefit backdated only to the date of the grant of ELR, rather than the application for ELR. This is because ELR is granted from the date of the Home Office decision whereas the 'recognition' of refugee status dates back to the original asylum application.

Leave 'in line'

1.94   If a child is born in the UK to parents with limited leave to enter or remain in the UK such as ELR, s/he does not automatically become a British citizen by virtue of being born here. (A separate application for leave to remain in line with the parents' leave can be made if this is to the advantage of the child. Such leave would usually be granted.) The Immigration Rules state that such a child does not need to obtain leave to remain unless s/he is travelling outside the UK and intends to return.[93] It has been suggested that such a child is therefore not a person subject to immigration control within the IAA 1999 s115(9) definition because s/he does not need leave to enter or remain in the UK. Similarly, in a homelessness application under the Housing Act 1996, such a child could be an eligible person who could give the parent priority. Newly-arrived dependants from outside the UK will need leave to enter until they are granted ELR. In either case, a local authority (social services) can be approached for housing and support under Children Act 1989 s17 if there is a child in need and housing or benefits have not been provided, because no such exclusion applies.

---

92   IAA 1999 s115(9)(a).
93   HC 395 paras 304–309.

Cases where the ELR document has expired

1.95 A person who has been granted limited leave to enter or remain in the UK such as a spouse during the first year of marriage, a student, or someone with ELR can apply to the Home Office for such leave to be extended or varied. The application must be made before the leave expires in order to retain a right of appeal under IA 1971. These applicants have leave to stay in the UK (on the same terms as their previous leave) while the application is being considered. For example, if they previously had ELR, they retain it until 28 days after a further decision is made. Such applicants are not PSICs within the meaning of IAA 1999 s115(9)(a). The letter with the original grant of leave and proof that they have applied for a variation in time (eg, solicitor's letter) should be sufficient evidence to demonstrate that they have ELR and that they retain any entitlement to social security benefits and housing as homeless people.

Indefinite leave to remain

1.96 ILR, which is also known as 'settled status' or 'settlement' can be granted in cases where the applicant had some other form of limited leave to enter or remain for a specified period. ILR is also granted to asylum-seekers who are recognised as refugees under the Refugee Convention.

Family reunion

1.97 If a husband or wife, or child under 18, who is outside the UK, wants to join someone who has been recognised as a refugee in the UK, s/he has a right to leave to enter or remain in the UK under the Immigration Rules, on proof of identity and of a relationship pre-dating the asylum claim. Other members of an extended family may be granted leave to enter or remain if the relationship is recognised by the Home Office. This is not required by the Refugee Convention but is contained in the UNHCR Handbook's guidelines. If the marriage post-dates the grant of refugee status, the refugee may also need to consider the ordinary rules for a spouse who wants leave, eg, that s/he can be maintained and accommodated without recourse to public funds. In ELR cases, family reunion is usually granted after four years from the grant of ELR, but can be applied for before this, eg, on Human Rights Convention grounds. The applicant would usually need to satisfy all the requirements of the Immigration Rules other than settlement. In exceptional compassionate circumstances the maintenance and accommodation rules may be waived. The family should be entitled to benefits and other welfare provision on arrival in the UK. In practice, the documentation may mistakenly include a condition prohibiting recourse to public funds. In such cases, it is advisable to refer them back to the port to amend it immediately.

Unfavourable decisions

Refusal of asylum

1.98   If the Home Office considers that the asylum-seeker does not meet the Refugee Convention criteria, a decision that asylum is refused ('the pre-decision letter') will be sent to the applicant and any legal representative, followed by a determination letter with reasons for the decision (see paras 1.80–1.85 above). Alternatively, s/he may be advised of the decision at a Home Office interview. Under IAA 1999 s75 the Home Office will serve a 'one-stop notice' on the applicant requesting him/her to raise any additional grounds such as an application under article 3 of the Human Rights Convention, the Immigration Rules or concessions. The determination of asylum may include a decision in relation to the additional grounds raised.

1.99   The consequences of the refusal of refugee status include:

–   Asylum support or interim support ends within 14 days of the asylum determination being received (after allowing two days for delivery by first class post), unless the supported person appeals or makes an article 3 claim.[95] Families continue to receive support as long as there is a dependent child under 18 in the UK.
–   The asylum-seeker has ten working days from the date of receiving the determination within which to appeal. The appeal must raise any other claims separately, eg, an article 3 claim, or a claim that the appellant falls within one of the concessions, in the course of the appeal.[96]

---

95   IAA 1999 s94.
96   Ibid, s74 and Immigration and Asylum Appeals (One-Stop Procedure) Rules 2000 SI No 2244.

- In-country applicants may have any existing leave to enter or remain in the UK curtailed. If the asylum-seeker enters an appeal, the immigration service will consider whether to detain or grant temporary admission. If temporary admission is granted, a form IS96 is issued. If temporary admission is refused, s/he will be detained under IA 1971.
- Directions for the removal of the applicant from the UK may be issued by the immigration service. The effect of an appeal against a refusal of asylum is that no removal directions may be given and that any existing directions are suspended pending the determination of the appeal.[97]

Remedies

Appeals

1.100   There is a time limit of ten working days (from receiving the determination containing reasons for refusal of refugee status) within which to appeal to the adjudicator. Time runs from the second day following the date of determination. If that appeal is unsuccessful there is a further appeal on a point of law to the Immigration Appeal Tribunal (IAT), with leave. Again, the time limit is ten days.

1.101   The Home Secretary has wide powers to certify an appeal as 'fast-track' under IAA 1999 Sch 4 para 9 if s/he decides that there is no fear of persecution under the Refugee Convention or that such a fear is manifestly unfounded, or if notification of proposed removal directions has been given, or if s/he believes the claim is vexatious or fraudulent. Certified appeals may be heard within five days of the Home Office sending the appeal papers to the adjudicator (but this is rare in practice) and a decision should be given within ten days of the hearing. Assuming that the certificate has been upheld on appeal, there is no right of further appeal to the IAT.

1.102   The law and procedure governing asylum and immigration appeals was overhauled by IAA 1999 Part IV and Sch 4, which established a one-stop appeal at which all arguments relating to removal and human rights must be raised.[98] Under the Immigration and

---

97 Ibid, Sch 4 para 10.
98 Ibid, ss74–77.

Asylum Appeals (One-Stop Procedure) Regulations, a 'one-stop' notice is served in two circumstances:

– Under IAA 1999 s74, where an applicant and his/her dependants have an in-country right of appeal (other than asylum or HRA appeals) they will receive a one-stop notice at the same time as receiving a notice refusing the in-country application. The applicant and dependants have ten working days to serve a statement of additional grounds on the Home Office. This must include all their reasons for seeking to remain in the UK (including any asylum or HRA reasons).

– Under IAA 1999 s75 a one-stop notice is served on the applicant and dependants who have applied for asylum or for leave to enter or to remain in the UK on HRA grounds. Again, they must respond with any additional grounds including HRA grounds within ten working days. The notice will be served by the Home Office before making a decision on the original asylum or HRA claim. Section 75(1) applies to illegal entrants and overstayers.

1.103   The intention is to prevent a series of appeals. If a person who has been refused asylum has failed to raise HRA arguments by this stage, s/he should not be allowed to raise them at a later stage (but see para 1.50). If the adjudicator dismisses the appeal, there is a further appeal to the IAT (unless the claim has been certified as unfounded). There may then be an application for judicial review or, in a limited number of cases, an appeal to the Court of Appeal.

1.104   The effect of an appeal to the adjudicator against a refusal of asylum in in-country cases is that the appellant's leave and conditions of leave are extended (see para 1.22 above). Port applicants are entitled to have temporary admission extended until their appeal is determined. Asylum support and interim support continue pending the appeal determination. An asylum-seeker who enters an appeal may be detained or granted temporary admission pending the appeal.

Removal directions

1.105   The circumstances in which a person who is not a British citizen may be removed from the UK are set out in IAA 1999 s10. A person who is subject to immigration control may be removed from the UK with no right to appeal if s/he entered the UK as an illegal entrant or has breached a condition of limited leave. Before making any such directions, the immigration service should take the HRA and compassionate circumstances into consideration.[99] There is a possible challenge by way of an appeal to the adjudicator against the directions, on the ground that there was no power to give them,[100] which may pre-empt any judicial review. Commentators have suggested there may also be scope for an appeal under IAA 1999 s65.

Unsuccessful asylum appeals

1.106 Where an appeal to the adjudicator is unsuccessful, and leave to appeal, or the substantive appeal, to the IAT has been refused, an asylum-seeker may be able to apply for judicial review or appeal to the Court of Appeal. An asylum-seeker without a dependent child stops being treated as an 'asylum-seeker' for the purposes of receiving asylum or interim support 14 days after 'the day on which the appeal is disposed of'.[101] 'Appeal' includes any appeal to the Court of Appeal. Childless asylum-seekers who remain in the UK to pursue a judicial review or otherwise may be eligible for NASS 'hard cases' support provided under IAA 1999 s4.[102] Those who have a need for care and attention arising for a reason other than their destitution, eg, age or ill-health, may be entitled to community care help.[103] An asylum-seeker with a dependent child is classed as an 'asylum-seeker' entitled to receive asylum or interim support, for as long as the child is under 18 and in the UK.[104]

Complaints

1.107 The main sources of complaint by immigration specialists on behalf of their clients are delay and poor decision-making. The IND Complaints Unit will not consider complaints about these issues, instead it investigates formal complaints about the conduct of IND staff. The Unit liaises with the Complaints Audit Committee, an independent committee appointed by the Home Secretary to monitor IND's complaints procedures. The IND also has 'user panels' and an IND Customer Service Charter. The ICD Briefing and Complaints Section deals with complaints about issues affecting the ICD. The

---

99 HC 395 paras 395A and 395B, as amended.
100 IAA 1999 s66.
101 Ibid, s94(3)(b).
102 See para 3.169.
103 See para 7.121 and *R v Wandsworth LBC ex p O* (2000) 3 CCLR 237, CA.
104 IAA 1999 s94(5).

Immigration Law Practitioners' Association (ILPA)[105] participates in ICD/IND liaison and user group meetings and circulates its correspondence in monthly mailings.

1.108   If there is no response to complaints about delays, the asylum-seeker's MP could be asked to write to the Home Secretary. A further complaint can be made to the Parliamentary Ombudsman via the MP by completing an application form.[106] The Ombudsman upheld a complaint by Bosnian refugees who were prevented from travelling to see a dying mother or attending her funeral by delay in the processing of applications for travel documents and ILR. The IND made an ex gratia payment to cover the family's administrative costs and paid £750 for the distress caused.[107]

1.109   There have been successful judicial reviews of delay in decision-making in certain circumstances where there is substantial delay and real prejudice has resulted. The High Court decided that the Home Office's delay was unlawful in a case where an asylum appeal had been allowed, but for over six months the IND had not issued documents confirming refugee status and indefinite leave to remain.[108]

1.110   The Race Relations Act (RRA) 1976 has been amended by the Race Relations (Amendment) Act 2000 to make racial discrimination by government departments unlawful and impose a positive duty to promote racial equality. There is an exemption for immigration purposes which limits the definition of racial discrimination to cases of discrimination on grounds of race or colour only. The legislation does not make it unlawful for a relevant person to discriminate against another person on grounds of nationality or ethnic or national origins in carrying out immigration and nationality origins. The exemption of the Home Office from liability for race discrimination was controversial and so RRA 1976 s19E provides for the appointment of a person to monitor the operation of the exemption.

1.111   The amended Act does extend IAA 1999 s65 (which currently gives a right of appeal in cases of human rights breaches) to cover racial discrimination. It provides for a right to appeal to the special adjudicator where the Home Office or immigration service has

---

105   See Appendix H.
106   Office of the Parliamentary Commissioner for Administration, Mill Bank Tower, Mill Bank, London SW1P 4QP; tel: 0845 015 4033; email: opca-enqu@ombudsman.org.uk.
107   Parliamentary Ombudsman complaint C1141/00/95.
108   *R v Secretary of State for the Home Department ex p Mersin* CO/4433/99, 25 May 2000, unreported.

racially discriminated in a decision about a person's right to enter or remain in the UK. If racial discrimination is proven, a claim for damages can be made in the county court.

Rights and duties of asylum-seekers pending a decision[109]

Monitoring and offences

1.112   IAA 1999 Part VI introduces a number of new criminal penalties connected to the provision of support. These are discussed in more detail in chapter 4. There is some common ground between the responsibilities of an asylum-seeker in relation to the asylum claim and those which relate to the support claim. It may be an offence not to notify NASS of a change of address.[110] In the same way, a failure to notify the IND of a change of address may jeopardise the asylum claim, eg, it may prevent the applicant from responding to requests for further information and lead to a negative decision.

1.113   The Act also introduces new powers for information sharing and monitoring of asylum-seekers. These are discussed in chapter 4.

Right to work

1.114   A concession outside the Immigration Rules allows an asylum-seeker permission to work if s/he is still awaiting a decision six months after the asylum application.[111] A similar concession was extended to asylum applicants whose appeals are pending.[112] The asylum-seeker can apply in person or by letter to the Home Office in in-country cases, or by letter to the immigration officer at the port in the case of port applicants. Permission to work is usually only granted to the principal asylum-seeker. A dependant will need to show particular circumstances to justify a grant of the right to work, eg, s/he has a useful skill or the main applicant is unable to work. Where the asylum-seeker has a job offer it may be granted during the first six months.

---

109   See chapters 3–5 for rights to IAA 1999 Part VI support.
110   IAA 1999 ss105(1)(c) and 106(1)(c).
111   At the time of writing, the government had announced a review of the right to work provisions.
112   *R v Secretary of State for the Home Department ex p Jammeh* (1998) 10 Admin LR 1 per Owen J; reversed in CA at [1998] INLR 701; [1999] IMM AR 1 but, in practice, asylum-seekers granted permission can retain it pending an appeal.

Permission to work may be endorsed on the SAL1 and SAL2. The difficulties which asylum-seekers face in obtaining National Insurance numbers are discussed in chapter 2.

1.115   AIA 1996 s8 made it a criminal offence to employ anyone who does not have the right to work in the UK. It is a defence for the employer to show that s/he has obtained evidence of the right to work, such as a National Insurance number[113] and was not aware that the employee was working illegally. Although there has been only one prosecution under s8, it was not repealed by the IAA 1999 as the government had proposed (when in opposition). Instead, s22 of the 1999 Act adds s8A to the AIA 1996. Section 8A requires the Home Secretary to issue a statutory 'code of practice' to advise employers how to comply with s8 without discriminating on grounds of race.

1.116   Since s8 was introduced, a number of asylum-seekers and other immigrants have complained that they believe they have been discriminated against when seeking employment. There is no explicit provision to make less favourable treatment on grounds of immigration status unlawful. Under RRA 1976 s4(1) racial discrimination in recruitment, whether in refusing to offer a job or in recruitment procedures, is unlawful.[114] Racial discrimination may be direct discrimination 'on racial grounds'[115] or indirect discrimination, applying a condition or requirement which an employer 'cannot show to be justifiable irrespective of the colour, race, nationality or ethnic or national origins of the person to whom it is applied'.[116] An employer who only applied the s8 requirements to black staff would be directly discriminating. The Court of Appeal has decided that it is not unlawful racial discrimination to ask all non-British or non-EEA citizens to produce evidence of the right to work.[117] So the requirement to produce a National Insurance number, for example, which indirectly discriminates against asylum-seekers, can be justified because of s8 and other statutory requirements. This may be a potential area for HRA challenges.

---

113 Employers may produce any one of the documents listed in the Immigration (Restrictions on Employment) Order 1996 SI No 3225.

114 The Commission for Racial Equality (CRE) provides advice and pursues complaints about race discrimination in the provision of services, see Appendix H.

115 RRA 1976 s1(1)(a).

116 Ibid, s1(1)(b).

117 *Dhatt v McDonalds Hamburgers Ltd* (1991) IRLR 130, CA.

Right to education[118]

1.117 Unaccompanied children claiming asylum and the children of asylum-seekers are entitled to a school place and free education up to the age of 18, provided that their education in the UK starts before the age of 16.[119] Children who arrive in the UK at 16 or over may receive education at the discretion of the local education authority. Social services have duties under the Children Act in relation to unaccompanied minors which would encompass assisting them with obtaining education.[120] Any decision on admissions will be subject to HRA and RRA 1976 considerations.

1.118 An asylum-seeker is usually treated as an overseas student for the purposes of fees for higher and further education (including part-time courses) with grants only available on a discretionary basis. The Further Education Funding Council (FEFC) (now the Learning and Skills Council) issued guidance on 16 March 2000 which said that for the purposes of further education institutions, an asylum-seeker in receipt of support under the AS Regs or Interim Regs would be treated as if s/he was in receipt of income support, ie, as home students exempt from fees. The FEFC treats unaccompanied minors between the ages of 16–18 as home students and they are not liable to be charged by further education institutions.

1.119 Students usually need to be ordinarily resident in the UK for three years, with ELR or ILR, to qualify for a higher education grant. The residence requirement does not apply to those who are recognised as refugees.[121] EEA nationals and their children who have been resident in the EEA for three years other than for the purposes of education are also exempt.

Right to NHS treatment

1.120 Asylum-seekers are entitled to free NHS treatment on the basis that they are 'ordinarily resident' in the UK.[122] Ordinary residence is defined in *Shah v Barnett LBC*[123] as where a person's abode is 'adopted

---

118 See chapter 4 for details of other education benefits.
119 See Education Act 1996 s10 for the general duty and DfEE Code of Practice on School Admissions, Annex B, www.dfee.gov.uk/sacode/index.htm.
120 See chapter 7.
121 Education (Fees and Awards) Regulations 1997 SI No 1972 as amended and Education (Student Support) Regulations 1999 SI No 496.
122 NHS (Charges to Overseas Visitors) Regulations 1989 SI No 306, as amended by NHS (Charges to Overseas Visitors) (Amendment) Regulations 1994 SI No 1535.
123 [1983] 1 All ER 226, HL.

voluntarily and for settled purposes as part of the regular order of one's life for the time being whether for long or short duration'.

Common problems

Legal advice and access to immigration advisers

Advice for those considering an asylum or article 3 claim

1.121   Asylum-seekers are entitled to obtain immigration advice and representation from any source, but there is a shortage of competent advice. Part V of the IAA 1999 was introduced to protect asylum-seekers and other immigrants from unscrupulous advisers. It is an offence for anyone to provide immigration advice in the course of business, whether or not for profit unless s/he is exempted by or registered with the Immigration Services Commissioner,[124] or authorised to do so by a body such as the Law Society or the Bar Council.[125] Organisations advising about asylum support issues should ensure that they do not give advice on immigration issues unless they are registered or have an exemption.

1.122   The Immigration Advisory Service and the Refugee Legal Centre are funded by the Home Office to provide legal advice and representation to asylum-seekers.[126] The Legal Services Commission funds solicitors and voluntary organisations to provide advice and controlled representation in asylum and immigration cases through exclusive contracting arrangements.

1.123   People in the UK who are making a claim for asylum or under article 3 of the Human Rights Convention, should be referred to an immigration specialist. A destitute single adult who is subject to immigration control but is not an asylum-seeker is not entitled to benefits or other welfare provision unless s/he has community care needs.[127] Advisers should be cautious of proposing an asylum or article 3 claim as a solution to homelessness or the lack of any income. Although it may be a route to support for a temporary period, an inappropriate claim may lead to existing leave being terminated, detention or removal from the UK. An asylum claim could

---

124   See Commissioner's website for code of practice and complaints procedure: www.oisc.org.uk.
125   IAA 1999 s84.
126   IA 1971 s23.
127   IAA 1999 Part VI.

damage credibility in relation to any other Home Office application for leave to remain in the UK, eg, through ELR. Alternatives to consider are a National Assistance Act 1948 application following *R v Wandsworth LBC ex p O*[128] and/or a HRA 1998 challenge (see paras 7.124 and 8.78).

Immigration advice pending a decision or appeal

1.124 It is important for non-immigration specialists to be aware of the short deadlines for producing evidence in support of an asylum claim and the risk of a refusal of asylum on technical 'non-compliance' grounds. Without quick access to competent immigration advice, an asylum-seeker may be unable to present an application that demonstrates that refugee status or ELR should be granted. The short appeal deadlines and the certification of appeals further reduce the chance of a fair consideration of the claim. Dispersal and/or difficulty financing travel to advisers may indirectly violate asylum-seekers' human rights by preventing them from effectively exercising their rights under the Refugee Convention or the various articles of the Human Rights Convention.

Contacting the Home Office

1.125 Non-immigration specialists should be cautious about contact with the IND because inappropriate contact may delay the processing of a claim or prejudice an application. It is appropriate for the client's immigration adviser to contact the IND rather than an adviser dealing with support only. The main public contact point is the Public Enquiry Office or Immigration and Nationality Enquiry Bureau (INEB).[129] In the past, it has been notoriously difficult to get a reply within a reasonable time or at all, but improvements have now been made. Local authorities and statutory agencies have dedicated contact numbers.

Documentation and problems with proving identity or age

1.126 IND documents are often misunderstood or rejected by council officers or other officials who are not trained in immigration law. If there is evidence that an asylum claim has been made, a local

128 (2000) 3 CCLR 237.
129 See Appendix H.

authority has a duty to provide emergency support under the Interim Regs reg 4[130] while further inquiries are being made. Although the Secretary of State has a duty to inquire into and establish age under IAA 1999 s94(7), social services may need to consider age to fulfil their duties under the Children Act 1989 s17 or s20. The Home Office can make a 'without prejudice' agreement to treat an asylum-seeker as a minor until it has concluded its inquiries.

1.127   If the applicant has no evidence of identity at all, a letter with a signed photo attached confirming that a solicitor is acting for the person in the photograph may ensure that the local authority makes a decision. Arguably, there is no legal requirement to provide this as a pre-condition of IAA 1999 Part VI support.

1.128   Immigration documents often contain mistakes relating to the applicant's name or date of birth. If these are contained in the final grant of refugee status or ELR, it may take some time for the Home Office to correct them, causing delay before the applicant can get access to benefits. If mistakes are not remedied, the applicant is likely to have difficulty getting a National Insurance number and may face accusations of fraud if the Home Office document is inconsistent with other documents. Therefore, any mistakes spotted before the final decision should be drawn to the Home Office's attention. A judicial review or complaint about IND delay in remedying mistakes could be considered where the applicant is prejudiced.

1.129   Limited evidence of identity, before or after an asylum decision, combined with short residence in the UK inhibits the ability to obtain a driving licence or bank account and interferes with other rights which British nationals have. In the case of driving licences, where the asylum-seeker, refugee or person with ELR does not have the relevant identification documents, write to the Driving Vehicle Licensing Agency (DVLA), to ask the secretary of state to exercise discretion in the stipulation of acceptable documents.[131] In the case of other public authorities, there may be scope for a request to exercise discretion to accept more limited evidence of identity in view of the Human Rights Convention 'anti-discrimination' article 14 combined with other relevant articles, eg, if article 8 rights are being interfered with. Internal complaints procedures could be considered.

---

130 See further para 4.9.
131 Road Traffic Act 1988 s97(1).

Variation of leave

1.130　If a person subject to immigration control with limited leave has applied to vary the original leave to enter or remain in the UK, s/he will not be issued with new documentation. However, s/he will have valid leave to enter/remain in the UK on the same terms as the original leave until the application has been processed (see para 1.22 above). It may save time for the immigration representative to provide a letter explaining this if the local authority or Benefits Agency are in doubt.

'Mixed' families

1.131　Members of the same family may have a mixture of immigration applications and decisions. A husband may be granted ELR or full refugee status but the wife or dependants who have arrived in the UK separately may have an outstanding asylum claim. It is worth checking the immigration documents to work out the status of each family member before advising about their potential support entitlements. One family member may be entitled to claim benefits or asylum support for the whole household. The question of 'mixed families' is discussed in more detail in the support chapters.

1.132　Where an asylum-seeker is granted ELR, the grant will include any dependent children. If those children reach 18 after leave is granted, evidence of identity, relationship and that the parent has been granted ELR should be accepted as evidence that the child also has ELR and is not a person subject to immigration control for the purposes of IAA 1999 s115. The child on reaching 18 does not need a separate document to prove immigration status and is entitled to claim social security and other benefits.

Common Home Office documents

1.133　These include:

- Letter of appointment at the ASU: delays in issuing SALs have meant that some asylum-seekers only have a letter inviting them to an interview about the asylum claim. If Home Office staff or immigration officers do not have time to establish identity at the port, the asylum-seeker will receive an appointment for an ASU or substantive asylum interview at a later date.

- IS96: a form indicating a grant of temporary admission. It will usually give the asylum-seeker's full name and date of birth and the date when temporary admission ends. It is given to those who do not have any other valid leave to enter or remain in the UK such as port applicants and illegal entrants.
- SAL1: this shows that the asylum-seeker has applied for asylum at the port of entry. If s/he has not satisfied the immigration officer as to identity, the form will state 'claims to be' before the name of the applicant. It will have a photograph of the asylum-seeker attached to the front of it and the photographs of any dependants attached to the back. A SAL1 or SAL2 shows that the Home Office has recorded a claim for asylum. It is generally accepted by other bodies as evidence of identity. Prior to 3 April 2000, a SAL 1 was treated as evidence that the asylum-seeker claimed asylum 'on arrival' and was entitled to income support. In practice, an asylum-seeker may have claimed 'on arrival' for benefit purposes but have a SAL2 and vice versa. It is usual for the asylum-seeker to surrender his/her SAL when a favourable or unfavourable decision on the claim has been made.
- SAL2: an asylum-seeker who has applied for asylum in-country should be given this. For asylum-seekers who arrived in the UK on or after 3 April 2000, the distinction between a SAL1 and SAL2 has no significance for the purposes of entitlement to benefits.
- SEF: a self-completion questionnaire for the asylum-seeker to give details of the ground(s) on which s/he is applying for asylum.
- ICD.1029: a refusal of refugee status without reasons.
- ICD.0725: a grant of refugee status.
- ICD.0716: a grant of ELR following a refusal of refugee status.
- BKL 5: this indicates a grant of ILR following ELR.
- ICD.0009: this indicates the grant of ELR outside the Immigration Rules.
- IS83: this indicates removal directions issued under IA 1971 Sch 2.

Benefits

For complete chapter contents, see overleaf

2.1   **Introduction**

2.8   A brief history

No recourse to public funds • Urgent cases payments • Habitual residence test • 'In-country' asylum-seekers are PFAs excluded from benefits • Transitional protection for asylum-seekers receiving benefits on 5 February 1996 • Child benefit entitlement removed • Benefits for asylum-seekers replaced with asylum support

2.16   The legal framework

2.22   **Entitlement to benefit**

2.25   Which benefit?

Contributory benefits • Non-contributory benefits

2.27   Is the claimant in a class which is excluded from entitlement?

Is the claimant a PSIC? • European nationals • People deported to the UK

2.32   Is the claimant a PSIC in a category which is not excluded?

PSICs who are entitled to means-tested benefits • PSICs who are entitled to non-means-tested benefits/social fund payments • Meaning of 'lawfully present' • Meaning of 'lawfully working' • Meaning of 'family member'

2.44   Is the claimant entitled to benefit because of transitional protection?

Transitional protection and means-tested benefits • When does transitional protection end? • Transitional protection and non-means-tested benefits • Meaning of 'on arrival'

2.57   Ordinary residence and habitual residence tests

Non-means-tested benefits: the six-month rule • Means-tested benefits: the habitual residence (HR) test • Who is exempt from the HR test? • Meaning of 'habitual residence'

2.65   Entitlement to contributory benefits

2.66   **Administration, claims and payments**

2.67   Claims for IS and income-based JSA

The evidence requirement • The National Insurance number (NINO) requirement

2.77   Delays in processing the claim where there is an urgent need

Crisis loans • Interim payments • Community care assistance

2.80   Urgent cases payments

Who will be paid at the UCP rate? • Who can be included in the benefit claim – mixed status households

Introduction

2.1   Some asylum-seekers are entitled to claim social security benefits. Advisers should check the benefits position of an asylum-seeker or any member of the household, before considering entitlement to asylum support or interim support.[1]

2.2   Asylum-seekers who are entitled to claim benefit include those who claimed asylum 'on arrival' before 3 April 2000 and those who were receiving benefits on 4 February 1996 provided that they are still awaiting the first asylum decision. Other asylum-seekers and persons subject to immigration control (PSICs) are entitled to certain benefits if they are covered by European Community law or reciprocal arrangements with other countries.

2.3   Immigration and Asylum Act (IAA) 1999 s115 provides that asylum-seekers and other PSICs are ineligible for non-contributory benefits as from 3 April 2000. On that date, the Social Security (Immigration and Asylum) Consequential Amendments Regulations (SSIA Regs) 2000[2] came into force.[3] The regulations provide transitional protection for some asylum-seekers who were eligible for benefit before 3 April. They also list the miscellaneous categories of PSICs who are entitled to benefits, mainly because of international agreements.

2.4   The mechanism for excluding various classes of PSICs from benefits has been a series of amendments to the social security regulations, which need unravelling to work out who is entitled to benefits. This can be a complex exercise, beginning with a test of immigration status and nationality. Claimants may also need to satisfy residence and presence tests.

2.5   The chapter begins by setting the scene for the current legal position with a brief history which explains commonly-used terms followed by an outline of the legal framework. Then, the chapter goes through the stages for working out who is still eligible for benefit, discussing the law in difficult areas.

2.6   The second half of the chapter considers making a claim (admini-

---

1   There is a quick guide to benefit entitlement at para 2.22 below. See table at para 3.9 for asylum support and interim support entitlement.
2   SI No 636.
3   Immigration and Asylum Act 1999 (Commencement No 3) Order 2000 SI No 464.

stration and payment) and remedies. It addresses the common difficulties in making a claim experienced by those with an outstanding immigration claim as well as by those who have been granted refugee status or exceptional leave. Finally, it gives an overview of potential challenges, from complaints about service delivery to appealing against benefit refusals.

2.7 The internet is a useful source of current social security materials such as regulations, DSS guidance and circulars, and commissioners' decisions.[4] The annotated version of the legislation is widely used by welfare benefits advisers and tribunal chairmen.[5] The Child Poverty Action Group (CPAG) publishes the accessible welfare benefits handbook. Their *Migration and Social Security Handbook* contains a detailed explanation of immigration and social security law including EC law.

A brief history

No recourse to public funds

2.8 The immigration rules introduced a condition that certain applicants for leave to enter or remain in the UK, had 'no recourse to public funds' as an early step in discouraging PSICs such as students and visitors from claiming benefits.[6] Initially, they were still entitled to claim benefit, but this could result in an unfavourable Home Office decision on their immigration application. Since 1980 if a person without recourse to public funds claims social security benefits, the Department for Social Security (DSS) has the power to reclaim the money from a sponsor who has signed an agreement to maintain and accommodate the sponsored person.[7] A sponsor who has given a valid written undertaking, and whose failure to maintain and accommodate leads to payment of income support (IS) or asylum support, is liable to be prosecuted.[8]

4 www.dss.gov.uk and see Appendices.
5 Social Security Legislation (Sweet & Maxwell, 2000).
6 HC 395, para 6. See para 1.20.
7 Now SSCBA 1992 s146.
8 Social Security Administration Act 1992 s105 and IAA 1999 s107.

Urgent cases payments

2.9   Income support is calculated by comparing a claimant's income with his/her 'applicable amount' of benefit.[9] 'Urgent cases payments' (UCPs) of IS, were paid to prescribed categories of 'persons from abroad' (PFAs) including asylum-seekers. Their 'applicable amount' was 90 per cent of IS.[10] The Income Support (General) Regulations (IS Regs) 1987[11] were later amended so that the applicable amount of IS was nil for all PFAs except for some asylum-seekers.[12] Urgent cases payments are now paid only to a limited class of 'asylum-seekers' and PSICs with dead sponsors or interrupted funds. The term 'PFA' now refers only to people who have failed the habitual residence test.

Habitual residence test[13]

2.10   The 'habitual residence test' was introduced to discourage European nationals from coming to Britain as 'benefit tourists' but its impact was felt by British nationals returning from abroad. Those who fail the test are classified as PFAs whose 'applicable amount' for IS, housing benefit (HB) or council tax benefit (CTB) purposes is nil. Certain claimants such as those with full refugee status are exempt from the test.[14]

'In-country' asylum-seekers are PFAs excluded from benefits

2.11   On 5 February 1996 the then Conservative government introduced the Social Security (Persons From Abroad) Miscellaneous Amendment Regulations 1996[15] amending the definition of asylum-seeker so that it excluded those who had claimed asylum 'in-country' or had received a determination of their claim. This prevented asylum-seekers from receiving IS, HB and CTB unless they had claimed asylum 'on arrival'. The Court of Appeal decided that the regulations were unlawful on the basis that they would make an asylum-seeker's rights of appeal against a refusal of asylum worthless because s/he

---

9   SSCBA 1992 s124(4).
10   Social Security Act 1986; IS reg 21(3). See para 2.80.
11   SI No 1967.
12   IS Regs 1987 regs 21(3), 70(3A), Sch 7. See also Housing Benefit (General) Regulations (HB Regs) 1987 SI No 1971 reg 7A and Council Tax Benefit (General) Regulations (CTB Regs) 1992 SI No 1814 reg 4A.
13   See para 2.59.
14   See para 2.60.
15   SI No 30.

would have no means of support.[16] Simon Brown LJ's judgment may still be useful to refer to in cases of healthy single asylum-seekers who are refused asylum support after an unsuccessful appeal. In one much quoted extract he said:

> ... the 1996 Regulations necessarily contemplate for some a life so destitute that to my mind no civilised nation can tolerate it. So basic are the human rights here at issue, that it cannot be necessary to resort to the [European Convention on Human Rights] to take note of their violation.

2.12   The Asylum and Immigration Act 1996 re-introduced the regulations from 24 July 1996. They operated by allowing benefit to 'asylum-seekers' and not to other PFAs. For these purposes 'asylum-seekers' meant those who claimed asylum 'on arrival' in the UK, 'other than on re-entry' and who had not received a decision on their asylum claim. This group remains entitled to urgent cases payments of IS, provided that the asylum claim was before 3 April 2000. Other immigrants with limited leave to enter or remain fell within the PFA definition, and so were excluded from entitlement.

Transitional protection for asylum-seekers receiving benefits on 5 February 1996[17]

2.13   Saving provisions provided transitional protection for asylum-seekers (or sponsored immigrants) who were receiving IS, HB or CTB on 4 February 1996 and had not received an asylum decision (or had an asylum appeal pending on 5 February). They can continue receiving benefit until the next negative decision. In relation to other non-contributory benefits, a claimant's entitlement continues 'until such time as his entitlement to that benefit is reviewed'.

Child benefit entitlement removed

2.14   An immigration test was also introduced for PSICs including asylum-seekers to exclude them from child benefit from 7 October 1996. Again, there was some transitional protection.

Benefits for asylum-seekers replaced with asylum support

2.15   In 1998 the Labour government decided to abolish entitlement to

---

16   *R v Secretary of State for the Department of Social Security ex p JCWI and B* [1996] 4 All ER 385.

17   Transitional protection is explained at paras 2.44–2.50.

benefits for all asylum-seekers, and to replace it with the asylum support scheme.[18] On 3 April 2000, IAA 1999 s115 removed entitlement to specified benefits[19] from any PSIC within the s115(9) definition. Prescribed categories of PSICs who are not excluded are set out in a Schedule to the Regulations.[20] Many PSICs are excluded from benefit by s115(9), but only asylum-seekers as defined by s94 of the Act are eligible for the safety-net of asylum or interim support.

The legal framework

2.16   The remaining rights of asylum-seekers and other immigrants to social security come from three main sources: domestic social security legislation, European Community (EC) law,[21] and reciprocal agreements[22] entered into by the UK and other countries. These provisions should be interpreted in the light of the Human Rights Act (HRA) 1998 and the European Convention on Human Rights ('Human Rights Convention'). The UK has ratified the European Convention on Social and Medical Assistance (ECSMA) and the Council of Europe Social Charter (CESC), which are reflected in domestic legislation.[23]

2.17   The relevant social security statutes are the Social Security Contributions and Benefits Act (SSCBA) 1992 (for rules of entitlement), the Social Security Administration Act 1992 and the Social Security Act 1998 (for the administration of the scheme). The Child Support, Pensions and Social Security Act 2000 contains the revised decision-making and appeals framework for HB and CTB. The bulk of social security law however is contained in secondary legislation. This allows the secretary of state considerable flexibility to change the law in response to case-law or political developments. The detailed

18 Home Office White Paper, *Fairer, Faster and Firmer – A Modern Approach to Immigration and Asylum* (CM 4018), 17 July 1998, para 8.21.
19 See IAA 1999 s115(1).
20 Regulations made under IAA 1999 s115(3) and (4). The SSIA Regs came into force on 3 April 2000, with a schedule of those PSICs who are entitled to certain benefits.
21 EC Reg 1408/71 co-ordinates social security systems within the European Economic Area (EEA), prohibiting discrimination against EEA nationals who are exercising their rights to freedom of movement to work. This allows EEA nationals and their family members to qualify for benefits in the UK on the same basis as British nationals. See para 2.29 below.
22 DSS Overseas Benefits Section, tel: 0191 218 7777 for details of reciprocal agreements.
23 See Appendix C and para 2.34 below.

rules relating to each benefit are contained in regulations.[24] Decisions of the social security commissioners are binding on the decision-maker and form part of social security law.

2.18 Social security decisions, previously made by adjudication officers, are now made by the Secretary of State for Social Security who is represented by 'decision-makers' (ie, the Benefits Agency staff who were formerly adjudication officers). Social fund decisions are made by 'appropriate officers'. These changes were introduced by the Social Security Act 1998 which made major changes to the administration of benefits and appeals. The Adjudication Officers' Guidance was replaced by the Decision-Makers' Guidance (DMG), which is useful to refer to, although it does not always represent an accurate statement of the law.

2.19 The Benefits Agency is an executive agency of the DSS, which administers social security benefits. In London local offices accept benefit claims but decision-making and administration is often performed in offices outside London. Decisions on eligibility for job seeker's allowance (JSA) are made by the Employment Service, part of the Department of Education and Employment (DfEE) on behalf of the DSS.[25] The Contributions Agency (now part of the Inland Revenue) administers national insurance payments and contributions. The Inland Revenue administers working families' tax credit and disabled person's tax credit, within which the Tax Credit Office processes claims. (Family credit and disability working allowance, which tax credits replaced, were administered by the Benefits Agency.) Local authorities administer HB and CTB.

2.20 The Appeals Service (formerly the Independent Tribunal Service) considers appeals against refusals of social security benefit and its jurisdiction is to be extended to HB and CTB appeals as from 2 July 2001.

2.21 Social security benefits may be broadly categorised as 'contributory', where entitlement is based on a national insurance record, or 'non-contributory'. Non-contributory benefits may be means-tested, such as IS, or non-means-tested such as disability living allowance, where the condition of eligibility is a degree of disability.

---

24 Eg, IS Regs, HB Regs.
25 The Department of Work and Pensions was formed on 8 June 2001 from parts of the former DSS, DfEE and Employment Service. Job Centre Plus is planned to combine the Employment Service with parts of the Benefits Agency, providing a single point of contact for those claiming IS, JSA, maternity and disability benefits. Any references should be read accordingly. See www.dss.gov.uk.

Entitlement to benefit[26]

2.22 The table is a guide to the main classes of PSICs who are entitled to benefits.[27] It should be used in conjunction with the more detailed explanation of entitlement below.

Type of benefit	Persons entitled to benefit
Means-tested benefits: – IS – income-based JSA – HB – CTB	*Asylum-seekers awaiting a first Home Office decision* (can claim UCPs for themselves and any dependant) (a) Asylum-seekers who claimed asylum 'on arrival' on or before 2 April 2000. (b) Asylum-seekers who claimed asylum in-country within three months of a 'country of upheaval' declaration.[28] (c) Asylum-seekers who were receiving benefit on 4 February 1996 and are covered by transitional protection.[29] *Other PSICs* (d) A person who is 'lawfully present' in the UK and is a national of a country which has ratified the European Convention on Social and Medical Assistance (ECSMA) or the Council of Europe Social Charter (CESC). The habitual residence test must also be satisfied. (e) A person who has been sponsored (in a written undertaking) to enter the UK and who has lived in the UK for five years or whose sponsor has died. (f) A person with limited leave to enter or remain in the UK, who has 'no recourse to public funds' and whose funding from abroad has stopped temporarily. Entitlement is for a maximum of 42 days in a period of limited leave.

26 See para 2.15 above.
27 Note that EEA nationals and their family members are also entitled to claim benefits. An asylum-seeker may be or become a family member of an EEA national, eg, by marriage.
28 Applies only to Sierra Leone in-country asylum claims between 16 May 1997 and 16 August 1997 and the Democratic Republic of the Congo (formerly Zaire) in-country claims between 1 July 1997 and 1 October 1997.
29 Also covers those with an asylum appeal pending on 5 February 1996 which has not yet been decided. The extent of transitional protection is explained at para 2.44 below.

	Asylum-seekers and others who have received a favourable Home Office decision (g) A person who has been granted refugee status (benefit can be backdated to date of asylum application). (h) A person who has been granted exceptional leave to remain (benefit can be backdated to grant of leave) or indefinite leave to remain.
Non means-tested benefits and social fund payments: – attendance allowance – child benefit – disability living allowance – disabled person's tax credit – invalid care allowance – severe disablement allowance – social fund payment – working families' tax credit	*Asylum-seekers awaiting a Home Office decision and other persons subject to immigration control* (for (a) to (c) this includes an asylum-seeker who is appealing or whose appeal has been dismissed) (a) A national of Algeria, Morocco, Slovenia, Tunisia or Turkey who is 'a worker' or family member of a worker. (b) People covered by a reciprocal agreement (see para 2.34). (c) An asylum-seeker or other person with transitional protection which covers those receiving benefit before 5 February 1996 (7 October 1996 for child benefit). Entitlement is lost if after 2 April 2000 the claim for asylum is refused. (d) People subject to a written sponsorship undertaking as described above (excepting tax credits). *Asylum-seekers and others who have received a favourable decision* (e) People with exceptional or indefinite leave to remain.
Contributory benefits, eg: – incapacity benefit – JSA – maternity allowance	There is no immigration test. Entitlement is based solely on the claimant's contribution record and other conditions such as pregnancy or incapacity for work

2.23   The three basic steps in assessing whether an asylum-seeker or other PSIC is entitled to benefit are:

- consider 'which benefit';
- consider whether or not s/he is in an excluded class as explained below;[30]
- if there is no exclusion, then consider the residence requirements.[31]

2.24   The claimant must also meet ordinary eligibility criteria, eg, a means test to qualify for IS, an 'actively seeking work' test to qualify for income-based JSA.

Which benefit?

Contributory benefits

2.25   Asylum-seekers and other PSICs are not excluded by IAA 1999 s115 from claiming *contributory* benefits. Section 115 does not apply to benefits such as incapacity benefit (IB), maternity allowance (MA) and contribution-based JSA.[32] In practice, few asylum-seekers will have worked for long enough to have been paid or credited with sufficient contributions to qualify for these insurance-based benefits.[33]

Non-contributory benefits

2.26   Apart from the exceptions listed below at para 2.32, any PSIC under s115(9) is excluded from income-based JSA, the following non-contributory benefits and tax credits:[34]

(a) attendance allowance,
(b) severe disablement allowance,
(c) invalid care allowance,
(d) disability living allowance,
(e) income support,

---

30 Note that the wording of the regulations covering entitlement to the various non-contributory benefits changes slightly according to the benefit in question (see, eg, Social Security (Persons from Abroad) Miscellaneous Amendment Regulations 1996 SI No 30, reg 12(1), (2) and (3)). A claimant may be excluded from IS but not from HB.
31 The Benefits Agency asks claimants if they have been absent from the UK during the previous two years and applies the HR test to those who have been abroad, unless an exemption applies (see para 2.60).
32 This refers to contribution-based JSA, not income-based JSA.
33 See further para 2.65.
34 IAA 1999 s115(1).

(f) working families' tax credit,
(g) disabled person's tax credit,
(h) a social fund payment,
(i) child benefit,
(j) housing benefit, or
(k) council tax benefit.

Is the claimant in a class which is excluded from entitlement?

2.27 Rather than simply listing the benefits and stating who is *entitled*, the SSIA Regs stipulate who is 'excluded' and who is 'not excluded'. Following this structure, here is a suggested approach to assessing who comes within the excluded categories:

– Is the claimant a PSIC within the meaning of IAA 1999 s115(9)?
– If s/he is a PSIC, does s/he fall within a prescribed category which is not excluded from certain benefits?
– If not, is s/he entitled to benefit because of transitional protection?

Is the claimant a PSIC?[35]

2.28 A PSIC is defined by IAA s115(9) as a person who is not an EEA national and who:

(a) Requires leave to enter or remain in the UK but does not have it. (This includes most asylum-seekers – temporary admission does not amount to leave to enter or remain for the purposes of Immigration Act 1971 s3. Some asylum-seekers may have had limited leave to enter the UK and have made an asylum claim before this expired.)

(b) Has leave to enter or remain in the UK which is subject to a condition that s/he does not have recourse to public funds. (Eg, visitors, students, au pairs, work permit holders, business and self-employed people, fiancé(e)s, artists and writers.[36] The provision only applies if the Home Office actually imposed a condition. If leave was granted before 1997 there may be no condition.)

(c) Has leave to enter or remain in the UK given as a result of a maintenance undertaking. (This is limited to a *written* undertaking given by another person under the immigration rules

35 The meaning of PSIC for social security purposes is different from the ordinary immigration law meaning (see para 1.14).
36 See paras 1.25–1.26 for definition of 'recourse to public funds'.

para 6 to be responsible for that person's maintenance and accommodation, eg, where an elderly dependent relative has been sponsored to come to the UK and the sponsor signed an undertaking in the prescribed form (currently RON 112 or SET(F)).

(d) Has leave to enter or remain only as a result of Sch 4 para 17 (ie, people who have their leave extended while they appeal against a refusal to grant or vary leave).

European nationals[37]

2.29 Nationals of an EEA country and their family members in the UK are not treated as PSICs excluded from benefits by s115. They can receive benefits provided they pass other eligibility rules such as the habitual residence test. The EEA[38] includes the countries of the European Union (Austria, Belgium, Denmark, Finland, France, Germany, Greece, Italy, Luxembourg, the Netherlands, Portugal, Republic of Ireland, Spain, Sweden, the UK) plus Iceland, Liechtenstein and Norway.

2.30 The Immigration (European Economic Area) Regulations 2000[39] outline the scheme under which EEA nationals and their family members can claim rights of entry into or residence in the UK. EEA nationals entitled to remain in the UK include 'workers', 'self-employed persons', 'providers and recipients of services'[40] as well as 'self-sufficient persons' including students and certain pensioners. Regulation 6 defines 'family member' generally as including the spouse, descendants of the EEA national who are under 21 or dependent on the EEA national or his/her spouse, or a dependent relative in the ascending line (grandparents) of the EEA national or his/her spouse. The definition of family member is more limited in the case of students, retired and self-sufficient persons.

People deported to the UK

2.31 The Income-Related Benefits and JSA (Amendment) Regulations 2000[41] provide that persons who are not PSICs and who have been

---

37 A detailed discussion of the rights of EEA nationals is beyond the scope of this book. See further *Migration and Social Security Handbook* (CPAG).

38 An EEA state is defined by IAA 1999 s167 as 'a State which is a contracting Party to the Agreement on the European Economic Area signed at Oporto on 2nd May 1992 as it has effect for the time being'.

39 SI 2000 No 2326 came into force on 2 October 2000 replacing the Immigration (European Economic Area) Order 1994 SI No 1895.

40 As defined by EU Treaty arts 39, 43 and 50 respectively.

41 SI No 979.

deported, expelled or removed *from* another country *to* the UK are eligible for IS, JSA, HB and CTB and that they are not subject to the habitual residence test, by amending the various regulations providing for those benefits.

Is the claimant a PSIC in a category which is not excluded?

2.32 Some groups of immigrants are not excluded from benefits, even though they are PSICs. SSIA Regs reg 2 sets out the persons who are not excluded from specified benefits. These are:

- persons specified in the Schedule to the regulations;[42]
- others covered by reciprocal agreements;[43]
- transitional cases.[44]

2.33 The body of the SSIA Regs amend existing social security regulations, eg, the IS Regs, to give effect to reg 2. The Schedule to the regulations is divided into Part I, which lists PSICs who are 'not excluded' from means-tested benefits and Part II which lists a more limited category of those who are entitled to non-means-tested benefits. Both Parts cover the social fund.

PSICs who are entitled to means-tested benefits

2.34 The following PSICs are entitled to claim income-based JSA, IS, social fund payment, HB or CTB.[45] (Note that there are other categories who are entitled to claim.)

- A person whose leave to enter or remain in the UK is subject to a 'no recourse to public funds' condition, whose funding from abroad has stopped temporarily. Benefit can only be paid under this heading for a maximum of 42 days in any one period of leave.
- A person whose leave to enter or remain in the UK was based on an undertaking by a sponsor and who has been here for five years or whose sponsor has died within five years. The five years runs from the date of entry to the UK or of the undertaking, whichever is the later.

---

42 SSIA Regs reg 2(1) and (2).
43 See SSIA Regs reg 2(3). DMG para 070310 or the DSS Overseas Benefits Directorate (tel 0191 218 7777) can provide an up-to-date list.
44 SSIA Regs reg 2(5).
45 Ibid, Sch Part I.

- A national of a country which has ratified[46] ECSMA.[47]
- A national of a state which has ratified the CESC and who is 'lawfully present' in the UK.[48] This includes nationals of EEA countries plus Cyprus, Czech Republic, Hungary, Malta, Poland, Slovakia and Turkey.[49]

PSICs who are entitled to non-means-tested benefits/social fund payments

2.35   The following PSICs can claim attendance allowance, severe disablement allowance, invalid care allowance, disability living allowance, social fund payment or child benefit:[50]

- Non-EEA nationals who are family members of EEA nationals who are lawfully in the UK.[51]
- 'A person who is lawfully working in Great Britain and is a national of a state with which the Community has concluded an agreement under Article 310 of the Treaty of Amsterdam . . . '[52] or a family member who is living with him/her. The EEA has agreements with Algeria, Morocco, Slovenia, Tunisia and Turkey. A Turkish national who has worked anywhere in the EEA is eligible even if s/he has not been employed in the UK.[53] For the definition of 'lawfully working' and 'family member' see para 2.40 onwards.
- Sponsored immigrants (even if they have not been in the UK for five years and/or their sponsor is alive).

Meaning of 'lawfully present'

2.36   The meaning of 'lawfully present' is a key issue for asylum-seekers from non-EEA countries which have ratified the CESC.[54] There are various arguments to support the view that an asylum-seeker with

---

46   Before 3 April 2000 nationals of countries which had merely signed and not ratified ECSMA or CESC were eligible for IS, HB, CTB and income-based JSA if they had limited leave not subject to a public funds condition. Eligibility in these cases ceased from 3 April 2000.
47   See Appendix C for list of ratifications.
48   See para 2.36.
49   See Appendix C for list of ratifications.
50   SSIA Regs Sch Part II.
51   EEA nationals are also entitled.
52   SSIA Regs Sch Part II.
53   *Surul* (Case C-262/96).
54   At the time of writing the Court of Appeal was due to consider the issue in *Kaya v Haringey LBC*. See also para 6.16.

temporary admission is 'lawfully present' and so entitled to IS, income-based JSA, HB or CTB (and housing as homeless). DSS guidance suggests that asylum-seekers are not 'lawfully present' if they have restrictions on their stay in the UK, ie, have not been given leave to enter or remain in the UK, but simply have temporary admission.[55]

2.37   There is some guidance on the interpretation of the term in CESC, ECSMA[56] and EC law. Article 13 of CESC provides, 'the right to social and medical assistance to nationals of other parties to the agreement who are lawfully within [the UK], in accordance with their obligations under the European Convention on Social and Medical Assistance'. Article 1 of ECSMA provides that nationals of the other contracting parties who are 'lawfully present within [the UK] shall be entitled to social and medical assistance on the same terms as [the UK's] own nationals'. Article 11 deals with residence rather than presence and provides that residence shall be considered lawful '. . . so long as there is in force in his case a permit or any such permission as is required by the laws and regulations of the country concerned to reside therein. Failure to renew any such permit, if due solely to the inadvertence of the person concerned, shall not cause him to cease to be entitled to assistance.' Residence becomes unlawful from the date of a deportation order 'unless a stay of execution is granted'.

2.38   In a different context, the European Court of Justice (ECJ) considered a situation where an EEA national was granted temporary admission for seven months but was not granted 'leave to enter or remain'.[57] The court described to 'leave to enter or remain' in UK law as 'a legal fiction', finding that a grant of temporary admission was a decision concerning entry.

2.39   The Court of Appeal has now decided in the context of a homelessness appeal that an asylum-seeker who does not have leave to enter the UK, but only has temporary admission, is not 'lawfully present'.[58] This decision is binding for the purposes of any asylum-seeker with temporary admission, unless there is a future separate appeal to the House of Lords.

---

55 For explanation of temporary admission/leave to enter or remain see paras 1.62 onwards. IND form IS96 is proof of temporary admission.
56 See Appendix C.
57 *R v Home Secretary ex p Yiadom* (Case C-357/98) (2000) *Times* 16 November, ECJ.
58 *Kaya v Haringey LBC, Secretary of State for Social Security as Intervenor* (2001) 1 May, unreported, CA.

Meaning of 'lawfully working'

2.40   A 'worker' in the context of EC case-law is not simply an EEA national who is in employment. The ECJ has considered the meaning of 'worker' in the context of EC Regulation 1612/68 which provides for freedom of movement and equal treatment of EEA nationals who are 'workers'. 'A worker' is someone who is working or *has been* working in part-time or full-time work provided it is not so irregular and limited that it is a 'marginal and ancillary' activity. If s/he has stopped work it must be due to involuntary unemployment/lay-off or to undertake relevant training.[59] An au pair who had worked for five weeks, with pay of £35 for a 13-hour week plus board and lodging was found to be a worker.[60]

2.41   The right to equal treatment for workers in social security matters under co-operation agreements between the EEA and other states extends to Turkish nationals by virtue of the EEC-Turkey Association Agreement and EEA Council Decision 3/80.[61]

2.42   ECJ judgments have established a wide definition of 'worker' in the context of the co-operation agreements which covers most of those who have stopped lawfully working for a valid reason.[62] Nationals of Algeria, Morocco, Slovenia, Tunisia, or Turkey are to be treated as 'a worker' (eligible for benefits) if:

–   they have permission to enter Britain and are working here with no restriction on their right to work; or

–   they have stopped working in the UK due to sickness, pregnancy,

59   For further discussion of 'worker' see *Levin v Secretary of State for Justice* (Case 53/81) [1982] ECR 1035; *Kempf v Staatssecretaris van Justitie* (Case 139/85) [1986] ECR 1741; *Raulin v Minister van Onderwijs en Wetenschappen* (Case 357/89) [1992] ECR I-1027 and DMG para 071916.

60   CIS 12909/1996.

61   In *Surul* (Case C-262/96), the ECJ considered the principle of equal treatment and co-ordination in social security matters which apply to EEA workers by virtue of EEC Reg 1408/71. It decided that the same 'freedom of movement' principles applied to Turkish workers, their families and survivors by virtue of Council Decision 3/80. The definition of 'worker and 'family member' was considered, and the court noted that the Decision 3/80 definition of 'worker' corresponds to the concept of worker contained in Reg 1408/71 Art 1(a) and that the term 'member of family' has the meaning given to it by Reg 1408/71 Art 1(f). See also social security commissioner's decision CFC/2613/1997.

62   See *Kziber* (Case C-18/90) [1991] ECR I-199; *Yousfi v Belgium* (Case C-58/93) [1994] ECR I-1353; *Krid v Caisse Nationale d'Assurance Veillesse des Travailleurs Salariés* (Case C-103/94) [1995] ECR I-719; *Hallouzi-Choho v Bestuur van de Sociale Verzekeringsbank* (Case C-126/95) [1996] ECR I-4807; *Babahenini* (Case C-113/97) [1998] ECR I-183.

reaching pension age, widowhood, a work-related accident or disease, unemployment or to look after children.

Meaning of 'family member'

2.43 'Member of the family' of a worker under the co-operation agreements or Turkish Association Agreement is not defined in domestic law for the purposes of non-means-tested benefits. The DSS Decision Makers' Guidance[63] suggests that 'it should be given its normal everyday usage, for example, a married or unmarried couple and any children who normally live with them'. Where this does not cover a family member, eg, adult siblings or same-sex couples, use could be made of the HRA 1998, and article 8 of the Human Rights Convention.

Is the claimant entitled to benefit because of transitional protection?

2.44 There is transitional protection enabling asylum-seekers who were entitled to or receiving benefits on 2 April 2000 to retain entitlement until the first negative decision on their asylum claim.[64] The regulations build on the existing transitional protection provided by the Asylum and Immigration Act 1996.[65] The table provides a quick guide to who is covered by transitional protection and is followed by more detailed commentary.

Transitional protection and means-tested benefits

2.45 Transitional protection applies to those who are defined as 'asylum-seekers' within the meaning of the IS, HB and CTB Regs. They are eligible to claim income-based JSA, IS, HB, CTB and a social fund payment if they were eligible for or receiving benefit on 2 April 2000.

– An asylum-seeker who made a claim for asylum 'on arrival'[67] in the UK on or before 2 April 2000 and whose claim has been recorded by the Home Secretary. Note that the requirement is an asylum claim before 3 April, not a benefit claim. The

---

63 DMG 3/99.
64 SSIA Regs reg 2.
65 Social Security (Persons From Abroad) Miscellaneous Amendment Regs 1996 SI No 30 reg 12, which also amended the substantive regulations.
66 Social Security Administration Act 1992 s25 interpreted in CIS 1015/95.
67 See para 2.51 for meaning of 'on arrival'.

Type of benefit	Persons covered by transitional protection	When transitional protection ends
Means-tested benefits: – IS – income-based JSA – HB – CTB – social fund payments	(a) asylum-seekers who claimed asylum 'on arrival' in the UK after 4 February 1996 and before 2 April 2000; (b) asylum-seekers who claimed asylum within three months of a 'country of upheaval' declaration and before 3 April 2000; (c) asylum-seekers who were receiving IS, HB or CTB on 4 February 1996 and their dependants.	(a) when the claim for asylum is recorded by the Home Secretary as decided or abandoned; (b) when the claim for asylum is recorded by the Secretary of State as decided or abandoned; (c) on the first unfavourable decision after 4 February 1996, including an appeal decision if the appeal was entered before 5 February 1996.
Non means-tested benefits: – attendance allowance – disability living allowance – invalid care allowance – severe disablement allowance	A person from abroad who was in receipt of or entitled to or receiving the benefit on 4 February 1996 and any dependants as at 3 April 2000.	(a) the claim for asylum (if any) is recorded by the Secretary of State as having been decided or abandoned, *or* (b) the entitlement to benefit is revised or superseded.
Child benefit	A person from abroad who was in receipt of child benefit on 7 October 1996.	(a) the claim for asylum (if any) is recorded by the Home Secretary as having been decided or abandoned, *or* (b) the entitlement to benefit is reviewed, revised or superseded. The birth of an additional child does not end entitlement.[66]

asylum-seeker may claim benefit for the first time after 2 April 2000. Entitlement survives a break in the claim.

- A person who claimed asylum from a country which the Home Secretary has declared to be a 'country of upheaval' within three months of the declaration.[68]
- An asylum-seeker who was entitled to or receiving IS, HB or CTB on 4 February 1996 due to the transitional protection afforded to those who were receiving benefit immediately before 5 February 1996.[69] A social security commissioner has decided that an appeal is determined within the meaning of IS Regs reg 70(3A)(b)(ii) as soon as the next decision after 5 February 1996, not (as was argued) when it is finally determined, eg, after the Immigration Appeal Tribunal refers it back to another adjudicator for reconsideration.[70] A member of the asylum-seeker's family is also covered by this transitional protection. Entitlement survives a break in the claim (see para 2.47). Therefore, in a case of relationship breakdown where the wife was receiving benefit on 4 February 1996, the husband can claim. Similarly a child who leaves school can make a claim for IS in his/her own right.

When does transitional protection end?

2.46   Benefit entitlement ends when the claim of asylum is recorded by the Home Secretary as decided (other than on appeal) or abandoned.[71] Therefore, it ends if an asylum-seeker withdraws the asylum claim or receives a decision refusing asylum. In the context of the old provisions which used the term 'determined', this applied even where the asylum-seeker had not received the notification or the Home Office later reconsidered the decision (in *Salem*).[72] It has been argued that the decision in *Salem* was incorrect (leave to appeal to the House of Lords was given but not pursued). In the context of asylum support and interim support, entitlement ends when the supported person receives an asylum decision *with reasons for the refusal of asylum.*[73]

---

68 Declarations were made in relation to the Democratic Republic of the Congo and Sierra Leone in May and July 1997 respectively. See table at para 2.22 above.
69 See *R v Secretary of State for Social Security ex p T* [1997] COD 480, CA; *R v Secretary of State for Social Security ex p Vijeikis* 5 March 1998, CA, unreported.
70 CIS/3418/1998, starred decision no 31/00.
71 SSIA Regs reg 12(4) and (7).
72 *R v Home Secretary ex p Salem* [1999] 1 AC 450; [1999] QB 805, CA.
73 This is discussed in detail in paras 1.80–1.85.

2.47   In the case of asylum-seekers receiving benefit on 4 February 1996 (because of pursuing an asylum appeal/awaiting a first decision), it ends on recording of the first unfavourable decision after that date, including an appeal decision if the appeal was entered before 5 February 1996. However, the Court of Appeal has now decided that entitlement survives a break in the claim.[74] Therefore, an asylum-seeker may end the benefit claim to work and reclaim at a later date.

2.48   Where transitional protection flows from an 'on arrival' asylum claim made before 3 April 2000 or a 'country of upheaval' claim, it does not extend to family members who make their own claim, eg, on death or separation unlike the protection to those receiving benefits on 4 February 1996. Transitional protection continues until the first negative asylum decision.

Transitional protection and non-means-tested benefits

2.49 A 'person from abroad' who was in receipt of or entitled to benefit under Social Security (Persons from Abroad) Miscellaneous Amendments Regulations 1996[75] reg 12(3) (attendance allowance, disability living allowance, severe disablement allowance and invalid care allowance) on 5 February 1996 or child benefit on 7 October 1996 and 3 April 2000 retains transitional protection after 2 April 2000 until:

(a) his claim for asylum (if any) is recorded by the Secretary of State as having been decided or abandoned; or
(b) his entitlement to that benefit claim is revised or superseded . . .'[76]

The transitional protection also covers persons who were members of the asylum-seeker's family on 3 April 2000.[77]

2.50   In *R v Chief Adjudication Officer ex p B*,[78] the Court of Appeal adopted a limited approach to the wording of reg 12(3) in the context of child benefit, deciding that a time-limited award is renewed upon expiry and not just on review (revision/supersession). The decision applies to disability living allowance, family credit, attendance allowance, invalid care allowance, severe disablement allowance and disability working allowance with dicta distinguishing the wording 'ending protection on review' from that which applies to other benefits. In

74 See *Yildiz v Secretary of State for Social Security* C/2000/3093, 28 February 2001, CA.
75 SI No 30.
76 SSIA Regs reg 12(10).
77 Ibid, reg 12(11).
78 [1999] 1 WLR 1695.

Yildiz v Secretary of State for Social Security, the Court of Appeal decided that reg 12(1) and (2) should be interpreted differently. In *R v Chief Adjudication Officer ex p B* the Court of Appeal decided that transitional protection is lost when a review is carried out or when a time-limited award is renewed upon expiry. In *R v Adjudication Officer ex p Velasquez*[79] the Court of Appeal held that transitional protection only applied to those entitled to *and receiving* benefit on 7 October 1996.

Meaning of 'on arrival'

2.51   An asylum-seeker who 'submits on arrival (other than on his re-entry[80]) in the UK . . . a claim for asylum on or before 2nd April 2000' is still eligible to claim IS, HB or CTB after that date, if s/he has not had a negative decision on the asylum claim.[81] Even if an asylum-seeker has been refused benefit or has a SAL2 rather than a SAL1, it is worth checking whether s/he falls within the current interpretation of 'on arrival'.

2.52   With no guidance from the Court of Appeal, the social security commissioners have failed to reach a consensus on the meaning of 'on his arrival' in IS Reg 70(3A). Commissioners are not bound by other commissioners' decisions although they are expected normally to follow them in the interests of certainty.[82]

2.53   Commissioner Howell QC attempted to tackle the problem of a series of inconsistent commissioners' decisions by reviewing all of them in CIS 3867/98.[83] He adopted the 'factual test' of 'on arrival'. He decided that commissioners who applied a test of whether the claim for asylum had been made within the port of entry even if this was after passing through immigration control (CIS 1137/97 and CIS 4341/98) were mistaken and the appropriate test was an 'immigration control' test (CIS 143/97 and CIS 3231/97).

> It follows in my judgment that the reference in reg 70(3A)(a) to a person submitting a claim for asylum on his arrival (other than on his re-entry) in the United Kingdom is concerned with the nature of the application made to be allowed into the United Kingdom at the point

---

79   (1999) *Times* 30 April, CA.
80   In CIS/2760/1999 (27 June 2000) it was held that 're-entry' included a case where a student returned to the UK after a three-week absence and claimed asylum due to receiving information which put him in fear of his life.
81   SSIA Regs reg 12(4), see para 2.44 onwards.
82   R(I) 12/75.
83   30 September 1999.

where a recently-arrived passenger submits, or should submit, himself to examination by an immigration officer at his or her port of first entry into this country.

The commissioner found in both this case and in the later CIS 3646/98[84] that clandestine entrants who had claimed asylum after passing through the port in a lorry had not claimed 'on arrival'.

2.54   In CIS 3803/98,[85] however, Commissioner Sanders decided that where a Libyan asylum-seeker was too ill to claim asylum when he reached Heathrow due to torture in Libya, this was an exceptional case in which he might fall within the 'on arrival' definition if the facts of his illness could be proven.

2.55   In 50/99, CIS 4341/98 the applicant for asylum had passed through immigration control at Gatwick with an agent without claiming asylum but attempted to claim asylum two hours later with the help of a man from the Third World Refugee Bureau, after waiting in the arrivals hall. Commissioner Williams rejected the 'as soon as reasonably practicable' test but, applying a measure of flexibility to the test of 'on arrival' (see also CIS 2719/97 and 4117/97) found that the claimant had claimed 'on arrival'. The DSS Decision Makers' Guidance accepts that an asylum-seeker who is prevented by ill-health from applying for asylum at immigration control but applies as soon as reasonably practicable falls within the 'on arrival definition'.[86]

2.56   The conflicting decisions leave representatives to argue from fact and principle unless a case reaches the Court of Appeal. There is scope to argue that 'on arrival' includes claims made within the port of entry, even after clearing immigration control or, to a very limited extent that it means 'as soon as reasonably practicable' following the exceptional circumstances test of CIS 3803/98. There is less authority for arguing that clandestine entrants, eg, travelling out of the port hidden in a lorry, have claimed 'on arrival'. The HRA 1998 should now be taken into consideration in any decisions interpreting the regulations.

84   5 January 2000.
85   7 July 1999.
86   DMG 31041.

Ordinary residence and habitual residence tests

2.57 Even if a claimant is not excluded from non-contributory benefits by virtue of the *immigration* test introduced by IAA 1999 s115, s/he will still need to pass any *residence* test which applies to the benefit claimed.

Non-means tested benefits: the six-month rule

2.58 There is a six months' (182 days) residence requirement for those claiming attendance allowance, disability living allowance, invalid care allowance, child benefit, severe disablement allowance and guardian's allowance. In the case of child benefit there are some exceptions to the six-month rule but these are unlikely to apply in the case of asylum-seekers.

Means-tested benefits: the habitual residence (HR) test

2.59 The requirement that a benefit claimant is either habitually resident or treated as habitually resident in the common travel area (the UK, Isle of Man, Republic of Ireland or the Channel Islands) applies to the following benefits:

- IS/income-based JSA;[87]
- HB and CTB.[88]

Who is exempt from the HR test?

2.60 A claimant who has lived outside the common travel area in the two years prior to the claim will be subject to the habitual residence test unless s/he comes within one of these exemptions:

- People who have been granted exceptional leave to enter or remain in the UK or are recognised as refugees in the UK are not subject to the HR test.[89] It would follow that asylum-seekers are also exempt and in practice the test is not applied to them.
- People who left Montserrat after 1 November 1995 due to the volcanic eruption there.

---

87 IS Regs reg 21(3), JSA Regs reg 85.
88 HB Regs/CTB Regs reg 7A(4)(e).
89 IS Regs reg 21(3) and (3F), 85(4) and (4A), JSA Regs reg 7A(4)(e) and (5), HB Regs.

- EEA nationals, if they come within the definition of 'a worker', and their family members.[90] An EEA national who is not working will be subject to the habitual residence test, eg, a Somali refugee who is a Dutch national and comes to the UK with her children as a work-seeker fleeing domestic violence in Holland.
- People deported or legally removed *to the UK* from another country.[91]

Meaning of 'habitual residence'

2.61   A claimant who fails the HR test is a 'person from abroad' who is not entitled to benefits until s/he has established HR. The Benefits Agency applies the HR test to claimants who have not lived in the UK (or common travel area[92]) throughout the past two years. They are subject to the HR test when they claim IS, income-based JSA or HB. If the claimant has a partner, consider transferring the main claimant if s/he passes, or is exempt from the test.

2.62   Each claim should be considered on its own merits, taking account of the facts at the date of the claim. If a claimant fails the test, consider repeat applications at regular intervals and an appeal against each individual negative decision.

- The claimant must have a 'settled intention' to reside in the UK. Events before and after arrival here can be used to demonstrate this. These would include circumstances and arrangements made before arrival in the UK and steps taken after arrival to settle here, eg, children attending school, registering with GPs and other organisations.
- A claimant will need to be resident in UK for an 'appreciable period' unless s/he is returning to the UK after a temporary absence abroad, in which case s/he is 'habitually resident' on the first day back in the UK.

2.63   The meaning of HR has been reviewed by the ECJ in *Swaddling v Adjudication Officer*[93] and by the House of Lords in *Nessa*.[94] In *Swaddling* the ECJ decided that an EEA national who has come to

---

90   See paras 2.29 and 2.40 for the definition of 'worker' and 'family member'.
91   See para 2.31.
92   The common travel area is the UK, the Republic of Ireland, the Channel Islands, and the Isle of Man.
93   *Swaddling v Adjudication Officer* (Case C90/97) [1999] All ER (EC) 217.
94   *Nessa v Chief Adjudication Officer* [1999] 1 WLR 1937.

the UK after working in Europe should not need to be in the UK for an appreciable period before being able to establish HR. The DSS then issued guidance[95] which states that the national of any country who is returning to the UK to 'pick up the pieces of their former life' is habitually resident as soon as s/he arrives in the UK, ie, does not need to be in the UK for an appreciable period. Commissioner Mesher has commented that the guidance incorrectly interprets *Swaddling*.[96] He confirmed that an EEA national who has worked/ been insured in the EEA and so falls within EC Reg 1408/71 cannot be excluded from benefit on the basis that the 'appreciable period' requirement is not met. He confirmed that the length of a person's residence in the UK will merely be one factor to consider in deciding whether s/he has a settled intention to remain here, and that in some circumstances other factors could mean that the person concerned was habitually resident on arrival.

2.64 Mrs Nessa came to the UK after living in Bangladesh all her life and appealed against a DSS decision that she was not habitually resident. In *Nessa*, the House of Lords attempted to distinguish her circumstances from those in *Swaddling*. The court held that a period of actual residence can be required for those who do not fall within *Swaddling*, ie, who have not worked in the EEA, although the appreciable period could be as short as one month. Lord Slynn stated:

> . . . as a matter of ordinary language a person is not habitually resident in any country unless he has taken up residence and lived here for a period . . . It is a question of fact to be decided on the date when the determination has to be made on the circumstances of each case whether and when the habitual residence had been established. Bringing possessions, doing everything necessary to establish residence before coming, having a right of abode, seeking to bring family, 'durable ties' with the country of residence have to be taken into account. The requisite period is not a fixed period. It may be longer when there are doubts. It may be short . . .

Commissioner Jacobs has accepted in the case of two appellants that no appreciable period is necessary to establish habitual residence.[97]

95 AM(AOG) 109.
96 CIS 15484/96, 20 July 1999.
97 CIS/1304/1997 and CJSA/5394/1998.

Entitlement to contributory benefits

2.65   An asylum-seeker excluded from non-contributory benefits may be eligible for a contributory benefit if s/he has lived and worked in the UK, or is a survivor of someone who has. This is outside the scope of the book. If it appears that an asylum-seeker may be eligible, reference should be made to the detailed rules.[98]

Administration, claims and payments

2.66   Asylum-seekers and other PSICs often experience practical difficulties with the initial claim for benefits. An asylum-seeker becomes entitled to Income Support (IS) after a favourable asylum decision, and asylum or interim support ends 14 days after Home Office notification of the decision. There is no duty to offer asylum or interim support if the household is excluded because of eligibility for IS.[99] Many asylum-seekers are left with no means of support because of Home Office delays in issuing documents and Employment Service delays in issuing a national insurance number.[100] Advisers should consider legal challenges to a delay or refusal to pay benefit, including judicial review applications in such cases. Some of the common issues are considered here.

Claims for IS and income-based JSA

The evidence requirement

2.67   To make a valid claim for IS or income-based JSA, the claimant must satisfy 'the evidence requirement'. (Claims for other benefits should be treated as valid from the date a letter of claim is received by the Benefits Agency.) The evidence requirement means the application form must be completed in full and accompanied by other evidence requested,[101] ie:

---

98   See current *Welfare Benefits Handbook* (CPAG, annual).
99   A destitute asylum-seeker or dependant of an asylum-seeker can claim asylum or interim support if only part of the household is eligible for social security benefit.
100   Social services help may be available in the case of children or people with community care needs (see para 7.121 onwards).
101   Social Security (Claims and Payments) Regulations 1987 No 1968 reg 4(1A), (1B).

- payslips;
- proof of other income (this will be form ASD 35[102] provided by NASS in the case of an asylum-seeker who has been receiving asylum support from NASS);
- proof of any savings or payment from an insurance policy;
- proof of service charges or ground rent.

2.68   If the form is not properly completed and the evidence requirement is not met, the Benefits Agency should contact the claimant allowing one month from the date of the claim to remedy the problem. If the evidence requirement is not met within that period, the claim may be rejected.[103]

2.69   Where asylum-seekers are unable to meet the evidence requirement within the specified period, or at all, they can ask the Benefits Agency for an exemption, for an extension of the one-month period, or to get the information on their behalf.

2.70   If a claimant cannot meet the evidence requirement, a request can be made for exemption on any of the following grounds:[104]

- a physical, mental learning or communication difficulty where it is not reasonably practicable for the claimant to find someone else to assist, eg, isolated asylum-seeker with mental health needs who cannot read or write English;
- the information required does not exist or could not be obtained except with a serious risk of physical or mental harm to the claimant, eg, documents are in the country of origin;
- a third party has the information and it is not reasonably practicable to obtain it.

The National Insurance number (NINO) requirement

2.71   The requirement to have a NINO (or be applying for one) as a precondition of a claim[105] is one of the main causes of delay for asylum-seekers claiming IS for the first time. A NINO is now required for HB, CTB and child benefit claims, except in the case of hostel-dwellers.[106] To avoid this delay, advisers should consider whether an

---

102 See Appendix D.
103 Ibid, reg 6(1A) and (4AB).
104 Ibid, reg 4(1B).
105 Social Security Administration Act 1992 s1(1A).
106 HB Regs reg 2B, CTB Regs reg 2B.

asylum-seeker can obtain a NINO prior to any claim for benefit. Asylum-seekers who have the right to work but are not eligible for benefit can apply for a NINO if they have a job offer or are registered with an employment agency, although priority is given to processing 'benefits-inspired applications', ie, NINO applications by benefit claimants. (It appears that 'employment inspired applicants' are dealt with by a separate section of the DSS.) The applicant must apply to the Benefits Agency for a NINO interview, to complete form CA5400.

2.72   Where a claimant has provided the information needed to process his/her application for a NINO, it may be possible to challenge any delay in awarding benefit pending the NINO allocation. Social Security Administration Act 1992 s1 provides that in addition to any other conditions, entitlement to benefit is dependent on the claim being made in a prescribed manner.

2.73   To qualify for benefit the claimant must provide in respect of every person of 16 and over covered by the claim either:

(a) . . .
   (i)   a statement of the person's national insurance number, an information or evidence establishing that that number has been allocated to the person; or
   (ii) information or evidence enabling the national insurance number that has been allocated to that person to be ascertained, or
(b)   the person makes an application for a national insurance number to be ascertained which is accompanied by information or evidence enabling such a number to be so allocated.[108]

2.74   The evidence required to obtain a NINO is evidence of identity, eg, birth certificate, SAL,[109] passport, national identity card, driving licence, utility bills, tenancy agreement. In practice, originals of documents are required. In addition, the Benefits Agency may refuse to accept evidence of immigration status and identity other than a Home Office letter confirming status, eg, not passports with entry stamps.

2.75   Before a decision on their immigration status, asylum-seekers may have sent the originals of documents proving identity to the Home Office, which is likely to keep them until an asylum decision is

---

108   Social Security Administration Act 1992 s1(1B).
109   Standard Acknowledgement letter provided by the Home Office, see Appendix D.

made. To obviate this difficulty, claimants can ask the Benefits Agency to endorse photocopies of original documents when they first visit the local office with these. If the original documents are later lost or sent to another agency, the photocopies should be relied on. The Benefits Agency is likely to argue that the IS and DCI (Departmental Central Index) Sections are discrete and the originals must be provided again.

2.76 After a decision of exceptional leave or full refugee status, a common problem is an error in the spelling of names or the order of names, which the Home Office may take months to correct. There have been a number of cases in which claimants have been refused benefits because they do not have a NINO and refused asylum support because they are no longer asylum-seekers. In such cases interim payments and social fund payments are also often refused. It may be possible to challenge a refusal of IS by arguing that the claimant has met the Social Security Administration Act 1992 s1(1B)(b) requirement if s/he has applied for a NINO, giving all the necessary evidence. Arguably, the Benefits Agency should accept the Home Office's confirmation that the Home Secretary is satisfied as to the claimant's identity. In practice, they often do not, but there is scope for judicial review and/or complaints.

Delays in processing the claim where there is an urgent need

Crisis loans

2.77 A claimant could consider an application[110] to the Benefits Agency for a discretionary social fund 'crisis loan' while the claim is being processed. Such claims are governed by the Social Fund Directions and the Social Fund Guide. Unlike budgeting loans and community care grants, it is not a pre-condition that the claimant is in receipt of IS/income-based JSA. Crisis loans must be to help meet expenses in an emergency to avoid serious damage or serious risk to the health and safety of the claimant or a member of the household. There is no definition of an emergency and the High Court has ruled that need and priority of an application should be considered before budgetary considerations.[111] It is arguable that asylum-seekers are entitled to crisis loans because they do not fall within the categories of persons

110 Form SF400 or SF401.
111 *R v Social Fund Inspector ex p Taylor* [1998] COD 152, QBD.

from abroad excluded from eligibility. However, it is a requirement of such a loan that the claimant will have the means to repay, and so it would be necessary to show that the claimant will be awarded income, eg, cash as part of an interim support or Children Act 1989 s17 payment or that s/he will be eligible for benefit in future. A claimant who failed the HR test could argue that s/he would be in a position to repay the loan in at least three to six months' time. If a crisis loan is refused, a revision within 28 days and written reasons for the decision should be requested.

Interim payments[112]

2.78   There is an entitlement to an interim payment of benefit if the claimant is, or may be, entitled to benefit or a tax credit, but it is not possible for the claim to be dealt with immediately. The Benefits Agency may refuse an interim payment on the basis that the claimant must meet the NINO requirement. Any such refusal can be challenged where all 'the necessary information' has been provided to enable a NINO to be allocated (see paras 2.69–2.76 above). Therefore, if there is a delay in paying IS to an asylum-seeker who has been granted exceptional leave, for example, an interim payment could be requested. If that is refused and income is urgently needed a judicial review application should be considered.

Community care assistance

2.79   A request to the local authority's social services department for a community care assessment may be appropriate as an emergency measure if the claimant has a health need or has children (see further chapter 7).

Urgent cases payments

2.80   Asylum-seekers and other persons subject to immigration control who are eligible for IS or income-based JSA by virtue of IS Reg 70(3) (or JSA Regs[113] reg 147) are paid at a reduced rate known as urgent cases payment (UCP). The applicable amount is calculated as 90 per

112 Social Security (Payments on account, Overpayments and Recovery) Regulations 1988 No 664 reg 2.
113 Jobseeker's Allowance Regulations 1996 SI No 207.

cent of the personal allowance plus full personal allowances for children, any premiums and housing costs.[114]

2.81 The income and capital rules which apply to UCPs are stricter than those which normally apply to IS.[115] If the claimant has any capital s/he will not be eligible – the normal capital limit and rules about disregarded capital do not apply. This means that if a claimant receives arrears of disability benefits or has savings, s/he will not be entitled to any UCP until the money has been spent or accounted for. Arrears of UCPs or concessionary UCPs are not taken into account as capital.

Who will be paid at the UCP rate?

2.82 Those entitled to IS because they are nationals of an EEA country or because of a reciprocal agreement will receive benefit at the normal rate: 100 per cent of IS. The PSICs who will be paid at the UCP rate are:

– asylum-seekers entitled to benefit by virtue of transitional protection;
– PSICs (such as students and visitors) who have limited leave but are temporarily without funds;
– PSICs (such as elderly dependent relatives) whose sponsor has died within five years of their date of entry or the date of the undertaking, whichever is later.

Who can be included in the benefit claim – mixed status households

2.83 An asylum-seeker who is eligible for IS at the UCP rate can claim for a dependant under IS Reg 70 regardless of the partner's immigration status. Therefore, if an asylum-seeker is entitled to IS because she claimed asylum on arrival before 3 April 2000, she can add her husband or children who arrive in the UK after 3 April 2000 to the claim. Transitional protection will enable them to continue receiving IS at the UCP couple rate until there is a relevant change of circumstances, eg, a refusal of the asylum claim.

2.84 The right to include persons subject to immigration control as dependants only applies to asylum-seekers claiming UCPs. Any other claimant who is entitled to benefits cannot include a person

114 IS Regs reg 71; JSA Regs reg 148.
115 IS Regs reg 72; JSA Regs reg 149.

subject to immigration control in the claim. Therefore, if the asylum-seeker is granted exceptional leave to remain but her partner's asylum claim is outstanding, she cannot claim for him while he is excluded from benefits by IAA 1999 s115. An asylum-seeker with an outstanding asylum claim and who is entitled to IS could however claim for a partner with exceptional leave to remain (at UCP rate).

Whether to claim IS or income-based JSA

2.85   For an asylum-seeker who has not yet had a decision on his/her asylum claim, the question of whether to claim IS or income-based JSA has important consequences, although the rate of payment is the same for both benefits. If s/he has stopped working in employed earner's employment due to loss of the job and is making a claim for UCP, there is a choice between claiming IS or income-based JSA.

Advantages of claiming income-based JSA

2.86   An asylum-seeker can claim income-based JSA if s/he has permission to work from the Home Office.[117] S/he will need to comply with a jobseeker's agreement and show that s/he is actively seeking work. There is also the requirement to sign on fortnightly at the local job centre. An advantage of claiming JSA is that if the asylum-seeker gets work; and then stops working due to unemployment, sickness or pregnancy, s/he will be credited with National Insurance contributions. This will allow him/her to start a contribution record. There is no immigration test for contributory benefits so an asylum-seeker with sufficient contributions could receive incapacity benefit or JSA even after a negative decision on his/her asylum claim. An asylum-seeker who is granted leave to remain in the UK will also benefit from starting to build up a contribution record. This is most likely to benefit single asylum-seekers or childless couples who have no difficulty in presenting themselves as actively seeking work.

Advantages of claiming IS

2.87   Until an asylum-seeker has the right to work, s/he will not be eligible to claim income-based JSA. The advantage of a claim for IS is that the asylum-seeker will not have to sign on or demonstrate that s/he is actively seeking work. Complying with the jobseeker's agreement

117   JSA reg 147(3).

may be difficult for those who are beginning to learn spoken and written English. The cost of seeking work may also be a problem since benefit is being paid at 90 per cent. If the claimant has dependent children, then a contributory benefit such as JSA will not meet the family's essential living needs if JSA stops after a negative decision. If the claimant has no realistic prospect of obtaining work and so will not develop a contribution record, the administrative burden of claiming income-based JSA is unlikely to outweigh any advantage

Treatment of asylum/interim support income

Before the asylum decision

2.88 It is possible for one household member to receive asylum support for essential living needs, while another member claims benefits. If a claimant's partner receives asylum support, this does not count as income for the purposes of income-based JSA or IS.[118] This means that asylum support in kind can be paid to the partner to cover his/her essential living needs and those of any dependants while the claimant receives IS.

2.89 Asylum support is treated as income for the purposes of HB and CTB.[119] The full asylum support payment whether in cash or in kind will be treated as income when assessing the amount of benefit. This even includes the payments of £50 in cash vouchers which an asylum-seeker can claim every six months.

Housing benefit non-dependant deductions[120]

2.90 There is no provision to exempt asylum-seekers or those they live with from non-dependant deductions. This means that where an asylum-seeker stays as the guest of someone claiming HB/CTB, the host will be subject to a reduction in his/her benefit, assuming a contribution from the asylum-seeker. This applies whether the asylum-seeker household is in receipt of asylum support for living expenses, of interim support or has no income at all. There is an argument that non-dependent deductions should not be levied because an asylum-seeker is 'temporary' according to government

---

118   IS Regs reg 21ZB(5) as amended by SSIA Regs reg 3(6)(c).
119   HB Regs reg 33(4) as amended by SSIA reg 6(4), CTB reg 24(5) as amended by SSIA reg 7(4)(b).
120   See para 3.128 re council tax liability of supported persons.

statements (see para 4.52). The claimant could apply to the local authority to exercise its discretion to award a discretionary housing payment under the Child Support, Pensions and Social Security Act 2000 ss69 and 70 and the Discretionary Financial Assistance Regulations 2000. This will replace 'extra benefit in exceptional circumstances'[120a] from 1 July 2001. A local authority may make a discretionary housing payment to recipients of HB/CTB outside of the HB/CTB schemes where the claimants 'appear to such an authority to require some further financial assistance (in addition to the benefit or benefits to which they are entitled) in order to meet housing costs'.[121] Where a discretionary housing payment is refused the remedy is an internal review only.

After the asylum decision

2.91   Any asylum or interim support income received during the 14-day grace period after the Home Office has made a decision on the asylum application will be treated as income for IS purposes.[122]

2.92   Where a recognised refugee makes a backdated claim for IS or income-based JSA, any payments of asylum support or interim support will be deducted from the award.[123]

Favourable and unfavourable Home Office decisions

2.93   Asylum support or interim support entitlement ends when an asylum claim is 'determined' for the purposes of IAA 1999 s94(3). A claim is determined at the end of the 'prescribed period'. The prescribed period is 14 days which starts either:

– on the date the applicant is notified of the decision which is two days after posting if the decision is sent by first class post; or
– on the date the appeal is disposed of.

2.94   This means asylum-seekers will only receive interim or asylum support for 14 days after notification of a favourable or unfavourable decision on the asylum claim. During this time they will need to sort out any benefit claim and make alternative housing arrangements. The 14-day period is not long enough to process an IS or HB claim in

120a HB reg 61(2), CTB Regs.
121   reg 2(1)(b).
122   IS reg 40(4)(b).
123   IS reg 21ZB, Sch 1B, para 18a.

most cases. In London the average time for processing an application for a NINO (which is treated as a prerequisite of an IS or HB claim) is two to three weeks. In order to advise those faced with this difficulty, advisers will need to be familiar with the evidence and NINO requirements (see para 2.69 onwards), rules about interim or other urgent payments, and should consider urgent applications for judicial review (see para 2.78). If all else fails, community care help should be sought in cases involving children[124] or adults with needs arising from age, ill-health, pregnancy, etc (see para 2.79).

2.95   If a household has been receiving asylum support from NASS, the asylum-seeker should be issued with a termination of support letter when a final decision is made on the asylum claim. Form ASD 35,[125] which should be issued by NASS when support stops, gives details of the Home Office decision, the names of household members and the period and value of asylum support. It contains a photograph of the main applicant for support. Adult dependants will receive a shorter letter giving details of support received.

Grant of refugee status

2.96   If an asylum-seeker is recognised as a refugee,[126] s/he is entitled to IS or income-based JSA, HB and CTB from the date of the asylum claim.[127] The refugee must apply for backdated IS (not income-based JSA), HB and CTB within 28 days of the date on which s/he receives notification that the Home Secretary has recognised him/her as a refugee. There is no provision to extend this period even if there would normally be 'good cause for a late claim'. If the asylum-seeker fails to make a valid claim within the 28 days s/he will lose the right to backdated benefit. No backdated IS will be paid for any period before 5 February 1996.

2.97   If the refugee is a childless claimant who is eligible for income-based JSA but not IS, s/he *must* submit a separate claim for back-dated IS *within 28 days*. The arrears will be paid at 100 per cent of the IS applicable amount rather than the UCP rate. Therefore, if the refugee was previously receiving IS at the 90 per cent UCP rate, s/he is entitled to make a backdated claim for the missing 10 per cent.[128]

---

124   Children Act 1989 s17.
125   See Appendix D.
126   Ibid, Form ICD.0725.
127   IS reg 21ZA and SSIA regs 3, 6 and 7.
128   SSIA reg 3(5) amending IS reg 21ZB.

2.98   The claim for backdated HB/CTB should be made to the authority in whose area the refugee is living at the time s/he claims the benefit. That authority should then determine HB/CTB for the whole period.[129] Asylum-seekers will only be eligible for backdated HB and CTB if they have a liability for rent/council tax. There is an exemption from council tax liability for those who are living in accommodation provided under the asylum or interim support duty.

Grant of 'exceptional leave to remain' (ELR)

2.99   Unlike the recognition of refugee status, a grant of exceptional leave to enter or remain in the UK takes effect from the date of the decision. This means that an asylum-seeker who is granted indefinite or exceptional leave to remain is eligible to claim benefits from the date of the ILR or ELR decision but cannot claim for any earlier period.

2.100   Claimants with ELR are sometimes refused benefits because Benefits Agency or local authority decision-makers misinterpret the immigration documents. ELR may initially be granted for a period of one year, but should not be confused with other forms of limited leave. In such cases, advisers can refer to IAA s115(9) which describes the categories of PSICs and in particular s115(9)(a) which defines a PSIC as a person who 'requires leave to enter or remain in the United Kingdom but does not have it'.

VOLO (Variation of Leave Order) cases[130]

2.101   A person with leave to enter or remain in the UK who applies for it to be extended or varied before it expires, should be treated as having leave on the same terms until the application is decided.[131] Where such an application has been made, a claimant with ELR which has expired should be treated as having ELR (and as entitled to benefits) until a Home Office decision has been made to grant or refuse the application. Evidence that a relevant application has been made could be provided in the form of a letter from an immigration representative. A letter of acknowledgement from the Home Office or dated receipt from the Home Office should also be acceptable.

129   HB reg 2A as amended by SSIA reg 6(5).
130   See para 1.22.
131   IA 1971 s3A as amended by IAA 1999 s3. Section 3A replaced the Variation of Leave Order (VOLO) 1976 SI No 1572 for all cases where an application to vary leave was made on or after 2 October 2000. See Immigration (Variation of Leave) (Amendment) Order 2000 SI No 2445.

Mixed families[132]

2.102 A claimant who is entitled to benefit as an asylum-seeker with transitional protection can claim means-tested benefits for him/herself and any dependants.[132a] A claimant with ELR or full refugee status cannot claim benefit for a dependant who is a PSIC, excluded from benefits by IAA s115. The asylum support adjudicators have considered a case where a wife had been granted ELR and was receiving IS of £87.83 per week for herself and her eight-year-old son.[133] Her husband had joined her after 3 April 2000 and claimed asylum (and asylum support from NASS). The adjudicator found that the husband was not excluded from claiming asylum support, since his wife could not claim IS for him as her dependant. However, the NASS 'threshold' for support for that size of household was £83.97 and so he would probably be refused support on the ground that he was not destitute within the meaning of IAA 1999 s95.

Children born in the UK without leave

2.103 An asylum-seeker who is granted exceptional leave or refugee status may have a child born in the UK who has not yet applied for or been granted leave to remain here. Such a child is not a British citizen but does not need to obtain leave to enter or remain in the UK unless s/he leaves the UK with an intention to re-enter.[134] It seems that such a child is not excluded from any benefit claim because s/he does not fall within the IAA 1999 s115 definition of PSIC. A child born in the UK would normally be granted 'leave in line' with the leave granted to the parents if the parents apply to have the position regularised.

Community care grants

2.104 Asylum-seekers who are granted ELR or refugee status may be eligible for a community care grant payment from the Benefits Agency to enable them to set up home after receiving the favourable decision on their asylum claim. Social Fund Direction 4(a)(v) provides for the

---

132 See NASS policy bulletin 11.
132a See Asylum Support Adjudicator Decision ASA 00/08/0037.
133 ASA 00/09/0054.
134 HC 395 paras 305–308, see para 1.94.

payment of a community care grant to help a person 'set up home in the community as part of a planned resettlement programme following a period during which s/he has been without a settled way of life'. Social fund guidance[135] suggests that those who have been 'staying in temporary accommodation provided by the Home Office pending a decision on their application for asylum in this country' may fall within the definition of 'unsettled way of life'.

2.105   Although the provision is aimed at asylum-seekers who have been receiving support from NASS, there is no reason why it should not apply equally to those who were receiving interim support from local authorities. Many single asylum-seekers dependent on interim support receive all their support in kind with no cash payments. This should strengthen their claim for a community care grant. There may also be asylum-seekers who have been living 'an unsettled way of life' while staying with various friends and relatives who should be considered for a grant. The guidance states that the list at para 3070 is not exhaustive.[136]

Unfavourable Home Office decisions

2.106   An asylum-seeker whose application for asylum is refused, and who is not granted any other form of leave such as ELR, loses any entitlement to benefit unless s/he falls within a class of PSICs who are not excluded from benefits (see para 2.27 above), eg, family members of EEA nationals. Asylum-seekers may be eligible for asylum support or interim support pending an asylum appeal or, in the case of families, for as long as they have dependent children under 18 living with them in the UK. The procedure is for 'disbenefited' claimants to obtain a form to claim NASS support.[137] NASS have made arrangements with local authorities to assist with the completion of these forms in the case of families with dependent children. Single asylum-seekers who lose IS after an unsuccessful asylum appeal, or other unsuccessful applicants for leave to enter or remain in the UK, may be entitled to claim help under the community care provisions explained in chapter 7.

---

135   Social Fund Guidance manual, para 3070.
136   Ibid, para 3071.
137   See para 3.97.

Remedies[138]

2.107 The Social Security Act 1998 overhauled the social security adjudication and appeals system and reduced the time limit for appeals from three months to one month. The rules governing appeals are contained in the Social Security and Child Support (Decisions and Appeals) Regulations 1999 SI No 991 (SSCSDA Regs).

2.108 From 2 April 2001, HB and CTB appeals are governed by the Child Support, Pensions and Social Security Act 2000. The Act replaces the existing system of HB reviews to bring the local authority decision-making framework in line with other social security benefits.[139] There are transitional regulations[140] which provide that outstanding council tax benefit and HB decisions and appeals will be transferred to the new system from 1 April 2001 and 2 April 2001 respectively. The substantive regulations were not available at the time of writing, but the main changes are:

– local authorities make decisions on claims instead of determinations;
– internal reviews are replaced by revision, supersession and appeal to an appeal tribunal with new time limits;
– appeal from the tribunal on a point of law is to the social security commissioners, and from there to the Court of Appeal.

2.109 The information about remedies in relation to social security decisions will therefore apply to HB and CTB claims and appeals. Where HB has been incorrectly refused, the claimant should bring a separate HB appeal even if there is a social security appeal on the same issue, eg, the HR test, or the meaning of 'lawfully present'.

Challenging a decision

Revision and supersession of decisions

2.110 The Social Security Act 1998 replaced the procedure of challenging a decision by requesting a 'review' with 'revision and supersession'

---

138 A detailed explanation of the social security appeals system is outside the scope of this book and advisers may wish to refer to the publications listed in Appendix H.
139 HB and CTB Circular A37/2000.
140 HB and CTB (Decisions and Appeals) Savings and Transitional Provisions Regulations 2000.

of decisions. A revision is more advantageous to the claimant because, unlike supersession, payment is backdated to the original decision.

'Any grounds' revision

2.111   Where a claimant is refused benefit s/he can request a written state-ment of reasons for the decision. A claimant may request a 'revision' of a decision on 'any grounds' within one month of the original decision.[141] This time limit is extended by 14 days if written reasons for the decision are requested. It runs from the date of receiving decisions in HB cases.

2.112   The time limit can be extended within 13 months if: the applica-tion has merit; there are special circumstances which meant that it was not practicable to request a revision within the time limit; and if it reasonable to grant the request.[142]

'Any time' revision

2.113   A claimant can request a revision at any time if there is an official error, such as an error of law or evidence of entitlement which another office failed to provide, or if there is no right of appeal against the decision.

Supersession

2.114   A claimant can ask for the decision of the decision-maker, the appeal tribunal or the commissioner to be superseded if there are no grounds for it to be revised. The grounds for supersession include an error of law, ignorance or mistake of relevant facts, or a change of circumstances.[143] A revision can be sought of the supersession decision, or an appeal, if it is a decision from which an appeal lies.

Appeals

2.115   The social security appeal tribunal does not have jurisdiction to hear appeals about certain matters. These are set out in SSCSDA Regs Sch 2 (see also DMG). Benefit decisions which are not appealable include:

 – reciprocal agreements with countries outside the UK;

141   SSCSDA reg 3(1)(b).
142   Ibid, reg 4.
143   Social Security Act 1998 s10.

- a child's temporary absence abroad for child benefit purposes;
- authorisation on the application of social security schemes to employed or self-employed people and members of their families moving within the EC;[144]
- whether to pay expenses to any person under Social Security Administration Act 1992 s180 (travelling expenses to benefits offices).

2.116   An appeal can be brought at the same time as a request for a revision, but this is not essential because the decision will automatically be reconsidered when an appeal is entered. If the Benefits Agency revises the decision, the appeal is treated as lapsed.

2.117   A valid appeal must be received by the relevant Benefits Agency office within one month of the date of the original decision, or of the written statement of receiving reasons for the decision.[145] Where a statement of reasons was requested by the claimant but has not been sent, an additional 14 days may be added to the one-month time limit.

2.118   For an appeal to be valid, it must be signed by the claimant, or by his/her appointee or a legal representative (if authorised in writing by the claimant). It should include enough details about the decision which is being appealed against for it to be identifiable, ie, the benefit which is the subject matter of the appeal and the date of the decision. It should include the grounds for the appeal. The appeal should be on the appropriate appeal form (GL24) although this is not essential.

2.119   After an appeal is accepted as valid, the Benefits Agency will prepare the decision-maker's submissions and send these and an inquiry form (TAS 1) to the appellant and representative, if any. An oral hearing must be requested by completing and returning the form TAS 1 to the local appeals service within 14 days of receipt. Otherwise the appeal may be considered without an oral hearing. If an interpreter is needed, it should be requested at this stage. An appeal can be struck out if the form is not returned.

Late appeals

2.120   Time can be extended for the appeal within 13 months (one month plus 12 months of the original decision) if there are reasonable prospects of success and it is 'in the interests of justice' for a late appeal to be

---

144   Council Reg 1408/71 arts 22(1) and 55(1).
145   SSCSDA reg 31(1)(a).

allowed, ie, death or serious illness of spouse or dependant, disruption of the post, or wholly exceptional circumstances.[146] Where the
deadline for an appeal has been missed, a fresh claim, a revision or
supersession should be considered. There is no time limit for
supersession.

Emergencies[147]

2.121   The ordinary procedure for challenging social security decisions is by
an appeal to the social security appeal tribunal and from there to the
commissioner. This is unsuitable in most cases involving asylum-
seekers and PSICs, because it is too slow. Where a case is urgent, a
letter can be written to the Appeals Service to ask a chairman of the
tribunal to exercise the discretion to allow an expedited appeal. In
particularly urgent cases where the claimant has no other means of
support, judicial review may be appropriate, whether of the original
decision or of the refusal to exercise the discretion to expedite the
hearing. A letter before action to the DSS Solicitor (Treasury Solicitor)
may be effective (see Appendix H for address). In some cases, eg,
delay in obtaining NINO, the use of internal complaints procedures
by writing to customer services may produce a quick response.

Challenging an appeal tribunal decision

2.122   If an appeal is unsuccessful, the appellant may request full written
reasons for the decision within one month of the hearing. There is a
right to appeal to the commissioner for social security and child support if the tribunal has made 'an error of law'.

The meaning of 'error of law' has been interpreted by the
commissioners in R(A) 1/72 and R(SB) 11/83 as meaning:

– where the law was misinterpreted or incorrectly applied;
– a lack of evidence to support the decision;
– perversity;
– breach of the rules of natural justice;
– inadequate findings of fact or reasons.

2.123   Leave to appear may be sought from the chairman of the tribunal
within a month of the appeal or receipt of the written decision by
either the appellant or the Home Secretary. An out-of-time applica-

---

146   Ibid, reg 32(4–6).
147   See also paras 2.77–2.79.

tion for leave may be sought within one year of the appeal decision if there are 'special reasons'.

2.124   The appellant's grounds of appeal must be attached to the application for leave. If leave is refused a renewed application can be made to the social security commissioner. If leave is granted there are 42 days to serve a notice of appeal. The commissioner can correct irregularities in the notice. There is an appeal from the social security commissioner to the Court of Appeal, again, on the ground of error of law.

2.125   A certificate for public funding for representation is not generally available for commissioner appeals. This may be a breach of the HRA 1998 and article 6 of the Human Rights Convention. Funding has been granted in cases involving complex EC law issues and should be available in cases based on HRA arguments. Commissioners' decisions are binding on the social security tribunal but not on other commissioners.

Complaints and compensation[148]

2.126   A complaint and/or request for an ex gratia or extra-statutory payment would be appropriate where a claimant has suffered due to the Benefits Agency's administrative delays, inefficiency or negligent advice.[149] Examples include a failure to offer interpreting facilities, incorrect advice that an applicant is not eligible for benefits, delays in processing NINO applications. Benefits Agency complaints should be made at first instance to the office supervisor and then up though the customer service manager of the Benefit Agency office, the District Manager and the Chief Executive of the Benefits Agency. A letter from a local MP to support the complaint usually ensures a response. If redress is not provided, a complaint could be made to the Parliamentary Ombudsman.

---

148 See Appendix H for relevant addresses. However, see also note 25 re changing titles of Agencies.
149 Claims for compensation for maladministration are dealt with by the Benefits Agency Chief Executive, Quarry House, Quarry Hill, Leeds, LS2 7UA.

CHAPTER 3

Asylum support eligibility

For complete chapter contents, see overleaf

Introduction

3.1   The 'asylum support' scheme, which was established by Immigration
and Asylum Act (IAA) 1999 Part VI is outlined in this chapter and in
chapter 4. The scheme replaced mainstream welfare provision with a
safety-net of minimal living expenses and/or housing for asylum-
seekers and their dependants. The Asylum Support Regulations (AS
Regs) 2000,[1] made under powers in IAA 1999 Sch 8, contain the
details of the scheme.

3.2   Decisions about *eligibility* for asylum support are made by the
National Asylum Support Service (NASS). NASS is part of the Home
Office's Immigration and Nationality Directorate (IND) and so
decisions about asylum support are formally made by the Home
Secretary. NASS assesses whether a destitute asylum-seeker is *eligible*
for 'asylum support'. *Provision* of support is then arranged, through
contracts with the private and public and voluntary sectors.

3.3   Chapter 3 explains who is eligible for asylum support, assessment
procedures, refusal or withdrawal of support and remedies. It ends by
considering other forms of support for those who are not eligible for
Part VI asylum support. Chapter 4 considers service provision including the kind and level of support provided and adequacy of accommodation. It then looks at ancillary procedures and criminal offences.

3.4   'Asylum support' is distinguished here from 'interim support'
provided by local authorities, (normally social services), under the
Asylum Support (Interim Provisions) Regulations 1999,[2] which we
refer to as 'the Interim Regs'. Interim support is discussed in detail in
chapter 5.

3.5   The Asylum Support Adjudicators consider appeals against the
refusal or withdrawal of asylum support. Their decisions are to be
published on a website.[3] NASS has produced an internal instruction
manual in the form of policy bulletins covering eligibility and
administration of the scheme, which are referred to where relevant.
The instructions are not publicly available but NASS will provide
specific information under the Data Protection Act 1998[4] and may
charge for it.

1   SI No 704.
2   SI No 3056.
3   See Appendix H.

Key features of the asylum support scheme

3.6   The main features of the asylum support scheme as provided by IAA
       1999 Part VI and the AS Regs 2000 are:

- The Home Secretary *may* provide support for 'asylum-seekers and
  their dependants' who appear to be destitute or to be likely to
  become destitute within a period prescribed as 14 days, or 56 days
  if they are already receiving asylum support.[5]

- The Home Secretary *must* provide support if the asylum-seeker
  has dependent children and the household is destitute, since
  the family is excluded from Children Act 1989 s17 help.[6]
  Unaccompanied asylum-seekers under 18 are not eligible for
  asylum support but can obtain social services help under s20 of
  the Children Act 1989.[7] After 18 they may be entitled to continue
  receiving 'advice, befriending and assistance' under Children Act
  1989 s24.

- 'Asylum-seeker' and 'dependant' are defined by IAA 1999 s94(1).

- IAA 1999 s95 (under which the AS Regs 2000 were made) provides that a person is destitute if s/he does not have adequate
  accommodation or cannot meet other 'essential' living needs for
  him/herself and any dependants.[8]

- Whether a person is 'destitute' is to be decided by the Home
  Secretary whose functions are carried out by decision-makers at
  NASS. Temporary support may be provided under IAA 1999 s98,
  by voluntary sector reception assistants, while NASS considers
  whether a household is eligible for s95 support.

- 'Support' means both accommodation adequate to the household's needs, and essential living expenses. Essential living needs
  will normally be provided for mainly in kind, with a cash element,
  unless there are exceptional circumstances.[9]

- In providing support, NASS must have regard to certain factors
  (the household's actual and potential resources and the cost
  of provision) and is required to disregard other matters (any

---

4 Code of Practice on Access para 7.
5 IAA 1999 s95(1) and AS reg 7.
6 IAA 1999 s122.
7 Some local authorities consider that support is provided under Children Act
   1989 s17 (see chapter 7).
8 IAA 1999 s95(3) and AS regs 5, 8 and 9.
9 IAA 1999 s96 and AS reg 10.

preference as to the location of accommodation, its nature and its fixtures and fittings) but this does not prevent individual circumstances from being taken into account.[10]

– Regulation 20 provides that support *may* be suspended or discontinued if the supported person or any dependant has (i) broken conditions of support, (ii) committed a criminal offence under Part VI of the Act, (iii) made himself 'intentionally destitute', (iv) left the authorised address, or (v) been away from the address without permission for longer than seven consecutive days or 14 days in a six-month period.

Asylum support or interim support?

3.7   Responsibility for destitute asylum-seekers is shared between NASS and local authorities. NASS did not have capacity to assess and arrange support for all asylum-seekers on 3 April 2000, the date when the AS Regs came into force. As a result, local authorities were asked to continue providing for certain categories of asylum-seekers under the Interim Regs. NASS initially provided asylum support to destitute asylum-seekers who had claimed asylum 'on arrival' in the UK on or after 3 April 2000. In Scotland and Northern Ireland all asylum-seekers who applied for asylum after 2 April 2000 were eligible for NASS support, whether they were 'on-arrival' or 'in-country' applicants.

3.8   Destitute asylum-seekers who claimed asylum in-country on or after 3 April 2000 continued to be eligible to claim interim support from local authorities only, rather than NASS. Later, in-country applicants were eligible for NASS support, depending on where they were living in England and Wales, and the date of their asylum claim (see table below). Those who were being supported by local authorities or who claimed asylum before the relevant dates remained their responsibility under the Interim Regs[11] (see chapter 5).

3.9   The Home Secretary made directions[12] stating when NASS would assume responsibility for providing support to newly presenting

10   AS regs 12 and 13.
11   The Asylum Support Adjudicator has confirmed that the household must have been *in receipt of*, not merely eligible for, local authority support under National Assistance Act 1948 s21 or Children Act 1989 s17. See ASA 00/11/0118.
12   Directions No 1 (made on 13 March 2000), No 2, No 2A (made on 10 April 2000) and No 3 (made on 11 July 2000) under IAA 1999 Sch 15, para 14(1).

Asylum-seekers who are eligible to claim asylum support from NASS	Asylum-seekers who are eligible to claim interim support from a local authority
Applied for asylum on arrival in the UK on or after 3 April 2000	Applied for asylum on arrival before 3 April 2000, received negative asylum decision (and so lost eligibility for benefits) before 25 September 2000
Applied for asylum in-country on or after 3 April 2000 while living in Scotland or Northern Ireland	
Applied for asylum in-country on or after 3 April 2000, was detained at Oakington detention centre and then released	
Living in the area of Kent County Council or Medway Council and applied for asylum in-country or received notice of a refusal of asylum (and so lost entitlement to income support) on or after 17 April 2000	All in-country applicants who claimed asylum in England or Wales before 24 July 2000 (except for those living in Kent who were only eligible to claim interim support before 17 April 2000)
In-country asylum-seekers living in London who claimed asylum on or after 24 July 2000	
In-country asylum-seekers living in the North East, Yorkshire, Humberside and Wales who claimed asylum on or after 31 July 2000	In-country asylum-seekers living in the North East, Yorkshire, Humberside or Wales who claimed asylum before 31 July 2000
In-country applicants living in the West Midlands and Sussex who claimed asylum on or after 29 August 2000	In-country asylum-seekers living in the West Midlands or Sussex who claimed asylum before 29 August 2000
All 'disbenefited' cases in England and Wales who were notified of a refusal of asylum on or after 25 September 2000,[14] ie, applicants who are refused income support due to a negative decision on their asylum claim (applies to on-arrival and country of upheaval cases only)	Disbenefited 'in-country' asylum-seekers who have lost entitlement to benefits, eg, those who have been receiving benefit since before 5 February 1996

asylum-seekers. The timetable was also announced in parliamentary statements.[13] The relevant date is the date of the claim for asylum, not the date of the claim for support. Unless otherwise stated, the time-table assumes either that the asylum claim has not yet been decided or that there is an outstanding asylum appeal.

3.10   Unaccompanied asylum-seeker children under 18 are not eligible for asylum support, but are entitled to social services help under the Children Act 1989.[15] There has been some debate about cases where a destitute asylum-seeker is eligible for NASS support but is 'in need of care and attention' because of community care needs.[16] In *Westminster CC v NASS*,[16a] the Court of Appeal upheld a decision by NASS that social services were responsible for housing a disabled asylum-seeker with community care needs. Households with s21 needs may prefer to seek a community care assessment and services.

Mixed households[17]

3.11   Eligibility for support is more complicated if an asylum-seeker comes to the UK to join a household which is already in receipt of interim support (chapter 5) or income support (chapter 2). If the later arrival comes within the definition of 'dependant' for interim support purposes, for example, s/he will not normally be eligible for asylum support but will be eligible for interim support. This is explained in the relevant chapters.

---

13   *Hansard*, HC Debates cols 556–558W, 16 March 2000; HC Debates col 6, 10 April 2000.

14   Although the direction was made to transfer disbenefited cases on 25 September 2000, the arrangements for access to NASS support are slightly different for this category. If they have a dependent child, they must approach the local authority (which acts as an agent for NASS) for assistance with making the claim. See further para 3.97.

15   There is some debate about whether this should be under s17 or s20 of the Children Act 1989. See further chapter 7.

16   Within the meaning of National Assistance Act 1948, s21. See chapter 7.

16a *Westminster CC v National Asylum Support Service* CO/4738/2000, 27 February 2001, QBD; (2001) 4 CCLR 143, CA.

17   There is a comprehensive outline of the correct approach to mixed households in NASS Policy Bulletin 11.

Eligibility for support

3.12   Under IAA 1999 s95(1):

> The Secretary of State may provide, or arrange for the provision of support for–
>
> (a) asylum-seekers, or
> (b) dependants of asylum-seekers,
>
> who appear to the Secretary of State to be destitute or to be likely to become destitute within such a period as may be prescribed.

3.13   Both the IAA and the AS Regs are drafted so that the provision of support is a power rather than a duty. Since there was a clear parliamentary intention to establish an entitlement to support,[17a] this should not have any effect on most applications for support. It may have some implications where there is a judicial review of decisions relating to support provision.[18]

3.14   There is a slightly different test of eligibility for temporary support under IAA 1999 s98 which is provided pending a decision on full s95 asylum support. Temporary support may be provided for:

> (a) asylum-seekers or
> (b) dependants of asylum-seekers,
>
> who it appears to the Secretary of State may be destitute.[19]

3.15   An asylum-seeker is eligible for temporary support if the household appears to have an immediate need for housing and support. Therefore, an asylum-seeker who appears likely to become destitute within 14 days, but not immediately, is entitled to asylum support under s95(1)(b) but not to temporary support under s98. The difference is not significant because temporary support is provided as a stop-gap until there is time to carry out a full assessment, and in every other respect the test of eligibility is the same – ss95(2)–(11) apply to an assessment of the temporary support duty.[20]

3.16   There are three basic steps in assessing whether an applicant is eligible for s95 asylum support:

- Is the applicant an 'asylum-seeker' or the 'dependant' of an asylum-seeker?

17a See, for example, Lord Williams of Mostyn, *Hansard*, HL Debates, 28 July 1999 cited in *Westminster V NASS*, CO/4738/2000, 27 February 2001, QBD.
18 See further remedies at para 3.140 below.
19 IAA 1999 s98(1).
20 Ibid, s98(3).

- Is the applicant excluded from support?
- Is the household destitute, ie, without a home or living expenses?

Is the applicant an 'asylum-seeker' or the 'dependant of an asylum-seeker'?

3.17   Only asylum-seekers and their dependants as defined by s94(1) may receive asylum support. Other categories of immigrants are not eligible, even if they are completely destitute, because IAA 1999 Part VI excludes 'persons subject to immigration control' from social security benefits and most other welfare provision. If they have a dependant 'child in need' they could apply for help under Children Act 1989 s17. Anyone with a need related to age, disability, illness or pregnancy, ie, not solely in need due to lack of accommodation and income, may be eligible for help under National Assistance Act 1948 s21 (see further chapter 7).

3.18   In the context of asylum support, the terms 'asylum-seeker' and 'dependant of an asylum-seeker' have a different meaning from their ordinary immigration law meaning.[21]

Meaning of 'asylum-seeker'

3.19   An 'asylum-seeker' for asylum support purposes is a person aged 18 or over who has 'made a claim for asylum which has been recorded by the Secretary of State but which has not been determined'.[22] A claim for asylum includes an appeal. A child under 18 who claims asylum in his/her own right is an 'asylum-seeker' for immigration law purposes only. If the child is in the UK without his/her parents and has an outstanding asylum application as an 'unaccompanied minor' s/he is entitled to housing and support under the Children Act 1989 and not under the s95 asylum support provisions.

3.20   A claim for asylum for support purposes is defined as either 'a claim that it would be contrary to the UK's obligations under the Refugee Convention, or under article 3 of the Human Rights Convention for that person to be removed from or required to leave the United Kingdom'.[23] Asylum-seekers who lose an ordinary claim for refugee status under the Refugee Convention may be able to make a

21 Ibid, s94(1).
22 Ibid, s94(1).
23 Ibid, s94(1).

free-standing article 3 claim or may raise article 3 arguments in the appeal.[24]

3.21   Where an ordinary asylum or other immigration application has been refused and an article 3 claim is being made (which allows a claim for asylum support), it is important that it is made at the earliest possible opportunity.[25] As part of the current procedure for appealing against a refusal of asylum, the asylum-seeker should state any additional Human Rights Convention grounds for wishing to stay in the UK.

3.22   Human Rights Convention points must be considered at any 'one-stop' appeal. The Human Rights Act (HRA) 1998 and Convention do not preclude an asylum-seeker from making a fresh article 3 claim after the appeal. However, in the absence of any new circumstances, the Home Office could simply refuse such a claim and rely on IAA 1999 s74(7) to refuse an appeal. The applicant is treated as an asylum-seeker entitled to support provided there is an article 3 claim 'which has not been determined'. If the article 3 claim had been refused at the appeal it seems to follow that the applicant would fall outside this definition. There may be exceptional circumstances which would require consideration of a fresh article 3 claim after an unsuccessful appeal, eg, if the political situation in the country of origin changed radically or if the applicant had suddenly developed a life-threatening medical condition.

3.23   The article 3 claim must be a claim which has been recorded by the Home Secretary (ie, the Home Office) to trigger an asylum support duty.[26] The meaning of this has not yet been decided by the courts and a solicitor's letter received by the IND should therefore satisfy the requirement.

Date of determination[27]

3.24   The 'date of determination' is not simply the date of the asylum decision or the date on which an asylum-seeker receives the decision. It is a date prescribed for the purposes of IAA 1999 s94(3) by the AS Regs. In a household without dependent children under 18, any asylum-seeker stops being an 'asylum-seeker' for support purposes 14 days after the Home Secretary notifies the asylum claimant of the

---

24 See chapter 1.
25 See further para 1.48.
26 IAA 1999 s94(1).
27 See para 1.80 for detailed explanation of 'date of determination'.

asylum decision or, if there is an appeal, 14 days after any appeal is disposed of.[28]

3.25   If the decision has been sent to the asylum-seeker or his/her representative by post, it is assumed it has been received on the second day after the day it was posted.[29] This applies even if it has been posted to the asylum-seeker's representative but not received by the asylum-seeker. Since asylum support stops 14 days later unless there is an appeal, it is important for representatives to pass on notification promptly. Asylum-seekers will need to keep in touch with their immigration advisers, which may be difficult, particularly for those who are living in dispersal areas, since the AS Regs do not make any extra provision for this expense.[30]

Meaning of 'determination'[31]

3.26   The determination is not the 'pre-decision letter' notifying the asylum-seeker that refugee status has been refused without reasons. The determination is the letter giving full reasons for the refusal and allowing an appeal or the appeal decision itself.

Households with dependent children

3.27   If an asylum-seeker has a dependent child under 18, s/he continues to be treated as an 'asylum-seeker' for as long as the child is under 18 and they both remain in the UK.[32] The meaning of dependent child is explained below. This means that 'failed' asylum-seeker households with dependent children are entitled to asylum support, rather than help under Children Act 1989 s17, for as long as the family is in the UK. If the asylum-seeker has been refused asylum and has either failed to appeal or appealed unsuccessfully, s/he will stop being treated as an asylum-seeker for support purposes if the child leaves the UK or reaches 18. S/he will otherwise only cease to be an asylum-seeker for support purposes if asylum or exceptional leave to enter or remain in the UK is granted, in which case the 14-day prescribed period applies (see para 3.24).

---

28   AS reg 2(2).
29   IAA 1999 s94(9).
30   Although the LSC makes some provision for travel to solicitors. See further para 3.67.
31   See further para 1.80.
32   IAA 1999 s94(5).

Meaning of 'dependant'

3.28 'Dependant' in relation to an asylum-seeker or supported person has a particular meaning for asylum support purposes which is set out in IAA 1999 s94 and AS reg 2(4). The definition is differently drafted in the Interim Regs, which allow for a wider category of dependants. Where additional family members arrive to join an applicant receiving interim support, they would be expected to apply for interim support as part of that household if they were eligible.[33] There may be limited circumstances in which they would be eligible for asylum support, eg, an adult disabled family member might arrive in the UK, claim asylum and form a separate household from the household in receipt of interim support.

3.29 The definition of dependant can be important, eg, in cases where family members arrive in the UK separately. If a family member is not treated as a dependant s/he could be dispersed to a different part of the UK from other relatives claiming NASS support.

Whose dependant?

3.30 The claim for asylum support can be made either by the asylum-seeker or by any dependant.[34] 'Dependant' is defined by AS reg 2(4) as the dependant of 'an asylum-seeker, the supported person or an applicant for asylum support'. Where the applicant for support is him/herself a dependant of the asylum-seeker, his/her dependants must also be dependants of the asylum-seeker to fall within the AS reg 2(4) definition. Unlike the position under the Interim Regs, a dependant of a dependant does not otherwise come within the definition. So if the asylum-seeker is in detention and his/her 17-year-old daughter makes a claim for support as his/her dependant, it appears that s/he cannot claim support for his/her own dependant, eg, husband or son, unless he is also a dependant of the asylum-seeker.

Categories of dependants

3.31 The categories of dependants are:

Husband or wife

3.32 The regulations use the term 'spouse' which is limited to a 'married

---

33 AS reg 4(4)(a).
34 Ibid, reg 3(1).

couple', defined as 'a man and woman who are married to each other and are members of the same household'.[35]

3.33   A husband or wife, unlike a partner in an unmarried couple, will be treated as a dependant even if the couple have not been living together before they applied for support together. In cases where a husband or wife arrives in the UK after a spouse who is receiving asylum support, a new application for support could be made. Both husband and wife may have made an asylum claim in their own right in which case they may need to provide evidence of the marriage to NASS. If the spouse is treated as a dependant for the purposes of the husband's or the wife's asylum claim, then the evidence accepted by the IND should be accepted by NASS.

Dependent child under 18

3.34   The child must be under 18 on the date of the application for asylum support or on the date when s/he joined a supported household. S/he will qualify as a dependant if:

- s/he is a child of the applicant or of the applicant's spouse and dependent on the applicant; or
- s/he is a member of the close family of the applicant or the applicant's spouse provided the child has been living as part of the applicant's household since birth or for six of the 12 months before this application for support.

3.35   Therefore, 'dependant' includes all close blood relatives of the husband or wife who are under 18 at the date of their claim regardless of length of residence. It appears that a child who has been adopted, whether formally or informally, should come within the definition of 'close family'. Dependant includes any child, related or unrelated, who has been living as part of the household for six months in the year preceding the claim for support provided they are under 18 at the date they ask to be included in the claim. Where a couple are unmarried, it could be argued that the child of a dependant partner is a member of the asylum-seeker's close family.

Disabled family member over 18

3.36   The family member will qualify as a dependant if s/he is 'in need of care and attention from the applicant or a member of his household by reason of a disability', and:

---

35   Ibid, reg 2(1).

– s/he is a child of the applicant or of the applicant's spouse and dependent on the applicant; or
– s/he is a member of the close family of the applicant or the applicant's spouse provided s/he has been living as part of the applicant's household since birth or for six of the 12 months before this application for support.

3.37   Therefore, an adult who has a disability or mental health condition can be treated as part of the household, despite the fact that s/he is over 18.[36] The term 'in need of care and attention' comes from National Assistance Act 1948 s21(1)(a).[37] In cases where there is a dispute, it may be helpful to refer to case-law interpreting s21(1)(a).

Unmarried couples

3.38   An unmarried couple means a heterosexual couple who can show they have been living together for two of the three years before the application for support or before the joint application if they arrived in the UK separately. 'Unmarried couple' is defined as 'a man and woman who though not married to each other, are living together as if married'.[38]

3.39   There have now been several asylum claims in which the Home Office has granted refugee status or exceptional leave to enter or remain on the basis of persecution on the ground of sexuality. The exclusion of same-sex couples therefore appears irrational and open to a judicial review with HRA arguments under Human Rights Convention articles 8 and 14 (breach of right to respect for family life and discrimination on the grounds of sexual orientation).

3.40   Some unmarried partners with long-term relationships may not satisfy the 'two out of the last three years' rule, eg, where they have been separated in civil war or while fleeing from their country of origin. If an unmarried heterosexual partner is not treated as a dependant then a HRA challenge arguing article 8 and article 14 (discrimination on the basis of unmarried status) may be appropriate.

Supported as a dependent child before the IAA 1999 came into force

3.41   Anyone who is living as part of the applicant's household and was receiving assistance from a local authority under Children Act 1989 s17 immediately before 6 December 1999 (the date when the Interim

36   Ibid, reg 2(4)(e).
37   See para 7.47.
38   AS reg 2(1).

Regs came into force) will qualify as a dependant. This category ensures that children whose parents were receiving social services' help because they were under 18, can be supported as dependants rather than adult children being required to make separate claims for support in their own right.[39] In most cases such households would continue to be eligible for interim support rather than asylum support. This (like clause (h) which applies to Scotland and Northern Ireland) is a 'mopping up' clause in anticipation of interim support cases being transferred to the asylum support scheme.

Treated as a dependant by the IND

3.42   Anyone who has made a claim for leave to enter or remain in the UK, or for variation of any such leave, which is being considered on the basis that s/he is dependent on the asylum-seeker, will automatically be treated as a dependant of the asylum-seeker for asylum support purposes.[40] This can be demonstrated by the applicant's immigration documents. If the asylum-seeker has a Home Office standard acknowledgement letter (SAL), the photographs and details of dependants will normally appear on the back of the SAL. This category extends to dependants for the purposes of the immigration claim even if they would otherwise be excluded from qualifying as dependants for support purposes, eg, same-sex partners.

'The relevant time'

3.43   Whether the family member is 'a dependant' should be judged at 'the relevant time', which is the date of the application for asylum support. Where another family member arrives in the UK or joins the supported household after arrival, the relevant time is the date of joining a person who is already a supported person.[41]

Problems arising from who can be treated as 'a dependant'

3.44   Regulation 2(5) raises some practical and Human Rights Convention, article 8 (right to respect for family life) questions because of the limits on who can be classed as a dependant. For example, it seems to exclude a dependent sibling of the asylum-seeker's partner if s/he has not been living with the household for the previous six months.

---

39   Ibid, reg 2(4)(g).
40   Ibid, reg 2(4)(i).
41   Ibid, reg 2(6).

There is a solution to these difficulties when the family member qualifies as a 'dependant' because s/he is treated as dependant for the purposes of the asylum claim.[42] However, this may not assist if family members have arrived in the UK at different times and/or if there is more than one claim for asylum.

3.45 The effects of AS reg 2 can be seen in an appeal to the Asylum Support Adjudicator[43] brought by an Afghan asylum-seeker who wanted to be treated as part of the same household as his three nephews aged between 23 and 29. NASS had withdrawn support under AS reg 20(1) on the grounds that the uncle had breached the conditions subject to which support was provided, ie, he had failed to travel to Hull, and because the nephews were not members of his immediate family. One of the nephews was in Kent, suffering from depression and anxiety, the other two had previously been dispersed to Wolverhampton. The appellant argued that he had a 'reasonable excuse' for refusing to be dispersed alone. The Asylum Support Adjudicator allowed the appeal, accepting the argument that he had a family duty and a cultural duty to care for and support his nephews who spoke no English, and noted that all of them had been in the UK for less than three weeks at the date of NASS's decision.

3.46 Refugee organisations lobbied for the IAA 1999 definition of dependant to encompass the extended family arrangements which exist in many refugee households. The provisions were amended to reflect this in part, but they still exclude household members from the definition. For example, an asylum-seeker might regard younger brothers and sisters from whom s/he had temporarily been separated as part of the household. In such cases there are two possible approaches. One option is to negotiate with NASS for the household to be supported or accommodated together, even though NASS may process two separate applications. An asylum support appeal would only be available if the asylum-seeker refuses to be dispersed to a part of the UK away from the family member or leaves accommodation to be near a family member, and if NASS then withdraws support under AS reg 20(1). If the householders are accommodated separately in different parts of the UK, a judicial review of the adequacy of the accommodation offered could be considered relying on the HRA, arguing that dispersal is a breach of the article 8 right to respect for family life (see para 8.55 onwards).

---

42 Ibid, reg 2(4)(i).
43 ASA 00/11/0110.

Who can apply for support?

3.47   The person applying for support may be either the asylum-seeker or his/her dependant(s). The explanatory notes to the Act (at para 270) give the example of a dependant claiming support if the asylum-seeker is in detention. There are a number of other circumstances where the dependants may need to claim or continue to receive support while temporarily or even permanently separated from the asylum-seeker. A dependent wife can claim support for herself and her dependent children after a relationship breakdown, although she should be advised of the implications for her immigration status.

Is the applicant excluded from support?[44]

3.48   An asylum-seeker is excluded from consideration for asylum support or temporary support if the whole household is *eligible to claim* **means-tested social security benefits or local authority support under the Interim Regs. The relevant social security benefits are income support, income-based jobseeker's allowance, housing benefit and council tax benefit. The exclusion applies even if a local authority has refused, suspended or terminated interim support unless refusal is due to ineligibility rather than, say, intentional destitution (see para 3.112 below). An applicant is also excluded if at the time of the asylum support application, NASS decides s/he does not come within the definition of 'asylum-seeker' or 'dependant on an asylum-seeker' which is explained above.**

Exclusion of single adult asylum-seekers

3.49   An adult asylum-seeker may be excluded from asylum support even if he is homeless and not actually receiving any interim support or benefits. See para 8.77 on advising adults in this position.

Exclusion of families

3.50   An asylum-seeker can claim asylum support even if one or more dependants are eligible for means-tested social security benefits. If an asylum-seeker is in receipt of social security benefits and is joined by dependants for social security purposes, the benefits can be

---

44   AS reg 4. NASS Policy Bulletin 11 also provides an outline. See also refusal or termination of support at para 3.99 below.

increased. If a non-asylum-seeker is in receipt of benefits, s/he cannot include a new asylum-seeker dependant. Such a dependant could apply for asylum support and the benefits would be taken into account as resources. Therefore, an application will not necessarily be excluded on the ground that some, but not all, of the household are eligible for means-tested benefits. This enables an asylum-seeker to claim asylum support including housing for the whole family including family members who are already in the UK receiving benefits.

3.51   The applicant for support still needs to satisfy the strict test of destitution. NASS decided that an asylum-seeker was excluded from support because his wife, who had exceptional leave to remain, was receiving £87.83 income support per week for herself and her son aged eight. In appeal number 00/09/0054, the Asylum Support Adjudicator noted that the household's income was more than the £83.97 per week essential living needs provided by NASS to a family of that size. So although NASS had incorrectly decided that her husband was excluded from asylum support, the Home Secretary was directed to revise the decision (and by implication decide that the applicant was not destitute).

Is the applicant destitute?

3.52   An applicant will be destitute *either* if s/he does not have access to 'adequate accommodation' *or* if s/he cannot meet the 'essential living needs' of him/herself and any dependant(s).[45] Therefore, an asylum-seeker may be living with friends and simply need help with living expenses, or s/he may have enough money to cover living expenses but need help with housing. The prescribed matters which the Home Secretary must consider in assessing destitution are contained in the AS Regs.

3.53   The steps in the assessment process are as follows:

– What income and assets are available to the applicant during the prescribed period?
– Can the applicant meet the essential living needs of the asylum-seeker and any dependant(s)?
– Does the applicant have adequate accommodation for him/herself and any dependants?

45 IAA 1999 s95(3).

- Can the applicant meet essential living needs and secure adequate accommodation until after the end of the prescribed period?

What income and assets are available to the applicant?[46]

3.54   Asylum support provided by NASS[47] or temporary support provided by reception assistants[48] must be ignored in assessing resources.

3.55   Any income, support or assets which the asylum support applicant, the supported person or any dependant has or 'might reasonably be expected to have' in the prescribed period must be taken into account. This includes assets outside the UK if they are available or might reasonably be expected to become available.[49]

3.56   It is difficult to see how notional help from friends and family can be assessed in practice and there is no specific provision for this in the regulations themselves. The explanatory notes to the Act (para 282) suggest that this includes resources to which an asylum-seeker might be expected to have access, eg, from friends and family in the UK. The Home Office Consultation paper[50] says this applies to cases where support is *being provided* by **friends and relatives or other sources. The intention seems to be to take account of support that family and friends are willing and can reasonably afford to provide. This should be distinguished from the emergency support which family or friends cannot really afford, but may offer on a humanitarian basis to prevent physical or mental injury. The schedule to the regulations asks applicants to provide information about any support that friends or relatives are giving at the time of application, as well as any financial support that friends or relatives can give.**

3.57   A Zimbabwean asylum-seeker who was released from Oakington successfully appealed against NASS's decision that she was not destitute because she had £100 in travellers' cheques.[51] The Asylum Support Adjudicator accepted evidence that the money was not available to her – she could not cash the cheques because her passport was held by the Immigration Service and she had no money to contact them and retrieve it.

---

46   AS reg 6.
47   IAA 1999 s95.
48   Ibid, s98.
49   AS reg 6(4).
50   NASS 'Consultation Document on the Main Regulations under Part VI of the Immigration and Asylum Act 1999', November 1999, para 21 (www.homeoffice.gov.uk/ind/assd/assd.htm).
51   ASA 00/09/0065.

3.58   There have been a number of asylum support appeals in cases where the asylum-seeker has arrived in the UK with savings over NASS's limits, and asylum support has been refused. Where the application for asylum support is for living expenses only, NASS will refuse support if the asylum-seeker's assets exceed the relevant asylum support amount for 14 days' living expenses. Where the application is for accommodation and living expenses, there are fixed amounts depending on the household size.

3.59   Where the asylum-seeker arrives in the UK with savings and spends some of the money, the approach taken to date by the Asylum Support Adjudicators has been to allow only small amounts to be spent on clothing, particularly in cases where the appellant is unable to produce receipts. A 37-year-old Iranian woman who arrived in the UK with her seven-year-old daughter and without luggage was refused asylum support for living expenses because she had £258.34. In her written appeal she explained she had spent £223 on buying basic clothes for herself and her child.[52] The Adjudicator decided that £40 for the mother and £30 for the daughter would have been realistic for basic clothing. Since the asylum support she would have received for essential living needs for 14 days was £126.28, he found that she was not destitute at the date of the application and dismissed her appeal. It is regrettable that the appellant was not represented at an oral hearing where evidence could have been given about the difficulties which a newly arrived asylum-seeker might have in obtaining cheap replacement clothes in London.

3.60   In a case where a Zimbabwean woman who had spent £109 on warm clothes was refused asylum support for subsistence and accommodation, the Chief Adjudicator 'was prepared to accept that a sum of £50 for warm clothing should have been taken into account in assessing the appellant's available means'.[53] In that case the appellant was successful because this left her with less than the £267.68 allowed by NASS for 14 days' food and accommodation.

Resources which must be taken into account

3.61   Only those assets listed in AS reg 6(5) can be taken into account:

(a)   cash;
(b)   savings;
(c)   investments;

---

52   ASA 00/10/0070.
53   ASA 00/05/0010.

(d) land;

(e) cars or other vehicles; and

(f) goods held for the purposes of a trade or other business.

3.62   The NASS application form requires the person claiming support
to notify NASS of all the household's assets and then explain why
they are not 'available' to him/her, eg, assets which are abroad. An
asylum-seeker is eligible for support while s/he takes steps to recover
property not currently available. Where assets are realised the Home
Secretary may recover sums paid in support.[54]

Resources which are not taken into account

3.63   NASS will not take into account jewellery, personal clothing, medical
items, and bedding.[55] The claimant is expected to inform NASS if the
value of jewellery owned by the household is more than £1,000 in
total. Jewellery includes watches. Jewellery is not an asset for the
purposes of AS reg 6(5). If jewellery is converted into cash, it would
then become an asset and the supported person would have a duty to
report it to NASS as a change of circumstances within AS reg
15(2)(b). The guidance notes on the asylum support application form,
which are attached to the regulations, explain this.

Can the applicant meet essential living needs?

3.64   NASS has produced a table showing the thresholds it expects will
meet an asylum-seeker's essential living needs. NASS will only
decide that the household is destitute if its resources or income fall
below the threshold. It appears that NASS has applied the thresholds
fairly rigidly. There have been appeals to the Asylum Support Adjudicator in cases where support has been refused because the household
had savings slightly above the threshold. There is no authority in the
Act or the regulations for applying fixed thresholds. There are clear
arguments that each case should be looked at on its merits, eg, a
newly arrived asylum-seeker in London would normally need more
than £267.68 to secure accommodation and subsistence for 14 days.
Evidence of the cost of housing and essential living needs should be
provided at appeals to support the argument that, eg, a single person
over 25 may be destitute within 14 days even if he has resources of
slightly more than £267.68.

54 AS reg 17.
55 See AS Regs Sch, note.

3.65   The table shows the amounts NASS expects will meet a new applicant's essential living needs.[56]

	Subsistence-only applicants		Applicants in need of housing and subsistence	
	Assets	Weekly income	Assets	Weekly income
Single person aged 25 or over	£73.08	£36.54	£267.68	£133.84
Single person aged 18 to 24	£57.90	£28.95	£252.50	£126.25
Couple	£114.74	£57.37	£503.94	£251.97
Lone parent	£73.08	£36.54	£267.68	£133.84
Child aged 16 and 17	£63.50	£31.75	£258.10	£129.05
Child aged under 16	£61.90	£30.95	£247.80	£123.90

3.66   There are no items specified which NASS *must* take into account to decide whether living needs are met. A number of items *may not* be taken into account by virtue of IAA 1999 s95(7) and AS reg 9:

(a) the cost of faxes;
(b) computers and the cost of computer facilities:
(c) the cost of photocopying;
(d) travel expenses [except for the initial journey to the address where support is provided];
(e) toys and other recreational items;
(f) entertainment expenses.

3.67   The cost of faxes, copying and travel may all be incidental to and necessary for a supported person's claim for asylum or appeal. The Consultation Paper[57] suggests that 'Legal expenses associated with the asylum-seekers' asylum claim may be provided through the Legal Aid Scheme'. Legal Services Commission (LSC) funding has been extended to cover the expense of reasonable travel to a solicitor's office as a legal help disbursement.[58] Thresholds at which asylum support entitlement is calculated are no more than 70 per cent of income support levels.[59] It may be difficult for an asylum-seeker who is working on a low income, just below asylum support threshold, to finance travel to his/her legal representative. In many parts of the UK

56 Based on NASS Policy Bulletin 4.
57 See para 14, note 5.
58 Amended LSC Contract Specification on disbursements, r2.13.
59 Asylum support is actually less than 70% of income support because it was calculated without taking premiums into account.

there is a shortage of immigration lawyers and so long-distance travel is required.[60] If the cost of travel to solicitors is not available, it may be possible to use Human Rights Convention arguments either in relation to NASS or the LSC.[61]

3.68   It has been suggested that the exclusion of toys from the assessment of essential living needs may constitute a breach of the UN Convention on the Rights of the Child.[62]

3.69   In considering whether a person's clothing needs are met, his personal preference as to clothing is excluded. A distinction is then drawn between 'his personal preference as to clothing' and 'his individual circumstances'.[63] It could be argued that individual circumstances include clothing required by cultural and religious norms.

3.70   If the Home Secretary decides that an applicant is destitute, whether because s/he cannot meet his/her essential living needs or has inadequate accommodation, the question of income and assets will be considered to decide what level and kind of support should be provided.[64]

Does the applicant have 'adequate accommodation' for the household?

For the purposes of this section, a person is destitute if–
(a) he does not have adequate accommodation or any means of
    obtaining it (whether or not his essential living needs are met)[65]

3.71   An applicant is destitute if s/he is homeless, ie, if s/he has no accommodation at all or no means of obtaining any adequate accommodation.[66] This means adequate accommodation for both the applicant and any dependant(s).[67]

3.72   The question of whether the asylum-seeker *has* 'adequate accommodation' when NASS is assessing whether or not the household is eligible for support,[68] is different from the question of whether the accommodation which NASS *provides* for asylum-seeker households

60 The LSC has details of the location of solicitors and not-for-profit agencies with immigration law franchises.
61 See para 8.98.
62 See also para 4.58 and chapter 8.
63 AS reg 9(2).
64 Ibid, reg 12. See para 4.76.
65 IAA 1999 s95(3).
66 Ibid.
67 Ibid, s95(4) and AS reg 8(3)(f).
68 Ibid, s95(6).

is adequate.[69] The meaning of 'adequate accommodation' in the context of housing provided by NASS is discussed in the next chapter.[70]

The meaning of 'adequate accommodation'

3.73 The approach to assessing whether asylum-seekers have adequate accommodation is similar to the test of homelessness in Housing Act 1996 ss175–177.[71] The main difference is that an asylum-seeker is not treated as destitute due to 'no enforceable right to occupy' the accommodation.[72] A homeless applicant who has an eviction order to take effect within 28 days is 'threatened with homelessness' and entitled to assistance. An applicant for asylum support may have to wait until 14 days before the eviction order before s/he is awarded support because that is the prescribed period under AS reg 7(a).

3.74 The IAA emphasises the policy aim that asylum-seekers should have 'no-choice' about their accommodation, but the regulations include many elements of the approach to the test of 'accommodation which is reasonable to continue to occupy' which has been developed in homelessness law. Both the IAA 1999 and the AS Regs borrow from the structure and terminology of Housing Act 1996 Part VII. Since the legislation is in many respects silent on the definition of adequacy, both the HRA and parliamentary materials may be used to assist interpretation.[72a]

3.75 To decide whether accommodation is adequate, the Home Secretary *must* have regard to prescribed matters and *may not* have regard to matters listed at IAA 1999 s95(6) or to other prescribed matters. The AS Regs include factors which must be taken into account. There are no factors which may not be taken into account as yet contained in regulations.

Factors which may not be considered

3.76 There are four specified factors which should not be taken into consideration by NASS in deciding whether an asylum-seeker's accommodation is adequate:[73]

69 Ibid, s97.
70 See para 4.17 onwards.
71 See discussion in chapter 6/refer to homelessness case-law, the latest DoE/DoH Code of Guidance and practitioner texts such as Arden and Hunter, *Homelessness and Allocations* (6th edn, LAG, forthcoming 2001).
72 IAA 1999 s95(6).
72a Ministerial statements were cited in *Westminster v NASS*, CO/4738/2000, 27 February 2001, QBD, relying on *Pepper v Hart* [1993] AC 593.
73 IAA 1999 s95(6).

(a)   there is no enforceable right to occupy the accommodation;
(b)   all or part of the accommodation is shared;
(c)   the accommodation is temporary;
(d)   the location of the accommodation.

3.77   These factors will need to be interpreted broadly to make sense of the provisions, eg, if an applicant has no enforceable right to occupy accommodation under s95(6)(a), s/he may not be able to secure entry to it, which is a relevant matter under AS reg 8(d). The government gave various assurances when the matter was debated:

> We would not ignore real or serious overcrowding or the fact that a large number of people were relying on very limited shared sanitary or cooking facilities . . . Some accommodation would be overcrowded even if it were in single person occupancy because there is not enough room for a large family . . . If there were overcrowding, it would be a relevant consideration because the accommodation would not then be adequate. On a slightly different point, some accommodation in Birmingham might well be adequate but it might not be suitable if it were unsafe if it were in an area where there had been racial attacks. Those are the kind of factors we would wish to take into account.[74]

3.78   Since the Asylum and Immigration Appeals Act 1993, an asylum-seeker eligible to apply for housing as homeless is not homeless if 'he has any accommodation in the United Kingdom, however temporary available for his occupation'. This definition was incorporated into Housing Act 1996 s186. The Court of Appeal in *Lismane v Hammersmith & Fulham LBC*[75] decided that an asylum-seeker who was living in accommodation in an appalling state of repair was homeless despite the 'however temporary' limitation. It may be useful to refer to *Lismane* should a similar question arise in relation to adequacy of an asylum-seeker's accommodation given the wording of IAA 1999 s95(6)(a).[76]

Factors which must be considered[77]

3.79   The AS Regs require the Home Secretary to take the following matters into account in deciding whether anyone in the household applying for asylum support is destitute because s/he does not have adequate accommodation:

74   Lord Williams of Mostyn, *Hansard*, HL Debates, cols 1159 and 1160, 20 October 1999.
75   See para 6.23.
76   See Appendix A.
77   AS reg 8(3).

(a) whether it would be reasonable for the person to continue to occupy the accommodation;
(b) whether the accommodation is affordable;
(c) whether it is emergency accommodation provided as s98 temporary support while a claim of support is being considered;
(d) whether the person can secure entry to the accommodation;
(e) where the accommodation is a vehicle or caravan, whether the applicant has a place where it can be parked and lived in;
(f) whether the accommodation is available for occupation by the person's dependants together with him;
(g) whether it is probable that the person's continued occupation of the accommodation will lead to domestic violence against him or any of his dependants.

3.80   The housing needs of both the applicant and any dependant(s) should be considered.[78] Where the family is living separately but wants to live as one household, it can be argued that the applicant is destitute because s/he does not have adequate accommodation for all those who come within the definition of dependant (see para 3.28 above).

3.81   The 'reasonable to continue to occupy' consideration is qualified by AS reg 7(4): ' . . . regard may be had to the general circumstances prevailing in relation to housing in the district of the local housing authority where the accommodation is'. Both concepts are taken from homelessness legislation.[79] This allows NASS to consider the asylum-seeker's housing situation in the light of the local housing situation. For example, NASS could not rely on AS reg 7(4) to decide that it is reasonable for an asylum-seeker to continue to occupy a bed and breakfast hotel, in an area where there is a plentiful supply of empty council housing.

3.82   In deciding whether the accommodation is affordable, the Home Secretary must have regard to income or assets which are available or might be expected to be available, the cost of the accommodation and the applicant's other reasonable living expenses.[80] Affordability is a concept used by Housing Act 1996 s177(3), and the Code of Guidance para 13.8. In general, the factors referred to in the AS Regs are the same and so homelessness case-law will again be useful.

3.83   Emergency accommodation provided under the s98 'temporary

78 IAA 1999 s95(4) and AS reg 3(f).
79 See further Housing Act 1996 s175(3) and paras 13.7–13.9 of Code of Guidance on Housing Act 1996, Parts VI and VII revised 7 March 1997. A long-awaited amended Code of Guidance was due to be published in 2001.
80 AS reg 5.

support' duty is not taken into account in assessing whether or not an applicant is destitute.

3.84   Other factors which NASS takes into account when considering whether accommodation is reasonable to continue to occupy are listed in the notes which form a schedule to the AS Regs. These are racial harassment or attacks, physical violence, sexual abuse or sexual harassment or harassment because of the asylum-seeker's religion.

3.85   Domestic violence means violence or threats of violence which are likely to be carried out from a close family member or someone who was formerly a close family member.[81] Although the homelessness provisions[82] relate to domestic violence from an associated person, this definition in practice may not be very different from 'close family member'. The remainder of the AS Regs' definition is in the same terms, so homelessness case-law will be useful in interpreting the provision.

3.86   An asylum-seeker may choose to stay in accommodation which would be inadequate under reg 8 and still receive support, provided that it is not unaffordable. S/he will not be permitted to stay in the emergency accommodation provided as temporary support under s98, eg, to avoid dispersal.

Can the applicant meet essential living needs and secure adequate accommodation for the prescribed period?

3.87   Support may be provided for asylum-seekers or their dependants who 'appear to the Secretary of State to be destitute or to be likely to become destitute'[83] within a specified period. Two different periods are prescribed by the regulations, depending on whether the applicant is making a new claim or is already in receipt of support:

- *New applications*: The prescribed period is '14 days beginning with the day on which the question falls to be determined' in relation to an application for support where the asylum-seeker is not already receiving support at the time of assessment.[84]
- *Supported households*: In a case where the applicant is already receiving asylum support but there is a change of circumstances

81   Ibid, reg 8(6).
82   Housing Act 1996 ss177–178.
83   IAA 1999 s95(1).
84   AS reg 7(a).

such as an additional family member joining the household or a partner getting a job, the relevant period is '56 days beginning with the day on which that question falls to be determined'.[85]

3.88   The assessment of destitution is an ongoing assessment while support is provided to the 'supported person(s)'. The supported person has a duty to report changes of circumstances such as income or assets becoming available.[86]

3.89   An asylum-seeker should only have support withdrawn if s/he had sufficient resources to support him/herself and his/her dependants for more than 56 days from the date on which destitution is reconsidered by NASS. This allows a supported asylum-seeker to obtain very short-term employment without loss of accommodation and support. Regulation 10 allows an asylum-seeker who has an income or is working, to make contributions to his/her support. There is no parallel provision in the Interim Regs.

Procedures for assessing eligibility

3.90   The procedures for assessing asylum support have serious implications for the asylum-seeker's immigration claim as well as eligibility for support and the type of support provided. Any information given to NASS may be passed on to a wide range of agencies from the police, government departments and local authorities, to private landlords and the post office. There is a risk of prosecution in cases of failure to provide accurate information or notify relevant changes of circumstances.[87]

3.91   The Asylum Support Adjudicator has considered an appeal against refusal of support where a minor had given an incorrect name and date of birth, which were recorded on her SAL1.[88] The appeal was dismissed because as a minor she was not entitled to support. The adjudicator commented that if NASS had been aware of her true name and age when she applied for support, support could have been refused on the ground that she had committed an offence under IAA 1999 s105(1)(a). 'The offence in question would have been making a statement or representation which the appellant knew to be

---

85   Ibid, reg 7(b).
86   Ibid, reg 15.
87   See further chapter 4.
88   ASA 00/09/0061.

false in a material particular with a view to obtaining support for herself.'

Application for asylum support

3.92   The procedure for applying for support is to complete an application form NASS1. Copies of the form are available by telephoning or writing to NASS.[89] There are 17 pages of notes explaining to the applicant how the form should be completed. These form a schedule to the AS Regs.[90] The form should be faxed to NASS followed by a hard copy, supporting documents and four photographs in the post. NASS initially stated that it aimed to make a decision within two working days of receiving the NASS1 form. Few applications were being decided in less than two to three weeks at the time of writing. Some applicants had remained in their emergency accommodation for months while awaiting an offer of s95 support.

3.93   A voluntary sector reception assistant can help new asylum-seekers to complete the NASS1 form and provide an interpreter if necessary. Applicants can otherwise complete the form themselves or with the help of a solicitor or legal representative. Legal Help funded by the Community Legal Service (CLS) should be available for this process, under the contract for housing, immigration, welfare benefits or 'tolerance'.

Asylum-seekers awaiting an asylum decision

3.94   Newly-arrived and newly-presenting asylum-seekers and their dependants who are in need of support are entitled to help from voluntary sector reception assistants who assess eligibility for, and arrange, temporary support including accommodation under s98 while the application to NASS is being considered.[91]

3.95   Voluntary sector organisations[92] are being funded by NASS under IAA 1999 Part VI to provide reception services and emergency accommodation to destitute asylum-seekers while the asylum claim is being assessed. The reception assistants are an integral part of the network of the one-stop services which also provide support and advice to asylum-seekers who are receiving s95 support.

89 See Appendices for NASS details.
90 SI 2000 No 704.
91 For details of the one-stop service voluntary organisations providing reception assistants see Appendix F.
92 Including the Refugee Council, Refugee Action, Refugee Arrivals Project, Migrant Helpline, the Scottish Refugee Council and the Welsh Refugee Council.

3.96　　Where special needs are identified, the applicant should be referred to a local authority (social services department) for an assessment of community care needs. The reception assistant is expected to refer the asylum-seeker to the Medical Foundation for the Care of Victims of Torture where appropriate.

Asylum-seekers whose claim for asylum has been refused on or after 25 September 2000 and who have appealed

3.97　　'Disbenefited'[93] former asylum-seekers living with a child under 18 should approach their local authority, or the placing authority if they have been housed as homeless in another area. The authority acts as agent for NASS, assisting with completion of the form and assessing the adequacy of accommodation. The local authority can provide emergency subsistence while NASS considers the application.

3.98　　Other disbenefited former asylum-seekers (who are entitled to support until their asylum appeal is determined) are expected to telephone NASS to obtain a form by post. NASS's arrangements for emergency provision are explained in NASS Policy Bulletin 53.

Refusal, suspension or termination of support

3.99　　NASS's procedure when refusing support is to send the applicant a refusal letter and a reasons letter, together with a notice of appeal form and explanatory letter.[94] If this procedure is not followed an applicant may have a valid ground for requesting an extension of the deadline of two days for submitting an appeal to the Asylum Support Adjudicator.

3.100　　NASS has a discretion to refuse support if it has previously been suspended or withdrawn under AS reg 20 and there is no material change of circumstances. In exercising this discretion, as a public authority, NASS would need to take HRA and Human Rights Convention considerations into account. A material change of circumstances is one of those listed at AS reg 15.[95] In such a case NASS need not consider a further application 'unless the Secretary of State considers there are exceptional circumstances which justify it being entertained'.

93　See para 3.9, end of table.
94　NASS Policy Bulletin 12.
95　See Appendix A.

3.101   Asylum support may be suspended or discontinued if any one of the following apply:[96]

   (a) suspected breach of asylum support condition without reasonable excuse;
   (b) suspected offence in relation to obtaining support;
   (c) intentional destitution;
   (d) one or more of supported household not living at authorised address;
   (e) unauthorised absence from authorised address for 7 consecutive nights or 14 nights in a 6-month period.

Suspected breach of conditions

3.102   IAA 1999 provides for support to be provided subject to conditions, which must be set out in writing and given to the supported person.[97] Sch 8 para 5 allows for regulations which make support subject to compliance with conditions.[98] Support may be withdrawn where there are reasonable grounds to suspect that the supported person or any dependant has failed to comply with any condition subject to which support is provided. Support can only be withdrawn under s20(1)(a) if the suspected breach is 'without reasonable excuse'. The conditions will normally include the duty to notify a change of circumstances as specified by AS reg 15.[99] Failure to do so is also a criminal offence.[100]

3.103   Many of the appeals to the Asylum Support Adjudicators are cases where NASS has withdrawn support on the ground that the asylum-seeker has breached conditions without reasonable excuse. The condition that support is provided subject to the requirement to live at, or travel, to a specified address seems to be a common reason for NASS deciding to withdraw support. There have been a number of appeals where asylum-seekers have refused to be dispersed out of London or have left accommodation due to racial harassment. Such appeals have been an indirect way of challenging the adequacy of accommodation or support after it has been refused. The difficulty of using this method of challenging the adequacy of accommodation, rather than judicial review is that if the appeal is unsuccessful, NASS

---

96 AS reg 20(1).
97 IAA 1999 s95(9)–(11).
98 AS reg 19.
99 See Appendix A.
100 IAA 1999 ss105(d) and 106(c). See para 4.113.

has discretion not to consider a further application for support unless there has been a material change of circumstances.

3.104   The Asylum Support Adjudicator has considered the meaning of 'without reasonable excuse' in the context of various asylum-seekers who have left accommodation due to racial harassment and refused to return. NASS have approached such cases by arguing that the asylum-seekers are in breach of a condition to return to the accommodation. In ASA 00/08/0033, a case where an asylum-seeker had suffered serious racial harassment, the factual background included:

– verbal abuse of the appellant who also had an egg and banana skin thrown at him,
– a British National Party demonstration outside the accommodation followed by the assault of two asylum-seekers nearby after which the appellant had acted as interpreter for one of the victims;
– the robbery and assault of an asylum-seeker occupying the same accommodation;
– local and national media coverage;
– offers of support by the police and service provider.

3.105   The Adjudicator decided 'in looking at questions of reasonableness I should be concerned not with the general efforts made to combat racial harassment but with how the situation affects this appellant in particular'. She followed *R v Brent LBC ex p McManus*,[101] a judicial review by a family who were found to be intentionally homeless after fleeing the psychological effects of sectarian violence in Northern Ireland. In *McManus* the High Court that decided the correct approach was to investigate the individual circumstances, and that the council was wrong simply to take account of the prevailing situation of violence in Belfast. Looking at the asylum-seeker's circumstances, the Adjudicator decided 'in this case the appellant did have reasonable excuse . . . very real fear of risk of attack'.

3.106   The Adjudicator went on to set out an approach to racial harassment which has been followed in other asylum support appeals, stating: 'no matter how ethnically and culturally mixed the local population may be, there is unlikely to be any area of the UK in which freedom from racial harassment can be guaranteed. In reaching a decision I have therefore had regard to the nature, degree, frequency, persistence and organisation of the harassment involved and its

101   (1993) 25 HLR 643.

immediacy to the appellant'. In other asylum support appeals, this approach has resulted in a decision that racial harassment is not generally a reasonable excuse for leaving accommodation. In ASA 00/09/0044, the Chief Asylum Support Adjudicator approached an appeal involving racial harassment by applying the strict House of Lords approach to the definition of refugee.[102] It is respectfully submitted that the courts' approach to an asylum-seeker refusing to return to a particular address because of racial harassment should be different from the approach to fear of persecution, justifying the grant of refugee status. The *Horvath* approach sets the test of reasonable excuse at too high a level. In ASA 00/09/0044, the appellant was a torture survivor who had left accommodation after racist abuse, which he did not understand at the time, and incidents of racial harassment affecting other occupiers. The adjudicator stated ' . . . there exists sufficient protection against racial harassment in this country in the form of a system of criminal law which makes violent attacks by persecutors punishable and a reasonable willingness to enforce that law on the part of law enforcement agencies . . . I am satisfied that the police have provided protection to the appellant when called upon to do so'.

3.107   An asylum-seeker can challenge a decision by NASS to withdraw support for breach of conditions if s/he was not provided with a written copy of the conditions and/or they were not translated or interpreted. Advisers could ask NASS to produce a copy of any conditions signed by the applicant. Asylum Support Adjudicators have confirmed the importance of conditions being provided to the supported person before NASS can withdraw support for a breach of conditions. In cases where support has been withdrawn due to a failure to travel to a dispersal area, appeals have succeeded where there is no evidence of the travel information and warning being communicated to the applicant. NASS policy bulletins 17 and 25 on the procedure to be followed in failure to travel cases require a letter warning of the consequences to be signed by the applicant and returned to NASS. An appeal was allowed where the NASS letter had not been adequately communicated to an Albanian single parent, who had a sick child and who could not read English.[103]

3.108   There have been a series of appeals relating to a Liverpool hostel which operated a regime so rigid that the asylum-seekers staged a

---

102   *Horvath v Home Secretary* [2000] 3 WLR 379, HL.
103   ASA 00/09/0046.

protest and a walk-out. Their support was withdrawn after they refused to comply with a NASS warning that it was a condition of support that they return to the accommodation. One of the appeals was successful on the ground that the warning letter had been sent to the incorrect address.[104] In another appeal the Chief Asylum Support Adjudicator found a breach of article 3 of the Human Rights Convention: 'I am satisfied on the evidence before me that the requirement to take meals only at the rigidly enforced times, the non-existing facilities for the preparation of food if meals were missed, with the resultant effects on the health and well-being of the appellant, a possible heart patient, represents a violation of article 3'. The Adjudicator concluded that the appellant had reasonable excuse not to return until the result of NASS's investigations had been notified to him and his grievances addressed.

3.109   A case decided under National Assistance Act 1948 s21 provides useful guidance on the approach which NASS should take in cases under reg 20(1)(a). The question of withdrawing s21 help from a 'disruptive' asylum-seeker was considered by the Court of Appeal in *R v Kensington and Chelsea RLBC ex p Kujtim*.[105] The court decided that, first, a fair thorough investigation must be carried out, taking account of the asylum-seeker's current needs before ending assistance. This investigation should allow the asylum-seeker to respond to the allegations. Secondly, a refusal to comply with requirements must be 'persistent and unequivocal'.

Suspected criminal offence under IAA 1999 Part VI

3.110   Support may be withdrawn where the Home Secretary has reasonable grounds to suspect that the supported person or any dependant has committed an offence under IAA 1999 Part VI. These offences are discussed in more detail at para 4.114. The relevant offences are:

- where false or dishonest representations were made to obtain support; or
- where an applicant has caused delay or obstruction of asylum support functions. Representations include an omission such as a failure to notify a change of circumstances.

104 ASA 00/11/0102.
105 [1999] 4 All ER 161, (1999) 2 CCLR 340, CA, discussed further at para 7.80.

3.111   The Asylum Support Adjudicator has stated that although the standard of proof for failing to disclose a material fact is a civil balance of probability, it requires a high degree of probability bearing in mind the seriousness of the consequences.[106] The burden of proof is on the Home Secretary. The circumstances surrounding the completion of the form must be looked at.[107]

Intentional destitution

3.112   An applicant is 'intentionally destitute' if s/he is 'destitute as a result of an act or omission deliberately done by him or any dependant of his without reasonable excuse while in the United Kingdom'.[108]

3.113   IND guidance to the Interim Regs dated 19 November 1999 suggests that an asylum-seeker will be 'intentionally destitute' if [he] has 'deliberately squandered his resources'.[109]

3.114   An Iranian asylum-seeker has won an appeal against a decision by NASS that he was intentionally destitute.[110] He had arrived in the UK with £979.96, which he had borrowed to get here, and then he had sent the money back to his sick father. The Asylum Support Adjudicator applied social security case-law[111] and decided that 'to reach a finding of intentional destitution, it must be shown that the appellant knew of the rules which he is alleged to have circumvented'. The appellant was not intentionally destitute because he had not received a clear warning from NASS about the consequences of any future disposal of funds. See also para 3.109 above.

3.115   The Court of Appeal granted permission to apply for judicial review of a decision that an asylum-seeker was intentionally destitute under the Interim Regs, in a case where he had left his accommodation before the IAA 1999 came into force.[112] It was argued that a finding of intentional destitution might cause indefinite destitution and so violate Mr Fetiti's Human Rights Convention rights (articles 3, 6, 8 and 14).

3.116   The definition of intentional destitution is slightly broader than intentional homelessness, which does not expressly include the

---

106   ASA 00/06/0012.
107   See also ASA 00/09/0061.
108   AS reg 20(2).
109   Para 13, see Appendix B.
110   ASA 00/06/0020.
111   CIS 124/1990.
112   *R (on the Application of Fetiti) v Islington LBC* C/00/2748, 19 October 2000, unreported.

conduct of other household members. Homelessness case-law has approached the conduct of other household members by considering whether they have acquiesced in the acts which have led to the loss of the accommodation.[113] Intentional homelessness leads to a more limited housing duty being owed to the family who can still access other forms of housing. The difficulty with a finding of intentional destitution is that it would result in no asylum support duty at all being owed to the applicant who would simply have 14 days' notice to quit the accommodation. The courts should give the regulations a reading which is compatible with the HRA 1998 to avoid a breach of article 2 or 3. If one of the supported persons is under 18, a local authority may have duties to the family under the Children Act 1989.[114] If the applicant is 'in need of care or attention' for a reason that does not arise solely out of the physical effects of destitution, eg, where there are also other factors such as age, disability, illness, mental illness or pregnancy, s/he may be entitled to help under National Assistance Act 1948 s21.[115]

Temporary or permanent absence from the 'authorised address'

3.117   Asylum support may cease if any member of the household moves or is temporarily away from his/her address without permission. This requirement underlines the monitoring role of NASS as part of the Home Office's IND. An asylum-seeker who moves house is also required to inform the Home Office or the port of entry for immigration purposes and his/her IS96 and/or SAL will be amended to show the new address.

3.118   If a supported person leaves his/her accommodation for longer than seven days consecutively or 14 days in total during a six-month period without permission, support can be withdrawn.

3.119   In ASA 00/11/0100 the Asylum Support Adjudicator found that the Home Secretary had a discretion when deciding whether or not to terminate support under AS reg 20(1)(d) and (e), which made the approach to considering those grounds analogous to the 'reasonable excuse' approach to reg 20(1)(a). 'It is equally open to an appellant under subparagraph (d) or (e) as under paragraph (a) to seek to

---

113   See, eg, *R v North Devon DC ex p Lewis* [1981] 1 WLR 328, QBD.
114   See paras 8.61–8.69.
115   *R v Wandsworth LBC ex p O* (2000) 3 CCLR 237, CA. See para 8.50.

discharge the burden of proof upon him by showing that his actions were reasonable in the circumstances.'

3.120   There have been a number of asylum support appeals against decisions to discontinue support where asylum-seekers have left accommodation because of racial harassment and/or because they believed it was inadequate. The adjudicators have taken a robust approach towards absence from accommodation, requiring asylum-seekers to prove reasonable excuse on a balance of probabilities. In one of the series of appeals arising from a walk-out of asylum-seekers from a Liverpool hostel (referred to at para 3.108 above), the Chief Asylum Support Adjudicator found the regime at the hostel was so harsh and rigid that it amounted to inhumane and degrading treatment within the meaning of article 3 and the asylum-seeker 'had reasonable excuse not to return to the authorised address.

3.121   IAA 1999 s125 gives a power to obtain a warrant to enter the supported household's home using reasonable force. A warrant will be granted where there is a reasonable belief that one or more of the supported household is not living in accommodation provided by NASS (see further para 4.99).

3.122   Whether the asylum-seeker is staying in accommodation s/he has found or in accommodation organised by NASS, it is referred to as the 'authorised address'. The supported person is required to notify NASS if the household moves to a new address even if it is provided by friends or family.

3.123   Since asylum-seeker households are subject to dispersal around the UK, it is not unlikely that they will need to be absent from accommodation at some point, eg, to visit friends or legal representatives in other parts of the country. The asylum-seeker can write to NASS to request permission to be absent, to avoid a breach of AS reg 20(1)(e). The regulation does not specify that permission must be obtained in advance, although supported persons should be advised to do so. Where necessary, there is an argument that permission should be granted retrospectively, eg, if the asylum-seeker needs to travel urgently to visit a sick relative.

Other grounds for withdrawal of support

3.124   Asylum support will also be refused or discontinued in the following circumstances:

- the supported person ceases to be 'an asylum-seeker' or dependant of 'an asylum-seeker';
- there is a change of circumstances so that the supported household is no longer destitute (eg, due to income over the NASS threshold becoming available).

3.125   An asylum-seeker is only entitled to support for as long as s/he comes within the s94(1) definition of asylum-seeker explained at the start of the chapter. Entitlement to support ends if the asylum-seeker withdraws the asylum claim or if the claim is refused and there is no outstanding appeal. Entitlement also ends if there is a favourable decision on the asylum claim.

3.126   The asylum-seeker and any dependant(s) who are refused or granted full refugee status or exceptional leave to enter/remain in the UK become ineligible for support 14 days after the Home Secretary has notified them of the decision. If the asylum-seeker has appealed against a negative decision, s/he becomes ineligible 14 days after the appeal is disposed of. The decision must be in writing and is deemed to be received on the second day after it was posted either to the asylum-seeker's last known address or to the representative.[116] It is important to note that where asylum is refused, the 14-day period runs from the date of receiving the full decision letter with reasons, not from the date of the 'pre-decision' letter stating that the asylum application has been refused. See para 5.118.

3.127   In the case of a favourable decision this allows very limited time for a supported person to transfer to mainstream welfare support, eg, to apply as homeless or obtain income support. Tactics for addressing these issues are discussed at para 2.67–2.80).

3.128   If an asylum-seeker is granted full refugee status s/he can claim backdated income support. S/he can also claim for housing benefit and council tax benefit to meet any past rent or council tax liability.[117] The claims must be made within 28 days of receiving the status decision.

116   IAA 1999 s94(3) and (9).
117   Asylum-seekers supported in s95 accommodation are not liable for council tax. The owner is liable (Local Government Finance Act 1992 s8 and the Council Tax (Liability for Owners) (Amendment) (England) Regulations 2000 SI No 537).

3.129   Where an asylum-seeker is refused asylum, s/he remains 'an asylum-seeker' eligible for Part VI asylum support as long as the household includes a dependent child under 18 (see para 3.27 above). If there is no dependent child, community care provision or 'hard cases' support may be available as a last resort (see para 3.167 below).

Effect of withdrawal of support

3.130   There is no prescribed notice period for withdrawal of support except that support continues for 14 days after notification of the asylum decision. Any notice to quit may be limited to seven days.[118]

New applications after withdrawal of support[119]

3.131   Where an award of asylum support has been suspended or discontinued under reg 20, no further application will be considered unless:

  - there has been a material change of circumstances of the kind which the asylum-seeker would have to report if s/he were receiving support, eg, arrival of a new household member (see para 4.91);
  - the Home Secretary considers there are exceptional circumstances.

3.132   The Home Secretary may allow a fresh application but then decide that an applicant is not eligible for support.[120]

3.133   There have been a number of unsuccessful asylum support appeals where the asylum-seeker has arrived in the UK with savings over the limit for support. In such cases the Asylum Support Adjudicators have suggested that there will be a change of circumstances, justifying a further claim for support, when the savings have reduced to below the destitution threshold.

Notices to quit and security of tenure

3.134   Where a supported person is in accommodation provided by NASS, AS reg 22 suggests that a notice to quit may be served without regard to security of tenure provisions which would normally apply.

3.135   Schedule 14 of the Act contains provisions to prevent tenancies provided under IAA 1999 Part VI from becoming secure or assured

118   AS reg 22.
119   Ibid, reg 21.
120   Ibid, reg 21(3).

tenancies.[121] The schedule also makes any tenancy or licence granted under IAA 1999 Part VI an 'excluded tenancy or licence' for the purposes of the Protection from Eviction Act 1977.[122] As a result, a household in NASS accommodation has very limited protection against landlord harassment or eviction. These provisions may be in breach of the HRA and Human Rights Convention on the ground that they discriminate between different classes of occupier on the basis of asylum-seeker status.[123]

3.136   The conditions of a reg 22 notice are:

  – withdrawal of asylum support due to reg 20 (see para 3.99 onwards);
  – asylum claim or appeal has been determined;
  – supported person no longer destitute;
  – supported person to be moved to other accommodation.

3.137   The notice to quit must be in writing and the notice period must normally be not less than seven days. The seven-day period must run until 14 days after the asylum-seeker receives the decision, where there has been an asylum decision or appeal. Where the decision is posted, the 14 days runs from the second day after the IND posted the decision on the asylum claim.

3.138   A period of less than seven days' written notice is allowed if 'the circumstances of the case are such that the notice period is justified'.[124] It was held to be arguable in *R v Newham LBC ex p Ojuri*[125] that a housing authority was under a public duty to act reasonably in terminating temporary accommodation provided to a homeless person with dependent children under Housing Act 1996 s188. In the circumstances of that case, the High Court decided that a 28-day period was reasonable. In *R v Secretary of State for the Environment ex p Shelter and Refugee Council*,[126] it was decided that local authorities were under a public law duty to act reasonably in evicting asylum-seekers from accommodation in cases where the statutory duty to provide accommodation had been withdrawn. Subject to consideration of individual cases, the court suggested that at least 28 days was generally appropriate.

---

121 IAA 1999 Sch 14, paras 81 and 88.
122 Ibid, para 73.
123 *Larkos v Cyprus* (1999) 7 BHRC 244. See chapter 8.
124 AS reg 22(4).
125 (1999) 31 HLR 631.
126 [1997] COD 49.

3.139   If it is found that NASS is allowing a notice period of less than seven days, representatives may wish to consider Human Rights Convention arguments in relation to respect for private and family life, peaceful enjoyment of possessions, discrimination, etc (articles 8 and 14, and Protocol 1) (See chapter 8). A short notice period is probably only lawful in limited cases, eg, where the basis of the decision is that the supported household has adequate accommodation otherwise available.

Remedies

Appeals to the Asylum Support Adjudicator

3.140   A unique appeals system has been developed to review decisions made by NASS. IAA 1999 s102 gives the Asylum Support Adjudicators jurisdiction to hear appeals where the Home Secretary refuses or terminates asylum support under IAA 1999 s95. The concept of 'adjudicator' is borrowed from immigration law. Asylum Support Adjudicators are appointed and financed by the Home Secretary. This appears to interfere with the article 6 right to a fair hearing in the light of the Scottish sheriffs' case of *Ruxton v Starrs*.[127] The question of whether article 6(1) applies to asylum support appeals has been considered by the Chief Asylum Support Adjudicator who decided that this was a matter for the higher courts, but the article contained minimum standards of fairness which should be applied to adjudicators' decisions.[128]

3.141   The Home Office anticipated 1,600 appeals in the first year of the new support scheme. Between April and December 2000, only 139 appeals were received. Of 24,000 applications to NASS for support, 0.1 per cent of applications were refused.

3.142   There have been difficulties for appellants, unable to attend hearings because of NASS initial refusals or delays in paying travel costs in advance. Of those who have attended, most were unrepresented. The Home Secretary has been represented by NASS decision-makers, or in some appeals by a solicitor and/or counsel. Yet a CLS certificate for public funding for representation is not currently available to asylum-seekers in asylum support appeals. It may be possible

---

127   2000 SLT 42.
128   ASA 00/09/0063.

to obtain 'exceptional public funding' under Access to Justice Act 1999 s6(8)(b) on the ground of 'overwhelming importance to the client', and possibly 'significant wider public interest'.[129]

3.143 Legal help under a contract for housing, immigration, welfare benefits or 'tolerance' can be used to advise and assist appellants. Another serious obstacle to asylum-seekers wishing to exercise their appeal rights or attend an oral hearing is that there is no statutory provision for emergency or other support while the appeal is being decided.

3.144 The majority of appeals have involved:

– a breach of the conditions subject to which support is provided, in particular a failure to travel to a dispersal area;
– leaving accommodation 'without reasonable excuse', mainly in cases of racial harassment;
– applicants who are excluded from support, eg, due to interim support entitlement;
– applicant not destitute due to resources above NASS thresholds.

3.145 The detailed rules governing appeals are contained in the Asylum Support (Appeals) Procedure Rules 2000[130] ('the Appeals Rules'). The rules came into force on 3 April 2000 and only apply to appeals against decisions by NASS. They do not provide for appeals against a local authority decision in relation to interim support, which must be challenged by judicial review.

3.146 It is only possible to appeal against a refusal or termination of support, not against the type, level or adequacy of support. This leaves many decisions outside the jurisdiction of the Adjudicator. In such cases judicial review will be the appropriate remedy, eg, of the Home Secretary's decision not to provide 'adequate accommodation'.

3.147 The preamble to the Appeals Rules states that they are made 'having regard to the desirability of securing, so far as is reasonably practicable, that appeals are brought and disposed of with the minimum delay'. The appeals procedure is designed as a fast-track procedure, with an Asylum Support Adjudicator's decision within nine working days of the original decision. The speed is necessary where

129 Such applications should be submitted on the usual forms to the Head Office, LSC Policy and Legal Department, 85 Gray's Inn Road, London WC1X 8TX with an application letter explaining that the application is for exceptional funding.
130 SI No 541.

appellants are destitute but makes it harder to obtain legal representation. Appellants have also had difficulties in obtaining assistance
from NASS to travel to oral hearings.

3.148   In many appeals to date, the decision has been reviewed by NASS
and overturned on receipt of the appeal and so the appeal has been
withdrawn.

3.149   Oral hearings are heard in public in Croydon[131] by the Chief
Asylum Support Adjudicator, deputy-chief Asylum Support Adjudicator or one of a team of Adjudicators. A public record of their judgments can be inspected at the office and is due to be published on the
internet. As with social security commissioners' decisions, important
decisions are 'starred'.

Grounds for appeal

3.150   The applicant for asylum support may appeal to an Adjudicator if the
Home Secretary decides:

– that the applicant does not qualify for support under IAA 1999
  s95; or
– to stop providing support before that support would otherwise
  have come to an end.[132]

Appeal procedure[133]

3.151   A notice of appeal must be completed and signed by the applicant
or his/her representative. The appropriate form is attached as a
schedule to the Appeals Rules. If the applicant wants an oral
hearing it should be requested on this form. An oral hearing
may mean the appeal takes longer than if it is decided on the
papers.

3.152   The notice of appeal must be received by the Adjudicator not later
than two days after the day the appellant received the asylum support
decision.

3.153   The Adjudicator may extend the time limit if s/he considers it is in
the interests of justice to do so or if the appellant or his/her representative was prevented from appealing in time 'by circumstances
beyond his control'. The adjudicator extended the time limit in a

---

131 Christopher Wren House, 113 High Street Croydon CR1 1GQ, tel 020 8688
     3977.
132 IAA 1999 s103.
133 See n130 above.

case where the asylum-seeker was not informed of the right of appeal.[134]

3.154　　The adjudicator must fax the notice of appeal to the Home Secretary on the date of receipt of the appeal or the following day. The Home Secretary may decide to withdraw his/her decision after receipt of the appeal.

3.155　　The Home Secretary must send the appeal bundle by fax or by hand to the adjudicator on the day after the adjudicator received notice of the appeal. It must be sent to the appellant or his/her representative by first class post or fax on the same day.

3.156　　The day after the Home Secretary sends the appeal bundle to the adjudicator is 'consideration day'. On that day the adjudicator must decide whether there should be an oral hearing. If the appeal is to be decided without a hearing it should be decided on the consideration day or as soon as possible thereafter and not later than four days after the consideration day.

3.157　　There must be an oral hearing if the appellant has requested one in the notice of appeal or if the adjudicator considers it necessary to dispose of the appeal justly. In an early appeal where the appellant's solicitor explained in the appeal notice that there was no request for an oral hearing because the appellant had no money to travel there, the adjudicator ordered an oral hearing and directed NASS to provide funds for travel.[135] If there is to be an oral hearing the adjudicator should set a day for it not later than four days after the consideration day. The adjudicator must give notice of an oral hearing to the appellant and the Home Secretary. If the appellant wants to provide additional evidence after entering the notice of appeal s/he must send it to both the adjudicator and to NASS.

Travel expenses

3.158　After some initial debate, NASS agreed to finance travel to asylum support appeals. A failure to facilitate travel has been accepted as a good reason to order an adjournment of an appeal.[136] In the same case, the chief asylum support adjudicator ordered a rehearing of the appeal before a different adjudicator where inadequate travel arrangements were made by NASS. The hearing had gone ahead without the appellant and had been dismissed. Although there was

134　ASA 00/07/0030.
135　ASA 00/07/0027.
136　ASA 00/11/0106.

no express provision to order a re-hearing the adjudicator took an imaginative approach, deciding that she had a duty to interpret Appeal Rule 19(2) so that it was compatible with the article 6 right to a fair hearing. The appellant later won his appeal.

3.159   If either the Home Secretary or the appellant do not attend the oral hearing, the appeal can be considered in their absence provided a notice of the date, time and place of hearing has been served. There are some simple rules governing evidence.[137] The adjudicator can take into account matters which s/he considers relevant even if they arose after the date of the decision. Evidence may be given by witnesses on oath. The appellant and Home Secretary are entitled to receive and consider copies of any documents if they have not received them in advance. The appeal hearing will usually be a public hearing and it should be recorded. The appellant may ask the adjudicator to exercise his/her power to exclude members of the public from a hearing.

3.160   The adjudicator must inform the appellant or his/her representative of the decision at the end of the hearing. If neither party is present the adjudicator should send his/her decision to the appellant on the same day, with a 'reasons statement' not later than two days after the appeal.

3.161   The adjudicator may:

– dismiss the appeal and uphold the decision of the Home Secretary;
– allow the appeal and substitute his decision for that of the Home Secretary, ie, grant asylum support to the appellant;[138]
– allow part of the appeal, eg, decide that the appellant is entitled to subsistence, but uphold the decision that s/he is not entitled to accommodation.

3.162   In a number of appeals the adjudicators have remitted the decision back to the Home Secretary with directions, eg, to make further inquiries, to redraft the decision letter, to provide support pending a further decision.

3.163   If an appeal is dismissed a further application for support will not be considered unless there is a material change of circumstances.[139]

3.164   If an appeal is dismissed, the appellant may be able to bring judicial review proceedings on ordinary administrative law principles. A judicial review has been brought of an adjudicator's decision

---

137   AS reg 10, see Appendix A.
138   IAA 1999 s103(3).
139   Ibid, s103(6).

in a case where an asylum-seeker had left accommodation due to racial harassment.[140]

Judicial review

3.165 The Home Secretary is the defendant in any judicial review of an Asylum Support Adjudicator's decision or of a NASS decision about service provision. To challenge an Asylum Support Adjudicator decision or to challenge a NASS decision about the type or level of support, the appropriate remedy is judicial review. A letter before action should be sent to NASS and to the Treasury Solicitor[141] (in Scotland, the Home Secretary is represented by the Scottish office). A CLS certificate of public funding for representation may be available. Cases may involve HRA arguments, making it easier to obtain public funding.

3.166 The provision of asylum support under the Act is a power, not a duty, except in relation to applicants with dependent children.[142] However, it is clear from the parliamentary debates that the intention was to establish a discretion which parliament intended to be exercised (see para 3.13). A failure to provide support to a person who qualifies, or a failure to otherwise comply with the regulations would almost certainly result in the Administrative Court granting relief. If necessary, HRA arguments could be used to interpret the exercise of the discretion. It may also be helpful to draw a comparison with the interim scheme where support is mandatory.

Applicants who are ineligible for asylum support under IAA 1999 Part VI

3.167 If an ex-asylum-seeker stops receiving NASS asylum support or local authority Interim Regs support, s/he may be entitled to help under the restrictive 'hard cases' support scheme or under community care provisions. See also chapters 7 and 8.

---

140 See June 2001 *Legal Action* 16 for further discussion about the ASA's jurisdiction.
141 See Appendix H for details.
142 IAA 1999 s122.

Households with children

3.168   IAA 1999 s122 only excludes households from Children Act 1989 help if there are no other Children Act needs or if support is being offered or arranged. This is explained at para 7.58 onwards. Where a person is 'subject to immigration control' and the household contains children under 18, the family may be eligible for Children Act 1989 s17 help if NASS refuses or withdraws support.

'Hard cases' support

3.169   When the IAA 1999 was debated, concern was expressed about destitute ex-asylum-seekers whose claims for asylum had been refused but who were pursuing a judicial review of the decision or were unable to leave the UK. The government indicated that it proposed a 'hard cases' fund to be administered by the voluntary sector.

3.170   In the absence of an organisation willing and able to take on this task, NASS decided to administer a scheme known as 'hard cases' support, provided under IAA 1999 s4. The terms of this scheme are contained in Annex A to a NASS letter dated 17 April 2000.[143] Provision is in the form of board and lodging outside London with no cash or vouchers.

3.171   The criteria for eligibility are that:

- the applicant no longer falls within the definition of asylum-seeker and his/her asylum claim has been refused;
- the applicant has received support from NASS or local authority support under the Interim Regs;
- the applicant appears to be destitute;
- the applicant cannot get support from another source such as friends, family or a local authority under community care provisions.

3.172   An applicant who is eligible under these criteria will not usually receive support unless either it is physically impracticable for him/her to travel to any other country or unless there are exceptional circumstances.

3.173   The procedure for applying for hard cases support is a letter to NASS explaining why the ex-asylum-seeker is eligible. The few former asylum-seekers who qualify for support will be expected to

143   See Appendix B.

attend monthly reviews. If there is insufficient evidence that they have taken steps to leave the country, 'hard cases support will be terminated'. If support is not provided or is refused, the appropriate remedy is a judicial review.

Ex-asylum-seekers 'in need of care and attention'

3.174   A person who is subject to immigration control (which includes a former asylum-seeker) is not entitled to residential accommodation under NAA 1948 s21(1):

> . . . if his need for care and attention has arisen solely –
> (a) because he is destitute; or
> (b) because of the physical effects, or anticipated physical effects, of his being destitute.[144]

3.175   *R v Wandsworth LBC ex p O*[145] was the first case to consider the effect of IAA 1999 s116. The Court of Appeal considered the case of a destitute person subject to immigration control, in need of care and attention, whose reasons for needing care and attention did not arise solely because of the (anticipated) physical effects of destitution. Where there was at least a minimal presence of other factors such as illness, old age or disability, etc, s/he would qualify for help under NAA 1948 s21(1).[146] In such cases where a single adult is excluded from benefits and asylum support and/or has been refused interim support, a request for a community care assessment could be made if there is a need for care and attention arising to some extent from age, disability, pregnancy, mental health or other reason which is not solely due to the physical or anticipated physical effects of destitution.

Destitute, childless ex-asylum-seekers with no means of support

3.176   Single adult asylum-seekers who do not have community care needs but wish to remain in the UK to pursue a judicial review of a negative asylum appeal decision are not eligible for hard cases support or community care provision. In such cases, it may be possible to apply for judicial review of the 'hard cases' criteria on the basis that to

---

144   IAA 1999 s116 amending National Assistance Act 1948, s21.
145   (2000) 3 CCLR 237, CA.
146   See para 8.46.

refuse any form of support is a breach of article 2, 6 or 8 of the Human Rights Convention.

3.177   In the light of the judicial statements made in cases such as *R v Secretary of State for Social Security ex p B*,[147] *R v Hammersmith and Fulham LBC ex p M*,[148] *R v Kensington and Chelsea RLBC ex p Kujtim*,[149] and *R v Wandsworth LBC ex p O*[150] it may be possible for an asylum-seeker or former asylum-seeker who is left completely destitute by NASS or by the local authority to challenge the decision. This applies whether or not the applicant has a meritorious judicial review application of the immigration decision and whether or not leaving the UK would frustrate the right to pursue the judicial review application.

147   [1997] 1 WLR 275, CA.
148   (1998) 30 HLR 10, CA.
149   [1999] 4 All ER 161, CA.
150   (2000) 2 CCLR 237, CA.

CHAPTER 4

Asylum support: service provision and ancillary matters

For complete chapter contents, see overleaf

4.103 Criminal offences

False or dishonest representations • Delay or obstruction • Failure of sponsor to maintain

Introduction

4.1   This chapter explains service provision under the asylum support scheme, including accommodation.[1] Immigration and Asylum Act (IAA) 1999 ss96–98 provide the framework for the ways in which the Home Secretary may offer support to asylum-seekers who are eligible under IAA 1999 s95 because they are destitute. More detailed provisions about support are included in the Asylum Support Regulations ('AS Regs') 2000.[2]

4.2   If a duty to provide asylum support is accepted under IAA 1999 s95, the Home Office's National Asylum Support Service (NASS) will make arrangements for accommodation and/or living expenses through its contracts with public, private and voluntary sector suppliers.

4.3   As well as asylum support provision, there is an outline of related welfare provision which a supported person can expect to receive, such as health and education benefits.

4.4   The chapter goes on to consider important ancillary matters, in particular, criminal offences, related to the provision of asylum support. These apply to both asylum and interim support. IAA 1999 Part VI support is provided subject to conditions and other legal obligations with serious human rights and civil liberties implications.

4.5   The arrangements for supporting asylum-seekers are described in NASS policy bulletins which contain NASS's procedures and its interpretation of the law.[3]

4.6   A supported person cannot appeal to the Asylum Support Adjudicators on the grounds of inadequate service provision. An appeal may only be considered where support is refused outright or withdrawn and where there is a pending asylum claim. Any legal challenge to service provision would usually be an application for judicial review. Adjudicator decisions have addressed questions which are relevant to the provision of support, eg, whether an asylum-seeker who is being racially harassed has a reasonable excuse for leaving accommodation. Although such decisions are not binding on the Administrative Court, they are a relevant consideration for NASS in deciding what kind of support to provide,

---

1 Chapter 3 explains who is *eligible* for asylum support.
2 SI No 704 (see Appendix A), made under IAA 1999 s95(12) and Sch 8.
3 See para 3.5.

eg, whether accommodation is adequate. The decisions are to be made available on a website.[4]

Key features

4.7 The key features of service provision under the AS Regs and IAA 1999 Part VI are:

- When an asylum-seeker applies for support under the AS Regs, and has nowhere to live or no resources, s/he may initially receive 'temporary support' under IAA 1999 s98 while the application is considered.
- If NASS decides that the applicant is 'destitute', s95(1) provides that support may be offered to the asylum-seeker and any dependants.[5]
- Section 95 gives the Home Secretary a *power* rather than a duty to provide support, but there is a *duty* under s122 to offer support to dependent children.
- Support is provided in the form of essential living needs and/or adequate accommodation as defined by s96(1). This subsection also covers travel to bail hearings and limited expenses connected to the asylum claim such as travel to IND interviews and appeal hearings, but not travel to solicitors.
- Unless there are exceptional circumstances, support must not be wholly or mainly in cash.[6] AS Regs Sch para 10 proscribes the cash value of the vouchers which may be provided to different classes of asylum-seeker and also limits the value of vouchers redeemable for cash to £10 for an individual or £20 for a couple per week as a general rule. The Home Secretary has the power to introduce an order to repeal s96(3), allowing asylum-seekers to be supported by cash payments.[7]
- The s95 power to provide support must be met by having regard to 'the desirability, in general, of providing accommodation in areas in which there is a ready supply of accommodation'. The policy is to disperse asylum-seekers around the UK to 'cluster' areas. In

---

4 See Appendix H for address.
5 See chapter 3 for meaning of 'destitute', 'asylum-seeker' and 'dependant'.
6 IAA 1999 s96(3).
7 Ibid, s96(5). Widespread opposition to the voucher scheme led to a government review in autumn 2000.

some cases, households may be able to challenge dispersal if the accommodation is not 'adequate' because of the location. The Home Secretary cannot take into account 'preferences' as to locality[8] but should take personal circumstances into account.

– Section 96(1) allows for accommodation and living expenses to be provided separately. If asylum-seeker households have accommodation with friends or relatives, they can apply to NASS for living expenses only. This option is not available to asylum-seekers receiving support from local authorities under the Asylum Support (Interim Provisions) Regulations 1999[9] unless they have dependent children. The scheme also has flexibility in allowing income and assets to be taken into account in assessing the level of support. A household may have a small income such as part-time earnings but still be eligible for some help with living expenses.

Forms of support

4.8   If an asylum-seeker is receiving housing and/or subsistence after applying to NASS, it may be temporary support,[10] asylum support[11] or hard cases support.[12] Hard cases support is explained in chapter 3.

Temporary support

4.9   The Home Secretary may provide 'temporary support' under IAA 1999 s98 only until a decision is reached on eligibility for full asylum support under s95.[13] Temporary support may be provided for:

(a) asylum-seekers or
(b) dependants of asylum-seekers,
who it appears to the Secretary of State may be destitute.[14]

4.10   Temporary support is arranged by reception assistants who are employed by voluntary organisations such as the Refugee Council,

8   Ibid, s97.
9   SI No 3056.
10 IAA 1999 s98.
11 Ibid, s95.
12 Ibid, s4.
13 See para 3.14 re temporary support eligibility.
14 IAA 1999 s98(1).

funded by the Home Office.[14a] They also help asylum-seekers who claimed asylum at the port to complete an application for full asylum support. Temporary support is in 'emergency accommodation' provided by voluntary organisations funded by the Home Office.[15] It was initially suggested that the emergency accommodation would be for a couple of days. At the time of writing asylum-seekers were spending weeks, pending arrangements to transfer them to the dispersal areas. The schedule to the regulations suggests that temporary support could be provided for up to three months in a case where an applicant has assets but needs time to realise them.[16] NASS's practice is to temporarily disregard an asset if it is clearly going to take time to realise (such as property). If it is clear that the applicant is taking reasonable steps to dispose of the premises, then the land/property is disregarded for 13 weeks. Note that, during this time, an asylum-seeker would not be housed in emergency accommodation, but dispersed in the usual way.

4.11 Temporary support is not generally available where asylum support has been refused and an applicant has appealed to the Asylum Support Adjudicator. In such cases community care provision should be considered (see para 3.174). In exceptional circumstances, reception assistants may be asked to arrange support for asylum-seekers whose s95 support has ended, eg, where they have left accommodation due to racial harassment and their complaints are being investigated.

4.12 There is no definition of what constitutes 'temporary support' in the Act itself. The explanatory notes to the Act suggest it 'may take any form'.[17] Section 96 stipulates how support under s95 may be provided and includes the requirement that accommodation should be adequate to the household's needs. It seems that s96 does not extend to the 'temporary support' duty under s98, which is expressly distinguished from the s95 duty.[18] If an asylum-seeker's temporary support is poor quality accommodation or insufficient subsistence, the Human Rights Act (HRA) 1998, community care provision and environmental housing powers should be considered.[19]

14a There is a separate procedure for 'disbenefited applicants', see para 3.98, although this may change.
15 AS Regs Sch, note 6A.
16 Ibid, note 8.
17 IAA 1999 explanatory notes, para 307.
18 Ibid, s98(2).
19 See chapters 6–8.

4.13   It may be possible to bring a judicial review of the (Home Secretary's) decision to provide inadequate temporary support by using the HRA, eg, under article 8 of the Human Rights Convention if the family are separated or under article 2 or 3 if the accommodation is so poor that it presents a serious risk to health.

4.14   As with accommodation provided under the full support duty, although there are no IAA 1999 requirements for good standards in emergency accommodation, ordinary environmental health law provisions will apply. These are explained at para 6.156 onwards. A visit by the local environmental officer may lead to repairs by the landlord, although the temporary period in emergency accommodation means there may not be time for enforcement action.

Type and level of asylum support

4.15   Once NASS decides that a household is destitute within the meaning of s95, it should arrange for the applicant to be offered full asylum support. Section 96 sets out the 'ways in which support may be provided'. These are limited to provision of:

– accommodation adequate for the household's needs;
– essential living needs;
– expenses connected to the asylum claim;
– expenses of attending bail hearings;
– other forms of support if there are exceptional circumstances.

4.16   Before deciding what form of support to provide or to continue to provide, NASS must take certain matters into account and ignore others.[20] The applicant's resources must be taken into account in deciding the kind and level of support.[21] The supported person's compliance with any conditions subject to which support is provided may be taken into account.[22]

Adequate accommodation

Under the new arrangements, asylum-seekers who are destitute will receive good-quality accommodation appropriate to their needs.[23]

---

20   IAA 1999 s97(1), (2) and (4).
21   AS Regs reg 12.
22   Ibid, reg 19.
23   Home Secretary, Jack Straw MP, HC Debates, col 980, 9 November 1999.

Accommodation will be offered on a no-choice basis just as it may be in respect of UK residents who present themselves as homeless, usually where accommodation is more readily available outside London and the south-east. That does not mean that asylum-seekers will be placed in isolated or derelict accommodation. Accommodation is likely to be in clusters, taking account as far as possible of support available from existing communities.[24]

4.17   A report in the *Observer* on 28 May 2000 stated that asylum-seekers in Liverpool were being housed in the Landmark, a crumbling 15-storey tower block abandoned by the council as unfit for its own tenants.[25] Shelter's report, *Far From Home*[26] highlighted the inadequacies of accommodation provided under the IAA 1999 both in and out of London. Of 154 properties occupied by asylum-seeker households, the majority were not safe from fire.

4.18   Where the Home Secretary decides that an applicant for support is destitute due to having no adequate accommodation under IAA 1999 s95(3)(a), s/he may provide accommodation which appears 'to be adequate for the needs of the supported person and his dependants (if any)'.[27] Section 97 then sets out the factors which must and may not be taken into account in providing housing.

4.19   Accommodation may be provided on a self-contained, bed and breakfast, full- or half-board basis, in a hostel, flat or house without regard to the asylum-seeker's 'preference'. In practice, the constant (political) emphasis on ignoring 'preference' appears to have limited statutory effect, since individual circumstances will be relevant (see para 4.24 below).

4.20   There is limited guidance on the standard of accommodation which should be provided to supported persons. Both the Act and the regulations use the word 'adequate' rather than 'suitable'. This reflects the 'no-choice' policy intention. Ministers have repeatedly suggested that the 'no-choice' approach to the housing of asylum-seekers is the same as the 'one offer' approach to the housing of homeless families. In evidence to the Special Standing Committee considering the bill, the Home Secretary, Jack Straw MP said, 'We

24 Ministerial statement, second reading of the IAA 1999, HC Debates, col 45, 22 February 1999.
25 NASS announced that the property would be inspected and it appears that some works may have been carried out. The asylum-seekers who are housed there were reluctant to take legal action.
26 *Far from Home: the housing of asylum-seekers in private rented accommodation*, Garvie (January 2001, Shelter publications).
27 IAA 1999 s96(1)(a).

have tried broadly to replicate the arrangements for people who are homeless but lawfully resident here whereby people have the one offer of accommodation and no more'.[28]

4.21   There is some support for challenging offers of inadequate accommodation to asylum-seekers on grounds similar to those used to challenge offers of unsuitable accommodation to homeless persons.[29] Home Office minister Barbara Roche MP gave this answer to a parliamentary question:

> The accommodation provider will have a contract with the National Asylum Support Service. They will ensure that the accommodation is 'suitable' in that it will be of an adequate standard; the relevant standard. The relevant standards are the same applied by local authorities when re-housing any homeless residents.[30]

4.22   NASS should take into account individual circumstances such as the location of other family members, education, medical and other social welfare needs when reaching a decision about where to accommodate a supported household.

Factors which may not be taken into account

4.23   In exercising his/her power to provide accommodation, the Home Secretary may not have regard to, 'any preference that the supported person or his dependants (if any) may have as to the locality in which the accommodation is to be provided'.[31]

4.24   Section 97 provides for regulations to prescribe factors which must or may not be taken into account. The AS Regs exclude from consideration any preference as to the 'nature of accommodation' to be provided and as to 'the nature and standard of fixtures and fittings'.[32] However, the regulation continues, ' . . . this shall not be taken to prevent the person's individual circumstances as they relate to accommodation needs being taken into account'. The government has drawn a distinction between preference and individual circumstances with assurances such as, ' . . . it is not required to have regard to preferences but we can have regard to circumstances. So we can look at the background circumstances of a group of asylum-seekers to disperse all those with a common ethnic, linguistic or territorial

---

28   25 March 1999.
29   Housing Act 1996 Part VII.
30   HC Written Answers, Vol 348, col 593, 20 April 2000.
31   IAA 1999 s97(2).
32   AS reg 13(2).

origin to a place common to all of them. That is looking at the circumstances and not preferences'.[33] This clearly requires NASS to take into account the location of other family members, education, medical and other social welfare needs.

Factors that must be taken into account

> When exercising his power under section 95 to provide accommodation, the Secretary of State must have regard to –
> (a) the fact that the accommodation is to be temporary pending determination of the asylum-seeker's claim;
> (b) the desirability, in general, of providing accommodation in areas where there is a ready supply of accommodation; and
> (c) such other matters as may be prescribed.[34]

4.25   The notion that the accommodation would be temporary was still a policy aspiration rather than a fact when the AS Regs came into force on 3 April 2000. The average time for processing an initial decision was an estimated 13 months but many claims had been outstanding for years.[35] If s97(1)(a) is relied on in defence to a challenge of adequacy, statistics could be obtained to show that the provision of support is not temporary. At the time of writing no matters had been prescribed.

Challenging dispersal

4.26   If an asylum-seeker refuses to travel to accommodation in a dispersal area, NASS may withdraw support. The remedy will then be an appeal to the Asylum Support Adjudicator. If such an appeal is unsuccessful, further support may be refused. It is therefore preferable to challenge dispersal directly by judicial review on the basis that the accommodation is not 'adequate'. The difficulty here is that a supported household may receive a couple of days' notice of a requirement to travel to the dispersal area, which leaves very little time to apply for permission for judicial review. Clients should be clearly warned of the consequences of failure to travel. It may be necessary

---

33 HL Debates, cols 1200–1201, 20 October 1999.
34 IAA 1999 s97(1).
35 The government aimed to make initial decisions on asylum applications for asylum within two months, determining appeals within a further four months by April 2001. It claimed to be meeting this target for families by Autumn 2000. The figures are misleading because they include up to 40% of negative decisions based on alleged 'non-compliance' with technical requirements (see para 1.79).

for them to move briefly to the dispersal area pending the initial judicial review application.

4.27   Section 97(1) sets out the presumption in favour of dispersing asylum-seekers around the UK. An asylum-seeker can challenge dispersal if accommodation has been offered, without taking into account individual circumstances and/or if the accommodation offered is not adequate for the household within the meaning of s96(1)(a). Dispersal was (indirectly) considered in asylum support appeal ASA 00/11/0095. The adjudicator decided that an elderly disabled couple, with adult children in London, had a reasonable excuse not to travel to NASS accommodation in a dispersal area. NASS had referred to its policy bulletins 30 and 31, which outline its approach to such cases. NASS allows a limited definition of 'close family tie' as a basis for refusal to travel outside London, where there are exceptional circumstances. The adjudicator considered there was a close family tie and exceptional circumstances. Considering the effect of article 8 right to respect for family life, she decided that dispersal was 'a legitimate aim' but that, in this case, the decision to disperse was neither necessary nor proportionate, following the approach in *Secretary of State for the Home Department v Abdi*.[36]

4.28   Detailed questions about the household's needs are asked in the NASS1 application form, which forms part of the AS Regs. It is worth reading the headings of the Schedule to the regulations (note 11): 'Ethnic Group and Religion, Health, Disability, Dietary needs, Any other information'. NASS has confirmed that it takes these factors into account as relevant considerations in determining the nature and location of accommodation. For example, under 'Ethnic Group and Religion' the note begins 'You should tell us your ethnic group and religion because it will help us to identify a suitable area for any accommodation we may give you'.

4.29   The following parliamentary statements by government ministers may be useful in supporting challenges to NASS decisions on adequacy of accommodation:

> The legislation does not allow us to take asylum-seekers' preferences as to location of accommodation into consideration. But if there is a particular reason . . . why an individual, or one of his dependants needs to be placed in a certain area, for example for ease of access to a specialised hospital to meet specific health needs, that will be taken into consideration by the directorate before reaching a decision.[37]

36   [1996] Imm AR 148, CA.
37   Lord Williams of Mostyn, *Hansard*, HL Debates, col 1163, 20 October 1999.

We shall have regard to any special needs, not least the safety, welfare and protection of children. Obviously we shall apply our minds to the maintenance of public health and work closely with local authorities, health authorities and public bodies to ensure that proper account is taken of these matters . . . As part of the arrangements we are making for the provision of accommodation and support, we shall be ensuring that the necessary translation services are made available . . . With regard to education, it is the Government's clear aim to ensure that all children of school age have proper access to the educational system that the Secretary of State would operate the dispersal policy with regard 'to any special needs, not least the safety, welfare and protection of children'.[38]

'Disbenefited' cases

4.30   Where asylum-seekers who are in receipt of social security benefits and/or housing as homeless receive a negative decision on their asylum claim on or after 25 September 2000, they are referred to as 'disbenefited' asylum-seekers. If they have an outstanding appeal or have children under 18, they are entitled to NASS support. It is NASS's policy not to disperse families in this category if they have dependent children who have been in school in the area where they live for a year or more. Single people will need to demonstrate 'exceptional compelling or compassionate reasons' for remaining in the area where they are settled. A similar phrase was used in the IND guidance on the operation of the local authority dispersal scheme[39] which suggests that 'a close family member' may constitute exceptional circumstances.

4.31   When the IAA 1999 was being debated, the Home Secretary made a parliamentary concession that families who were settled should not be dispersed (see para 4.36 and Appendix E). Barbara Roche MP later announced the policy on disbenefited asylum-seekers:

Any asylum-seeker who is in receipt of social security benefits and whose asylum claim is recorded as refused on or after 25 September 2000 and who would otherwise be destitute may seek support from the National Asylum Support Service (NASS) . . . Asylum-seekers who are no longer entitled to social security benefits after 25 September and who apply for a full support package from NASS are likely to be offered accommodation outside the south-east. However NASS will give due consideration to cases where there are exceptional compelling or compassionate reasons why an asylum-seeker should

38 Ibid.
39 IND Guidance, 19 November and 1 December 1999, see Appendix B.

be allowed to remain in the area in which he was living at the time the social security benefits were stopped. In cases where families have children who attended a particular school for at least 12 months, we will give consideration to enabling those asylum-seeker families to remain in their existing accommodation so that the education of those families is not unduly disrupted . . .[40]

4.32   It is arguable that asylum-seekers who have settled in an area over a long period, forming family and social ties, should not be dispersed, both on the basis of individual circumstances, HRA considerations and the discriminatory nature of such a policy. Evidence to support the argument could include medical and psychological needs, family and community ties, language needs, religious worship, and the effect on any children who have not been at school for a year. It would also be appropriate to consider whether there is a relevant asylum-seeker community in the area where the client is to be dispersed. If the dispersal interferes with article 8 or other qualified Convention rights, NASS would need to demonstrate that the policy is proportionate and legitimate.

Grounds for challenge

4.33   Possible grounds for challenging an offer of accommodation in the dispersal areas include:

Health

4.34   Accommodation which does not meet the supported household's physical or mental health needs, or with disrepair which makes it a significant risk to health, seems to fall outside the definition of 'adequate'. Shared accommodation may be inadequate if sharing adversely affects health or interferes with the family's right to respect for family life under article 8. Accommodation may be inadequate if the supported person needs to be near friends, family or members of the same refugee community for practical or emotional support.[41]

Access to immigration advice/interpreters

4.35   The shortage of immigration lawyers in the dispersal areas has been widely reported and may obstruct the asylum-seeker's right to pursue his/her asylum claim or appeal resulting in a breach of article 3 or

40   *Hansard*, HC Debates, col 766W, 26 January 2001.
41   See ASA 00/11/0095.

article 8.[42] A Law Society survey in autumn 2000 found that 62 per cent of 168 Community Legal Service (CLS) immigration firms had at some point not had the capacity to take on cases of asylum-seekers. The Legal Services Commission (LSC) has taken steps to address the shortage such as incentives to contractors and the funding of training courses run by the Immigration Law Practitioners' Association (ILPA). The LSC could be asked for details of the availability of immigration advice in the dispersal area, ie, numbers of immigration law franchises and legal help contracts. There is some funding for legal representatives to travel to advise asylum-seekers. In many of the dispersal areas there are limited interpreting and translation services in languages spoken by asylum-seekers.

Family settled in one area

4.36   Where a family has lived in a particular area for over a year, there is support from parliamentary statements[43] that they should not be moved, particularly if the children are settled in school:

> If people have waited for some time for the processing of a claim – whether it is genuine or unfounded; the circumstances of the transfer from their country are often traumatic, – and have settled in an area, I, my hon Friend the Under-Secretary and the officials in the department have no interest in gratuitously disrupting reasonably settled lives.[44]

Racial harassment

4.37   The approach of NASS and the Asylum Support Adjudicator to racial harassment is explained at para 3.104. Some of the asylum-seekers dispersed out of London to deprived inner-city areas have experienced serious racial harassment and local authorities have been forced to move them elsewhere. In a case where an asylum-seeker family was experiencing persistent harassment, evidence was obtained from the children's school, the family doctor, and local newspaper reports to demonstrate that the accommodation was inadequate because of the risk of harassment. In cases involving proposed accommodation, inquiries about the ethnicity of the area and statistics for racially motivated offences could be made of

---

42 The LSC has details of immigration franchises around the UK.
43 See also para 5.76.
44 Home Secretary, Jack Straw MP, *Hansard*, HC Debates, col 985, 9 November 1999.

agencies such as the local authority, the police and local Commission for Racial Equality.

Specialist medical needs

4.38   The availability of specialist support from organisations such as the Medical Foundation for the Care of Victims of Torture should be taken into account when decisions are taken about where asylum-seekers should be accommodated. This is documented in correspondence between the Medical Foundation and the Home Office and in the parliamentary debates on the Act:

> I pay tribute to the very fine work of the Medical Foundation for the Care of Victims of Torture. Where it is clear that someone needs specialised services which cannot be delivered other than through a body of that sort, and the location of that body does not fit in with our normal cluster arrangements, we shall consider the possibility of finding accommodation adjacent to those services . . .[45]

4.39   The Asylum Support Adjudicators have refused appeals against a withdrawal of support where asylum-seekers had refused to travel to the dispersal areas because they were on the waiting list for Medical Foundation treatment.[46] The approach of the adjudicators has been to distinguish the case of an asylum-seeker who is awaiting treatment from those where treatment has started. Adjudicator Brass has confirmed, 'arrangements are in place whereby the Secretary of State will offer accommodation in or near the London area to those asylum-seekers who are in receipt of treatment from the foundation'.[47] In the first such appeal[48] NASS had given an undertaking to consider moving the appellant nearer to London when counselling commenced (or, if appointments were infrequent, to pay travel costs). Where a doctor has referred an asylum-seeker to the Medical Foundation for consideration or where an in-country asylum-seeker is receiving on-going treatment, NASS may consider deferring dispersal. NASS has internal guidance governing these cases.[49]

45   Lord Williams of Mostyn, *Hansard*, HC Debates, col 1112, 21 July 1999.
46   ASA 00/09/0049 and ASA 00/09/00.
47   ASA 00/09/0049.
48   ASA 00/09/0044.
49   NASS will pay for travel costs from a dispersal area to the Medical Foundation. NASS Policy Bulletins 19 and 21 cover provision in cases where the supported person is receiving Medical Foundation treatment.

HIV status

> We have not selected particular areas for those with HIV infection. Instead when asylum-seekers make an application for asylum they are invited to indicate whether they have any special needs. Consideration is given on a case-by-case basis to those needs both in terms of the accommodation and support package and the proximity to any medical treatment which may be required.[50]

4.40 Asylum-seekers with AIDS or HIV status could obtain evidence of appropriate treatments and trials from specialist HIV agencies. It would also be relevant to obtain evidence of where other people with AIDS and HIV are settled to ensure the asylum-seeker can obtain appropriate treatment and support. Where their medical condition is symptomatic, a request to social services for a community care assessment and provision may ensure that they are provided with accommodation which meets their medical needs (see chapter 7).

Effect of refusing an offer of accommodation

4.41 In cases where an asylum-seeker has refused an initial offer of accommodation, support can be refused (AS Reg 19) or withdrawn on the ground of breach of conditions. The AS Regs provide:

Suspension or discontinuation of support
20 (1) Asylum support for a supported person and his dependants (if any), or for one or more dependants of a supported person, may be suspended or discontinued if – . . .
(c) the Secretary of State has reasonable grounds to suspect that the supported person has intentionally made himself and his dependants (if any) destitute . . .

4.42 This clearly relates to cases where the person who has refused an offer is already a 'supported person'. A supported person is someone who is receiving support under IAA 1999 s95.[51] This does not include those receiving temporary support arranged by reception assistants under s98. Nor does it include those who have applied to NASS for support after initially being self-supporting, eg, those staying with friends and relatives. In such cases the effect of refusing an offer is that as long as that accommodation is available, NASS would not have a duty to make an offer of different accommodation unless the

---

50 Barbara Roche MP, Under-Secretary of State for the Home Office in response to a parliamentary question, *Hansard*, HC Debates, col 378, 17 April 2000.
51 IAA 1999 s94(1).

original accommodation was not 'adequate'. If an applicant refuses an offer and then reapplies at a later stage, NASS would only have a duty to make an offer of different accommodation if there is a material change of circumstances, eg, an application for vouchers, only where the applicant can stay in London with friends.

4.43   A refusal of an offer may lead to a finding of 'intentional destitution' if the asylum-seeker is a supported person, eg, being transferred from accommodation arranged by NASS to alternative accommodation. In exercising the discretion to treat a supported person as 'intentionally destitute', NASS has a duty as a public authority under HRA 1998 s6 to take the Human Rights Convention into account. In such cases there is no appeal to an Asylum Support Ajudicator to challenge the adequacy of accommodation. The appropriate remedy is an application for judicial review.

4.44   After support has been suspended or terminated, NASS can refuse to consider another application for support unless there has been a change of relevant circumstances.[52] These circumstances are the reg 15 changes which there is a duty to report (see para 4.103) such as births, deaths and marriages. The Home Secretary may consider an application if there are 'exceptional circumstances' to justify a further application being made.

4.45   Where the household contains children under 18, the family might be able to obtain assistance under Children Act 1989 s17 if NASS withdraws support. A local authority cannot provide Children Act help under s17 if the Home Secretary is offering or arranging adequate accommodation and/or essential living needs.[53] The wording of IAA 1999 s122 suggests that there is a continuing duty to offer adequate accommodation and living expenses to families with children under 18, but no duty to actually provide accommodation if an offer is refused:

> (3) If it appears to the Secretary of State that adequate accommodation is not being provided for the child, he must exercise his powers under section 95 by offering, and if his offer is accepted by providing or arranging for the provision of, adequate accommodation for the child as part of the eligible person's household.
>
> (4) If it appears to the Secretary of State that essential living needs of the child are not being met, he must exercise his powers under section 95 by offering, and if his offer is accepted by providing or

---

52 AS reg 21.
53 IAA 1999 s122(3)–(5). Circumstances may in future be prescribed where s122(5) does not apply: IAA 1999 s122(11).

arranging for the provision of, essential living needs for the child as part of the eligible person's household.

4.46 The government made it clear in response to questions about the exclusion of children from s17 duties that the social services safety net would remain:

> Even in those rare circumstances in which a person refuses an offer that is considered to be reasonable and a reasonable discharge of the Secretary of State's duty the children would become the responsibility of the Social Services department . . . The only duties under the Children Act being transferred from the local authority social services department to the Asylum Support Directorate at the Home Office are those in respect of accommodation and essential living needs. The local social services department's much wider duty in respect of the welfare of children remains continuous . . .[54]

Section 4 accommodation and Oakington

4.47 When a claim for asylum is made, the Home Office will usually consider whether to detain the applicant or grant 'temporary admission'.[55] The grant of temporary admission may be subject to residence conditions under the Immigration Act 1971.

4.48 IAA 1999 s4 gives the Home Secretary the power to provide or arrange for the provision of facilities for the accommodation of persons –

(a) temporarily admitted to the United Kingdom under paragraph 21 of Schedule 2 to the 1971 Act;
(b) released from detention under that paragraph; or
(c) released on bail from detention under any provision of the Immigration Acts.

4.49 Hard cases support is provided under s4. This is board and lodging provided to some childless asylum-seekers whose claim for asylum and appeal has been refused.[56]

4.50 Oakington Detention Centre is an old RAF base in Cambridge which is used to provide temporary accommodation for up to 400 asylum-seekers including families. When s4 was debated it was at first implied that it was needed to provide the power to establish facilities such as Oakington. Then on 2 November 1999, Lord Williams of Mostyn said:

---

54 Home Secretary, Jack Straw MP, *Hansard*, HC Debates, col 464, 16 June 1999.
55 See further para 1.62.
56 See para 3.169.

I stress that the facility at Oakington is based on existing detention powers . . . it is designed to deal with claims where it appears that a rapid decision can be made . . . applicants will be required to stay at Oakington under existing immigration powers to detain.[57]

4.51   An asylum-seeker can be required to stay at Oakington and observe a curfew as a condition of his/her temporary admission pending a rapid decision on the asylum claim or a transfer to NASS accommodation. If the condition is breached, the asylum-seeker risks being detained in prison or an ordinary detention centre. Oakington is designed to house asylum-seekers with 'unmeritorious' claims while quick decisions are made. There is no regulation of support provision or the suitability of accommodation at Oakington by the IAA 1999. Asylum-seekers who are resident there have access to state-funded immigration advice from the Immigration Advice Service or the Refugee Legal Centre.

Essential living needs

Level of support

The proposed provision is set at 70 per cent of the equivalent income support because the asylum support system is intended to be on a short-term basis, a safety net arrangement, and it should be possible to live on these amounts for short periods only.[58]

4.52   Where the household has no other income, the levels for maximum asylum support are set by the AS Regs at approximately 70 per cent of income support levels (excluding premiums) at the time the Act came into force. Apart from the planned temporary nature of support, the explanation given for setting asylum support at a figure 30 per cent below the official poverty line was that asylum-seekers would not have overheads such as the need to replace household items or utility bills.[59] 'The accommodation will contain domestic utensils and equipment necessary for a decent level of existence including linen, pots and pans, cutlery, crockery and so forth. In addition, council tax will be paid and the utilities – gas, electricity and water – will be paid also.'[60] Where accommodation is provided by NASS, it is the landlord

---

57 *Hansard*, HL, Vol 606, col 733, 2 November 1999.
58 Home Secretary, Jack Straw MP, *Hansard*, Vol 333, col 475, 15 June 1999.
59 *Asylum-seekers Support, An information document setting out proposals for the new support scheme*, Home Office, March 1999, para 4.19.
60 Lord Williams of Mostyn, *Hansard*, HL Debates, col 251, 29 June 1999.

and not the asylum-seeker who is liable for council tax (see para 3.128).

4.53   If a supported household is not being provided with the above, it may be possible to challenge the level of support provided (see below). This may be appropriate where a supported household is not living in accommodation provided by NASS and is responsible for utility bills.

4.54   The standard levels of support are included as a table in the regulations.[61]

Qualifying couple (*married/unmarried, both must be 16 or over, one over 18*)	£57.37
Lone parent aged 18 or over	£36.54
Single person aged 25 or over	£36.54
Single person aged at least 18 but under 25	£28.95
Person aged at least 16 but under 18 (except a member of a qualifying couple)	£31.75
Person aged under 16	£30.95[62]

4.55   When specifying these levels of support, AS reg 10 states asylum support may be expected to be provided at these levels *as a general rule*. This allows scope for greater or lesser amounts to be provided where appropriate. The government suggested that regulations would be made under the IAA 1999 to specify the circumstances in which the Home Secretary could make payments to meet special needs, eg, where a medical condition gives rise to special needs.[63] Similarly IAA 1999 Sch 8 allows for regulations to provide for particular items falling outside the definition of 'essential living needs'. There are no such regulations to date – the AS Regs do not expressly make any such provision. NASS has introduced a one-off maternity payment.[64] The s96(1)(b) provision for essential living needs would allow NASS to make payment at an appropriate level, eg, a higher payment may be appropriate if an asylum-seeker has a need for additional heating or a special diet due to a medical condition. Asylum-seekers with health needs could argue for support to be provided at a higher level.

61   See AS reg 10.
62   Increased from £26.60 on 4 December 2000. Asylum Support (Amendment) Regulations 2000 SI No 3053.
63   IAA 1999 Sch 8, paras 3 and 4, and explanatory notes para 281.
64   NASS Policy Bulletin 37.

4.56   Although there is no inflation-linked provision for annual increases in asylum, there was a government commitment 'to make regular annual reviews of the level at which support is provided to asylum-seekers'.[66]

4.57   Households receiving local authority support under the Asylum Support (Interim Provisions) Regulations 1999[67] may be paid at different rates.[68]

Forms of support

Excluded items

4.58   Support may be given 'by providing what appear to the Secretary of State to be essential living needs of the supported person and his dependants'.[69] These are prescribed by AS reg 9(4)[70] and exclude the cost of faxes, computer facilities, photocopying, travel (except to bail hearings, Home Office interviews/appeals and the initial journey to NASS accommodation), toys and entertainment expenses. The most controversial item on this list is toys. The purpose of including toys on the list is to underline the Home Secretary's view that they are not an essential living need for the provision of public funds. However, it has been suggested that the exclusion may breach the UN Convention on the Rights of the Child.[71] The Home Office has suggested that the supported person would have to use his/her £10 per week cash to cover any excluded expenses.[72]

The voucher scheme[73]

> . . . children are denied equality in the playground and are pointed at as the voucher children. We regard that as fundamentally unacceptable and inhumane . . . Article 3 of the convention on the rights of the child states: 'In all actions concerning children, whether

66   Lord Williams of Mostyn, *Hansard*, HL Debates, col 1164, 20 October 1999 and see note 33.
67   SI No 3056.
68   See para 5.53.
69   IAA 1999 s96(1)(b).
70   See paras 4.52.
71   See chapter 8.
72   See, eg, 'Consultation Documents on the Main Regulations under Part VI of the Immigration and Asylum Act 1999', NASS, November 1999, para 14 and 'Asylum-seekers Support, An information document setting out proposals for the new support scheme', Home Office, March 1999, para 4.21.
73   At the time of writing the government was conducting a review of the voucher scheme.

undertaken by public or private social welfare institutions, courts of law, administrative authorities or legislative bodies, the best interest of the child shall be a primary consideration.' We feel that the provisions will not be in the best interest of the child. Article 2 of the same convention declares: 'States Parties shall respect and ensure the rights set forth in the present Convention to each child within their jurisdiction without discrimination of any kind'.[74]

4.59   Asylum support must be not be provided wholly or mainly in cash unless the individual circumstances are exceptional.[75] This provision is based on the government's view that provision in kind would deter 'abusive' asylum claims. The regulations provide that asylum support will usually be provided in the form of vouchers which can be exchanged for goods or services and a maximum of £10 per week, per supported person, in cash. The vouchers are issued to the support applicant and are non-transferable. They are distributed through the Post Office where the £10 cash element can be converted into money.

4.60   The Home Office entered a contract for the provision of vouchers with a company called Sodexho Pass International which has experience of operating similar schemes in other parts of Europe. Its scheme is generally more flexible than the ad hoc schemes operated by local authorities supporting asylum-seekers, which have often been limited to one or two large supermarket chains. Sodexho also has contracts with independent retailers including second-hand shops and some specialist food-shops. The smallest denomination voucher is 50 pence.

4.61   Many of the problems which are inherent in a voucher scheme, and explain the widespread public opposition to it, remain. Asylum-seekers are unable to purchase food at the cheapest outlets such as markets. Some are unable to purchase items dictated by their culture, or religion or medical condition. The Home Office does not allow cash change when items are purchased with vouchers. Organisations running charity shops such as Oxfam, where asylum-seekers could purchase second-hand clothes, campaigned for the voucher scheme to be withdrawn or at least change to be allowed. Evidence supplied by Oxfam and other agencies to the Home Office review of the voucher scheme could be obtained to support a claim that an individual household should receive provision in cash on the basis of 'exceptional circumstances' (see para 5.55).

74   UNHCR submission to the Immigration and Asylum Bill Special Standing Committee, *Hansard*, HC Debates, col 143, 16 March 1999.
75   IAA 1999 s96(3).

4.62   In evidence to the Parliamentary Special Standing Committee, Kent County Council stated that the existing scheme was detrimental to community relations, creating tensions between asylum-seekers and other shoppers. The United Nations High Commission for Refugees (UNHCR), quoted above at para 4.59, was particularly concerned about the stigmatising effect, especially on children, in the light of the International Covenant on Civil and Political Rights and the International Covenant on Economic, Social and Cultural Rights. Although the UK is a party to both conventions, unlike the Human Rights Convention, they are not part of domestic law.[76]

4.63   The Home Secretary has retained the power to replace support in kind with support in the form of cash.[77] There is scope for this if the voucher scheme proves to be a failure whether due to legal challenges or political pressure. There is potential for a challenge to the voucher scheme if there is evidence of adverse effect on the health and/or welfare of supported households. This could take the form of a judicial review supported by human rights arguments. Another approach would be to complain to an MP, perhaps after collecting evidence of adverse effect from a number of households in a particular locality. The Home Office is subject to the new Race Relations (Amendment) Act 2000, which prevents public bodies from discriminating on racial grounds. Where immigration functions are involved, unlawful discrimination on 'racial grounds' is limited to colour and race, so that it is not unlawful to discriminate 'on grounds of nationality or ethnic or national origins'.

Other forms of support and welfare provision

Expenses connected with the asylum claim or bail hearings[78]

4.64   The supported person may be provided with expenses other than legal expenses, which are incurred in connection with the asylum claim.[79] This covers the cost of travel to interviews at the Home Office or port of entry, and arguably to appeal hearings. It also covers travel to appointments at the Medical Foundation for a medical assessment connected to the claim[80] and arguably should cover other similar

76   See further para 8.101.
77   IAA 1999 s96(5).
78   Ibid, s96(1)(c)–(e).
79   Ibid, s96(1)(c).
80   NASS Policy Bulletin 19.

medical appointments. The IAA 1999 explanatory notes at para 300 suggest that it would include the cost of preparing and copying documents. AS reg 9(4)(c) specifically excludes photocopying costs from the assessment of an asylum-seeker's essential living needs when considering whether s/he is destitute. The LSC will finance the cost of travel to a solicitor as a Legal Help disbursement.

4.65   The asylum-seeker and his/her dependants should receive travel costs to enable them to attend bail hearings of either an asylum-seeker or dependant who is detained under any provision of the Immigration Acts.[81] This is aimed at enabling the whole supported household to travel back to the dispersal area after a court hearing.

Exceptional circumstances

4.66   Support may be provided in other ways if the circumstances of a particular case are exceptional.[82] Although this is a discretion rather than a duty, it could be read in conjunction with the HRA 1998 to extend the limited provision provided by the IAA and AS Regs. It should allow more extensive provision in the form of cash or by other means where a supported person has a physical disability or HIV positive status if this gives rise to additional costs.[83]

Funeral costs

4.67   NASS has refused to pay for the funeral costs of an asylum-seeker who died while receiving NASS support on the ground that there was no power to provide for him/her because s/he was no longer an asylum-seeker within the meaning of s94(1). If the dependant of a supported person dies, an application for a funeral payment could be made on the basis of exceptional circumstances under s96(3).

Six-monthly lump sum[84]

4.68   After six months of receiving support, each supported person is eligible to claim a payment of £50 in vouchers, which can be exchanged for cash. It is up to each household to make a claim as the payment is

81 IAA 1999 s96(1)(d) and (e).
82 Ibid, s96(3).
83 Disabled asylum-seekers are excluded from the eligibility for disability living allowance which enables other disabled people to cover extra costs: IAA 1999 s115(1)(d).
84 AS reg 11.

not awarded automatically. This payment will be repeated every six months for as long as support is received. This means that a family with a dependent child under 18 will be eligible for it for as long as they are in the UK receiving support, even after an unsuccessful appeal.

4.69   The Secretary of State may refuse to make the payment if s/he believes the supported person is responsible without reasonable excuse for the delay in 'the determination of his claim for asylum'.[85]

Maternity payment

4.70   A supported person may claim a one-off maternity payment of £300 within two weeks of the birth of a child (NASS Policy Bulletin 37).

Education and leisure

4.71   AS reg 14 makes a provision for 'services' to asylum-seekers in the form of education including English language classes and 'developmental activities' such as sport but only 'for the purpose of maintaining good order' among supported persons.

4.72   Asylum-seeker children are entitled to primary and secondary education under the Education Act 1996 s10, which places a duty on local education authorities to secure adequate places in primary and secondary schools for children residing temporarily or permanently in their area. Department of Education and Science circulars state that these duties 'are not qualified by the immigration status of parents'.[86] There is guidance in the Department of Education and Employment (DfEE) Code of Practice on School Admissions, Annex B.[87]

4.73   The Parents Charter 1994 advises parents: 'You have a right to a school place for your child from age 5 to age 16 and a school or college place for him or her from 16 to 18. These places are provided free of charge. You have a duty to make sure that your child goes to school until he or she is 16. You can say which school you would prefer your child to go to'.[88] The Education Act 1996 requires local education authorities and governors of maintained schools to admit children to the school of their choice, subject to resource consider-

---

85   Ibid, reg 11(6).
86   Department of Education and Science Circulars 11/88 and 6/93.
87   www.dfee.gov.uk/sacode/index.htm.
88   'Our children's education: The updated Parents' Charter 1994', DfEE, p9.

ations. Judicial review could be considered in a case where a local education authority failed to provide adequate school places for asylum-seeker children, or failed to allow asylum-seekers to exercise parental choice in selecting a school for their child.

4.74   Local education authorities must provide free school meals to children of asylum-seekers receiving asylum support under IAA 1999 Part VI.[89] DfEE *Guidance on Support of Asylum Seeking and Refugee Families* covers entitlement for children receiving interim support. School uniform grants remain discretionary, but arguably could fall within a local authority's duties under Children Act 1989 s17.

Health costs

4.75   If a household is in receipt of asylum support, certain health benefits are passported.[90] The supported person needs to apply to NASS for a certificate HC2 which allows free prescription, dental treatment, sight tests, wigs and fabric supports. Applications should be renewed every six months. Vouchers for the cost of glasses or contact lenses and travel costs to and from hospital may also be available. Where these items have already been paid for, a refund can be claimed within three months.

Setting the level of support

4.76   The Home Secretary may decide that an asylum-seeker is destitute due to inadequate resources or accommodation even though the household has some income or assets. In deciding what kind and level of support to offer, AS reg 12 repeats the list of relevant factors at AS reg 6(4).[91] Any income, assets or support of the applicant or his/her dependant(s) may be taken into account in deciding what kind of support should be offered and at what level. Support provided under the Act is excluded but other resources are relevant, whether in or outside the UK, if they might reasonably be expected to be available to the household.

Contributions to support

4.77   An asylum-seeker may have some resources but still be eligible for

---

89   IAA 1999 Sch 14, para 117 amends the Education Act 1996 s512(3).
90   AS Regs Sch.
91   See Appendix A.

support. AS reg 12 should be read in conjunction with reg 16 which works in a similar way to the old civil legal aid scheme (now CLS certificate of funding for representation) where an assisted person would make periodic contributions while receiving full legal aid. Prompt payment of contributions may be made a condition of continued asylum support.[92]

4.78   Where an asylum-seeker has resources, the Home Secretary can:

– set the asylum support at a level to reflect the resources; or
– set the asylum support at the standard level but require the supported person to make payments to NASS in the form of 'contributions'.[93]

Overpayments

4.79   Where asylum support has been overpaid due to an error by NASS, the Act allows for the Home Secretary to recover the overpayment as a debt.[94] It can also be recovered by deductions from the asylum support.[95]

4.80   Section 114 limits recovery to an overpayment which is the result of 'an error on the part of the Secretary of State'. Where overpayment is due to a criminal misrepresentation by the applicant or a third party, recovery may be ordered by the court, even if there is no finding of fraud.[96] It may be arguable that the overpayment provisions are inapplicable in a case where the overpayment is due to an innocent error on the part of the applicant and/or where there are no court proceedings.

Breach of conditions[97]

4.81   Support may be provided subject to written conditions.[98] The extent to which the household has complied with any conditions is specified as a factor which can be taken into account in deciding the level or kind of support to be provided.[99] A breach of conditions also allows support

---

92   IAA 1999 s95(9) and AS reg 16(4).
93   AS reg 16.
94   IAA 1999 s114 or AS reg 17.
95   AS reg 18.
96   IAA 1999 s112.
97   AS reg 19, see also para 3.102.
98   IAA 1999 s95(9) and (1).
99   AS reg 19(1)(b).

to be withdrawn.[100] An example of this is that NASS's internal instructions provide that travel to accommodation in the dispersal areas is a condition of support. If an asylum-seeker fails to travel, NASS may terminate support on the basis that conditions have been breached.

4.82   A strict approach to conditions could make the asylum support regime punitive in relation both to the terminating of support and to the type of support offered. There is no express provision that the conditions must be reasonable. The qualification that conditions have been breached 'without reasonable excuse' applies explicitly in cases of suspension or termination of support due to breach of conditions.

4.83   The question of when support should be withdrawn due to a breach of conditions is discussed in detail in other chapters. *R v Kensington and Chelsea RBC ex p Kujtim*[101] requires that community care help for destitute asylum-seekers should only be withdrawn after a thorough investigation. The Court of Appeal also indicated that a discharge of duty could only occur after a persistent refusal to comply with requirements and a warning letter. It is arguable that NASS should take these considerations into account when exercising its discretion to reduce the level of support or change the form of support.

4.84   The IAA 1999 explanatory notes suggest that 'individuals who vandalised the property they had been allocated' could be in breach of conditions where consideration would be given to the level and nature of future support.[102] Are supported households who have misbehaved to be placed in less desirable accommodation or get fewer food vouchers? In practice it is difficult to see how NASS could offer asylum support of less than 70 per cent of income support without violating articles 2 or 3 of the Human Rights Convention.

Remedies and complaints

Problems with accommodation

4.85   Problems with the standard of NASS accommodation and harassment or similar complaints are discussed in chapter 6 at para 6.149 onwards.

---

100 Ibid, reg 19(1)(a), see para 3.102.
101 *R v Kensington and Chelsea RLBC ex p Kujtim* [1999] 4 All ER 161; (1999) 2 CCLR 340, CA.
102 IAA 1999 explanatory notes, para 284.

Judicial review

4.86   The Asylum Support Adjudicator does not have jurisdiction to hear appeals about the adequacy of accommodation or the kind and level of support provided.

4.87   If a supported household is provided with accommodation which is not adequate, an application for judicial review should be made of the decision by the Home Secretary (ie, by NASS decision-makers) to provide that accommodation, on the basis that s/he has failed to take into account relevant circumstances or has acted unlawfully. NASS will be represented in any such action by the Treasury Solicitor who should be notified of any hearing.[103]

4.88   A supported person may wish to bring a challenge on the basis that the level or kind of support is inappropriate, eg, that support should be provided in cash rather than in kind due to exceptional circumstances or that more vouchers are needed because of special needs such as a diabetic diet. Again, judicial review would be the appropriate remedy.

Procedures and ancillary matters

4.89   NASS's provision of support under IAA 1999 is linked to the Home Office's immigration control functions by new powers contained in Part VI of the Act. Support is provided subject to conditions and asylum-seekers may be prosecuted if they fail to report a relevant change of circumstances. The provisions explained below apply to both interim support and asylum support. There are wide powers to obtain and exchange information, and to enter premises. A number of new criminal offences aim to deter fraud and misrepresentation by asylum-seekers or those who seek to profit from them.

Procedures for provision of support under IAA 1999 Part VI

4.90   Asylum support may be provided subject to conditions. A written copy of these conditions should be provided to the supported per-

---

103   Treasury Solicitor, 25 Queen Anne's Gate, London SW1; tel 0209 210 3039; fax 0207 210 3433.

son.[104] The conditions should be translated into the asylum-seeker's first language where necessary or translated if appropriate. In relation to accommodation, conditions are likely to be in the form of a licence agreement. In relation to living expenses, the conditions will be based on the duty to notify change of circumstances, eg, if the asylum-seeker gets a job or moves house.

Duty to notify of change of circumstances

4.91 The supported person or a dependant must notify the Home Secretary, without delay, of any relevant change of circumstances. There are 18 relevant changes listed in AS reg 15(2) which range from pregnancy to death.[105] If a person (not simply the applicant) does not notify relevant changes s/he faces suspension or termination of support and/or prosecution.

4.92 In summary, the relevant changes of circumstances in relation to the supported person or a dependant are:

- a new dependant arrives in the UK;
- new assets;
- gaining/losing employment;
- marriage/divorce/cohabitation/separation;
- name change;
- pregnancy/childbirth;
- leaving school;
- sharing accommodation with someone new;
- moving house/leaving accommodation;
- hospital/prison admission;
- leaving the UK;
- death.

4.93 There is a power to make further inquiries and request further information from the supported person or his/her dependants if the Home Secretary considers that it affects the future provision of asylum support.[106]

---

104 IAA 1999 s95(9)–(11).
105 See Appendix A.
106 AS reg 15(3).

Home Office powers to obtain information and enter premises

4.95   These powers have serious civil liberties implications both in relation to the supported person and those who accommodate him/her including friends, relatives or voluntary sector organisations. There may be scope for challenges to these parts of the Act on the basis that they are incompatible with the Human Rights Convention, article 8, and Protocol 1, article 1.

Exchange of information about asylum-seekers

4.96   Information held by the police, the National Criminal Intelligence Service, the national crime squad, or Customs and Excise can be supplied to the Home Office for use in the provision of support to asylum-seekers.[107] Similarly the Home Office can pass on information to those agencies.[108] The aim is to obtain information from other agencies, including contractors, to identify and prosecute those who use the asylum support scheme for the purposes of fraud.[109]

Warrants under IAA 1999 s125

4.97   The Home Secretary has the power to obtain a warrant to enter accommodation which NASS has provided to a supported household. The warrant can be executed 'at any reasonable time . . . using reasonable force'. A justice of the peace may grant a warrant to a person authorised in writing by the Home Secretary, if satisfied that there is reason to believe that:

   (a) the supported person or any dependants of his for whom the accommodation is provided is not resident in it,
   (b) the accommodation is being used for any purpose other than the accommodation of the asylum-seeker or any dependants of his, or
   (c) any person other than the supported person and his dependants (if any) is residing in the accommodation.

4.98   This is a draconian power which allows the grant of a warrant in a

---

107   IAA 1999 s20.
108   IAA 1999 s21.
109   Mike O'Brien, Under-Secretary of State for the Home Department, *Hansard*, HC Debates, col 499, 16 June 1999.

very wide range of circumstances. The provision may breach article 1 of Protocol 1 and article 8 of the Human Rights Convention.[110]

Information from property owners[111]

4.99   The power to obtain a warrant to forcibly enter asylum-seekers' homes is complemented by a power to obtain information about where supported persons live. Section 126 enables the Home Secretary to obtain information from friends, relatives or others providing accommodation to asylum-seekers who are receiving vouchers only from NASS. Information may be required from any person appearing to the Home Secretary to have any interest or be involved in any way in the management or control of the accommodation.

4.100   The Home Secretary can demand 'such information with respect to the premises and the persons occupying them as he may specify'. The only limitation is that information obtained may only be used in the exercise of his functions under IAA 1999 Part VI (the support provisions). This provides the limited consolation that any information is used in relation to asylum support decisions, not in relation to ordinary immigration decisions such as the asylum claim, detention, deportation, etc.

Information from postal services[112]

4.101   The Home Secretary may track down persons who have moved while receiving asylum support by requiring postal services to give details of any forwarding address. The terms of the power are that the information is:

(a) for use in the prevention, detection, investigation or prosecution of criminal offences under this Part;

(b) for use in checking the accuracy of information relating to support provided under this Part;

(c) for any other purpose relating to the provision of support to asylum-seekers.

4.102   Unlike s126, there is no limit on the use of the information obtained, provided it is obtained for one of the above purposes.

---

110   See chapter 8.
111   IAA 1999 s126.
112   Ibid, s127.

Therefore, such information could be passed on to those responsible for deciding the asylum claim.

Criminal offences

4.103 A series of new criminal offences which relate to the provision of asylum support are established by IAA 1999 ss105–108. Prosecution will be in the magistrates' court. The most serious offence has a maximum sentence of seven years' imprisonment.

4.104   It is not merely the asylum-seeker or applicant for support who is liable to prosecution. Any person or body corporate, such as a private landlord or housing association, may be found guilty of the offence. This renders an asylum-seeker's representative, friend, relative or housing provider potentially liable if s/he fails to pass on information.

4.105   In the case of a body corporate, it will be liable if an offence has been committed with the consent or connivance of an officer (director, manager, secretary or similar) or due to his/her neglect. Both the relevant officer and the organisation may be prosecuted and sentenced.[113]

False or dishonest representations[114]

4.106 The first two offences in Part VI cover misrepresentations or failure to notify a change of circumstances. The wording builds on the misrepresentation provisions governing homeless and housing register applicants.[115] There is no express requirement in the IAA 1999 to explain to every applicant his/her duties and potential liability in ordinary language, as required by the Housing Act 1996. The Asylum Support Adjudicator considered the effect of s105(1) in an asylum support appeal where support had been withdrawn after a young asylum-seeker gave incorrect information about her age and identity. The adjudicator decided that no offence had been committed under s105(1)(a), because there had been no warning.[116]

4.107   A distinction is drawn between false and dishonest representations. 'False representations'[117] are where the aim is 'obtaining

113 Ibid, s109.
114 Ibid, ss105 and 106.
115 Housing Act 1996 ss171 and 124.
116 ASA 00/09/0061.
117 IAA 1999 s105.

support for himself or any other person'. The offence is triable in the magistrates' court with a sentence of up to three months and/or a fine of up to scale 5 (currently £2,000).

4.108   'Dishonest representations'[118] are where the aim is 'obtaining any benefit or other payment or advantage for himself or any other person' and the conduct must be dishonest. The sentence if tried in the magistrate's court is up to six months' imprisonment and/or the statutory maximum fine. In the case of more serious offences it can be tried in the Crown Court with imprisonment of up to seven years and/or a fine.

4.109   The s106 'dishonest misrepresentations' offence is aimed at serious and calculated fraud 'such as where someone makes a plan to extract as much from the Home Office as possible by deception'.[119] Section 105 in contrast is aimed at false misrepresentations to obtain asylum support. In either case the person may be guilty of an offence under any one of four heads:

- making a statement or representation knowing it is false;
- producing or arranging for the production of false documents or information;
- failing to notify a change of relevant circumstances when required to do so in accordance with any provision made by or under Part VI (this is qualified by 'without reasonable excuse' in the case of false representations only);
- knowingly causing another person's failure to notify a change of relevant circumstances (without reasonable excuse in the case of s105).

4.110   Perhaps the most significant of the above for a supported person is s105(c) which makes it an offence not to notify a relevant change of circumstance 'when required to do so'. AS reg 15 imposes an onerous requirement to notify specified changes of circumstances 'without delay' (see paras 4.91 and 4.92). Asylum-seekers should be informed of these when they claim support. If there are any prosecutions under this clause, one possible defence may be that the relevant circumstances and the duty to notify were not explained to the supported person in his/her first language.

---

118   Ibid, s106.
119   Ibid, explanatory notes, para 322.

Delay or obstruction

4.111   Section 107 introduces a vague and broad offence of 'delay or ob-struction without reasonable excuse' which is punishable in the magistrates' court by a fine of up to scale 3 (£1,000). Any person may be guilty of this if s/he:

(a) intentionally delays or obstructs a person exercising functions conferred by or under this Part; or
(b) refuses or neglects to answer a question, give any information or produce any document when required to do so in accordance with any provision made by or under this Part.

4.112   There is considerable scope for prosecuting asylum-seekers and their associates under this provision. The broad framing of the provision may indicate an aim of deterrence rather than conviction.

Failure of sponsor to maintain

4.113   Section 108 introduces the offence of a refusal or neglect of a sponsor to maintain his/her spouse or dependent relative. The failure must result in asylum support being provided and there is a defence of 'reasonable excuse' or being on strike. Sponsorship is discussed at para 1.24. The provision is aimed at cases where someone obtains leave to enter the UK on the basis of sponsorship and subsequently claims asylum. The sentence is up to three months' imprisonment and/or a fine up to level 4 (£1,500).

Interim support

For complete chapter contents, see overleaf

Introduction

5.1   Interim support is the 'interim scheme' of support provided by local authorities under the Asylum Support (Interim Provisions) Regulations 1999[1] ('Interim Regs'). This is distinguished here from asylum support provided by the National Asylum Support Service (NASS) under the Asylum Support Regulations 2000[2] ('AS Regs'). A destitute asylum-seeker who is ineligible for social security benefits[3] can claim either asylum support or interim support, depending on the date of the asylum claim.

5.2   Until 6 December 1999 local authorities had a duty to look after destitute single asylum-seekers under National Assistance Act 1948 s21 as interpreted by *R v Hammersmith and Fulham LBC ex p M.*[4] Asylum-seeker households with dependent children were supported under Children Act 1989 s17.

5.3   When the IAA 1999 became law, NASS was not ready to support all destitute asylum-seekers. IAA 1999 s95(13)[5] provided for regulations to be made under Sch 9 of the Act. These established a scheme of support for an 'interim period' beginning on 6 December 1999, which could continue until 1 April 2002. This scheme required local authorities[6] to continue supporting destitute asylum-seekers, allowing NASS to gradually assume responsibility for new cases.

5.4   Both the asylum support and the interim support schemes originate in IAA 1999 Part VI. The schemes provide a bare safety-net of support to destitute asylum-seekers and their dependants. Despite the similarities, there are differences in the tests of eligibility, procedures, service provision and remedies. Unlike the AS Regs, the Interim Regs do not extend to Scotland or Northern Ireland.

5.5   This chapter provides a self-contained outline of interim support,

---

1   SI No 3056.
2   SI No 704.
3   See chapter 2 for details of which asylum-seekers are eligible for social security benefits.
4   (1997) 1 CCLR 85, CA.
5   IAA 1999 s170 provided for s95(13) and Sch 9 to take effect from 6 December 2000.
6   'Local authority' is defined by Interim reg 2(1) as a county or metropolitan district council, a district council with the functions of a county council, a London borough council, the Common Council of the City of London or the Council of the Isles of Scilly (in England) and a county or county borough council (in Wales).

referring to chapters 3 and 4 where the provisions are similar. After explaining who is eligible for interim support, it describes procedures and service provision, including the meaning of 'adequate accommodation' and challenges to dispersal. It then considers grounds on which local authorities may refuse or withdraw support and remedies. The new offences connected with the provision of Part VI support apply to both asylum and interim support and are explained in chapter 4.[7]

Legal framework

5.6　On 6 December 1999, asylum-seeker adults and families being supported by local authorities under National Assistance Act 1948 s21 or the Children Act 1989, were deemed to be transferred to the interim support scheme.[8] The new scheme is administered along similar lines to the previous community care arrangements. Unaccompanied asylum-seeker children under 18 continue to be provided for under the Children Act 1989.

5.7　On the same date, the Interim Regs, which set out the terms of the interim support scheme, came into force. The Home Secretary then made a series of directions under IAA 1999 Sch 15, para 14(1) specifying when the interim period specified by reg 2(5) would end. The directions ended local authorities' responsibility to support the various categories of asylum-seekers on specified dates.[9] National Assistance Act 1948 s21 was amended by IAA 1999 s116 so that 'persons subject to immigration control' were excluded from eligibility. This was limited to cases where needs arose *solely* as a result of destitution (or the likely physical effects of destitution). Destitute asylum-seeker families must be provided with housing and living expenses under s95 of the Act, rather than under Children Act 1989 s17 for families eligible for IAA 1999 support.[10]

5.8　The Home Office Immigration and Nationality Directorate (IND) has produced useful guidance on the Interim Regs dated 19 November 1999 and 1 December 1999 respectively[11] ('IND guidance'). There is also guidance issued to local authorities by the Local Government

---

7　Paras 4.103–4.113.
8　Interim reg 11.
9　See paras 3.7–3.9.
10　IAA 1999 s122, Interim reg 12.
11　See Appendix B.

Association[12] ('LGA guidance') which governs procedures for the dispersal of asylum-seekers out of the south-east to other parts of the UK. The IAA 1999 explanatory notes also offer some assistance in interpreting the provisions. The decisions of the Asylum Support Adjudicators offer guidance on questions of eligibility for support,[13] although their jurisdiction is limited to appeals against NASS decisions and so the case-law is not directly binding on local authorities. NASS has a set of internal policy bulletins or instructions containing the Home Secretary's interpretation of the law.[14]

Key features

5.9 Key features of the interim support scheme include:

- Asylum-seekers and their dependants are 'eligible' for support if they 'appear to be destitute or to be likely to become destitute within 14 days'.[15]
- A person is destitute if s/he does not have adequate accommodation or cannot meet other 'essential' living needs.[16]
- The local authority has to decide whether a person is 'eligible'[17], ie, 'the authority to whom a claim for support is made, except where a claim is transferred by a local authority in accordance with regulation 9'.
- Support means a package of accommodation and essential living needs, including some asylum travel expenses and exceptional expenses.[18] Families with dependent children, who have accommodation, can be supported by a 'split package' of living expenses. Childless asylum-seekers must receive accommodation *and* living expenses.
- In deciding what support to provide, the local authority is required to have regard to some matters (the household's actual and potential resources, their welfare, and the cost of provision) and is required to disregard other matters (any preference as to the location of accommodation, its nature and its fixtures and fittings).[19]

12 Ibid.
13 See para 3.140 onwards.
14 See para 3.5. The policy bulletins are primarily for the use of case-workers.
15 Interim reg 2(1).
16 IAA 1999 s95.
17 Interim reg 3(2).
18 Ibid, reg 5(1)(3) and (4).
19 Ibid, reg 6.

– Regulation 7 provides that support *must* be refused if the person has made him/herself 'intentionally destitute'.[20] The regulations prevent asylum-seekers from claiming interim support from a second local authority.[21] They also bar a claim from a second local authority where a claim for National Assistance Act 1948 s21 assistance had been made in the previous year.[22]

– There is a power to suspend or discontinue support if the assisted person 'leaves accommodation provided as part of such support for more than seven consecutive days without reasonable excuse'.[23] Regulation 8 also provides that support can be suspended or discontinued if the assisted person is intentionally destitute under s7(1).[24]

– The interim scheme allows local authorities to 'disperse' asylum-seekers, ie, transfer responsibility for supporting and housing them, by agreement.[25]

Interim support or asylum support?

5.10   The first step in advising an asylum-seeker who needs support is to consider which scheme applies. Is the local authority or NASS responsible for support? There is a table at para 3.9 showing which asylum-seekers are eligible to claim asylum support from NASS and which are eligible to claim interim support from a local authority. Unaccompanied asylum-seekers who are under 18 are not eligible but can claim help under the Children Act 1989.

Who is eligible to claim interim support?

– Asylum-seekers who were receiving local authority support (under the Children Act 1989 or National Assistance Act 1948) on 5 December 1999.

---

20   Ibid, reg 7(1)(a).
21   Ibid, reg 7(1)(b).
22   Ibid, reg 7(1)(c).
23   Ibid, reg 8(2)(b).
24   See chapter 3 re Asylum Support Adjudicator decisions on the termination of support.
25   Interim reg 9.

- In-country asylum-seekers who claimed asylum anywhere in England or Wales after 2 April 2000 and before 24 July 2000. (Asylum-seekers who made an in-country claim in Kent must have claimed before 17 April 2000.)
- In-country asylum-seekers living in Humberside, the North-East, Wales or Yorkshire who claimed asylum before 31 July 2000.
- In-country asylum-seekers living in Sussex or the West Midlands who claimed asylum before 29 August 2000.
- Asylum-seekers who were in receipt of social security benefits and were refused asylum before 25 September 2000 ('disbenefited' asylum-seekers).

5.11   Although the Interim Regs[26] provide that the interim scheme ends on 1 April 2002, the Act itself does not specify an end-date. The government has suggested that all asylum-seekers will either receive a decision on their claim or be transferred to the NASS asylum support scheme before 2002. Alternatively, the Home Secretary could introduce further regulations to continue the interim scheme for any asylum-seekers who are still receiving interim support on 1 April 2002.

5.12   The AS Regs came into force on 3 April 2000 and NASS assumed responsibility for asylum-seekers who claimed asylum 'on arrival' on or after 3 April 2000. At first, asylum-seekers who had applied for asylum 'in-country' after 3 April 2000 continued to be the responsibility of local authorities. After 3 April 2000, eligibility for interim support gradually ceased for new in-country applicants as the NASS scheme was phased in.[27] The timetable is based on directions made by the Home Secretary.[28] The relevant date is the date of the claim for asylum, not the date of the claim for support. Therefore, if an asylum-seeker living in London claimed asylum in-country before 3 April 2000 but became destitute in June 2000, s/he was entitled to local authority for support, not to NASS support. The normal eligibility rules described below also need to be satisfied.

26 Ibid, reg 2(5).
27 HC Written Answers col 515, 11 July 2000.
28 Directions No 1 (13 March 2000), No 2, No 2A (10 April 2000) and No 3 (11 July 2000) under IAA 1999 Sch 15, para 14(1).

Assessing eligibility for interim support

5.13   The Interim Regs require local authorities to provide support to 'eligible persons'.[29] Eligible persons are 'asylum-seekers' or 'their dependants' who 'appear to be destitute or likely to become destitute' within 14 days.[30] Either the 'asylum-seeker' or 'their dependant' can make the claim for support. It may be necessary or desirable for the dependant to make the claim, eg, for a wife to make a claim if her husband is in hospital. The terms 'asylum-seeker' and 'dependant' have specific meanings for support purposes, which are different from their ordinary immigration law meanings (see also chapter 3). Those who are ineligible for support are listed at paras 5.91–5.122.

Meaning of 'asylum-seeker'[31]

5.14   Eligibility for interim and asylum support only lasts for as long as a person is an 'asylum-seeker' as defined by IAA 1999 s94(1). An asylum-seeker for support purposes is a person of 18 or over who has made a claim for asylum under the Refugee Convention or a claim under article 3 of the Human Rights Convention,[32] which has not yet been determined (see para 5.16).

5.15   An asylum-seeker with a dependent child under 18 is defined as an 'asylum-seeker' for support purposes for as long as the child is under 18 and they both stay in the UK.[33] This means that even if the asylum claim or appeal is unsuccessful, an asylum-seeker with a child can continue to receive interim support. This applies for as long as the family stays in the UK even if they have no legal right to remain.

When is an asylum claim 'determined'?

5.16   A claim for asylum is 'determined' 14 days after notification of the asylum decision.[34] The determination is the full reasoned decision, not the pre-decision letter, which simply states that asylum has been

29 Interim reg 3(1).
30 IAA 1999 Sch 9, para 2; Interim reg 2(1) and (6).
31 The s94(1) definition of asylum-seeker is discussed in more detail at para 3.19.
32 By virtue of IAA 1999 s167(1) 'Refugee Convention' means the Geneva Convention relating to the Status of Refugees 1951 and 1967 Protocol, and 'Human Rights Convention' means the European Convention for the Protection of Human Rights and Fundamental Freedoms.
33 IAA 1999 s94(5).
34 Ibid, s94(3)(a).

refused.[35] If an asylum-seeker appeals against a negative decision, the claim is 'determined' 14 days after the appeal is disposed of.[36] Unless an asylum decision is notified in person, the 14 days starts on the second day after the day the Home Secretary posts it to the asylum-seeker and his/her legal representative.[37]

Meaning of 'dependant'

5.17   The 'dependant' of an asylum-seeker is defined by IAA 1999 s94(1) and prescribed by the Interim Regs.[38] The Interim Regs definition is slightly different from 'dependant' in the AS Regs.[39] The individual clauses defining 'dependant' are discussed in detail in chapter 3 and it may be useful to cross-refer to them.[40]

5.18   Under Interim reg 2(1) 'dependant', in relation to an asylum-seeker, an assisted person or a person claiming support, means a person in the UK who:

(a) is his spouse [ie, husband or wife];
(b) is a child of his or his spouse who is under 18 and dependent[41] on him;
(c) is under 18 and is a member of his, or his spouse's close family;
(d) is under 18 and had been living as part of his household:
   (i)   for at least six of the 12 months before the day on which his claim for support was made; or
   (ii) since birth [this includes a child who is not dependent on the asylum-seeker and/or is not his/her own child. It would include, eg, younger half-brothers and sisters of the asylum-seeker];
(e) is in need of care and attention[42] from him or a member of his family by reason of a disability and would not fall within sub-paragraph (c) or (d) but for the fact that he is not under 18 [the

---

35 The meaning of determination is explained at para 5.16.
36 IAA 1999 s94(3)(b).
37 Ibid, s94(9).
38 Interim reg 2.
39 The main difference is AS reg 2(1)(5) which provides that only a dependant of the asylum-seeker can be treated as a dependant for asylum support purposes.
40 See para 3.28.
41 'Dependent' is undefined, but there is no requirement of financial dependence, see, eg, *R v Camden LBC ex p Diirshe* CO/5069/99, 24 February 2000, QBD, unreported.
42 'In need of care and attention' is a term borrowed from National Assistance Act 1948 s21 (see further chapter 7).

effect of this is that the disabled person must also be either a member of the asylum-seeker's or his/her spouse's close family or s/he must have lived with the asylum-seeker for six of the previous 12 months];

(f) had been living with him as a member of an unmarried couple for at least two of the three years before the day on which his claim for support was made [this provision applies only to a partner who has lived with the asylum-seeker for the relevant period. Unlike the similar provision in AS reg 2(1), the definition appears wide enough to cover same-sex couples. This is supported by the IND guidance of 19 November 1999 which refers to 'partners' (see Appendix B)];

(g) is a person living as part of his household who was receiving assistance under section 17 of the Children Act 1989 immediately the beginning of the interim period [ie, 6 December 1999];

(h) has made a claim for leave to enter or remain in the UK or for a variation of any such leave which is being considered on the basis that he is dependent on the asylum-seeker; or

(i) in relation to an assisted person or a person claiming support who is himself a dependant of an asylum-seeker, is the asylum-seeker [so where the dependant of an asylum-seeker, eg, the wife, is the person claiming support, the husband is classified as a 'dependant' for interim support purposes. This applies in cases such as where a wife rather than the asylum-seeker (husband) makes the claim for interim support, eg, where the asylum-seeker is in detention].

5.19   Anyone who is a dependant for the purposes of the asylum-seeker's claim for asylum is a dependant for interim support purposes.[43] However it is possible to be a dependant for support purposes but to have separate claims for asylum, eg, a man and a woman in an unmarried couple may have both made a claim for asylum. Unlike the asylum support position, a dependant for asylum support purposes does not need to be a dependant of the asylum-seeker either for the purposes of the asylum application or within the Interim Regs definition of dependant of an asylum-seeker. 'Dependant' extends to a dependant of the assisted person, who may be a dependant of the asylum-seeker's dependant, but not of the asylum-seeker. For example, where the asylum-seeker has a daughter who is part of the supported household and the daughter has a child, the new child is a 'dependant' of the grandfather for support purposes.

---

43 Interim reg 2(1)(h).

Test of 'destitution'

5.20   A local authority must reach its own decision on whether or not an asylum-seeker together with any of his/her dependant(s) appears to be destitute or appears likely to become destitute within 14 days.[44] The definition of destitution contained in IAA 1999 s95(3)–(8) applies to interim support cases.[45] The AS Regs contain a detailed list of prescribed matters to be taken into account in assessing destitution, but it does not apply to the interim scheme and there is no such list in the Interim Regs.

5.21   The government decided to allow local authorities to apply their experience in assessing destitution, following case-law developed under National Assistance Act 1948 s21(1)(a). This began with *R v Hammersmith and Fulham LBC ex p M*.[46] The Court of Appeal upheld the decision that destitute asylum-seekers, in danger of suffering illness as the result of their inability to obtain food and shelter, could be in need of care and attention within the meaning of s21. Later court decisions have established that a person could still be in need of care and attention because of destitution even though s/he was able to meet some needs, eg, accommodation but not food,[47] or was entitled to work but unemployed.[48] This is the approach to destitution which appears to have been adopted in IAA 1999 s95, since a person is destitute *either* if s/he does not have adequate accommodation, or any means of obtaining it, *or* if s/he cannot meet essential living needs.

5.22   It is arguable that the test 'asylum-seeker or their dependants who appear to be destitute or likely to become destitute in 14 days'[49] is a broader test than the ordinary National Assistance Act 1948 s21 test of 'in need of care and attention' which addresses the immediate need. Local authorities making decisions under the Interim Regs should ensure that they are considering whether the asylum-seeker is likely to become destitute *in the next 14 days*.

5.23   There are also differences between the test of destitution which

---

44   Ibid, reg 3(2).
45   See IAA 1999 Sch 9, para 3 and explanatory notes, para 291.
46   (1997) 1 CCLR 85, CA. See para 5.2.
47   *R v Newham LBC ex p Gorenkin* (1998) 1 CCLR 309, QBD.
48   *R v Newham LBC ex p Plastin* (1998) 1 CCLR 304; cf *R v Southwark LBC ex p Hong Cui* (1999) 2 CCLR 86.
49   Interim reg 2(1).

local authorities should apply and the test which NASS should apply. The detailed provision on matters to be taken into account by NASS in assessing destitution under the AS Regs does not apply to local authority decisions on interim support. The AS Regs, unlike the Interim Regs, extend the prescribed period[50] in which an applicant is 'likely to become destitute' from 14 days to 56 days in cases where an asylum-seeker is already receiving support. In a case where a supported asylum-seeker received £1,000 from the Criminal Injuries Compensation Authority, the council decided he was not destitute for interim support purposes because this was enough to house and support him for over 14 days. He had to reapply for interim support after the capital had reduced. If he had been supported by NASS he could have argued that £1,000 was not enough to cover the longer 56-day period prescribed by the AS Regs. However, the factors set out in IAA 1999 Part VI, which apply to the test of destitution for asylum support purposes, are relevant considerations for a local authority assessment of whether an applicant is destitute.

Assessment procedures

5.24   The LGA has produced detailed guidance on the interim support scheme for local authorities.[51] The LGA guidance covers assessment procedures and dispersal. It can be argued that local authorities should have regard to the terms of the LGA interim scheme, at least in the context of dispersal, because the IND guidance of 19 November 1999 and, more particularly, 1 December 1999 refers to the LGA scheme.[52] The authority for this is IAA 1999 Sch 9, para 9(7). This requires local authorities to take into account the Home Secretary's guidance when transferring a claim for support to another authority. There is also a public law duty to have regard to the LGA guidance as a relevant consideration which a reasonable authority should take into account.

5.25   If there is evidence of special needs, such as a physical or mental illness, the LGA guidance provides that a local authority should ensure that the asylum-seeker is assessed by a qualified social worker before considering dispersal.

50   IAA 1999 s95(1).
51   See LGA website: www.opengov.lga.uk.
52   See Appendix B.

Evidence of asylum-seeker status

5.26   When an asylum-seeker makes a claim for interim support, s/he will be asked to provide evidence of identity and immigration status. It is common for problems to arise both at this stage and when eligibility is reviewed during the course of the claim.

5.27   The asylum-seeker will be asked for his/her Home Office documents (see para 1.133). S/he will be expected to provide one or more of the following:[53]

SAL2

5.28   The 'standard acknowledgement letter' (SAL) 2 is treated as evidence that the asylum-seeker is an 'in-country' applicant with an outstanding asylum claim. It has a photograph of the asylum-seeker and anyone who is a dependant for the purposes of the asylum claim.

SAL1

5.29   This shows that the asylum-seeker has claimed asylum at the port of entry. It has a photograph of the asylum-seeker and anyone who is a dependant for the purposes of the asylum claim. In a limited number of cases it may not mean that the asylum-seeker has claimed 'on arrival' for income support (IS) purposes, eg, s/he may have returned to the port after clearing immigration control.[54] If an asylum-seeker claimed asylum before 3 April 2000 but has a SAL1, s/he will also need to provide a letter from the Benefits Agency refusing IS.

IND Form IS96

5.30   This shows that the asylum-seeker has been given temporary admission by an immigration officer. It does not include a photograph indicating identity. An asylum-seeker who was not granted any other form of leave to enter the UK may be given an IS96 either when s/he claims asylum as an illegal entrant or in the course of enforcement procedures by the Immigration Service. If the asylum-seeker has the right to work, this may be recorded on the IS96.

---

53   These documents are the basic documents which an asylum-seeker is likely to have but the Home Office uses a variety of other reference and form numbers to refer to documents and these may change.
54   See further para 2.51.

IND Asylum Screening Unit letter or solicitor's letter

5.31 If an asylum-seeker does not have a SAL1, SAL2 or IS96 the local authority will usually request some other evidence of asylum-seeker status. If the asylum-seeker is a recent arrival this could be an IND appointment letter for the Home Office Asylum Screening Unit (ASU), which is an initial interview at the IND to establish identity and take fingerprints. An asylum-seeker who has made a claim for asylum may have to wait a considerable period even to get an ASU appointment letter. In such cases, one form of identity suggested by local authorities is a letter from a solicitor or 'bona fide representative' with a photograph of the applicant and his/her full name.

Common problems with documentation

5.32 Asylum-seekers often have limited documentation and there are difficulties in obtaining information quickly from the Home Office. Many applicants arrive in the UK without any evidence of their true identity. There is a duty to provide interim support to a destitute asylum-seeker under Interim reg 4 even if s/he cannot prove his/her identity. This was conceded by Camden LBC's social services department after a successful application for leave for judicial review in *R v Camden LBC ex p Diirshe*.[55] There is no statutory requirement for documentation such as a solicitor's letter. Despite this, many authorities still insist at least on a solicitor's letter identifying the applicant before they will assist. The Legal Services Commission has said that the legal help scheme may be used to fund the work required for a solicitor to provide a letter. If assistance is refused because the applicant has no documentation, advisers may wish to consider judicial review or use of local authority complaints procedures (see paras 5.123–5.131).

5.33 Where an asylum-seeker receiving interim support has a SAL, it will usually be stamped by the local authority providing support. The SAL will be checked for any such stamp when a new claim is made. This is because there is generally no interim support duty where the asylum-seeker has applied to another local authority on the ground of destitution in the previous 12 months (see para 5.96 below).

5.34 The local authority may periodically ask an assisted person for evidence that his/her asylum claim or appeal has not yet been decided. Although an authority could request the information directly from

55 CO/5069/99, 24 February 2000, QBD, unreported.

the Home Office, Interim reg 8(1) and (2) entitles them to require this information from the assisted person. The asylum-seeker may have difficulty in obtaining such a letter from his/her immigration representative. Non-immigration specialists should be cautious about advising on immigration law. IAA 1999 Part V makes it a criminal offence for individuals or organisations to give immigration advice unless they are registered or exempted within the meaning of the Act.

Assessment of resources

5.35   When assessing whether an asylum-seeker is eligible for interim support, a local authority should consider what type of support to provide. In assessing what type and level of support to provide, the local authority should consider the individual circumstances of the case, and its decisions may be open to challenge if it has failed to do so. Relevant and irrelevant matters are set out in the Interim reg 6(1), but should not be regarded as an exhaustive list:

> In providing support, the local authority are to have regard to:
> (a) income which the assisted person has or his dependants (if any) have, or might reasonably be expected to have;
> (b) support which is or assets which are, or might reasonably be expected to be, available to the assisted person, or to his dependants (if any):
> (c) the welfare of the assisted person and his dependants (if any); and
> (d) the cost of providing support.

5.36   The regulations do not specifically require that the resources of other relatives in the UK should be taken into account but this is the intention of reg 6(1)(b). The IND guidance of 19 November 1999[56] suggests at para 18 that the Interim Regs 'enable' local authorities to take into account support in kind from friends or family. A reasonable approach would be to treat support provided by relatives and friends who are reasonably able to provide it as a relevant consideration. This should be distinguished from support which has been provided to the asylum-seeker household as an emergency measure to avert real suffering where relatives and friends are not reasonably able, or willing, to continue to provide it.

5.37   The matters to which local authorities are to have regard, anticipate that different types of support will be provided depending on the assisted person's existing assets. This allows the asylum-seeker or

56   See Appendix B.

any dependant to have some income, eg, part-time earnings, but still be eligible for interim support, at a proportionately lower level.

5.38   Many local authorities apply a strict test to the question of income or resources which the assisted person might reasonably be expected to have. In some cases, local authorities have decided that an asylum-seeker is not destitute on the basis that s/he has been in the UK for a considerable period and should be able to get a job and support the household. Such decisions are open to challenge where the authority has failed to take into account relevant circumstances including any childcare responsibilities, whether the applicant has a right to work/national insurance number, the asylum-seeker's ability to speak English, physical and mental health needs, whether the asylum-seeker has a reasonable prospect of obtaining work given local employment practices, likely earnings level for the individual asylum-seeker, etc. Some authorities use fraud investigation teams to carry out home visits to inspect the assisted household's belongings.[57]

'Mixed households'[58]

5.39   Asylum-seeker households often include people who have arrived in the UK at different times and/or do not have the same immigration status. For example, a family could include a father who claimed asylum 'on arrival' before 3 April 2000 and is entitled to IS, his adult daughter who claimed in-country on 3 April 2000 and is entitled to interim support, and siblings who arrived later and were directed to NASS at the airport. An asylum-seeker will be entitled to interim support even if one or more family members are receiving benefits (or working) if there is not enough income or accommodation for the whole household, ie, if the person claiming interim support is destitute. There are gaps in provision for mixed households and it may be necessary to ask the courts to interpret the regulations in the light of the article 8 right to family life.

5.40   A proposed approach to mixed households is as follows:

–   Consider which household members want to be accommodated together as a family.
–   Check whether any household members can claim IS, housing benefit or housing as homeless for themselves with the other

57   In some cases home visits may constitute a breach of Human Rights Convention article 8 and Protocol 1, article 1, See further chapter 8.
58   NASS Policy Bulletin 11 contains a clear explanation of mixed households.

family members as dependants.⁵⁹ A family may be entitled to housing as homeless if there is a family member with priority need who is receiving IS and so in Class I.⁶⁰

- If no-one is entitled to mainstream benefits and housing or if only some of the household members are eligible, consider whether a household member who isn't receiving IS is eligible to claim interim support with the other family members as dependants.
- If no one is eligible for interim support with the other family members as dependants, consider whether a household member is eligible to claim asylum support from NASS with other family members as dependants.
- If there is no eligibility for asylum support (eg, where household members are 'persons subject to immigration control' but not asylum-seekers under IAA 1999 s94) consider whether social services have a duty to provide community care help under Children Act 1989 s17 or National Assistance Act 1948 s21.⁶¹

Subsistence-only claims

5.41   Where the asylum-seeker's household includes a dependant under 18, a family with accommodation may request interim support for subsistence only, eg, if they are staying with friends.⁶² This is a means of avoiding dispersal if the asylum-seeker can find suitable accommodation with friends, family or community members. In such cases the local authority should carry out a home visit to assess whether the accommodation 'meets the standard of the assessing local authority'.⁶³ In such cases, the household will be eligible for support to cover essential living needs.

5.42   The Interim Regs limit the amount of cash which can be paid to a childless asylum-seeker to £10 per person per week, unless there are exceptional circumstances, but there is power to provide support to families exclusively in the form of cash. Alternatively, the local authority may provide cash and/or vouchers. There was no power to provide support in the form of cash under National Assistance Act

59   See chapters 2 and 6.
60   Homelessness (England) Regulations 2000 SI No 701, reg 3(i).
61   See further chapter 7.
62   Interim reg 5(2)(c). Single asylum-seekers or those without dependent children cannot make a 'subsistence only' claim and the local authority has to provide support as a package of housing and subsistence.
63   LGA guidance, para 5.1.

1948 s21.[64] There are strong arguments that support should be provided exclusively or mainly in cash. It may be possible to challenge
local authorities who provide support in the form of vouchers on
Human Rights Convention grounds (articles 3 and 14). Evidence of
the effect of difficulties or discrimination experienced by the household in question when using vouchers as well as general evidence
could be used. A number of agencies such as Oxfam and the Medical
Foundation for the Care of Victims of Torture submitted evidence of
problems with vouchers to the Home Office's review of the voucher
scheme in December 2000 (see para 5.55).

5.43   The applicant for support may be asked to sign a form stating that
s/he has not been working. This should be translated as a matter of
good practice. IAA 1999 s95(9)–(11) provides that if support is provided subject to conditions, they must be set out in writing and a copy
given to the supported person.

Assessment procedure for accommodation under the LGA dispersal scheme[65]

5.44   When the Interim Regs came into force on 6 December 1999, the
LGA established a procedure for transferring responsibility for support between local authorities.[66] Where an asylum-seeker presents to
a London borough which then considers dispersal, under the LGA
guidance the borough is required to complete an assessment form
containing specified information. Where an asylum-seeker presents
with a special need, an assessment should be carried out by a qualified social worker and a care package agreed before a dispersal
request is made by the local authority. The LGA procedure requires
the social worker's report to be appended to the dispersal referral
form. Under the procedure, a physical or mental health need is not
usually a reason which would allow an asylum-seeker to require
accommodation in London except in a case of a particular need
which could only be met in London, eg, for support from the Medical
Foundation for Care of the Victims of Torture. However, where an
asylum-seeker has community care needs, there may be a duty to
provide accommodation under National Assistance Act 1948 s21, in

64 *R v Secretary of State for M and K* (1998) 1 CCLR 495, CA.
65 The various types of dispersal and grounds for challenging dispersal are
    explained at para 5.74 below. This section deals with the procedure.
66 LGA guidance. See para 5.76.

which case the asylum-seeker has a right to choose accommodation (see para 7.77). The LGA guidance requires the receiving authority to make arrangements for the receiving local authority to meet the supported person's psychological and emotional needs.

5.45   The procedure for dispersal requires the London Asylum-seekers Consortium to use the information provided on the referral form and obtain accommodation from one of the regional consortia. The receiving authority should then assume responsibility for the household. In many cases no accommodation has been available in the dispersal areas and so the London borough has housed asylum-seekers in London or through their own sources. This part of the procedure is also used in relation to the dispersal of asylum-seekers who are being housed as homeless under Housing Act 1996.[67]

Service provision

Type of support

5.46   Local authorities must provide 'temporary support' under IAA 1999 s98, until a decision has been made about eligibility, at which point full interim support must be provided or refused. There is no express duty under the interim scheme to support an applicant who is challenging a refusal of support by judicial review. In such cases, an application could be made to the court for interim relief.

Temporary support

5.47   A local authority must provide a form of emergency interim support known as 'temporary support' while it considers whether or not an applicant is eligible for interim support.[68] The IND guidance of 19 November 1999 explains:

> . . . this ensures that immediate assistance can be given to an asylum-seeker and his dependants pending determination of his eligibility for support; this might turn on whether or not he really is an asylum-seeker, whether he is really destitute or whether he falls within a category for whom support must be refused.

5.48   As with homelessness applications, some local authorities refuse

---

67   See para 6.4.
68   Interim reg 4; IAA 1999 explanatory notes, para 290.

help until the applicant has 'proved' s/he is eligible. It may take some time for an asylum-seeker to obtain all the necessary documents. In such circumstances, an application for judicial review of the refusal to provide temporary support may be appropriate. A letter before action threatening such an application must be sent. Leave was granted to apply for judicial review in the case *of R v Camden LBC ex p Diirshe*[69] but the local authority conceded the reg 4 duty before the full hearing.[70]

5.49   Support must be provided in cases where a local authority is attempting to transfer a claim out of London or the south-east under the dispersal scheme, pending the transfer. This applies if the local authority has decided to transfer the duty for support and disperse under Interim reg 9. Temporary support (s98) or full support (s95) must be provided by the authority to which the claim is made until it has been transferred under reg 9. It must also be provided by the local authority which has accepted the transfer pending full interim support.

5.50   The test of what is adequate temporary support is subjective. It must 'appear to the local authority by whom it is provided to be adequate for the needs of the person claiming support and his dependants (if any)'.[71] There is no definition of 'adequate', which is discussed below in relation to full interim support. Under the Housing Act 1996, both temporary accommodation and permanent accommodation provided to homeless people must be 'suitable'. When the IAA 1999 was debated, the government resisted pressure to provide that asylum-seekers should be accommodated in 'suitable' accommodation or to provide a detailed test of 'adequate' in the Act. However, ministers drew an analogy with provision for homeless people when describing the proposed provision for asylum-seekers.[72]

Full interim support

5.51   If the local authority decides that the asylum-seeker is an 'eligible person' (see para 5.11 above), it must provide interim support consisting of 'accommodation' and 'essential living needs'.[73] The asylum-seeker or his/her dependant who has applied for support then

---

69 CO/5069/99, 24 February 2000, QBD, unreported.
70 See also para 5.32 above.
71 Interim reg. 4(f).
72 See chapter 4.
73 Interim regs 3 and 5.

becomes an 'assisted person'.[74] The type of provision which a local authority can provide depends on whether or not the household includes dependent children. If the household includes a dependent child and has housing, it can provide essential living needs only.

5.52   Interim support, like asylum support, can be provided subject to conditions, eg, not to cause a nuisance in the accommodation provided. A breach of the conditions may entitle the local authority to suspend or terminate provision. A written copy of any conditions must be given to the assisted person.[75] Similarly where there are language difficulties, conditions should be translated or interpreted to the assisted person and his/her dependants. The effect of a breach of conditions is explained below (see para 5.101 onwards).

5.53   Unlike the AS Regs, there are no figures for the level at which support must be provided under the Interim Regs. In April 2000 some adult asylum-seekers were receiving only £25 per week each in food vouchers (and no cash) whereas in other areas the figure was nearer £35. This level of support was lower than the amounts that are set by the AS Regs. The Home Office Consultation Paper states: 'There will be no upper limit set to the amount of support authorities could provide at the present time; this is to reflect the different levels and manner in which support is being provided . . . authorities would be advised of the amount the Secretary of State considers appropriate for support to asylum-seekers overall'.[76] Most local authorities use the Home Office grant figures as a guide for the total cost of accommodation and living expenses. In April 2000, these were set at £150 per week for single asylum-seekers and £220 for families.

Vouchers and level of support

5.54   Local authorities have their own voucher schemes, which are more limited than NASS's scheme. In many areas, asylum-seekers on interim support can only exchange their vouchers at one outlet of a major supermarket chain and may only buy food, toiletries or clothes. There is scope for challenging the means and level of provision by judicial review where this is inadequate to meet the household's essential living needs (see paras 4.52–4.57). There may be cases

---

74 Ibid, reg 2(1).
75 IAA 1999 s95(9)–(11) and Interim reg 5(6).
76 *Asylum-seeker Support: Proposed Interim Arrangements under Schedule 8 of the Immigration and Asylum Bill*, Consultation Paper issued by the Home Office, 20 August 1999.

where it can be argued that support should be provided to childless asylum-seekers in the form of cash on the grounds of exceptional circumstances under Interim reg 5(5)(b).

5.55 NASS support levels are set at 70 per cent of IS, without taking premiums into account. IS is set at 'the official poverty line'. The Human Rights Convention, articles 2 and 3, and NASS levels of support are relevant considerations when a local authority is deciding at what level to provide subsistence. Local authorities must also ensure that the welfare of the assisted person and any dependants is taken into account.[77] The cost of providing support is also a relevant consideration but generally the voucher scheme is more expensive to administer than cash. Considerable evidence about the difficulties and discriminatory nature of the vouchers was presented to the Home Office review of the voucher scheme in December 2000.[78] Problems reported by asylum-seekers include harassment at supermarket check-outs and difficulties in obtaining a diet specific to religious or cultural needs.

Families

5.56 If the household includes a child under 18, interim support can either be provided as a full package of accommodation and living expenses or as a 'split' package in the form of either accommodation or living expenses. This enables families to live with relatives or community members while claiming interim support for living expenses. A considerable proportion of assisted households have chosen this option in order to avoid dispersal out of the south-east.

5.57 As discussed above, local authorities can provide support to families in the form of cash only. They have the power, but not the duty, to provide essential living needs in cash where there are children under 18 in the household. The IND Guidance of 19 November 1999 states: 'there is no limit on the proportion of support which may be given by way of cash payments for families, although under regulation 6 authorities are required to have regard to the cost of providing support . . . '.[79] A local authority may decide to provide support 'in kind' by full or half-board, by meals-on-wheels, or to use a combination of food vouchers and cash.

---

77 Interim reg 6(1)(c).
78 See, eg, *Token Gestures*, December 2000. Oxfam, tel 01865 3136000.
79 Para 15, see Appendix B.

5.58   School-age children whose parents are asylum-seekers receiving interim support are entitled to free school meals.[80]

Single asylum-seekers and childless couples

5.59   If the assisted household consists solely of one or more adults aged 18 or over, there is no power to provide a 'split package', unless there are 'exceptional circumstances'. In order to receive any interim support, the adult asylum-seeker must be housed under the interim scheme. In such cases the cash element of the essential living needs can be no more than £10 per person per week unless there are 'exceptional circumstances'.[81] The rest of the provision must be in kind, and is usually in the form of food vouchers. 'Exceptional circumstances' are not defined in the statutory provisions or guidance. In the context of asylum support, the explanatory notes at para 281 suggest that such exceptional payments could be made in the case of medical conditions.

Travel expenses

5.60   There is very limited provision for the funding of travel expenses. The local authority must fund 'reasonable travel expenses' to enable the asylum-seeker to attend an asylum interview or asylum appeal.[82] Unlike the AS Regs, the Interim Regs do not expressly exclude travel expenses from the definition of essential living needs. A failure to provide an asylum-seeker with travel expenses to attend an interview could amount to a breach of article 3 if it means the asylum-seeker cannot exercise the right to claim asylum.[83] Under the legal help scheme the LSC will finance reasonable travel expenses of asylum-seekers to attend solicitors' appointments.[84]

Adequate accommodation and dispersal

5.61   The local authority must provide eligible persons with, '[a]ccommodation appearing to the local authority by whom it is provided to be adequate for the needs of the assisted person and his dependants'.[85] Dispersal and 'adequate accommodation' are also considered in detail in chapter 4.

---

80   IAA 1999 Sch 14 amends Education Act 1996 s512 (requirement to provide free school meals).
81   Interim reg 5(5)(b).
82   Ibid, reg 5(3).
83   See further chapter 8.
84   LSC Contract Specification on disbursements r2.13.

5.62   It was anticipated that the Home Secretary would make regulations under the IAA 1999 to define 'adequate' but to date there is no
detailed provision. The government has clearly stated in the course of
debates and parliamentary questions that 'adequate accommodation'
under the IAA 1999 has the same meaning as 'suitable' in the homelessness context, but that asylum-seekers' accommodation is 'temporary'. Under Housing Act 1996 s188 interim accommodation
provided to homeless persons while inquiries are made must be
'suitable' within the meaning of s206(1).[86] Interim reg 6(1)(c) provides that a local authority is to have regard to welfare when providing
support, which would include accommodation. The meaning of 'adequate' and the relevance of the parliamentary material in the absence
of detailed regulations are considered below and in chapter 4.

5.63   The test of adequacy of accommodation under the Interim Regs is
virtually the same as the test for asylum support purposes. The
Interim Regs add the requirement that the assisted person's welfare
and the cost of accommodation are relevant factors. The scheme of
dispersal under the interim support scheme is distinct from NASS
dispersal, but government statements on where accommodation is
provided are relevant to both interim support and asylum support.[87]
Parliamentary materials are referred to because of the lack of statutory material or guidance on the meaning of 'adequate'.

5.64   In providing support, which of course includes accommodation, a
local authority must have regard to: 'the welfare of the assisted person and his dependants (if any)'.[88] There is no definition of 'welfare'
and no reason why it should not allow a wide range of arguments
about the well-being of the assisted person and his/her family members from a social, educational, medical, cultural or other perspective.
Case-law under Children Act 1989 s1, which makes the welfare of
a child paramount in relation to many of the decision-making
processes under that Act, may be helpful.

5.65   The cost of support is also a relevant factor under reg 6(1)(d).

5.66   Housing provided under the Interim Regs should be offered on a
'no choice' basis in line with the stated policy aims of the IAA 1999,
incorporated in Interim reg 6(2):

In providing accommodation under these Regulations, the local

---

85   Interim reg. 5(1)(a).
86   See chapter 6.
87   See further para 4.29.
88   Interim reg 6(1)(c).

authority are not to have regard to any preference that the assisted person or his dependants (if any) may have as to:

(a) the locality in which the accommodation is to be provided;
(b) the nature of the accommodation to be provided; or
(c) the nature and standard of fixtures and fittings in the accommodation.

Preference or individual circumstances?

5.67   Despite the emphasis on 'no choice' accommodation, a local authority must examine the individual circumstances of each assisted person when deciding on the nature and location of accommodation offered. There is authority for this in the IND Guidance, the LGA guidance and government statements made during the parliamentary stages of the bill. During the course of the Immigration and Asylum Bill, House of Commons Special Standing Committee (18 March 1999), Home Office minister Mike O'Brien MP agreed that an asylum-seeker's preference should be distinguished from his/her individual circumstances.

5.68   At the second reading of the bill in the House of Lords, the government spokesman, Lord Williams of Mostyn stated:

> We then come to the question of preferences. I agree that when one looks at the language of the Bill one questions why it is in that form. It is because it is not required to have regard to preferences, but we can have regard to circumstances. So we can look at the background circumstance of a group of asylum-seekers to disperse all those with a common ethnic, linguistic or territorial origin to a place common to all of them. That is looking at circumstances and not preferences.[89]

5.69   There is parliamentary authority for the proposition that accommodation for asylum-seekers should be provided on the same terms as accommodation that is provided to homeless people under Housing Act 1996 Part VII. 'If they seek accommodation provided by the state, they should be in the same positions as homeless people in this country and be given one choice'.[90] 'We have tried broadly to replicate the arrangements for people who are homeless but lawfully resident here, whereby people have the one offer of accommodation and no more'.[91]

5.70   At the second reading of the bill, on behalf of the government, Lord Williams of Mostyn gave a detailed statement in response to a proposed amendment to the Immigration and Asylum Bill

---

89   *Hansard*, HL Debates, cols 1200–1201, 20 October 1999.
90   Mike O'Brien, Special Standing Committee, 18 March 1999.
91   Home Secretary, Jack Straw MP, Special Standing Committee, 25 March 1999.

which aimed to ensure that if asylum-seekers were dispersed, needs such as counselling, and their children's educational needs would be taken into account. His statement contained a series of assurances in relation to the provision of accommodation.[92]

5.71   In *R v Waltham Forest LBC ex p Haile*[93] the local authority conceded that it was unlawful to disperse an asylum-seeker without considering the impact of dispersal on the welfare of the asylum-seeker and his/her family. This consideration had to be given by the local authority itself. The concession was made after the High Court had granted permission to apply for judicial review and after the Home Secretary had been joined to the proceedings.

5.72   It is arguable that 'adequate accommodation' is accommodation in areas where educational needs can be met, such as language support. The 'public health' assurance could be used to support representations where asylum-seekers with infectious health conditions such as hepatitis B, or those recovering from TB, are accommodated in shared hostel or bed and breakfast accommodation.

5.73   Accommodation where there is inadequate provision of competent immigration advice or language and translation facilities may also be considered inappropriate. There is evidence from the Refugee Council to suggest that in many of the dispersal areas there are limited interpreting and translation services in languages spoken by asylum-seekers. NASS monitors information about asylum-seekers sent to its 'cluster areas' and the languages spoken in those areas. Such information makes it clear that there is a chronic shortage of immigration advice and representation in most of the dispersal areas.[94]

Types of dispersal

5.74 To advise an asylum-seeker who is challenging a dispersal decision, or in a case where dispersal has already taken place, it is useful to analyse the form of dispersal. Dispersal may take any of the following forms:

- *self-dispersal*: where the asylum-seeker travels to the region before applying for support.
- *local authority voluntary dispersal outside the Interim Regs*: where a local authority makes its own arrangements, with a housing provider or authority to house the asylum-seeker in that area. The

---

92 See para 4.29. *Hansard*, HL Debates, col 1163, 20 October 1999.
93 CO/4756/99, unreported.
94 Details of advisers with an immigration franchise can be obtained from the LSC.

original local authority usually retains responsibility for supporting the asylum-seeker. This applies to all cases of dispersal before
the interim scheme was introduced on 6 December 1999, to dis-
persals to Scotland after 6 December 1999 and to individual
arrangements made from 6 December onwards outside reg 9. It is
used predominantly by London boroughs but also in cases where
an authority outside the south-east has responsibility for the
asylum-seeker but has dispersed him/her within the cluster area,
eg, from Manchester to Oldham.

– *local authority voluntary dispersal under Interim reg 9*: discussed
below. Note that dispersal of asylum-seekers eligible for housing
as homeless operates in a similar way, with reference to the LGA
guidance.[95]

– *NASS dispersal under the AS Regs*: discussed in chapter 4.

5.75   The Interim Regs provide a voluntary rather than a statutory
scheme for the dispersal of asylum-seekers.

A local authority may transfer a claim for support made to them, or
responsibility for providing support, to another local authority on such
terms as may be agreed between the two authorities.[96]

5.76   The LGA reached agreement on a voluntary dispersal scheme for
authorities to disperse asylum-seekers from London and the south-
east.The LGA guidance has a statutory basis in IAA 1999 Sch 9, para
9(7) which states: 'In exercising any power under the regulations to
refer or transfer, a local authority must have regard to such guidance
as may be issued by the Secretary of State with respect to the exercise
of the power'. The IND guidance of 1 December 1999 expressly refers
to the LGA guidance. Local authorities dispersing asylum-seekers
should have regard to the terms of the LGA interim scheme, in
the light of the Home Office guidance of 19 November and, more
particularly 1 December 1999.

Challenging dispersal[97]

If someone has waited a year or two years in a particular area, it would
be unacceptable to require that person to move in order to meet a

95 For details of the scheme of dispersal under the Housing Act 1996, see paras
    6.71–6.76.
96 Interim reg 9.
97 Dispersal may be inappropriate if an asylum-seeker has community care needs.
    See para 5.44.

national dispersal policy. Typically such a person will have made arrangements for schooling, health care and so on. Financial responsibility will move to the Home Office, but we will not move people who are settled for the time being and whose cases have frankly taken too long to be dealt with.[98]

5.77 The first potential ground for a challenge will be where a local authority has failed to carry out an adequate assessment of the household's individual circumstances, taking into account the questions of adequacy of accommodation and the welfare of the household as required by Interim reg 6(1)(c). Welfare clearly includes the welfare of the children and their educational needs. The ministerial statement above supports the argument that a family which is settled in a particular area should not be dispersed, especially where the children are settled in school.

5.78 Barbara Roche MP has made a parliamentary statement on behalf of the Home Office concerning asylum-seekers settled in a particular area in the context of disbenefited asylum-seekers who became NASS's responsibility from 25 September 2000.[99] It was announced that, in general, families with dependent children who have been in school for 12 months will not be dispersed. Others will be dispersed unless they can show exceptional compelling or compassionate reasons considered on their merits.

5.79 There is little justification for a local authority to take a different approach to asylum-seekers settled in its area. It is also arguable that there is no justification for the distinction drawn between families and childless applicants. In the case of a single asylum-seeker who has settled in an area over a long period, the authority should consider whether a dispersal would interfere with the Human Rights Convention in view of health needs, relatives, community ties and support, and/or religious worship in the authority's area. In the case of both childless asylum-seekers and families, the authority should take into account IND guidance 'to ensure there are no exceptional reasons why the asylum-seeker should remain in the authority'.

5.80 A decision by a local authority in Kent or in London to disperse an asylum-seeker can be challenged if there are 'exceptional reasons' for the asylum-seeker and/or any dependants to stay in the south-east. The IND guidance of 1 December 1999 explains how dispersal

---

98 Home Secretary, Jack Straw MP, *Hansard*, HC Debates col 983, 9 November 1999.
99 *Hansard*, HC Debates col 766W, 26 January 2001, reproduced at para 4.31.

should operate and the meaning of 'exceptional reasons'. Even if there is no obvious procedural error in the decision, the authority may not have taken into account circumstances which could amount to 'exceptional reasons' as suggested by the guidance, ie:

(a) particular medical needs which can only be met locally (for example, access to the Medical Foundation for Care of Victims of Torture); or
(b) close family members already living in the area.

5.81   'Particular medical needs' means needs such as for HIV treatment, counselling or treatment of a rare disease which could only be met in a centre for excellence. There are a number of conditions and diseases for which medical treatment is only available in London or other major cities. Asylum-seekers with HIV/AIDS may need to live in or near London or other major cities to access appropriate medical treatment and support.[100]

5.82   Decisions of local authorities to disperse asylum-seekers with HIV throughout the dispersal areas can be challenged if individual circumstances, the 'welfare' consideration or the LGA guidance have not been taken into account. Asylum-seekers who are receiving specialist counselling for post-traumatic stress disorder may not be able to access this treatment in some of the dispersal areas. Another example where dispersal may be unlawful is where an asylum-seeker has reached a critical stage in his/her medical treatment and the move could damage his/her health. A local authority accepted that an asylum-seeker in a late stage of pregnancy and receiving regular hospital check-ups due to an apparent abnormality of the foetus should not be dispersed at that stage in her pregnancy.

5.83   There is no definition of 'close family members' in the guidance. In the context of many asylum communities, it will be appropriate to argue for a subjective interpretation of the phrase according to the asylum-seeker's own definition. S/he may treat a cousin once or twice removed or a half-brother who is part of an extended family as a 'close family member'. A relevant consideration is that many asylum-seekers have lost their immediate family members in civil war. Where the only surviving relative is a cousin twice removed, s/he may amount to a close family member if, eg, a close relationship has developed. In *Surdonja v Ealing LBC*,[101] the Court of Appeal

100   Contact Terence Higgins Trust for up-to-date information, tel: 020 7831 0330.
101   [2000] 3 WLR 481, CA.

considered the meaning of family associations in the context of homelessness law and stated, ' . . . the actual closeness of the family association may count for more than the precise degree of consanguinity'.

5.84 In the context of 'living in the area' it is consistent with the guidance to treat 'the area' as the south-east since that is the area from which dispersal takes place within the regulations. Alternatively, it could be argued that 'the area' is Kent, a particular London borough or greater London, depending on the circumstances of the case.

5.85 Medical reasons and close relatives are not intended to be an exhaustive list of 'exceptional reasons'. A combination of factors may amount to 'exceptional' or may demonstrate that the asylum-seeker needs to stay in the south-east for 'welfare' reasons. In *R v Hammersmith and Fulham LBC ex p Isik*[102] the Court of Appeal granted permission to apply for judicial review of a decision to disperse a Turkish Kurdish family to Hull after it had been refused by the High Court. Mr and Mrs Isik had refused to move out of London because their two young daughters were settled in school and they relied on a network of community support. They had lived in London for over a year. Shortly before the substantive hearing, the council offered the family accommodation in London.

5.86 A local authority which decides to disperse a household out of London without taking the welfare of each household member into account will be vulnerable to judicial review. Where an Eritrean asylum-seeker refused dispersal out of London because he needed support from the Eritrean community due to moderate mental health needs and limited knowledge of English, the authority accepted that it was not reasonable to refer him to an area where there were no other members of his community and no one who spoke the same language.

Adequacy of accommodation

5.87 There are no regulations governing standards of accommodation provided under the interim support scheme, apart from the 'welfare' requirement in reg 6(1)(c). It has been suggested that 'accommodation should be habitable, and of a standard sufficient to maintain the overall well-being of the asylum-seeker'.[103]

102 C/2000/2450, CA, permission hearing 15 August 2000, final hearing 19 September 2000 (unreported).

103 *Asylum-seeker Support: Proposed Interim Arrangements under Schedule 8 of the Immigration and Asylum Bill*, Consultation Paper issued by the Home Office, 20 August 1999.

5.88   Paragraph 4 of the IND guidance of 1 December 1999[104] states that where an asylum-seeker is dispersed to a receiving authority, that authority should take into account the following circumstances when deciding what accommodation to offer:

– the cultural background and language of the asylum-seeker;
– any particular needs regarding the type of accommodation required (for example, family accommodation, special needs or disabilities);
– the particular characteristics of the locality in which accommodation is situated;
– the accessibility of support structures – whether voluntary or statutory (in general, such support structures should be within easy reach of the accommodation by public transport.

5.89   Where an authority has failed to take into account any such relevant factors affecting the adequacy of the accommodation, the decision may be open to challenge by judicial review.

5.90   The LGA guidance appends 'the Chartered Institute of Environmental Health (CIEH) Good Practice principles on asylum-seekers' accommodation'. The guidelines recommend liaison between social services, housing and environmental health departments in each local authority area where accommodation is provided to asylum-seekers. They stress that where there is an existing 'Houses in Multiple Occupation registration scheme' under the Housing Act 1996, this would also apply to houses in multiple occupation occupied by asylum-seekers.

Refusal, suspension and termination of interim support[105]

5.91   The Interim Regs distinguish between refusal of support at the initial application stage, and suspension or termination of support where an asylum-seeker was receiving interim support. So reg 7 applies to new

---

104 Provided for by IAA 1999 Sch 19, para 7.
105 See para 4.103 for an outline of the new criminal offences connected with the provision of support where an assisted person has failed to notify a change of circumstances or made misrepresentations. These apply to both interim support and asylum support.

applications, whereas reg 8 applies where an assisted person is being supported and has, eg, breached conditions or left accommodation provided.

5.92   Under the AS Regs, NASS has a *discretion* to refuse or withdraw support. Under Interim reg 7 a local authority has a *duty* to refuse, suspend or terminate support in specified circumstances. The only exception is where the authority 'did not or could not with reasonable diligence have known about the circumstances'.[106] The exercise of this duty could leave healthy single adult asylum-seekers completely destitute because they cannot rely on a community care safety-net. If support is not provided, a local authority may be interfering with a household's rights under the Human Rights Convention.

Refusal of support[107]

5.93   A local authority must refuse support to a new applicant under reg 7 where it knows or should have known about the following circumstances:

Intentional destitution

5.94   This is defined as 'where the person claiming support has intentionally made himself and his dependants (if any) destitute'.[108] A person is 'intentionally destitute' if s/he is or appears to be likely to become destitute within 14 days 'as a result of an act or omission deliberately done or made by him or any dependant of his without reasonable excuse while in the United Kingdom'. Case-law on intentional destitution is discussed in detail in chapter 3, including decisions of the Asylum Support Adjudicators, which are relevant in considering the meaning of 'intentional destitution' and 'reasonable excuse'. In ASA 00/11/0106 the adjudicator decided that an asylum-seeker had a reasonable excuse not to return to a hostel with a harsh regime, when his grievances had not been addressed by NASS and the outcome reported to him.

---

106 Interim reg 7(3).
107 See also chapter 3 which considers refusal or termination of asylum support on grounds of intentional destitution, breach of conditions and leaving accommodation.
108 Interim reg 7(1)(a).

5.95   The IND guidance[109] suggests that this provision could be used where an asylum-seeker 'has deliberately squandered his resources'. Where a local authority is considering exercising this discretion it would be required to take into account articles 2 and 3 of the Human Rights Convention if the asylum-seeker could be left completely destitute as a result of the withdrawal of support. Interim reg 12 provides that a family is not entitled to help under Children Act 1989 s17 if they are entitled to interim support. If support is withdrawn from a family with a dependent child, IAA 1999 s122(9)–(10) provides that only the authority in the area where the accommodation was provided may provide Children Act help. This prevents the family from obtaining s17 help from a different local authority. During parliamentary debates, the government insisted that it was not its intention that the IAA 1999 would remove the Children Act safety-net from asylum-seekers.[110]

Previous application to another authority

5.96   A local authority must refuse to provide interim support if the asylum-seeker has applied to a different local authority for interim support or support under National Assistance Act 1948 s21 or Children Act 1989 s17 during the previous 12 months.[111] The provision is aimed at preventing an asylum-seeker 'shopping around' local authorities for the best support package. Most local authorities stamp the asylum-seeker's SAL, providing evidence of when and where any claim for assistance was made.

5.97   The prohibition results in a number of practical problems and raises human rights issues. When an asylum-seeker arrives in the UK, it may be some time before s/he locates other members of his/her family such as siblings from whom s/he has been separated in flight. An asylum-seeker may need to move to a new area to give or receive support from family members. The provision appears to prevent an asylum-seeker from making a new claim in a different area, even in exceptional circumstances. It may be possible to resolve this problem where there is more than one family member in the asylum-seeker household by changing the claimant. Therefore, where an asylum-seeker husband was claiming help under Children

---

109 19 November 1999, para 13. See Appendix B.
110 See para 4.46 and Jack Straw MP, *Hansard*, HC Debates cols 410 and 464, 16 June 1999.
111 Interim reg 7(1)(b) and (c).

Act 1989 s17 for his family in Ealing and they needed to move nearer
to support his disabled mother-in-law who lived alone in Croydon, his
wife could make the interim support claim to the London borough of
Croydon.

Entitlement to IS

5.98 An asylum-seeker who is eligible for IS is ineligible for interim support.[112] However, it is possible for one member of the household to
receive IS and another to receive interim support (see para 5.39).

No asylum claim

5.99 Interim reg 7(1)(e) emphasises that interim support must be refused
'where neither the person claiming support nor any of his dependants is an asylum-seeker or has made a claim for leave to enter or
remain in the United Kingdom, or for variation of any such leave
which is being considered on the basis that he is dependent on an
asylum-seeker'. Even if the claim for asylum under the Refugee Convention has been refused, an assisted person may have an 'asylum
claim' under article 3 of the Human Rights Convention, ie, that to
remove him/her from the UK would result in torture or inhuman
or degrading treatment. The IAA 1999 requires an article 3 claim to
be raised at least in the course of the asylum-seeker's 'one-stop'
appeal, but it is arguable that it can be raised at a later date if necessary, eg, if circumstances change. The meaning of asylum claim, article 3 claims and the one-stop appeal process is explained fully in
chapter 1.

5.100 Regulation 7(e) should not affect a family with a dependent child
under 18 because the applicant continues to be treated as an asylum-
seeker eligible for interim support until his/her departure from the
UK.[113] The effect of reg 7(e) is that support should be refused to other
households where there is no outstanding asylum claim or appeal,
even if the asylum-seeker or dependant has applied to remain in the
UK on other grounds, such as compassionate grounds. Advice for
those who are not eligible for interim support is discussed below at
paras 5.117–5.120.

112 Ibid, reg 7(d).
113 IAA 1999 s94(1) and (5).

212 Support for asylum-seekers / chapter 5

Suspension and termination of support

Breach of conditions or absence from accommodation

5.101 Regulation 8(1) places a duty on local authorities to 'discontinue' interim support if they discover that any of the grounds for refusal of support set out in Interim reg 7(1) applies (see paras 5.93–5.100). There is also a *power* to suspend or discontinue interim support in either of the following circumstances:

(a) where the assisted person, or any dependant of his, fails without reasonable excuse to comply with any condition subject to which the support is provided;[114]

(b) where the assisted person, or any dependant of his, leaves accommodation provided as part of such a support for more than seven consecutive days without reasonable excuse.[115]

5.102 The IND guidance of 19 November 1999 states that a local authority could choose not to apply the seven-day requirement or could extend it.[116]

5.103 Support may be provided subject to conditions.[117] Any such conditions must be set out in writing.[118] A copy of the conditions must be given to the supported person.[119] It follows that a termination of support on the ground of breach of conditions would be unlawful where an assisted person has not been properly informed of the conditions of support. The LGA guidance indicates that there should be an induction of those offered support when they are provided with accommodation and a service agreement with an interpreter. The service agreement should be translated into the supported person's first language. If these conditions have not been met, this could be used as a ground on which to challenge the reasonableness of a termination of support for breach of conditions.

5.104 The Asylum Support Adjudicators have considered a number of cases where asylum-seekers have left accommodation, either because they believed it to be inadequate or because of racial harassment. In these appeals, NASS had withdrawn support under AS reg 20(1)(b) and (e) on the ground of a breach or a suspected breach of the

---

114 Interim reg 8(2)(a).
115 Ibid, reg 8(2)(b).
116 Para 16, see Appendix B.
117 IAA 1999 s95(9).
118 Ibid, s95(10).
119 Ibid, s95 (11).

condition to live at/return to the accommodation or on the ground that the asylum-seeker had left the accommodation without permission. Although the wording of the Interim Regs and the AS Regs is not identical, the approach of the adjudicators is relevant to local authority decision-making.[120]

5.105 The Court of Appeal has considered the duties of a local authority which stopped providing residential accommodation in a case where an asylum-seeker had allegedly been violent and disruptive. *R v Kensington and Chelsea RLBC ex p Kujtim*[121]outlines the correct approach to the exercise of discretion under National Assistance Act 1948 s21. It is reasonable to apply the same approach to assessments under the IAA 1999 and the Interim Regs. The court stressed that a local authority should only treat its duty as discharged if there had been a *persistent and unequivocal* refusal to comply with requirements rather than a single transgression.

5.106 In his judgment, Potter LJ stated:

> . . . if an applicant assessed as in need of Part III accommodation either unreasonably refuses to accept the accommodation provided or if, following its provision, by his conduct he manifests a persistent and unequivocal refusal to observe the reasonable requirements of the local authority in relation to the occupation of such accommodation, then the local authority is entitled to treat its duty as discharged and to refuse to provide further accommodation.

He went on to say that a fresh duty to provide accommodation would arise if the applicant can demonstrate that 'there is no longer reason to think that he will persist in his refusal to observe the reasonable requirements of the local authority in respect of the provision of such accommodation'.[122]

5.107 A local authority which is considering a decision to stop providing interim support should follow the well-established approach to public decision-making which is simply re-stated in *Kujtim*. Before reaching a decision, it is essential that the authority carries out a thorough investigation, taking into account the applicant's current needs. The applicant should have a chance to put his/her side of the case. As in homelessness applications, a 'CID type' inquiry is not necessary,[123] ie, the authority does not have to carry out police-style investigations.

120 See paras 3.102–3.124 for fuller discussion and case references.
121 (1999) 2 CCLR 340, CA.
122 Ibid at 354, paras 32–33 and headnote.
123 *Lally v Kensington and Chelsea RLBC* (1980) *Times* 27 March, QBD.

5.108   In *R (on the application of Fetiti) v Islington LBC*,[125] the council had refused to provide interim support to an asylum-seeker who had left accommodation provided under the old National Assistance Act provisions and then re-applied after the Interim Regs came into force. The Court of Appeal granted permission to apply for judicial review on the basis that the applicant was not receiving support at the date of decision and so his support could not be suspended or discontinued. In response to the council's second argument, that Mr Fetiti was intentionally destitute, it was argued that this was not possible since he left the accommodation before the regulations came into force. It was also argued that to remove the right to interim support would result in indefinite destitution, in breach of Human Rights Convention articles 3 and 8(1) and that the effect of this was discriminatory under article 14.

5.109   The consultation paper on interim support suggests that asylum-seekers would be excluded from support if they 'deliberately abuse the support made available to them, for example, by a serious breach of tenancy conditions'.[126] It gives as an example of a serious breach of conditions 'any asylum-seeker who has proved to be an exceptionally bad tenant, for example, by vandalising the accommodation'. ASA 00/09/0063 is an asylum support appeal in which an alleged serious breach of conditions was considered. The asylum-seeker's support was withdrawn after he was imprisoned for alleged threats to kill and assaults on another resident with a hot teapot and a metal pole. The Asylum Support Adjudicator balanced the breach of the occupancy agreement against Human Rights Convention considerations and upheld NASS's decision to withdraw support. The alleged conduct had been witnessed by staff and residents who had felt threatened by it. However, the appellant appeared in handcuffs at the hearing, unrepresented and there was no medical evidence or detailed evidence as to the reasons for his conduct.

5.110   See para 5.56 above for cases where a local authority suspends or discontinues interim support to an asylum-seeker with a dependent child.

5.111   If a local authority terminates support for an adult asylum-seeker, s/he is likely to have no other source of support available. Since

125 C/00/2748, 19 October 2000, CA, unreported. The case settled after the grant of permission.
126 *Asylum-seeker Support: Proposed Interim Arrangements under Schedule 8 of the Immigration and Asylum Bill*, Consultation Paper issued by the Home Office, 20 August 1999.

'suspension or discontinuation' of support is discretionary the local authority should exercise the discretion consistently with their Human Rights Act (HRA) 1998 obligations. This might preclude the authority from terminating support where to do so would make the asylum-seeker destitute, in breach of Human Rights Convention article 3 or possibly article 2 (see paras 8.13 and 8.14).

5.112 It should be possible to challenge decisions to suspend or discontinue support under Interim reg 8(2)(a) if conditions are unreasonable or have not been explained to the assisted person, using ordinary administrative law principles.

5.113 The provision to terminate support where an asylum-seeker is absent from the accommodation is in slightly different terms in the AS Regs, which require the asylum-seeker to obtain permission for absence. A number of circumstances can be foreseen where an asylum-seeker might leave the accommodation temporarily, eg, to visit family or community members in another part of the country or for hospital in-patient treatment. Such cases should fall within the reasonable excuse exemption. Again, local authorities' discretion in the application of this provision and their interpretation of 'without reasonable excuse' should be considered from a HRA perspective.

Termination of support after asylum or appeal decision

Favourable decisions

5.114 An asylum-seeker who is granted full refugee status or exceptional leave to enter or remain will cease to be an 'asylum-seeker' and so the household becomes ineligible for support 14 days after the Home Secretary has notified the applicant of the decision. (The exception to this would be where the Home Office appeals against a successful asylum appeal.) The decision must be in writing and is treated as received on the second day after it was posted either to the asylum-seeker's last known address or to his/her representative, provided it was sent by first class post.[127] If an asylum-seeker has successfully appealed against a negative decision on his/her asylum claim, s/he becomes ineligible for interim support 14 days after s/he is notified of the appeal decision. Again, the 14 days run from the second day after the decision was posted.

127   IAA 1999 s94(3) and (9).

5.115   The prescribed period allows limited time for the asylum-seeker to find alternative accommodation and income. Tactics for addressing these issues are discussed in more detail at paras 2.93–2.106.

5.116   Where the household includes a child under 18, who is a child in need, an application could be made for assistance under Children Act 1989 s17 until the family have arranged benefits and housing (see paras 7.61–7.67).

Unfavourable decisions

5.117   An asylum-seeker who is refused asylum but whose household includes a dependent child under 18, continues to be treated as an asylum-seeker eligible for interim support for as long as the asylum-seeker and the child are in the UK and the child is under 18, even if all rights to challenge the asylum decision have been exhausted.[128]

5.118   Any other asylum-seeker (where there is no child under 18) who has received a negative decision on the initial claim for asylum stops being treated as an asylum-seeker eligible for assistance when the asylum claim is 'determined'.[129] The claim is only determined at the end of a 14-day period which begins when the Home Secretary 'notifies' the asylum-seeker of the decision.[130] This notice of the decision is not the 'pre-decision' letter informing the applicant that the claim for asylum has been refused.[131] It is the full decision letter containing reasons for the refusal, which also triggers the right of appeal. The 14-day period starts on the second day after a written decision was posted. If the asylum-seeker appeals within this period, s/he will continue to be defined as an asylum-seeker, eligible for interim support until 14 days after the appeal is disposed of.

5.119   An asylum-seeker who is not eligible for interim support may be eligible for help under National Assistance Act 1948 s21 if s/he is in need of care and attention for a reason which is not solely due to destitution.[132] If s/he has no special needs it may be possible to bring some form of HRA 1998 challenge. An asylum-seeker who is pursuing a judicial review after an unsuccessful asylum appeal may be eligible for hard cases support.

128 Ibid, s94(5).
129 Ibid, s94(1).
130 Ibid, s94(3).
131 See para 1.80 which explains the distinction between the pre-decision letter and the notification of the decision on the asylum claim.
132 See further para 7.68 onwards and *R v Wandsworth LBC ex p O* (2000) 3 CCLR 237, CA.

5.120   Even if an asylum-seeker's claim for asylum as a refugee under the Refugee Convention has been refused, s/he may have a claim under article 3 of the Human Rights Convention if removal from the UK would result in torture or inhuman or degrading treatment. It is essential that any asylum-seeker whose refugee claim is unsuccessful is referred to an immigration specialist for advice about whether a claim should be made under article 3.

'Hard cases' support[133]

5.121   A childless adult asylum-seeker who is no longer eligible for interim support after a refusal of asylum and an unsuccessful appeal may not be able to leave the UK immediately for practical reasons. S/he may wish to remain in the UK to pursue a judicial review application. NASS administers a scheme known as 'hard cases' support which provides limited assistance (board and lodging only, outside London) in very limited circumstances. The criteria are set out in an IND letter dated 17 April 2000.[134] The scheme as initially established appears to offer less assistance than the community care provisions, as interpreted by the Court of Appeal in *R v Wandsworth LBC ex p O*.[135] In *R v Home Secretary ex p Gebregziabher*, Admin Ct, unreported, permission to apply for judicial review was granted on 11 October 2000 after NASS refused 'hard cases' support to a healthy single man who had no travel documents to travel back to Ethiopia. The case was settled before the substantive hearing.

5.122   The procedure for applying for hard cases support is to write to the Operations Team, NASS, Quest House, Cross Road, Croydon, CR9 6EL.

Remedies

5.123   There is no statutory procedure for appealing against a refusal of interim support or inadequate provision. The Asylum Support Adjudicators do not have jurisdiction to consider interim support cases. Existing remedies for challenging a local authority decision apply. The statutory procedure for complaining about social services provision does not extend to interim support.

---

133 See para 3.169 for a full discussion of the hard cases grant.
134 See Appendix B.
135 (2000) 3 CCLR 237, CA.

5.124   Where asylum-seekers experience disrepair in accommodation provided under the Interim Regs, ordinary private law repairing provisions and environmental health law duties will apply. These are explained at paras 6.149–6.158. Asylum-seekers in accommodation provided under IAA 1999 Part VI are excluded from protection from illegal eviction and harassment by Sch 14, para 73. Tenancies granted by private landlords are not capable of being assured tenancies under the Housing Act 1988 by virtue of para 88. Paragraph 81 amends the Housing Act 1985 so that public sector housing provided under IAA 1999 Part VI cannot be a secure tenancy. Similar provisions apply to Scotland. Clearly, there are Human Rights Convention article 8 implications if an asylum-seeker has no protection against eviction/harassment (see chapter 8).

Complaints

5.125   The LGA guidance on interim support (see Appendix B) makes specific provision for complaints by the assisted person about a breach of the 'service agreement'. This is a contract which should be signed by the assisted person and housing provider on the commencement of their licence. This would apply to cases where there has been a dispersal, whether under the Interim Regs or under homelessness provision. At first instance a complaint about inadequate provision is to the service provider who is providing or arranging accommodation. If the assisted person feels that the service provider has failed to comply with the agreement, s/he can complain directly to the asylum-seekers consortia. The procedure anticipates legal action if the complaint is not resolved promptly.

5.126   Local authorities are required to have procedures to complain about social services functions by virtue of the Local Authority Social Services Act 1970. At the time of writing, the provision of interim support was not one of the functions, which are specified at Sch 1. Similarly, the Secretary of State for Health's default powers to intervene in a case where the specified functions are not properly exercised do not appear to apply. This would not preclude an assisted person from making a complaint under the local authority's ordinary complaints procedure.

5.127   Where a local authority appears to be acting unlawfully, a complaint could be made to its monitoring officer. The monitoring officer has a duty under Local Government and Housing Act 1989 s5 to report to the full council if the authority is acting in contravention of the law or a code of practice or if there is maladministration. The monitoring officer has powers to stop action or to suspend it until the report has been considered. A referral to the monitoring officer may place political pressure on the local authority and should ensure that the action in question is reviewed at a senior management level.

5.128   If the local authority fails to resolve the complaint, a further complaint to the local government ombudsman could be considered. The independent housing ombudsman could be used for complaints about service provision by housing providers who are registered social landlords. Both have powers to recommend compensation. An ombudsman complaint is likely to take at least a year and so has limited value in resolving urgent problems of individual provision.

Judicial review

5.129   Decisions of local authorities in relation to eligibility for interim support, the type of support, refusal, suspension and discontinuation of support are administrative decisions which can be challenged by judicial review. The assisted person or a representative body bringing any such challenge will need to demonstrate that any other remedy such as a complaints procedure has been exhausted or is inappropriate in view of the urgency. To succeed in a judicial review, the applicant will need to show that the local authority has not followed the correct procedures, that it has not applied the Act and regulations correctly or that it has made a decision which is perverse. Decisions about interim support, as decisions of a public body, should be compliant with the HRA.[136]

5.130   A letter before action should be sent to the local authority before an application for permission is issued. Usually this will be combined with an application for interim relief in the form of housing and/or subsistence until the application is heard. The application will usually be considered at first instance as a paper application. If permission to apply for judicial review is refused, there is a right of appeal to the Court of Appeal.

136 See para 8.48 onwards.

CHAPTER 6

Housing rights

For complete chapter contents, see overleaf

Introduction

6.1   The Immigration and Asylum Act (IAA) 1999 is a further step in the removal of asylum-seekers and other persons from abroad from the scope of statutory provision for social housing, in parallel with their exclusion from entitlement to social security benefits. Broadly, the Act excludes asylum-seekers and other persons subject to immigration control from entitlement to assistance as homeless persons under Housing Act (HA) 1996 Part VII, and to the allocation of social housing under HA 1996 Part VI. With very limited exceptions, those who claimed asylum in the UK from 3 April 2000 are not entitled to assistance under the HA 1996, until a favourable decision is made on their application. However, entitlement remains for limited categories of asylum-seekers. There is transitional protection for some asylum-seekers, and there is a restoration of entitlement to those granted refugee status or leave to remain. This chapter therefore considers the entitlement to housing assistance for those with asylum decisions pending, and those who are the subject of favourable decisions. The limited remedies available to asylum-seekers faced with disrepair, insanitary housing and harassment are also considered.

6.2   The IAA 1999 also removes from asylum-seekers rights of security of tenure and to protection from eviction where they are housed under the Act. These aspects are considered in chapters 4 and 5 in relation to the 'adequacy' of accommodation and the dispersal provisions.

6.3   This chapter begins with an examination of the elements of statutory provision for the homeless with particular reference to the rights of asylum-seekers. The allocation of accommodation is then similarly treated. There is an analysis of the effects upon accommodation rights of changes in immigration status. The Homes Bill, before parliament at the time of writing, will make changes to homelessness and allocation law: a summary of the material changes appears at paras 6.92–6.103 below. The chapter concludes with a description of remedies available to asylum-seekers for poor housing conditions and harassment.

Homelessness and allocation under the HA 1996

6.4   The HA 1996 makes provision for securing accommodation for homeless people (Part VII) and for allocating long-term social housing to people (Part VI).¹ Part VII² places duties on local authorities to assess certain homeless applicants, and to secure accommodation for applicants meeting qualifying criteria for a limited period. Part VI³ establishes a framework within which local authorities must allocate tenancies of their own housing stock and that of registered social landlords (including most housing associations).

6.5   The HA 1996 contains a series of restrictions on the rights of persons from abroad, including asylum-seekers. Sections of the IAA 1999 contain a parallel series of wider restrictions, and repeal the corresponding sections in the HA 1996: however, at the time of writing, the repeal has not yet been implemented, and the respective provisions have to be read together.

6.6   For those advising asylum-seekers, most problems concern two areas – whether people qualify for assistance and accommodation and, in relation to the homeless, the nature of the assistance that is provided.

Homelessness: does the local authority have a duty to assist?

6.7   Duties under Part VII are triggered when a person applies to a housing authority and the housing authority has reason to believe that s/he 'may be' homeless or threatened with homelessness.⁴

6.8   In respect of such a person the housing authority is required to 'make such inquiries as are necessary to satisfy themselves' whether or not the person is *eligible, homeless, in priority need*, and *intentionally homeless*; the authority may also inquire about whether s/he has any *local connection*. Whether any duty is owed by the authority to the person depends on the outcome of these inquiries.

Eligibility

6.9   Eligibility is restricted on the ground of immigration status, and in the case of asylum-seekers and their dependants, additionally on the ground of accommodation available. The restrictions leave two groups of asylum-seekers eligible:

1 For a full treatment of these statutory provisions and their associated case-law, see Arden & Hunter, *Homelessness & Allocations* (6th edn, LAG, forthcoming).
2 In force 27 January 1997.
3 In force 1 April 1997.
4 HA 1996 s183.

- those given 'transitional protection' from the previous statutory scheme – a group that will diminish in time;
- those eligible because of their nationality.

In addition there are those who acquire eligibility through a favourable decision being made on their asylum application.

Ineligiblity through immigration status

6.10   The restrictions on the ground of immigration status operate by making a general exclusion from eligibility, and then 're-including' people falling in specified classes.

6.11   An applicant who is a person from abroad is ineligible if s/he is a person subject to immigration control within the meaning of the Asylum and Immigration Act (AIA) 1996 unless s/he falls within one of certain categories specifically accorded eligibility.[5] People who are not subject to immigration control may nonetheless be ineligible if they are subject to, and do not satisfy, the habitual residence test.

6.12   By AIA 1996 s13(2), a person is subject to immigration control if s/he is a person who under the Immigration Act (IA) 1971 requires leave to enter or remain in the UK (whether or not such leave has been given). By IA 1971 ss2 and 3, all people require leave to enter or remain except:

- British citizens;
- Commonwealth citizens with right of abode;
- citizens of the Republic of Ireland;
- citizens of European Economic Area (EEA) states who are 'workers', self-employed or providing services[6] and their family members.

6.13   It should be noted that this is a wider category than the definition of 'persons subject to immigration control' who are excluded from entitlement to benefits and other welfare provision by IAA 1999 s115: the category includes all those requiring leave to enter or remain, whether or not they are subject to a condition requiring that they have no recourse to public funds.

---

5   Ibid, s185(2).
6   IA 1988 s7(1); see paras 1.18–1.19. These provisions parallel those applicable to social security benefits which are discussed in detail in paras 2.22, 2.23, 2.33–2.35.

6.14   The categories specifically accorded eligibility are Classes A to I in Homelessness (England) Regulations 2000 reg 3:[7]

Class A: Persons recorded as being refugees.

Class B: Persons with exceptional leave to remain (ELR) whose leave does not exclude them from recourse to public funds.

Class C: Persons with a current leave to enter or remain which is not subject to any limitation or condition and who are habitually resident in the common travel area, other than sponsored immigrants who have been here for less than five years and whose sponsor is still alive.

Class D: Persons who left Montserrat after 1 November 1995 because of a volcanic eruption.

Class E: Persons who are habitually resident in the common travel area and who are either (i) lawfully present and a national of a state which has *ratified* the European Convention on Social and Medical Assistance (ECSMA) or the Council of Europe Social Charter (CESC), or (ii) who continue to be owed a duty that arose prior to 3 April 2000, under HA 1985 Part III (old homelessness scheme) or HA 1996 Part VII (new homelessness scheme) and who are nationals of a state which is a *signatory* to ECSMA or CESC. See the table in Appendix C for the states which are covered. The scope of this class may be limited – see para 6.16 below.

Class F: Asylum-seekers whose claims have been recorded by the Home Secretary as having been made on arrival (other than on re-entry) and which have not been recorded as having been decided (other than on appeal) or abandoned.

Class G: Persons who have been recorded by the Home Secretary as having claimed asylum within three months of an upheaval declaration and whose claims have not been recorded as having been decided (other than on appeal) or abandoned.

Class H: Asylum-seekers who made a 'relevant claim' for asylum on or before 4 February 1996 and who were, on 4 February 1996, entitled to housing benefit under Housing Benefit (General) Regulations 1987 reg 7A (the regulation that deals with persons from abroad). A 'relevant claim' for asylum is one:

7   SI No 701; see Appendix A. The same regulations are applied to Wales by the Homelessness (Wales) Regs 2000 SI No 1079.

a) on which no initial decision has been recorded and which is not recorded as abandoned, or

b) on which there has been an initial refusal decision made before 5 February 1996, but there is an appeal still pending made either before 5 February 1996 or within the relevant time limits.[8]

Class I: Persons receiving income-based jobseekers' allowance (JSA) or income support (IS) (except those with limited leave to enter or remain subject to a condition that they have no recourse to public funds but who receive benefit because of a temporary interruption in the receipt of funds from abroad).

6.15 'Asylum-seekers' in Classes F, G and H are only eligible if, additionally, they are 18 or over, and have their asylum claim recorded by the Home Secretary as being made before 3 April 2000, and that claim must not have been determined.[9] Those with asylum claims made on or after 3 April 2000 fall within the scope of National Asylum Support Service (NASS) assistance.

6.16 Considering the categories 're-included' in relation to asylum-seekers, it is to be noted that asylum-seekers may be rendered eligible under Classes F, G and H, but also under Classes E and I. However, in the case of Class E, asylum-seekers can only qualify under the subsisting homelessness duty *limb* (reg 3(3)(e)(ii)) since asylum-seekers have been found not to be 'lawfully present'.[10] It is to be noted also that the homelessness eligibility of asylum-seekers ends with the first decision on the asylum application: unlike asylum support, it is not extended during an appeal or by there being dependent children in the household. Furthermore, doubt has been cast on whether these regulations are effective in re-including categories of asylum-seekers: IAA 1999 s117(4) prevents people who are subject to immigration control under IAA 1999 s115 being re-included in this way. People may be taken out of the scope of s115 for particular purposes by regulations made under s115(3) and (4), but the Homelessness (England) Regulations 2000 are not made under s115(3) and (4); they are made under powers given to the

---

8 Homelessness (England) Regs 2000 reg 3(2).
9 Ibid, reg 2.
10 *Kaya v Haringey LBC* (2001) 1 May, CA (unreported).

Home Secretary by HA 1996 s185(2). Thus it is arguable that the regulations are ultra vires.[11]

6.17   Those not subject to immigration control may nonetheless be ineligible if they do not satisfy the habitual residence test. As noted above, certain people are not subject to immigration control, ie:

a)   British citizens;
b)   Commonwealth citizens with right of abode;
c)   citizens of the Republic of Ireland;
d)   citizens of EEA states who are 'workers', self-employed or providing services,[12] former 'workers' and their family members.

Of these, people falling within a), b) and c) are ineligible unless:[13]

– they are 'habitually resident' in the common travel area (the UK, Channel Islands, Isle of Man and Republic of Ireland); or
– they are receiving IS or income-based JSA; or
– they left Montserrat after 1 November 1995 because of a volcanic eruption.

6.18   For the meaning of 'habitually resident' see paras 2.61–2.64. Note that this exclusion does not affect asylum-seekers since they are among the categories of persons subject to immigration control.

Ineligibility through accommodation being available

6.19   There is a further hurdle placed in the path of asylum-seekers who surmount the eligibility criteria based on immigration status, above.

6.20   By HA 1996 s186, an asylum-seeker or a dependant of an asylum-seeker who is otherwise eligible is to be considered ineligible for assistance if s/he has any accommodation in the UK, however temporary, available for his/her occupation.[14] This applies only to asylum-seekers, and persons within classes A to E and I above are not affected unless they are asylum-seekers.

11   This was argued in the county court in *Kaya* (ibid) but the Court of Appeal did not consider the issue.
12   See paras 1.18–1.19, 2.29, 2.30, 2.35–2.43.
13   HA 1996 s185(3) and Homelessness (England) Regs 2000 reg 4 (see Appendix A).
14   HA 1996 s186(1).

6.21   Under s186 a person is an asylum-seeker from the point when his/her claim for asylum is recorded by the Home Secretary until the point where the claim is recorded by the Home Secretary as having been finally determined or abandoned.[15]

6.22   A dependant is a spouse, or a child of the asylum-seeker under 18 years, who does not him/herself have right of abode or indefinite leave to remain in the UK.[16] A person is a dependant of an asylum-seeker from the point s/he is recorded by the Home Secretary as being a dependant until the point when the Home Secretary records that s/he is no longer a dependant, or the point when the claim for asylum of the asylum-seeker whose dependant s/he is recorded as has finally been determined or abandoned.[17]

6.23   The impact of s186 is limited by the effect of HA 1996 s175(3). In *Lismane v Hammersmith and Fulham LBC*[18] the Court of Appeal held that an asylum-seeker who occupied temporary accommodation, which was clearly unsuitable for her needs, would qualify for housing assistance notwithstanding the provisions of HA 1996 s186(1) – a determination of her eligibility did not exclude the application of s175(3), which required a consideration of whether the accommodation was such that it was reasonable for her to continue to occupy it.

6.24   Furthermore, it appears that HA 1996 s186 will be repealed.[19] If the government does decide to repeal s186, whether the occupation of some form of accommodation is a bar to assistance will, for eligible asylum-seekers as for other applicants, depend on the test of homelessness under s175 (see paras 6.29–6.32 below).

Assessing eligibility

6.25   The above rules are complex and confusing: there follows a 12-step guide to establish if an asylum-seeker is eligible for assistance as a homeless person. References in *italics* are to the detailed provisions above.

---

15   Ibid, s186(2); see paras 2.46–2.47 for the meaning of these terms.
16   Ibid, s186(4).
17   Ibid, s186(3).
18   (1999) 31 HLR 427.
19   IAA 1999 s117(5) repeals HA 1996 s186, but has not yet come into force. IAA 1999 (Commencement No 3) Order 2000 SI No 464 implements IAA 1999 Part VI with the exception of s117(5).

Question	Yes	No
1. Is the asylum-seeker getting IS or means-tested JSA? *(see para 6.14, Class I)*	Go on to 12	Go on to 2
2. Has the claim for asylum been determined? *(see para 6.21)*	Go on to 3	Go on to 8
3. Has it been determined by a grant of refugee status? *(see para 6.14, Class A)*	Eligible	Go on to 4
4. Has it been determined by a grant of ELR (with no condition preventing recourse to public funds attached)? *(see para 6.14, Class B)*	Eligible	Go on to 5
5. Has it been refused, and no appeal lodged?	Ineligible	Go on to 6
6. Has it been refused, an appeal lodged, and the appeal refused?	Ineligible	Go on to 7
7. Is it a claim which was refused before 5 February 1996 and in which an appeal was lodged within the time limits which is still pending? *(see para 6.14, Class H)*	Go on to 12	Ineligible
8. The person has a pending asylum application: was it made before 5 February 1996? *(see para 6.14, Class H)*	Go on to 12	Go on to 9
9. Was the asylum application made by a person from Sierra Leone or the Congo (formerly Zaire) within three months of 1 July 1997 (Sierra Leone) or 16 May 1997 (Congo)? *(see para 6.14, Class G)*	Go on to 12	Go on to 10
10. Was the asylum application made on arrival? *(see para 6.14, Class F)*	Go on to 11	Ineligible
11. Was the asylum application made before 3 April 2000? *(see para 6.15)*	Go on to 12	Ineligible
12. Does the asylum-seeker have any accomodation, however temporary, available for his/her occupation and which it is reasonable for him/her to continue to occupy? *(see paras 6.19–6.24)*	Ineligible	Eligible

Ineligible applicants

6.26   Asylum-seekers who are homeless but ineligible under the above provisions should seek assistance with accommodation from NASS (see chapter 3), or from the local authority social services department under the Interim Regulations (see chapter 5) or community care legislation (see chapter 7). The table at para 3.9 will help identify whether a person falls under NASS asylum support or local authority interim support. The table at para 7.52 will help identify whether a person is entitled to assessment for community care services.

6.27   The local authority's duties to provide appropriate advice and assistance to secure accommodation for applicants who are intentionally homeless or not in priority need[20] do not apply to applicants who are ineligible.

6.28   A person who is ineligible to apply may nonetheless be accommodated if there is another member of the household (or another person with whom s/he may reasonably be expected to live) who is eligible to apply. To qualify for assistance the eligible person will have to be homeless without regard to the accommodation needs of ineligible household members (see para 6.31 below) and in priority need without reliance upon ineligible household members (see paras 6.34–6.37 below). However, where the eligible person does so qualify, the duty upon the local authority is to secure accommodation for the eligible applicant and anyone who can reasonably be expected to live with him/her – including household members who are themselves ineligible (see para 6.52 below).

Homelessness

6.29   After considering eligibility, the local authority should consider whether an applicant is homeless or threatened with homelessness. To be considered homeless[21] a person must have no accommodation available for his/her occupation in the UK or elsewhere which s/he is entitled to occupy because:

a)   s/he has a legal interest (including ownership, a lease or a tenancy); or

b)   s/he has a licence; or

c)   s/he has a right to occupy under a court order; or

d)   a statute or rule of law states that s/he can occupy or prevents another person from recovering possession from him/her.

6.30   A person may also be homeless because:

e)   his/her home is a boat, caravan or similar and s/he has nowhere to moor or park it; or

f)   although s/he has accommodation under a) to d) above, s/he cannot secure entry to it; or

20 HA 1996 ss190, 192.
21 Ibid, s175.

g) although s/he has accommodation under a) to d) above, it would not be reasonable for him/her to continue to occupy it.

A person is threatened with homelessness if it is likely that he will become homeless within 28 days.

6.31   Particular issues need to be considered in deciding whether asylum-seekers are homeless or threatened with homelessness:

- The standard of homelessness is in effect made more stringent for asylum-seekers and their dependants by HA 1996 s186 (discussed at paras 6.20–6.24), excluding from assistance any person who has 'any accommodation however temporary available for his occupation'. Strictly, this requirement would exclude asylum-seekers from eligibility rather than result in their being considered 'not homeless'.
- The definition of homelessness refers to the availability of accommodation in the UK 'or elsewhere': in practice, asylum-seekers with pending applications or appeals will not be considered to have accommodation available in the country they have fled from, although this may be an issue if they have entered the UK from a third country where they have accommodation. If a person cannot afford to travel to the accommodation which it would otherwise be reasonable for him/her to continue to occupy, then that factor would make it unreasonable to occupy the accommodation.[22]
- Accommodation will only be considered to be available for occupation if it is available for occupation by the applicant and any other person who usually resides with him/her as a family member or any other person who might reasonably be expected to reside with him/her. However (and this has particular importance for asylum-seekers who are joined in the UK by, or who are themselves joining, other family members), it should be noted that any ineligible person is to be disregarded in deciding whether an applicant is homeless or threatened with homelessness.[23] Thus, to qualify as homeless, an applicant must be without accommodation for him/herself and *eligible* members; the accommodation needs of ineligible persons are ignored in deciding whether the eligible applicant has accommodation available for occupation. For example, accommodation will not 'cease to be available' to an applicant in circumstances where s/he has a right to occupy it but

22 *Nipa Begum v Tower Hamlets LBC* (2000) 32 HLR 445.
23 HA 1996 s185(4).

is not permitted (say, under the terms of the tenancy agreement) to have living with him/her family members who themselves are ineligible for assistance. Similarly, it will not be unreasonable for an applicant to continue to occupy accommodation if it is suitable for single occupation but too small for him/her to live in with family members who themselves are ineligible for assistance. Similar rules apply to proving priority need – see para 6.35 below. However, where the eligible applicant does so qualify as homeless and in priority need, the duty upon the local authority is to secure accommodation for the eligible applicant and anyone who can reasonably be expected to live with her/him – including household members who are themselves ineligible (see para 6.52 below).

6.32   Where an applicant is not homeless under these rules, but being joined in the accommodation by an ineligible spouse, partner or dependants results in the accommodation becoming inadequate (eg, overcrowded), then the household will be eligible for accommodation under the asylum support provisions. Assistance is provided depending on whether the existing accommodation is 'adequate', applying IAA 1999 ss95–96 and Asylum Support Regulations 2000 (AS Regs) reg 8.[24]

Priority need

6.33   Only those applicants with a priority need for accommodation fall within the local authority's duty to secure accommodation. The following have a priority need for accommodation:[25]

a)   a pregnant woman or a person with whom she resides or might reasonably be expected to reside;

b)   a person with whom dependent children reside or might reasonably be expected to reside;

c)   a person who is vulnerable as a result of old age, mental illness, handicap or physical disability or other special reason, or with whom such a person resides or might reasonably be expected to reside;

d)   a person who is homeless or threatened with homelessness as a result of an emergency such as flood, fire or other disaster.

24   SI No 704; see Appendix A.
25   HA 1996 s189.

6.34   Particular issues need to be considered in deciding whether asylum-seekers have a priority need.

6.35   As with the test of homelessness an applicant is not entitled to rely on persons who are ineligible for housing assistance to establish a priority need.[26] Thus, an eligible applicant who has living with him a pregnant wife or dependent children who are themselves ineligible cannot rely on their residence with him to give him a priority need for accommodation. (In the example of the pregnant wife, once the child is born in the UK the father would be in priority need, since the child would not be ineligible.[27]) Similarly, an applicant who lives with and cares for an elderly or disabled person who is her/himself ineligible for housing assistance will not thereby acquire priority need.

6.36   Where an applicant is not in priority need under these rules, but being joined in the accommodation by an ineligible spouse, partner or dependants results in the accommodation becoming inadequate (eg, overcrowded), then the household will be eligible for accommodation under the asylum support provisions. Assistance is provided depending on whether the existing accommodation is 'adequate', applying AS Regs reg 8.[28]

6.37   Asylum-seekers who have no dependent children or no eligible dependent children may themselves qualify as being in priority need in their own right. Many asylum-seekers will satisfy the test of being vulnerable as a result of old age, mental illness, handicap or physical disability or other special reason. A person is 'vulnerable' when he is 'homeless, less able to fend for himself than an ordinary homeless person so that injury or detriment to him will result when a less vulnerable man would be able to cope without harmful effects'.[29] It is to be construed in a housing context, and thus means less able to fend for oneself in finding and keeping accommodation.[30] While lack of English[31] or lack of money will not by itself amount to vulnerability, a combination of factors is capable of amounting to 'other special reason'.[32] Asylum-seekers who fall short of 'mental illness or handicap or physical disability' are nonetheless likely to exhibit a variety of

---

26   Ibid, s185(4).
27   See para 1.94.
28   See Appendix A.
29   *R v Camden LBC ex p Pereira* (1999) 31 HLR 317, CA.
30   *R v Kensington and Chelsea RLBC ex p Kihara* (1996) 29 HLR 147, CA; *R v Bath CC ex p Sangermano* (1984) 17 HLR 94; *R v Lambeth LBC ex p Carroll* (1987) 20 HLR 142.
31   *R v Bath CC ex p Sangermano* (1984) 17 HLR 94.
32   *R v Kensington and Chelsea RLBC ex p Kihara* (1996) 29 HLR 147, CA.

factors which would be relevant to 'other special reason', such as post-traumatic stress disorder, the effects of torture and detention, and the loss of family members.

6.38   Children born in the UK are not 'persons subject to immigration control': they do not require leave to enter or remain, and so are not excluded from eligibility. Dependent children cannot make an application as homeless in their own right,[33] but their birth or presence in the household may give rise to priority need, where one of the adults in the household is eligible.

6.39   Asylum-seekers who are 16 or 17 years old are likely to be vulnerable if they are 'at risk' or less able to fend for themselves than other young people.[34] Lack of family contact and support and previous social services care[35] are likely to be relevant factors in the cases of young asylum-seekers. Those who have been looked after by the local authority may additionally qualify for assistance with accommodation under Children Act (CA) 1989 s24 (see paras 7.102–7.108) or, from 1 October 2001, under the Children (Leaving Care) Act 2000 (see para 7.105).

6.40   Again, where the eligible homeless applicant is in priority need, the duty upon the local authority is to secure accommodation for the eligible applicant and anyone who can reasonably be expected to live with her/him – including household members who are themselves ineligible (see para 6.52 below).

6.41   If an applicant is homeless or threatened with homelessness, but not in priority need, only limited duties are owed to her/him (see para 6.56 below).

Intentional homelessness

6.42   A person becomes intentionally homeless if s/he deliberately does or fails to do anything in consequence of which s/he ceases to occupy accommodation which is available for his/her occupation and which it would have been reasonable for him/her to continue to occupy.[36] The act or omission will not be considered 'deliberate' if the person

---

33   *R v Oldham MBC ex p Garlick* [1993] AC 509, 25 HLR 319, HL.
34   DoE/DoH Code of Guidance on Housing Act 1996 Parts VI and VII, paras 14.10, 14.11 (nb, the Code of Guidance is currently under review); DETR Guidance, 12 April 2000.
35   Whether provided under CA 1989 s17 or s20 – see paras 7.98–7.108.
36   HA 1996 s191(1).

was unaware of any relevant fact and acted or failed to act in good faith.[37]

6.43 In relation to asylum-seeker applicants it should be noted that a person may be intentionally homeless by leaving accommodation abroad,[38] although in practice local authorities are unlikely to conclude that an asylum-seeker is intentionally homeless for leaving accommodation in the country s/he is fleeing from, while an asylum application is pending.

6.44 Findings of intentional homelessness are likely to be more common where asylum-seekers have left accommodation in areas they have been dispersed to, either before or after a decision on their asylum application. It should be noted that the test of whether or not such a person is intentionally homeless is different from the test of 'intentional destitution' that would be applied if the person were to re-apply to NASS or for local authority interim support: 'intentional homelessness' refers only to the act or omission of the applicant, while 'intentional destitution' may arise from the act or omission of any dependant.[39]

6.45 Applicants who are in priority need but intentionally homeless are owed only limited duties.[40] The authority must secure suitable accommodation for such period as it considers reasonable for the applicant to find accommodation him/herself and provide 'appropriate' advice and assistance to the applicant in his/her own attempts to find suitable accommodation.

6.46 Applicants found intentionally homeless but not in priority need are entitled only to 'appropriate' advice and assistance.

Local connection

6.47 The local connection provisions are considered below (paras 6.66–6.76).

37 Ibid, s191(2).
38 Ibid, s175(1).
39 Ibid, s191; AS Regs reg 20(2); Asylum Support (Interim Provisions) Regs 1999 SI No 3056 reg 7(2); see paras 3.112–3.116.
40 HA 1996 s190.

Homelessness: what are the duties owed?

Temporary accommodation pending decision

6.48   A person who applies as homeless to a local authority may be entitled to temporary accommodation while the authority enquires into his/her case. By HA 1996 s188(1):

> If the local housing authority have reason to believe that an applicant may be homeless, eligible for assistance and have a priority need, they shall secure that accommodation is available for his occupation pending a decision as to the duty (if any) owed . . .

6.49   Such accommodation must be suitable[41] for the applicant and anyone else who can reasonably be expected to live with the applicant (including 'ineligible persons' – see para 6.52 below). The extent to which particular temporary accommodation must suit an applicant's needs will vary according to how long it is occupied.[42] Bed and breakfast accommodation is commonly used despite guidance that it should only be considered as a 'last resort' and that it is unsuitable for families with children.[43] The particular circumstances of asylum-seekers may render such accommodation unsuitable even in the short-term, but compelling evidence would be required to challenge such a decision.[44] The practice of local authorities to simply allocate whatever accommodation is available on the day an applicant becomes homeless, without regard to individual needs, is unlawful.[45]

6.50   The authority may not refer the applicant to another authority for accommodation under this section, but may nonetheless itself find temporary accommodation for the applicant outside its own area.

The 'full housing duty'

6.51   If the authority is satisfied that an applicant is homeless, eligible, in priority need and not intentionally homeless then a duty arises to ensure that accommodation is available to the applicant.[46] The only exception to a positive duty on the authority to secure accommoda-

---

41   Ibid, ss205(1), 206(1); *R v Ealing LBC ex p Surdonja* (1999) 31 HLR 686.
42   *R v Exeter CC ex p Gliddon* (1984) 14 HLR 103.
43   DoE/DoH Code of Guidance on Housing Act 1996 Parts VI and VII, para 20.2.
44   *R v Newham LBC ex p Sacupima* [2001] 33 HLR 1 and 18.
45   Ibid.
46   HA 1996 s193(2).

tion is where the authority is satisfied that other suitable accommodation is available in its district which the applicant can take up with advice and assistance from the authority;[47] the Homes Bill proposes to abolish this exception – see para 6.99 below.

6.52 The duty is to secure that accommodation is available for the applicant and anyone else who usually resides with the applicant as a family member, or anyone else who can reasonably be expected to live with the applicant.[48] 'Anyone else' here includes persons subject to immigration control who would fail the eligibility requirement in HA 1996 s185: once an applicant is owed the housing duty, that duty extends to securing accommodation for the whole of his/her household whether or not they are eligible.

6.53 The duty continues for a minimum period of two years, but may be renewed if the criteria (see para 6.51 above) are still satisfied.[49] Many local authorities will in practice make offers of long-term accommodation through the housing register within the initial two-year period. The Homes Bill proposes to end the two-year limit – see para 6.97 below.

6.54 The accommodation secured must be 'suitable' – see paras 6.57–6.65 below.

Other housing duties

6.55 If an applicant is homeless and in priority need, but found intentionally homeless, the authority has a duty to:[50]

(a) secure that accommodation is available for his occupation for such period as they consider will give him a reasonable opportunity of securing accommodation for his occupation, and

(b) provide him with such advice and assistance as they consider appropriate in the circumstances in any attempts he may make to secure that accommodation becomes available for his occupation.

Accommodation secured under s190(2)(a) must be 'suitable' (see paras 6.59–6.65 below).

6.56 If an applicant is homeless (whether or not intentionally), but not

---

47 Ibid, s197.
48 Ibid, s176.
49 The Homes Bill, before parliament at the time of writing, proposes to abolish the minimum period.
50 HA 1996 s190.

in priority need, the authority owes the 'advice and assistance' duty described in s190(2)(b).[51] The Homes Bill proposes to add a power (not a duty) for the authority to secure accommodation for such applicants who are not intentionally homeless. Such applicants will in most cases be eligible for housing benefit. It should be noted that NASS guidance[52] states that such applicants will be expected to take advantage of such advice and assistance, and to take reasonable steps to find alternative accommodation, before they will be entitled to the provision of accommodation by NASS.

Suitability of accommodation

6.57   Accommodation secured by the local authority must be suitable[53] for the applicant and anyone else who usually resides with the applicant as a family member, or anyone else who can reasonably be expected to live with the applicant.[54] Again, 'anyone else' here includes persons who would fail the eligibility requirement in HA 1996 s185.

6.58   In determining what is suitable, the authority must have regard to HA 1996 Parts IX, X and XI (slum clearance, overcrowding and houses in multiple occupation).[55] Lord Hoffmann in *Awua v Brent LBC*[56] observed that, '[t]his points to suitability being primarily a matter of space and arrangement, though no doubt other matters (such as whether the occupant can afford the rent) may also be material'. In *R v Newham LBC ex p Sacupima*[57] the Court of Appeal held that the location of accommodation was relevant to its suitability.

6.59   The circumstances of asylum-seekers may give rise to special consideration in relation to suitability. For example, the courts have quashed suitability decisions where an asylum-seeker refused a basement estate flat which reminded her of a prison where she had been tortured,[58] and where an asylum-seeker refused an offer where she would be in contact with Turkish and Kurdish communities in

---

51 Ibid, ss190(3), 192.
52 NASS Policy Bulletin 11.
53 HA 1996 ss193, 206.
54 Ibid, s176.
55 Ibid, s210.
56 [1996] 1 AC 55; (1996) 27 HLR 453.
57 (2001) 33 HLR 18.
58 *R v Brent LBC ex p Omar* (1991) 23 HLR 446.

circumstances where she had a genuine terror of such contact and where her daughter's mental health would be damaged by acceptance.[59]

6.60 So far as is reasonably practicable, authorities must accommodate the homeless person within their own district.[60] Authorities should have regard to the importance of housing homeless people as close as possible to where they previously lived so that they can keep the same schools, doctors, social workers, etc.[61] These requirements are modified in the case of asylum-seekers.

Suitability of accommodation for asylum-seekers

6.61 In addition to the above factors, local authorities are directed to consider particular factors in relation to asylum-seekers when considering suitability of accommodation.[62] The authority:

(a) shall also have regard to the fact that the accommodation is to be temporary pending determination of the applicant's claim for asylum; and

(b) shall not have regard to any preference that the applicant, or any person who might reasonably be expected to reside with him, may have as to the locality in which the accommodation is to be secured.

6.62 Section 210(1A) has the effect that the accommodation must be suitable as temporary accommodation. The decision in *Lismane v Hammersmith and Fulham LBC*[63] would however still apply to this accommodation (see para 6.23 above). Section 210(1A) excludes mere accommodation preferences from consideration. It does not however permit the housing authority to disregard real welfare considerations which relate to the location of accommodation, for example, its proximity to medical assistance, social support and the like.

6.63 It is arguable that where the applicant is an eligible person who is not an asylum-seeker and s/he is to be housed with family or household members who are asylum-seekers, the authority in considering the provision of accommodation should not apply the restrictions on suitability applicable to asylum-seeker applications (s210 as

---

59 *R v Haringey LBC ex p Karaman* (1997) 29 HLR 366.
60 HA 1996 s208.
61 Code of Guidance paras 21.15–2.19.
62 HA 1996 s210(1A), as amended by Homelessness (Asylum-seekers) (Interim Period) (England) Order 1999 SI No 3126; see Appendix A.
63 (1999) 31 HLR 427.

amended) and should secure accommodation in its district so far as is reasonably practicable.[64] This issue has yet to be decided by the courts.

6.64   The requirement upon local authorities to house homeless people within their area where practicable (see para 6.60 above) is modified in the case of asylum-seekers: the requirement is removed where another housing authority has agreed in writing that the first authority can secure accommodation for all or an agreed number of asylum-seekers in its area.[65] Nonetheless, the requirements as to suitability (as modified in the case of asylum-seekers) still apply.

6.65   If there is no agreement in writing with another housing authority, authorities can still house asylum-seeker applicants outside their area, but will need to be satisfied that it was not reasonably practical to house them within the area.[66]

Referral of the housing duty to another authority

Referral of persons who are not asylum-seekers

6.66   In the case of homeless applicants who are not asylum-seekers, where a person is owed the full housing duty, the authority can transfer the duty to house to another housing authority, by 'referring' the case.[67] The 'conditions for referral' are given in HA 1996 s198(2):

> (2)   The conditions for referral of the case to another authority are met if –
>
> (a) neither the applicant nor any person who might reasonably be expected to reside with him has a local connection with the district of the authority to whom his application was made,
>
> (b) the applicant or a person who might reasonably be expected to reside with him has a local connection with the district of that other authority, and
>
> (c) neither the applicant nor any person who might reasonably be expected to reside with him will run the risk of domestic violence in that other district.

6.67   The term 'local connection' is defined in HA 1996 s199 and the duties on referring and target authorities are set out more fully in HA

---

64   HA 1996 s208(1); it is submitted that s208(1A) should not apply in such cases.
65   Ibid, s208(1A).
66   Ibid, s208.
67   Ibid, s198(1).

1996 s200. The Homes Bill proposes to add a provision that the conditions for referral will not be met where the applicant or a household member has suffered violence in the target authority area and it is probable that a return to the area will lead to further violence – see para 6.100 below.

6.68   Asylum-seekers who are granted refugee status or ELR are likely to be particularly affected by the 'local connection' provisions. Typically, a person has been dispersed under NASS asylum support or local authority interim support, and that accommodation is terminated upon the change of immigration status, whereupon the person applies to a London local authority. If accepted as owed the full housing duty by the London authority, that person would stand to be referred back to the dispersal area authority for housing if s/he could not establish that s/he or anyone who could reasonably be expected to reside with him/her (a) had a local connection with the London borough in question, and, (b) where there is no such connection, had no local connection with the area of the authority to which s/he had been dispersed. In either case, local connection is defined by HA 1996 s199: a person has a local connection with an authority area if s/he meets one of four criteria:

– s/he is or was in the past usually resident in it, and her/his residence is or was of her/his own choice;
– s/he is employed in it;
– s/he has family associations;
– there are special circumstances.

6.69   These criteria are developed in the Code of Guidance chapter 16, and the Local Authority Association Joint Local Connection Agreement contains guidelines for resolving disputes between local authorities as to where homeless persons have local connections. The criteria and the guidance are not to be applied rigidly however, so that the ordinary meaning of the term 'local connection' is lost.[68]

6.70   In the typical case of people granted refugee status or ELR, referred to above, it should be noted that 'normal residence' must be of choice, and accommodation provided under the dispersal provisions of the IAA 1999 or the referral provisions of the HA 1996 is unlikely to have been of the asylum-seeker's choice.[69] Guidance to

68 *R v Eastleigh BC ex p Betts* [1983] 2 AC 613; (1983) 10 HLR 97, HL.
69 See by analogy residence following service in the armed forces, considered in *R v Vale of White Horse DC ex p Smith and Hay* (1984) 17 HLR 160, QBD.

local authorities suggests that 'normal residence' will be established by residence for six months of the last 12 months, and that 'family associations' will exist where there are parents, adult children, brothers or sisters residing for at least five years in the area in question. The criterion of 'other special circumstance' leaves open a wide range of considerations that may give rise to a local connection.

Referral of asylum-seekers

6.71   In the case of homeless applicants who are asylum-seekers, the position is modified. Provision for asylum-seekers under NASS asylum support and local authority interim support includes machinery for the dispersal of applicants to accommodation outside London and the south east.[70] Parallel provision has been made for applicants as homeless under the HA 1996 by extending the referral conditions in s198. The conditions for referral made it difficult for housing authorities to refer persons from abroad elsewhere, even when such persons had no connection with the housing authority's area. The reason for this was that such persons would also often not have a local connection with any other housing authority. Such persons had to remain the responsibility of the housing authority to whom they applied and this was perceived as imposing a disproportionate burden on housing authorities in London and those near ports of entry to the UK.[71] Accordingly, s198 was amended.[72]

6.72   These amendments make it possible to refer asylum-seekers to other housing authorities:

– irrespective of whether the asylum-seeker or any person residing with her/him has a local connection with the area of *any* local authority; and
– irrespective of any preference that the asylum-seeker or a person residing with him/her might express.

6.73   The only conditions for referral in the case of asylum-seekers are that the two housing authorities concerned have agreed in writing that a referral should take place and neither the asylum-seeker nor any person who might reasonably be expected to reside with him/her

---

70   See paras 4.17–4.25, 5.61–5.76.
71   *R v Hillingdon LBC ex p Streeting* [1980] 1 WLR 1425 at 1429.
72   IAA 1999 s169(2) and Sch 15, para 13, and Homelessness (Asylum-seekers) (Interim Period) (England) Order 1999 SI No 3126 – amending s198 by adding s198(4A) and (4B).

runs the risk of domestic violence[73] in the district of the other authority. The Homes Bill proposes to widen 'domestic violence' to include
other 'violence' – see para 6.100 below.

6.74   In deciding whether or not to refer, the housing authority concerned will be expected to act rationally in a public law sense.
That probably means that it would have to have regard at least to
relevant considerations such as a need for local medical treatment or
reliance upon support from locally-resident family members that
might make it unreasonable to refer the asylum-seeker to another
authority.[74]

6.75   The authority to which an asylum-seeker is referred would also
have to act rationally in that sense and would also be under the
duty to provide 'suitable accommodation' under ss206 and 210, as
amended (see paras 6.57–6.65 above).

6.76   It should be noted that the referral provisions apply only to applicants owed the full housing duty, and not to applicants in temporary
accommodation pending decision.[75] Accommodation provided under
HA 1996 s188 must be provided by the housing authority itself,
although it can nevertheless be outside the housing authority's own
district (see paras 6.48–6.50).

Homelessness: applications and decisions

Applications

6.77   A homeless person may apply to any local housing authority (borough
councils in cities, and district councils elsewhere). A person does not
have to apply to the authority where s/he is or was last living; however,
upon a decision being made on the application, an authority may refer

---

73 Defined in HA 1996 s177.
74 See guidance on Homelessness (Asylum-seekers) (Interim Period) (England)
    Order 1999 SI No 3126 issued by the DETR on 22 November 1999 under
    HA 1996 s182. The following guidance issued to local authorities is relevant to
    the implementation of these provisions: 'Guidance Note to Local Authorities in
    England and Wales – Interim Arrangements for Asylum-seeker Support' (Local
    Government Association); letter from Home Office Immigration and Nationality
    Directorate to all chief executives of local authorities in England and Wales re
    IAA 1999 and Asylum Support (Interim Provisions) Regs 1999, dated 19
    November 1999.
75 See guidance issued by the DETR dated 22 November 1999 to the Homelessness
    (Asylum-seekers) (Interim Period) (England) Order 1999 SI No 3126.

the applicant to another authority for housing – see paras 6.66–6.76 above. Authorities will not in practice accept applications where an applicant has an application pending with another authority.

Decisions

6.78   Authorities must make inquiries and on their completion notify the applicant in writing of their decision, with reasons for any adverse finding.[76] The decision letter must advise the applicant of his/her right to request a review and of the time-limit for doing so.[77] These requirements apply to decisions about homelessness, eligibility, priority need, intentional homelessness and local connection, but they do not apply to a decision that an offer of accommodation is suitable. For remedies available in the case of an adverse homelessness decision, see paras 6.104–6.108 below.

Allocation

What is allocation?

6.79   HA 1996 Part VI governs the 'allocation' of housing accommodation by local housing authorities.

6.80   A housing authority 'allocates' accommodation when it selects a person to be a secure or introductory tenant of council accommodation; nominates a person to be a secure or introductory tenant of other accommodation (eg, owned by a body that can grant a secure or introductory tenancy, such as a housing action trust); or nominates a person to be an assured tenant of a registered social landlord.[78] Note, however, that the grant of a tenancy by a local authority (but not the nomination of a person to be an assured tenant of a registered social landlord), which is made in order to provide accommodation under the asylum support provisions of IAA 1999 is not an allocation under HA 1996 Part VI.[79] For the granting of tenancies or other rights of occupation in local authority housing stock falling outside the scope of allocation under HA 1996 Part VI, see paras 6.113–6.115 below.

---

76 HA 1996 s184.
77 Ibid, s184(5).
78 Ibid, s159.
79 HA 1985 Sch 1 para 4A, as amended by IAA 1999 Sch 14 para 81.

6.81   The allocation of accommodation must take place in accordance with rules as to priorities and procedure devised by the housing authority and set out in its 'allocation scheme'.[80] The schemes are usually 'points based'. Published allocation schemes usually also set out policy on the *transfer* of local authorities' own tenants, although the power to transfer arises under HA 1985 s21, and not under HA 1996 Part VI.[81]

6.82   Every housing authority is required to maintain a register of 'qualifying persons' known as the 'housing register'.[82] Allocations may only be made to persons on the register. The Homes Bill proposes to abolish both the housing register requirement, and the concept of qualifying persons, although ineligible persons will still be excluded – see paras 6.101–6.103 below.

Qualifying persons

6.83   A housing authority may only allocate accommodation to 'qualifying persons'.[83] Most asylum-seekers are not qualifying persons and so cannot be re-housed through the housing register unless and until they are granted refugee status or ELR in the UK.

6.84   Housing authorities have a broad discretion to decide what classes of people are, or are not, 'qualifying persons', but are subject to regulations made by the Home Secretary[84] prescribing people who may or may not be qualifying persons, and to a code of guidance.[85] Thus, the inclusion or exclusion of persons from abroad for the purposes of allocation of public housing is regulated along similar lines to the scheme for homeless people described at paras 6.9–6.25 above. There is a general exclusion of all persons subject to immigration control, modified by the 're-inclusion' of people falling within classes specified in regulation.

6.85   Persons subject to immigration control within the meaning of the AIA 1996 can only be qualifying persons if they come within a prescribed class.[86] Persons who are not subject to immigration control

---

80 HA 1996 s167.
81 It is proposed in the Homes Bill that transfers be brought within the scope of HA 1996 Part VI– see paras 6.96–6.103 below.
82 HA 1996 s162.
83 Ibid, s161.
84 Ibid, s161(3).
85 Code of Guidance on HA 1996 Parts VI and VII.
86 HA 1996 s161(2).

may nonetheless be ineligible if they are subject to, and do not satisfy, the habitual residence test.[87]

6.86   By AIA 1996 s13(2), a person is subject to immigration control if s/he is a person who under the IA 1971 requires leave to enter or remain in the UK (whether or not such leave has been given). By IA 1971 ss2 and 3, all persons require leave to enter or remain except:

a)   British citizens;
b)   Commonwealth citizens with right of abode;
c)   citizens of the Republic of Ireland;
d)   citizens of EEA states who are workers, self-employed or providing services[88] and their family members.

6.87   It should be noted that this is a wider category than the definition of 'persons subject to immigration control' who are excluded from entitlement to benefits and other welfare provision by IAA 1999 s115. The category includes all those requiring leave to enter or remain, whether or not they are subject to a condition requiring that they have no recourse to public funds.

6.88   The categories specifically accorded eligibility are Classes A to E in Allocation of Housing (England) Regulations 2000 reg 4:[89]

Class A: Persons recorded as being refugees.

Class B: Persons with ELR whose leave does not exclude them from recourse to public funds.

Class C: Persons with current leave to enter or remain which is not subject to any limitation or condition (ie, those with settled status) and who are habitually resident in the common travel area, other than sponsored immigrants who have been here for less than five years and whose sponsor is still alive.

Class D: Persons who left Montserrat after 1 November 1995 because of a volcanic eruption.

Class E: Persons who are habitually resident in the common travel area and who are either (i) lawfully present and a national of a state which has *ratified* the ECSMA or the ESC, or (ii) who continue to be owed a duty that arose prior to 3 April 2000, under HA 1985 Part III (old homelessness scheme)

87 See paras 2.59–2.64.
88 See paras 1.18–1.19, 2.29, 2.30, 2.35–2.43.
89 SI 2000 No 702; see Appendix A. The same regulations are applied to Wales by the Homelessness (Wales) Regs 2000 SI No 1079.

or HA 1996 Part VII (new homelessness scheme) and who are nationals of a state which is a *signatory* to ECSMA or ESC (see Appendix C for table of states covered).

6.89 It should be noted that, in contrast to the homelessness provisions, no specific class of asylum-seekers is 're-included', and thus all asylum-seekers are excluded from qualification for the allocation of public housing, unless they fall within the subsisting homelessness duty *limb* of Class E (reg 4(e)(ii)) since asylum-seekers have been found not to be 'lawfully present' (see para 6.16 above).

6.90 The Allocation of Housing (England) Regulations 2000 are subject to the same question mark over their authority as the equivalent homelessness regulations – see para 6.16 above. The regulations are made under HA 1996 s161, and their scope is similarly proscribed.[90]

6.91 As with the homelessness provisions, a person who is *not* subject to immigration control may nonetheless be ineligible if s/he is not 'habitually resident'.[91] It has been noted at para 6.86 that certain persons are not subject to immigration control. Of these, people falling within a), b) and c) are ineligible unless:[92]

– they are 'habitually resident' in the common travel area (the UK, Channel Islands, Isle of Man and Republic of Ireland); or
– they left Montserrat after 1 November 1995 because of a volcanic eruption.

6.92 For the meaning of 'habitually resident' see paras 2.59–2.64. Note that this exclusion does not affect asylum-seekers since they are among the categories of persons subject to immigration control.

6.93 Children born in the UK are not 'persons subject to immigration control': they do not require leave to enter or remain, and so are not excluded from eligibility. There is nothing in HA 1996 Part VI to exclude children from applying to go on the housing register, although local authority allocation schemes may exclude them.

6.94 Housing authorities exercising allocation functions are required to have regard to guidance issued by the Home Secretary.[93] The DoE/DoH Code of Guidance on HA 1996 Parts VI and VII contains helpful guidance as to the meaning of eligibility for allocation purposes at chapter 4.

90 By HA 1996 s161(2A), inserted by IAA 1999 s117(3).
91 HA 1996 s161(3) and Allocation of Housing (England) Regs 2000 SI No 702 reg 6.
92 HA 1996 s185(3) and Homelessness (England) Regs 2000 SI No 701 reg 4.
93 HA 1996 s169.

6.95   Once a person has been accepted onto the housing register, the local authority's allocation scheme will apply to determine whether and when accommodation is offered, and what that accommodation will be. In assessing the needs of applicants, eg, in relation to household size, local authorities have a wide discretion: they are not required to have regard to whether household members are eligible or ineligible, and most do not in practice do so. The rules concerning who is or is not a qualifying person do not apply to household members of a registered applicant when the authority is considering the applicant's needs.[94] If a local authority allocation policy were to fail to take account of ineligible household members, it would be in breach of its obligation under s167(2)(c) to give preference under its allocation scheme to families with dependent children.[95]

The Homes Bill

6.96   At the time of writing the Homes Bill was before parliament. Its provisions include modifications of both Part VI (allocation) and Part VII (homelessness) of the HA 1996. The changes which are material to the account given above of these statutory schemes may be summarised as follows.

Changes to homelessness provisions

6.97   The duty to secure accommodation for a two-year period (s193(3) and (4)) is to be abolished.

6.98   The other circumstances whereby the authority's duty ends (s193(5)–(8)) are to remain, but are supplemented. The duty will end if a final offer under Part VI is refused, if the applicant accepts the offer of an assured tenancy by a private landlord, or if the applicant accepts an assured shorthold tenancy. Refusal of an assured shorthold tenancy by the applicant will not end the duty.

6.99   The availability of 'other suitable accommodation' in its district will no longer absolve the authority of its duty to secure accommodation (s197 abolished).

6.100   'Domestic violence' in the contexts of accommodation not being

94   *R v Tower Hamlets LBC ex p Kimvono* (2000) 5 December, QBD; February 2001 *Legal Action* 27.
95   Ibid.

reasonable to continue to occupy (s177) and of referral to another
authority (s198) is to be widened to include other 'violence'.

Changes to allocation provisions

6.101 The obligation to maintain a housing register, the inclusion only of
qualifying persons, and the review procedure for register disputes
(ss161–165) are all to be abolished.

6.102 They are replaced by a requirement on the authority to consider
applications; all persons are to be eligible unless specified as
ineligible. The existing provisions as to ineligibility of persons subject to immigration control are repeated, with a power to the Home
Secretary to specify in regulations classes of eligible and ineligible
persons, subject to a requirement that no one to whom IAA 1999
s115 applies may be made eligible by regulation.

6.103 The rules as to persons to whom a reasonable preference is to be
given in the allocation of accommodation (s167) are revised. Transfers requested by council tenants are to be 'allocations' within the
scope of HA 1996 Part VI.

Remedies in homelessness and allocation cases

Challenging homelessness decisions

6.104 Detailed provisions about the review of homelessness decisions and
appeal to the county court are set out in HA 1996 ss202–204, and the
Allocation of Housing and Homelessness (Review Procedures) Regulations 1999.[96] A brief summary is given here.

6.105 The applicant has a right to request a review of decisions made by
local authorities concerning[97] eligibility; whether duties to secure
accommodation, advise and assist[98] are owed, and what those duties
are; whether the applicant is to be referred to another authority; and
whether or not accommodation is suitable.

6.106 The review must be requested within 21 days of the decision. The
review must be carried out by a more senior officer and be completed
within 56 days of the request. The applicant must be notified of the

96   SI No 71.
97   HA 1996 s202.
98   Ie, duties under HA 1996 ss190–193 and 195–197.
99   Ibid, s204(1).

decision on review. If the decision on review is adverse, the applicant has a right of appeal on a point of law to the county court.[99] The applicant has 21 days from the review decision (or from the expiry of the 56 days if no decision is made within that time) to lodge the appeal.

6.107   Not all decisions made on homelessness applications carry a right to review and appeal. Most importantly, decisions about the provision of temporary accommodation pending assessment[100] and pending review or appeal[101] carry no right to review or appeal. Such decisions may be challenged by way of judicial review.

6.108   While there is a right to a statutory review of a suitability decision, an applicant may not both accept an offer of accommodation and seek a review of its suitability.[102] Where accommodation is offered under HA 1996 s193(5), it is implied that the authority has decided it is suitable, although good practice requires that the applicant be given express notification of such a decision.[103] The consequence of refusing the offered accommodation and relying on a request for review is that the authority will be entitled to consider itself no longer under any duty to assist him/her.[104] Thus, when an offer is made, an applicant must either accept it, or seek a review with the risk that, if the decision is upheld on review, the applicant will be left with nothing.[105]

Challenging allocation decisions

6.109   There is a statutory right to review of a decision of a housing authority as to whether or not to include a person on the housing register. Detailed provisions as to the review procedure are set out in HA 1996 ss164–165, and the Allocation of Housing and Homelessness (Review Procedures) Regulations 1999. A brief summary is given here.

6.110   If a housing authority refuses to put someone on the housing register, or removes a person from the housing register, 'they shall notify him of their decision and of the reasons for it'.[106] That

---

100   Ibid, s188.
101   Ibid, s204(4).
102   *Alghile v Westminster City Council* [2001] EWCA CIV 363, (overruling *R v Kensington and Chelsea RLBC ex p Byfield* (1999) 31 HLR 913).
103   Ibid.
104   HA 1996 s193(5).
105   *Alghile v Westminster City Council* [2001] EWCA CIV 363.
106   HA 1996 s164(1).

notice must inform the person of his/her right to seek a review of the decision and of the time-limit for seeking the review (21 days or such longer period as the authority may allow in writing).[107]

6.111 A review decision may be challenged by an application for judicial review. There is no right of appeal to the county court as with homelessness decisions. Note that the review procedure is confined to decisions about whether to include a person on the register. Other decisions of local authorities in relation to allocation, including the lawfulness or otherwise of allocation schemes, may only be challenged by judicial review.

6.112 There may be an issue about whether the review procedure – comprising a statutory internal review supplemented by the availability of judicial review limited to a point of law – complies with article 6 of the European Convention on Human Rights (see chapter 8). The review procedure (along with the housing register requirement) is set to be abolished under the Homes Bill (see above).

The use of social housing as accommodation for asylum-seekers

6.113 It has been seen that HA 1996 Parts VI and VII as routes into social housing are blocked for most asylum-seekers and people from abroad. This does not mean, however, that local authorities cannot use their own housing stock to accommodate such persons. The requirement that all lettings be through HA 1996 Part VI is confined to allocation by local authorities of secure or introductory tenancies and nomination by local authorities to registered social landlords for letting on assured tenancies. It does not embrace:

a) the grant of or nomination to a tenancy or licence by a local authority which is exempt from security;[108]

b) the nomination of a person to a tenancy or licence which is exempt from assured status.[109]

6.114 Lettings under a) which are exempt from security include a tenancy or licence granted to provide accommodation under IAA 1999

---

107 Ibid, s164(2) and (3).
108 The classes of occupation exempt from security are defined by HA 1985 Sch 1.
109 The classes of occupation exempt from assured status are defined by HA 1988 Sch 1.

Part VI[110] – that is, accommodation for asylum-seekers through NASS or under the Interim Regs. Note, however, that there is no parallel provision exempting tenancies or licences granted by registered social landlords from assured status, and so a local authority may not house asylum-seekers by nomination to a housing association. It may, however, lease accommodation from a registered social landlord to provide temporary accommodation.[111] Both NASS[112] and local authorities[113] may require registered social landlords to provide 'reasonable assistance' in providing accommodation under IAA 1999 Part VI. Similarly, a county council (social services authority) may require such assistance from a district council (housing authority) in its area.[114] Neither the exemption from security of accommodation for asylum-seekers nor the powers to require assistance extend to accommodation provided for other persons subject to immigration control. Leasing from housing associations or private landlords may however be used to accommodate such persons.

6.115   These provisions are complemented by IAA 1999 s118, which requires that housing authorities avoid 'so far as practicable' granting tenancies or licences to persons subject to immigration control as defined by IA 1971 ss2 and 3 (see para 6.86 above), unless they do so to provide accommodation for asylum-seekers under IAA 1999 s95 or for persons falling within classes specified by the Home Secretary. The classes specified[115] are the same as those applying to allocation under HA 1996 Part VI (see para 6.88 above) with the addition of classes comprising:

- those owed a duty under National Assistance Act (NAA) 1948 s21 (see paras 7.44–7.57, 7.68–81);
- those owed a duty under CA 1989 s17 (see paras 7.58–7.67, 7.97–108);
- those owed housing duties under homelessness legislation (see paras 6.7–6.56);
- those entitled to assistance under the interim provisions (see chapter 5);

---

110   HA 1985 Sch 1 para 4A, as amended by IAA 1999 Sch 14 para 81.
111   HA 1985 Sch 1 para 6.
112   IAA 1999 s100.
113   Ibid, Sch 9 para 11, and Asylum Support (Interim Provisions) Regs 1999 SI No 3056 reg 10.
114   Ibid.
115   Ibid, s118(1)(a) and Persons Subject to Immigration Control (Housing Authority Accommodation and Homelessness) Order 2000 SI No 706.

– students in accommodation provided under arrangements between colleges and local authorities.

Successions and assignments

6.116 Successions to and assignments of tenancies are unaffected by immigration status. The rules which exclude asylum-seekers from housing allocation do not apply to successions and assignments. In local authority housing stock, successions and assignments are excluded from the scope of allocation under Part VI[116] and, in that they do not involve the 'grant' of rights of occupation by a local authority, are not embraced by the restrictions in IAA 1999 s118, above.

Effects of changes in immigration status

6.117 This section describes the consequences for the provision of assistance under HA 1996 Parts VI and VII and for other housing rights of changes in the status of asylum-seekers. The following changes of status are considered:

– the grant of refugee status or ELR;
– the refusal of an asylum application or an appeal;
– the asylum-seeker and others reaching 18 years of age.

Grant of refugee status or ELR

6.118 A successful asylum application will conclude with a decision by the Home Secretary or at the conclusion of an appeal to grant the applicant refugee status or ELR (see paras 1.86–1.97).

6.119 People who have refugee status or ELR are eligible to apply for assistance under HA 1996 Parts VI and VII.

6.120 Where the person is in accommodation provided by NASS or under local authority interim support at the point when such a decision is made, the provision of accommodation will cease 14 days from the date of notification of the Home Secretary's decision or, where an appeal has been made, from the appeal decision.

6.121 The power to provide assistance under the Asylum Support and

116 HA 1996 s160.

Interim Regs schemes ends 14 days after the determination of the claim for asylum. Where the person and his/her dependants are in NASS accommodation, they will be expected to leave the accommodation at the end of the 14-day period. Where the person is in accommodation provided under the Interim Regs the local authority must cease assistance at the end of the 14-day period.[117] In the latter case, it may be that, if the local authority has a duty under the HA 1996 to secure accommodation for the person, it will decide to maintain him/her in the present accommodation under that duty, in place of its duty under the Interim Regs.

6.122   Where the household of the person whose asylum claim has been determined includes persons with their own asylum claims which remain pending, then the continuation of accommodation under the asylum support scheme for the latter will depend upon whether the former is entitled to accommodation for the whole household under the homelessness provisions (see paras 6.31, 6.37 and 6.52 above).

6.123   Where the asylum-seeker whose claim is determined is supported with accommodation by the local authority under community care legislation (usually NAA 1948 s21 or CA 1989 s17), then, unless the asylum-seeker requires residential care, the social services department is likely to take steps to terminate that support and transfer responsibility to the housing department. However, there is no requirement to end support within 14 days as is the case with asylum support. The local authority should not terminate support until satisfied that, as the case may be, the applicant's needs are otherwise being met[118] or that the child is no longer a child in need.[119] The change of circumstances occasioned by a grant of refugee status or ELR in such circumstances should give rise to a formal review of the community care or CA 1989 assessment and revision of the care plan before any changes are made to service provision. Precipitate termination of community care services in such cases could be challenged by judicial review.

6.124   Where an asylum-seeker is granted refugee status or ELR and s/he has been staying with relatives (with or without provision for essential living needs by NASS or the local authority), s/he remains entitled to occupy that accommodation until his/her licence to do so is terminated by the tenant or owner.

---

117 Asylum Support (Interim Provisions) Regs 1999 SI No 3056 reg 8(1) – see Appendix A.
118 NAA 1948 s21.
119 CA 1989 s17.

6.125   The asylum-seeker upon notification of a grant of refugee status or ELR should at once apply to the local authority to register on the housing register. As soon as s/he is informed that his/her accommodation provided by NASS or the local authority is to be terminated, s/he should apply to the local housing authority for assistance under HA 1996 Part VII as a homeless person.

6.126   Asylum-seekers granted refugee status or ELR should not leave their accommodation provided by NASS or the local authority or by relatives until it is terminated. If they do, they risk a finding of intentional homelessness upon their applying for assistance as homeless persons. This is particularly likely to occur where asylum-seekers who have been dispersed are granted status and thereupon return to London and apply to local authorities as homeless persons.

6.127   A person granted refugee status or ELR whose accommodation has been terminated by NASS or the local authority or by relatives will be 'threatened with homelessness' as soon as s/he is within 28 days of the date when s/he has to leave the accommodation, and 'homeless' on the day s/he does have to leave. Such an applicant will be eligible for assistance. If s/he is in priority need, the local authority will have a duty to secure interim accommodation for him/her and anyone who can reasonably be expected to live with him/her,[120] pending the conclusion of inquiries (see paras 6.48–6.50 above).

6.128   If the applicant cannot satisfy the authority that s/he may be in priority need, there is no duty to secure interim accommodation. However, the authority is still under a duty to make inquiries into the applicant's circumstances and to make a decision on the application.[121] If it is decided that the applicant does not have a priority need, the authority must provide appropriate advice and assistance to the applicant's attempts to secure accommodation him/herself. In practice, this usually means advice and information about private sector housing, and may include a scheme for providing deposits and rent in advance. Before any decision is made on the application, the authority has a duty to make advice and information available.[122] Such a person, even though not eligible for accommodation as a homeless person, should nonetheless make a housing register application. S/he will also be eligible for housing benefit.

6.129   On the conclusion of inquiries, the local authority will make

120   HA 1996 s188.
121   Ibid, s184.
122   Ibid, s179(1).

decisions upon whether the applicant is homeless, eligible for assistance, in priority need, intentionally homeless and about local connection, and depending on those decisions, duties to secure accommodation may follow: see paras 6.7–6.56 above.

6.130   A common practical problem arises when a decision is made by the Home Secretary or on appeal granting refugee status or ELR, but the decision is not formally communicated to the applicant. Typically, the consequence is that asylum support accommodation is terminated, but on approaching the local authority, the applicant is told that s/he will not be assisted until s/he can produce the standard documentation (form ICD.0725 – previously GEN23 – for refugee cases, or Home Office letter granting ELR for a specified period – see paras 1.80–1.97). The remedies for the applicant are by way of judicial review, either of the failure of the Home Office or appellate authority to issue a decision, or of the local authority for breach of its duty under HA 1996 ss184 and 188. The second option will be preferable in most cases: the threshold is a low one – it is only necessary to give the local authority 'reason to believe' that the applicant 'may' be eligible for assistance. Parallel problems arise in claming benefits (see paras 2.93–2.102), and housing authorities frequently refuse to assist applicants unless they can show proof of benefit entitlement or of the allocation of a National Insurance number. Given the time taken to process benefit claims and NI number applications, such requirements arguably place the threshold under HA 1996 s188 too high. It should be recalled that people with refugee status or ELR are not subject to the habitual residence test.

Refusal of an asylum application or an appeal

6.131   An unsuccessful asylum application concludes with a refusal decision by the Home Secretary, or a refusal on appeal. In a few cases, such a refusal of an asylum application is subsequently superseded by a decision to grant ELR, in which case the consequences of refusal discussed below are also superseded.

6.132   Applicants who are subject to such a refusal are not entitled to assistance under HA 1996 Part VI (allocation) or Part VII (homelessness), unless:

– they fall within Class E (habitually resident citizens of states who are signatories or ratifiers of two European treaties (see above, paras 6.14 and 6.16 (homelessness) and 6.88 (allocation))); or

- they fall within Class I for homelessness only (receiving IS or means-tested JSA (see above, para 6.14).

6.133   Those who as a result of refusal cease to be qualifying persons under HA 1996 Part VI will have their names removed from the housing register on 28 days' notice.[123] The effect of refusal on rights to remain in different categories of accommodation are considered below.

Where the person is in accommodation provided under the asylum or interim support schemes

6.134   Where the person is in accommodation provided by NASS or under the Interim Regs at the point when such a decision is made, the provision of accommodation will end 14 days from the date of the Home Secretary's decision or, where an appeal has been made, from the appeal decision. The accommodation provider will be told to issue a seven-day notice to quit.[124] There is one exception which applies to an applicant who has either:

- been refused and has not appealed; or
- has exhausted his/her appeal rights; or
- has withdrawn his/her claim for asylum

and whose household includes a dependent child under 18 years of age.

6.135   In such cases accommodation will only cease if leave to remain is granted, or if the child reaches 18, leaves the household, ceases to be dependent, or leaves the UK.[125] Thus, accommodation for households with dependent children continues under the asylum support scheme until they leave the UK.

6.136   Unsuccessful asylum-seekers without dependent children required to leave asylum support accommodation will be made homeless. If their need for accommodation has arisen solely because of destitution or because of the physical effects or anticipated physical effects of destitution, they will be excluded from assistance with accommodation under NAA 1948 s21, and their only prospect of government assistance is under the hardship provisions of the asylum support scheme (see paras 3.169–3.173). Conversely, those

123 Ibid, s165(3), and Allocation of Housing (England) Regs 2000 SI No 702 reg 8 – see Appendix A.
124 NASS Policy Bulletin 22.
125 IAA 1999 s94(5), (6).

who have a need for accommodation which does not arise solely because of destitution or its physical effects, should at once apply to the social services department for assistance (see paras 7.27–7.30, 7.68–7.81).

Where the person refused is in accommodation secured under HA 1996 Part VII

6.137   When an asylum-seeker who is being provided with assistance under HA 1996 Part VII as a homeless person has his/her application for asylum refused by the Home Secretary, the local authority ceases to be under a duty to provide that assistance (save for Class E cases – see paras 6.14 and 6.16 above).[126] Note that, unlike accommodation under the asylum support scheme, Part VII assistance does not continue until the determination of an appeal, and does not continue if the household contains dependent children.

6.138   Where a person continues to be assisted by the local authority, having originally been provided with assistance under the old homelessness scheme[127] before AIA 1996 s9(2) came into force (19 August 1996),[128] the exclusion of ineligible persons does not apply, and the local authority's duty continues.[129] This is because the duty to secure accommodation for the unintentionally homeless in priority need under HA 1985 Part III[130] was not time-limited. Thus, an applicant to a local authority originally assisted to secure accommodation under the 1985 Act, who subsequently loses that accommodation and whose circumstances have otherwise not changed will be entitled to continuing assistance under the 1985 Act provisions.

6.139   Whether or not the termination of the duty under the homelessness provisions results in loss of accommodation, and whether this is sooner or later, will depend on the accommodation the person has. Such accommodation may be temporary and excluded from any security of tenure, or it may be a tenancy attracting a degree of security (see para 6.148 below).

6.140   Where the person is in temporary accommodation provided by a local authority, s/he will be entitled to reasonable notice.[131] According

---

126   HA 1996 s193(6)(a).
127   HA 1985 Part III.
128   Now repealed by IAA 1999 s169(1), (3), Sch 14 paras 108, 110–112, Sch 16.
129   *R v Hackney LBC ex p K* (1998) 30 HLR 760.
130   HA 1985 s65(2) (now repealed).
131   *R v Secretary of State for the Environment ex p Shelter* [1997] COD 49, QBD.

to the Code of Guidance, the period 'should not, reasonably, be less than the period normally given to someone who is found to be intentionally homeless':[132] that is, 'such period as they [the local authority] consider will give him a reasonable opportunity of securing accommodation for his occupation'.[133] Arguably, in the case of refused asylum-seekers, given that they will not be entitled to housing benefit, that period should be longer than the 28 days used as a 'rule of thumb' by most local authorities.

Where the person whose asylum application is refused has a tenancy

6.141　Where the person has an assured tenancy (shorthold or otherwise) or a secure tenancy, ordinary housing law applies. Changes in immigration status do not affect security of tenure.[134] The person will be entitled to remain until a possession order is obtained and lawfully executed. The fact that refused asylum-seekers cease to be entitled to housing benefit and so may be unable to pay the rent does not alter this position.

6.142　A tenant who has lost housing benefit as a result of a refusal of his/her asylum application is likely to face possession proceedings on the ground of rent arrears. If the tenancy is secure, or if it is assured (but not if it is a shorthold tenancy and not if possession is sought on Ground 8 of HA 1988 Sch 2), a possession order will only be made if the judge considers it reasonable to do so. A possession order may be avoided by arguing that there is an obligation on social services to assist[135] and an application for such assistance has been made, or that in a case where an asylum appeal is pending, a successful appeal resulting in the grant of refugee status would mean an entitlement to arrears of housing benefit, and that the court should not decide the possession proceedings until the outcome of the appeal is known.

Asylum support where other accommodation lost

6.143　Where a person who has been accommodated outside the asylum support scheme loses that accommodation or it becomes inadequate or impractical to continue to occupy, s/he can apply for accommodation under the asylum support scheme.

132　Para 12.38.
133　HA 1996 s190(2)(a); *R v Newham LBC ex p Ojuri (No 5)* (1999) 31 HLR 631.
134　*Akinbolu v Hackney LBC* (1997) 29 HLR 259.
135　See paras 7.25–7.40.

6.144   Where the person has no dependent child in his/her household, support will continue to be available until a decision is made on the asylum application without an appeal; or until a decision is made on appeal, or until the asylum application is withdrawn. An application for support can be made while support is available.

6.145   Where the person has a dependent child, support will only cease to be available if leave to remain is granted, or if the child reaches 18, leaves the household, ceases to be dependent, or leaves the UK.[136] An application for support can be made while support is available.

6.146   See paras 5.10–5.12 for whether the application is made to NASS or to the local authority under the interim scheme.

The asylum-seeker and others reaching 18 years of age

6.147   Unaccompanied asylum-seekers aged under 18 are the responsibility of the social services department. When they reach 18 responsibility for accommodating them may change (see paras 7.98–7.108, 7.122–7.125). They may in limited cases be eligible in their own right for assistance as homeless persons.

Housing conditions and protection from eviction and harassment

Security of tenure

6.148   The ordinary law relating to the recovery of possession of land applies to tenants who are asylum-seekers or other persons subject to immigration control, just as it applies to other tenants.[137] Changes in a person's immigration status do not affect the rights of such tenants in relation to security of tenure and protection from eviction. This applies to those tenants who acquired their tenancy through arrangements made before 6 December 1999 or who have acquired their tenancy since that date otherwise than through arrangements made by NASS or the local authority. A tenancy or licence granted by a local authority to provide accommodation under NASS asylum support or local authority interim support is not a secure tenancy or

---

136   IAA 1999 s94(5), (6).
137   *Akinbolu v Hackney LBC* (1997) 29 HLR 259.

licence under the HA 1985,[138] and where granted by a private landlord or housing association is not an assured tenancy under the HA 1988.[139] Recovery of possession of accommodation provided under the asylum support scheme is described at paras 3.134–3.139.

Housing conditions[140]

6.149 Many asylum-seekers are housed in sub-standard accommodation.[141] The contractual basis of accommodation provision by NASS is an 'occupancy agreement' which the supported person should have been asked to sign when s/he moved into the accommodation provided on behalf of NASS by a contractor. It should contain details of the landlord's obligations to maintain and manage the property. It may contain an express contractual duty to maintain the accommodation or carry out repairs.

6.150 The housing provider will also have entered a contract with NASS which should contain terms about the condition of the property.[142] Contractors who are providing accommodation on behalf of NASS, are expected, as a term of their contract, to have an internal complaints procedure to enable the supported person(s) to make a complaint about harassment or about the service provided, eg, where utilities are not provided, furniture is missing, or the property is in disrepair. The housing provider should respond to the complaint within seven days and record the outcome in a logbook. If the supported person is not satisfied, it is the function of the landlord to make a referral to the nearest one-stop service for advice and advocacy, and from there to NASS.

6.151 IAA 1999 s96 provides for accommodation 'appearing to the Secretary of State to be adequate' for the needs of the supported person and any dependants. 'Adequate' suggests that the accommodation should be in basic repair and (in a non-technical sense) fit for human habitation with basic facilities such as adequate space, and with water, heating, sanitation and cooking facilities in proper working order. It is part of NASS's role to inspect accommodation to ensure

---

138 HA 1985 Sch 1 para 4A, as amended by IAA 1999 s169(1) and Sch 14 para 81.
139 HA 1988 Sch 1 para 12A, as amended by IAA 1999 s169(1) and Sch 14 para 88.
140 See further *Repairs: Tenants' Rights*, Appendices (LAG, 1999).
141 See *Far From Home: the housing of asylum-seekers in private rented accommodation*, Garvie (Shelter Publications, January 2001).
142 Housing providers are asked by the Home Office to sign the Official Secrets Act and may not disclose the location of properties let through the NASS scheme.

contracts are being fulfilled.[143] Commentators have pointed out the difficulty of the Home Office carrying out a function more suited to the local authority housing and environmental health departments with local knowledge of landlords. NASS has a contract with the Property Advisors to the Civil Estate to inspect properties to ensure that the physical standard of accommodation provided complies with the terms of the contract. This programme of inspections is supplemented by NASS's Performance Monitoring Inspections Team. Its role is 'to ensure that accommodation providers are complying with the contract requirements for effective housing management and access to support services'.

6.152   The courts seem likely to treat an occupation agreement entered into under IAA 1999 as a licence to occupy accommodation rather than a tenancy. Landlord and Tenant Act 1985 s11 implies an obligation upon the landlord to repair into a tenancy but not into a licence.

6.153   This does not mean that property owners have no legal duties to asylum-seeker occupiers. Licensors of dwellings may have retained sufficient control of the dwelling to be liable to the occupiers in negligence for personal injury or property damage, or to justify an implied term as to repair or fitness of purpose, depending on the circumstances of the case. In *Greene v Chelsea BC*,[144] the council exercised statutory powers to requisition housing accommodation. Those powers made it impossible to grant occupiers a tenancy, only a licence. When one occupier was injured after a ceiling collapsed, the council was held liable in negligence. It had been informed about the bulging ceiling but had failed to repair it. The case is significant because landlords do not usually owe a duty of care in negligence to licensees.

6.154   It has been held to be an implied term, on the facts and in a case relating to business premises, that the premises would be fit for their purposes.[145]

6.155   Even if a county court action is available, there are difficulties for an asylum-seeker in bringing it, because s/he will not generally have any security of tenure. An award of compensation could temporarily remove eligibility for support because the household would have some money. Unless an emergency injunction is available another

143 Bob Eagle, Director of NASS, 25 March 1999 in his submissions to the Special Standing Committee on the Immigration and Asylum Bill.
144 [1954] 2 QB 127.
145 *Wetter Electric Ltd v Welsh Development Agency* [1983] 1 QB 796 (slightly doubted in *Morris-Thomas v Petticoat Lane Rentals* (1986) 53 P & CR 238).

problem is that occupation of the accommodation is intended to be short-term. An asylum-seeker may prefer to use the speedier Environmental Protection Act 1990 procedures.

Accommodation which is prejudicial to health

6.156   If an asylum-seeker is placed in accommodation which is 'prejudicial to health', in a poor state of repair, lacking adequate amenities or means of escape from fire, a request could be made to the local authority's environmental health officer (EHO) to inspect with a view to taking action under Environmental Protection Act 1990 s80 if the accommodation appears to be prejudicial to health or a nuisance. The EHO should also act if the accommodation is 'unfit' under the HA 1985, which covers overcrowding, adequate fire escapes and serious disrepair. If the landlord refuses to do repairs after the local authority has served a notice, the authority can take enforcement action, doing the works itself and recouping the cost from the landlord. If the EHO will not act promptly or at all, an asylum-seeker could consider a judicial review of the EHO's decision. The EHO will not take action where the landlord is the same local authority.

6.157   In cases where the EHO will not act, the asylum-seeker can take individual action under Environmental Protection Act 1990 s82, by serving a 21-day standard notice[146] at the landlord's registered office, supported by evidence of the prejudice to health. If the landlord does not do the necessary repair works to 'abate the nuisance' within 21 days, the asylum-seeker can start a fast-track procedure to prosecute the landlord in the magistrates' court. Community Legal Service Legal Help funding will be needed for an independent EHO's report to support the action. This may be justified by demonstrating that the local authority EHO will not intervene.

6.158   Many asylum-seekers are housed by private sector landlords. If an asylum-seeker is considering action to enforce repairs, advice should be given about the risk of the landlord responding with possession proceedings to which there may be no defence if there is only a licence agreement or an assured shorthold tenancy. Furthermore, asylum-seekers do not have protection from harassment and illegal eviction under the Protection from Eviction Act 1977[147] – see below.

---

146   See further *Repairs: Tenants' Rights*, Appendices (LAG, 1999).
147   Accommodation provided under IAA 1999 Part VI is an excluded tenancy or licence under Protection from Eviction Act 1977 s3A, as amended by IAA 1999 s169(1) and Sch 14 para 73.

Harassment and domestic violence

6.159   The statutory protection from harassment afforded to tenants and licensees has been taken away from asylum-seekers.[148] The recourse of asylum-seekers suffering harassment is to complain to the accommodation provider under its complaints procedure, or direct to NASS, or to the police. Asylum-seekers who experience harassment by landlords pressurising them to leave without court action should also be advised to contact the local authority tenancy relations officer.

6.160   The contract between NASS and the accommodation provider requires the latter to have a complaints procedure to deal with allegations of harassment, in the same way as complaints about sub-standard accommodation (see para 6.150 above). The supported person can contact NASS directly if s/he has been harassed by the housing provider.

6.161   NASS's policy guidance[149] states that its role in investigating racial harassment is to establish whether it is appropriate to provide alternative accommodation because there is a significant risk of violence occurring if the person were to remain there. It goes on to say that 'the responsibility for tackling harassment lies with the police and the relevant local authority'. The guidance lists the various legal remedies which asylum-seekers who are suffering racial harassment can pursue. NASS's approach has been to consider whether there is an immediate and significant risk to the household.

6.162   If a supported person needs to leave NASS accommodation due to domestic violence or racial or other harassment, s/he should make an immediate complaint to the housing provider. Internal instructions specifically provide for consideration of a move in such circumstances. If NASS does not provide alternative accommodation, judicial review (of the decision not to provide adequate accommodation) would be the appropriate remedy. There have been a number of appeals to the Asylum Support Adjudicator where NASS has terminated support in cases of racial harassment on the ground that the asylum-seeker has breached a condition of support by failing to travel back to the accommodation from which s/he fled. These are discussed at paras 3.102 onwards.

---

148   Protection from Eviction Act 1977 s3A, as amended by IAA 1999 s169(1) and Sch 14 para 73.
149   NASS Policy Bulletin 18.

Chapter 7

Community care services for asylum-seekers

For complete chapter contents, see overleaf

Introduction

7.1   Prior to the Immigration and Asylum Act (IAA) 1999, community care services provided by local authorities constituted the principal source of accommodation and subsistence for destitute asylum-seekers. A central purpose of the Act was to establish a separate system for providing such support for asylum-seekers – the National Asylum Support Service (NASS) and, until NASS could be fully implemented, support under the Interim Regs[1] – and correspondingly to withdraw community care services from asylum-seekers. The IAA creates a series of exclusions, disentitling persons subject to immigration control from rights to assessment and the provision of community care services. However, these exclusions are not comprehensive, and substantial areas remain where persons subject to immigration control continue to be eligible for community care services.

7.2   This chapter comprises an overview of the way in which the community care scheme now fits in with the asylum support scheme, with a summary of who is excluded from community care services and who is included. There then follows a detailed examination of:

- what 'community care services' means;
- the machinery of assessment;
- the exclusions affecting persons subject to immigration control; and
- the nature of services available.

In each case services under the National Health Service and Community Care Act (NHSCCA) 1990 and services under the Children Act (CA) 1989 are considered separately.

7.3   The chapter concludes with an examination of problems arising upon changes of status, and an outline of remedies available.

Overview

Community care services

7.4   Community care services comprise a range of means of providing for the needs of people through social services departments of local authorities and in some cases through health authorities. Needs

---

1   Asylum Support (Interim Provisions) Regs 1999 SI No 3056.

which can be met include accommodation, subsistence, and support services. In practice local authorities do use their powers and duties under the community care statutes (particularly the National Assistance Act (NAA) 1948 and the CA 1989) to provide accommodation and subsistence for individuals. But in general the statutes do not contain defined rights for individuals to such provision in specified circumstances such as are found in benefits or homelessness law. Rather, the statutes usually give local authorities general duties and powers to promote the welfare of people in their area, and define ways in which they may meet those responsibilities. Whether or not an individual has recourse to the courts when a local authority fails to make provision will usually depend on whether the authority has complied with its responsibilities in a public law sense.

7.5   Asylum-seekers have, by means of IAA 1999 Part VI, been excluded from community care services to a considerable extent, but there remain important categories where eligibility for assistance remains.

Who is excluded?

7.6   *Asylum-seeker families with children* receive accommodation and essential living needs from NASS under the Asylum Support Regulations (AS Regs)[2] or from local authorities under the Interim Regs, and continue to do so even after a refusal of the asylum claim. But if entitlement to such provision ends for any reason, see paras 7.61–7.62. Also, if the family includes an adult or child who has needs over and above the provision of adequate accommodation and for essential living needs, see para 7.60.

7.7   *Destitute adult asylum-seekers* also receive accommodation and essential living needs from NASS under the AS Regs or from local authorities under the Interim Regs. If they are without dependent children, this provision continues until a final decision is made upon their application for asylum (including by way of appeal). However, if they have needs for services which arise other than solely from destitution, see paras 7.68–7.81. If they require services on leaving mental hospital, see paras 7.94–7.96. If they require services on reaching the age of 18 after having been in local authority care, see paras 7.102–7.108.

7.8   *Adults without children whose asylum claims have been finally rejected.*

2   SI No 704.

Asylum support ends for such adults upon a final adverse decision being made upon the application for asylum or exceptional leave to remain (see paras 3.124–3.129, 5.114–5.120), save for support available in limited circumstances under the hardship scheme (see paras 3.169–3.173, 5.121–5.122). The IAA 1999 and the regulations made under it deprive such adults of resort to assistance under the community care provisions unless they fall within the categories referred to in para 7.7. It may be arguable that this statutory framework infringes the European Convention on Human Rights – see paras 8.31–8.33.

Who is included?

7.9   *Unaccompanied asylum-seeker children* are exclusively the responsibility of local authorities under CA 1989 Part III (see paras 7.102–7.108) and are not covered by NASS or the Interim Regs.

7.10   *Families with children where asylum support provision stops.* If services under NASS or the Interim Regs are suspended or discontinued for any reason (for example, because it is decided that the asylum-seeker became 'intentionally destitute') then the children become eligible for assistance under CA 1989 Part III – and under CA 1989 s17 that can and usually should include assistance for the whole family (see paras 7.61–7.62).

7.11   *Families with children whose needs go beyond asylum support provision.* Accommodation under NASS and the Interim Regs must be 'adequate' for the needs of the family, and essential living needs must be met. However, where the family includes a 'child in need' for the purposes of CA 1989 s17, that child may have needs for community care services over and above adequate accommodation and essential living needs, and in that case the local authority must comply with a request for an assessment of the child's needs and complete a care plan providing for services to be put in place (see para 7.60).

7.12   *Adult asylum-seekers with needs arising other than solely through destitution.* Adult asylum-seekers and other persons subject to immigration control (whether or not looking after children) who have a need for services which derives at least in part from a cause other than simple lack of accommodation and subsistence (such as pregnancy, old age, physical or mental illness, or disability) are eligible for assistance under the community care regime, including accommodation, basic living requirements, welfare needs including domiciliary help and counselling, and emergency assistance where necessary (see paras 7.68–7.81). They should apply to the social services department of the local authority, and not to NASS.[3]

7.13   *Adults leaving mental hospital.* Whether or not his/her current needs arise through destitution alone, an asylum-seeker who has been detained for treatment under the Mental Health Act (MHA) 1983 is entitled to services including accommodation, subsistence, and support (see paras 7.94–7.96 below).

7.14   *Adults who have (as children) been in local authority care.* Such children are entitled to support on leaving care and there is no exclusion of persons from abroad from services under CA 1989 s24, nor under the Children (Leaving Care) Act 2000 (see paras 7.102–7.108, 7.122–7.125).

Assessments and remedies

7.15   Access to community care services is via an assessment of need, following the making of a decision as to the provision of services based upon the results of the assessment, usually called a 'care plan' (see paras 7.25–7.40).

7.16   If a local authority fails or refuses to complete an assessment of need or a care plan in respect of a child or adult then, unless the person concerned is plainly ineligible for assistance, the most appropriate remedy is likely to be judicial review proceedings to ensure that the local authority carries out its duty. If the assessment of need or care plan is unsatisfactory, the appropriate remedy will be either pursuing a formal complaint through the Social Services Complaints Review Panel to obtain a different decision from the local authority, or judicial review to correct errors of law, including failures to comply with the assessment procedures set out in the Policy Guidance and the Children Act 1989 Guidance and Regulations (see further paras 7.126–7.130).

What are community care services?

7.17   Community care services are defined[4] as those services which a local authority may provide or arrange to be provided under:

---

3   *Westminster CC v NASS* [2001] EWHC Admin 138, QBD (Admin Ct); upheld by CA, see (2001) 4 CCLR 143.
4   NHSCCA 1990 s46(3).

- NAA 1948 Part III (residential accommodation for persons in need and a range of services for disabled people, including those available under Chronically Sick and Disabled Persons Act (CSDPA) 1970 s2[5] and Health Services and Public Health Act (HSPHA) 1968 s45 (a range of services for the elderly);
- National Health Service Act (NHSA) 1977 s21 and Sch 8 (a range of services for the social care and aftercare of the ill); and
- MHA 1983 s117 (a wide range of accommodation and other after-care services for mentally ill persons discharged from detention in hospital).

7.18   Services under CA 1989 Part III (a very wide range of services which can include accommodation, cash, and assistance in kind) are not 'community care services' as defined by statute.[6] Nonetheless, many services for children under Part III are analogous to adult services under the NHSCCA 1990 and many of the procedures are very similar, so they are generally considered to be part of 'community care' in a broader sense.

Which local authority to approach?

7.19   Most community care services are administered by the social services department of the local authority. Where there is not a unitary local authority for an area, the social services department will be part of the county council. Some services (under MHA 1983 s117 and the NHSA 1977) also involve health authorities in responsibility for service provision.

7.20   Particular social services departments are driven by shortage of resources to dispute with social services departments in other areas whether a particular individual in need of services is or is not their responsibility. For most community care services what decides this issue is where the individual is considered to be 'ordinarily resident'. A person will be ordinarily resident in an area if s/he can show a regular habitual mode of life in a particular place, the continuity of which has persisted despite any temporary absences.[7]

---

5   These qualify as 'community care services' because they are provided under NAA 1948 s29 (which is within NAA 1948 Part III); *R v Kirklees MBC ex p Daykin* (1998) 1 CCLR 512, QBD.
6   NHSCCA 1990 s46.
7   *Shah v Barnet LBC* [1983] 1 All ER 226. Note there is no statutory definition of the term 'ordinarily resident'.

7.21   Importantly for asylum-seekers, ordinary residence will not be acquired where residence has not been voluntarily adopted, or where there has been no settled purpose in living in a particular residence.[8] Many asylum-seekers will accordingly not acquire ordinary residence in any local authority area. But where they do it is important to note that once provided with accommodation under NAA 1948 s21 (see paras 7.68–7.81), the person remains ordinarily resident in the area of the authority where s/he was living before that accommodation was provided.[9] In the case of provision under CA 1989 s17 (see paras 7.97–7.108), this position is reversed and the duty is owed by an authority to children 'within their area'.[10] Thus, consider a case where authority A provides accommodation to an asylum-seeker in the area of authority B: an adult asylum-seeker who was ordinarily resident in the area of authority A remains the responsibility of authority A if s/he loses the accommodation; an adult asylum-seeker who had not established ordinary residence in area A may become the responsibility of authority B upon losing the accommodation; an asylum-seeker who is an unaccompanied minor may become the responsibility of authority B upon losing the accommodation.[11]

7.22   In considering the provision of accommodation under NAA 1948 s21 (see paras 7.68–7.81), a local authority's duty to provide accommodation[12] extends to those who are ordinarily resident in its area, but also to those who are not ordinarily resident in any area but are living in its area when the need arises, and to those (whether or not ordinarily resident anywhere) who are in urgent need.[13] In addition to these duties, the authority has a power to provide for a person who is ordinarily resident in the area of another authority if that authority agrees.[14]

7.23   Disputes about ordinary residence in relation to NAA 1948 s21 are settled by referral to the Secretary of State;[15] otherwise such disputes may be settled by the courts.[16]

7.24   Ordinary residence is not generally relevant in deciding which

8   Ibid.
9   NAA 1948 s24(5).
10   CA 1989 s17(1)(a); *R v Lambeth LBC ex p Caddell* [1998] 1 FLR 235.
11   The rules about ordinary residence are different in the case of provision under MHA 1983 s117 – see s117(3).
12   See paras 7.72–7.73.
13   NAA 1948 s24(3); Approvals and Directions (LAC(93)10).
14   Ibid, s24(4).
15   Ibid, s32(3).
16   *R v Kent CC ex p Salisbury and Pierre* (2000) 3 CCLR 38, QBD.

local authority should conduct an assessment. The need for assessment is triggered by an application by a person to an authority or by that authority becoming aware that an individual may have a need for community care services which the authority has a power to provide. The authority cannot generally refuse to assess because a person is not ordinarily resident in its area.[17]

Assessing applicants for community care services

7.25   In order to make decisions about whether or not to provide community care services, local authorities follow a prescribed procedure for conducting an assessment and preparing a care plan. A person seeking such services triggers this procedure by requesting the authority to carry out an assessment of need and complete a care plan. The assessment of need identifies which needs the local authority considers ought to be met. The care plan then sets out how the local authority has decided to meet the needs assessed.

7.26   In urgent cases, the local authority may make emergency provision for a person's needs pending the outcome of the assessment process.[18]

Assessment for services under the NHSCCA 1990

7.27   When a local authority is aware that a person may be in need of community care services which it has a power to provide, it has a duty to carry out an assessment and a duty to make a decision on the basis of the assessment as to whether there are needs which call for the provision of services.[19] The failure of a local authority in either duty can be challenged by way of judicial review proceedings. In practice, the matter is invariably resolved speedily, at or around the stage of applying for permission in such proceedings.

7.28   The threshold test for assessment (whether there 'may be' a need for services) is very low and the consequent duty to assess is absolute (in other words, does not depend on whether resources are available to carry out assessments, or on whether the local authority would be likely to provide relevant services).[20] Accordingly, it may be difficult

17   *R v Berkshire CC ex p P* (1998) 1 CCLR 141, QBD.
18   NHSCCA 1990 s47(5).
19   Ibid, s47.
20   *R v Bristol CC ex p Penfold* (1998) 1 CCLR 315, QBD.

for a local authority to justify delay in completing an assessment for any reasons other than professional reasons inherent in the assessment process itself.[21]

7.29   If, during the assessment of need, it appears to the local authority that the person concerned is disabled, the local authority is required to make a decision as to the services the person requires as mentioned in Disabled Persons (Services, Consultation and Representation) Act 1986 s4, without his/her requesting the authority to do so.[22] This simply means that the local authority has to assess the person's needs for services under CSDPA 1970 s2. Furthermore, the local authority must inform him/her that it will be carrying out this assessment and of his/her rights under that Act, the most important of which is the right to have account taken of the ability of any carer to continue to provide care on a regular basis.[23]

7.30   If at any time during the assessment, it appears to the local authority that the person concerned might need health services or housing services, the local authority must notify the district health authority or local housing authority and invite them to assist, as far as is reasonable in the circumstances, in the making of the assessment. (In unitary authorities, the social services authority will also be the housing authority.) In making any decision as to the provision of services, the local authority must take into account any services which are likely to be made available by that district health authority or the local housing authority.[24] Conversely, of course, the local authority would have to take into account the fact that services might not be likely to be forthcoming from the district health authority or local housing authority, which could increase the needs that the local authority would have to consider meeting. For example, if a person has a community care need for housing which is not likely to be provided by the housing department in the near future, or the person is excluded from local authority housing by eligibility rules (see paras 6.10–6.25, 6.83–6.95), then the local authority has at least to consider exercising its community care powers to provide at least temporary housing, and may be under a duty to do so.[25]

21   *R v Kirklees MBC ex p Daykin* (1998) 1 CCLR 512, QBD.
22   NHSCCA 1990 s47(2).
23   Disabled Persons (Services, Consultation and Representation) Act 1986 s8.
24   NHSCCA 1990 s47(3).
25   See *R v Tower Hamlets LBC ex p Bradford* (1998) 1 CCLR 294, QBD; *R v Wigan MBC ex p Tammadge* (1998) 1 CCLR 581, QBD; *R v Lambeth LBC ex p K* (2000) 3 CCLR 141, QBD; *R v Bristol CC ex p Penfold* (1998) 1 CCLR 315, QBD; *R v Kensington and Chelsea RLBC ex p Kujtim* (1999) 2 CCLR 340, CA.

Assessment for services under the CA 1989

7.31   The CA 1989 does not expressly impose a duty upon local authorities to conduct assessments of need, such as applies in the case of adults by virtue of NHSCCA 1990 s47. The duty to assess is found in the mandatory guidance and regulations[26] made under the CA 1989, and has been recognised as being implicit in the CA 1989 by a series of decisions in the courts.[27] The procedure for conducting assessments is also derived from the guidance. The guidance is issued under the Local Authority Social Services Act (LASSA) 1970 (see paras 7.35–7.38) and is thus substantially binding.

7.32   Volume 2 of the guidance contains the following relevant provisions summarised here:

a) The definition of 'need' in s17(10) of the Act is deliberately wide to reinforce the emphasis on preventative support and services to families. The child's needs will include physical, emotional and educational needs according to his or her age, sex, race, religion, culture and language and the capacity of the current carer to meet those needs. The Act requires each authority to decide its own level and scale of services appropriate to the children in need within its area, however, a local authority cannot lawfully substitute any other definition of 'need', for example, by confining services to children at risk of significant harm (paragraph 2.4).

b) In assessing individual need, authorities must assess the existing strengths and skills of the families concerned and help them overcome identified difficulties and enhance strengths. Sometimes the needs will be found to be intrinsic to the child; at other times however it may be that parenting skills and resources are depleted (paragraph 2.5).

c) Good practice requires that the assessment of need should be undertaken in an open way and should involve those caring for the child, the child and other significant persons. Families with a child in need, whether the need results from family difficulties or the child's circumstances, have the right to receive sympathetic support and sensitive intervention (paragraph 2.7).

d) In making an assessment, the local authority should take account of the particular needs of the child – that is, in relation to health, development, disability, education, religious persuasion, racial

---

26 See CA 1989 Sch 2; Children Act 1989 Guidance and Regulations, Vols 2 and 3.
27 *R v Tower Hamlets LBC ex p Bradford* (1998) 1 CCLR 294; *R v Lambeth LBC ex p K* (2000) 3 CCLR 141; *R v Wigan MBC ex p Tammadge* (1998) 1 CCLR 581.

origin, cultural and linguistic background and so on (paragraph 2.8).

e) Assessment must identify and find a way to provide as helpful a guide as is possible to the child's needs (paragraph 2.9). Once the need has been identified a plan for the best service provision will be required (paragraph 2.10).

Volume 3 contains further provisions relevant to assessments:

a) Assessments must cover the child's needs, the parent's abilities, the wishes and views of the child, and all factors relevant to the welfare of the individual child (paragraphs 2.21–2.22; see also paragraphs 2.56–2.57).

b) There is no prescribed format for a child care plan, but there should be such a plan recorded in writing, containing the child's and his or her family's social history and a number of key elements including the child's identified needs, how those needs might be met, the timescale, the proposed services, a contingency plan, details of the roles all relevant persons are to play, the extent to which the wishes and views of the child, his or her parents and anyone else with a sufficient interest in the child have been obtained and acted upon and explanations of why wishes or views have been discounted, dates for reviews and so forth (paragraph 2.62).

7.33　　　Assistance under CA 1989 s17 may be provided unconditionally or subject to conditions as to the repayment of the assistance or of its value (in whole or in part).[28] Before giving any assistance, or imposing any conditions, the local authority has to have regard to the means of the child and his/her parents.[29] Charges cannot be made to persons in receipt of income support or family credit (now replaced by working families tax credit).

Assessment procedures: directions and guidance

7.34　In carrying out assessments, local authorities are regulated by directions and guidance issued by central government. There are no directions specific to NHSCCA 1990 assessments.[30] However, LASSA 1970 s7 provides that local authorities shall, in the exercise of their social services functions, including the exercise of any discretion conferred

28　CA 1989 s17(7).
29　Ibid, s17(8).
30　The Home Secretary has power to issue such directions (s47(4)) but none has yet been issued.

by any relevant legislation, act under the general guidance of the Secretary of State. 'Social services functions'[31] include the assessment procedures and the provision of all community care services, and services under CA 1989 Part III. Guidance issued under LASSA 1970 s7 is known generally as 'statutory guidance' or 'mandatory guidance' and comprises a series of circulars issued to local authorities, and the volumes of guidance issued under CA 1989.

7.35   Guidance issued under LASSA 1970 s7 is in substance compelling. The duty under s7 to 'act under' this guidance requires local authorities to follow the path charted by the Secretary of State's guidance, with liberty to deviate from it where the local authority judges on admissible grounds that there is good reason to do so, but without the freedom to take a substantially different course.[32]

7.36   Most guidance that the practitioner comes across is not issued under LASSA 1970 s7. For the most part this is 'departmental guidance' or 'practice guidance', such as *The Managers' Guide, The Practitioners' Guide*, and so forth. The local authority must have regard to this guidance,[33] and cannot act contrary to the guidance because it does not agree with it. That would, in effect, be to disregard it.[34]

7.37   The main general guidance issued by the Secretary of State under LASSA 1970 s7 so far as concerns community care services is the circular *Community Care in the Next Decade and Beyond.*[35] This is commonly referred to as the 'Policy Guidance'. So far as concerns children, the principal guidance under s7 is the five-volume *The Children Act 1989 Guidance and Regulations*.

7.38   The Policy Guidance on assessment procedures includes the following (summarised here):

a) The individual service user and normally, with his or her agreement, any carers should be involved throughout the assessment and care management process and should feel that the process is aimed at meeting their wishes (paragraph 3.16).

b) The local authority is required to publish readily accessible information about care services, criteria and policies to enable users and carers to exercise choice and participate properly (paragraph 3.18).

c) The assessment and care management process should take into account particular risk factors for service users, carers and the

31 Defined in LASSA 1970 Sch 1.
32 *R v Islington LBC ex p Rixon* (1998) 1 CCLR 119, QBD.
33 Ibid.
34 *R v North Derbyshire HA ex p Fisher* (1998) 1 CCLR 150, QBD.
35 HMSO, November 1990.

community generally: abilities and attitudes; health (especially remediable conditions or chronic conditions requiring continuing healthcare) and accommodation and social subordinates (paragraph 3.19).

d) Once needs have been assessed, the services to be provided or arranged and the objectives of any intervention should be agreed in the form of a care plan which, so far as possible, should preserve or restore normal living (paragraph 3.24).

e) The aim should be to secure the most cost-effective package of services that meets the user's care needs, taking account of the user's and carer's own preferences. Where agreement between all the parties is not possible, the points of difference should be recorded (paragraph 3.25).

f) Decisions on service provision should include clear agreement about what is going to be done, by whom and by when (paragraph 3.26).

g) It is necessary to assess the needs of carers and the ability of carers to continue to cope (paragraphs 3.27–3.29).

h) Care needs should be reviewed at regular intervals and should be reviewed if it is clear that community care needs have changed (paragraph 3.51).

Further and more detailed guidance is contained in the *Managers' Guide*[36] and the *Practitioners' Guide.*[37]

7.39   The *Children Act 1989 Guidance and Regulations* contain detailed provisions as to what assessments and care plans should contain and how they should be carried out, in particular in Volumes 2 and 3 (see para 7.32). The guidance is quite similar to the adult guidance in the Policy Guidance (see para 7.38 above).

Where a need is identified, does a local authority have to meet it?

7.40   Local authorities have a duty to provide some community care services and a discretion as to whether to provide others. A duty can exist in relation to services under CSDPA 1970 s2 and NAA 1948 s21. In such cases, once a local authority has decided that a need for a community care service exists, it has a duty to take steps to meet that need. Where, however, provision is discretionary, the authority must consider whether or not to meet the need. In deciding whether or not a need exists, the local authority must apply the language of the

36 *Care Management and Assessment – Managers' Guide* (HMSO, 1991).
37 *Care Management and Assessment – A Practitioners' Guide* (HMSO, 1991) – also commonly known as 'the Practice Guidance'.

relevant statute, but in doing so may have regard to its own local policy, or 'eligibility criteria'. Eligibility criteria are a system of placing individuals in a hierarchy of categories (or 'bands') according to levels of difficulty or levels of risk of harm if services are not provided. Eligibility criteria are published and vary from one local authority to another. Notwithstanding the banding under eligibility criteria, the authority must consider each individual case.[38]

Exclusion of persons subject to immigration control from community care services

7.41 The IAA 1999[39] excludes certain persons subject to immigration control from certain community care services. Not all persons subject to immigration control are excluded, and the exclusion operates only in relation to certain services. An overview of who is (and who is not) excluded is given at paras 7.6–7.14 above. A table designed to assist in identifying whether or not an individual is excluded appears at para 7.52 below.

7.42 If a person is excluded by the Act, there is no duty on the local authority to assess, since the duty to carry out a community care assessment only arises in relation to a person for whom a local authority may provide or arrange for the provision of community care services[40] and the Act removes the power of local authorities to provide services to persons excluded and receiving asylum support.[41]

Excluded NHSCCA 1990 services

7.43 The exclusion operates only in relation to services under three provisions of the community care statutes:

 - NAA 1948 s21 (residential accommodation);
 - HSPHA 1968 s45 (a range of services for the elderly); and
 - NHSA 1977 Sch 8 para 2 (a range of services for the social care and aftercare of the ill).

Thus there is no exclusion in relation to services under the remaining provisions:

38 *R v Islington LBC ex p Rixon* (1998) 1 CCLR 119.
39 ss116–117.
40 NHSCCA 1990 s47(1); the effect of CA 1989 guidance is the same.
41 IAA 1999 ss116–117.

- NAA 1948 s29 including services under CSDPA 1970 s2 (a wide range of services for the disabled);
- MHA 1983 s117 (a very wide range of services for the aftercare of mentally ill persons discharged from detention).

People excluded from NHSCCA 1990 services

7.44 In the case of each of the three community care services where the exclusion operates, the exclusion from eligibility is limited to persons subject to immigration control as defined by IAA 1999 s115 who are also people whose need for the service in question has arisen solely because they are destitute, or because of the physical effects or anticipated physical effects of their destitution.[42]

7.45 It should be noted that in relation to housing and social security benefits, the definition of 'persons subject to immigration control' in IAA 1999 s115 has the effect of 're-including' as eligible for housing and benefits classes of people prescribed in regulations, who would otherwise be ineligible under s115. However, in relation to community care services, no such regulations have been made, and thus all 'persons subject to immigration control' stand to be excluded. That is, a person is excluded if s/he is not a national of a European Economic Area state and if s/he:

    a) requires leave to enter or remain in the United Kingdom but does not have it; or

    b) has leave to enter or remain in the United Kingdom which is subject to a condition that he or she does not have recourse to public funds; or

    c) has leave to enter or remain in the United Kingdom given as a result of the maintenance undertaking (a written undertaking given by another person in pursuance of the immigration rules, to be responsible for that person's maintenance and accommodation); or

    d) has leave to enter or remain in the United Kingdom pending the conclusion of an appeal.[43]

7.46 As mentioned above, a person is only excluded from the three prescribed community care services, if, in addition to being a person to whom IAA 1999 s115 applies, his/her need for assistance has arisen

---

42 Ibid.
43 IAA 1999 s115(9), Sch 4 para 17; see paras 1.14–1.26.

solely because s/he is destitute, or because of the physical effects, or anticipated physical effects, of his/her being destitute.

7.47   The statutory criteria for residential accommodation under NAA 1948 s21 include needing 'care and attention . . . not otherwise available' by reason of 'age, illness, disability or any other circumstances'. Before the IAA 1999, the courts held that destitution and the other difficulties that faced many asylum-seekers at that time could be 'any other circumstances', giving rise to a threat of illness and therefore a need for 'care and attention'.[44] It was accordingly established that destitution can be an element in determining whether a need for residential accommodation under NAA 1948 s21 exists, and the same consideration would appear to apply to other community care services.

7.48   IAA 1999 ss116–117 ensure, therefore, that people falling within s115 may not be provided with community care services under NAA 1948 s21, Health Services and Public Health Act (HSPHA) 1968 s45 or National Health Service Act (NHSA) 1977 Sch 8 para 2 if their need arises *solely* because of destitution or because of the physical effects, or anticipated physical effects of destitution.

7.49   However, destitution can still be a component, even the major component, of the need for community care services. Provided that a person has a need for community care services distinguishable from his/her requirement for accommodation and essential living needs, it does not matter that that need is exacerbated by destitution or its effects. The person is only excluded if destitution is the *sole* element in the need.[45]

7.50   This is the effect of the decision of the Court of Appeal in *R v Wandsworth LBC ex p O*,[46] the leading case on the interpretation of these provisions. It is worthwhile setting out the relevant passage from the leading judgment of Simon Brown LJ in full:

> In what circumstances, then, is it to be said that destitution is the sole cause of need? The local authorities contend that the approach should be this. First ask if the applicant has (a) somewhere to live ('adequate accommodation') and (b) means of support (the means to 'meet his other essential living needs') [see section 95(3) of the Act of 1999]. Assuming the answer is 'No' to each of those questions, ask next whether, but for those answers, he would need section 21 assistance.

44   *R v Westminster City Council ex p M, P, A and X* (1997) 1 CCLR 69, QBD.
45   *R v Wandsworth LBC ex p O* [2000] 1 WLR 2539; (2000) 3 CCLR 237, CA.
46   Ibid at 2548D–E; at 246D–G.

If not, he does not qualify. In other words, it is only if an applicant would still need assistance even without being destitute that he is entitled to it.

The applicants contend for an altogether different approach. They submit that if an applicant's need for care and attention is to any material extent made more acute by some circumstance other than mere lack of accommodation and funds, then, despite being subject to immigration control, he qualifies for assistance. Other relevant circumstances include, of course, age, illness and disability, all of which are expressly mentioned in section 21(1) itself. If, for example, an immigrant, as well as being destitute, is old, ill or disabled, he is likely to be yet more vulnerable and less well able to survive than if he were merely destitute.

Given that both contended-for constructions are tenable, I have not the least hesitation in preferring the latter. The word 'solely' in the new section is a strong one and its purpose there seems to me evident. Assistance under the Act of 1948 is, it need hardly be emphasised, the last refuge of the destitute. If there are to be immigrant beggars on our streets, then let them at least not be old, ill or disabled.

7.51 It should be noted that people who have needs that do not arise solely from destitution, and who therefore potentially qualify for these community care services, include not only asylum-seekers, but all other persons subject to immigration control, including applicants for exceptional leave to remain, people lawfully here with leave and people unlawfully here,[47] and whether or not they are pursuing some form of immigration appeal.

Community care or asylum support?

7.52 Advisers will commonly be faced with the question of whether a local authority has any responsibility to assess the needs of an applicant for community care services. The following steps should be followed to answer this question:

Question	Yes	No
1 May the person have a need for any community care service? *(see paras 7.17–7.18)*	Go on to 2	No duty
2 Is the applicant a person subject to immigration control as defined by IAA 1999 s115? *(see para 7.45)*	Go on to 3	Section 47 duty exists

47 *R v Wandsworth LBC ex p O* [2000] 1 WLR 2539; (2000) 3 CCLR 237, CA.

Question	Yes	No
3 Is the community care service for which the person may have a need an excluded service (under ss116–117)? *(see para 7.43)*	Go on to 4	Section 47 duty exists in respect of that service; for needs for other services go on to 4
4 Does the need for any such service arise to any extent from a cause other than destitution or the anticipated physical effects of destitution? *(see paras 7.46–7.51)*	Section 47 duty exists	No duty (unless statutory provisions can be interpreted to create such a duty by the application of Human Rights Act 1998 *(see paras 8.4–8.5)*

7.53   Advisers will also frequently face the question of whether and to what extent an applicant's needs for accommodation and essential living needs fall to be met under a local authority's community care responsibilities, or under NASS. There is a lack of clarity here. The Court of Appeal in *R v Wandsworth LBC ex p O*[48] appears to have taken the view that, providing destitution (or the physical effects or anticipated physical effects of destitution) is not the sole cause of need, the person concerned falls within the community care regime, even though his/her destitution could be met in other ways, for example, under the Interim Regs or under NASS provision. That would mean that all his/her needs including accommodation and essential living needs would have to be met under community care provisions and not under the support provisions. It should be emphasised however that the Court of Appeal was not directly concerned with this issue. It should be noted that in relation to CA 1989 provision, the IAA 1999 specifically provides that local authorities may not make provision under CA 1989 s17 where there is NASS provision or where the Secretary of State is liable to make provision under NASS (see paras 7.58–7.67). The fact that there is no equivalent in the IAA 1999 in relation to community care services provision might be construed as supporting the Court of Appeal's position.

48 Ibid.

7.54   Since the *ex p O* case, the point has been directly considered by the court in *Westminster City Council v NASS*.[49] In this case, the court decided that where an asylum-seeker's needs for services under NAA 1948 s21 arose not solely from destitution, the responsibility to meet those needs lay with the local authority under the community care regime and not with NASS. The court considered that if responsibility for meeting the needs of such a person belonged to NASS, the amendment[50] to the NAA 1948 preserving entitlement in the case of such a person would have no meaning.[51]

7.55   In that case, neither party contended that responsibility for support might be shared between NASS and the local authority.[52] The alternative view is that the provision of accommodation and essential living needs under NAA 1948 s21 is a 'safety net' provision, which only arises to the extent that there is a need for care and attention 'not otherwise available', and so a person's needs for adequate accommodation and essential living needs should be met under NASS or the Interim Regs, while any needs for community care services going beyond adequate accommodation and essential living needs are for the local authority to assess and meet.

7.56   Where an applicant has an urgent need and is not excluded from community care provision, it is arguable that the local authority has a responsibility to make urgent temporary provision under NAA 1948 s21, pending completion of the NASS and NHSCCA 1990 assessments. NASS and the local authority under the Interim Regs also have responsibility for making temporary provision (see paras 4.9–4.14, 5.46–5.53).

7.57   In practice there should not be such a potential 'demarcation dispute' in cases involving the Interim Regs rather than NASS, since the social services department of the local authority would be responsible whether services were to be provided under community care powers and duties, or under the Interim Regs.

Exclusion from CA 1989 services

7.58   There are exclusions from eligibility for assistance under CA 1989 s17 affecting those eligible under both NASS and the Interim Regs

---

49 [2001] EWHC Admin 138, QBD (Admin Ct) and confirmed by CA at (2001) 4 CCLR 143.
50 By IAA 1999 s116, inserting s21(1A) into the NAA 1948; see paras 7.41, 7.44–7.51.
51 See also, the Court of Appeal discussion at (2001) 4 CCLR 143.
52 Contrast the position in relation to services under the CA 1989 – see para 7.60, 7.64.

schemes. In effect, almost all asylum-seeker families with children are excluded from the provision of accommodation and subsistence under the CA 1989, save for unaccompanied minors, whose needs are provided for almost entirely under the Act.

7.59   IAA 1999 s122 provides that local authorities must not exercise their powers under CA 1989 s17 to provide accommodation or essential living needs in respect of dependent children whose needs in those respects are or could be met by the Home Secretary (ie, NASS) acting under IAA 1999 s95 to provide support for the family as a whole.[53] This exclusion can be disapplied in certain cases by regulations,[54] although none have as yet been made.

7.60   If, after being provided with accommodation and essential living needs by the Home Secretary, the child remains a child in need for other reasons, for example, connected with his/her disability, then the local authority still has power to meet those needs, under CA 1989 s17. It is thus clearly envisaged that a child in need may have its (and its family's) needs for accommodation and its essential living needs met under NASS (by the Home Office) and other needs met simultaneously by the local authority under CA 1989 s17.

7.61   If the child's family has had support withdrawn, for whatever reason, then the local authority regains its powers under CA 1989 s17 in respect of the child. If accommodation has been provided under asylum support and is withdrawn, it is only the local authority for the area in which the accommodation is located that regains power to assist under s17.[55] It is not clear whether this means, for example, that a family in London applying for asylum support and refusing accommodation offered in Cleveland, would have to seek assistance under the CA 1989 from social services in Cleveland; it is arguable that accommodation 'offered' differs from accommodation 'provided', and the wording of IAA 1999 s122 would appear to support this.[56]

7.62   IAA 1999 is silent as to whether those powers to assist under the CA 1989 include the power to make provision for the whole family, but support for the whole family, provided with a view to safeguarding or promoting the welfare of the child, would seem to be at least possible[57] and almost always desirable because of the general duty

---

53   IAA 1999 s122(5).
54   Ibid, s122(11).
55   Ibid, s122(8)–(10).
56   See, in particular, ibid, s122(3) and (4).
57   Because of CA 1989 s17(3).

to keep families together.[58] Contentious cases might occur where one or more of the adults caused support to be withdrawn by breaching conditions or becoming intentionally destitute, but common humanity, let alone article 8 of the Human Rights Convention, suggests that families should be maintained together unless the proximity of the parents by itself would actually harm the children.[59]

7.63   It should be noted, however, that families with dependent children will not cease to be eligible for support merely because their asylum claim has been determined by the Home Secretary, or on appeal if there is an appeal. For support purposes an asylum-seeker is to be treated[60] as continuing to be an asylum-seeker so long as s/he has a dependent child under 18 years in his/her household and they are both in the UK.

7.64   The position is similar under the Interim Regs. By reg 12, a person entitled to support under the Interim Regs is not entitled to assistance under CA 1989 s17. Assistance under s17 is restrictively defined[61] as assistance by way of the provision of accommodation or of any essential living needs. This enables local authorities to use their powers under s17 to meet the needs of children in need, other than those met by the provision of accommodation and essential living needs to the whole family under the Interim Regs.

7.65   As with NASS asylum support, if support under the Interim Regs is withdrawn and as a result families cease to be entitled to it, the prohibition on assistance under CA 1989 s17, found in reg 12, disappears. In the case of the Interim Regs, the revival of s17 assistance is not limited to the local authority for the area where accommodation under those regulations was being provided.

7.66   Again, as with NASS asylum support, support under the Interim Regs will not be withdrawn merely because the asylum claim has been determined by the Home Secretary, or on appeal if there is an appeal. For support purposes an asylum-seeker is to be treated as continuing to be an asylum-seeker so long as s/he has a dependent child under 18 years in his/her household and they are both in the UK.

7.67   Unaccompanied children are not excluded at all from the provisions of the CA 1989. They continue to be dealt with entirely under

---

58 Ibid, s17(1); see *R v Barnet LBC ex p Guleed* (2001) 4 CCLR 33.
59 *R v Barnet LBC ex p Foran* (1999) 2 CCLR 329; *cf R v Hammersmith and Fulham LBC ex p Damoah* (1999) 2 CCLR 18; *R v Barnet LBC ex p Guleed* (2001) 4 CCLR 33.
60 IAA 1999 s94(5).
61 Reg 2(4).

the CA 1989 regime and not under the support provisions found in IAA 1999 (see paras 7.102–7.108).

The nature and extent of community care services

Services under the NHSCCA 1990 subject to exclusions

Residential accommodation under NAA 1948 s21

7.68   Asylum-seekers and other persons subject to immigration control who have needs which derive at least in part from causes other than destitution or the physical effects of destitution (for example, because they are elderly, handicapped, disabled, physically or mentally ill, or pregnant) will be entitled to have their needs for accommodation and subsistence met by the local authority social services department under NAA 1948 s21.

7.69   Local authorities have powers to provide residential accommodation under NAA 1948 s21, and those powers are converted into duties by, and in the circumstances set out in, the Approvals and Directions made under s21 by the Secretary of State for Social Services.[62] Persons subject to immigration control are excluded from these services in the circumstances described above (see paras 7.43–7.51).

7.70   Most commonly, the duty arises under NAA 1948 s21(1)(a) and para 2(1)(b) of the Approvals and Directions, in respect of 'persons aged 18 or over who by reason of age, illness, disability or any other circumstances are in need of care and attention not otherwise available to them'. The structure of these provisions warrants careful note as the duty is to provide 'residential accommodation' to those (not, as may be expected, in need of *accommodation*, but to those) in need of *care and attention* not otherwise available to them. In particular circumstances, an authority may be under a duty to provide accommodation to a person who, at the point of assessment, has accommodation available– see paras 7.72–7.73.

7.71   Where residential accommodation is provided, there is a duty to meet needs for food and other welfare services, where required.[63] No assistance can be given however in the form of cash.[64]

---

62 See Appendix A.
63 See NAA 1948 s21(5) and Approvals and Directions para 4.
64 *R v Secretary of State for Health ex p M and K* (1998) 1 CCLR 495.

7.72   The case of *R v Westminster City Council ex p M, P, A & X*[65] established that destitute asylum-seekers, in danger of suffering illness as
the result of their inability to obtain shelter and food, could be in
need of care and attention for the purposes of these provisions. Later
cases established that a person could still need care and attention
(and thus give rise to a duty to provide accommodation) because of
destitution even though s/he was able to meet some needs (for
example, accommodation but not food)[66] or was entitled to work but
not able to find work.[67]

7.73   The rationale of the courts' approach to provision under NAA 1948
s21 appears to have been adopted in IAA 1999 which provides that
a person is destitute either if s/he does not have adequate accommodation or any means of obtaining it (whether or not his/her other
essential needs are met), or if s/he has adequate accommodation or
the means of obtaining it, but cannot meet other essential living
needs.[68]

7.74   For the duty under NAA 1948 s21 to arise in relation to a person
subject to immigration control (see para 7.45) the need for care and
attention must not arise solely because of destitution or the physical
effects of destitution.[69] There would, therefore, have to be another
element present, of the kind mentioned in s21, ie, age, illness,
disability or other circumstance giving rise to a need for care and
attention (see para 7.70).

7.75   The Approvals and Directions set out a number of types of cases
where there is a duty or power to provide residential accommodation.
Local authorities will also have published eligibility criteria under
NHSCCA 1990 s46 and the Policy Guidance by reference to which
social workers decide whether a 'need' for residential accommodation exists. If the criteria are too stringent, having regard to the statutory framework, judicial review is possible. Once a local authority has
assessed a need for residential accommodation as existing, then it
must meet the need.[70]

---

65   (1997) 1 CCLR 69 at 85.
66   *R v Newham LBC ex p Gorenkin* (1998) 1 CCLR 309.
67   *R v Newham LBC ex p Plastin* (1998) 1 CCLR 304; *cf R v Southwark LBC ex p
        Hong Cui* (1999) 2 CCLR 86.
68   IAA 1999 s95(3).
69   Ibid, s116.
70   *R v Kensington and Chelsea RLBC ex p Kujtim* (1999) 2 CCLR 340; *R v Islington
        LBC ex p Batantu* (2000) 8 November, QBD, January 2001 *Legal Action* 28.

7.76   'Residential accommodation' can be accommodation in an institution, a hostel or an ordinary house or flat.[71] It should be suitable, which in this context requires the local authority to have regard to the welfare of all persons for whom accommodation is provided, and to provide different descriptions of accommodation suited to different descriptions of persons.[72] It must meet whatever needs have been assessed as existing.[73] The authority should strive to meet the assisted person's preferences within its available resources.[74] It has to plan how best to meet the needs assessed and how best to meet preferences in accordance with the provisions of the Policy Guidance (see para 7.38).

7.77   Where the NAA (Choice of Accommodation) Directions 1992 conditions are met, the assisted person has the right to choose his/her 'preferred accommodation'. The conditions summarised here are that:[75]

a) the preferred accommodation appears to the local authority to be suitable in relation to the person's needs as assessed by them;
b) the cost of making arrangements at the preferred accommodation would not require the authority to pay more than they would usually expect to pay having regard to the assessed needs;
c) the preferred accommodation is available;
d) the persons in charge of the preferred accommodation provide it subject to the authority's usual terms and conditions.

If the accommodation would require the authority to pay more than it would usually expect to pay, third parties are permitted to 'top up' with the difference.[76]

7.78   It is important to note that, while an authority absolutely must meet assessed needs, the way in which the authority meets those needs is largely a matter for the authority to decide, although it must strive to meet service provision preferences within available resources.[77] This is in stark contrast to the support system under the

---

71 *R v Newham LBC ex p Medical Foundation for the Care of Victims of Torture* (1998) 1 CCLR 227; *R v Bristol City Council ex p Penfold* (1998) 1 CCLR 315.
72 NAA 1948 s21(2).
73 *R v Avon CC ex p M* (1999) 2 CCLR 185; *R v Richmond LBC ex p H* (2000) 20 July, QBD, January 2001 *Legal Action* 28.
74 Policy Guidance para 3.25.
75 Reg 3.
76 Reg 4.
77 Policy Guidance para 3.25.

IAA 1999 wherein it is repeatedly stressed that no regard is to be had to an applicant's preferences.

7.79　　Residential accommodation can be provided by the local authority entering into arrangements with the private sector, under NAA 1948 s26. Alternatively, it can be provided by the local authority using accommodation held for that purpose under NAA 1948 s21 itself. The local authority can grant licences of its own housing stock for this purpose.[78]

7.80　　It is only in an exceptional case that a local authority is entitled to treat its duty under s21 as discharged, so that it does not have to offer further accommodation. In *R v Kensington and Chelsea RLBC ex p Kujtim*,[79] the Court of Appeal emphasised that it was essential that local authorities should not reach the conclusion that their duty to provide residential accommodation was discharged unless satisfied that an applicant has unreasonably refused to accept accommodation provided, or that a service user has persistently and unequivocally refused to comply with the local authority's requirements (for example as to behaviour), coupled with a careful consideration of his/her current needs and circumstances.

7.81　　A local authority may charge for accommodation provided under s21. There is a detailed scheme of means testing and regulation.[80] These charging provisions are not usually relevant to asylum-seekers with limited resources.

Services for the elderly under HSPHA 1968 s45

7.82　　Asylum-seekers and other persons subject to immigration control who have needs which derive at least in part from causes other than destitution or the physical effects of destitution (for example, because they are elderly, handicapped, disabled, physically or mentally ill) will be eligible for services under HSPHA 1968 s45.

7.83　　Compared with its effect on NAA 1948 s21, discussed above, the exclusion of certain persons subject to immigration control will have little impact in relation to services under HSPHA 1968 s45, since

---

78　The proscription on local authorities granting tenancies and licences to persons subject to immigration control imposed by IAA 1999 s118 is lifted for the purposes of NAA 1948 s21 by Persons Subject to Immigration Control (Housing Authority Accommodation and Homelessness) Order 2000 SI No 706 reg 4(1)(a).

79　[1999] 4 All ER 161; (1999) 2 CCLR 340.

80　See NAA 1948 s22, National Assistance (Assessment of Resources) Regulations 1992 SI No 2977 and *Charging for Residential Accommodation Guide* (LAC (95)7 – as frequently amended).

there will be few people (if any) with a need for these services for whom destitution is the only cause of that need.

7.84   The services provided under HSPHA 1968 s45[82] are miscellaneous services which local authorities are empowered to provide for the elderly, in accordance with approvals and directions made under that section, which are found in Circular LAC 19/71. The services include meals on wheels and recreation, in the home or elsewhere, social work assistance, practical assistance and adaptations in the home and warden services.

7.85   Almost by definition, it might be thought, a person likely to qualify for this kind of service would not be in need solely by reason of destitution, but also by reason of old age.

Services for the sick under the NHSA 1977

7.86   Asylum-seekers and other persons subject to immigration control who have needs which derive at least in part from causes other than destitution or the physical effects of destitution (for example, because they are elderly, handicapped, disabled, physically or mentally ill) will be eligible for services under the NHSA 1977.

7.87   The services provided under NHSA 1977 Sch 8 para 2 relate to services that local authorities may, and in some cases must, provide for the prevention of illness, the care of people suffering from illness and the aftercare of people who have been suffering from illness. Provision is made in accordance with approvals and directions.[83] The kinds of services involved are day centres and similar facilities, social services support, social and recreational facilities. Provision is discretionary.

7.88   Again, almost by definition, it might be thought, a person likely to qualify for these kinds of services would not be in need solely by reason of destitution, but also by reason of past or present illness, and thus the limited exclusion of persons subject to immigration control described at paras 7.41–7.51 is likely to have little impact.

Services under the NHSCCA 1990 which are not subject to exclusions

7.89   There is no exclusion of asylum-seekers or other persons subject to immigration control from services under NAA 1948 s29,[84] CSDPA

82 See Appendix A.
83 Ibid.
84 LAC (93)10.

1970 s2[85] and MHA 1983 s117.[86] Of these three sets of provisions, only MHA 1983 s117 offers the possibility of the provision of assistance with accommodation and subsistence.

NAA 1948 s29 and CSDPA 1970 s2

7.90 These enactments apply only to substantially disabled persons: 'persons aged 18 or over who are blind, deaf or dumb, or who suffer from mental disorder of any description and other persons aged 18 or over who are substantially and permanently handicapped by illness, injury, or congenital deformity or such other disabilities as may be prescribed by the Minister'.

7.91 The services under NAA 1948 s29 are provided in accordance with approvals and directions made under that section[87] and, again, each local authority will have its own published eligibility criteria. The services provided include social work assistance, different types of day centres, holiday homes, travel, and warden schemes.

7.92 The services under CSDPA 1970 s2 are set out in the section itself and include practical assistance in the home, various kinds of leisure provision, home adaptations, telephones and meals. The assessment process was considered by the House of Lords in *R v Gloucestershire CC ex p Barry*.[88] The conclusion was that, in assessing needs and whether it was necessary to meet them, local authorities are entitled and obliged to have regard to current standards of living, the nature and extent of the disability, the extent and manner to which quality of life would be improved and the cost of providing the service in the context of the resources available to the local authority. The relative cost is to be weighed against the relative benefit and the relative need for that benefit, in the light of the local authorities' published community care criteria.

7.93 Additionally, in the case of persons from abroad, the local authority will inevitably have to pay particular attention to the effect on such persons of destitution.

MHA 1983 s117

7.94 There is no exclusion so far as concerns services under MHA 1983 s117. These services are 'aftercare' services provided for persons

---

85 See Appendix A.
86 Ibid.
87 Ibid.
88 [1997] AC 584; (1997) 1 CCLR 40.

who cease to be detained under the treatment provisions of the MHA 1983.[89] They include 'social work, support in helping the ex-patient with problems of employment, accommodation or family relationships, the provision of domiciliary services and the use of day centre and residential facilities'.[90] They also include the provision of residential accommodation and charges cannot be made.[91] Responsibility for the provision of services rests jointly upon the health and social services authorities.

7.95   Essentially, before a mentally-ill person is discharged from detention there has to be a multidisciplinary assessment of his/her needs, subsequent to discharge, completed by relevant medical and social services officers.[92]

7.96   So far as concerns all of these services, people subject to immigration control are eligible for assistance on the same basis as British citizens. The only additional factor likely to arise, is that the destitution of people from abroad may result in needs existing which would not otherwise have existed and may increase the needs that fall to be met under the community care scheme if physical or mental damage is to be avoided.

Services for children

7.97   The IAA 1999 marks a new departure in taking the subsistence and accommodation needs of children living with their families who are asylum-seekers outside the scope of the CA 1989. Apart from this exclusion, services for children are almost exclusively provided under the CA 1989. An exception is made in respect of children who are disabled[93] who are eligible for all of the services within CSDPA 1970

---

89 S117 applies only to those detained under the treatment sections of the Act (ss3, 37 and 41) but not to those detained under s2 – detention for assessment for a period not exceeding 28 days.

90 *Clunis v Camden and Islington HA* (1998) 1 CCLR 215 at 225GH.

91 *R v Richmond LBC ex p Watson* (1999) 2 CCLR 402, QBD and [2001] 1 All ER 436, CA.

92 *The Care Programme Approach* (HC(90)23/LASSL(90)23); *Guidance on the Discharge of Mentally Disordered People and their Continuing Care in the Community, Building Bridges: A Guide to Arrangements for the Inter-Agency Working for Care and Protection of Severely Mentally Ill People* (LASSL(94)4/HSG(94)27); *R v Ealing LBC ex p Fox* [1993] 3 All ER 170; *R v Mental Health Review Tribunal ex p Hall* (1999) 2 CCLR 361, QBD and 383, CA.

93 As defined by NAA 1948 s29.

s2[94] (as to which, see paras 7.90–7.93). Provision for unaccompanied children who claim asylum is made entirely under the CA.

Children in need

7.98 Local authorities have powers and duties under CA 1989 Part III[95] in relation to 'children in need'. A child is defined as a person under 18 years of age.[96] The term 'child in need' is defined in CA 1989 s17(10) as being a child who is:

- unlikely to achieve or maintain, or to have the opportunity of achieving or maintaining, a reasonable standard of health[97] or development[98] without the provision for him/her of services by the local authority under CA 1989 Part III; or
- likely to suffer significant impairment of health or development, or further impairment, without the provision for him/her of services by the local authority under CA 1989 Part III; or
- disabled: that is a child who is blind, deaf or dumb or who suffers from mental disorder of any kind or who is substantially and permanently handicapped by illness, injury or congenital deformity.

Children of families of asylum-seekers lacking accommodation and the means of support are likely to fall within the scope of this definition.

Services for children in need living with their families

7.99 The services provided can include assistance in kind and also cash.[99] All of the services can be provided for the child or, where appropriate, for the child and his/her family.[100] Assistance in kind can include accommodation.[101] Where a child is homeless, the local authority is

94 See CSDPA 1970 s28A; *R v Bexley LBC ex p B* (2000) 3 CCLR 15.
95 See Appendix A.
96 CA 1989 s105(1).
97 'Health' means physical or mental health.
98 'Development' includes physical, intellectual, emotional, social or behavioural development.
99 CA 1989 s17(6).
100 Ibid, s17(3).
101 *Att-Gen ex rel Tilley v Wandsworth LBC* [1981] 1 WLR 854; *R v Tower Hamlets LBC ex p Monaf* (1988) 20 HLR 529; *R v Northavon DC ex p Smith* [1994] 2 AC 402; *R v Tower Hamlets LBC ex p Bradford* (1998) CCLR 294; *R v Hammersmith and Fulham LBC ex p Damoah* (1999) 2 CCLR 18; *R v Lambeth LBC ex p K* (2000) 3 CCLR 141.

under a duty to provide assistance, but there is no absolute duty under s17 to house homeless children together with their families. Rather, local authorities must take such steps as are reasonably practicable to enable a child to live with his/her family where it is necessary to promote and safeguard the child's welfare.[102] Local authorities can grant tenancies or licences to accommodate families under s17.[103] Local authorities must make such provision as they consider appropriate in respect of advice, social activities, travel for the purpose of using services, and holidays.[104]

7.100   Prior to the IAA 1999, local authorities provided destitute asylum-seeker families with accommodation, food and other basic necessities under CA 1989 s17 on a very large scale. The great advantage of the CA 1989 regime is its flexibility. Once the authority has decided to provide assistance there is no limit to the type of assistance that can be provided or the way in which it can be provided.

7.101   However, it is a flexibility that cuts both ways. Assistance under CA 1989 s17 confers no right to particular accommodation and services. A local authority can discharge its duties in a variety of ways as appropriate in the circumstances. Thus it may satisfy a need for accommodation by securing accommodation itself, or by providing assistance to parents to secure accommodation in the private rented sector. The assistance must, however, be effective.[105]

Services for unaccompanied asylum-seeker children

7.102   This covers children under 18 years of age who arrive in the UK, claim asylum and are without close adult family members either accompanying them or already present in the UK and whom they can join. Such children are the responsibility of the social services department of the local authority in whose area they are for the time

102   CA 1989 s17 and Sch 2 Part I para 10; *R v Barnet LBC ex p Foran* (1999) 2 CCLR 329; *R v Hammersmith and Fulham LBC ex p Damoah* (1999) 2 CCLR 18; *R v Barnet LBC ex p Guleed* (2001) 4 CCLR 33, CA.
103   The proscription on local authorities granting tenancies and licences to persons subject to immigration control imposed by IAA 1999 s118 is lifted for the purposes of children in need by Persons Subject to Immigration Control (Housing Authority Accommodation and Homelessness) Order 2000 SI No 706 reg 4(1)(b), although the availability of accommodation for such grants will be restricted by the requirement that allocations be made in accordance with HA 1996 Part VI – see paras 6.79–6.95.
104   CA 1989 s17 and Sch 2 Part I para 8.
105   *R v Barking and Dagenham LBC ex p Ebuki* (2000) 5 December, QBD (Admin Ct).

being, and should on arrival be referred immediately to the social services department for an assessment and for the immediate provision of assistance. Assistance provided ranges from accommodation and food to foster carers, leisure, language help and trauma counselling. Such children should be treated no differently from UK children who have been taken into care except, of course, that they may need extra help.

7.103   Assistance is provided to such children under CA 1989 s20. The authority must provide accommodation to any child in need who appears to require it as a result of there being no one who has parental responsibility for him/her, being lost or abandoned, or the child's carers being prevented for the time being from providing suitable accommodation or care. In addition to providing accommodation, the authority must maintain the child.[106] Provision must so far as practicable have regard to the wishes of the child[107] but otherwise local authorities are given a wide discretion as to how they discharge their duty.[108] Where the authority is also providing accommodation for a sibling, the children should be accommodated together.[109] Fostering arrangements with a family of the same refugee community are common.

7.104   Assessment takes place under CA 1989 Sch 2 Part 1 para 3, and subject to the guidance referred to at paras 7.31–7.33. Provision must be reviewed regularly.[110]

7.105   Provision for children looked after by local authorities will be modified by the commencement on 1 October 2001 of the Children (Leaving Care) Act 2000. The Act will improve provision for children aged 16 and 17 years who have been looked after by the authority for at least 13 weeks since their fourteenth birthday. For such children, the local authority which last looked after the child will have a responsibility to provide maintenance, accommodation and other support unless or until it is satisfied that it is not necessary to provide such support to promote the child's welfare. The Act also makes provision for the assessment of need, the preparation of a 'pathway plan' and the appointment of a personal adviser, for such children. Financial support of such children (unless they are parents or disabled) will be wholly the responsibility of the local authority and entitlement to state

106   CA 1989 s23(1).
107   Ibid, s22(4), (5).
108   Ibid, s23(2).
109   Ibid, s23(7).
110   Ibid, s26, and Review of Children's Cases Regulations 1991 SI No 895.

benefits will correspondingly be removed. Provision under the Act (save in relation to education training and employment) does not extend beyond the child's eighteenth birthday. Needs not met under the new Act may still be met under CA 1989 s24, described at paras 7.122–7.125.

7.106   When the asylum-seeker reaches his/her eighteenth birthday, entitlement to support under CA 1989 ss17 and 20 ceases, but support may continue under CA 1989 s24 – see paras 7.122–7.125.

7.107   Where a child, having arrived as an unaccompanied minor, has adult family members who arrive in the UK or are located, the child is likely to be accommodated with them. The local authority is under a duty[111] to make arrangements for such a child to live with his/her parent or anyone with parental responsibility,[112] or 'a relative friend or other person connected with him', subject to considerations of practicality and welfare. Where such an adult is an asylum-seeker, the child will become the responsibility of NASS or the local authority under the Interim Regs if s/he is a 'dependant' of the adult, as defined by IAA 1999 s94(1) and the AS Regs or Interim Regs (see paras 3.28–3.46, 5.17–5.19). In such circumstances, the local authority may not[113] continue to provide support under CA 1989 s17, but its duties under ss20, 23 and 24 are unaffected. In practice this means that the accommodation and maintenance of the child remains the responsibility of the social services department under CA 1989 until the child is accommodated and maintained under NASS provision or the Interim Regs.

7.108   For the consequences for unaccompanied asylum-seeker children of decisions being made on their applications, see paras 7.113 and 7.118, and for the consequences of their reaching 18 years of age, see paras 7.122–7.125.

Effects of changes of status

7.109   This section describes the consequences for the provision of services under the community care statutes and the CA 1989 of changes in the status of asylum-seekers. The following changes of status are considered:

---

111   Ibid, s23(4), (5).
112   Defined by ibid ss2, 3.
113   IAA 1999 s122.

- the grant of refugee status or exceptional leave to remain;
- the refusal of an asylum application or an appeal;
- the asylum-seeker and others reaching 18 years of age.

The grant of refugee status or exceptional leave to remain

7.110 A successful asylum application will conclude with a decision by the Home Secretary or at the conclusion of an appeal to grant the applicant refugee status or exceptional leave to remain in the UK (ELR) – see paras 1.86–1.97.

7.111 People who have refugee status or ELR are entitled to assistance under Housing Act (HA) 1996 Parts VI and VII. The asylum-seeker upon notification of a grant of refugee status or ELR should at once apply to register on the housing register of the local authority, and upon becoming homeless or threatened with homelessness apply for assistance under Part VII as a homeless person (see paras 6.7–6.95). Such people will also be entitled to work and to state benefits.[114] If not working they should immediately apply for income support or job-seeker's allowance, and housing benefit and council tax benefit, as appropriate.

7.112 Where the asylum-seeker whose claim is determined is supported with accommodation and subsistence by the local authority under community care legislation (usually NAA 1948 s21 or CA 1989 s17), then – unless the asylum-seeker requires residential care – the social services department is likely to take steps to terminate that support and transfer responsibility to the housing department, its own benefit department and to the Benefits Agency. However, there is no requirement to end support within 14 days as is the case with asylum/interim support. The local authority should not terminate support until satisfied that, as the case may be, the applicant's needs are otherwise being met[115] or the child is no longer a child in need.[116] The change of circumstances occasioned by a grant of refugee status or ELR should give rise to a formal review of the community care or CA assessment and revision of the care plan before any changes are made to service provision. Peremptory termination of community care services in such cases could be challenged by judicial review.

114 ELR in such circumstances does not usually have attached to it a condition that the person does not have recourse to public funds.
115 NAA 1948 s21.
116 CA 1989 s17.

7.113   Unaccompanied asylum-seeker children who are the subject of positive decisions on their applications will not have their support under the CA 1989 terminated in consequence. Those 16 years old or over may qualify for means-tested jobseeker's allowance or income support, including arrears if granted refugee status (see paras 2.96–2.101).

7.114   As with the shift from asylum support provision, there is commonly a practical problem when a decision is made by the Home Secretary or on appeal granting refugee status or ELR, but the applicant has not yet received documents proving his/her new immigration status. The social services department may in such circumstances terminate assistance, but on approaching the local authority or the Benefits Agency, the applicant is told that s/he will not be assisted until s/he can produce the standard documentation (form ICD.0725 – previously GEN23 – for refugee cases, or a Home Office letter granting ELR for a specified period (see paras 1.80–1.85). There are similar problems where such people apply for benefits and have to wait while a National Insurance number is allocated (see paras 2.96–2.101 for difficulties in processing benefits claims). The remedies for the applicant are by way of judicial review, either of the failure of the Home Office or appellate authority to issue the documentation, or of the local authority social services department for breach of its duties under NAA 1948 s21 or under CA 1989 s17. The second option will be preferable in most cases for the reasons stated at para 7.112.

7.115   The same problems and possible remedies will be relevant to people who are granted refugee status or ELR having previously been assisted under asylum or interim support. Where such people experience difficulty in proving their new status so as to be able to obtain housing under HA 1996 Part VII or benefits, they will be able to seek assistance from the local authority social services department under NAA 1948 s21 or CA 1989 s17, as appropriate, since their exclusion from such services will have ended with their grant of status.

Refusal of an asylum application or an appeal

7.116   An unsuccessful asylum application concludes with a refusal decision by the Home Secretary, or a refusal on appeal. Two questions arise:

  – What will be the effect of such a decision on services already being provided to the applicant?

– In what circumstances will such a decision lead to an applicant being entitled to community care services because of the withdrawal of other means of support?

7.117   In answer to the first question, services already provided to an asylum-seeker under the community care statutes and the CA 1989 are unaffected by a decision to refuse the asylum application, whether that decision is made by the Home Secretary or on appeal.

7.118   In the case of unaccompanied asylum-seeker children, the answer to both questions is that negative decisions on their applications will have no effect. The support described above (paras 7.102–7.108) continues after a negative asylum decision so long as the child remains under 18 and in the UK.

7.119   In answer to both questions, as far as adults whose households include dependent children are concerned, asylum support will continue following an adverse asylum decision unless the youngest child reaches 18, or the dependent child leaves the household or the UK, or unless leave to remain is granted.

7.120   That leaves adults without dependent children in their household, who will cease to be entitled to assistance under the asylum support scheme when their asylum application is refused without an appeal being made, or where all appeal rights have been exhausted.

7.121   Such adults will be entitled to services under NAA 1948 s29 including CSDPA 1970 s2 (services for the disabled) and under MHA 1983 s117 (aftercare services for discharged mental patients). They will also be entitled to services under NAA 1948 s21 (residential accommodation and support), HSPHA 1968 s45 (services for the elderly), and NHSA 1977 Sch 8 para 2 (services for those who are ill), provided their need for those services does not arise solely because of destitution or because of the physical effects or anticipated physical effects of destitution.[117] It may also be arguable that, even if they do not satisfy this proviso, they are eligible for services under NAA 1948 s21 since to deny them such services would infringe their convention rights under the Human Rights Act 1998 (see para 8.63).

The asylum-seeker and others reaching 18 years of age

7.122   Unaccompanied asylum-seekers aged under 18 are excluded from support under the asylum support scheme,[118] and are the

117   IAA 1999 ss116–117 – see above.
118   Ibid, s94(1).

responsibility of the social services department who may support them under CA 1989 s17 or take them into care under CA 1989 s20 (see paras 7.102–7.108). Where a child has been in care or provided with accommodation under s17 or s20, the local authority remains under a duty under CA 1989 s24 'to advise, assist and befriend' that child after the care or provision ceases. This applies to children who are under 21 and who received such care or provision at any time while they were 16 or 17.[119] The term 'in care' covers a variety of provision, from short-term fostering to children's homes. The 'assistance' to be provided may be in kind or, in exceptional circumstances, in cash.[120] Assistance in kind can include provision of accommodation.[121]

7.123   Local authorities commonly take the view that s24 duties are limited to those who have been in care under s20, and do not extend to those assisted under s17, but this is incorrect.[122]

7.124   If an asylum-seeker child (unaccompanied or not), on reaching his/her eighteenth birthday, has had his/her asylum application refused and has exhausted the appeal rights, then s/he will not be entitled to assistance from NASS. S/he may be entitled to assistance with accommodation under NAA 1948 s21, if – as is likely to be the case – his/her need for assistance arises other than solely because of destitution or the physical effects of destitution (see paras 7.44–7.51 above).

7.125   If an asylum-seeker child (unaccompanied or not), on reaching his/her eighteenth birthday, has a pending asylum application or appeal, then s/he may be eligible for support from NASS. In the case of unaccompanied children, the social services department is advised to arrange for a NASS application to be made two weeks before the child reaches his/her eighteenth birthday, and should provide evidence of destitution, including evidence of support provided under CA 1989 s24.[123] NASS has agreed to defer dispersal of asylum-seekers who are taking or about to take final school examinations when they

119 CA 1989 s24(2).
120 Ibid, s24(7).
121 *Att-Gen ex rel Tilley v Wandsworth LBC* [1981] 1 WLR 854.
122 CA 1989 s24 applies to people under 21 who have at any time while 16 or 17 been 'looked after' by a local authority; 'looked after' means (s22(1)) in care or provided with accommodation in the exercise of functions which are the responsibility of the social services committee under the Local Government and Social Services Act 1970; such functions include functions under CA 1989 s17 (LASSA 1970 Sch).
123 NASS Policy Bulletin 29.

turn 18.[124] However, local authorities retain a duty to assist such young people under CA 1989 s24, and it is arguable that they should provide for their needs under these duties rather than refer them to NASS.

Community care challenges

7.126 In practice, many challenges to a failure by a local authority to carry out an assessment or provide a community care service are likely to be by way of judicial review, on the basis that the local authority has misconstrued its statutory powers or acted irrationally or unfairly.

7.127 If there is a generalised breakdown of local authority provision, then it is possible to ask the Home Secretary to exercise his/her default powers under LASSA 1970 s7D. It is rare for the existence of default powers to constitute an alternative remedy to judicial review.[125]

7.128 Otherwise, many decisions can be challenged by way of the complaints procedures, which local authorities are required to set up under LASSA 1970 s7B and the Local Authority Social Services (Complaints Procedure) Order 1990.[126] Complaints ultimately result, if successful, in recommendations being made by the Social Services Complaints Review Panel. Although not binding, local authorities must have good reason for not complying with such recommendations.[127] The complaints procedure is well-suited to cases where there is a dispute about the detail of service provision, ie, whether accommodation is suitable, whether food is suitable, whether enough food or enough suitable clothing has been provided, etc. The complainant can attend the Social Services Complaints Review Panel and present his/her predicament orally to the panel.

7.129 The complaints procedure is suitable where the issue relates to questions of fact and degree. It is not likely to constitute an alternative remedy to judicial review where a discrete issue of law arises.[128]

---

124 Ibid.
125 *R v Devon CC ex p Baker* [1995] 1 All ER 73; *R v Leicester Guardians* [1899] 2 QB 632; though not unknown: *R v Westminster City Council ex p P* (1998) 1 CCLR 486.
126 SI No 2244.
127 *R v Avon CC ex p M* (1999) 2 CCLR 185.
128 *R v Devon CC ex p Baker* [1995] 1 All ER 73; *R v Sutton LBC ex p Tucker* (1998) 1 CCLR 251.

7.130   The local government ombudsman[129] has power to intervene in community care cases, although in this context s/he will often not be able to act quickly enough. There can, however, sometimes be considerable advantages in involving the local government ombudsman as s/he has power:

- to recommend that compensation is paid;
- to carry out investigations and ascertain facts which it might be difficult to ascertain in the course of judicial review;
- to review local authority procedures in the round;
- in effect to force local authorities to change procedures and to report back to demonstrate that change has occurred.[130]

The ombudsman can also be brought in if the local authority fails to implement the complaints procedure correctly or promptly.

---

129 For address, see Appendix H.
130 See, eg, *Investigation into Complaint No 97/A/2959 against Hackney LBC*.

CHAPTER 8

Asylum support and the Human Rights Act

For complete chapter contents, see overleaf

Introduction

8.1   The Human Rights Act (HRA) 1998 incorporates the rights set out in the European Convention on Human Rights ('the Convention') into UK law. It does not replace or supersede any existing rights, but rather supplements them, in some areas creating discrete new rights.[1] The Act consists of a series of provisions describing how the Convention is incorporated into UK law, followed by a Schedule setting out the articles which comprise the Convention rights incorporated. The Act came into force on 2 October 2000.

8.2   This chapter gives an outline of the HRA and the Convention, concentrating on those aspects relevant to the law in relation to support for asylum-seekers, and then looks at particular problem areas where there may be opportunities for challenges based upon the infringement of Convention rights. Extracts from the HRA appear in Appendix A and further resources are listed at Appendix H.

Outline of the HRA 1998 and the Convention

How the HRA applies to UK law

8.3   There are four ways in which the HRA applies to UK law:

  – influencing interpretation of the law;
  – introducing machinery to regulate primary and secondary legislation;
  – regulating the actions of public authorities;
  – creating an individual right of action in the courts.

Interpretation of the law

8.4   The HRA requires courts to interpret all legislation so as to be compatible with the Convention, so far as it is possible to do so.[2] The courts must assume that parliament intended that all legislation be compatible with the Convention, and this applies to all legislation whether enacted before or after 2 October 2000.[3] Ministers introducing new legislation to parliament are required to make a

---

1   HRA 1998 s11.
2   Ibid, s3(1).
3   Ibid, s3(2).

declaration as to its compatibility with Convention rights:[4] the Home Secretary declared that the Immigration and Asylum Act (IAA) 1999 was compatible with the Convention.

Regulation of primary and secondary legislation

8.5   In interpreting legislation, the courts may find that it is not possible to interpret legislation so as to be compatible with the Convention, because the legislation is contrary to the Convention. Where this occurs in relation to secondary legislation, the courts can strike the legislation down, unless primary legislation prevents them from doing so.[5] Where it occurs in relation to primary legislation, the higher courts (the House of Lords, the Judicial Committee of the Privy Council, the Court of Appeal, the High Court and – in Scotland – the High Court of Justiciary) cannot strike legislation down, but can make a 'declaration of incompatibility' in relation to a particular statute.[6] This declaration does not invalidate the statute, which remains in force,[7] but it is intended that a declaration will prompt the government to legislate to correct the defect in the statute, though there is no mechanism to ensure that this happens. Primary legislation consists of Acts of Parliament, also known as statutes (eg, the IAA 1999). Secondary legislation, also known as subordinate or delegated legislation, refers to law made by ministers under powers granted by Acts of Parliament, usually comprised in statutory instruments containing sets of regulations (eg, the Asylum Support Regulations 2000).

Regulation of the actions of public authorities

8.6   The HRA makes it unlawful for public authorities to act in a way which is incompatible with the Convention,[8] unless the authority is *required* to act in that way by primary legislation. The term 'public authorities' is widely defined to include any court or tribunal and 'any person certain of whose functions are functions of a public nature'.[9] This definition includes virtually all the bodies that make decisions in relation to asylum support: the Home Office and its agencies,

---

4   Ibid, s19.
5   Ibid, s3.
6   Ibid, s4.
7   Ibid, s4(6).
8   Ibid, s6(1) and (2).
9   Ibid, s6(3); on the meaning of 'public authority' in this context, see also *Hansard*, HL Debates col 1231, 3 November 1997.

(including the National Asylum Support Service (NASS) and the Asylum Support Adjudicator); the Department of Social Security and its agencies including the Benefits Agency; local authorities; and the Lord Chancellor's Department, including the courts and the Appeals Service.

8.7   In some cases, whether a body is acting as a public authority is more questionable. Consider, for example, where NASS provides accommodation under contract with a private landlord. NASS is exercising public functions when it enters into a contract with a housing provider, and when it decides that that particular accommodation is adequate for an asylum-seeker, but it is more questionable whether the provider is exercising public functions when it enters an occupancy agreement with the asylum-seeker.[10] Again, where the Home Secretary has contracted with voluntary organisations to provide temporary accommodation and support pending assessment,[11] it may be argued that where decisions about the nature and extent of such support are delegated to those organisations, they are decisions of a public nature.[12]

An individual right of action in the courts

8.8   Where individuals believe that their Convention rights have been infringed by a public authority, they can bring proceedings in respect of that breach in the courts, and can rely on their Convention rights in defending proceedings brought against them by public authorities.[13] Proceedings brought by an individual do not have to be wholly based on the assertion of Convention rights, but where those proceedings are brought by way of judicial review, the individual must be a 'victim' of the unlawful act complained of.[14] Convention rights may be brought in alongside other causes of action or bases of defence in all kinds of proceedings involving public authorities. Proceedings brought under the HRA must be commenced within a year of the act complained of,[15] and may only be brought in relation to acts of public authorities taking place after 2 October 2000. The assertion of Con-

10 See, eg, *R v Servite Houses and Wandsworth LBC ex p Goldsmith and Chatting* (2000) 3 CCLR 325.
11 Pursuant to IAA 1999 s98 – see paras 4.9–4.14.
12 *Donoghue v Poplar HARCA Ltd and Secretary of State for the Environment*, June 2001 *Legal Action* 23.
13 HRA 1998 s7(1).
14 Ibid, s7(3).
15 Ibid, s7(5).

vention rights as a defence may, in contrast, relate to an alleged breach of rights taking place before the commencement date.[16]

Convention rights

8.9 The Convention sets out a series of human rights. These are contained in 14 articles and a set of protocols. The HRA does not incorporate all of the articles and protocols: only articles 2–12 and 14; articles 1–3 of protocol 1, and articles 1 and 2 of protocol 6 as read with articles 16–18 of the Convention.

8.10 The articles are framed in wide terms and use concepts which appear broad and sweeping in their scope. However, some of the rights are limited and others are qualified. All are subject to interpretation: the interpretation developed by the European Court of Human Rights (ECtHR), the European Commission of Human Rights and the Committee of Ministers of the Council of Europe, in the form of case-law, must be taken into account by courts and tribunals in the UK in implementing the HRA.[17] However, the binding nature of previous decisions of the ECtHR and Commission is tempered by the principle of the Convention being a 'living instrument': Convention rights are to be interpreted according to current conditions. The older the decision, the less reliable it is as a guide to interpretation.

Three categories of Convention rights

8.11 The rights apply in three different ways, according to the nature of the right.

– **Absolute rights**: these cannot be restricted in any circumstances and are to be applied without consideration of balancing with the general public interest (articles 2, 3, 4(1) and 7).
– **Limited rights**: these can be the subject of a specific derogation entered by a government, but may not otherwise be restricted (articles 4(2) and (3), 5 and 6).
– **Qualified rights**: these are rights in respect of which the articles include clauses which restrict the rights by allowing consideration of certain categories of public interest (articles 8–12, and

16 Ibid, s22(4).
17 Ibid, s2.

protocol 1, articles 1–3). See paras 8.21–8.27 below for how qualification works in practice.

The articles describing the Convention rights

8.12   The most relevant articles of the Convention are set out in Appendix
A. This chapter concentrates on those articles that are likely to be of
relevance to decision-making on asylum-seeker support issues.

Article 2 – Right to life (absolute right)

8.13   1.   Everyone's right to life shall be protected by law. No one shall be
deprived of his life intentionally save in the execution of a sentence of a court following his conviction of a crime for which this
penalty is provided by law.

2.   Deprivation of life shall not be regarded as inflicted in contravention of this article when it results from the use of force which is
no more than absolutely necessary:

a.   in defence of any person from unlawful violence;

b.   in order to effect a lawful arrest or to prevent the escape of a
person lawfully detained;

c.   in action lawfully taken for the purpose of quelling a riot or
insurrection.

Article 2 extends to a requirement to take reasonable measures to
protect life.

Article 3 – Prohibition of torture (absolute right)

8.14   No one shall be subjected to torture or to inhuman or degrading
treatment or punishment.

–   'Torture' has been defined[18] as 'deliberate inhuman treatment
causing intense physical and mental suffering'.

–   'Inhuman treatment' has been defined[19] as 'treatment that causes
intense physical and mental suffering'.

–   'Degrading treatment' has been defined[20] as 'treatment that
arouses in the victim a feeling of fear, anguish and inferiority
capable of humiliating and debasing the victim and possibly
breaking his/her moral resistance'.

–   Such treatment will not fall within the scope of article 3 unless it

18   *Ireland v UK* (A/25) (1978) 2 EHRR 25.
19   Ibid.
20   Ibid.

attains a minimum threshold of severity. The threshold is to be determined on a case-by-case basis, having regard to all the circumstances.

Article 6(1) – Right to a fair trial (limited right)

8.15 So far as civil proceedings are concerned, the article provides that:

> In the determination of his civil rights and obligations . . . everyone is entitled to a fair and public hearing within a reasonable time by an independent and impartial tribunal established by law. Judgment shall be pronounced publicly . . . [except in prescribed circumstances].

Article 8 – Right to respect for private and family life (qualified right)

8.16
1. Everyone has the right to respect for his private and family life, his home and his correspondence.
2. There shall be no interference by a public authority with the exercise of this right except such as is in accordance with the law and is necessary in a democratic society in the interests of national security, public safety or the economic well-being of the country, for the prevention of disorder or crime, for the protection of health or morals, or for the protection of the rights and freedoms of others.

– Article 8(1) is qualified by article 8(2).
– Respect for private life, for family life, for home and for correspondence are each to be considered as discrete rights.

Article 9 – Right to freedom of thought, conscience and religion (qualified right)

8.17
1. Everyone has the right to freedom of thought, conscience and religion; this right includes the freedom to change his religion or belief and freedom, either alone or in community with others and in public or in private, to manifest his religion or belief, in worship, teaching, practice and observance.
2. Freedom to manifest one's religion or beliefs shall be subject only to such limitations as are prescribed by law and are necessary in a democratic society in the interests of public safety, for the protection of public order, health or morals, or for the protection of the rights and freedoms of others.

– Article 9(1) is qualified by article 9(2).
– This qualification only applies to the *manifestation* of religious belief: the right to *hold* a religious belief is unqualified. Further-

more, this qualification, unlike that under article 8, does not entitle public authorities to rely on arguments about the economic well-being of the country to justify interference with the right. Also, the courts are directed by HRA 1998 s13 to have 'particular regard to the importance' of this Convention right in cases involving the exercise of freedom of thought, conscience and religion by religious organisations.

Article 14 – Prohibition of discrimination

8.18   The enjoyment of the rights and freedoms set forth in this Convention shall be secured without discrimination on any ground such as sex, race, colour, language, religion, political or other opinion, national or social origin, association with a national minority, property, birth or other status.

– This is not a free-standing right. Rather it refers to discrimination in relation to the application of the other Convention rights. It is only necessary to show that the subject matter of a case falls within the ambit of another Convention right:[21] there will be a breach of the Convention if discrimination is shown, even if there is no breach of the particular Convention right to which it attaches.[22]

– The phrase 'or other status' has been interpreted to include sexual orientation, marital status, and illegitimacy. It is arguable that 'asylum-seeker' may form such a category.

– Whether the prohibition on discrimination can be limited or restricted will depend on the article under consideration; article 14 does not itself fall within one of the three categories of Convention rights (see para 8.11 above). In practice, the court would consider whether there was an objective and reasonable justification for discrimination, and whether differential treatment was proportionate to the aim pursued.

Protocol 1, Article 1 – Protection of property (qualified right)

8.19   Every natural or legal person is entitled to the peaceful enjoyment of his possessions.

This right is qualified:

---

21 *X v Germany* (1976) 19 YB 276; *Schmidt and Dahlstrom v Sweden* (1979–80) 1 EHRR 632.
22 *Belgian Linguistics Case (No 2)* (1979–80) 1 EHRR 252.

No one shall be deprived of his possessions except in the public interest and subject to the conditions provided for by the law and by the general principles of international law. The preceding provisions shall not, however, in any way impair the right of a State to enforce such laws as it deems necessary to control the use of property in accordance with the general interest or to secure the payment of taxes or other contributions or penalties.

'Possessions' includes an interest in land, and so the article may be raised where action by a public authority deprives a person of a tenancy.

Protocol 1, Article 2 – Right to education (qualified right)

8.20   No person shall be denied the right to education.

- The acts of public authorities in relation to education must 'respect the rights of parents to ensure ... education and teaching is in conformity with their own religious and philosophical convictions'.
- The HRA[23] includes a caveat that the requirement in this sentence is accepted only in so far as it is compatible with the provision of efficient instruction and training and with the avoidance of unreasonable public expenditure.
- The article has been interpreted to concern primarily primary and secondary education, rather than higher education.[24]

Scope and application of qualified rights

8.21   Strictly, the wording of each article itself contains an exhaustive description of the grounds on which the particular right may be qualified. In practice, the approach of the ECtHR has been to establish a broader set of principles applied generally to the interpretation of qualified rights such as articles 8 and 9 and protocol 1, articles 1 and 2 above. A fivefold test is applied. The limitation or restriction of qualified rights will only be upheld if the public body seeking to restrict or limit them can show:

- that it is in accordance with the law, *and*
- that it pursues a legitimate aim, *and*
- that it is necessary and proportionate, *and*

23   Sch 3, part II.
24   *X v UK* [1975] DR 50.

- that it is not discriminatory,
  or
- that it falls within 'a margin of appreciation'.

It is in accordance with the law

8.22   Any limitation or restriction of a Convention right must first be 'prescribed by law', which means that domestic law permits or requires it. Second, the limitation or restriction in domestic law must be 'accessible', which means those affected by it must be able to find out about it. Third, it must be clearly and precisely expressed so that the individual can know in advance the application of domestic law in the particular case.

It pursues a legitimate aim

8.23   Any limitation or restriction must fall within the ambit of the qualification stated in the clauses of the particular article of the Convention, and must be an effective means of achieving that aim.

It is necessary and proportionate

8.24   Any limitation or restriction must be 'necessary in a democratic society'. This means that the limitation or restriction fulfills a pressing social need, and is proportionate to the aim of responding to that need. This is perhaps the most important and fundamental principle of interpretation of Convention rights: it encapsulates the approach of the ECtHR which is to seek a 'fair balance' between the rights of the individual and the rights of the community. An act of a public authority which is lawful and which interferes with a Convention right in pursuance of a legitimate aim, will only be upheld if it can be shown that the extent of the interference is no more than is strictly necessary to achieve that aim. Application of the principle involves asking whether the legitimate aim being pursued could be achieved by any means which are less restrictive of individual rights. Furthermore, the more important the right is to the individual, the less likely it is that interference with it will be justified.

It is not discriminatory

8.25   A limitation or restriction must not be discriminatory, which means that a person is not treated less favourably than another in a similar or analogous situation[25] where there is 'no objective and reasonable justification' for so doing. Whether there is such a justification depends on the aim and effect of the act, and whether there is a reasonable relationship between the means employed and the aim sought to be realised.[26]

It is within a 'margin of appreciation'

8.26   The test of whether a restriction or limitation is prescribed by law is entirely objective: the other tests require a measure of judgment. The ECtHR will assume that the public authorities of the individual state are best placed to apply the tests of whether an act is 'legitimate', 'necessary', and 'proportionate'. The court will supervise the assessment made by the domestic authority but will not substitute its own assessment for that of the domestic authority unless it is 'manifestly without reasonable foundation'.[27] This is known as the 'margin of appreciation'. The domestic authority is assumed to be best placed to 'appreciate' correctly the weight to be given to local factors qualifying Convention rights. Just how much local discretion is allowed depends on the context – the more intimate and personal the right, the narrower will be the margin of appreciation; the more matters of domestic public policy are concerned, the wider the margin of appreciation. States are given a wide margin of appreciation in spheres of welfare provision. In essence, respect for national differences between member states is balanced against the protection of universal individual rights.

8.27   The margin of appreciation is a feature of the application of the Convention by the ECtHR to the actions of public authorities in signatory states. It is not a feature of the application of the Convention and the HRA by UK courts to the actions of UK public authorities. The UK courts must determine whether an act is 'legitimate', 'necessary', and 'proportionate', without considerations of subsidiarity intervening. This is not to say that in scrutinising the decisions of public authorities the UK courts can be expected to 're-make' every decision under challenge. Nor, on the other hand, is the court's role limited to overruling irrationality in the *Wednesbury*[28] sense. Rather, it is to be

---

25 *Marckx v Belgium* (1979–80) 2 EHRR 330.
26 *Belgian Linguistics Case (No 2)* (1979–80) 1 EHRR 252.
27 *Palumbo v Italy*, February 2001 *Legal Action* 28–29.
28 *Associated Provincial Picture Houses v Wednesbury Corporation* [1948] 1 KB 223, CA.

expected that courts will intervene in the merits of decisions by applying the tests of legitimacy, necessity and proportionality to a greater
or lesser extent depending on criteria such as the importance of the
right, the extent of the interference alleged, the accountability of the
decision-maker and the vulnerability of the individual,[29] in line with
the broad purpose of the HRA.

Convention rights and asylum support

8.28   This section looks at areas of the provision of support for asylum-
seekers in which articles of the Convention are or may be engaged.
Given that both the asylum support scheme and the HRA are rela-
tively new and to a great extent untested, the purpose is to highlight
areas of the scheme which may give rise to challenges based on the
infringement of Convention rights, and to consider the scope of such
challenges.

8.29   The nature of statutory provision for asylum-seekers is intrinsic-
ally likely to raise questions of infringement of human rights. The
political purpose of the enactments and regulations has been to bear
down upon and minimise the level of provision for asylum-seekers
with a view to deterring them from making their applications to the
UK. Legislation to remove and restrict provision for a category of
persons according to their immigration status tends to run up against
the guarantee of fundamental human rights under the Convention.
The government in framing legislation has had to consider carefully
whether convention rights are infringed, but the resulting official line
is bound to be challenged by litigation brought under the HRA or
turning on its provisions. We will look at a series of possible areas of
challenge.

8.30   The particular points examined are:

– whether the whole scheme for asylum support may be open
  to challenge as an infringement of Convention rights (see paras
  8.31–8.33);
– whether the disqualification of categories of people from being
  'applicants' for accommodation is discriminatory (see para 8.34);

---

29   *R v Home Secretary ex p Mahmood* (2001) *Times* 9 January; *R v Home Secretary ex p
Isiko* (2001) *Times* 20 February; *R v Home Secretary of State ex p Javed* [2001]
EWHC Admin 7.

- whether different treatment of married, unmarried and same-sex couples infringes Conventions rights (see paras 8.36–8.39);
- whether restrictive definitions of 'dependants' infringe article 8, with particular reference to adopted children, children born outside marriage, and disabled people and their carers (see paras 8.40–8.47);
- whether decisions about adequate accommodation infringe Convention rights (see paras 8.48–8.54);
- whether decisions on dispersal and location of accommodation infringe Convention rights (see paras 8.48–8.51, 8.55–8.60);
- whether decisions about essential living needs infringe Convention rights (see paras 8.48–8.51, 8.61–8.66);
- whether decisions resulting in destitution infringe Convention rights (see paras 8.67–8.72);
- whether procedures for the summary recovery of possession of accommodation provided under asylum support infringe Convention rights (see paras 8.73–8.76);
- whether ancillary powers given to the Home Secretary to force entry to premises under warrant, and to gather and disseminate information, breach Convention rights (see paras 8.77–8.79);
- whether lack of independent and impartial decision-making infringes article 6(1), looking particularly at the asylum support adjudicator, and homelessness and allocation decisions (see paras 8.80–8.86);
- whether the rules of the scheme restrict access to justice so as to infringe article 6(1) (see paras 8.87–8.92);

Does the whole scheme infringe Convention rights?

8.31   It may be suggested that the whole statutory framework on which provision for asylum-seekers and other persons subject to immigration control is based is incompatible with Convention rights, although the public authorities concerned are likely to be able to defeat such an argument with some ease. IAA 1999 ss115–122, and Housing Act (HA) 1996 s185 exclude from basic welfare provision a large category of people on the basis of their immigration status, and in some cases can lead to a person being left destitute indefinitely. Schemes of needs-based state welfare provision have been found to engage the right to respect for private life under article 8. If article 8 is engaged, it can be argued that these statutes are discriminatory by basing provision upon status, contrary to article 14. It would then be for the public authorities to establish that such discrimination has a reasonable and necessary justification and that the interference with the right to private life was necessary in a democratic society 'in the interests of national security, public safety or the economic well-being of the country, for the prevention of disorder or crime, for the protection of health or morals, or for the protection of the rights and freedoms of others'. 'Necessary' in this context requires an examination of whether the discrimination is proportionate to the ends served. It may well be thought that the government would have little difficulty in satisfying these requirements in the context of the scheme as a whole.

8.32   Particular elements of the scheme may be open to challenge on the same grounds. An instance is the modification of Housing Acts 1985 and 1988 to prevent accommodation provided under the asylum support provisions from attracting secure or assured status respectively.[30] These provisions may infringe article 14 read with article 8. In a challenge it would be for the government to show that there was a reasonable and objective justification for the difference in treatment of asylum-seekers compared with other housing applicants.[31]

8.33   A further example is HA 1996 s185(4), which excludes consideration of ineligible family members in deciding whether an applicant is in priority need. This may be incompatible with article 8. It would be for the government to show that there was a reasonable and proportionate justification for this interference with family life.

Capacity to make applications

8.34   Housing authorities have often refused to accept applications for accommodation from children and mental patients. Before the commencement of the HRA, the courts implied into the statutory provisions as to the making of applications under the homelessness legislation a requirement that an applicant meet a 'threshold of capacity' (ie, be capable of a certain level of understanding), so excluding most dependent children and certain mental patients.[32] It may be expected that there will be a challenge to such exclusion, arguing that a decision by a public authority as to who can and who cannot be an applicant engages (at least, if not infringes) the right to respect for private life under article 8, and that the exclusion of categories of

---

30 IAA 1999 Sch 14.
31 See the ECtHR's analysis in *Larkos v Cyprus* (1999) 7 BHRC 244.
32 *R v Oldham MBC ex p G and R v Tower Hamlets LBC ex p Begum* [1993] AC 509.

persons such as these is discriminatory in breach of article 14. By analogy, failure to secure access to legal remedies for a person failing a test of competence has been found to breach article 8 by failing to secure for such a person respect for private life.[33]

Decisions about family members

8.35   The statutory provision for asylum-seekers involves public authorities making decisions in a number of contexts about who does and who does not belong to family units or households, decisions which have consequences for whether or not support is provided, and how it is provided. The legal framework and the decisions made under it tend to require consideration of article 8, the right to respect for private and family life. These issues arise in particular in the definitions of dependants in Asylum Support Regulations[34] reg 2 and Asylum Support (Interim Provisions) Regulations[35] reg 2, and also in the interpretation of the phrase 'member of the family' in relation to social security entitlement for 'workers' of EEA states (see paras 2.34–2.35). The following particular aspects of the scheme are likely to give rise to challenges.

Couples

8.36   In the case of both asylum support[36] and interim support,[37] provision is extended to the dependants of asylum-seekers; the definition of dependants includes married couples and unmarried couples. For asylum support purposes, the definition of both 'married couple' and 'unmarried couple' is confined to relationships between a man and a woman; same-sex couples are excluded. In the case of unmarried couples, a member of such a couple will only be considered a dependant of the other if they have been living together for at least two of the past three years.[38] Consequences of these definitions may be that provision is made for one member of the couple but not the other, or that applications are dealt with separately so that, for

---

33 *X and Y v Netherlands* (1985) 8 EHRR 235.
34 Asylum Support Regulations (AS Regs) 2000 SI No 704.
35 Asylum Support (Interim Provisions) Regulations 1999 SI No 3056 (Interim Regs).
36 AS Regs reg 2(1).
37 Interim Regs reg 2(1).
38 AS Regs reg 2(4)(f); Interim Regs reg 2(1)(f).

example, one member of the couple may be dispersed and the other not.

8.37   So far as same-sex couples are concerned, such relationships are not recognised as covered by the concept of family life under article 8.[39] However, interference with the rights of a same-sex couple may infringe the right to respect for private life under the same article.[40] It should also be recalled that the Convention is a 'living instrument' and the extension of the concept of 'family life' to same-sex relationships may only be a matter of time.[41]

8.38   Unmarried heterosexual couples are not excluded from the concept of family life, but whether 'family life' exists in the case of a particular couple will be a question of fact 'depending upon the real existence in fact of close personal ties'.[42] To establish this the court will look at relevant factors including whether the couple live together, the length of the relationship, whether there are children and other evidence of the couple's commitment to each other.[43] The restriction on the definition of dependency in the AS Regs to couples who have lived together for two of the last three years may be found to be arbitrary and inconsistent with the Convention right, in particular in its application to asylum-seekers. The exigencies of flight from persecution commonly involve couples being split up and only being reunited after considerable periods of time.

8.39   In either case, article 8 may come into play in challenging a decision by NASS or a local authority to exclude consideration of a member of an unmarried couple or of a same-sex couple from provision in response to a particular asylum-seeker's application for assistance.

Dependants and households

8.40   The problem for public authorities of who should be housed with an eligible applicant is likely to engage the right to respect for the home, private and family life under article 8. The definitions of dependants in the AS Regs[44] and the Interim Regs[45] seek to prescribe categories of

39   See, eg, *X and Y v UK* (1983) 32 DR 220; *Kerkhoven v Netherlands*, Commission decision of 19 May 1992.
40   *X and Y v UK* (1983) 32 DR 220.
41   See, eg, the approach adopted by Lord Clyde in *Fitzpatrick v Sterling Housing Association* (2000) 32 HLR 178, at 199–200.
42   *K v UK* (1986) 50 DR 199 at 207.
43   *Kroom v Netherlands* (1995) 19 EHRR 263; *X , Y and Z v UK* (1997) 24 EHRR 143.
44   AS Regs reg 2.
45   Interim Regs reg 2.

persons who will be considered as comprising a family or household and in so doing may breach article 8 in particular cases. Applicants to local authorities under HA 1996 Parts VI and VII are subject to a wide discretion exercised by the authority, in the case of homeless applicants in deciding who usually resides with an applicant as a family member or who can or cannot be reasonably expected to reside with an applicant,[46] and in the case of housing register applicants in the treatment of families and households in the local allocation scheme.

8.41   For example, problems may be expected with the inclusion or exclusion of adopted children or the children of unmarried partners.

Adopted children

8.42   The relationship of adoptive parent and adopted child falls within the concept of family life,[47] and thus a refusal to consider adopted children as 'close family members' of an asylum-seeker would breach article 8.

Children born outside marriage

8.43   In interpreting 'family life' the ECtHR has upheld the rights of children born outside marriage to be treated no differently from children born within marriage. Thus, a child should not be included or excluded from the category of 'close family members' on the basis of whether or not the parents are married. However, this does not preclude determination of the existence of 'family life' in cases of unmarried couples as a question of fact and degree. For example, if an asylum-seeker was living with or joined by his/her unmarried partner and a child of the partner (but not of the asylum-seeker), and on application for assistance, the child was not considered to be a dependant of the asylum-seeker, the question of whether or not article 8 was breached would be determined by the facts of the relationship between the asylum-seeker and the child. However, the interpretation of 'family life' is also to a degree purposive, and includes the concept of a right to develop normal family relationships,[48] and thus it might be argued that factors involving the future of the relationship between the asylum-seeker and the child should be considered, and not just the history of the relationship to date.[49]

---

46   HA 1996 s176.
47   *X v Belgium* (1975) 7 DR 75; *X v France* (1982) 31 DR 241.
48   *Marckz v Belgium* (1979) 2 EHRR 330.
49   See in particular *Söderbäck (Per) v Sweden* (33124/96) 22 October 1997.

Disabled persons and their carers

8.44   The position of disabled people and their carers may also give rise to challenges. Under both asylum support and interim support, a disabled person may be treated as a dependant of an asylum-seeker if the asylum-seeker or a member of his/her household or family provides care services, and meets particular conditions (see paras 3.36 and 5.18). Conversely, a disabled asylum-seeker will not usually be able to obtain support for a person who arrives with him/her as a carer. The inflexibility of these rules, which make no allowance for the nature of particular relationships, may give rise to an infringement of the right to respect for private life under article 8.

Other 'family members'

8.45   The households of asylum-seekers may include other individuals who fall outside the definition of 'close family members' (see paras 3.35 and 5.19), eg, siblings or grandchildren who are not covered by the provisions bringing within the scope of the term 'dependant' those under 18 who have lived with the asylum-seeker for the past six months, or who are disabled. Whether or not the exclusion of such individuals from consideration as dependants constitutes a breach of the right to family or private life is again likely to be a question of fact and degree in the individual case. The court may be expected to look at all the circumstances of the family, its history and prospects, and the evidence of close relationship and dependency. The ECtHR has shown itself willing to extend the concept of 'family life' to a wider group of family members where formal relationship is allied to practical support and dependency. For example, it has accepted that article 8 is engaged in a case of siblings where deportation would mean separation of the applicant from his ten siblings,[50] and in a case of grandparents and grandchildren where there were regular contact and visits.[51]

8.46   The arbitrary division of households and families may also be a consequence of Interim Regs reg 7(1)(c), requiring local authorities to refuse applications for support where an applicant has in the previous 12 months applied to another authority for assistance under National Assistance Act (NAA) 1948 s21 or Children Act (CA) 1989 s17 (see paras 5.96–5.97). For example, an asylum-seeker making an

---

50   *Boughanemi v France* (1996) 22 EHRR 228; see also *Moustaquim v Belgium* (A/193) 18 February 1991.
51   *Price v UK* (1988) 55 DR 224; see also *Boyle v UK* (1994) 19 EHRR 179 – a case of uncle and nephew.

emergency application for assistance shortly after arrival to one local authority may be prevented from being united with other family members already present in the area of another authority. It should be noted that this regulation does not prevent an authority assisting a person who has previously applied to another authority for support under the Interim Regs.

8.47   Challenges in this area are most likely to arise in relation to decisions of NASS or local authorities to refuse applications for assistance from 'dependants' of asylum-seekers or to refuse to take particular family or household members into account in making provision for accommodation and essential living needs. A refusal by NASS of assistance on the application of a person claiming to be the dependant of an asylum-seeker would be challenged by way of an appeal to the Asylum Support Adjudicator; otherwise such decisions are challengeable by judicial review.

Decisions about the nature and extent of asylum support

8.48   The implementation by NASS and local authorities of the scheme for asylum support involves the greatest element of discretion when it comes to decisions about what support is to be provided and where. In practice, these public authorities are charged with contracting for accommodation and devising means of providing support, and matching these up with the particular circumstances of applicants. It is a process that will naturally give rise to challenges. The key yardsticks for measuring the discharge of these functions are the terms 'adequate accommodation', and provision for 'essential living needs', and the relevance of the HRA is likely to be in bringing to bear the Convention rights as an aid to interpretation of what these terms mean, and whether a public authority has discharged its obligations in a particular case. Thus, the mostly likely context is judicial review of:

– a decision to refuse assistance because an applicant is judged to have adequate accommodation or support already, or to have left without reasonable excuse accommodation judged to be adequate;[52] or

---

52 An appeal to the ASA may be appropriate in NASS cases before judicial review is considered because in general, judicial review is only available where other statutory remedies have been exhausted. Where this category of decision is made by a local authority, there is no statutory appeal, and judicial review is likely to be appropriate immediately (see paras 8.93–8.100 below).

- a decision that a particular offer of accommodation discharges the authority's obligation to provide adequate accommodation; or
- a decision that adequate accommodation may be provided by dispersal of the applicant; or
- a decision that a particular level of support with essential living needs is appropriate; or
- a decision that a particular case does not fall within the ambit of 'exceptional circumstances'.

8.49   It has been established that article 8 might place positive obligations on the state to adopt particular measures to ensure respect for private life.[53] However, Convention rights do not extend to a requirement that states have legislation ensuring that a person has a home,[54] nor to a positive obligation to provide alternative accommodation of an applicant's own choosing.[55]

8.50   However, it may be argued that interference with the right to respect for private life might arise in a case where a public authority required a person to live in an area in which they had chosen not to live. This might apply in cases where a person is dispersed by NASS pursuant to IAA 1999 s97(1) (see paras 4.17–4.40) and Interim Regs reg 9 (see paras 5.61–5.86). It might also apply to cases where an applicant under HA 1996 Part VII is accommodated outside the area of the authority, or referred to another authority under the local connection provisions (see paras 6.66–6.76). The operation of Interim Regs reg 7(1)(c), requiring local authorities to refuse applications for support where an applicant has in the previous 12 months applied to another authority for assistance under NAA 1948 s21 or CA 1989 s17, may also give rise to such a challenge (see paras 5.96–5.97).

8.51   Where a public authority has promised re-housing but failed to provide it, the Convention right to respect for home may be infringed. The court found so at first instance in *R v Newham LBC ex p Al-Nashed and Bibi*,[56] a case where the local authority had promised the applicants that they would be provided with a secure home after a period in temporary accommodation, but where the applicants remained in the temporary accommodation some years later.

---

53   *Botta v Italy* (153/1996/772/973) 24 February 1998.
54   *X v FRG* (159/56) (1956) 1YB 202; *Burton v UK* (1996) 22 EHRR CD 135; *Velosa Barretto v Portugal*, 26 October 1995, ECtHR, unreported.
55   *Burton v UK* (1996) 22 EHRR CD 135; *Buckley v UK* (1997) 23 EHRR 101.
56   28 July 2000, QBD, unreported.

Adequacy of accommodation

8.52 There is little guidance as to the interpretation of the term 'adequate', defining the standard of accommodation applicable to asylum-seekers under the asylum support and interim support schemes (see paras 4.17–4.25 and 5.61–5.76). Adverse effects of inadequate accommodation upon occupiers may amount to an interference with respect to private or family life, or, in an extreme case, to inhuman and degrading treatment contrary to article 3;[57] examples are:

- accommodation that is so small that the sharing of rooms interferes with the welfare and development of children;
- accommodation to which occupiers have great difficulty in gaining access or in using because of age or infirmity;
- accommodation where disrepair or conditions prejudicial to health prevent the occupiers pursuing a normal way of life, or interfere with family relations or development;
- accommodation where one family or household has to share with another;
- accommodation where conditions and rules are imposed that are oppressive.

8.53 Most such accommodation will not be provided directly by public authorities, but rather by providers pursuant to contracts with public authorities. However, this should not prove an obstacle to an action being brought or defence being mounted on the basis of Convention rights. It is arguable that the public authority bears responsibility for the conditions in accommodation provided under such contracts, and for the actions of those managing such accommodation.[58]

8.54 The absence of facilities and the imposition of strict rules in accommodation may give rise to inhuman or degrading treatment so as to infringe article 3, in particular since the rules are backed by withdrawal of support for those who breach conditions under which accommodation is provided. In such cases, assistance may be derived from cases concerning conditions for prisoners.[59] It is arguable that in relation to conditions, a lower threshold of inhuman and degrading

---

57 See, eg, case ASA 00/11/006 described at para 3.158.
58 *Cyprus v Turkey* [1982] 4 EHRR 482, and *Ireland v UK* (1979–80) 2 EHRR 25 in the context of article 3; *Donoghue v Poplar HARCA Ltd and Secretary of State for the Environment*, June 2001 *Legal Action* 23.
59 Eg, *Cyprus v Turkey* [1982] 4 EHRR 482; *Greek Case* (1969) 12 Yearbook 1.

treatment should apply to those required to live in particular accommodation without being lawfully detained, and that harsh conditions and regimes are inappropriate.

Dispersal and location of accommodation

8.55   Decisions to disperse applicants to accommodation outside London and the south-east under the asylum support and interim support schemes (see paras 4.26–4.40 and 5.74–5.86) and decisions to refer homeless applicants to another authority or house in another authority's area (see paras 6.66–6.76) may constitute an interference with Convention rights. There may be an interference with the right to respect for family and private life and the home (article 8) in cases where a dispersal or referral decision results in:

– the loss of an applicant's existing home;[60]
– the loss of family contact, support or care;[61]
– removal of a person from access to medical treatment unavailable in the target area;[62]
– removal of a person from essential social support or services not available in the target area;
– removal of children from educational services in circumstances where their welfare or development would be prejudiced, or from specialist educational services not available in the target area.

8.56   It is to be noted in this context that the right to respect for private life includes respect for a person's moral and physical integrity,[63] which will be relevant where dispersal decisions mean loss of medical treatment or care, or loss of other sources of support which have an adverse impact on the person's health or welfare.

8.57   A dispersal decision which deprives a person of proper medical

---

60 *R (on the application of Johns and McLellan) v Bracknell Forest DC* (2001) *Daily Telegraph* 13 February, QBD (Admin Ct).
61 Eg, in ASA 00/11/0095, the ASA found that a decision to disperse an elderly disabled Polish couple away from their son and other family members breached article 8: the ASA found dispersal to be founded on a legitimate aim, but the particular decision to be neither necessary nor proportionate.
62 The ECtHR has found a breach of Convention rights in cases where deportation has resulted in loss of medical treatment unavailable in the target country (*D v UK* (1997) 24 EHRR 423).
63 *X and Y v Netherlands* (1985) 8 EHRR 235.
64 This proposition was expressly not excluded as a possibility in *Tanko v Finland* (23634/94) unreported.

care[64] or results in the withdrawal of treatment[65] may, in serious cases, amount to inhuman or degrading treatment contrary to article 3. By analogy with prisoner cases,[66] there may be a positive duty to ensure adequate medical treatment for those required to live in particular accommodation or in a particular location.

8.58   Asylum-seekers subject to dispersal decisions after a period of living in the UK (commonly those whose entitlement to benefits has ended following an adverse decision) may have acquired possessions and be unable to take them with them to the offered accommodation. This may constitute an infringement of Convention rights under protocol 1, article 1, the right to peaceful enjoyment of possessions. The HRA may be used to support a challenge to the dispersal decision, or to an argument that the provision of assistance should include the transporting of the applicant's possessions to the new location.

8.59   Dispersal decisions may result in the removal of an asylum-seeker from an area where s/he can practice his/her religion to one in which s/he cannot. Such a decision may engage article 9, which protects, among other things, the individual's freedom to worship or practice or teach religion in community with others. Home Office guidance[67] accepts that where an asylum-seeker can only practice his/her religion in a certain area then consideration should be given to allocating accommodation in that area.

8.60   There may be an interference with a person's right to fair determination of civil rights and obligations under article 6(1) if a decision to disperse or refer an applicant results in loss of access to competent immigration advice and to interpreters. In many of the target areas for dispersal, specialist immigration advisers are few or oversubscribed, and interpreting services unavailable (see para 4.35). For the application of article 6(1) generally, see below at paras 8.80–8.92. It should be noted that decisions about immigration and nationality have not hitherto been considered to fall within the scope of civil rights and obligations.[68]

Types and levels of provision for essential living needs

8.61   It has been seen that levels and types of support are to an extent prescribed by regulation, and to an extent left to the discretion of

---

64   *D v UK* (1997) 24 EHRR 423.
65   *Hurtado v Switzerland* (A/280-A) (1994) unreported.
67   NASS Policy Bulletin 30, para 8.31.
68   See in particular *P v UK* (1987) 54 DR 211 in relation to asylum-seekers.

NASS and local authorities. Under asylum support, AS Regs reg 10 sets out maximum levels of support calculated at 70 per cent of income support rates, but these are guideline rates only and support may be provided in a particular case at levels above or below this (see paras 4.52–4.57). 'Essential living needs' are to be met, but regulations prohibit allowance for excluded items (see para 4.58). Support must not be provided wholly or mainly in cash except in exceptional circumstances (see paras 4.59–4.63). Under the Interim Regs, no figures are prescribed even as a guideline.

8.62   The guideline of 70 per cent of income support rates may infringe Convention rights, in particular, the right under article 8 to respect for private or family life, read with the proscription of discrimination under article 14. The justification for the guideline is that a rate lower than income support levels is warranted because the period during which support is provided will be temporary and accommodation provided will include furniture, equipment, and outgoings including fuel charges (see para 4.52). It may be that the level of support provided to asylum-seekers will be lower than that available to people in similar circumstances receiving income support and housing benefit. There may also be cases where the guideline figures are provided notwithstanding that in fact a person remains in accommodation for a long period, or the accommodation does not include furniture equipment and services. In such cases it is arguable that articles 8 and 14 are breached.

8.63   It may similarly be argued that articles 8 and 14 are breached in cases where the package of support services provided to asylum-seekers is less than that which is or would be available to destitute people entitled to assistance under NAA 1948 s21 or CA 1989 s17.

8.64   Given the expressed rationale for the guideline rates, decisions by NASS or local authorities to provide support at *lower* rates may engage article 8 and breach article 14.

8.65   The requirement that support be wholly or mainly in kind rather than in cash has been implemented through a voucher system. Such a system may engage article 8 and breach the Convention right by amounting to discrimination contrary to article 14. A scheme which provides vouchers for asylum-seekers compared with cash for benefit claimants may be discriminatory, and result in active discrimination experienced by asylum-seekers in using vouchers. The problems and inequities inherent in the voucher scheme are described elsewhere (see paras 4.59–4.63). Convention rights might be engaged if it could be shown in a particular case that the voucher scheme either affected supported persons adversely, or was prejudicial to the effective delivery of support.

8.66   In these and similar cases, Convention rights are likely to arise as an aid to interpretation of the responsibilities of public authorities in Asylum Support Adjudicator or judicial review proceedings challenging particular support provision decisions.

Decisions resulting in destitution

8.67   The withdrawal of asylum support will in certain cases leave a person destitute and without recourse to any means of support. This will occur in cases where *either*:

- an adverse decision is made on the asylum application and either no appeal made, or all appeal rights (not including judicial review) have been exhausted; *or*
- a person has been refused support as a result of 'intentional destitution' or support has been suspended or discontinued; *and*
- the person's household does not include a dependent child under 18 years of age;[69] *and*
- the person has a need for care and attention which arises *solely* from destitution or the physical effects or anticipated physical effects of destitution; *and*
- the person is not supported under the 'hard cases' provisions (see paras 3.169–3.173).

8.68   Such cases may give rise to a challenge under articles 2, 3 or 8 of the Convention. The route to a challenge may be by judicial review of a decision to refuse assistance under the hard cases provisions, on the grounds that:

- the criteria adopted by the Home Secretary pursuant to IAA 1999 s4 for eligibility for hard cases support[70] are incompatible with the Convention articles; and/or

---

69 While such people supported under NASS or the Interim Regs may lose that support through, eg, intentional destitution, they should not be destitute as a result since they would qualify for assistance under CA 1989 s17. However, this was not acknowledged by government spokesmen in the course of the passage of IAA 1999 through parliament, and it was suggested that children might be taken into care in such cases. This would however be contrary to s17 – see, eg, *R v Barnet LBC ex p Guleed* (2001) 4 CCLR 33.

70 Contained in the Home Office letter of 3 April 2000.

- the forms of support prescribed by the Home Secretary (described in the same letter) are incompatible with the Convention articles; and/or
- the application of the criteria or the form of provision made in a particular case breaches the articles.

8.69   Alternatively, challenge may be by way of judicial review of a decision to refuse, suspend or discontinue support under AS Regs reg 20 or Interim Regs regs 7 and 8, on the basis that the exercise of discretion to refuse, suspend or discontinue must be exercised compatibly with Convention rights. In the case of the Interim Regs, local authorities are told they *must* discontinue support to the 'intentionally destitute'. Any challenge would therefore be to the compatibility of the regulations themselves with the Convention (see paras 5.91–5.95).

8.70   There are difficulties with arguments that such cases fall within the scope of article 3, the prohibition on torture, inhuman or degrading treatment or punishment. There is authority for the proposition that, in exceptional cases, article 3 can impose an obligation on states to take steps or refrain from taking steps so as to avoid extreme hardship causing illness.[71] It has been accepted that the development of particular practices by public authorities can amount to a breach of article 3,[72] but maybe only where the consequent treatment is intentional.[73] Treatment in any case would have to exceed a minimum threshold of severity. Because article 3 is an absolute right, it may be expected that the courts will be reluctant to extend the categories of case already recognised as falling within it, particularly if the facts of a case can more appropriately be considered under another Convention right.

8.71   Safeguarding physical integrity has been accepted by the courts as an element in the right to respect for private life under article 8. There is no minimum threshold of severity such as required under article 3. The protection of physical integrity under article 8 is subject to the balancing of the rights of the individual with public interests, and indeed it may be this factor which has led to an apparent greater

71 *D v UK* (1997) 24 EHRR 423; *Keenan v UK* (2001) *Times* 18 April.
72 *East African Asians v UK* (1981) 3 EHRR 76 (refusal of UK residence to East African UK passport holders).
73 *Adbulaziz, Cabales and Balkandali v UK* (1985) 7 EHRR 471.
74 *Costello-Roberts v UK* (1993) 19 EHRR 112; *A v UK* (25599/94) 18 September 1997.

willingness by the ECtHR to lay down markers. The court has interpreted this aspect of article 8 to include a positive obligation on states to protect children from excessive corporal punishment[74] or from sexual abuse.[75]

8.72   The ECtHR has rejected attempts to extend Convention rights to include a right to be provided with accommodation.[76] However, there may be room for development in particular cases. In 1999, the court speculated that a refusal by public authorities to provide assistance with accommodation to a person suffering from a severe disease so as to enable him to be discharged from hospital might in certain circumstances infringe the right to respect for private life under article 8.[77] A challenge to the compatibility with Convention rights of the provisions excluding from assistance under NAA 1948 s21 those asylum-seekers whose rights to assistance under asylum support provisions have ended may have a prospect of success given the attitude of the Court of Appeal in *O v Wandsworth LBC*.[78] Permission was granted by the Court of Appeal in such a case raising articles 3 and 8.[79]

Summary recovery of possession of asylum support accommodation

8.73   Tenancies or licences provided under IAA 1999 Part VI are deprived of statutory protection against summary eviction. They are neither secure nor assured (see para 6.148), and are excluded from the procedures required to recover possession under the Protection from Eviction Act 1977 (see paras 3.134–3.139). Tenure of such accommodation may be ended by a notice to quit of at least seven days, or less where a shorter period is justified.[80] The provisions may infringe article 8, the right to respect of family and private life and the home, and protocol 1, article 1, the right to peaceful enjoyment of possessions.[81] The right under article 6(1) to a fair hearing before an impartial tribunal may also be infringed. In the context of any of

75 *Stubbings v UK* (1996) 23 EHRR 213.
76 *X v FRG* (159/56) (1956) 1YB 202; *Burton v UK* (1996) 22 EHRR CD 135; *Buckley v UK* (1997) 23 EHRR 101; *Velosa Barretto v Portugal*, 26 October 1995, ECtHR, unreported; *Chapman and Others v UK* (2001) *Times* 30 January.
77 *Marzari v Italy* [1999] 28 EHRR CD 175.
78 [2000] 4 All ER 590.
79 *R v Islington LBC ex p Fetiti* C/00/2748, 19 October 2000, CA, unreported.
80 IAA 1999 Sch 8 para 9 and AS Regs reg 22.
81 See, eg, *R (on the application of Johns and McLellan) v Bracknell Forest DC* (2001) *Daily Telegraph* 13 February, QBD (Admin Ct).

these articles, there may also be a breach of article 14, since the legislation deprives people of rights they would otherwise enjoy by reason of their membership of a group – asylum-seekers. The ECtHR has found that rules about protection from eviction may not be discriminatory.[82]

8.74   Eviction may breach article 8(1) by interference with family or private life, or the home. 'The home' seems most obviously relevant, but there may be no such interference where the right to occupy has been legally ended,[83] eg, by a notice to quit. In deciding whether the regime for summary possession against asylum-seekers breaches article 8, a court would have to consider whether first the statutory framework and second the particular decision to evict was legitimate, necessary in a democratic society and proportionate. It is at least strongly arguable that precipitate evictions of asylum-seekers are not necessary for any of the reasons stated in article 8(2). In an appropriate case an action might be brought for an injunction to stay an eviction. The authorities referred to at para 3.138 would be relevant. Where a supplier of asylum support accommodation has evicted asylum-seekers arbitrarily, taking advantage of the removal of statutory protection from eviction, the public authority contracting for and arranging the accommodation (NASS or the local authority) is likely to be fixed with responsibility for the infringement of Convention rights.[84]

8.75   In relation to protocol 1, article 1, arguments about deprivation and peaceful enjoyment of possessions are likely to weigh on both sides – both the tenant's right to unhampered occupation and the landlord's right to recover property. The ECtHR has accorded a wide margin of appreciation to states to balance these factors in the general interest.[85] It has also said that individuals are entitled to expect a coherent system to achieve that balance and 'a clear practical and effective opportunity to challenge an administrative act that was a direct interference with [any] right of property'.[86]

8.76   In relation to article 6(1), it is arguable that the termination of rights of occupation of accommodation is a determination of civil rights and obligations, entitling people to have the issue dealt with by

---

82   *Larkos v Cyprus* [1998] EHRLR 653.
83   *S v UK* (1986) 47 DR 274.
84   *Young, James and Webster v UK* (1982) 4 EHRR 38.
85   *Spadea and Scalabino v Italy* (1996) 21 EHRR 482.
86   *De La Pradelle v France* (A/253-B) 1992, unreported.

an independent tribunal. However, since, in most cases there would be no defence to the claim to possession, the termination would not be decisive for rights and obligations, and as this means there is no issue to be tried, article 6(1) would not be engaged.[87] In such a case, a public authority will be expected to meet a high standard of procedural fairness in applying the law. A court would look closely at whether an interference breaching article 8(1) was in accordance with the law as required by article 8(2).[88]

Ancillary powers

8.77 The IAA 1999 gives a series of powers to the Home Secretary intended to assist in combating fraud and criminal activity. These include:

- a power to disclose information about asylum-seekers, and for others to disclose information to the Home Secretary (ss20, 21 – see para 4.96);
- a power to enter premises under a warrant (s125 – see paras 4.97–4.98);
- a power to obtain information from property owners and the postal services (ss126, 127 – see paras 4.99–4.100);

8.78 The exercise of these powers is likely to engage or infringe article 8, the right to respect for private life. By their application to asylum-seekers where they do not apply to other groups of people, they may infringe article 14, the proscription of discrimination. The application of article 8 to these powers will require consideration of whether their exercise is legitimate, necessary in a democratic society and proportionate (see paras 8.21–8.27 above). These criteria should be applied both to the scope of the powers as drafted in the Act, and to the particular facts of each case. The court will require that the Act contains sufficient safeguards to ensure that the powers are not exercised too broadly.[89] Thus, for example, it may be argued that the lack of any limit on the use to which information obtained under IAA 1999 s127 (information from postal services) may be put means that it exceeds what is necessary and proportionate to achieve the purpose of the section. In dealing with the particular case, the key issue will be

---

87 *Ringeisen v Austria* (1979–80) 1 EHRR 455.
88 *Buckley v UK* (1996) 23 EHRR 101.
89 *Funke v France* (1993) 16 EHRR 297.

whether the public authority in taking the particular action under these powers has properly assessed the risk of crime occurring and limited the action to that which is necessary to combat that risk.[90] Thus, warrants issued under IAA 1999 s125 may be drawn too widely, or inquiries addressed to property owners under s126 may go beyond what is required to achieve the legitimate purpose. The exchange of information under IAA 1999 ss20 and 21 which infringes article 8(1) will need to be justified under one of the reasons in article 8(2). In a case where the interference is serious in its implications for the individual, the court is likely to consider the passing of information justified only where there is a 'pressing need' to do so.[91]

8.79   Additionally, the power to enter under warrant (IAA 1999 s125) may infringe protocol 1, article 1, the right to peaceful enjoyment of possessions, and article 6(1), the right to determination of civil rights and obligations in a public hearing. In relation to protocol 1, article 1, occupation of accommodation under a tenancy licence or contract constitutes a property right falling within the scope of the article.[92] The decision to apply for or grant or execute a warrant may infringe the Convention right if it does not strike a correct balance between the rights of the individual and the general interests of the community.[93]

Procedural fairness and article 6

8.80   Article 6(1) of the Convention, so far as civil proceedings are concerned, provides a right to a fair and public hearing within a reasonable time by an independent and impartial tribunal established by law. The right to a hearing in public is qualified in specified circumstances. More significantly for our purposes, the right is confined to the determination of a person's 'civil rights and obligations'.

8.81   The phrase 'civil rights and obligations' includes all litigation between private individuals, but only some disputes between individuals and public bodies. It includes those disputes between individuals and public bodies that are *decisive* of *private* rights and obligations. It embraces only those rights which already exist or are recognised in domestic law. In a case where one party is the state

90 *Niemietz v Germany* (1993) 16 EHRR 97; *McLeod v UK* [1999] EHRLR 125.
91 *R v A Local Authority in the Midlands ex p LM* [2000] 1 FLR 612, QBD.
92 *DP v UK* (1986) 51 DR 195; *Association of General Practitioners v Denmark* (1989) 62 DR 226.
93 *Sporrong and Lonnroth v Sweden* (1983) 5 EHRR 35.

and the other is an individual, the court will examine the context and weigh up the public and private aspects. In this book we are concerned with the provision of welfare support by the state, be it by way of asylum support, benefits, housing or community care services. Perhaps the best indicator of the approach taken by the ECtHR to 'civil rights and obligations' in this context is the court's classification of social security benefits. The position initially adopted by the court was that determination of entitlement to state benefits was within the scope of article 6(1) where benefit entitlement bore upon the individual's means of subsistence and was determined by reference a private right, such as a contract of employment.[94] Subsequently, the court extended its position and decided that a non-contributory means-tested welfare benefit deriving solely from statute was within the scope of article 6(1).[95] The position is different where a scheme of welfare payments which is discretionary or ex gratia is concerned. Determinations under such schemes do not fall within the scope of article 6(1).[96]

8.82   The rights and remedies in relation to asylum support, benefits, housing and community care services raise a series of issues about procedural fairness, which are now considered in turn. Whether or not such issues fall within the determination of 'civil rights and obligations' will be considered in each case.

Lack of independent and impartial decision-making

8.83   Adjudication and review procedures established in relation to the provision considered in this book include several examples where independence and impartiality are questionable.

Asylum support adjudication

8.84   IAA 1999 s102, establishes a system of Asylum Support Adjudicators (ASAs) to hear appeals against decisions of the Home Secretary that a person does not qualify for asylum support. Adjudicators are appointed by the Home Secretary.[97] If the appeal is refused, there is no further right of appeal, although judicial review proceedings will be available. There are three points to consider.

---

94 *Feldbrugge v Netherlands* (1986) 8 EHRR 425, a case concerning sickness benefit.
95 *Salesi v Italy* (1998) 26 EHRR 187; see also *Gustafson v Sweden* (1998) 25 EHRR 623.
96 *Machatova v Slovak Republic* [1997] 24 EHRR CD 44.
97 IAA 1999 Sch 10 para 1.

– *Does the determination by the ASA constitute a determination of a civil right or obligation?* There is as yet no authority to establish whether or not decisions about qualification for asylum support fall within the scope of 'civil rights and obligations'. As described above, the issue is whether or not the determination is decisive of private law rights. Applying the analogy with benefits outlined at para 8.81 above to asylum support determinations, it is to be noted that asylum support under IAA 1999 Part VI is discretionary, except in cases involving dependent children, where it is mandatory.[98] It may be argued that the extensive detailed provisions of the scheme under Part VI, including as they do specific qualifying criteria, mean that Part VI has more of the character of a mandatory scheme than a discretionary one, and should fall within article 6(1).[99] The Home Office is of the view that asylum support under Part VI does not engage article 6(1) because it considers support does not fall within 'civil rights and obligations'.[100] The Chief ASA has reserved her position on when asylum support provision decisions determine 'civil rights and obligations', but has accepted that article 6 and the other Convention rights constitute a set of 'minimum standards' that should be applied to asylum support decision-making.[101]

– *Is the ASA impartial and independent?* The ASA carries out a quasi-judicial function and makes decisions authorised by statute.[102] However, the fact that s/he is appointed by the Home Secretary, and is required to conduct proceedings according to rules made by the Home Secretary, will mean that the requirement for impartiality and independence is not satisfied.[103]

– *Is the defect cured by the availability of judicial review?* Where, as in the case of asylum support, a determination is made by an administrative tribunal which is not independent or impartial, the ECtHR will accept that article 6(1) is complied with if there is a right of appeal or review to a court or tribunal which does meet the

---

98 Ibid, ss95(1), 122(3),(4).

99 *Gustafson v Sweden* (1998) 25 EHRR 623, a case involving a criminal injuries compensation scheme where qualifying conditions were clearly defined by statute.

100 NASS Policy Bulletin 30, para 8.6.

101 ASA 00/09/0063.

102 IAA 1999 s103(3).

103 *Bryan v UK* (1996) 21 EHRR 342; *Chapman v UK* (2001) *Times* 30 January; *Scanfuture v Secretary of State for Trade* (2001) *Times* 26 April.

requirements of independence and impartiality.[104] Judicial review
is confined to issues of law. It may be used to challenge a decision
if it was perverse, irrational, if it had no basis on the evidence, or if
it had been made without regard to relevant factors or with regard
to irrelevant factors. Judicial review cannot be used to re-examine
issues of fact. If there were no issue of law, judicial review would
not be available. If there were an issue of law, then unless the
scope of judicial review was sufficient to cover all matters challenged in the ASA's decision, its availability might not serve to
cure the ASA's failure to comply with article 6(1).[105] Thus, the
defect may not be cured in cases where the result of a successful
judicial review must be to remit the case for reconsideration
by the ASA (rather than for the court to substitute its own
decision).[106]

Review of homelessness decisions

8.85   HA 1996 s202, provides for review of certain homelessness decisions
by 'a person of appropriate seniority' not involved in the original
decision. Regulations specify that it is the authority's responsibility to
carry out the review.[107] A judge has suggested that authorities should
consider appointing an independent and impartial official to conduct
reviews[108] but it remains to be seen whether this advice is followed.
There is no entitlement to an oral hearing. If the decision is upheld
on review, there is a right of appeal on a point of law to the county
court. There are again three questions to consider:

– *Does a decision on a homelessness application constitute a determination of a civil right or obligation?* Applying the principles and
  case-law referred to at para 8.84 above, it may be that the answer
  to this question is 'yes'. The subject matter of reviews under
  s202 on its face comprises statutory duties, and not a discretionary
  scheme. The provision of accommodation to categories of person

104 *Albert and Le Compte v Belgium* (1983) 5 EHRR 533.
105 *Bryan v UK* (1996) 21 EHRR 342.
106 *Kingsley v UK* (35605/97) (2001) *Times* 9 January; *Chapman v UK* (27238/95)
    (2001) *Times* 30 January; however, where decisions are made on policy grounds,
    judicial review may be sufficient to cure the defect – see *R v Secretary of State for
    the Environment Transport and the Regions ex p Holding and Barnes plc* (2001)
    Times 10 May.
107 Allocation of Housing and Homelessness (Review Procedures) Regulations 1999
    SI No 71.
108 *Adan v Newham LBC*, December 2000 *Legal Action* 29 per HHJ Laurie.

according to need may be considered to be akin to a scheme of means-tested welfare benefits. There is no authority on the point.[109]

- *Is the review officer impartial and independent?* In practice most reviews are undertaken by another (and more senior) officer of the department which took the original decision. Such a review would breach article 6(1).

- *Would the defect be cured by an appeal to the county court?* The jurisdiction of the county court in homelessness appeals is analogous to judicial review, and the points made in para 8.84 above apply.

Review of housing allocation decisions

8.86   Decisions by local authorities to exclude or remove a person from the housing register are subject to review by the authority.[110] The procedure is governed by regulations[111] which specifically give the local authority responsibility for conducting the review. There is no right to an oral hearing and no statutory appeal. Again there are three questions to consider:

- *Does a decision on a housing register application constitute a determination of a civil right or obligation?* Again, applying the principles and case-law referred to at para 8.84 above, it may be that the answer to this question is 'yes'. The admission or otherwise of 'qualifying persons' to the housing register is, at least in part, the discharge of a statutory duty[112] rather than a discretionary scheme. The allocation of social housing to categories of person according to need may be considered to be akin to a scheme of means-tested welfare benefits. Again, there is no authority on the point.

- *Is the review officer impartial and independent?* In practice most reviews are undertaken within the housing department. Such a review would breach article 6(1).

- *Would the defect be cured by judicial review proceedings?* The points made above at para 8.84 in relation to judicial review apply. The availability of judicial review would only cure the defect if the

---

109 At county court level it has been accepted that a local authority review was determinative of an applicant's civil rights – see *Melim v Westminster City Council*, February 2001 *Legal Action* 29.

110 HA 1996 s164.

111 Allocation of Housing and Homelessness (Review Procedures) Regulations 1999 SI No 71.

112 HA 1996 s163(1).

issues arising from the local authority's decision were confined to issues of law falling within the scope of judicial review.

Access to justice

8.87 Several features of the provision for asylum-seekers have an impact on access to justice.

Dispersal and travel costs

8.88 There are concerns that the dispersal of asylum-seekers will deprive them of access to competent lawyers. Where an asylum-seeker has a lawyer, dispersal may place him/her at such a distance that s/he cannot effectively continue to give instructions and receive advice and representation. Where an asylum-seeker does not have a lawyer, dispersal may place him/her in a part of the country where expertise among lawyers about asylum cases is sparse and numbers of competent lawyers inadequate to meet demand. The Legal Help scheme may cover reasonable costs of travel to a solicitor (see para 3.67). If payment of such costs is not available to an asylum-seeker, article 6(1) may be infringed. Article 6(1) is only engaged where there is a 'determination' of a Convention right. In this case, a determination may be a refusal (relying on AS Regs reg 9) to meet the cost of such travel as part of an assessment of essential living needs.

8.89 Access to justice issues have also been raised by the creation in the ASA of a system of adjudication by appeal hearing in circumstances where appellants have no means to pay for the cost of travel to the hearing venue. A decision reached where the appellant has been unable to attend for this reason may infringe the right to a fair hearing under article 6(1), and the ASA has adjourned or re-heard appeals in such cases.

Time limits

8.90 An appeal against a refusal or termination of asylum support to the ASA[113] (see paras 3.140–3.164) must be brought no later than two days after the applicant received the adverse decision. The ASA has a discretion to extend the time limit where it is in the interests of justice to do so.[114] There will be many cases where remoteness from sources of advice, lack of English or lack of literacy, or lack of money will prevent

113 Under IAA 1999 s102.
114 See, eg, para 3.153.

appellants meeting the time limit. The time limit arguably infringes the Convention right to a fair hearing, and the ASA should have regard to such infringement in exercising his/her discretion. If a late appeal is not accepted, judicial review may include reliance upon breach of article 6(1).

'Equality of arms'

8.91   The right to a fair and public hearing within a reasonable time under article 6(1) includes a right for a person to present his/her case and evidence 'under conditions that do not place him at a substantial disadvantage vis-à-vis his opponent',[115] though this does not necessarily mean a right to representation if the opponent is legally represented (see para 8.92 below). There is a presumption in favour of full disclosure of documents relevant to the case.[116] A party must be given an opportunity to comment on documentary evidence[117] and cross examine witnesses. These rights will be relevant to the conduct of hearings before the ASA (see paras 3.151–3.157).

Absence of public funding for legal representation.

8.92   The Legal Help scheme is available to provide advice and assistance free of charge in respect of all legal issues arising relating to provision for asylum-seekers described in this book. Asylum-seekers will rarely be outside the scope of the means test governing entitlement under the scheme. Public Funding is available for proceedings in the courts arising out of these legal issues, subject to a means and merits test. Neither Legal Help nor Public Funding is available to pay the cost of legal representation at hearings of the social security and housing benefit appeal tribunals, before ASAs, under HA review procedures, or (subject to exceptions) before the social security commissioners. All these hearings will concern determinations of Convention rights, and so the right to a fair hearing under article 6(1) may be engaged. The ECtHR has accepted that an absence of legal aid may lead to an infringement of article 6(1). The court will need to consider whether the applicant would be able to present his/her case properly and satisfactorily without a lawyer.[118] The ECtHR considers that legal aid will only be required to secure effective

115 *Dombo-Beheer BV v Netherlands* (1994) 18 EHRR 213.
116 *McMichael v UK* (1995) 20 EHRR 205.
117 *Feldbrugge v Netherlands* (1986) 8 EHRR 425.
118 *Airey v Ireland* (1979–80) 2 EHRR 305.

access to the court where the assistance of a lawyer is 'indispensable' because of the complexity of the procedure or of the case, or where representation is prescribed in domestic law.[119] Where a particular tribunal or hearing has been devised with procedures intended to be used by the appellant without representation, the requirements of article 6(1) may be met.

Proceedings and remedies

Proceedings

8.93   A decision or action (or inaction) on the part of a public authority giving rise to a breach of the Convention should first be met by an assertion of the Convention right and a request for remedial action. It should be recalled that it is unlawful for a public authority to act in a way which is incompatible with a Convention right, unless it is required to do so by primary legislation.[120] The assertion of Convention rights is thus not confined to litigation, and may form the basis of a range of alternative forms of recourse, such as requests for review, complaints to ombudsmen and the local authority's monitoring officer, complaints under the social services complaints procedure, applications to arbitration schemes, and so forth.

8.94   A breach of the Convention may, by itself, be a basis for litigation.[121] The appropriate proceedings are likely to be a judicial review of the act (or inaction) constituting the breach. Judicial review is generally available where other remedies have been exhausted or are not appropriate. Judicial review proceedings may only be brought by a 'victim' of the act.[122] The time limit for commencing proceedings is one year from the date of the act complained of; the court may extend the time limit in exceptional circumstances, and a shorter time limit may apply if specified in relation to the procedure in question.[123]

8.95   A breach of the Convention may also form part of another kind of claim or part of a defence to a claim, and indeed may be relied upon in any proceedings.

8.96   Thus, considering examples that may arise in relation to issues covered by this book, it would be possible to raise a breach of the Convention:

119 Ibid.
120 HRA 1998 s6(1).
121 Ibid, s7(1)(a).
122 Ibid, s7(4).
123 Ibid, s7(5).

- in judicial review proceedings challenging decisions of public authorities under the IAA 1999 and its subordinate legislation, the Social Security Acts, the HA 1996 and community care legislation;
- in appeals to the ASA;
- in appeals to social security appeal tribunals or the social security commissioners;
- in HA appeals in the county court;
- in defending possession proceedings.

8.97   In considering both claims and defences, it is important to recall that a remedy in the courts will only be available to the extent that the action of a public authority is found to be unlawful. As noted above, under HRA 1998 s6(2), an act will not be unlawful if it results from primary legislation, and either the authority could not have acted differently, or the primary legislation could not be read to be compatible with a Convention right. Although the higher courts have the power to make declarations of incompatibility in relation to primary legislation, such a declaration will not be a remedy in the particular case. Thus, for example, a decision by NASS to refuse to accept a member of an unmarried couple as a dependant of an asylum-seeker would be based on regulations[124] made under IAA 1999 s94. If such a decision were challenged by way of judicial review, the High Court would be charged with interpreting the regulations so as to be compatible with the Convention and, if that were not possible, would be able to strike down the regulations. By contrast a decision by a local authority to refuse assistance under NAA 1948 s21 to a person subject to immigration control whose needs arose solely from destitution would be based on primary legislation.[125] The High Court could seek to interpret the exclusion so as to be compatible with the Convention. If that was not possible, the court could not overrule the decision, which would remain a lawful decision. The limit of the court's power would be to make a declaration of incompatibility under HRA 1998 s4.

8.98   Prior to incorporation of the Convention by the HRA 1998, alleged breaches could only be adjudicated in the ECtHR in Strasbourg. Now the such cases can be brought in the UK courts, but proceedings in the ECtHR will still be appropriate where:

---

124 AS Regs reg 2(4) and (5).
125 The amendment of NAA 1948 s21 made by IAA 1999 s116, adding s21(1A) and (1B).

- no effective remedy for an alleged breach of a Convention right is provided in domestic law;
- statutory or common law in the UK is incompatible with the Convention, particularly where there has been a declaration of incompatibility by the UK courts, but the government has failed to legislate to rectify the defect.

The procedure is lengthy and beset by delays, which may make it of marginal use to asylum-seekers.

Remedies

8.99 Where a court finds a breach of the Convention, it may grant such relief or remedy or make such order within its powers as it considers just and appropriate.[126] Article 13 of the Convention guarantees an effective remedy. That article is not incorporated by the HRA 1998, but the government in passing the bill committed itself to ensuring that remedies and relief should be effective.[127]

8.100 Where the particular court has the relevant powers, this will include the payment of damages, but only where such an award is in the view of the court necessary, having regard to other relief available and the consequences for the aggrieved person.[128] Damages under the HRA 1998 must take account of the principles on which damages are awarded by the ECtHR. Damages are available, as in domestic law, for actual financial loss, for non-pecuniary losses, and for costs and expenses. Under non-pecuniary losses, the ECtHR has awarded damages for pain, anxiety, distress, feelings of injustice and humiliation. Most HRA litigation will take the form of judicial review proceedings. A claim for judicial review may include a claim for damages, but may not seek damages alone.[129] Damages may be awarded in judicial review proceedings if the court is satisfied that, if the claimant had begun an ordinary action for damages at the same time as the judicial review proceedings, damages would have been awarded in those proceedings.[130] Since the HRA creates a free-standing right to bring proceedings,[131] this should be no impediment.

---

126 HRA 1998 s8(1).
127 Lord Chancellor, *Hansard*, HL Debates col 479, 18 November 1997.
128 HRA 1998 s8(3).
129 CPR r54.3(2).
130 Supreme Court Act 1981 s31(4).
131 HRA 1998 s7(1).

Other international instruments

8.101   The UK has ratified a number of other international conventions that are relevant to human rights. The provisions of these conventions cannot be relied upon directly in litigation. However, where legislation has been enacted after a relevant convention has been ratified, the courts will endeavour to construe it consistently with the relevant convention.[132]

8.102   The instruments of particular relevance to the issue covered in this book are:

- International Covenant on Economic, Social and Cultural Rights;
- International Covenant on Civil and Political Rights 1966 (particularly articles 1–3, 12 and 14);
- UN Convention on the Rights of the Child 1989 (particularly articles 1–6, 14, 16, 20, 22, 26–31, 39);
- European Social Charter 1961 (particularly articles 1, 12 and 19);
- European Convention on Social and Medical Assistance 1953 (particularly articles 1, 11–14, and 18–19).

132 *R v Home Secretary ex p Brind* [1991] 1 AC 696.

APPENDICES

A   **Extracts from legislation**

B   **Directions and guidance**

Guidance on Interim Provisions (19 November 1999 and 1 December 1999) (Immigration and Nationality Directorate (National Asylum Support Service))

Criteria for Eligibility for Hard Cases Support (17 April 2000) (NASS)

Guidance on Interim Arrangements for Asylum-seeker Support Annex 6 (Accommodation standards) (Local Government Association)

Guidance on Homelessness (Asylum-seekers) (Interim Period) (England) Order 1999 SI No 3126 (22 November 1999) (DETR)

Secretary and State's Approvals and Directions under National Assistance Act 1948 ss21(1) and 29, paras 1 and 4 (LAC(93)10)

C   **International instruments**

European Convention on Social and Medical Assistance articles 1, 11–14, 18, 19, annex extracts and protocol

Council of Europe Social Charter articles 1, 12–19

United Nations Convention on the Rights of the Child 1989

Membership of the European Union and European Economic Area, signatories/ratifications of the Council of Europe Social Charter and the European Convention on Social and Medical Assistance

D   **Home Office forms and decision letters**

Form ASD 35 – NASS letter issued on termination of support

SAL1 – standard acknowledgement letter issued at port

SAL2 – standard acknowledgement letter issued 'in-country'

IS96 – notice of temporary admission

ICD 0725 – letter granting indefinite leave to remain as a refugee

ICD 00716 – letter granting exceptional leave to remain

ICD 0009 – letter granting indefinite leave to remain after exceptional leave to remain

ICD 1029 – letter refusing refugee status without giving reasons ('pre-decision letter')

E   **Extract from *Hansard* debates**

F   **'One-stop' services and reception services**

G   **Main welfare entitlements and support**

H   **Resources**

Extracts from legislation

Immigration and Asylum Act 1999

PART VI: SUPPORT FOR ASYLUM-SEEKERS: INTERPRETATION
Interpretation of Part IV

94 (1) In this Part –

'adjudicator' has the meaning given in section 102(2);

'asylum-seeker' means a person who is not under 18 and has made a claim for asylum which has been recorded by the Secretary of State but which has not been determined;

'claim for asylum' means a claim that it would be contrary to the United Kingdom's obligations under the Refugee Convention, or under Article 3 of the Human Rights Convention, for the claimant to be removed from, or required to leave, the United Kingdom;

'the Department' means the Department of Health and Social Services for Northern Ireland;

'dependant', in relation to an asylum-seeker or a supported person, means a person in the United Kingdom who –

(a) is his spouse;

(b) is a child of his, or of his spouse, who is under 18 and dependent on him; or

(c) falls within such additional category, if any, as may be prescribed;

'the Executive' means the Northern Ireland Housing Executive;

'housing accommodation' includes flats, lodging houses and hostels;

'local authority' means –

(a) in England and Wales, a county council, a county borough council, a district council, a London borough council, the Common Council of the City of London or the Council of the Isles of Scilly;

(b) in Scotland, a council constituted under section 2 of the Local Government etc (Scotland) Act 1994;

'supported person' means –

(a) an asylum-seeker, or

(b) a dependant of an asylum-seeker,

who has applied for support and for whom support is provided under section 95.

(2) References in this Part to support provided under section 95 include references to support which is provided under arrangements made by the Secretary of State under that section.

(3) For the purposes of this Part, a claim for asylum is determined at the end of such period beginning –

(a) on the day on which the Secretary of State notifies the claimant of his decision on the claim, or

(b) if the claimant has appealed against the Secretary of State's decision, on the day on which the appeal is disposed of,

as may be prescribed.

(4) An appeal is disposed of when it is no longer pending for the purposes of the Immigration Acts or the Special Immigration Appeals Commission Act 1997.

(5) If an asylum-seeker's household includes a child who is under 18 and a dependant of his, he is to be treated (for the purposes of this Part) as continuing to be an asylum-seeker while –

(a) the child is under 18; and

(b) he and the child remain in the United Kingdom.

(6) Subsection (5) does not apply if, on or after the determination of his claim for asylum, the asylum-seeker is granted leave to enter or remain in the United Kingdom (whether or not as a result of that claim).

(7) For the purposes of this Part, the Secretary of State may inquire into, and decide, the age of any person.

(8) A notice under subsection (3) must be given in writing.

(9) If such a notice is sent by the Secretary of State by first class post, addressed –

(a) to the asylum-seeker's representative, or

(b) to the asylum-seeker's last known address,

it is to be taken to have been received by the asylum-seeker on the second day after the day on which it was posted.

PROVISION OF SUPPORT
Persons for whom support may be provided

95 (1) The Secretary of State may provide, or arrange for the provision of, support for –

(a) asylum-seekers, or

(b) dependants of asylum-seekers,

who appear to the Secretary of State to be destitute or to be likely to become destitute within such period as may be prescribed.

(2) In prescribed circumstances, a person who would otherwise fall within subsection (1) is excluded.

(3) For the purposes of this section, a person is destitute if –

(a) he does not have adequate accommodation or any means of obtaining it (whether or not his other essential living needs are met); or

(b) he has adequate accommodation or the means of obtaining it, but cannot meet his other essential living needs.

(4) If a person has dependants, subsection (3) is to be read as if the references to him were references to him and his dependants taken together.

(5) In determining, for the purposes of this section, whether a person's accommodation is adequate, the Secretary of State –

(a) must have regard to such matters as may be prescribed for the purposes of this paragraph; but

(b) may not have regard to such matters as may be prescribed for the purposes of this paragraph or to any of the matters mentioned in subsection (6).

(6) Those matters are –
(a) the fact that the person concerned has no enforceable right to occupy the accommodation;
(b) the fact that he shares the accommodation, or any part of the accommodation, with one or more other persons;
(c) the fact that the accommodation is temporary;
(d) the location of the accommodation.

(7) In determining, for the purposes of this section, whether a person's other essential living needs are met, the Secretary of State –
(a) must have regard to such matters as may be prescribed for the purposes of this paragraph; but
(b) may not have regard to such matters as may be prescribed for the purposes of this paragraph.

(8) The Secretary of State may by regulations provide that items or expenses of such a description as may be prescribed are, or are not, to be treated as being an essential living need of a person for the purposes of this Part.

(9) Support may be provided subject to conditions.

(10) The conditions must be set out in writing.

(11) A copy of the conditions must be given to the supported person.

(12) Schedule 8 gives the Secretary of State power to make regulations supplementing this section.

(13) Schedule 9 makes temporary provision for support in the period before the coming into force of this section.

Ways in which support may be provided

96 (1) Support may be provided under section 95 –
(a) by providing accommodation appearing to the Secretary of State to be adequate for the needs of the supported person and his dependants (if any);
(b) by providing what appear to the Secretary of State to be essential living needs of the supported person and his dependants (if any);
(c) to enable the supported person (if he is the asylum-seeker) to meet what appear to the Secretary of State to be expenses (other than legal expenses or other expenses of a prescribed description) incurred in connection with his claim for asylum;
(d) to enable the asylum-seeker and his dependants to attend bail proceedings in connection with his detention under any provision of the Immigration Acts; or
(e) to enable the asylum-seeker and his dependants to attend bail proceedings in connection with the detention of a dependant of his under any such provision.

(2) If the Secretary of State considers that the circumstances of a particular case are exceptional, he may provide support under section 95 in such other ways as he considers necessary to enable the supported person and his dependants (if any) to be supported.

(3) Unless the circumstances of a particular case are exceptional, support

provided by the Secretary of State under subsection (1)(a) or (b) or (2) must not be wholly or mainly by way of payments made (by whatever means) to the supported person or to his dependants (if any).

(4) But the Secretary of State may by order provide for subsection (3) not to apply –

   (a) in all cases, for such period as may be specified;
   (b) in such circumstances as may be specified;
   (c) in relation to specified categories of person; or
   (d) in relation to persons whose accommodation is in a specified locality.

(5) The Secretary of State may by order repeal subsection (3).

(6) 'Specified' means specified in an order made under subsection (4).

Supplemental

97 (1) When exercising his power under section 95 to provide accommodation, the Secretary of State must have regard to –

   (a) the fact that the accommodation is to be temporary pending determination of the asylum-seeker's claim;
   (b) the desirability, in general, of providing accommodation in areas in which there is a ready supply of accommodation; and
   (c) such other matters (if any) as may be prescribed.

(2) But he may not have regard to –

   (a) any preference that the supported person or his dependants (if any) may have as to the locality in which the accommodation is to be provided; or
   (b) such other matters (if any) as may be prescribed.

(3) The Secretary of State may by order repeal all or any of the following –

   (a) subsection (1)(a);
   (b) subsection (1)(b);
   (c) subsection (2)(a).

(4) When exercising his power under section 95 to provide essential living needs, the Secretary of State –

   (a) must have regard to such matters as may be prescribed for the purposes of this paragraph; but
   (b) may not have regard to such other matters as may be prescribed for the purposes of this paragraph.

(5) In addition, when exercising his power under section 95 to provide essential living needs, the Secretary of State may limit the overall amount of the expenditure which he incurs in connection with a particular supported person –

   (a) to such portion of the income support applicable amount provided under section 124 of the Social Security Contributions and Benefits Act 1992, or
   (b) to such portion of any components of that amount,

   as he considers appropriate having regard to the temporary nature of the support that he is providing.

(6) For the purposes of subsection (5), any support of a kind falling within section 96(1)(c) is to be treated as if it were the provision of essential living needs.

(7) In determining how to provide, or arrange for the provision of, support

under section 95, the Secretary of State may disregard any preference which the supported person or his dependants (if any) may have as to the way in which the support is to be given.

Temporary support

98 (1) The Secretary of State may provide, or arrange for the provision of, support for –
   (a) asylum-seekers, or
   (b) dependants of asylum-seekers,
   who it appears to the Secretary of State may be destitute.
   (2) Support may be provided under this section only until the Secretary of State is able to determine whether support may be provided under section 95.
   (3) Subsections (2) to (11) of section 95 apply for the purposes of this section as they apply for the purposes of that section.

SUPPORT AND ASSISTANCE BY LOCAL AUTHORITIES, ETC
Provision of support by local authorities

99 (1) A local authority may provide support for asylum-seekers and their dependants (if any) in accordance with arrangements made by the Secretary of State under section 95.
   (2) Such support may be provided by the local authority –
   (a) in one or more of the ways mentioned in section 96(1) and (2);
   (b) whether the arrangements in question are made with the authority or with another person.
   (3) The Executive may provide support by way of accommodation for asylum-seekers and their dependants (if any) in accordance with arrangements made by the Secretary of State under section 95, whether the arrangements in question are made with the Executive or with another person.
   (4) A local authority may incur reasonable expenditure in connection with the preparation of proposals for entering into arrangements under section 95.
   (5) The powers conferred on a local authority by this section include power to –
   (a) provide services outside their area;
   (b) provide services jointly with one or more bodies who are not local authorities;
   (c) form a company for the purpose of providing services;
   (d) tender for contracts (whether alone or with any other person).

Local authority and other assistance for Secretary of State

100 (1) This section applies if the Secretary of State asks –
   (a) a local authority,
   (b) a registered social landlord,
   (c) a registered housing association in Scotland or Northern Ireland, or
   (d) the Executive,
   to assist him to exercise his power under section 95 to provide accommodation.
   (2) The person to whom the request is made must co-operate in giving the Secretary of State such assistance in the exercise of that power as is reasonable in the circumstances.

(3) Subsection (2) does not require a registered social landlord to act beyond its powers.

(4) A local authority must supply to the Secretary of State such information about their housing accommodation (whether or not occupied) as he may from time to time request.

(5) The information must be provided in such form and manner as the Secretary of State may direct.

(6) 'Registered social landlord' has the same meaning as in Part I of the Housing Act 1996.

(7) 'Registered housing association' has the same meaning-
  (a) in relation to Scotland, as in the Housing Associations Act 1985; and
  (b) in relation to Northern Ireland, as in Part II of the Housing (Northern Ireland) Order 1992.

Reception zones
101 (1) The Secretary of State may by order designate as reception zones –
  (a) areas in England and Wales consisting of the areas of one or more local authorities;
  (b) areas in Scotland consisting of the areas of one or more local authorities;
  (c) Northern Ireland.
  [(2)–(18) *not reproduced.*]

APPEALS
Asylum support adjudicators
102 (1) There are to be adjudicators to hear appeals under this Part.

(2) A person appointed as an adjudicator under this Part is to be known as an Asylum Support Adjudicator (but is referred to in this Part as 'an adjudicator').

(3) Schedule 10 makes further provision with respect to adjudicators.

Appeals
103 (1) If, on an application for support under section 95, the Secretary of State decides that the applicant does not qualify for support under that section, the applicant may appeal to an adjudicator.

(2) If the Secretary of State decides to stop providing support for a person under section 95 before that support would otherwise have come to an end, that person may appeal to an adjudicator.

(3) On an appeal under this section, the adjudicator may –
  (a) require the Secretary of State to reconsider the matter;
  (b) substitute his decision for the decision appealed against; or
  (c) dismiss the appeal.

(4) The adjudicator must give his reasons in writing.

(5) The decision of the adjudicator is final.

(6) If an appeal is dismissed, no further application by the appellant for support under section 95 is to be entertained unless the Secretary of State is satisfied that there has been a material change in the circumstances.

(7) The Secretary of State may by regulations provide for decisions as to where

support provided under section 95 is to be provided to be appealable to an adjudicator under this Part.

(8) Regulations under subsection (7) may provide for any provision of this section to have effect, in relation to an appeal brought by virtue of the regulations, subject to such modifications as may be prescribed.

(9) The Secretary of State may pay any reasonable travelling expenses incurred by an appellant in connection with attendance at any place for the purposes of an appeal under this section.

Secretary of State's rules

104 (1) The Secretary of State may make rules regulating –
  (a) the bringing of appeals under this Part; and
  (b) the practice and procedure of the adjudicators.

(2) The rules may, in particular, make provision –
  (a) for the period within which an appeal must be brought;
  (b) as to the burden of proof on an appeal;
  (c) as to the giving and admissibility of evidence;
  (d) for summoning witnesses;
  (e) for an appeal to be heard in the absence of the appellant;
  (f) for determining an appeal without a hearing;
  (g) requiring reports of decisions of adjudicators to be published;
  (h) conferring such ancillary powers on adjudicators as the Secretary of State considers necessary for the proper discharge of their functions.

(3) In making the rules, the Secretary of State must have regard to the desirability of securing, so far as is reasonably practicable, that appeals are brought and disposed of with the minimum of delay.

OFFENCES
False representations

105 (1) A person is guilty of an offence if, with a view to obtaining support for himself or any other person under any provision made by or under this Part, he –
  (a) makes a statement or representation which he knows is false in a material particular;
  (b) produces or gives to a person exercising functions under this Part, or knowingly causes or allows to be produced or given to such a person, any document or information which he knows is false in a material particular;
  (c) fails, without reasonable excuse, to notify a change of circumstances when required to do so in accordance with any provision made by or under this Part; or
  (d) without reasonable excuse, knowingly causes another person to fail to notify a change of circumstances which that other person was required to notify in accordance with any provision made by or under this Part.

(2) A person guilty of an offence under this section is liable on summary conviction to imprisonment for a term not exceeding three months or to a fine not exceeding level 5 on the standard scale, or to both.

Dishonest representations

106 (1) A person is guilty of an offence if, with a view to obtaining any benefit or other payment or advantage under this Part for himself or any other person, he dishonestly –

    (a) makes a statement or representation which is false in a material particular;

    (b) produces or gives to a person exercising functions under this Part, or causes or allows to be produced or given to such a person, any document or information which is false in a material particular;

    (c) fails to notify a change of circumstances when required to do so in accordance with any provision made by or under this Part; or

    (d) causes another person to fail to notify a change of circumstances which that other person was required to notify in accordance with any provision made by or under this Part.

  (2) A person guilty of an offence under this section is liable –

    (a) on summary conviction, to imprisonment for a term not exceeding six months or to a fine not exceeding the statutory maximum, or to both; or

    (b) on conviction on indictment, to imprisonment for a term not exceeding seven years or to a fine, or to both.

  (3) In the application of this section to Scotland, in subsection (1) for 'dishonestly' substitute 'knowingly'.

Delay or obstruction

107 (1) A person is guilty of an offence if, without reasonable excuse, he –

    (a) intentionally delays or obstructs a person exercising functions conferred by or under this Part; or

    (b) refuses or neglects to answer a question, give any information or produce a document when required to do so in accordance with any provision made by or under this Part.

  (2) A person guilty of an offence under subsection (1) is liable on summary conviction to a fine not exceeding level 3 on the standard scale.

Failure of sponsor to maintain

108 (1) A person is guilty of an offence if, during any period in respect of which he has given a written undertaking in pursuance of the immigration rules to be responsible for the maintenance and accommodation of another person –

    (a) he persistently refuses or neglects, without reasonable excuse, to maintain that person in accordance with the undertaking; and

    (b) in consequence of his refusal or neglect, support under any provision made by or under this Part is provided for or in respect of that person.

  (2) A person guilty of an offence under this section is liable on summary conviction to imprisonment for a term not exceeding 3 months or to a fine not exceeding level 4 on the standard scale, or to both.

  (3) For the purposes of this section, a person is not to be taken to have refused or neglected to maintain another person by reason only of anything done or omitted in furtherance of a trade dispute.

[s109 *not reproduced*.]

EXPENDITURE
Payments to local authorities
110 (1) The Secretary of State may from time to time pay to any local authority or Northern Ireland authority such sums as he considers appropriate in respect of expenditure incurred, or to be incurred, by the authority in connection with –
   (a) persons who are, or have been, asylum-seekers; and
   (b) their dependants.

(2) The Secretary of State may from time to time pay to any-
   (a) local authority,
   (b) local authority association, or
   (c) Northern Ireland authority,
   such sums as he considers appropriate in respect of services provided by the authority or association in connection with the discharge of functions under this Part.

(3) The Secretary of State may make payments to any local authority towards the discharge of any liability of supported persons or their dependants in respect of council tax payable to that authority.

[(4)–(9) *not reproduced.*]

Grants to voluntary organisations
111 (1) The Secretary of State may make grants of such amounts as he thinks appropriate to voluntary organisations in connection with –
   (a) the provision by them of support (of whatever nature) to persons who are, or have been, asylum-seekers and to their dependants; and
   (b) connected matters.

(2) Grants may be made on such terms, and subject to such conditions, as the Secretary of State may determine.

Recovery of expenditure on support: misrepresentation etc
112 (1) This section applies if, on an application made by the Secretary of State, the court determines that –
   (a) a person ('A') has misrepresented or failed to disclose a material fact (whether fraudulently or otherwise); and
   (b) as a consequence of the misrepresentation or failure, support has been provided under section 95 or 98 (whether or not to A).

(2) If the support was provided by the Secretary of State, the court may order A to pay to the Secretary of State an amount representing the monetary value of the support which would not have been provided but for A's misrepresentation or failure.

(3) If the support was provided by another person ('B') in accordance with arrangements made with the Secretary of State under section 95 or 98, the court may order A to pay to the Secretary of State an amount representing the payment to B which would not have been made but for A's misrepresentation or failure.

(4) 'Court' means a county court or, in Scotland, the sheriff.

Recovery of expenditure on support from sponsor

113 (1) This section applies if –

    (a) a person ('the sponsor') has given a written undertaking in pursuance of the immigration rules to be responsible for the maintenance and accommodation of another person; and

    (b) during any period in relation to which the undertaking applies, support under section 95 is provided to or in respect of that other person.

(2) The Secretary of State may make a complaint against the sponsor to a magistrates' court for an order under this section.

(3) The court –

    (a) must have regard to all the circumstances (and in particular to the sponsor's income); and

    (b) may order him to pay to the Secretary of State such sum (weekly or otherwise) as it considers appropriate.

(4) But such a sum is not to include any amount attributable otherwise than to support provided under section 95.

(5) In determining –

    (a) whether to order any payments to be made in respect of support provided under section 95 for any period before the complaint was made, or

    (b) the amount of any such payments,

the court must disregard any amount by which the sponsor's current income exceeds his income during that period.

(6) An order under this section is enforceable as a magistrates' court maintenance order within the meaning of section 150(1) of the Magistrates' Courts Act 1980.

(7) In the application of this section to Scotland –

    (a) omit subsection (6);

    (b) for references to a complaint substitute references to an application; and

    (c) for references to a magistrates' court substitute references to the sheriff.

(8) In the application of this section to Northern Ireland, for references to a magistrates' court substitute references to a court of summary jurisdiction and for subsection (6) substitute –

    '(6) An order under this section is an order to which Article 98(11) of the Magistrates' Courts (Northern Ireland) Order 1981 applies.'

Overpayments

114 (1) Subsection (2) applies if, as a result of an error on the part of the Secretary of State, support has been provided to a person under section 95 or 98.

(2) The Secretary of State may recover from a person who is, or has been, a supported person an amount representing the monetary value of support provided to him as a result of the error.

(3) An amount recoverable under subsection (2) may be recovered as if it were a debt due to the Secretary of State.

(4) The Secretary of State may by regulations make provision for other methods of recovery, including deductions from support provided under section 95.

EXCLUSIONS
Exclusion from benefits

115 (1) No person is entitled to income-based jobseeker's allowance under the Jobseekers Act 1995 or to –
- (a) attendance allowance,
- (b) severe disablement allowance,
- (c) invalid care allowance,
- (d) disability living allowance,
- (e) income support,
- (f) working families' tax credit,
- (g) disabled person's tax credit,
- (h) a social fund payment,
- (i) child benefit,
- (j) housing benefit, or
- (k) council tax benefit,

under the Social Security Contributions and Benefits Act 1992 while he is a
person to whom this section applies.

(2) No person in Northern Ireland is entitled to –
- (a) income-based jobseeker's allowance under the Jobseekers (Northern
Ireland) Order 1995, or
- (b) any of the benefits mentioned in paragraphs (a) to (j) of subsection (1),

under the Social Security Contributions and Benefits (Northern Ireland) Act
1992 while he is a person to whom this section applies.

(3) This section applies to a person subject to immigration control unless he
falls within such category or description, or satisfies such conditions, as may
be prescribed.

(4) Regulations under subsection (3) may provide for a person to be treated for
prescribed purposes only as not being a person to whom this section
applies.

(5) In relation to the benefits mentioned in subsection (1)(f) or (g), 'prescribed'
means prescribed by regulations made by the Treasury.

(6) In relation to the matters mentioned in subsection (2) (except so far as it
relates to the benefits mentioned in subsection (1)(f) or (g)), 'prescribed'
means prescribed by regulations made by the Department.

(7) Section 175(3) to (5) of the Social Security Contributions and Benefits Act
1992 (supplemental powers in relation to regulations) applies to regulations
made by the Secretary of State or the Treasury under subsection (3) as it
applies to regulations made under that Act.

(8) Sections 133(2), 171(2) and 172(4) of the Social Security Contributions and
Benefits (Northern Ireland) Act 1992 apply to regulations made by the
Department under subsection (3) as they apply to regulations made by the
Department under that Act.

(9) 'A person subject to immigration control' means a person who is not a
national of an EEA State and who –
- (a) requires leave to enter or remain in the United Kingdom but does not
have it;
- (b) has leave to enter or remain in the United Kingdom which is subject to a
condition that he does not have recourse to public funds;

(c) has leave to enter or remain in the United Kingdom given as a result of a maintenance undertaking; or

(d) has leave to enter or remain in the United Kingdom only as a result of paragraph 17 of Schedule 4.

(10) 'Maintenance undertaking', in relation to any person, means a written undertaking given by another person in pursuance of the immigration rules to be responsible for that person's maintenance and accommodation.

Amendment of section 21 of the National Assistance Act 1948

116 In section 21 of the National Assistance Act 1948 (duty of local authorities to provide accommodation), after subsection (1), insert –

'(1A) A person to whom section 115 of the Immigration and Asylum Act 1999 (exclusion from benefits) applies may not be provided with residential accommodation under subsection (1)(a) if his need for care and attention has arisen solely –

(a) because he is destitute; or

(b) because of the physical effects, or anticipated physical effects, of his being destitute.

(1B) Subsections (3) and (5) to (8) of section 95 of the Immigration and Asylum Act 1999, and paragraph 2 of Schedule 8 to that Act, apply for the purposes of subsection (1A) as they apply for the purposes of that section, but for the references in subsections (5) and (7) of that section and in that paragraph to the Secretary of State substitute references to a local authority.'

Other restrictions on assistance: England and Wales

117 (1) In section 45 of the Health Services and Public Health Act 1968 (promotion by local authorities of the welfare of old people), after subsection (4), insert –

'(4A) No arrangements under this section may be given effect to in relation to a person to whom section 115 of the Immigration and Asylum Act 1999 (exclusion from benefits) applies solely –

(a) because he is destitute; or

(b) because of the physical effects, or anticipated physical effects, of his being destitute.

(4B) Subsections (3) and (5) to (8) of section 95 of the Immigration and Asylum Act 1999, and paragraph 2 of Schedule 8 to that Act, apply for the purposes of subsection (4A) as they apply for the purposes of that section, but for the references in subsections (5) and (7) of that section and in that paragraph to the Secretary of State substitute references to a local authority.'

(2) In paragraph 2 of Schedule 8 to the National Health Service Act 1977 (arrangements by local authorities for the prevention of illness and for care and after-care), after sub-paragraph (2), insert –

'(2A) No arrangements under this paragraph may be given effect to in relation to a person to whom section 115 of the Immigration and Asylum Act 1999 (exclusion from benefits) applies solely –

(a) because he is destitute; or

(b) because of the physical effects, or anticipated physical effects, of his being destitute.

(2B) Subsections (3) and (5) to (8) of section 95 of the Immigration and Asylum Act 1999, and paragraph 2 of Schedule 8 to that Act, apply for the purposes of subsection (2A) as they apply for the purposes of that section, but for the references in subsections (5) and (7) of that section and in that paragraph to the Secretary of State substitute references to a local social services authority.'

(3) In section 161 of the Housing Act 1996 (allocation of housing accommodation only to qualifying persons), after subsection (2), insert –
'(2A) Regulations may not be made under subsection (2) so as to include in a prescribed class any person to whom section 115 of the Immigration and Asylum Act 1999 (exclusion from benefits) applies.'

(4) In section 185 of the 1996 Act (persons from abroad not eligible for housing assistance), after subsection (2), insert –
'(2A) Regulations may not be made under subsection (2) so as to include in a prescribed class any person to whom section 115 of the Immigration and Asylum Act 1999 (exclusion from benefits) applies.'

(5) In the 1996 Act, omit section 186 (asylum-seekers and their dependants).

(6) In section 187(1) of the 1996 Act (provision of information by Secretary of State), in paragraph (a), for 'or has become an asylum-seeker, or a dependant of an asylum-seeker' substitute 'a person to whom section 115 of the Immigration and Asylum Act 1999 (exclusion from benefits) applies'.

Housing authority accommodation

118 (1) Each housing authority must secure that, so far as practicable, a tenancy of, or licence to occupy, housing accommodation provided under the accommodation provisions is not granted to a person subject to immigration control unless –
  (a) he is of a class specified in an order made by the Secretary of State; or
  (b) the tenancy of, or licence to occupy, such accommodation is granted in accordance with arrangements made under section 95.

(2) 'Housing authority' means –
  (a) in relation to England and Wales, a local housing authority within the meaning of the Housing Act 1985;
  (b) in relation to Scotland, a local authority within the meaning of the Housing (Scotland) Act 1987; and
  (c) in relation to Northern Ireland, the Executive.

(3) 'Accommodation provisions' means –
  (a) in relation to England and Wales, Part II of the Housing Act 1985;
  (b) in relation to Scotland, Part I of the Housing (Scotland) Act 1987;
  (c) in relation to Northern Ireland, Part II of the Housing (Northern Ireland) Order 1981.

(4) 'Licence to occupy', in relation to Scotland, means a permission or right to occupy.

(5) 'Tenancy', in relation to England and Wales, has the same meaning as in the Housing Act 1985.

(6) 'Person subject to immigration control' means a person who under the 1971 Act requires leave to enter or remain in the United Kingdom (whether or not such leave has been given).

(7) This section does not apply in relation to any allocation of housing to which Part VI of the Housing Act 1996 (allocation of housing accommodation) applies.

Homelessness: Scotland and Northern Ireland

119 (1) A person subject to immigration control –
- (a) is not eligible for accommodation or assistance under the homelessness provisions, and
- (b) is to be disregarded in determining for the purposes of those provisions, whether another person –
  - (i) is homeless or is threatened with homelessness, or
  - (ii) has a priority need for accommodation,

  unless he is of a class specified in an order made by the Secretary of State.
(2) An order under subsection (1) may not be made so as to include in a specified class any person to whom section 115 applies.
(3) 'The homelessness provisions' means –
- (a) in relation to Scotland, Part II of the Housing (Scotland) Act 1987; and
- (b) in relation to Northern Ireland, Part II of the Housing (Northern Ireland) Order 1988.
(4) 'Person subject to immigration control' has the same meaning as in section 118.

Other restrictions on assistance: Scotland

120 (1) In section 12 of the Social Work (Scotland) Act 1968 (general social welfare services of local authorities), after subsection (2) insert –

'(2A) A person to whom section 115 of the Immigration and Asylum Act 1999 (exclusion from benefits) applies is not to receive assistance under subsection (1) of this section (whether by way of residential accommodation or otherwise) if his need for assistance has arisen solely –
- (a) because he is destitute; or
- (b) because of the physical effects, or anticipated physical effects, of his being destitute.

(2B) Subsections (3) and (5) to (8) of section 95 of the Immigration and Asylum Act 1999, and paragraph 2 of Schedule 8 to that Act, apply for the purposes of subsection (2A) as they apply for the purposes of that section, but for the references in subsections (5) and (7) of that section and in that paragraph to the Secretary of State substitute references to a local authority.'
(2) In section 13A of that Act (provision of residential accommodation with nursing), after subsection (3) insert –

'(4) No arrangements under subsection (1) above may be given effect to in relation to a person to whom section 115 of the Immigration and Asylum Act 1999 (exclusion from benefits) applies solely –
- (a) because he is destitute; or
- (b) because of the physical effects, or anticipated physical effects, of his being destitute.

(5) Subsections (3) and (5) to (8) of section 95 of the Immigration and Asylum Act 1999, and paragraph 2 of Schedule 8 to that Act, apply for the purposes of subsection (4) above as they apply for the purposes of that

section, but for the references in subsections (5) and (7) of that section and in that paragraph to the Secretary of State substitute references to a local authority.'

(3) In section 13B of that Act (provision of care and after-care), after subsection (2) insert –

'(3) No arrangements under subsection (1) above may be given effect to in relation to a person to whom section 115 of the Immigration and Asylum Act 1999 (exclusion from benefits) applies solely –

(a) because he is destitute; or

(b) because of the physical effects, or anticipated physical effects, of his being destitute.

(4) Subsections (3) and (5) to (8) of section 95 of the Immigration and Asylum Act 1999, and paragraph 2 of Schedule 8 to that Act, apply for the purposes of subsection (3) above as they apply for the purposes of that section, but for the references in subsections (5) and (7) of that section and in that paragraph to the Secretary of State substitute references to a local authority.'

(4) In section 7 of the Mental Health (Scotland) Act 1984 (functions of local authorities), after subsection (2) insert –

'(3) No arrangements under paragraph (a) or (c) of subsection (1) above may be given effect to in relation to a person to whom section 115 of the Immigration and Asylum Act 1999 (exclusion from benefits) applies solely –

(a) because he is destitute; or

(b) because of the physical effects, or anticipated physical effects, of his being destitute.

(4) Subsections (3) and (5) to (8) of section 95 of the Immigration and Asylum Act 1999, and paragraph 2 of Schedule 8 to that Act, apply for the purposes of subsection (3) above as they apply for the purposes of that section, but for the references in subsection (5) and (7) of that section and in that paragraph to the Secretary of State substitute references to a local authority.'

(5) In section 8 of that Act (provision of after-care services), after subsection (3) insert –

'(4) After care services may not be provided under subsection (1) above in respect of any person to whom section 115 of the Immigration and Asylum Act 1999 (exclusion from benefits) applies solely –

(a) because he is destitute; or

(b) because of the physical effects, or anticipated physical effects, of his being destitute.

(5) Subsections (3) and (5) to (8) of section 95 of the Immigration and Asylum Act 1999, and paragraph 2 of Schedule 8 to that Act, apply for the purposes of subsection (4) above as they apply for the purposes of that section, but for the references in subsection (5) and (7) of that section and in that paragraph to the Secretary of State substitute references to a local authority.'

(6) In the Asylum and Immigration Appeals Act 1993, omit sections 4 and 5 and Schedule 1 (provisions relating to housing of asylum-seekers).

Other restrictions on assistance: Northern Ireland

121 (1) In Article 7 of the Health and Personal Social Services (Northern Ireland) Order 1972 (prevention of illness, care and after-care), after paragraph (2) insert –

'(3) No arrangements made under paragraph (1) may be given effect to in relation to a person to whom section 115 of the Immigration and Asylum Act 1999 applies solely –

(a) because he is destitute; or

(b) because of the physical effects, or anticipated physical effects, of his being destitute.

(3A) Subsections (3) and (5) to (8) of section 95 of the Immigration and Asylum Act 1999, and paragraph 2 of Schedule 8 to that Act, apply for the purposes of paragraph (3) as they apply for the purposes of that section, but for the references in subsections (5) and (7) of that section and in paragraph 2 of that Schedule to the Secretary of State substitute references to the Department.'

(2) In Article 15 of that Order (general social welfare), after paragraph (5) insert –

'(6) Assistance may not be provided under paragraph (1) in respect of any person to whom section 115 of the Immigration and Asylum Act 1999 applies if his need for assistance has arisen solely –

(a) because he is destitute, or

(b) because of the physical effects, or anticipated physical effects, of his being destitute.

(7) Subsections (3) to (8) of section 95 of the Immigration and Asylum Act 1999, and paragraph 2 of Schedule 8 to that Act, apply for the purposes of paragraph (6) as they apply for the purposes of that section, but for references to the Secretary of State in subsections (5) and (7) of that section and in paragraph 2 of that Schedule substitute references to the Department.'

(3) In the Asylum and Immigration Appeals Act 1993, omit sections 4 and 5 and Schedule 1 (provisions relating to housing of asylum-seekers).

Support for children

122 (1) In this section 'eligible person' means a person who appears to the Secretary of State to be a person for whom support may be provided under section 95.

(2) Subsections (3) and (4) apply if an application for support under section 95 has been made by an eligible person whose household includes a dependant under the age of 18 ('the child').

(3) If it appears to the Secretary of State that adequate accommodation is not being provided for the child, he must exercise his powers under section 95 by offering, and if his offer is accepted by providing or arranging for the provision of, adequate accommodation for the child as part of the eligible person's household.

(4) If it appears to the Secretary of State that essential living needs of the child are not being met, he must exercise his powers under section 95 by offering, and if his offer is accepted by providing or arranging for the provision of, essential living needs for the child as part of the eligible person's household.

(5) No local authority may provide assistance under any of the child welfare

provisions in respect of a dependant under the age of 18, or any member of his family, at any time when –

    (a) the Secretary of State is complying with this section in relation to him; or

    (b) there are reasonable grounds for believing that –

        (i) the person concerned is a person for whom support may be provided under section 95; and

        (ii) the Secretary of State would be required to comply with this section if that person had made an application under section 95.

  (6) 'Assistance' means the provision of accommodation or of any essential living needs.

  (7) 'The child welfare provisions' means –

    (a) section 17 of the Children Act 1989 (local authority support for children and their families);

    (b) section 22 of the Children (Scotland) Act 1995 (equivalent provision for Scotland); and

    (c) Article 18 of the Children (Northern Ireland) Order 1995 (equivalent provision for Northern Ireland).

  (8) Subsection (9) applies if accommodation provided in the discharge of the duty imposed by subsection (3) has been withdrawn.

  (9) Only the relevant authority may provide assistance under any of the child welfare provisions in respect of the child concerned.

  (10) 'Relevant authority' means –

    (a) in relation to Northern Ireland, the authority within whose area the withdrawn accommodation was provided;

    (b) in any other case, the local authority within whose area the withdrawn accommodation was provided.

  (11) In such circumstances as may be prescribed, subsection (5) does not apply.

Back-dating of benefits where person recorded as refugee

123 (1) This section applies if –

    (a) a person is recorded by the Secretary of State as a refugee within the meaning of the Refugee Convention; and

    (b) before the refugee was so recorded, he or his dependant was a person to whom section 115 applied.

  (2) Regulations may provide that a person mentioned in subsection (1)(b) may, within a prescribed period, claim the whole, or any prescribed proportion, of any benefit to which he would have been entitled had the refugee been so recorded when he made his claim for asylum.

  (3) Subsections (5) and (6) apply if the refugee has resided in the areas of two or more local authorities and he or his dependant makes a claim under the regulations in relation to housing benefit.

  (4) Subsections (5) and (6) also apply if the refugee has resided in the areas of two or more local authorities in Great Britain and he or his dependant makes a claim under the regulations in relation to council tax benefit.

  (5) The claim must be investigated and determined, and any benefit awarded must be paid or allowed, by such one of those authorities as may be prescribed by the regulations ('the prescribed authority').

(6) The regulations may make provision requiring a local authority who are not the prescribed authority to supply that authority with such information as they may reasonably require in connection with the exercise of their functions under the regulations.

(7) The regulations may make provision in relation to a person who has received support under this Part or who is a dependant of such a person –
   (a) for the determination, or for criteria for the calculation, of the value of that support; and
   (b) for the sum which he would be entitled to claim under the regulations to be reduced by the whole, or any prescribed proportion, of that valuation.

(8) The reductions permitted by subsection (7) must not exceed the amount of the valuation.

(9) 'Regulations' means –
   (a) in relation to jobseeker's allowance under the Jobseekers Act 1995, regulations made by the Secretary of State under that Act or the Social Security Administration Act 1992;
   (b) in relation to jobseeker's allowance under the Jobseekers (Northern Ireland) Order 1995, regulations made by the Department under that Order or the Social Security Administration (Northern Ireland) Act 1992;
   (c) in relation to a benefit under the Social Security Contributions and Benefits Act 1992, regulations made by the Secretary of State under that Act or the Social Security Administration Act 1992;
   (d) in relation to a benefit under the Social Security Contributions and Benefits (Northern Ireland) Act 1992, regulations made by the Department under that Act or the Social Security Administration (Northern Ireland) Act 1992.

MISCELLANEOUS
Secretary of State to be corporation sole for purposes of Part VI

124 (1) For the purpose of exercising his functions under this Part, the Secretary of State is a corporation sole.

(2) Any instrument in connection with the acquisition, management or disposal of property, real or personal, heritable or moveable, by the Secretary of State under this Part may be executed on his behalf by a person authorised by him for that purpose.

(3) Any instrument purporting to have been so executed on behalf of the Secretary of State is to be treated, until the contrary is proved, to have been so executed on his behalf.

Entry of premises

125 (1) This section applies in relation to premises in which accommodation has been provided under section 95 or 98 for a supported person.

(2) If, on an application made by a person authorised in writing by the Secretary of State, a justice of the peace is satisfied that there is reason to believe that –
   (a) the supported person or any dependants of his for whom the accommodation is provided is not resident in it,
   (b) the accommodation is being used for any purpose other than the accommodation of the asylum-seeker or any dependant of his, or

(c) any person other than the supported person and his dependants (if any) is residing in the accommodation,

he may grant a warrant to enter the premises to the person making the application.

(3) A warrant granted under subsection (2) may be executed –
    (a) at any reasonable time;
    (b) using reasonable force.

(4) In the application of subsection (2) to Scotland, read the reference to a justice of the peace as a reference to the sheriff or a justice of the peace.

Information from property owners

26 (1) The power conferred by this section is to be exercised with a view to obtaining information about premises in which accommodation is or has been provided for supported persons.

(2) The Secretary of State may require any person appearing to him –
    (a) to have any interest in, or
    (b) to be involved in any way in the management or control of,

such premises, or any building which includes such premises, to provide him with such information with respect to the premises and the persons occupying them as he may specify.

(3) A person who is required to provide information under this section must do so in accordance with such requirements as may be prescribed.

(4) Information provided to the Secretary of State under this section may be used by him only in the exercise of his functions under this Part.

Requirement to supply information about redirection of post

27 (1) The Secretary of State may require any person conveying postal packets to supply redirection information to the Secretary of State –
    (a) for use in the prevention, detection, investigation or prosecution of criminal offences under this Part;
    (b) for use in checking the accuracy of information relating to support provided under this Part; or
    (c) for any other purpose relating to the provision of support to asylum-seekers.

(2) The information must be supplied in such manner and form, and in accordance with such requirements, as may be prescribed.

(3) The Secretary of State must make payments of such amount as he considers reasonable in respect of the supply of information under this section.

(4) 'Postal packet' has the same meaning as in the Post Office Act 1953.

(5) 'Redirection information' means information relating to arrangements made with any person conveying postal packets for the delivery of postal packets to addresses other than those indicated by senders on the packets.

PART X: MISCELLANEOUS AND SUPPLEMENTAL
Interpretation

67 (1) In this Act –
'the 1971 Act' means the Immigration Act 1971;
'adjudicator' (except in Part VI) means an adjudicator appointed under section 57;

'Chief Adjudicator' means the person appointed as Chief Adjudicator under section 57(2);

'claim for asylum' (except in Parts V and VI and section 141) means a claim that it would be contrary to the United Kingdom's obligations under the Refugee Convention for the claimant to be removed from, or required to leave, the United Kingdom;

'the Commission' means the Special Immigration Appeals Commission;

'country' includes any territory;

'EEA State' means a State which is a Contracting Party to the Agreement on the European Economic Area signed at Oporto on 2nd May 1992 as it has effect for the time being;

'the Human Rights Convention' means the Convention for the Protection of Human Rights and Fundamental Freedoms, agreed by the Council of Europe at Rome on 4th November 1950 as it has effect for the time being in relation to the United Kingdom;

'the Immigration Acts' means –

(a) the 1971 Act;

(b) the Immigration Act 1988;

(c) the Asylum and Immigration Appeals Act 1993;

(d) the Asylum and Immigration Act 1996; and

(e) this Act;

'prescribed' means prescribed by regulations made by the Secretary of State;

'the Refugee Convention' means the Convention relating to the Status of Refugees done at Geneva on 28 July 1951 and the Protocol to the Convention;

'voluntary organisations' means bodies (other than public or local authorities) whose activities are not carried on for profit.

(2) The following expressions have the same meaning as in the 1971 Act –

'certificate of entitlement';

'entry clearance';

'illegal entrant';

'immigration officer';

'immigration rules';

'port';

'United Kingdom passport';

'work permit'.

Short title, commencement and extent

170 (1) This Act may be cited as the Immigration and Asylum Act 1999.

(2) Subsections (1) and (2) of section 115 come into force on the day on which the first regulations made under Schedule 8 come into force.

(3) The following provisions come into force on the passing of this Act –

(a) section 4;

(b) section 9;

(c) section 15;

(d) section 27;

(e) section 31;

(f) section 94;

(g) section 95(13);
(h) section 99(4) and (5);
(i) sections 105 to 109;
(j) section 110(1), (2) and (8) (so far as relating to subsections (1) and (2));
(k) section 111;
(l) section 124;
(m) section 140;
(n) section 145;
(o) section 146(1);
(p) sections 166 to 168;
(q) this section;
(r) Schedule 9;
(s) paragraphs 62(2), 73, 78, 79, 81, 82, 87, 88 and 102 of Schedule 14;
(t) paragraphs 2 and 13 of Schedule 15.

(4) The other provisions of this Act, except section 10 and paragraph 12 of Schedule 15 (which come into force in accordance with section 9), come into force on such day as the Secretary of State may by order appoint.

(5) Different days may be appointed for different purposes.

(6) This Act extends to Northern Ireland.

(7) Her Majesty may by Order in Council direct that any of the provisions of this Act are to extend, with such modifications (if any) as appear to Her Majesty to be appropriate, to any of the Channel Islands or the Isle of Man.

SCHEDULE 8: PROVISION OF SUPPORT: REGULATIONS
General regulation-making power

1 The Secretary of State may by regulations make such further provision with respect to the powers conferred on him by section 95 as he considers appropriate.

Determining whether a person is destitute

2 (1) The regulations may provide, in connection with determining whether a person is destitute, for the Secretary of State to take into account, except in such circumstances (if any) as may be prescribed –

(a) income which the person concerned, or any dependant of his, has or might reasonably be expected to have, and

(b) support which is, or assets of a prescribed kind which are, or might reasonably be expected to be, available to him or to any dependant of his,

otherwise than by way of support provided under section 95.

(2) The regulations may provide that in such circumstances (if any) as may be prescribed, a person is not to be treated as destitute for the purposes of section 95.

Prescribed levels of support

3 The regulations may make provision –

(a) as to the circumstances in which the Secretary of State may, as a general rule, be expected to provide support in accordance with prescribed levels or of a prescribed kind;

(b) as to the circumstances in which the Secretary of State may, as a general rule, be expected to provide support otherwise than in accordance with the prescribed levels.

Provision of items and services

4   The regulations may make provision for prescribed items or services to be provided or made available to persons receiving support under section 95 for such purposes and in such circumstances as may be prescribed.

Support and assets to be taken into account

5   The regulations may make provision requiring the Secretary of State, except in such circumstances (if any) as may be prescribed, to take into account, when deciding the level or kind of support to be provided –
   (a) income which the person concerned, or any dependant of his, has or might reasonably be expected to have, and
   (b) support which is, or assets of a prescribed kind which are, or might reasonably be expected to be, available to him or to any dependant of his,
   otherwise than by way of support provided under section 95.

Valuation of assets

6   The regulations may make provision as to the valuation of assets.

Breach of conditions

7   The regulations may make provision for the Secretary of State to take into account, when deciding-
   (a) whether to provide, or to continue to provide, support under section 95, or
   (b) the level or kind of support to be provided,
   the extent to which any condition on which support is being, or has previously been, provided has been complied with.

Suspension or discontinuation of support

8   (1) The regulations may make provision for the suspension or discontinuance of support under section 95 in prescribed circumstances (including circumstances in which the Secretary of State would otherwise be under a duty to provide support).
   (2) The circumstances which may be prescribed include the cessation of residence –
   (a) in accommodation provided under section 95; or
   (b) at an address notified to the Secretary of State in accordance with the regulations.

Notice to quit

9   (1) The regulations may provide that if –
   (a) as a result of support provided under section 95, a person has a tenancy or a licence to occupy accommodation,
   (b) one or more of the conditions mentioned in sub-paragraph (2) are satisfied, and
   (c) he is given such notice to quit as may be prescribed by the regulations,
   his tenancy or licence is to be treated as ending with the period specified in that notice, regardless of when it could otherwise be brought to an end.

(2) The conditions are that –
- (a) the support provided under section 95 is suspended or discontinued as a result of any provision of a kind mentioned in paragraph 8;
- (b) the relevant claim for asylum has been determined;
- (c) the supported person has ceased to be destitute;
- (d) he is to be moved to other accommodation.

Contributions to support

10 The regulations may make provision requiring a supported person to make payments to the Secretary of State, in prescribed circumstances, by way of contributions to the cost of the provision of that support.

Recovery of sums by Secretary of State

11 (1) The regulations may provide for the recovery by the Secretary of State of sums representing the whole or part of the monetary value of support provided to a person under section 95 where it appears to the Secretary of State –
- (a) that that person had, at the time when he applied for support, assets of any kind in the United Kingdom or elsewhere which were not capable of being realised; but
- (b) that those assets have subsequently become, and remain, capable of being realised.

(2) An amount recoverable under regulations made by virtue of sub-paragraph (1) may be recovered –
- (a) as if it were a debt due to the Secretary of State; or
- (b) by such other method of recovery, including by deduction from support provided under section 95 as may be prescribed.

Procedure

12 The regulations may make provision with respect to procedural requirements including, in particular, provision as to –
- (a) the procedure to be followed in making an application for support;
- (b) the information which must be provided by the applicant;
- (c) the circumstances in which an application may not be entertained;
- (d) the making of further enquiries by the Secretary of State;
- (e) the circumstances in which, and person by whom, a change of circumstances of a prescribed description must be notified to the Secretary of State.

SCHEDULE 9: ASYLUM SUPPORT: INTERIM PROVISIONS

1 (1) The Secretary of State may by regulations make provision requiring prescribed local authorities or local authorities falling within a prescribed description of authority to provide support, during the interim period, to eligible persons.

(2) 'Eligible persons' means –
- (a) asylum-seekers, or
- (b) their dependants,

who appear to be destitute or to be likely to become destitute within such period as may be prescribed.

(3) For the purposes of sub-paragraph (1), in Northern Ireland, a Health and Social Services Board established under Article 16 of the Health and Personal Social Services (Northern Ireland) Order 1972 is to be treated as a local authority.

2 (1) The regulations must provide for the question whether a person is an eligible person to be determined by the local authority concerned.

(2) The regulations may make provision for support to be provided, before the determination of that question, to a person making a claim for support under the regulations by the Secretary of State or such local authority as may be prescribed.

(3) 'The local authority concerned' has such meaning as may be prescribed.

3 Subsections (3) to (8) of section 95 apply for the purposes of the regulations as they apply for the purposes of that section, but for the references in subsections (5) and (7) to the Secretary of State substitute references to the local authority concerned.

4 The regulations may prescribe circumstances in which support for an eligible person –
(a) must be provided;
(b) must or may be refused; or
(c) must or may be suspended or discontinued.

5 The regulations may provide that support –
(a) is to be provided in prescribed ways;
(b) is not to be provided in prescribed ways.

6 The regulations may include provision –
(a) as to the level of support that is to be provided;
(b) for support to be provided subject to conditions;
(c) requiring any such conditions to be set out in writing;
(d) requiring a copy of any such conditions to be given to such person as may be prescribed.

7 The regulations may make provision that, in providing support, a local authority –
(a) are to have regard to such matters as may be prescribed;
(b) are not to have regard to such matters as may be prescribed.

8 The regulations may include provision –
(a) prescribing particular areas, or descriptions of area, (which may include a locality within their own area) in which a local authority may not place asylum-seekers while providing support for them;
(b) prescribing circumstances in which a particular area, or description of area, (which may include a locality within their own area) is to be one in which a local authority may not place asylum-seekers while providing support for them;
(c) as to the circumstances (if any) in which any such provision is not to apply.

9 (1) The regulations may make provision for the referral by one local authority to

another of a claim for support made under the regulations if the local authority to whom the claim is made consider that it is not manifestly unfounded but –

(a) they are providing support for a number of asylum-seekers equal to, or greater than, the maximum number of asylum-seekers applicable to them; or

(b) they are providing support for a number of eligible persons equal to, or greater than, the maximum number of eligible persons applicable to them.

(2) For the purposes of any provision made as a result of sub-paragraph (1), the regulations may make provision for the determination by the Secretary of State of –

(a) the applicable maximum number of asylum-seekers;

(b) the applicable maximum number of eligible persons.

(3) The regulations may make provision for any such determination to be made –

(a) for local authorities generally;

(b) for prescribed descriptions of local authority; or

(c) for particular local authorities.

(4) The regulations may provide that a referral may not be made –

(a) to a prescribed local authority;

(b) to local authorities of a prescribed description; or

(c) in prescribed circumstances.

(5) The regulations may make provision for the payment by a local authority of any reasonable travel or subsistence expenses incurred as a result of a referral made by them.

(6) The regulations may make provision for the transfer of a claim for support, or responsibility for providing support, under the regulations from one local authority to another on such terms as may be agreed between them.

(7) In exercising any power under the regulations to refer or transfer, a local authority must have regard to such guidance as may be issued by the Secretary of State with respect to the exercise of the power.

10 (1) The regulations may make provision for the referral of claims for support made to the Secretary of State to prescribed local authorities or local authorities of a prescribed description.

(2) The regulations may make provision for the payment by the Secretary of State of any reasonable travel or subsistence expenses incurred as a result of a referral made by him as a result of provision made by virtue of sub-paragraph (1).

11 (1) The regulations may make provision requiring prescribed local authorities or other prescribed bodies to give reasonable assistance to local authorities providing support under the regulations.

12 The regulations may make provision for the procedure for making and determining claims for support.

13 The regulations may make provision for an asylum-seeker or a dependant of an asylum-seeker who has received, or is receiving, any prescribed description of support from a local authority to be taken to have been accepted for support under the regulations by a prescribed local authority.

14   A person entitled to support under the regulations is not entitled to any prescribed description of support, except to such extent (if any) as may be prescribed.

15   'The interim period' means the period –
(a) beginning on such day as may be prescribed for the purposes of this paragraph; and
(b) ending on such day as may be so prescribed.

SCHEDULE 14 – CONSEQUENTIAL AMENDMENTS
. . .
The Protection from Eviction Act 1977
73   In section 3A of the Protection from Eviction Act 1977 (excluded tenancies and licences), after subsection (7), insert –
'(7A) A tenancy or licence is excluded if it is granted in order to provide accommodation under Part VI of the Immigration and Asylum Act 1999.'

The Housing Act 1985
81   In Schedule 1 to the Housing Act 1985 (tenancies which cannot be secure tenancies), after paragraph 4, insert –

'Accommodation for asylum-seekers
4A (1) A tenancy is not a secure tenancy if it is granted in order to provide accommodation under Part VI of the Immigration and Asylum Act 1999.
(2) A tenancy mentioned in sub-paragraph (1) becomes a secure tenancy if the landlord notifies the tenant that it is to be regarded as a secure tenancy.'

The Housing Act 1988
88   In Schedule 1 to the Housing Act 1988 (tenancies which are not assured tenancies), after paragraph 12, insert –

'Accommodation for asylum-seekers
12A (1) A tenancy granted by a private landlord under arrangements for the provision of support for asylum-seekers or dependants of asylum-seekers made under Part VI of the Immigration and Asylum Act 1999.
(2) 'Private landlord' means a landlord who is not within section 80(1) of the Housing Act 1985.'

SCHEDULE 15 – TRANSITIONAL PROVISIONS AND SAVINGS
. . .
Assistance under Part VII of the Housing Act 1996
13 (1)   The Secretary of State may by order provide for any provision of Part VII of the Housing Act 1996 (homelessness) to have effect in relation to section 185(2) persons, during the interim period, with such modifications as may be specified in the order.
(2) An order under this paragraph may, in particular, include provision –

  (a) for the referral of section 185(2) persons by one local housing authority to another by agreement between the authorities;
  (b) as to the suitability of accommodation for such persons;
  (c) as to out-of-area placements of such persons.
(3) 'Interim period' means the period beginning with the passing of this Act and ending on the coming into force of the repeal of section 186 of the Act of 1996 (asylum-seekers and their dependants) by this Act (as to which see section 117(5)).
(4) 'Local housing authority' has the same meaning as in the Act of 1996.
(5) 'Section 185(2) person' means a person who –
  (a) is eligible for housing assistance under Part VII of the Act of 1996 as a result of regulations made under section 185(2) of that Act; and
  (b) is not made ineligible by section 186 (or any other provision) of that Act.
(6) The fact that an order may be made under this paragraph only in respect of the interim period does not prevent it from containing provisions of a kind authorised under section 166(3)(a) which are to have continuing effect after the end of that period.

Provision of support

14 (1) The Secretary of State may, by directions given to a local authority to whom Schedule 9 applies, require the authority to treat the interim period fixed for the purposes of that Schedule as coming to an end –
  (a) for specified purposes,
  (b) in relation to a specified area or locality, or
  (c) in relation to persons of a specified description,
  on such earlier day as may be specified.
(2) The Secretary of State may, by directions given to an authority to whom an amended provision applies, provide for specified descriptions of person to be treated –
  (a) for specified purposes, or
  (b) in relation to a specified area or locality,
  as being persons to whom section 115 applies during such period as may be specified.
(3) Directions given under this paragraph may –
  (a) make such consequential, supplemental or transitional provision as the Secretary of State considers appropriate; and
  (b) make different provision for different cases or descriptions of case.
(4) 'Specified' means specified in the directions.
(5) 'Amended provision' means any provision amended by –
  (a) section 116;
  (b) section 117(1) or (2);
  (c) section 120; or
  (d) section 121.

Asylum Support (Interim Provisions) Regulations 1999 SI No 3056

Citation, commencement and extent

1 (1) These Regulations may be cited as the Asylum Support (Interim Provisions) Regulations 1999 and shall come into force on 6th December 1999.

(2) These Regulations do not extend to Scotland or Northern Ireland.

Interpretation

2 (1) In these Regulations –

'assisted person' means an asylum-seeker, or a dependant of an asylum-seeker, who has applied for support and for whom support is provided;

'dependant', in relation to an asylum-seeker, an assisted person or a person claiming support, means a person in the United Kingdom who –

(a) is his spouse;

(b) is a child of his, or of his spouse, who is under 18 and dependent on him;

(c) is under 18 and is a member of his, or his spouse's, close family;

(d) is under 18 and had been living as part of his household:

(i)   for at least six of the 12 months before the day on which his claim for support was made; or

(ii) since birth;

(e) is in need of care and attention from him or a member of his household by reason of a disability and would fall within sub-paragraph (c) or (d) but for the fact that he is not under 18;

(f) had been living with him as a member of an unmarried couple for at least two of the three years before the day on which his claim for support was made;

(g) is a person living as part of his household who was receiving assistance from a local authority under section 17 of the Children Act 1989 immediately before the beginning of the interim period;

(h) has made a claim for leave to enter or remain in the United Kingdom, or for variation of any such leave, which is being considered on the basis that he is dependent on the asylum-seeker; or

(i) in relation to an assisted person or a person claiming support who is himself a dependant of an asylum-seeker, is the asylum-seeker;

'eligible persons' means asylum-seekers or their dependants who appear to be destitute or to be likely to become destitute within 14 days;

'local authority' means –

(a) in England, a county council, a metropolitan district council, a district council with the functions of a county council, a London borough council, the Common Council of the City of London or the Council of the Isles of Scilly;

(b) in Wales, a county council or a county borough council.

(2) Any reference in these Regulations to support is to support under these Regulations.

(3) Any reference in these Regulations to assistance under section 21 of the National Assistance Act 1948 is to assistance, the need for which has arisen solely –
   (a) because of destitution; or
   (b) because of the physical effects, or anticipated physical effects, of destitution.
(4) Any reference in these Regulations to assistance under section 17 of the Children Act 1989 is to the provision of accommodation or of any essential living needs.
(5) The interim period begins on the day on which these Regulations come into force and ends on 1st April 2002.
(6) For the purposes of section 94(3) of the Immigration and Asylum Act 1999 (day on which a claim for asylum is determined), the period of 14 days is prescribed for any case to which these Regulations apply.

Requirement to provide support
3 (1) Subject to regulations 7 and 8 –
   (a) the local authority concerned, or
   (b) the local authority to whom responsibility for providing support is transferred under regulation 9,
   must provide support during the interim period to eligible persons.
(2) The question whether a person is an eligible person is to be determined by the local authority concerned.
(3) For the purposes of these Regulations, the local authority concerned are the local authority to whom a claim for support is made, except where a claim for support is transferred by a local authority in accordance with regulation 9, in which case the local authority concerned are the local authority to whom the claim is transferred.

Temporary support
4 (1) This regulation applies to support to be provided before it has been determined whether a person is an eligible person ('temporary support').
(2) Temporary support is to be provided to a person claiming support –
   (a) by the local authority to whom the claim is made until such time (if any) as the claim is transferred under regulation 9;
   (b) where the claim is so transferred, by the local authority to whom the claim is transferred.
(3) Temporary support must appear to the local authority by whom it is provided to be adequate for the needs of the person claiming support and his dependants (if any).

Provision of support
5 (1) Subject to paragraph (2), support is to be provided by providing –
   (a) accommodation appearing to the local authority by whom it is provided to be adequate for the needs of the assisted person and his dependants (if any) ('accommodation'); and
   (b) what appear to the local authority by whom it is provided to be essential living needs of the assisted person and his dependants (if any) ('essential living needs').

(2) Where an assisted person's household includes a child who is under 18 and a dependant of his, support is to be provided –
   (a) in accordance with paragraph (1);
   (b) by providing accommodation; or
   (c) by providing essential living needs.
(3) Support is to be provided to enable the assisted person (if he is the asylum-seeker) to meet reasonable travel expenses incurred in attending –
   (a) a hearing of an appeal on his claim for asylum; or
   (b) an interview in connection with his claim for asylum which has been requested by the Secretary of State.
(4) Where the circumstances of a particular case are exceptional, support is to be provided in such other ways as are necessary to enable the assisted person and his dependants (if any) to be supported.
(5) Support provided by way of payments made (by whatever means) to the assisted person and his dependants (if any) is not to exceed £10 per person in any one week, unless –
   (a) the assisted person's household includes a child who is under 18 and a dependant of his; or
   (b) the circumstances of a particular case are exceptional.
(6) A local authority may provide support subject to conditions.
(7) Such conditions are to be set out in writing.
(8) A copy of the conditions is to be given to the assisted person.

Matters to which the local authority are to have regard

6 (1) In providing support, the local authority are to have regard to –
   (a) income which the assisted person has, or his dependants (if any) have, or might reasonably be expected to have;
   (b) support which is, or assets which are, or might reasonably be expected to be, available to the assisted person, or to his dependants (if any);
   (c) the welfare of the assisted person and his dependants (if any); and
   (d) the cost of providing support.
(2) In providing accommodation under these Regulations, the local authority are not to have regard to any preference that the assisted person or his dependants (if any) may have as to –
   (a) the locality in which the accommodation is to be provided;
   (b) the nature of the accommodation to be provided; or
   (c) the nature and standard of fixtures and fittings in that accommodation.

Refusal of support

7 (1) Unless this paragraph does not apply, support must be refused in the following circumstances –
   (a) where the person claiming support has intentionally made himself and his dependants (if any) destitute;
   (b) where the person claiming support has made a claim for support to another local authority, except where the claim is one to which regulation 9 applies;
   (c) where the claim for support is made by a person to a local authority other than one to whom, in the previous 12 months, he has made a

claim for assistance under section 21 of the National Assistance Act 1948 or under section 17 of the Children Act 1989;

(d) where the person claiming support –

    (i) is an asylum-seeker within the meaning of paragraph (3A)(a) or (aa) of regulation 70 of the Income Support (General) Regulations 1987 who has not ceased to be an asylum-seeker by virtue of sub-paragraph (b) of that paragraph;

    (ii) is a person who became an asylum-seeker under paragraph (3A)(a) of regulation 70 of the Income Support (General) Regulations 1987 and who has not ceased to be an asylum-seeker by virtue of sub-paragraph (b) of that paragraph, as saved by regulation 12(1) of the Social Security (Persons from Abroad) Miscellaneous Amendments Regulations 1996;

    (iii) is not a person from abroad within the meaning of sub-paragraph (a) of regulation 21(3) of the Income Support (General) Regulations 1987 by virtue of the exclusions specified in that sub-paragraph;

(e) where neither the person claiming support nor any of his dependants is an asylum-seeker or has made a claim for leave to enter or remain in the United Kingdom, or for variation of any such leave, which is being considered on the basis that he is dependent on an asylum-seeker.

(2) For the purposes of paragraph (1)(a), a person has intentionally made himself destitute if he appears to be, or likely within 14 days to become, destitute as a result of an act or omission deliberately done or made by him or any dependant of his without reasonable excuse while in the United Kingdom.

(3) Paragraph (1) does not apply where the local authority concerned did not know, or could not with reasonable diligence have known, of any circumstance set out in that paragraph.

Suspension and discontinuation of support

8 (1) Support for the assisted person and his dependants (if any) must be discontinued as soon as the local authority by whom it is provided become aware of any circumstance which, if they had known of it when the claim was made, would have led to the claim being refused in accordance with regulation 7(1).

(2) Support may be suspended or discontinued –

(a) where the assisted person, or any dependant of his, fails without reasonable excuse to comply with any condition subject to which the support is provided;

(b) where the assisted person, or any dependant of his, leaves accommodation provided as part of such support for more than seven consecutive days without reasonable excuse.

Transfer of a claim for support or responsibility for providing support by a local authority

9 A local authority may transfer a claim for support made to them, or responsibility for providing support, to another local authority on such terms as may be agreed between the two authorities.

Assistance to those providing support

10 Reasonable assistance to a local authority providing support is to be given
by –

(a) any district council for an area any part of which lies within the area of
the local authority providing support, and

(b) any registered social landlord, within the meaning of Part I of the Housing Act 1996, which manages any house or other property which is in
the area of the local authority providing support,

who is requested to provide such assistance by the local authority providing
support.

Transitional provision

11 (1) Where an asylum-seeker or a dependant of an asylum-seeker is receiving
assistance from a local authority under section 21 of the National Assistance
Act 1948 or under section 17 of the Children Act 1989 immediately before
the beginning of the interim period, he is to be taken to have been accepted
for support by the local authority providing such assistance.

Entitlement to claim support

12 A person entitled to support under these Regulations is not entitled to
assistance under section 17 of the Children Act 1989.

Asylum Support Appeals (Procedure) Rules 2000 SI No 541

GENERAL
Title and commencement

1 These Rules may be cited as the Asylum Support Appeals (Procedure) Rules
2000 and shall come into force on 3rd April 2000.

Interpretation

2 (1) In these Rules –

'the Act' means the Immigration and Asylum Act 1999;

'adjudication' means a decision of an adjudicator made in accordance with
section 103(3) of the Act;

'appeal bundle' means a bundle prepared by the Secretary of State containing copies of the following documents –

(a) the form on which the appellant made a claim for support under section
95 of the Act, if the appeal is made under section 103(1) of the Act;

(b) any supporting documentation attached to that form;

(c) the decision letter; and

(d) other material relied on by the Secretary of State in reaching his
decision;

'appellant' means a person who appeals under section 103 of the Act against
a decision of the Secretary of State;

'bank holiday' means a day that is specified in, or appointed under, the Banking and Financial Dealings Act 1971;

'consideration day' has the meaning given to it by rule 4(4);

'decision letter' means a letter from the Secretary of State giving notice of a decision that gives rise to a right to appeal under section 103;

'excluded day' means a Saturday, a Sunday, a bank holiday, Christmas Day or Good Friday;

'member of the adjudicators' staff' means a person appointed by the Secretary of State under paragraph 5(1) of Schedule 10 to the Act;

'notice of appeal' has the meaning given to it by rule 3(1); and

'party' includes the appellant and the Secretary of State.

(2) Any reference in these Rules:

(a) to an adjudicator, in relation to the sending, giving or receiving of notices or other documents, whether by an adjudicator or a party to the appeal, includes a reference to a member of the adjudicators' staff;

(b) to an adjudicator, in relation to the receiving of a notice of appeal by him, includes a reference to the offices occupied by the adjudicators;

(c) to the appellant, in relation to the sending or giving of notices or other documents by the adjudicator or the Secretary of State, is also a reference to his representative, if he has one; and

(d) to a representative is to be construed in accordance with rule 15.

(3) For the purposes of these Rules, an appeal is determined when an adjudicator gives his adjudication.

PROCEDURE BEFORE DETERMINATION OF APPEAL
Notice of appeal

3 (1) A person who wishes to appeal under section 103 of the Act must give notice to an adjudicator by completing in full, and in English, the form for the time being issued by the Secretary of State for the purpose ('notice of appeal'); and any form so issued is to be in the form shown in the Schedule to these Rules or a form to like effect.

(2) The notice of appeal must be signed by the appellant or his representative.

(3) Subject to paragraph (4), the notice of appeal must be received by the adjudicator not later than 2 days after the day on which the appellant received the decision letter.

(4) The adjudicator may extend the time limit for receiving the notice of appeal (either before or after its expiry) if –

(a) he considers that it is in the interests of justice to do so; and

(b) he is satisfied that:

(i)   the appellant; or

(ii)   his representative (if he has one);

was prevented from complying with the time limit by circumstances beyond his control.

Procedure after receiving notice of appeal

4 (1) On the day that the adjudicator receives notice of appeal or, if not reasonably practicable, as soon as possible on the following day, he must send a copy of the notice of appeal or, if not reasonably practicable, as soon as possible on

the following day, and any supporting documents, to the Secretary of State by fax.

(2) On the day after the day on which the adjudicator receives notice of appeal, the Secretary of State must send the appeal bundle to the adjudicator by fax or by hand and to the appellant by first class post or by fax.

(3) On consideration day, the adjudicator must –

   (a) decide in accordance with rule 5 whether there should be an oral hearing;

   (b) set the date for determining the appeal in accordance with rule 6;

   (c) if there is to be an oral hearing, give notice to the Secretary of State and the appellant, in accordance with rule 7, of the date on which it is to be held.

(4) 'Consideration day' means the day after the day on which the Secretary of State sends the appeal bundle to the adjudicator in accordance with paragraph (2).

Whether there should be an oral hearing

5 (1) The adjudicator must decide to hold an oral hearing –

   (a) where the appellant has requested an oral hearing in his notice of appeal; or

   (b) if the adjudicator considers that it is necessary for the appeal to be disposed of justly.

(2) In all other cases, the appeal may be determined without an oral hearing.

Date for determination of appeal

6 (1) If there is to be an oral hearing, the hearing must be held and the appeal determined 4 days after consideration day.

(2) In all other cases, the appeal must be determined on consideration day, or as soon as possible thereafter, but in any event not later than 4 days after consideration day.

Notification of date of oral hearing

7   If there is to be an oral hearing, the adjudicator must send a notice to the appellant and to the Secretary of State informing them of the date, time and place of the hearing.

Further evidence provided before the determination of the appeal

8 (1) Where the appellant sends to the adjudicator evidence to which this paragraph applies, the appellant must at the same time send a copy of such evidence to the Secretary of State.

(2) Paragraph (1) applies to evidence which is sent after the appellant has sent notice of appeal to the adjudicator but before the appeal has been determined.

(3) Where the Secretary of State sends to the adjudicator evidence to which this paragraph applies, the Secretary of State must at the same time send a copy of such evidence to the appellant.

(4) Paragraph (3) applies to evidence which is sent after the Secretary of State has sent the appeal bundle to the adjudicator but before the appeal has been determined.

DETERMINATION OF APPEAL
Hearing of appeal in absence of either party

9 (1) If an appellant has indicated in his notice of appeal that he does not want to attend, or be represented at, an oral hearing, the hearing may proceed in his absence.

(2) Where –

(a) an appellant has indicated in his notice of appeal that he wants to attend, or be represented at, an oral hearing;

(b) he has been notified of the date, time and place of the hearing in accordance with rule 7; and

(c) neither he nor his representative (if he has one) attends the hearing;

the hearing may proceed in his absence.

(3) Where neither the Secretary of State nor his representative (if he has one) attends the hearing, it may proceed in his absence.

Evidence

10 (1) Paragraph (2) applies to all appeals.

(2) The adjudicator may take into account any matters which he considers to be relevant to the appeal (including matters arising after the date on which the decision appealed against was taken).

(3) Paragraphs (4) to (6) apply to oral hearings only.

(4) No person may be compelled to give any evidence or produce any document which he could not be compelled to give or produce on the trial of an action.

(5) The adjudicator may require any witness to give evidence on oath or affirmation, and for that purpose an oath or affirmation in due form may be administered.

(6) When the adjudicator takes into consideration documentary evidence at an oral hearing, a party present at the hearing is to be given an opportunity of inspecting and considering that evidence and taking copies if copies have not been provided previously to that party in accordance with these Rules.

Record of proceedings

11   A record of the proceedings at an oral hearing before the adjudicator is to be made.

Exclusion of public

12 (1) Subject to the provisions of this rule, oral hearings are to take place in public.

(2) Subject to the provisions of paragraph (3), the adjudicator may exclude a member of the public or members of the public generally from a hearing or from part of a hearing if, and to the extent that, he considers it necessary to do so in the public interest.

(3) But nothing in this rule is to prevent a member of the Council on Tribunals, a member of the Scottish Committee of that Council, the Chief Asylum Support Adjudicator or the Deputy Chief Asylum Support Adjudicator, in their capacity as such, from attending an oral hearing.

Adjudication

13 (1) Where an oral hearing is held –

  (a) the adjudicator must inform all persons present of his adjudication at the conclusion of the hearing;

  (b) if neither the appellant nor his representative (if he has one) is present at the conclusion of the hearing, the adjudicator must send notice of his adjudication on the same day to the appellant;

  (c) if the Secretary of State is not present at the conclusion of the hearing, the adjudicator must send notice of his adjudication on the same day to the Secretary of State; and

  (d) not later than 2 days after the day on which the appeal is determined, the adjudicator must send a reasons statement to the appellant and the Secretary of State.

 (2) Where there is no oral hearing, the adjudicator must on the day that the appeal is determined –

  (a) send notice of his adjudication to the appellant and the Secretary of State; and

  (b) send a reasons statement to them.

 (3) An adjudication takes effect from the day on which it is made.

 (4) A 'reasons statement' is a written statement giving reasons for the adjudication.

MISCELLANEOUS
Directions
14   The adjudicator may give directions on any matter arising in connection with an appeal if he considers it necessary or desirable to do so in the interests of justice.

Representation
15   A party to the appeal may be represented by any other person.

Withdrawal of decision
16 (1) Where the Secretary of State withdraws the decision which is appealed against, he must give notice to the adjudicator and the appellant forthwith.

 (2) Where the appellant withdraws his appeal, he must give notice to the adjudicator and the Secretary of State forthwith.

 (3) Where paragraph (1) or (2) applies, the appeal is to be treated for all purposes as at an end.

Notices
17   In the absence of express provision, any notice or other document required or authorised by these Rules to be sent or given by any party may be sent by first class post, by fax or by hand.

Time
18 (1) Subject to paragraph (2), for the purposes of these Rules, a notice or other document is to be taken to have been received on the day on which it was in fact received.

(2) Where a notice or other document is sent by first class post by the Secretary of State or by the adjudicator, it is to be taken to have been received 2 days after the day on which it was sent, unless the contrary is proven.

(3) Where reference is made in these Rules to a specified number of days after an event, the number of days is to be calculated from the expiry of the day on which the event occurred.

(4) Where these Rules provide that an act is to be done or to be taken to have been done –
   (a) not later than a specified number of days after an event; or
   (b) a specified number of days after an event;
   and that number of days –
   (c) expires on an excluded day, the act is to be taken to have been done as required if done on the next working day;
   (d) includes an excluded day, that day is to be discounted.

(5) Where these Rules provide that an act is to be done or to be taken to have been done on a certain day and that day is an excluded day, the act is to be taken to have been done as required if done on the next working day.

Irregularities

19 (1) Any irregularity resulting from failure to comply with these Rules before the adjudicator has determined the appeal is not by itself to render the proceedings void.

(2) But the adjudicator must, if he considers that either party may have been prejudiced, take such steps as he thinks fit to remove or reduce the prejudice.

SCHEDULE – RULE 3(1): ASYLUM SUPPORT ADJUDICATORS: NOTICE OF APPEAL

Section one: Give your personal details
Full Name
Date of Birth Nationality
Your NASS reference number

Section two
Give an address in the United Kingdom where we can contact you
Give a daytime fax or telephone number in the UK where we can contact you (if you have one)

Section three
Give the date of the decision letter against which you are appealing

Section four
Do you want an oral hearing of your appeal? Yes/No
Do you want to attend any oral hearing of your appeal? Yes/No
If you want to attend the hearing, will you need an interpreter? Yes/No
If so, in what language?
Are you to be represented in this appeal? Yes/No
If so you must give full details of your representative: name and address,

and telephone and fax numbers if available, together with any reference number the representative has given your case.

Will your representative attend any oral hearing of your appeal? Yes/No

Section five
What are the grounds of your appeal?
What matters in the decision letter do you dispute?
Signature
Date
[Appellant/Representative]
If you have further information which you would like the Adjudicator to take into account when making a decision about your appeal, you should send copies of any documents with this form.
Return this form to:
Asylum Support Adjudicator
Christopher Wren House
113 High Street
Croydon CR0 1GQ

Asylum Support Regulations 2000 SI No 704

GENERAL
Citation and commencement
1   These Regulations may be cited as the Asylum Support Regulations 2000 and shall come into force on 3rd April 2000.

Interpretation
2   (1) In these Regulations –
'the Act' means the Immigration and Asylum Act 1999;
'asylum support' means support provided under section 95 of the Act;
'dependant' has the meaning given by paragraphs (4) and (5);
'the interim Regulations' means the Asylum Support (Interim Provisions) Regulations 1999;
'married couple' means a man and woman who are married to each other and are members of the same household; and
'unmarried couple' means a man and woman who, though not married to each other, are living together as if married.
(2) The period of 14 days is prescribed for the purposes of section 94(3) of the Act (day on which a claim for asylum is determined).
(3) Paragraph (2) does not apply in relation to a case to which the interim Regulations apply (for which case, provision corresponding to paragraph (2) is made by regulation 2(6) of those Regulations).
(4) In these Regulations 'dependant', in relation to an asylum-seeker, a supported person or an applicant for asylum support, means, subject to paragraph (5), a person in the United Kingdom ('the relevant person') who –

(a) is his spouse;

(b) is a child of his or of his spouse, is dependant on him and is, or was at the relevant time, under 18;

(c) is a member of his or his spouse's close family and is, or was at the relevant time, under 18;

(d) had been living as part of his household –
    (i)   for at least six of the twelve months before the relevant time, or
    (ii)   since birth,
and is, or was at the relevant time, under 18;

(e) is in need of care and attention from him or a member of his household by reason of a disability and would fall within sub-paragraph (c) or (d) but for the fact that he is not, and was not at the relevant time, under 18;

(f) had been living with him as a member of an unmarried couple for at least two of the three years before the relevant time;

(g) is living as part of his household and was, immediately before 6th December 1999 (the date when the interim Regulations came into force), receiving assistance from a local authority under section 17 of the Children Act 1989;

(h) is living as part of his household and was, immediately before the coming into force of these Regulations, receiving assistance from a local authority under –
    (i)   section 22 of the Children (Scotland) Act 1995; or
    (ii)   Article 18 of the Children (Northern Ireland) Order 1995;
    or

(i) has made a claim for leave to enter or remain in the United Kingdom, or for variation of any such leave, which is being considered on the basis that he is dependant on the asylum-seeker;

and in relation to a supported person, or an applicant for asylum support, who is himself a dependant of an asylum-seeker, also includes the asylum-seeker if in the United Kingdom.

(5) Where a supported person or applicant for asylum support is himself a dependant of an asylum-seeker, a person who would otherwise be a dependant of the supported person, or of the applicant, for the purposes of these Regulations is not such a dependant unless he is also a dependant of the asylum-seeker or is the asylum-seeker.

(6) In paragraph (4), 'the relevant time', in relation to the relevant person, means –

(a) the time when an application for asylum support for him was made in accordance with regulation 3(3); or

(b) if he has joined a person who is already a supported person in the United Kingdom and sub-paragraph (a) does not apply, the time when he joined that person in the United Kingdom.

(7) Where a person, by falling within a particular category in relation to an asylum-seeker or supported person, is by virtue of this regulation a dependant of the asylum-seeker or supported person for the purposes of these Regulations, that category is also a prescribed category for the purposes of paragraph (c) of the definition of 'dependant' in section 94(1) of the Act and,

accordingly, the person is a dependant of the asylum-seeker or supported person for the purposes of Part VI of the Act.

(8) Paragraph (7) does not apply to a person who is already a dependant of the asylum-seeker or supported person for the purposes of Part VI of the Act because he falls within either of the categories mentioned in paragraphs (a) and (b) of the definition of 'dependant' in section 94(1) of the Act.

(9) Paragraph (7) does not apply for the purposes of any reference to a 'dependant' in Schedule 9 to the Act.

INITIAL APPLICATION FOR SUPPORT
Initial application for support: individual and group applications

3 (1) Either of the following –
   (a) an asylum-seeker, or
   (b) a dependant of an asylum-seeker,
   may apply to the Secretary of State for asylum support.

(2) An application under this regulation may be –
   (a) for asylum support for the applicant alone; or
   (b) for asylum support for the applicant and one or more dependants of his.

(3) The application must be made by completing in full and in English the form for the time being issued by the Secretary of State for the purpose; and any form so issued shall be the form shown in the Schedule to these Regulations or a form to the like effect.

(4) The application may not be entertained by the Secretary of State unless it is made in accordance with paragraph (3).

(5) The Secretary of State may make further enquiries of the applicant about any matter connected with the application.

(6) Paragraphs (3) and (4) do not apply where a person is already a supported person and asylum support is sought for a dependant of his for whom such support is not already provided (for which case, provision is made by regulation 15).

Persons excluded from support

4 (1) The following circumstances are prescribed for the purposes of subsection (2) of section 95 of the Act as circumstances where a person who would otherwise fall within subsection (1) of that section is excluded from that subsection (and, accordingly, may not be provided with asylum support).

(2) A person is so excluded if he is applying for asylum support for himself alone and he falls within paragraph (4) by virtue of any sub-paragraph of that paragraph.

(3) A person is so excluded if –
   (a) he is applying for asylum support for himself and other persons, or he is included in an application for asylum support made by a person other than himself;
   (b) he falls within paragraph (4) (by virtue of any sub-paragraph of that paragraph); and
   (c) each of the other persons to whom the application relates also falls within paragraph (4) (by virtue of any sub-paragraph of that paragraph).

(4) A person falls within this paragraph if at the time when the application is determined –
   (a) he is a person to whom interim support applies; or
   (b) he is a person to whom social security benefits apply; or
   (c) he has not made a claim for leave to enter or remain in the United Kingdom, or for variation of any such leave, which is being considered on the basis that he is an asylum-seeker or dependent on an asylum-seeker.

(5) For the purposes of paragraph (4), interim support applies to a person if –
   (a) at the time when the application is determined, he is a person to whom, under the interim Regulations, support under regulation 3 of those Regulations must be provided by a local authority;
   (b) sub-paragraph (a) does not apply, but would do so if the person had been determined by the local authority concerned to be an eligible person; or
   (c) sub-paragraph (a) does not apply, but would do so but for the fact that the person's support under those Regulations was (otherwise than by virtue of regulation 7(1)(d) of those Regulations) refused under regulation 7, or suspended or discontinued under regulation 8, of those Regulations;
   and in this paragraph 'local authority', 'local authority concerned' and 'eligible person' have the same meanings as in the interim Regulations.

(6) For the purposes of paragraph (4), a person is a person to whom social security benefits apply if he is –
   (a) a person who by virtue of regulation 2 of the Social Security (Immigration and Asylum) Consequential Amendments Regulations 2000 is not excluded by section 115(1) of the Act from entitlement to –
      (i) income-based jobseeker's allowance under the Jobseekers Act 1995; or
      (ii) income support, housing benefit or council tax benefit under the Social Security Contributions and Benefits Act 1992;
   (b) a person who, by virtue of regulation 2 of the Social Security (Immigration and Asylum) Consequential Amendments Regulations (Northern Ireland) 2000 is not excluded by section 115(2) of the Act from entitlement to –
      (i) income-based jobseeker's allowance under the Jobseekers (Northern Ireland) Order 1995; or
      (ii) income support or housing benefit under the Social Security Contributions and Benefits (Northern Ireland) Act 1992;

(7) A person is not to be regarded as falling within paragraph (2) or (3) if, when asylum support is sought for him, he is a dependant of a person who is already a supported person.

(8) The circumstances prescribed by paragraphs (2) and (3) are also prescribed for the purposes of section 95(2), as applied by section 98(3), of the Act as circumstances where a person who would otherwise fall within subsection (1) of section 98 is excluded from that subsection (and, accordingly, may not be provided with temporary support under section 98).

(9) For the purposes of paragraph (8), paragraphs (2) and (3) shall apply as if any reference to an application for asylum support were a reference to an application for support under section 98 of the Act.

DETERMINING WHETHER PERSONS ARE DESTITUTE
Determination where application relates to more than one person, etc

5 (1) Subject to paragraph (2), where an application in accordance with regulation 3(3) is for asylum support for the applicant and one or more dependants of his, in applying section 95(1) of the Act the Secretary of State must decide whether the applicant and all those dependants, taken together, are destitute or likely to become destitute within the period prescribed by regulation 7.

   (2) Where a person is a supported person, and the question falls to be determined whether asylum support should in future be provided for him and one or more other persons who are his dependants and are –
   (a) persons for whom asylum support is also being provided when that question falls to be determined; or
   (b) persons for whom the Secretary of State is then considering whether asylum support should be provided,

   in applying section 95(1) of the Act the Secretary of State must decide whether the supported person and all those dependants, taken together, are destitute or likely to become destitute within the period prescribed by regulation 7.

Income and assets to be taken into account

6 (1) This regulation applies where it falls to the Secretary of State to determine for the purposes of section 95(1) of the Act whether –
   (a) a person applying for asylum support, or such an applicant and any dependants of his, or
   (b) a supported person, or such a person and any dependants of his,

   is or are destitute or likely to become so within the period prescribed by regulation 7.

   (2) In this regulation 'the principal' means the applicant for asylum support (where paragraph (1)(a) applies) or the supported person (where paragraph (1)(b) applies).

   (3) The Secretary of State must ignore –
   (a) any asylum support, and
   (b) any support under section 98 of the Act,

   which the principal or any dependant of his is provided with or, where the question is whether destitution is likely within a particular period, might be provided with in that period.

   (4) But he must take into account –
   (a) any other income which the principal, or any dependant of his, has or might reasonably be expected to have in that period;
   (b) any other support which is available to the principal or any dependant of his, or might reasonably be expected to be so available in that period; and
   (c) any assets mentioned in paragraph (5) (whether held in the United Kingdom or elsewhere) which are available to the principal or any dependant of his otherwise than by way of asylum support or support under section 98, or might reasonably be expected to be so available in that period.

(5) Those assets are –
  (a) cash;
  (b) savings;
  (c) investments;
  (d) land;
  (e) cars or other vehicles; and
  (f) goods held for the purpose of a trade or other business.
(6) The Secretary of State must ignore any assets not mentioned in paragraph (5).

Period within which applicant must be likely to become destitute

7 The period prescribed for the purposes of section 95(1) of the Act is –
  (a) where the question whether a person or persons is or are destitute or likely to become so falls to be determined in relation to an application for asylum support and sub-paragraph (b) does not apply, 14 days beginning with the day on which that question falls to be determined;
  (b) where that question falls to be determined in relation to a supported person, or in relation to persons including a supported person, 56 days beginning with the day on which that question falls to be determined.

Adequacy of existing accommodation

8 (1) Subject to paragraph (2), the matters mentioned in paragraph (3) are pre-scribed for the purposes of subsection (5)(a) of section 95 of the Act as matters to which the Secretary of State must have regard in determining for the purposes of that section whether the accommodation of –
  (a) a person applying for asylum support, or
  (b) a supported person for whom accommodation is not for the time being provided by way of asylum support,
  is adequate.
  (2) The matters mentioned in paragraph (3)(a) and (d) to (g) are not so pre-scribed for the purposes of a case where the person indicates to the Secretary of State that he wishes to remain in the accommodation.
  (3) The matters referred to in paragraph (1) are –
  (a) whether it would be reasonable for the person to continue to occupy the accommodation;
  (b) whether the accommodation is affordable for him;
  (c) whether the accommodation is provided under section 98 of the Act, or otherwise on an emergency basis, only while the claim for asylum support is being determined;
  (d) whether the person can secure entry to the accommodation;
  (e) where the accommodation consists of a moveable structure, vehicle or vessel designed or adapted for human habitation, whether there is a place where the person is entitled or permitted both to place it and reside in it;
  (f) whether the accommodation is available for occupation by the person's dependants together with him;
  (g) whether it is probable that the person's continued occupation of the accommodation will lead to domestic violence against him or any of his dependants.

398 Support for asylum-seekers / Appendix A

(4) In determining whether it would be reasonable for a person to continue to occupy accommodation, regard may be had to the general circumstances prevailing in relation to housing in the district of the local housing authority where the accommodation is.

(5) In determining whether a person's accommodation is affordable for him, the Secretary of State must have regard to –

    (a) any income, or any assets mentioned in regulation 6(5) (whether held in the United Kingdom or elsewhere), which is or are available to him or any dependant of his otherwise than by way of asylum support or support under section 98 of the Act, or might reasonably be expected to be so available;

    (b) the costs in respect of the accommodation; and

    (c) the person's other reasonable living expenses.

(6) In this regulation –

    (a) 'domestic violence' means violence from a person who is or has been a close family member, or threats of violence from such a person which are likely to be carried out; and

    (b) 'district of the local housing authority' has the meaning given by section 217(3) of the Housing Act 1996.

(7) The reference in paragraph (1) to subsection (5)(a) of section 95 of the Act does not include a reference to that provision as applied by section 98(3) of the Act.

Essential living needs

9 (1) The matter mentioned in paragraph (2) is prescribed for the purposes of subsection (7)(b) of section 95 of the Act as a matter to which the Secretary of State may not have regard in determining for the purposes of that section whether a person's essential living needs (other than accommodation) are met.

(2) That matter is his personal preference as to clothing (but this shall not be taken to prevent the Secretary of State from taking into account his individual circumstances as regards clothing).

(3) None of the items and expenses mentioned in paragraph (4) is to be treated as being an essential living need of a person for the purposes of Part VI of the Act.

(4) Those items and expenses are –

    (a) the cost of faxes;

    (b) computers and the cost of computer facilities;

    (c) the cost of photocopying;

    (d) travel expenses, except the expense mentioned in paragraph (5);

    (e) toys and other recreational items;

    (f) entertainment expenses.

(5) The expense excepted from paragraph (4)(d) is the expense of an initial journey from a place in the United Kingdom to accommodation provided by way of asylum support or (where accommodation is not so provided) to an address in the United Kingdom which has been notified to the Secretary of State as the address where the person intends to live.

(6) Paragraph (3) shall not be taken to affect the question whether any item or

expense not mentioned in paragraph (4) or (5) is, or is not, an essential living need.

(7) The reference in paragraph (1) to subsection (7)(b) of section 95 of the Act includes a reference to that provision as applied by section 98(3) of the Act and, accordingly, the reference in paragraph (1) to 'that section' includes a reference to section 98.

PROVISION OF SUPPORT
Kind and levels of support for essential living needs

10 (1) This regulation applies where the Secretary of State has decided that asylum support should be provided in respect of the essential living needs of a person.

(2) As a general rule, asylum support in respect of the essential living needs of that person may be expected to be provided weekly in the form of vouchers redeemable for goods, services and cash whose total redemption value, for any week, equals the amount shown in the second column of the following Table opposite the entry in the first column which for the time being describes that person.

TABLE

Qualifying couple	£57.37
Lone parent aged 18 or over	£36.54
Single person aged 25 or over	£36.54
Single person aged at least 18 but under 25	£28.95
Person aged at least 16 but under 18 (except a member of a qualifying couple)	£31.75
Person aged under 16	£26.60

(3) In paragraph (1) and the provisions of paragraph (2) preceding the Table, 'person' includes 'couple'.

(4) In this regulation –
  (a) 'qualifying couple' means a married or unmarried couple at least one of whom is aged 18 or over and neither of whom is aged under 16;
  (b) 'lone parent' means a parent who is not a member of a married or unmarried couple;
  (c) 'single person' means a person who is not a parent or a member of a qualifying couple; and
  (d) 'parent' means a parent of a relevant child, that is to say a child who is aged under 18 and for whom asylum support is provided.

(5) Where the Secretary of State has decided that accommodation should be provided for a person (or couple) by way of asylum support, and the accommodation is provided in a form which also meets other essential living needs (such as bed and breakfast, or half or full board), the amounts shown in the Table in paragraph (2) shall be treated as reduced accordingly.

(6) The redemption value of the vouchers redeemable for cash which the Secretary of State may be expected to include in the asylum support provided for any week in accordance with paragraph (2) may, as a general rule, be

expected not to exceed £10 per person (or, as the case may be, £20 per qualifying couple).

Additional single payments in respect of essential living needs

11 (1) At the end of each qualifying period, the Secretary of State may as a general rule be expected to provide, or arrange for the provision of, additional support for an eligible person (in respect of his essential living needs) in the form of a single issue of vouchers redeemable for cash whose total redemption value equals £50.

(2) In paragraph (1) 'eligible person' means a person for whom asylum support has been provided for the whole of the qualifying period.

(3) Each of the following is a qualifying period –
   (a) the period of six months beginning with the day on which asylum support was first provided for the person; and
   (b) each period of six months beginning with a re-start day.

(4) Each of the following is a re-start day –
   (a) the day after the day on which the period mentioned in paragraph (3)(a) ends; and
   (b) the day after the day on which a period mentioned in paragraph (3)(b) ends.

(5) Paragraph (1) applies only if an application for the additional support is made to the Secretary of State by or on behalf of the eligible person.

(6) Where a person is, in the opinion of the Secretary of State, responsible without reasonable excuse for a delay in the determination of his claim for asylum, the Secretary of State may treat any qualifying period as extended by the period of delay.

Income and assets to be taken into account in providing support

12 (1) This regulation applies where it falls to the Secretary of State to decide the level or kind of asylum support to be provided for –
   (a) a person applying for asylum support, or such an applicant and any dependants of his; or
   (b) a supported person, or such a person and any dependants of his.

(2) In this regulation 'the principal' means the applicant for asylum support (where paragraph (1)(a) applies) or the supported person (where paragraph (1)(b) applies).

(3) The Secretary of State must take into account –
   (a) any income which the principal or any dependant of his has or might reasonably be expected to have,
   (b) support which is or might reasonably be expected to be available to the principal or any dependant of his, and
   (c) any assets mentioned in regulation 6(5) (whether held in the United Kingdom or elsewhere) which are or might reasonably be expected to be available to the principal or any dependant of his, otherwise than by way of asylum support.

Accommodation

13 (1) The matters mentioned in paragraph (2) are prescribed for the purposes of subsection (2)(b) of section 97 of the Act as matters to which regard may not be had when exercising the power under section 95 of the Act to provide accommodation for a person.

(2) Those matters are –

(a) his personal preference as to the nature of the accommodation to be provided; and

(b) his personal preference as to the nature and standard of fixtures and fittings;

but this shall not be taken to prevent the person's individual circumstances, as they relate to his accommodation needs, being taken into account.

Services

14 (1) The services mentioned in pararaph (2) may be provided or made available by way of asylum support to persons who are otherwise receiving such support, but may be so provided only for the purpose of maintaining good order among such persons.

(2) Those services are –

(a) education, including English language lessons,

(b) sporting or other developmental activities.

Change of circumstances

15 (1) If a relevant change of circumstances occurs, the supported person concerned or a dependant of his must, without delay, notify the Secretary of State of that change of circumstances.

(2) A relevant change of circumstances occurs where a supported person or a dependant of his –

(a) is joined in the United Kingdom by a dependant or, as the case may be, another dependant, of the supported person;

(b) receives or gains access to any money, or other asset mentioned in regulation 6(5), that has not previously been declared to the Secretary of State;

(c) becomes employed;

(d) becomes unemployed;

(e) changes his name;

(f) gets married;

(g) starts living with a person as if married to that person;

(h) gets divorced;

(i) separates from a spouse, or from a person with whom he has been living as if married to that person;

(j) becomes pregnant;

(k) has a child;

(l) leaves school;

m) starts to share his accommodation with another person;

(n) moves to a different address, or otherwise leaves his accommodation;

(o) goes into hospital;

(p) goes to prison or is otherwise held in custody;

    (q) leaves the United Kingdom; or

    (r) dies.

(3) If, on being notified of a change of circumstances, the Secretary of State considers that the change may be one –

    (a) as a result of which asylum support should be provided for a person for whom it was not provided before, or

    (b) as a result of which asylum support should no longer be provided for a person, or

    (c) which may otherwise affect the asylum support which should be provided for a person,

he may make further enquiries of the supported person or dependant who gave the notification.

(4) The Secretary of State may, in particular, require that person to provide him with such information as he considers necessary to determine whether, and if so, what, asylum support should be provided for any person.

Contributions

16 (1) This regulation applies where, in deciding the level of asylum support to be provided for a person who is or will be a supported person, the Secretary of State is required to take into account income, support or assets as mentioned in regulation 12(3).

(2) The Secretary of State may –

    (a) set the asylum support for that person at a level which does not reflect the income, support or assets; and

    (b) require from that person payments by way of contributions towards the cost of the provision for him of asylum support.

(3) A supported person must make to the Secretary of State such payments by way of contributions as the Secretary of State may require under paragraph (2).

(4) Prompt payment of such contributions may be made a condition (under section 95(9) of the Act) subject to which asylum support for that person is provided.

RECOVERY OF SUMS BY SECRETARY OF STATE
Recovery where assets become realisable

17 (1) This regulation applies where it appears to the Secretary of State at any time (the relevant time) –

    (a) that a supported person had, at the time when he applied for asylum support, assets of any kind in the United Kingdom or elsewhere which were not capable of being realised; but

    (b) that those assets have subsequently become, and remain, capable of being realised.

(2) The Secretary of State may recover from that person a sum not exceeding the recoverable sum.

(3) Subject to paragraph (5), the recoverable sum is a sum equal to whichever is the less of –

    (a) the monetary value of all the asylum support provided to the person up to the relevant time; and

(b) the monetary value of the assets concerned.

(4) As well as being recoverable as mentioned in paragraph 11(2)(a) of Schedule 8 to the Act, an amount recoverable under this regulation may be recovered by deduction from asylum support.

(5) The recoverable sum shall be treated as reduced by any amount which the Secretary of State has by virtue of this regulation already recovered from the person concerned (whether by deduction or otherwise) with regard to the assets concerned.

Overpayments: method of recovery

18   As well as being recoverable as mentioned in subsection (3) of section 114 of the Act, an amount recoverable under subsection (2) of that section may be recovered by deduction from asylum support.

BREACH OF CONDITIONS AND SUSPENSION AND DISCONTINUATION OF SUPPORT
Breach of conditions: decision whether to provide support

19 (1) When deciding –

(a) whether to provide, or to continue to provide, asylum support for any person or persons, or

(b) the level or kind of support to be provided for any person or persons, the Secretary of State may take into account the extent to which any relevant condition has been complied with.

(2) A relevant condition is a condition subject to which asylum support for that person or any of those persons is being, or has previously been, provided.

Suspension or discontinuation of support

20 (1) Asylum support for a supported person and his dependants (if any), or for one or more dependants of a supported person, may be suspended or discontinued if –

(a) the Secretary of State has reasonable grounds to suspect that the supported person or any dependant of his has failed without reasonable excuse to comply with any condition subject to which the asylum support is provided;

(b) the Secretary of State has reasonable grounds to suspect that the supported person or any dependant of his has committed an offence under Part VI of the Act;

(c) the Secretary of State has reasonable grounds to suspect that the supported person has intentionally made himself and his dependants (if any) destitute;

(d) the supported person or any dependant of his for whom asylum support is being provided ceases to reside at the authorised address; or

(e) the supported person or any dependant of his for whom asylum support is being provided is absent from the authorised address –

  (i)   for more than seven consecutive days and nights, or

  (ii) for a total of more than 14 days and nights in any six month period, without the permission of the Secretary of State.

(2) For the purposes of this regulation, a person has intentionally made himself

destitute if he appears to be, or to be likely to become within the period prescribed by regulation 7, destitute as a result of an act or omission deliberately done or made by him or any dependant of his without reasonable excuse while in the United Kingdom.

(3) For the purposes of this regulation, the authorised address is –

   (a) the accommodation provided for the supported person and his dependants (if any) by way of asylum support; or

   (b) if no accommodation is so provided, the address notified by the supported person to the Secretary of State in his application for asylum support or, where a change of his address has been notified to the Secretary of State under regulation 15, the address for the time being so notified.

Effect of previous suspension or discontinuation

21 (1) Where –

   (a) an application for asylum support is made,

   (b) the applicant or any other person to whom the application relates has previously had his asylum support suspended or discontinued under regulation 20, and

   (c) there has been no material change of circumstances since the suspension or discontinuation,

the application need not be entertained unless the Secretary of State considers that there are exceptional circumstances which justify its being entertained.

(2) A material change of circumstances is one which, if the applicant were a supported person, would have to be notified to the Secretary of State under regulation 15.

(3) This regulation is without prejudice to the power of the Secretary of State to refuse the application even if he has entertained it.

NOTICE TO QUIT

22 (1) If –

   (a) as a result of asylum support, a person has a tenancy or licence to occupy accommodation,

   (b) one or more of the conditions mentioned in paragraph (2) is satisfied, and

   (c) he is given notice to quit in accordance with paragraph (3) or (4),

his tenancy or licence is to be treated as ending with the period specified in that notice, regardless of when it could otherwise be brought to an end.

(2) The conditions are that –

   (a) the asylum support is suspended or discontinued as a result of any provision of regulation 20;

   (b) the relevant claim for asylum has been determined;

   (c) the supported person has ceased to be destitute; or

   (d) he is to be moved to other accommodation.

(3) A notice to quit is in accordance with this paragraph if it is in writing and –

   (a) in a case where sub-paragraph (a), (c) or (d) of paragraph (2) applies, specifies as the notice period a period of not less than seven days; or

   (b) in a case where the Secretary of State has notified his decision on the relevant claim for asylum to the claimant, specifies as the notice period a period at least as long as whichever is the greater of –

    (i)   seven days; or

    (ii) the period beginning with the date of service of the notice to quit and ending with the date of determination of the relevant claim for asylum (found in accordance with section 94(3) of the Act).

(4) A notice to quit is in accordance with this paragraph if –

    (a) it is in writing;

    (b) it specifies as the notice period a period of less than seven days; and

    (c) the circumstances of the case are such that that notice period is justified.

MEANING OF 'DESTITUTE' FOR CERTAIN OTHER PURPOSES

23 (1) In this regulation 'the relevant enactments' means –

    (a) section 21(1A) of the National Assistance Act 1948;

    (b) section 45(4A) of the Health Services and Public Health Act 1968;

    (c) paragraph 2(2A) of Schedule 8 to the National Health Service Act 1977;

    (d) sections 12(2A), 13A(4) and 13B(3) of the Social Work (Scotland) Act 1968;

    (e) sections 7(3) and 8(4) of the Mental Health (Scotland) Act 1984; and

    (f) Articles 7(3) and 15(6) of the Health and Personal Social Services (Northern Ireland) Order 1972.

(2) The following provisions of this regulation apply where it falls to an authority, or the Department, to determine for the purposes of any of the relevant enactments whether a person is destitute.

(3) Paragraphs (3) to (6) of regulation 6 apply as they apply in the case mentioned in paragraph (1) of that regulation, but as if references to the principal were references to the person whose destitution or otherwise is being determined and references to the Secretary of State were references to the authority or (as the case may be) Department.

(4) The matters mentioned in paragraph (3) of regulation 8 (read with paragraphs (4) to (6) of that regulation) are prescribed for the purposes of subsection (5)(a) of section 95 of the Act, as applied for the purposes of any of the relevant enactments, as matters to which regard must be had in determining for the purposes of any of the relevant enactments whether a person's accommodation is adequate.

(5) The matter mentioned in paragraph (2) of regulation 9 is prescribed for the purposes of subsection (7)(b) of section 95 of the Act, as applied for the purposes of any of the relevant enactments, as a matter to which regard may not be had in determining for the purposes of any of the relevant enactments whether a person's essential living needs (other than accommodation) are met.

(6) Paragraphs (3) to (6) of regulation 9 shall apply as if the reference in paragraph (3) to Part VI of the Act included a reference to the relevant enactments.

(7) The references in regulations 8(5) and 9(2) to the Secretary of State shall be construed, for the purposes of this regulation, as references to the authority or (as the case may be) Department.

[*Schedule not reproduced.*]

Social Security Administration Act 1992

PART I: CLAIMS FOR AND PAYMENTS AND GENERAL ADMINISTRATION OF BENEFIT NECESSITY OF CLAIM
Entitlement to benefit dependent on claim

1 (1) Except in such cases as may be prescribed, and subject to the following provisions of this section and to section 3 below, no person shall be entitled to any benefit unless, in addition to any other conditions relating to that benefit being satisfied –

(a) he makes a claim for it in the manner, and within the time, prescribed in relation to that benefit by regulations under this Part of this Act; or

(b) he is treated by virtue of such regulations as making a claim for it.

(1A) No person whose entitlement to any benefit depends on his making a claim shall be entitled to the benefit unless subsection (1B) below is satisfied in relation both to the person making the claim and to any other person in respect of whom he is claiming a benefit.

(1B) This subsection is satisfied in relation to a person if –

(a) the claim is accompanied by –

(i) a statement of the person's national insurance number and information or evidence establishing that that number has been allocated to that person; or

(ii) information or evidence enabling the national insurance number that has been allocated to the person to be ascertained; or

(b) the person makes an application for a national insurance number to be allocated to him which is accompanied by information or evidence enabling such a number to be so allocated.

[(1C) and (3) not reproduced.]

(4) In this section and section 2 below 'benefit' means –

(a) benefit as defined in section 122 of the Contributions and Benefits Act;

(aa) a jobseeker's allowance; and

(b) any income-related benefit.

(5) This section (which corresponds to section 165A of the 1975 Act, as it had effect immediately before this Act came into force) applies to claims made on or after 1st October 1990 or treated by virtue of regulations under that section or this section as having been made on or after that date.

(6) Schedule 1 to this Act shall have effect in relation to other claims.

Social Security (Immigration and Asylum) Consequential Amendments Regulations 2000 SI No 636

Persons not excluded from specified benefits under section 115 of the Immigration and Asylum Act 1999

2 (1) For the purposes of entitlement to income-based jobseeker's allowance, income support, a social fund payment, housing benefit or council tax benefit under the Contributions and Benefits Act, as the case may be, a person falling within a category or description of persons specified in Part I of the Schedule is a person to whom section 115 of the Act does not apply.

(2) For the purposes of entitlement to attendance allowance, severe disablement allowance, invalid care allowance, disability living allowance, a social fund payment or child benefit under the Contributions and Benefits Act, as the case may be, a person falling within a category or description of persons specified in Part II of the Schedule is a person to whom section 115 of the Act does not apply.

(3) For the purposes of entitlement to child benefit, attendance allowance or disability living allowance under the Contributions and Benefits Act, as the case may be, a person in respect of whom there is an Order in Council made under section 179 of the Social Security Administration Act 1992 giving effect to a reciprocal agreement in respect of one of those benefits, as the case may be, is a person to whom section 115 of the Act does not apply.

(4) For the purposes of entitlement to –
   (a) income support, a social fund payment, housing benefit or council tax benefit under the Contributions and Benefits Act, as the case may be, a person who is entitled to or is receiving benefit by virtue of paragraph (1) or (2) of regulation 12 of the Persons from Abroad Regulations is a person to whom section 115 of the Act does not apply;
   (b) attendance allowance, disability living allowance, invalid care allowance, severe disablement allowance, a social fund payment or child benefit under the Contributions and Benefits Act, as the case may be, a person who is entitled to or is receiving benefit by virtue of paragraph (10) of regulation 12 is a person to whom section 115 of the Act does not apply.

(5) For the purposes of entitlement to income support by virtue of regulation 70 of the Income Support Regulations (urgent cases), to jobseeker's allowance by virtue of regulation 147 of the Jobseeker's Allowance Regulations (urgent cases) or to a social fund payment under the Contributions and Benefits Act, as the case may be, a person to whom regulation 12(3) applies is a person to whom section 115 of the Act does not apply.

(6) For the purposes of entitlement to housing benefit, council tax benefit or a social fund payment under the Contributions and Benefits Act, as the case may be, a person to whom regulation 12(6) applies is a person to whom section 115 of the Act does not apply.

Amendment of the Income Support Regulations

3 (1) The Income Support Regulations shall be amended in accordance with the following provisions of this regulation.

(2) In regulation 2(1) (interpretation) –

  (a) after the definition of 'housing benefit expenditure' there shall be inserted the following definition –
  'Immigration and Asylum Act' means the Immigration and Asylum Act 1999;' and

  (b) the definition of 'immigration authorities' shall be omitted.

(3) In paragraph (3)(a) of regulation 4ZA, for the words ' regulation 70(3)(a)' there shall be substituted the words 'paragraph 1 of Part I of the Schedule to the Social Security (Immigration and Asylum) Consequential Amendments Regulations 2000'.

(4) In regulation 21 (special cases) –

  (a) in paragraph (1) for the words 'regulation 21ZA' there shall be substituted the words 'regulation 21ZB';

  (b) in paragraph (3) the first definition of 'person from abroad' shall be omitted;

  (c) in paragraph (3), after the opening words, there shall be inserted the following definition –
  'partner of a person subject to immigration control' means a person –

  (i)   who is not subject to immigration control within the meaning of section 115(9) of the Immigration and Asylum Act; or

  (ii) to whom section 115 of that Act does not apply by virtue of regulation 2 of the Social Security (Immigration and Asylum) Consequential Amendments Regulations 2000; and

  (iii) who is a member of a couple and his partner is subject to immigration control within the meaning of section 115(9) of that Act and section 115 of that Act applies to her for the purposes of exclusion from entitlement to income support;'; and

  (d) in paragraph (3) in the second definition of 'person from abroad' the word 'also' shall be omitted.

(5) For regulation 21ZA (treatment of refugees) after the heading there shall be substituted the following regulation –

'21ZB (1)   This paragraph applies to a person who has submitted a claim for asylum on or after 3rd April 2000 and who is notified that he has been recorded by the Secretary of State as a refugee within the definition in Article 1 of the Convention relating to the Status of Refugees done at Geneva on 28th July 1951 as extended by Article 1(2) of the Protocol relating to the Status of Refugees done at New York on 31st January 1967.

(2) Subject to paragraph (3), a person to whom paragraph (1) applies, who claims income support within 28 days of receiving the notification referred to in paragraph (1), shall have his claim for income support determined as if he had been recorded as a refugee on the date when he submitted his claim for asylum.

(3) The amount of support provided under section 95 or 98 of the Immigration and Asylum Act, including support provided by virtue of regulations made under Schedule 9 to that Act, by the Secretary of State in respect of

essential living needs of the claimant and his dependants (if any) as specified in regulations made under paragraph 3 of Schedule 8 to the Immigration and Asylum Act shall be deducted from any award of income support
due to the claimant by virtue of paragraph (2).'.

(6) In regulation 40 (calculation of income other than earnings) –
  (a) at the beginning of paragraph (4) there shall be inserted the words
    'Subject to paragraph (5)';
  (b) in paragraph (4) for the words following 'paragraph (1)' there shall be
    substituted the following sub-paragraphs –
    '(a) any payment to which regulation 35(2) or 37(2) (payments not
    earnings) applies; or
    (b) in the case of a claimant who is receiving support provided under
    section 95 or 98 of the Immigration and Asylum Act including support
    provided by virtue of regulations made under Schedule 9 to that Act, the
    amount of such support provided in respect of essential living needs of
    the claimant and his dependants (if any) as is specified in regulations
    made under paragraph 3 of Schedule 8 to the Immigration and Asylum
    Act;';
  (c) after paragraph (4) there shall be added the following paragraph –
    '(5) In the case of a claimant who is the partner of a person subject to
    immigration control and whose partner is receiving support provided
    under section 95 or 98 of the Immigration and Asylum Act including
    support provided by virtue of regulations made under Schedule 9 to that
    Act, there shall not be included as income to be taken into account
    under paragraph (1) the amount of support provided in respect of essen-
    tial living needs of the partner of the claimant and his dependants (if
    any) as is specified in regulations made under paragraph 3 of Schedule 8
    to the Immigration and Asylum Act.'.

(7) In regulation 70 (urgent cases) –
  (a) in paragraph (2) for sub-paragraph (a) there shall be substituted the
    following sub-paragraph –
    '(a) a claimant to whom paragraph (2A) applies (persons not excluded
    from income support under section 115 of the Immigration and Asylum
    Act);';
  (b) after paragraph (2) there shall be inserted the following paragraph –
    '(2A) This paragraph applies to a person not excluded from entitlement
    to income support under section 115 of the Immigration and Asylum
    Act by virtue of regulation 2 of the Social Security (Immigration and
    Asylum) Consequential Amendments Regulations 2000 except for a
    person to whom paragraphs 3 and 4 of Part I of the Schedule to those
    Regulations applies.'; and
  (c) paragraphs (3), (3A) and (3B) shall be omitted.

(8) In regulation 71 (applicable amounts in urgent cases) –
  (a) in paragraph (1)(d), for the words 'paragraph 17' there shall be substi-
    tuted the words 'paragraph 16A'; and
  (b) in paragraph (2), for the words 'paragraph (3)' in each place where they
    occur, there shall be substituted the words 'paragraph 2A'.

(9) In Schedule 1B (prescribed categories of person) –

(a) after paragraph 18, there shall be inserted the following paragraph –

'**18A** A person to whom regulation 21ZB (treatment of refugees) applies by virtue of regulation 21 ZB(2) from the date his claim for asylum is made until the date the Secretary of State makes a decision on that claim.';

(b) in paragraph 21, for the words 'regulation 70(3)' there shall be substituted the words 'regulation 70(2A)'.

(10) After paragraph 16 of Schedule 7 (applicable amounts in special cases) –

(a) in column (1) there shall be inserted the following paragraph –

'**Partner of a person subject to immigration control**

16A (a) A claimant who is the partner of a person subject to immigration control.

(b) Where regulation 18 (polygamous marriages) applies and the claimant is a person –

(i)   who is not subject to immigration control within the meaning of section 115(9) of the Immigration and Asylum Act; or

(ii)   to whom section 115 of that Act does not apply by virtue of regulation 2 of the Social Security (Immigration and Asylum) Consequential Amendments Regulations 2000; and

(iii)   who is a member of a couple and one or more of his partners is subject to immigration control within the meaning of section 115(9) of that Act and section 115 of that Act applies to her for the purposes of exclusion from entitlement to income support.';

(b) in column (2) there shall be inserted the following paragraph –

'**16A** (a) The amount applicable in respect of the claimant only under regulation 17(1)(a) plus that in respect of any child or young person who is a member of his family and who is not a person subject to immigration control within the meaning of section 115(9) of the Immigration and Asylum Act, and to whom section 115 of that Act does not apply for the purposes of exclusion from entitlement to income support, any amounts which may be applicable to him under regulation 17(1)(b), (c) or (d) plus the amount applicable to him under regulation 17(1)(e), (f) and (g) or, as the case may be, regulation 19 or 21.

(b) The amount determined in accordance with that regulation or regulation 19 or 21 in respect of the claimant and any partners of his and any child or young person for whom he or his partner is treated as responsible, who are not subject to immigration control within the meaning of section 115(9) of the Immigration and Asylum Act and to whom section 115 of that Act does not apply for the purposes of exclusion from entitlement to income support.'.

(11) In paragraph 17 of Schedule 7 (applicable amounts in special cases) for the words in column (1) there shall be substituted the words 'person from abroad' and for the words in column (2) there shall be substituted the word 'nil'.

(12) In paragraph 21 of Schedule 9 (treatment of income in kind) –

(a) in sub-paragraph (1) for the words 'Subject to sub-paragraph (2)' there shall be substituted the words 'Subject to sub-paragraphs (2) and (3)';

(b) in sub-paragraph (1) after the words 'except where' there shall be added the following words –
'regulation 40(4)(b) (provision of support under section 95 or 98 of the Immigration and Asylum Act including support provided by virtue of regulations made under Schedule 9 to that Act in the calculation of income other than earnings) or';

(c) after sub-paragraph (2) there shall be added the following sub-paragraph –
'(3) The first exception under sub-paragraph (1) shall not apply where the claimant is the partner of a person subject to immigration control and whose partner is receiving support provided under section 95 or 98 of the Immigration and Asylum Act including support provided by virtue of regulations made under Schedule 9 to that Act and the income in kind is support provided in respect of essential living needs of the partner of the claimant and his dependants (if any) as is specified in regulations made under paragraph 3 of Schedule 8 to the Immigration and Asylum Act.'.

(13) In paragraph 57 of Schedule 9 (disregards in the calculation of income other than earnings) and paragraph 49 of Schedule 10 (capital to be disregarded) for the words 'regulation 21ZA' there shall be substituted the words 'regulation 21ZB'.

Amendment of the Housing Benefit Regulations

6 (1) The Housing Benefit Regulations shall be amended in accordance with the following provisions of this regulation.

(2) In regulation 2(1) (interpretation) after the definition of 'housing association' there shall be inserted the following definition –
'Immigration and Asylum Act' means the Immigration and Asylum Act 1999;'.

(3) In regulation 7A (persons from abroad) –
(a) paragraphs (2), (3), (4)(a), (b), (c), (d), (e)(iv), (v) and (vi), (f) and (g), (4A), (5)(a), (b) and (c) and (5A) shall be omitted;
(b) in paragraph (6) the words 'Paragraphs (3)(b) and (4A)' shall be substituted by the words 'Paragraph 1 of Part I of the Schedule to, and regulation 2 as it applies to that paragraph of, the Social Security (Immigration and Asylum) Consequential Amendments Regulations 2000.'; and
(c) in paragraph (7) the definitions of the 'Common Travel Area' and the 'Convention relating to the Status of Refugees' shall be omitted.

(4) In paragraph (4) of regulation 33 (calculation of income other than earnings) for the words following 'paragraph (1)' there shall be substituted the following sub-paragraphs –
'(a) any payment to which regulation 28(2) (payments not earnings) applies; or
(b) in the case of a claimant who is receiving support under section 95 or 98 of the Immigration and Asylum Act including support provided by virtue of regulations made under Schedule 9 to that Act, the amount of such support provided in respect of essential living needs of the claim-

ant and his dependants (if any) as is specified in regulations made under paragraph 3 of Schedule 8 to the Immigration and Asylum Act.'.

(5) In Schedule A1 (treatment of claims for housing benefit by refugees) –

(a) in paragraph 1(1)(b) for the words following paragraph (ii) there shall be substituted the following words 'his claim for housing benefit shall be treated as having been made on the date specified in sub-paragraph (2)';

(b) in paragraph 1(2) for heads (a) and (b), there shall be substituted the following words –

'on the date on which his claim for asylum was recorded by the Secretary of State as having been made.';

(c) after paragraph 1 there shall be inserted the following paragraph –

'Appropriate authority to whom a claim for housing benefit by a refugee shall be made and time for making a claim

2A (1) A claim for housing benefit made by a refugee on or after 3rd April 2000 for the relevant period may be made to the appropriate authority for the area in which the dwelling which the claimant occupied as his home was situate and in respect of which he was liable to make payments.

(2) Where the claimant has occupied more than one dwelling as his home in the relevant period, only one claim for housing benefit shall be made in respect of that period and such a claim shall be made to the authority for the area in which the dwelling occupied by the refugee is situate and in respect of which he was liable to make payments when, after he is notified that he has been recorded by the Secretary of State as a refugee, he makes a claim for housing benefit.

(3) The appropriate authority to which a claim for housing benefit is made in accordance with this paragraph, shall determine the claimant's entitlement to that benefit for the whole of the relevant period.

(4) A claim for housing benefit to which this paragraph refers, shall be made within 28 days of a claimant receiving notification from the Secretary of State that he has been recorded as a refugee.

(5) Regulation 72(15) of these Regulations (backdating of claims) shall not have effect with respect to claims to which this Schedule applies.'; and

(d) paragraph 2 shall be omitted.

(6) In paragraph 21 of Schedule 4 (treatment of income in kind) after the words 'income in kind' there shall be added the following words –

'except where regulation 33(4)(b) (provision of support under section 95 or 98 of the Immigration and Asylum Act in the calculation of income other than earnings) applies'.

(7) In paragraph 62 of Schedule 4 and paragraph 51 of Schedule 5 for the words 'regulation 21ZA' there shall be substituted the words 'regulation 21ZB'.

Transitional arrangements and savings

12 (1) Paragraph (2) shall apply where, in relation to a claim for income support, a social fund payment, housing benefit or council tax benefit, as the case may be, a person has submitted a claim for asylum on or before 2nd April 2000 and is notified that he has been recorded by the Secretary of State as a refugee within the definition in Article 1 of the Convention relating to the Status of Refugees done at Geneva on 28th July 1951 as extended by Article 1(2) of the Protocol relating to the Status of Refugees done at New York on 31st January 1967.

(2) Where this paragraph applies –

    (a) regulation 21ZA of the Income Support Regulations (treatment of refugees) shall continue to have effect as if regulation 3(4)(a), (5) and (9) had not been made;

    (b) regulations 4(3C), 6(4D) and 19(8) of the Claims and Payments Regulations shall continue to have effect as if regulation 5 had not been made;

    (c) paragraphs 1 and 2 of Schedule A1, paragraph 62 of Schedule 4 and paragraph 51 of Schedule 5 to the Housing Benefit Regulations (treatment of claims for housing benefit by refugees) shall continue to have effect as if regulation 6(5) and (7) had not been made; and

    (d) paragraphs 1 and 2 of Schedule A1, paragraph 62 of Schedule 4 and paragraph 51 of Schedule 5 to the Council Tax Benefit Regulations (treatment of claims for council tax benefit by refugees) shall continue to have effect as if regulation 7(5) and (7) had not been made.

(3) Regulation 70 of the Income Support Regulations and regulation 147 of the Jobseeker's Allowance Regulations, as the case may be, shall apply to a person who is an asylum seeker within the meaning of paragraph (4) who has not ceased to be an asylum seeker by virtue of paragraph (5).

(4) An asylum seeker within the meaning of this paragraph is a person who –

    (a) submits on his arrival (other than on his re-entry) in the United Kingdom from a country outside the Common Travel Area a claim for asylum on or before 2nd April 2000 to the Secretary of State that it would be contrary to the United Kingdom's obligations under the Convent for him to be removed or required to leave, the United Kingdom and that claim is recorded by the Secretary of State as having been made before that date; or

    (b) on or before 2nd April 2000 becomes, while present in Great Britain, an asylum seeker when –

        (i) the Secretary of State makes a declaration to the effect that the country of which he is a national is subject to such a fundamental change of circumstances that he would not normally order the return of a person to that country; and

        (ii) he submits, within a period of three months from the date that declaration was made, a claim for asylum to the Secretary of State under the Convention relating to the Status of Refugees, and

        (iii) his claim for asylum under that Convention is recorded by the Secretary of State has having been made; and

    (c) in the case of a claim for jobseeker's allowance, holds a work permit or has written authorisation from the Secretary of state permitting him to work in the United Kingdom.

(5) A person ceases to be an asylum seeker for the purposes of this paragraph when his claim for asylum is recorded by the Secretary of State as having been decided (other than on appeal) or abandoned.

(6) For the purposes of regulation 7A of the housing Benefit Regulations and regulation 4A of the Council Tax Benefit Regulations, a person who is an asylum seeker within the meaning of paragraph (7) who has not ceased to be an asylum seeker by virtue of paragraph (8), is not a person from abroad within the meaning of paragraph (1) of those regulations.

(7) An asylum seeker within the meaning of this paragraph is a person who –
   (a) submits on his arrival (other than on his re-entry) in the United Kingdom from a country outside the Common Travel Area a claim for asylum on or before 2nd April 2000 to the Secretary of State that it would be contrary to the United Kingdom's obligations under the Convention for him to be removed or required to leave, the United Kingdom and that claim is recorded by the Secretary of State has having been made before that date, or
   (b) on or before 2nd April 2000 becomes, while present in Great Britain, an asylum seeker when –
      (i) the Secretary of State makes a declaration to the effect that the country of which he is a national is subject to such a fundamental change of circumstances that he would not normally order the return of a person to that country; and
      (ii) he submits, within a period of three months from the date that declaration was made, a claim for asylum to the Secretary of State under the Convention relating to the Status of Refugees; and
      (iii) his claim for asylum under that Convention is recorded by the Secretary of State has having been made.

(8) A person ceases to be an asylum seeker for the purposes of this paragraph when his claim for asylum is recorded by the Secretary of State as having been decided (other than on appeal) or abandoned.

(9) In paragraphs (4) and (7) 'the Common Travel Area' means the United Kingdom, the Channel Islands, the Isle of Man and the Republic of Ireland collectively and 'the Convention' means the Convention relating to the Status of Refugees done at Geneva on 28th July 1951 as extended by Article 2(1) of the Protocol relating to the Status of Refugees done at New York on 31st January 1967.

(10) Where, before the coming into force of these Regulations, a person has claimed benefit to which he is entitled or is receiving benefit by virtue of regulation 12(3) of the Persons from Abroad Regulations or regulation 14B(g) of the Child Benefit (General) Regulations 1976, as the case may be, those provisions shall continue to have effect, for the purposes of entitlement to attendance allowance, disability living allowance, invalid care allowance, severe disablement allowance or child benefit, as the case may be, until such time as –
   (a) his claim for asylum (if any) is recorded by the Secretary of State as having been decided or abandoned; or
   (b) his entitlement to that benefit is revised or superseded under section 9 or 10 of the Social Security Act 1998, if earlier,
   as if regulations 8, 9, 10 and 11 and paragraph (2) or paragraph (3), as the case may be, of regulation 13, had not been made.

(11) In the Persons from Abroad Regulations –

(a) in paragraph (1) of regulation 12, after the words 'shall continue to have effect' there shall be inserted the words '(both as regards him and as regards persons who are members of his family at the coming into force of these Regulations)'; and

(b) notwithstanding the amendments and revocations in regulations 3, 6 and 7, regulations 12(1) and (2) of the Persons from Abroad Regulations shall continue to have effect as they had effect before those amendments and revocations came into force.

SCHEDULE – PERSONS NOT EXCLUDED FROM CERTAIN BENEFITS UNDER SECTION 115 OF THE IMMIGRATION AND ASYLUM ACT 1999

Part I: Persons not excluded under section 115 of the Immigration and Asylum Act from entitlement to income-based jobseeker's allowance, income support, a social fund payment, housing benefit or council tax benefit

1 A person who –

(a) has limited leave (as defined in section 33(1) of the Immigration Act 1971) to enter or remain in the United Kingdom which was given in accordance with the immigration rules (as defined in that section) relating to –

(i) there being or there needing to be, no recourse to public funds, or

(ii) there being no charge on public funds,

during that period of limited leave; and

(b) having, during any one period of limited leave (including any such period as extended), supported himself without recourse to public funds, other than any such recourse by reason of the previous application of this sub-paragraph, is temporarily without funds during that period of leave because remittances to him from abroad have been disrupted, provided there is a reasonable expectation that his supply of funds will be resumed.

2 A person who has been given leave to enter or remain in, the United Kingdom by the Secretary of State upon an undertaking by another person or persons pursuant to the immigration rules within the meaning of the Immigration Act 1971, to be responsible for his maintenance and accommodation and who has not been resident in the United Kingdom for a period of at least five years beginning on the date of entry or the date on which the undertaking was given in respect of him, whichever date is the later and the person or persons who gave the undertaking to provide for his maintenance and accommodation has, or as the case may be, have died

3 A person who –

(a) has been given leave to enter or remain in, the United Kingdom by the Secretary of State upon an undertaking by another person or persons pursuant to the immigration rules within the meaning of the Immigration Act 1971, to be responsible for his maintenance and accommodation; and

(b) has been resident in the United Kingdom for a period of at least five years beginning on the date of entry or the date on which the undertaking was given in respect of him, whichever date is the later.

4   A person who is a national of a state which has ratified the European Convention on Social and Medical Assistance (done in Paris on 11th December 1953) or a state which has ratified the Council of Europe Social Charter (signed in Turin on 18th October 1961) and who is lawfully present in the United Kingdom.

Part II: Persons not excluded under section 115 of the Immigration and Asylum Act from entitlement to attendance allowance, severe disablement allowance, invalid care allowance, disability living allowance a social fund payment or child benefit

1   A member of a family of a national of a State contracting party to the Agreement on the European Economic Area signed at Oporto on 2nd May 1992 as adjusted by the Protocol signed at Brussels on 17th March 1993.

2   A person who is lawfully working in Great Britain and is a national of a State with which the Community has concluded an agreement under Article 310 of the Treaty of Amsterdam amending the Treaty on European Union, the Treaties establishing the European Communities and certain related Acts providing, in the field of social security, for the equal treatment of workers who are nationals of the signatory State and their families.

3   A person who is a member of a family of, and living with, a person specified in paragraph 2.

4   A person who has been given leave to enter, or remain in, the United Kingdom by the Secretary of State upon an undertaking by another person or persons pursuant to the immigration rules within the meaning of the Immigration Act 1971, to be responsible for his maintenance and accommodation.

Housing Act 1996

PART VII: HOMELESSNESS
Allocation only to qualifying persons

161 (1) A local housing authority shall allocate housing accommodation only to persons ('qualifying persons') who are qualified to be allocated housing accommodation by that authority.

(2) A person subject to immigration control within the meaning of the Asylum and Immigration Act 1996 is not qualified to be allocated housing accommodation by any authority in England and Wales unless he is of a class prescribed by regulations made by the Secretary of State.

(2A) Regulations may not be made under subsection (2) so as to include in a prescribed class any person to whom section 115 of the Immigration and Asylum Act 1999 (exclusion from benefits) applies.

(3) The Secretary of State may by regulations prescribe other classes of persons who are, or are not, qualifying persons in relation to local housing authorities generally or any particular local housing authority.

(4) Subject to subsection (2) and any regulations under subsection (3) a local

housing authority may decide what classes of persons are, or are not, qualifying persons.

(5) The prohibition in subsection (1) extends to the allocation of housing accommodation to two or more persons jointly if any of them is excluded from being a qualifying person by subsection (2) or regulations under subsection (3).

(6) The prohibition does not otherwise extend to the allocation of housing accommodation to two or more persons jointly if one or more of them are qualifying persons.

Application for assistance

183 (1) The following provisions of this Part apply where a person applies to a local housing authority for accommodation, or for assistance in obtaining accommodation, and the authority have reason to believe that he is or may be homeless or threatened with homelessness.

(2) In this Part –

'applicant' means a person making such an application,

'assistance under this Part' means the benefit of any function under the following provisions of this Part relating to accommodation or assistance in obtaining accommodation, and

'eligible for assistance' means not excluded from such assistance by section 185 (persons from abroad not eligible for housing assistance) or section 186 (asylum seekers and their dependants).

(3) Nothing in this section or the following provisions of this Part affects a person's entitlement to advice and information under section 179 (duty to provide advisory services).

Persons from abroad not eligible for housing assistance

185 (1) A person is not eligible for assistance under this Part if he is a person from abroad who is ineligible for housing assistance.

(2) A person who is subject to immigration control within the meaning of the Asylum and Immigration Act 1996 is not eligible for housing assistance unless he is of a class prescribed by regulations made by the Secretary of State.

(2A) Regulations may not be made under subsection (2) so as to include in a prescribed class any person to whom section 115 of the Immigration and Asylum Act 1999 (exclusion from benefits) applies.

(3) The Secretary of State may make provision by regulations as to other descriptions of persons who are to be treated for the purposes of this Part as persons from abroad who are ineligible for housing assistance.

(4) A person from abroad who is not eligible for housing assistance shall be disregarded in determining for the purposes of this Part whether another person –

(a) is homeless or threatened with homelessness, or

(b) has a priority need for accommodation.

Asylum-seekers and their dependants

186 (1) An asylum-seeker, or a dependant of an asylum-seeker who is not by virtue of section 185 a person from abroad who is ineligible for housing assistance, is not eligible for assistance under this Part if he has any accommodation in the United Kingdom, however temporary, available for his occupation.

(2) For the purposes of this section a person who makes a claim for asylum –
   (a) becomes an asylum-seeker at the time when his claim is recorded by the Secretary of State as having been made, and
   (b) ceases to be an asylum-seeker at the time when his claim is recorded by the Secretary of State as having been finally determined or abandoned.

(3) For the purposes of this section a person –
   (a) becomes a dependant of an asylum-seeker at the time when he is recorded by the Secretary of State as being a dependant of the asylum-seeker, and
   (b) ceases to be a dependant of an asylum-seeker at the time when the person whose dependant he is ceases to be an asylum-seeker or, if it is earlier, at the time when he is recorded by the Secretary of State as ceasing to be a dependant of the asylum-seeker.

(4) In relation to an asylum-seeker, 'dependant' means a person –
   (a) who is his spouse or a child of his under the age of eighteen, and
   (b) who has neither a right of abode in the United Kingdom nor indefinite leave under the Immigration Act 1971 to enter or remain in the United Kingdom.

(5) In this section a 'claim for asylum' means a claim made by a person that it would be contrary to the United Kingdom's obligations under the Convention relating to the Status of Refugees done at Geneva on 28th July 1951 and the Protocol to that Convention for him to be removed from, or required to leave, the United Kingdom.

Homelessness (Asylum-Seekers) (Interim Period) (England) Order 1999 SI No 3126

Citation, commencement and extent

1 (1) This Order may be cited as the Homelessness (Asylum-Seekers) (Interim Period) (England) Order 1999 and shall come into force on 6th December 1999.

(2) This Order extends to England only.

Modification of Part VII of the Housing Act 1996 for certain asylum-seekers

2   Part VII of the Housing Act 1996 (homelessness) shall have effect in relation to asylum-seekers who are section 185(2) persons with the modifications specified in the following provisions of this Order.

Referrals to other local authorities

3   In section 198 (referral of case to another local housing authority) –
   (a) in subsection (3), after 'this purpose', there shall be inserted ', and for
       the purpose of subsection (4A)(c),'; and
   (b) after subsection (4), there shall be inserted –
       '(4A) The conditions for referral of the case to another authority are also
       met if –
       (a) the local housing authority to whom the application has been made
       and another housing authority have agreed that the case should be
       referred to that other authority;
       (b) that other authority has provided written confirmation of the
       agreement to the local housing authority; and
       (c) neither the applicant nor any person who might reasonably be
       expected to reside with him will run the risk of domestic violence in the
       district of that other authority.
       (4B) When reaching the agreement referred to in subsection (4A)(a), the
       local housing authority to whom the application was made and the other
       authority need not have regard to –
       (a) any preference that the applicant, or any person who might reason-
       ably be expected to reside with him, may have as to the locality in which
       the accommodation is to be secured; or
       (b) whether the applicant, or any person who might reasonably be
       expected to reside with him, has a local connection with the district of
       any local housing authority.'.

Discharge of functions by local housing authorities

4   (1) In section 206 (discharge of functions by local housing authorities), after
     subsection (1), there shall be inserted –
         '(1A) In discharging their housing functions under this Part, a local
         housing authority shall have regard to the desirability, in general, of
         securing accommodation in areas in which there is a ready supply
         of accommodation.'.

Out-of-area placements

5   (1) In section 208 (discharge of functions: out-of-area placements), after subsec-
     tion (1), there shall be inserted –
     '(1A) Subsection (1) shall not apply where –

     (a) the local housing authority and another housing authority have agreed
         that the local housing authority may secure that accommodation is
         available for the occupation of all or an agreed number of asylum-
         seekers who are section 185(2) persons in that other authority's district;
         and
     (b) that other authority has provided written confirmation of the agreement
         to the local housing authority.'.

Suitability of accommodation

6   In section 210 (suitability of accommodation), after subsection (1), there
     shall be inserted –

'(1A) In determining for the purposes of this Part whether accommodation is suitable for an applicant, or any person who might reasonably be expected to reside with him, the local housing authority –

(a) shall also have regard to the fact that the accommodation is to be temporary pending the determination of the applicant's claim for asylum; and

(b) shall not have regard to any preference that the applicant, or any person who might reasonably be expected to reside with him, may have as to the locality in which the accommodation is to be secured.'.

The interim period

7   This Order shall cease to have effect on the date on which section 186 of the Housing Act 1996 (asylum-seekers and their dependants) is repealed by the Immigration and Asylum Act 1999 (as to which see section 117(5) of that Act).

Homelessness (England) Regulations 2000 SI No 701

Citation, commencement and extent

1   (1) These Regulations may be cited as the Homelessness (England) Regulations 2000 and shall come into force on 3rd April 2000.

(2) These Regulations extend to England only.

Interpretation

2   (1) In these Regulations –

'the 1971 Act' means the Immigration Act 1971;

'the 1995 Act' means the Jobseekers Act 1995;

'the 1996 Act' means the Housing Act 1996;

'asylum-seeker' means a person who is not under 18 and who made a claim for asylum which is recorded by the Secretary of State as having been made before 3rd April 2000 but which has not been determined;

'claim for asylum' means a claim that it would be contrary to the United Kingdom's obligations under the Refugee Convention for the claimant to be removed from, or required to leave, the United Kingdom;

'the Common Travel Area' means the United Kingdom, the Channel Islands, the Isle of Man and the Republic of Ireland collectively;

'the immigration rules' means the rules laid down as mentioned in section 3(2) of the 1971 Act (general provisions for regulation and control);

'limited leave' means leave under the 1971 Act to enter or remain in the United Kingdom which is limited as to duration; and

'the Refugee Convention' means the Convention relating to the Status of Refugees done at Geneva on 28th July 1951, as extended by Article 1(2) of the Protocol relating to the Status of Refugees done at New York on 31st January 1967.

(2) For the purposes of the definition of 'asylum-seeker', a claim for asylum is determined at the end of such period beginning –

    (a) on the day on which the Secretary of State notifies the claimant of his decision on the claim; or

    (b) if the claimant has appealed against the Secretary of State's decision, on the day on which the appeal is disposed of,

as may be prescribed under section 94(3) of the Immigration and Asylum Act 1999.

(3) For the purposes of regulations 3(1)(i) (Class I) and 4(d) –

    (a) 'an income-based jobseeker's allowance' means a jobseeker's allowance, payable under the 1995 Act, entitlement to which is based on the claimant satisfying conditions which include those set out in section 3 of the 1995 Act (the income-based conditions);

    (b) 'income support' has the same meaning as in section 124 of the Social Security Contributions and Benefits Act 1992 (income support); and

    (c) a person is on an income-based jobseeker's allowance on any day in respect of which an income-based jobseeker's allowance is payable to him and on any day –

        (i) in respect of which he satisfies the conditions for entitlement to an income-based jobseeker's allowance but where the allowance is not paid in accordance with section 19 of the 1995 Act (circumstances in which jobseeker's allowance is not payable); or

        (ii) which is a waiting day for the purposes of paragraph 4 of Schedule 1 to the 1995 Act (waiting days) and which falls immediately before a day in respect of which an income-based jobseeker's allowance is payable to him or would be payable to him but for section 19 of the 1995 Act.

Classes of persons subject to immigration control who are eligible for housing assistance

3 (1) The following are classes of persons prescribed for the purposes of section 185(2) of the 1996 Act (persons subject to immigration control who are eligible for housing assistance) –

    (a) Class A – a person recorded by the Secretary of State as a refugee within the definition in Article 1 of the Refugee Convention;

    (b) Class B –a person –

        (i) who has been granted by the Secretary of State exceptional leave to enter or remain in the United Kingdom outside the provisions of the immigration rules; and

        (ii) whose leave is not subject to a condition requiring him to maintain and accommodate himself, and any person who is dependent on him, without recourse to public funds;

    (c) Class C – a person who has current leave to enter or remain in the United Kingdom which is not subject to any limitation or condition and who is habitually resident in the Common Travel Area other than a person –

        (i) who has been given leave to enter or remain in the United Kingdom upon an undertaking given by another person (his 'sponsor') in writing in pursuance of the immigration rules to be responsible for his maintenance and accommodation;

(ii) who has been resident in the United Kingdom for less than five years beginning on the date of entry or the date on which the undertaking was given in respect of him, whichever date is the later; and

(iii) whose sponsor or, where there is more than one sponsor, at least one of whose sponsors, is still alive;

(d) Class D – person who left the territory of Montserrat after 1st November 1995 because of the effect on that territory of a volcanic eruption;

(e) Class E – a person who is habitually resident in the Common Travel Area and who –

(i) is a national of a state which has ratified the European Convention on Social and Medical Assistance done at Paris on 11th December 1953 or a state which has ratified the European Social Charter done at Turin on 18th October 1961 and is lawfully present in the United Kingdom; or

(ii) before 3rd April 2000 was owed a duty by a housing authority under Part III of the Housing Act 1985 (housing the homeless) or Part VII of the 1996 Act (homelessness) which is extant, and who is a national of a state which is a signatory to the European Convention on Social and Medical Assistance done at Paris on 11th December 1953 or a state which is a signatory to the European Social Charter done at Turin on 18th October 1961;

(f) Class F – a person who is an asylum-seeker and who made a claim for asylum –

(i) which is recorded by the Secretary of State as having been made on his arrival (other than on his re-entry) in the United Kingdom from a country outside the Common Travel Area; and

(ii) which has not been recorded by the Secretary of State as having been either decided (other than on appeal) or abandoned;

(g) Class G – a person who is an asylum-seeker and –

(i) who was in Great Britain when the Secretary of State made a declaration to the effect that the country of which that person is a national is subject to such a fundamental change in circumstances that he would not normally order the return of a person to that country;

(ii) who made a claim for asylum which is recorded by the Secretary of State as having been made within a period of three months from the day on which that declaration was made; and

(iii) whose claim for asylum has not been recorded by the Secretary of State as having been either decided (other than on appeal) or abandoned;

(h) Class H – person who is an asylum-seeker and –

(i) who made a relevant claim for asylum on or before 4th February 1996; and

(ii) who was, on 4th February 1996, entitled to benefit under regulation

7A of the Housing Benefit (General) Regulations 1987 (persons from abroad); and

(i) Class I – a person who is on an income-based jobseeker's allowance or in receipt of income support and is eligible for that benefit other than because –

(i) he has limited leave to enter or remain in the United Kingdom which was given in accordance with the relevant immigration rules; and

(ii) he is temporarily without funds because remittances to him from abroad have been disrupted.

(2) In paragraph (1)(h)(i) (Class H), a relevant claim for asylum is a claim for asylum which –

(a) has not been recorded by the Secretary of State as having been either decided (other than on appeal) or abandoned; or

(b) has been recorded as having been decided (other than on appeal) on or before 4th February 1996 and in respect of which an appeal is pending which –

(i) was pending on 5th February 1996; or

(ii) was made within the time limits specified in the rules of procedure made under section 22 of the 1971 Act (procedure).

(3) In paragraph (1)(i)(i) (Class I), 'relevant immigration rules' means the immigration rules relating to –

(a) there being or there needing to be no recourse to public funds; or

(b) there being no charge on public funds.

Descriptions of persons who are to be treated as persons from abroad ineligible for housing assistance

4 The following is a description of persons, other than persons who are subject to immigration control, who are to be treated for the purposes of Part VII of the 1996 Act (homelessness) as persons from abroad who are ineligible for housing assistance –

A person who is not habitually resident in the Common Travel Area other than –

(a) a worker for the purposes of Council Regulation (EEC) No 1612/68 or (EEC) No 1251/70;

(b) a person with a right to reside in the United Kingdom pursuant to the Immigration (European Economic Area) Order 1994 and derived from Council Directive No 68/360/EEC or No 73/148/EEC;

(c) a person who left the territory of Montserrat after 1st November 1995 because of the effect on that territory of a volcanic eruption;

(d) a person who is on an income-based jobseeker's allowance or in receipt of income support.

Prescribed period of notice where an authority proposes to cease securing accommodation under section 194

5 For the purposes of section 194(6) of the 1996 Act (notice of ceasing to exercise power to secure accommodation under section 194), the prescribed period is 28 days.

Period prescribed for the purpose of conditions for referral of an application

6   For the purposes of section 198(4)(b) of the 1996 Act (referral of case to another local housing authority), the prescribed period is the aggregate of –
(a) five years; and
(b) the period beginning on the date of the previous application and ending on the date on which the applicant was first placed in pursuance of that application in accommodation in the district of the authority to whom the application is now made.

Revocation

7   The following Regulations are revoked –

(a) the Homelessness Regulations 1996, in so far as they extend to England;
(b) regulations 4 and 5 of the Allocation of Housing and Homelessness (Amendment) Regulations 1997, in so far as they extend to England;
(c) regulation 3 of the Allocation of Housing and Homelessness (Amendment) (No. 2) Regulations 1997, in so far as they extend to England; and
(d) regulations 4 and 5 of the Allocation of Housing and Homelessness (Amendment) (England) Regulations 1999.

Allocation of Housing (England) Regulations 2000 SI No 702

Citation, commencement and extent

1   (1) These Regulations may be cited as the Allocation of Housing (England) Regulations 2000 and shall come into force on 3rd April 2000.
(2) These Regulations extend to England only.

Classes prescribed under section 161(2) who are qualifying persons

4   The following are classes of persons subject to immigration control prescribed for the purposes of section 161(2) of the Act (allocation only to qualifying persons) –
(a) Class A – a person recorded by the Secretary of State as a refugee within the definition in Article 1 of the Convention relating to the Status of Refugees done at Geneva on 28th July 1951 as extended by Article 1(2) of the Protocol relating to the Status of Refugees done at New York on 31st January 1967;
(b) Class B – a person –
(i) who has been granted by the Secretary of State exceptional leave to enter or remain in the United Kingdom outside the provisions of the immigration rules; and
(ii) whose leave is not subject to a condition requiring him to maintain and accommodate himself, and any person who is dependent on him, without recourse to public funds;

(c) Class C – a person who has current leave to enter or remain in the United Kingdom which is not subject to any limitation or condition and who is habitually resident in the Common Travel Area other than a person –

   (i) who has been given leave to enter or remain in the United Kingdom upon an undertaking given by another person (his 'sponsor') in writing in pursuance of the immigration rules to be responsible for his maintenance and accommodation;

   (ii) who has been resident in the United Kingdom for less than five years beginning on the date of entry or the date on which the undertaking was given in respect of him, whichever date is the later; and

   (iii) whose sponsor or, where there is more than one sponsor, at least one of whose sponsors, is still alive;

(d) Class D – a person who left the territory of Montserrat after 1st November 1995 because of the effect on that territory of a volcanic eruption;

(e) Class E – a person who is habitually resident in the Common Travel Area and who –

   (i) is a national of a state which has ratified the European Convention on Social and Medical Assistance done at Paris on 11th December 1953 or a state which has ratified the European Social Charter done at Turin on 18th October 1961 and is lawfully present in the United Kingdom; or

   (ii) before 3rd April 2000 was owed a duty by a housing authority under Part III of the Housing Act 1985 (housing the homeless) or Part VII of the Act (homelessness) which is extant, and who is a national of a state which is a signatory to the European Convention on Social and Medical Assistance done at Paris on 11th December 1953 or a state which is a signatory to the European Social Charter done at Turin on 18th October 1961.

Classes prescribed under section 161(3) who are qualifying persons

5   The following are prescribed classes of persons, other than persons who are subject to immigration control, who are qualifying persons in relation to a local housing authority for the purposes of section 161(3) of the Act (allocation only to qualifying persons) –

(a) Class F – a person who is aged 18 years or over and who is owed a duty by that authority under –

   (i) section 193 of the Act (duty to persons with priority need who are not homeless intentionally); or

   (ii) subsection (2) of section 195 of the Act (duties in case of threatened homelessness) where, in pursuance of the duty under that subsection, the authority secure that accommodation (other than that occupied by that person when he made his application for assistance under Part VII of the Act) is available for occupation by him;

(b) Class G – a person who is aged 18 years or over –

   (i) who, within the previous two years, has been owed a duty by that authority under section 192(2) or 197(2) of the Act (duty to persons

> not in priority need who are not homeless intentionally and duty where other suitable accommodation available); and
>
> (ii) who is not a person who has subsequently been owed a duty by that authority under section 190 of the Act (duties to persons becoming homeless intentionally);

(c) Class H – a person who left the territory of Montserrat after 1st November 1995 because of the effect on that territory of a volcanic eruption.

Classes prescribed under section 161(3) who are not qualifying persons

6   The following is a prescribed class of persons, other than persons who are subject to immigration control, who are not qualifying persons in relation to a local housing authority for the purposes of section 161(3) of the Act (allocation only to qualifying persons) –

Class I – a person who is not habitually resident in the Common Travel Area other than –

(a) a worker for the purposes of Council Regulation (EEC) No 1612/68 or (EEC) No 1251/70;

(b) a person with a right to reside in the United Kingdom pursuant to the Immigration (European Economic Area) Order 1994 and derived from Council Directive No 68/360/EEC or No 73/148/EEC;

(c) a person who left the territory of Montserrat after 1st November 1995 because of the effect on that territory of a volcanic eruption.

Information in the housing register

7   A local housing authority's housing register shall contain, in relation to each qualifying person –

(a) the name of the qualifying person;

(b) the number of other persons who normally reside with him as a member of his family or who might reasonably be expected to reside with him;

(c) the number of persons falling within paragraphs (a) and (b) above who are –

　　(i)　 under the age of 10 years;

　　(ii)　 expecting a child; or

　　(iii)　 aged 60 years or over;

(d) the address of the qualifying person;

(e) the date on which the qualifying person was put on the register; and

(f) the most recent date on which an entry on the register was amended.

Requirements before removing a person from the housing register

8   (1) Before removing a person from their housing register under section 163(5) of the Act (operation of housing register) a local housing authority shall give him notice in accordance with this regulation.

(2) A notice under this regulation shall –

(a) require the person to provide the authority with such information as they reasonably require to enable them to decide whether to remove him from the register;

(b) specify a period of not less than 28 days beginning with the day on which the person receives the notice within which the information must be provided; and

(c) inform the person that the authority may decide to remove him from their register if –
    (i) they do not receive the information within the specified period; or
    (ii) they consider that in the light of the information they receive within that period there are reasons why he should be removed.

(3) Notice required to be given to a person under this regulation shall be given in writing and, if not received by him, shall be treated as having been given if it is made available at the authority's office for a reasonable period for collection by him.

Revocation

9   The following Regulations are revoked –

(a) the Allocation of Housing Regulations 1996, in so far as they extend to England;

(b) regulations 2 and 3 of the Allocation of Housing and Homelessness (Amendment) Regulations 1997, in so far as they extend to England;

(c) the Allocation of Housing and Homelessness (Amendment) (No 2) Regulations 1997, in so far as they extend to England; and

(d) the Allocation of Housing and Homelessness (Amendment) (England) Regulations 1999.

Persons Subject to Immigration Control (Housing Authority Accommodation and Homelessness) Order 2000 SI No 706

Citation, commencement and extent

1 (1) This Order may be cited as the Persons subject to Immigration Control (Housing Authority Accommodation and Homelessness) Order 2000 and shall come into force on 3rd April 2000.

(2) This Order does not extend to Wales.

(3) Article 4 extends to England only.

(4) Articles 5 and 8 extend to Northern Ireland only.

(5) Articles 6 and 9 extend to Scotland only.

(6) Article 7 extends to Scotland and Northern Ireland only.

Interpretation

2   In this Order –

'the 1971 Act' means the Immigration Act 1971;

'the 1985 Act' means the Housing Act 1985;

'the 1995 Act' means the Jobseekers Act 1995;

'the 1999 Act' means the Immigration and Asylum Act 1999;

'asylum-seeker' means a person who is not under 18 and who made a claim for asylum which is recorded by the Secretary of State as having been made on or before 2nd April 2000 but which has not been determined;

'child in need' means a child –

(a) who is unlikely to achieve or maintain, or to have the opportunity of achieving or maintaining, a reasonable standard of health or development without the provision for him of services by a local authority under Part III of the Children Act 1989 (local authority support for children and families);

(b) whose health or development is likely to be significantly impaired, or further impaired, without the provision for him of such services; or

(c) who is blind, deaf or dumb or suffers from mental disorder of any kind or is substantially and permanently handicapped by illness, injury or congenital deformity or such other disability as may be prescribed by regulations made under section 17 of the Children Act 1989 (provision of services for children in need, their families and others);

'claim for asylum' means a claim that it would be contrary to the United Kingdom's obligations under the Refugee Convention for the claimant to be removed from, or required to leave, the United Kingdom;

'Common Travel Area' means the United Kingdom, the Channel Islands, the Isle of Man and the Republic of Ireland collectively;

'designated course' means a course of any kind designated by regulations made by the Secretary of State for the purposes of paragraph 10 of Schedule 1 to the 1985 Act (student lettings which are not secure tenancies);

'development' means physical, intellectual, emotional, social or behavioural development;

'educational establishment' means a university or institution which provides further education or higher education (or both); and for the purposes of this definition 'further education' has the same meaning as in section 2 of the Education Act 1996 (definition of further education) and 'higher education' means education provided by means of a course of any description mentioned in Schedule 6 to the Education Reform Act 1988 (courses of higher education);

'family', in relation to a child in need, includes any person who has parental responsibility for the child and any other person with whom he has been living;

'full-time course' means a course normally involving not less than 15 hours attendance a week in term time for the organised day-time study of a single subject or related subjects;

'health' means physical or mental health;

'the immigration rules' means the rules laid down as mentioned in section 3(2) of the 1971 Act (general provisions for regulation and control);

'limited leave' means leave under the 1971 Act to enter or remain in the United Kingdom which is limited as to duration;

'the Refugee Convention' means the Convention relating to the Status of Refugees done at Geneva on 28th July 1951 as extended by Article 1(2) of the

Protocol relating to the Status of Refugees done at New York on 31st January 1967;

'specified education institution' means –

(a) a university or other institution within the higher education sector within the meaning of section 91(5) of the Further and Higher Education Act 1992 (interpretation of Education Acts), in respect of a university or other institution in England, or section 56(2) of the Further and Higher Education (Scotland) Act 1992 (interpretation of Part II), in respect of a university or other institution in Scotland;

(b) an institution in England within the further education sector within the meaning of section 91(3) of the Further and Higher Education Act 1992;

(c) a college of further education in Scotland which is under the management of an education authority or which is managed by a board of management in terms of Part I of the Further and Higher Education (Scotland) Act 1992 (further education in Scotland);

(d) a central institution in Scotland within the meaning of section 135(1) of the Education (Scotland) Act 1980 (interpretation);

(e) an institution in England which provides a course qualifying for funding under Part I of the Education Act 1994 (teaching training);

(f) a higher education institution in Northern Ireland within the meaning of Article 30(3) of the Education and Libraries (Northern Ireland) Order 1993 (funding by Department of higher education); or

(g) an institution of further education in Northern Ireland within the meaning of Article 3 of the Further Education (Northern Ireland) Order 1997 (definition of 'further education').

Housing authority accommodation – England, Scotland and Northern Ireland

3   The following are classes of persons specified for the purposes of section 118(1) of the 1999 Act (housing authority accommodation) in respect of England, Scotland and Northern Ireland –

(a) Class A – a person recorded by the Secretary of State as a refugee within the definition in Article 1 of the Refugee Convention;

(b) Class B – a person –
   (i)   who has been granted by the Secretary of State exceptional leave to enter or remain in the United Kingdom outside the provisions of the immigration rules; and
   (ii) whose leave is not subject to a condition requiring him to maintain and accommodate himself, and any person who is dependent on him, without recourse to public funds;

(c) Class C – a person who has current leave to enter or remain in the United Kingdom which is not subject to any limitation or condition and who is habitually resident in the Common Travel Area other than a person –
   (i)   who has been given leave to enter or remain in the United Kingdom upon an undertaking given by another person (his 'sponsor') in writing in pursuance of the immigration rules to be responsible for his maintenance and accommodation;

    (ii)   who has been resident in the United Kingdom for less than five years beginning on the date of entry or the date on which the undertaking was given in respect of him, whichever date is the later; and

    (iii)   whose sponsor or, where there is more than one sponsor, at least one of whose sponsors, is still alive;

(d) Class D – a person who left the territory of Montserrat after 1st November 1995 because of the effect on that territory of a volcanic eruption;

(e) Class E – a person who is –

    (i)   a national of a state which has ratified the European Convention on Social and Medical Assistance done at Paris on 11th December 1953 or a state which has ratified the European Social Charter done at Turin on 18th October 1961;

    (ii)   lawfully present in the United Kingdom; and

    (iii)   habitually resident in the Common Travel Area;

(f) Class F – a person who is attending a full-time course at a specified education institution in a case where the housing accommodation which is or may be provided to him –

    (i)   is let by a housing authority to that specified education institution for the purposes of enabling that institution to provide accommodation for students attending a full-time course at that institution; and

    (ii)   would otherwise be difficult for that housing authority to let on terms which, in the opinion of the housing authority, are satisfactory.

Housing authority accommodation – England

4 (1) The following are classes of persons specified for the purposes of section 118(1) of the 1999 Act in respect of England –

(a) Class G – a person who is owed a duty under section 21 of the National Assistance Act 1948 (duty of local authorities to provide accommodation);

(b) Class H – person who is either a child in need or a member of the family of a child in need;

(c) Class I – person –

    (i)   who is owed a duty under section 63(1) (interim duty to accommodate in case of apparent priority need), 65(2) or (3) (duties to persons found to be homeless) or 68(1) or (2) (duties to persons whose applications are referred) of the 1985 Act;

    (ii)   who is owed a duty under section 188(1) (interim duty to accommodate in case of apparent priority need), 190(2) (duties to persons becoming homeless intentionally), 193(2) (duty to persons with priority need who are not homeless intentionally), 195(2) (duties in case of threatened homelessness) or 200(1), (3) or (4) (duties to applicant whose case is considered for referral or referred) of the Housing Act 1996; or

    (iii)   in respect of whom a local housing authority are exercising their power under section 194(1) (power exercisable after minimum period of duty under section 193) of the Housing Act 1996;

(d) Class J – an asylum-seeker to whom, or a dependant of an asylum-seeker to whom, a local authority is required to provide support in accordance with regulations made under Schedule 9 to the 1999 Act (asylum support: interim provisions);

(e) Class K – person who is attending a designated course, which is a full-time course, at an educational establishment in a case where the housing accommodation which is or may be provided to him by a local housing authority –

    (i)   is not and will not be let to him as a secure tenancy by virtue of paragraph 10 of Schedule 1 to the 1985 Act (student lettings which are not secure tenancies); and

    (ii) would otherwise be difficult for that local housing authority to let on terms which, in the opinion of the local housing authority, are satisfactory;

(f) Class L – person who has a secure tenancy within the meaning of section 79 of the 1985 Act (secure tenancies).

(2) 'Dependant', in relation to an asylum-seeker within paragraph (1)(d) (Class J), means a person in the United Kingdom who –

(a) is his spouse;

(b) is a child of his, or of his spouse, who is under 18 and dependent on him; or

(c) falls within such additional category as may be prescribed under section 94(1) of the 1999 Act (interpretation of Part VI – support for asylum-seekers), for the purposes of regulations made under Schedule 9 to the 1999 Act (asylum support: interim provisions), in relation to an asylum-seeker.

Revocation

10   The following Orders are revoked –

(a) the Housing Accommodation and Homelessness (Persons subject to Immigration Control) Order 1996, in so far as it extends to England and Scotland;

(b) the Homelessness (Persons subject to Immigration Control) (Amendment) Order 1997, in so far as it extends to England and Scotland;

(c) the Housing Accommodation and Homelessness (Persons subject to Immigration Control) (Amendment) Order 1998, in so far as it extends to England;

(d) the Housing Accommodation and Homelessness (Persons subject to Immigration Control) (Northern Ireland) Order 1998;

(e) the Housing Accommodation and Homelessness (Persons subject to Immigration Control) (Amendment) (Scotland) Order 1999; and

(f) the Housing Accommodation (Persons subject to Immigration Control) (Amendment) (England) Order 1999.

Children Act 1989

Provision of services for children in need, their families and others

17 (1) It shall be the general duty of every local authority (in addition to the other duties imposed upon them by this Part) –

(a) to safeguard and promote the welfare of children within their area who are in need; and

(b) so far as is consistent with that duty to promote the upbringing of such children by their families,

by providing a range and level of services appropriate to those children's needs.

(2) For the purpose principally of facilitating the discharge of their general duty under this section, every local authority shall have the specific duties and powers set out in Part I of Schedule 2.

(3) Any service provided by an authority in the exercise of functions conferred on them by this section may be provided for the family of a particular child in need or for any member of his family, if it is provided with a view to safeguarding or promoting the child's welfare.

(4) The Secretary of State may by order amend any provision of Part I of Schedule 2 or add any further duty or power to those for the tune being mentioned there.

(5) Every local authority –

(a) shall facilitate the provision by others (including in particular voluntary organisations) of services which the authority have power to provide by virtue of this section, or section 18, 20, 23 or 24; and

(b) may make such arrangements as they see fit for any person to act on their behalf in the provision of any such service.

(6) The services provided by a local authority in the exercise of functions conferred on them by this section may include giving assistance in kind or, in exceptional circumstances, in cash.

(7) Assistance may be unconditional or subject to conditions as to the repayment of the assistance or of its value (in whole or in part).

(8) Before giving any assistance or imposing any conditions, a local authority shall have regard to the means of the child concerned and of each of his parents.

(9) No person shall be liable to make any repayment of assistance or of its value at any time when he is in receipt of income support, working families' tax credit or disabled person's tax credit under Part VII of the Social Security Contributions and Benefits Act 1992 or of an income-based jobseeker's allowance.

(10) For the purposes of this Part a child shall be taken to be in need if –

(a) he is unlikely to achieve or maintain, or to have the opportunity of achieving or maintaining, a reasonable standard of health or development without the provision for him of services by a local authority under this Part;

(b) his health or development is likely to be significantly impaired, or further impaired, without the provision for him of such services; or

(c) he is disabled,
and 'family', in relation to such a child, includes any person who has parental responsibility for the child and any other person with whom he has been living.

(11) For the purposes of this Part, a child is disabled if he is blind, deaf or dumb or suffers from mental disorder of any kind or is substantially and permanently handicapped by illness, injury or congenital deformity or such other disability as may be prescribed; and in this Part –
'development' means physical, intellectual, emotional, social or behavioural development; and
'health' means physical or mental health.

Provision of accommodation for children: general

20 (1) Every local authority shall provide accommodation for any child in need within their area who appears to them to require accommodation as a result of –
  (a) there being no person who has parental responsibility for him;
  (b) his being lost or having been abandoned; or
  (c) the person who has been caring for him being prevented (whether or not permanently, and for whatever reason) from providing him with suitable accommodation or care.

  (2) Where a local authority provide accommodation under subsection (1) for a child who is ordinarily resident in the area of another local authority, that other local authority may take over the provision of accommodation for the child within –
  (a) three months of being notified in writing that the child is being provided with accommodation; or
  (b) such other longer period as may be prescribed.

  (3) Every local authority shall provide accommodation for any child in need within their area who has reached the age of sixteen and whose welfare the authority consider is likely to be seriously prejudiced if they do not provide him with accommodation.

  (4) A local authority may provide accommodation for any child within their area (even though a person who has parental responsibility for him is able to provide him with accommodation) if they consider that to do so would safeguard or promote the child's welfare.

  (5) A local authority may provide accommodation for any person who has reached the age of sixteen but is under twenty-one in any community home which takes children who have reached the age of sixteen if they consider that to do so would safeguard or promote his welfare.

  (6) Before providing accommodation under this section, a local authority shall, so far as if reasonably practicable and consistent with the child's welfare –
  (a) ascertain the child's wishes regarding the provision of accommodation; and
  (b) give due consideration (having regard to his age and understanding) to such wishes of the child as they have been able to ascertain.

  (7) A local authority may not provide accommodation under this section for any child if any person who –

(a) has parental responsibility for him; and
(b) is willing and able to –
    (i)   provide accommodation for him; or
    (ii)   arrange for accommodation to be provided for him,
objects.
[(8)–(10) not reproduced.]

(11) Subsections (7) and (8) do not apply where a child who has reached the age of sixteen agrees to being provided with accommodation under this section.

Advice and assistance for certain children

24 (1) Where a child is being looked after by a local authority, it shall be the duty of the authority to advise, assist and befriend him with a view to promoting his welfare when he ceases to be looked after by them.

(2) In this Part 'a person qualifying for advice and assistance' means a person within the area of the authority who is under twenty-one and who was, at any time after reaching the age of sixteen but while still a child –
(a) looked after by a local authority;
(b) accommodated by or on behalf of a voluntary organisation;
(c) accommodated in a registered children's home;
(d) accommodated –
    (i)   by any Health Authority, Special Health Authority, Primary Care Trust or local education authority; or
    (ii)   in any residential care home, nursing home or mental nursing home or in any accommodation provided by a National Health Service Trust, for a consecutive period of at least three months; or
(e) privately fostered,
but who is no longer so looked after, accommodated or fostered.

(3) Subsection (2)(d) applies even if the period of three months mentioned there began before the child reached the age of sixteen.

(4) Where –
(a) a local authority know that there is within their area a person qualifying for advice and assistance;
(b) the conditions in subsection (5) are satisfied; and
(c) that person has asked them for help of a kind which they can give under this section,
they shall (if he was being looked after by a local authority or was accommodated by or on behalf of a voluntary organisation) and may (in any other case) advise and befriend him.

(5) The conditions are that –
(a) it appears to the authority that the person concerned is in need of advice and being befriended;
(b) where that person was not being looked after by the authority, they are satisfied that the person by whom he was being looked after does not have the necessary facilities for advising or befriending him.

(6) Where as a result of this section a local authority are under a duty, or are empowered to advise and befriend a person, they may also give him assistance.

(7) Assistance given under subsections (1) to (6) may be in kind or, in exceptional circumstances, in cash.

(8) A local authority may give assistance to any person who qualifies for advice and assistance by virtue of subsection (2)(a) by –
  (a) contributing to expenses incurred by him in living near the place where he is, or will be –
    (i) employed or seeking employment; or
    (ii) receiving education or training; or
  (b) making a grant to enable him to meet expenses connected with his education or training.

(9) Where a local authority are assisting the person under subsection (8) by making a contribution or grant with respect to a course of education or training, they may –
  (a) continue to do so even though he reaches the age of twenty-one before completing the course; and
  (b) disregard any interruption in his attendance on the course if he resumes it as soon as is reasonably practicable.

(10) Subsections (7) to (9) of section 17 shall apply in relation to assistance given under this section (otherwise than under subsection (8)) as they apply in relation to assistance given under that section.

(11) Where it appears to a local authority that a person whom they have been advising and befriending under this section, as a person qualifying for advice and assistance, proposes to live, or is living, in the area of another local authority, they shall inform that other local authority.

(12) Where a child who is accommodated –
  (a) by a voluntary organisation or in a registered children's home;
  (b) by any Health Authority, Special Health Authority, Primary Care Trust or local education authority; or
  (c) in any residential care home, nursing home or mental nursing home or in any accommodation provided by a National Health Service Trust,
  ceases to be so accommodated, after reaching the age of sixteen, the organisation, authority or (as the case may be) person carrying on the home shall inform the local authority within whose area the child proposes to live.

(13) Subsection (12) only applies, by virtue of paragraph (b) or (c), if the accommodation has been provided for a consecutive period of at least three months.

(14) Every local authority shall establish a procedure for considering any representations (including any complaints) made to them by a person qualifying for advice and assistance about the discharge of their functions under this Part in relation to him.

(15) In carrying out any consideration of representations under subsection (14), a local authority shall comply with any regulations made by the Secretary of State for the purposes of this subsection.

Persons qualifying for advice and assistance [Sections 24, 24A–D substituted for s24 as originally enacted by Children (Leaving Care) Act 2000 s4(1) – not yet in force]

24 (1) In this Part 'a person qualifying for advice and assistance' means a person who –

(a) is under twenty-one; and

(b) at any time after reaching the age of sixteen but while still a child was, but is no longer, looked after, accommodated or fostered.

(2) In subsection (1)(b),'looked after, accommodated or fostered' means –

(a) looked after by a local authority;

(b) accommodated by or on behalf of a voluntary organisation;

(c) accommodated in a private children's home;

(d) accommodated for a consecutive period of at least three months –

(i) by any Health Authority, Special Health Authority, Primary Care Trust or local education authority, or

(ii) in any care home or independent hospital or in any accommodation provided by a National Health Service trust; or

(e) privately fostered.

(3) Subsection (2)(d) applies even if the period of three months mentioned there began before the child reached the age of sixteen.

(4) In the case of a person qualifying for advice and assistance by virtue of subsection (2)(a), it is the duty of the local authority which last looked after him to take such steps as they think appropriate to contact him at such times as they think appropriate with a view to discharging their functions under sections 24A and 24B.

(5) In each of sections 24A and 24B, the local authority under the duty or having the power mentioned there ('the relevant authority') is –

(a) in the case of a person qualifying for advice and assistance by virtue of subsection (2)(a), the local authority which last looked after him; or

(b) in the case of any other person qualifying for advice and assistance, the local authority within whose area the person is (if he has asked for help of a kind which can be given under section 24A or 24B).

Advice and assistance

24A (1) The relevant authority shall consider whether the conditions in subsection (2) are satisfied in relation to a person qualifying for advice and assistance.

(2) The conditions are that –

(a) he needs help of a kind which they can give under this section or section 24B; and

(b) in the case of a person who was not being looked after by any local authority, they are satisfied that the person by whom he was being looked after does not have the necessary facilities for advising or befriending him.

(3) If the conditions are satisfied –

(a) they shall advise and befriend him if he was being looked after by a local authority or was accommodated by or on behalf of a voluntary organisation; and

(b) in any other case they may do so.

(4) Where as a result of this section a local authority are under a duty, or are empowered, to advise and befriend a person, they may also give him assistance.

(5) The assistance may be in kind or, in exceptional circumstances, in cash.

(6) Subsections (7) to (9) of section 17 apply in relation to assistance given under this section or section 24B as they apply in relation to assistance given under that section.

Employment, education and training

24B (1) The relevant local authority may give assistance to any person who qualifies for advice and assistance by virtue of section 24(2)(a) by contributing to expenses incurred by him in living near the place where he is, or will be, employed or seeking employment.

(2) The relevant local authority may give assistance to a person to whom subsection (3) applies by –
  (a) contributing to expenses incurred by the person in question in living near the place where he is, or will be, receiving education or training; or
  (b) making a grant to enable him to meet expenses connected with his education or training.

(3) This subsection applies to any person who –
  (a) is under twenty-four; and
  (b) qualifies for advice and assistance by virtue of section 24(2)(a), or would have done so if he were under twenty-one.

(4) Where a local authority are assisting a person under subsection (2) they may disregard any interruption in his attendance on the course if he resumes it as soon as is reasonably practicable.

(5) Where the local authority are satisfied that a person to whom subsection (3) applies who is in full-time further or higher education needs accommodation during a vacation because his term-time accommodation is not available to him then, they shall give him assistance by –
  (a) providing him with suitable accommodation during the vacation; or
  (b) paying him enough to enable him to secure such accommodation himself.

(6) The Secretary of State may prescribe the meaning of 'full-time', 'further education', 'higher education' and 'vacation' for the purposes of subsection (5).

Information

24C (1) Where it appears to a local authority that a person –
  (a) with whom they are under a duty to keep in touch under section 23B, 23C or 24; or
  (b) whom they have been advising and befriending under section 24A; or
  (c) to whom they have been giving assistance under section 24B,
  proposes to live, or is living, in the area of another local authority, they must inform that other authority.

(2) Where a child who is accommodated –
  (a) by a voluntary organisation or in a private children's home;

(b) by any Health Authority, Special Health Authority, Primary Care Trust or local education authority; or

(c) in any care home or independent hospital or any accommodation provided by a National Health Service trust,

ceases to be so accommodated, after reaching the age of sixteen, the organisation, authority or (as the case may be) person carrying on the home shall inform the local authority within whose area the child proposes to live.

(3) Subsection (2) only applies, by virtue of paragraph (b) or (c), if the accommodation has been provided for a consecutive period of at least three months.

Representations: sections 23A to 24B

24D (1) Every local authority shall establish a procedure for considering representations (including complaints) made to them by –

(a) a relevant child for the purposes of section 23A or a young person falling within section 23C;

(b) a person qualifying for advice and assistance; or

(c) a person falling within section 24B(2),

about the discharge of their functions under this Part in relation to him.

(2) In considering representations under subsection (1), a local authority shall comply with regulations (if any) made by the Secretary of State for the purposes of this subsection.

Chronically Sick and Disabled Persons Act 1970

Provision or welfare services

2 (1) Where a local authority having functions under s29 National Assistance Act 1948 are satisfied in the case of any person to whom that section applies who is ordinarily resident in their area that it is necessary in order to meet the needs of that person for that authority to make arrangements for all or any of the following matters, namely –

(a) the provision of practical assistance for that person in his home;

(b) the provision for that person of, or assistance to that person in obtaining, wireless, television, library or similar recreational facilities;

(c) the provision for that person of lectures, games, outings or other recreational facilities outside his home or assistance to that person in taking advantage of educational facilities available to him;

(d) the provision for that person of facilities for, or assistance in, travelling to and from his home for the purpose of participating in any services provided under arrangements made by the authority under the said section 29 or, with the approval of the authority, in any services provided otherwise than as aforesaid which are similar to services which could be provided under such arrangements;

(e) the provision of assistance for that person in arranging for the carrying out of any works of adaptation in his home or the provision of any additional facilities designed to secure his greater safety, comfort or convenience;

(f) facilitating the taking of holidays by that person, whether at holiday homes or otherwise and whether provided under arrangements made by the authority or otherwise;

(g) the provision of meals for that person whether in his home or elsewhere;

(h) the provision for that person of, or assistance to that person in obtaining, a telephone and any special equipment necessary to enable him to use a telephone,

then, subject to the provisions of section 7(1) of the Local Authority Social Services Act 1970 (which requires local authorities in the exercise of certain functions, including functions under the said section 29, to act under the general guidance of the Secretary of State) and to the provisions of section 7A of that Act (which requires local authorities to exercise their social services functions in accordance with directions given by the Secretary of State) it shall be the duty of that Authority to make those arrangements in exercise of their functions under the said section 29.

Health Services and Public Health Act 1968 s45

Promotion, by local authorities, of the welfare of old people

45 (1) A local authority may with the approval of the Secretary of State, and to such extent as he may direct shall, make arrangements for promoting the welfare of old people.

[(2) *repealed*.]

(3) A local authority may employ as their agent for the purposes of this section any voluntary organisation or any person carrying on, professionally or by way of trade or business, activities which consist of or include the provision of services for old people, being an organisation or person appearing to the authority to be capable of promoting the welfare of old people.

(4) No arrangements under this section shall provide –

(a) for the payment of money to old people except in so far as the arrangements may provide for the remuneration of old people engaged in suitable work in accordance with the arrangements;

(b) for making available any accommodation or services required to be provided under the National Health Service Act 1977.

(4A) No arrangements under this section may be given effect to in relation to a person to whom section 115 of the Immigration and Asylum Act 1999 (exclusion from benefits) applies solely –

(a) because he is destitute; or

(b) because of the physical effects, or anticipated physical effects, of his being destitute.

(4B) Subsections (3) and (5) to (8) of section 95 of the Immigration and Asylum Act 1999, and paragraph 2 of Schedule 8 to that Act, apply for the purposes of subsection (4a) as they apply for the purposes of that section, but for the references in subsections (5) and (7) of that section and in that paragraph to the Secretary of State substitute references to a local authority.

Local Authority Social Services Act 1970

Local authorities to exercise social services functions under guidance of Secretary of State

7 (1) Local authorities shall, in the exercise of their social services functions, including the exercise of any discretion conferred by any relevant enactment, act under the general guidance of the Secretary of State.
[(2), (3) *repealed*.]

Directions by the Secretary of State as to exercise of social services functions

7A (1) Without prejudice to section 7 of this Act, every local authority shall exercise their social services functions in accordance with such directions as may be given to them under this section by the Secretary of State.

(2) Directions under this section–
(a) shall be given in writing; and
(b) may be given to a particular authority, or to authorities of particular class, or to authorities generally.

Note: Schedule 1 enactments conferring functions assigned to social services committee as follows:

- Children and Young Persons Act 1933 Pts III, IV
- National Assistance Act 1948 ss21 to 27, 29 and 30, 43 to 45, 48, 49, 56(3) except so far as it relates to an offence under s47(11)
- Disabled Persons (Employment) Act 1958 s3
- Mental Health Act 1959 s8 and the Registered Homes Act 1984 so far as its provisions relate to mental nursing homes
- Mental Health (Scotland) Act 1984 s10
- Health Visiting and Social Work (Training) Act 1962 s5(1)(b), and as extended by section 45(9) of the Health Services and Public Health Act 1968 s5(1)(c)
- Children and Young Persons Act 1963 Pt I
- Health Services and Public Health Act 1968 ss45, 65
- Social Work (Scotland) Act 1968 ss75(2) and 76(4)
- Family Law Reform Act 1969 s7(4)
- Children and Young Persons Act 1969, the whole Act except section 9 in so far as it assign functions to a local authority in its capacity of a local education authority.
- Chronically Sick and Disabled Persons Act 1970 ss1, 2, 18
- Local Authority Social Services Act 1970 ss6 and 7B

- Children Act 1975 Pt II
- Adoption Act 1976
- Supplementary Benefits Act 1976 Sch 5
- National Health Service Act 1977
- Residential Homes Act 1980 ss1 to 7
- Mental Health Act 1983 Pts II, III and IV, ss66, 67, 69(1), 114, 115, 116, 117, 130
- Registered Homes Act 1984 PtI
- Public Health (Control of Disease) Act 1984 s46(2) and (5)
- Housing Act 1985 s72(b)
- Children Act 1989, the whole Act, in so far as it confers functions on a local authority within the meaning of that Act.
- National Health Service and Community Care Act 1990 ss46, 47
- Education Act 1993 s166
- Carers (Recognition and Services) Act 1995 s1

National Health Service Act 1977

CO-OPERATION AND ASSISTANCE
Local social services authorities

21 (1) Subject to paragraphs (d) and (e) of section 3(1) above, the services described in Schedule 8 to this Act in relation to –
  (a) care of mothers and young children,
  (b) prevention, care and after care,
  (c) home help and laundry facilities,
  are functions exercisable by local social services authorities, and that Schedule has effect accordingly.

(2) A local social services authority who provide premises, furniture or equipment for any of the purposes of this Act may permit the use of the premises, furniture or equipment –
  (a) by any other local social services authority, or
  (b) by any of the bodies constituted under this Act, or
  (c) by a local education authority.
  This permission may be on such terms (including terms with respect to the services of any staff employed by the authority giving permission) as may be agreed.

(3) A local social services authority may provide (or improve or furnish) residential accommodation–
  (a) for officers employed by them for the purposes of any of their functions as a local social services authority, or
  (b) for officers employed by a voluntary organisation for the purposes of any services provided under this section and Schedule 8.

SCHEDULE 8: LOCAL SOCIAL SERVICES AUTHORITIES
Care of mothers and young children

1 (1) A local social services authority may, with the Secretary of State's approval, and to such extent as he may direct shall, make arrangements for the care of expectant and nursing mothers (other than for the provision of residential accommodation for them).

Prevention, care and after-care

2 (1) A local social services authority may, with the Secretary of State's approval, and to such extent as he may direct shall, make arrangements for the purpose of the prevention of illness and for the care of persons suffering from illness and for the after-care of persons who have been suffering and in particular for –

[(a) *repealed.*]

(b) the provision for persons whose care is undertaken with a view to preventing them from becoming ill, persons suffering from illness and persons who have been so suffering, of centres or other facilities for training them or keeping them suitably occupied and the equipment and maintenance of such centres;

(c) the provision, for the benefit of such persons as are mentioned in paragraph (b) above, of ancillary or supplemental services; and

(d) for the exercise of the functions of the Authority in respect of persons suffering from mental disorder who are received into the guardianship under Part II or III of the Mental Health Act 1983 (whether the guardianship of the local social services authority or of other persons).

Such an authority shall neither have the power nor be subject to a duty to make under this paragraph arrangements to provide facilities for any of the purposes mentioned in section 15(1) of the Disabled Persons (Employment) Act 1944.

(2) No arrangements under this paragraph shall provide for the payment of money to persons for whose benefit they are made except –

(a) in so far as they may provide for the remuneration of such persons engaged in suitable work in accordance with the arrangements, of such amounts as the local social services authority think fit in respect of their occasional personal expenses where it appears to that authority that no such payment would otherwise be made.

...

(2A) No arrangements under this paragraph may be given effect to in relation to a person to whom section 115 of the Immigration and Asylum Act 1999 (exclusion from benefits) applies solely –

(a) because he is destitute; or

(b) because of the physical effects, or anticipated physical effects, of his being destitute.

(2B) Subsections (3) and (5) to (8) of section 95 of the Immigration and Asylum Act 1999, and paragraph 2 of Schedule 8 to that Act, apply for the purposes of subsection (2a) as they apply for the purposes of that section, but for the references in subsections (5) and (7) of that section and in that paragraph to the Secretary of State substitute references to a local social services authority.

(3) The Secretary of State may make regulations as to the conduct of premises in which, in pursuance of arrangements made under this paragraph, are provided for persons whose care is undertaken with a view to preventing them from becoming sufferers from mental disorder within the meaning of that Act of 1983 or who are, or have been, so suffering, facilities for training them or keeping them suitably occupied.

(4A) This paragraph does not apply in relation to persons under the age of 18.

(4AA) No authority is authorised or may be required under this paragraph to provide residential accommodation for any person.

Home help and laundry facilities

3 (1) It is the duty of every local social services authority to provide on such a scale as is adequate for the needs of their area, or to arrange for the provision on such a scale as is so adequate, of home help for households where such help is required owing to the presence of a person who is suffering from illness, lying-in, an expectant mother, aged, handicapped as a result of having suffered from illness or by congenital deformity, and every such Authority has power to provide or arrange for the provision of laundry facilities for households for which home help is being, or can be, provided under this sub-paragraph.

Research

4 Without prejudice to any powers conferred on them by any other Act, a local social services authority may conduct or assist other persons in conducting research into matters relating to the functions of local social services authorities under this Schedule.

National Health Service And Community Care Act 1990

Assessment of needs for community care services

47 (1) Subject to subsections (5) and (6) below, where it appears to a local authority that any person for whom they may provide or arrange for the provision of community care services may be in need of any such services, the authority –

(a) shall carry out an assessment of his needs for those services; and
(b) having regard to the results of that assessment, shall then decide whether his needs call for the provision by them of any such services.

(2) If at any time during the assessment of the needs of any person under subsection (1)(a) above it appears to a local authority that he is a disabled person, the authority –

(a) shall proceed to make such a decision as to the services he requires as is mentioned in section 4 of the Disabled Persons (Services, Consultation and Representation) Act 1986 without his requesting them to do so under that section; and

(b) shall inform him that they will be doing so and of his rights under that Act.

(3) If at any time during the assessment of the needs of any person under subsection (1)(a) above, it appears to a local authority –

(a) that there may be a need for the provision to that person by such Health Authority as may be determined in accordance with regulations of any services under the National Health Service Act 1977, or

(b) that there may be the need for the provision to him of any services which fall within the functions of a local housing authority (within the meaning of the Housing Act 1985) which is not the local authority carrying out the assessment,

the local authority shall notify that Health Authority or local housing authority and invite them to assist, to such extent as is reasonable in the circumstances, in the making of the assessment; and, in making their decision as to the provision of services needed for the person in question, the local authority shall take into account any services which are likely to be made available for him by that Health Authority or local housing authority.

(4) The Secretary of State may give directions as to the manner in which an assessment under this section is to be carried out or the form it is to take but, subject to any such directions and to subsection (7) below, it shall be carried out in such manner and take such form as the local authority consider appropriate.

(5) Nothing in this section shall prevent a local authority from temporarily providing or arranging for the provision of community care services for any person without carrying out a prior assessment of his needs in accordance with the preceding provisions of this section if, in the opinion of the authority, the condition of that person is such that he requires those services as a matter of urgency.

(6) If, by virtue of subsection (5) above, community care services have been provided temporarily for any person as a matter of urgency, then, as soon as practicable thereafter, an assessment of his needs shall be made in accordance with the preceding provisions of this section.

(7) This section is without prejudice to section 3 of the Disabled Persons (Services, Consultation and Representation) Act 1986.

(8) In this section –

'disabled person' has the same meaning as in that Act; and

'local authority' and 'community care services' have the same meanings as in section 46 above.

Mental Health Act 1983

After-care

117 (1) This section applies to persons who are detained under section 3 above, or admitted to a hospital in pursuance of a hospital order made under section 37 above, or transferred to a hospital in pursuance of a hospital direction made under section 45A above or a transfer direction made under section 47 or 48 above, and then cease to be detained and (whether or not immediately after so ceasing) leave hospital.

(2) It shall be the duty of the Health Authority and of the local social services authority to provide, in co-operation with relevant voluntary agencies, after-care services for any person to whom this section applies until such time as the Health Authority and the local social services authority are satisfied that the person concerned is no longer in need of such services; but they shall not be so satisfied in the case of a patient who is subject to after-care under supervision at any time while he so remains subject.

(2A) It shall be the duty of the Health Authority to secure that at all times while a patient is subject to after-care under supervision –

(a) a person who is a registered medical practitioner approved for the purposes of section 12 above by the Secretary of State as having special experience in the diagnosis or treatment of mental disorder is in charge of the medical treatment provided for the patient as part of the after-care services provided for him under this section; and

(b) a person professionally concerned with any of the after-care services so provided is supervising him with a view to securing that he receives the after-care services so provided.

(2B) Section 32 above shall apply for the purposes of this section as it applies for the purposes of Part II of this Act.

(3) In this section 'the Health Authority' means the Health Authority and 'the local social services authority' means the local social services authority for the area in which the person concerned is resident or to which he is sent on discharge by the hospital in which he was detained.

National Assistance Act 1948

Duty of local authorities to provide accommodation

21 (1) Subject to and in accordance with the provisions of this Part of this Act, a local authority may with the approval of the Secretary of State, and to such extent as he may direct shall, make arrangements for providing:

(a) residential accommodation for persons aged eighteen or over who by reason of age, illness, disability or any other circumstances are in need of care and attention which is not otherwise available to them and

(aa) residential accommodation for expectant and nursing mothers who are in need of care and attention which is not otherwise available to them.

(1A) A person to whom section 115 of the Immigration and Asylum Act 1999 (exclusion from benefits) applies may not be provided with residential accommodation under subsection (1)(a) if his need for care and attention has arisen solely –

(a) because he is destitute; or

(b) because of the physical effects, or anticipated physical effects, of his being destitute.

(1B) Subsections (3) and (5) to (8) of section 95 of the Immigration and Asylum Act 1999, and paragraph 2 of Schedule 8 to that Act, apply for the purposes of subsection (1A) as they apply for the purposes of that section, but for the references in subsections (5) and (7) of that section and in that paragraph to the Secretary of State substitute references to a local authority.

(2) In making any such arrangements a local authority shall have regard to the welfare of all persons for whom accommodation is provided, and in particular to the need for providing accommodation of different descriptions suited to different descriptions of such persons as are mentioned in the last foregoing subsection.

(2A) In determining for the purposes of paragraph (a) or (aa) of subsection (1) of this section whether care and attention are otherwise available to a person, a local authority shall disregard so much of the person's capital as does not exceed the capital limit for the purposes of section 22 of this Act.

(2B) For the purposes of subsection (2A) of this section –

   (a) a person's capital shall be calculated in accordance with assessment regulations in the same way as if he were a person for whom accommodation is proposed to be provided as mentioned in subsection (3) of section 22 of this Act and whose ability to pay for the accommodation falls to be assessed for the purposes of that subsection; and

   (b) 'the capital limit for the purposes of section 22 of this Act' means the amount for the time being prescribed in assessment regulations as the amount which a resident's capital (calculated in accordance with such regulations) must not exceed if he is to be assessed as unable to pay for his accommodation at the standard rate;

   and in this subsection 'assessment regulations' means regulations made for the purposes of section 22(5) of this Act.

   [(3) *repealed.*]

(4) Subject to section 26 of this Act, accommodation provided by a local authority in the exercise of their functions under this section shall be provided in premises managed by the authority or, to such extent as may be determined in accordance with the arrangements under this section, in such premises managed by another local authority as may be agreed between the two authorities and on such terms as to the reimbursement of expenditure incurred by the said other authority, as may be so agreed.

(5) References in this Act to accommodation provided under this Part thereof shall be construed as references to accommodation provided in accordance with this and the five next following sections, and as including references to board and other services, amenities and requisites provided in connection with the accommodation except where in the opinion of the authority managing the premises their provision is unnecessary.

(6) References in this Act to a local authority providing accommodation shall be construed, in any case where a local authority agree with another local authority for the provision of accommodation in premises managed by the said other authority, as references to the first-mentioned local authority.

(7) Without prejudice to the generality of the foregoing provisions of this section, a local authority may –

   (a) provide, in such cases as they may consider appropriate, for the conveyance of persons to and from premises in which accommodation is provided for them under this Part of the Act;

(b) make arrangements for the provision on the premises in which accommodation is being provided of such other services as appear to the authority to be required.

(8) Nothing in this section shall authorise or require a local authority to make any provision authorised or required to be made (whether by that or by any other authority) by or under any enactment not contained in this Part of this Act, or authorised or required to be provided under the National Health Service Act 1977.

Welfare arrangements for blind, deaf, dumb and crippled persons, etc

29 (1) A local authority may, with the approval of the Secretary of State, and to such extent as he may direct in relation to persons ordinarily resident in the area of the local authority shall make arrangements for promoting the welfare of persons to whom this section applies, that is to say persons aged eighteen or over who are blind, deaf or dumb or who suffer from mental disorder of any description, and other persons aged eighteen or over who are substantially and permanently handicapped by illness, injury, or congenital deformity or such other disabilities as may be prescribed by the Minister.

[(2), (3) *repealed*.]

(4) Without prejudice to the generality of the provisions of subsection (1) of this section, arrangements may be made thereunder –

(a) for informing persons to whom arrangements under that subsection relate of the services available for them thereunder;

(b) for giving such persons instruction in their own homes or elsewhere in methods of overcoming the effects of their disabilities;

(c) for providing workshops where such persons may be engaged (whether under a contract of service or otherwise) in suitable work, and hostels where persons engaged in the workshops, and other persons to whom arrangements under subsection (1) of this section relate and for whom work or training is being provided in pursuance of the Disabled Persons (Employment) Act 1944 or the Employment and Training Act 1973 may live;

(d) for providing persons to whom arrangements under subsection (1) of this section relate with suitable work (whether under a contract of service or otherwise) in their own homes or elsewhere;

(e) for helping such persons in disposing of the produce of their work;

(f) for providing such persons with recreational facilities in their own homes or elsewhere;

(g) for compiling and maintaining classified registers of the persons to whom arrangements under subsection (1) of this section relate.

(4A) Where accommodation in a hostel is provided under paragraph (c) of subsection (4) of this section –

(a) if the hostel is managed by a local authority, section 22 of this Act shall apply as it applies where accommodation is provided under s21;

(b) if the accommodation is provided in a hostel managed by a person other

than a local authority under arrangements made with that person, subsections (2) to (4A) of section 26 of this Act shall apply as they apply
where accommodation is provided under arrangements made by virtue
of that section; and

(c) sections 32 and 43 of this Act shall apply as they apply where accommodation is provided under sections 21 to 26;

and in this subsection references to 'accommodation' include references to
board and other services, amenities and requisites provided in connection
with the accommodation, except where in the opinion of the authority managing the premises or, in the case mentioned in paragraph (b) above, the
authority making the arrangements their provision is unnecessary.

[(5) *repealed.*]

(6) Nothing in the foregoing provisions of this section shall authorise or
require –

(a) the payment of money to persons to whom this section applies, other
than persons for whom work is provided under arrangements made by
virtue of paragraph (c) or paragraph (d) of subsection (4) of this section
or who are engaged in work which they are enabled to perform in consequence of anything done in pursuance of arrangements made under
this section; or

(b) the provision of any accommodation or services required to be provided
under the National Health Service Act 1977.

(7) A person engaged in work in a workshop provided under paragraph (c) of
subsection (4) of this section, or a person in receipt of a superannuation
allowance granted on his retirement from engagement in any such workshop, shall be deemed for the purposes of this Act to continue to be ordinarily resident in the area in which he was ordinarily resident immediately
before he was accepted for work in that workshop; and for the purposes of
this subsection a course of training in such workshop shall be deemed to be
work in that workshop.

Human Rights Act 1998

SCHEDULE 1 – THE ARTICLES
PART I: THE CONVENTION: RIGHTS AND FREEDOMS
Article 2: Right to life

1   Everyone's right to life shall be protected by law. No one shall be deprived of
his life intentionally save in the execution of a sentence of a court following
his conviction of a crime for which this penalty is provided by law.

2   Deprivation of life shall not be regarded as inflicted in contravention of this
Article when it results from the use of force which is no more than absolutely necessary:

(a) in defence of any person from unlawful violence;

(b) in order to effect a lawful arrest or to prevent the escape of a person
lawfully detained;

(c) in action lawfully taken for the purpose of quelling a riot or insurrection.

Article 3: Prohibition of torture
No one shall be subjected to torture or to inhuman or degrading treatment or punishment.

Article 6: Right to a fair trial
1   In the determination of his civil rights and obligations or of any criminal charge against him, everyone is entitled to a fair and public hearing within a reasonable time by an independent and impartial tribunal established by law. Judgment shall be pronounced publicly but the press and public may be excluded from all or part of the trial in the interest of morals, public order or national security in a democratic society, where the interests of juveniles or the protection of the private life of the parties so require, or to the extent strictly necessary in the opinion of the court in special circumstances where publicity would prejudice the interests of justice.
2   Everyone charged with a criminal offence shall be presumed innocent until proved guilty according to law.
3   Everyone charged with a criminal offence has the following minimum rights:
   (a) to be informed promptly, in a language which he understands and in detail, of the nature and cause of the accusation against him;
   (b) to have adequate time and facilities for the preparation of his defence;
   (c) to defend himself in person or through legal assistance of his own choosing or, if he has not sufficient means to pay for legal assistance, to be given it free when the interests of justice so require;
   (d) to examine or have examined witnesses against him and to obtain the attendance and examination of witnesses on his behalf under the same conditions as witnesses against him;
   (e) to have the free assistance of an interpreter if he cannot understand or speak the language used in court.

Article 8: Right to respect for private and family life
1   Everyone has the right to respect for his private and family life, his home and his correspondence.
2   There shall be no interference by a public authority with the exercise of this right except such as is in accordance with the law and is necessary in a democratic society in the interests of national security, public safety or the economic well-being of the country, for the prevention of disorder or crime, for the protection of health or morals, or for the protection of the rights and freedoms of others.

Article 9: Freedom of thought, conscience and religion
1   Everyone has the right to freedom of thought, conscience and religion; this right includes freedom to change his religion or belief and freedom, either alone or in community with others and in public or private, to manifest his religion or belief, in worship, teaching, practice and observance.
2   Freedom to manifest one's religion or beliefs shall be subject only to such limitations as are prescribed by law and are necessary in a democratic society in the interests of public safety, for the protection of public order, health or morals, or for the protection of the rights and freedoms of others.

Article 10: Freedom of expression

1   Everyone has the right to freedom of expression. This right shall include freedom to hold opinions and to receive and impart information and ideas without interference by public authority and regardless of frontiers. This Article shall not prevent States from requiring the licensing of broadcasting, television or cinema enterprises.

2   The exercise of these freedoms, since it carries with it duties and responsibilities, may be subject to such formalities, conditions, restrictions or penalties as are prescribed by law and are necessary in a democratic society, in the interests of national security, territorial integrity or public safety, for the prevention of disorder or crime, for the protection of health or morals, for the protection of the reputation or rights of others, for preventing the disclosure of information received in confidence, or for maintaining the authority and impartiality of the judiciary.

Article 11: Freedom of assembly and association

1   Everyone has the right to freedom of peaceful assembly and to freedom of association with others, including the right to form and to join trade unions for the protection of his interests.

2   No restrictions shall be placed on the exercise of these rights other than such as are prescribed by law and are necessary in a democratic society in the interests of national security or public safety, for the prevention of disorder or crime, for the protection of health or morals or for the protection of the rights and freedoms of others. This Article shall not prevent the imposition of lawful restrictions on the exercise of these rights by members of the armed forces, of the police or of the administration of the State.

Article 14: Prohibition of discrimination

The enjoyment of the rights and freedoms set forth in this Convention shall be secured without discrimination on any ground such as sex, race, colour, language, religion, political or other opinion, national or social origin, association with a national minority, property, birth or other status.

Article 16: Restrictions on political activity of aliens

Nothing in Articles 10, 11 and 14 shall be regarded as preventing the High Contracting Parties from imposing restrictions on the political activity of aliens.

PART II: THE FIRST PROTOCOL
Article 1: Protection of property

Every natural or legal person is entitled to the peaceful enjoyment of his possessions. No one shall be deprived of his possessions except in the public interest and subject to the conditions provided for by law and by the general principles of international law. The preceding provisions shall not, however, in any way impair the right of a State to enforce such laws as it deems necessary to control the use of property in accordance with the general interest or to secure the payment of taxes or other contributions or penalties.

Article 2: Right to education

No person shall be denied the right to education. In the exercise of any functions which it assumes in relation to education and to teaching, the State shall respect the right of parents to ensure such education and teaching in conformity with their own religious and philosophical convictions.

SCHEDULE 2 – REMEDIAL ORDERS
Orders

1 (1) A remedial order may –
  (a) contain such incidental, supplemental, consequential or transitional provision as the person making it considers appropriate;
  (b) be made so as to have effect from a date earlier than that on which it is made;
  (c) make provision for the delegation of specific functions;
  (d) make different provision for different cases.

  (2) The power conferred by sub-paragraph (1)(a) includes –
  (a) power to amend primary legislation (including primary legislation other than that which contains the incompatible provision); and
  (b) power to amend or revoke subordinate legislation (including subordinate legislation other than that which contains the incompatible provision).

  (3) A remedial order may be made so as to have the same extent as the legislation which it affects.

  (4) No person is to be guilty of an offence solely as a result of the retrospective effect of a remedial order.

Procedure

2 No remedial order may be made unless –
  (a) a draft of the order has been approved by a resolution of each House of Parliament made after the end of the period of 60 days beginning with the day on which the draft was laid; or
  (b) it is declared in the order that it appears to the person making it that, because of the urgency of the matter, it is necessary to make the order without a draft being so approved.

Orders laid in draft

3 (1) No draft may be laid under paragraph 2(a) unless –
  (a) the person proposing to make the order has laid before Parliament a document which contains a draft of the proposed order and the required information; and
  (b) the period of 60 days, beginning with the day on which the document required by this sub-paragraph was laid, has ended.

  (2) If representations have been made during that period, the draft laid under paragraph 2(a) must be accompanied by a statement containing –
  (a) a summary of the representations; and
  (b) if, as a result of the representations, the proposed order has been changed, details of the changes.

Urgent cases

4 (1) If a remedial order ('the original order') is made without being approved in draft, the person making it must lay it before Parliament, accompanied by the required information, after it is made.

   (2) If representations have been made during the period of 60 days beginning with the day on which the original order was made, the person making it must (after the end of that period) lay before Parliament a statement containing –
   (a) a summary of the representations; and
   (b) if, as a result of the representations, he considers it appropriate to make changes to the original order, details of the changes.

   (3) If sub-paragraph (2)(b) applies, the person making the statement must –
   (a) make a further remedial order replacing the original order; and
   (b) lay the replacement order before Parliament.

   (4) If, at the end of the period of 120 days beginning with the day on which the original order was made, a resolution has not been passed by each House approving the original or replacement order, the order ceases to have effect (but without that affecting anything previously done under either order or the power to make a fresh remedial order).

Definitions

5 In this Schedule –
'representations' means representations about a remedial order (or proposed remedial order) made to the person making (or proposing to make) it and includes any relevant Parliamentary report or resolution; and
'required information' means –

   (a) an explanation of the incompatibility which the order (or proposed order) seeks to remove, including particulars of the relevant declaration, finding or order; and
   (b) a statement of the reasons for proceeding under section 10 and for making an order in those terms.

Calculating periods

6 In calculating any period for the purposes of this Schedule, no account is to be taken of any time during which –

   (a) Parliament is dissolved or prorogued; or
   (b) both Houses are adjourned for more than four days.

SCHEDULE 3 – DEROGATION AND RESERVATION
PART II: RESERVATION

At the time of signing the present (First) Protocol, I declare that, in view of certain provisions of the Education Acts in the United Kingdom, the principle affirmed in the second sentence of Article 2 is accepted by the United Kingdom only so far as it is compatible with the provision of efficient instruction and training, and the avoidance of unreasonable public expenditure.

Directions and guidance

Letter dated 19 November 1999 from National Asylum Support Service to all chief executives of local authorities in England and Wales

Dear Chief Executive

Immigration and Asylum Act 1999: the Asylum Support (Interim Provisions) Regulations 1999

1   The purpose of this letter is to explain the effect of new provisions regarding the support of asylum-seekers by local authorities in England and Wales that take effect from 6 December 1999.

2   The Immigration and Asylum Act 1999 ('The 1999 Act'), which received Royal Assent earlier this month contains new provisions regarding the support of asylum-seekers and their dependants pending the determination of the asylum claim. Part VI of the Act lays the ground for a new Home Office led National Asylum Support Service to be established, which will take the lead in all support for new asylum-seekers from 1 April 2000. The Act also contains important new provisions for the support of people applying for asylum before 1 April 2000 by local authorities. It should be read in conjunction with Part VI of, including Schedule 9 to, the 1999 Act and the Asylum Support (Interim Provisions) Regulations (SI 1999 No 3056) ('The Regulations'); a copy of the text of these Regulations accompanies this letter. These Regulations, and associated provisions, have effect from 6 December 1999.

3   The new interim provisions do not apply in Scotland or Northern Ireland, where existing arrangements for the support of asylum-seekers continue to have effect until the main new Part VI scheme comes into force.

4   The new provisions do not affect arrangements for the support of unaccompanied children under the age of 18 who seek asylum in this country. They will continue to be supported by local authorities under the relevant child welfare legislation.

5   Since 1996 people who have applied for asylum at the port of entry to this country have been entitled to claim social security benefits until the first negative decision on their asylum application. In general, those who apply for asylum 'in country' have not been entitled to social

security benefits and, where they are in need of support, have had to look to local authorities for support under social services legislation. Similarly asylum-seekers who applied at the port of entry and were initially in receipt of social security benefits, but who subsequently have a negative decision on their asylum application, have had to look to social services departments for support if they remain in this country pending the outcome of an appeal against that decision. The Government does not propose to change that basic distinction for people who apply for asylum before 1 April 2000. Local authorities will continue to be responsible only for those asylum-seekers who applied for asylum in country, and for others remaining here pending the outcome of an appeal.

6   Currently local authorities support asylum-seekers under section 21 of the National Assistance Act 1948 and section 17 of the Children Act 1989. These social services powers were never intended to give general support to people simply because they are destitute, and are not well suited to that function. Schedule 9 to the 1999 Act and regulations made under it therefore replace the duties owed to asylum-seekers under social services legislation with a new purpose-designed duty of support. The Regulations provide that asylum-seekers and their dependants who are currently supported under social services legislation will automatically transfer onto the new interim support arrangements set out in the regulations when they take effect on 6 December 1999; consequently individual asylum-seekers already accommodated under that legislation need not be aware of any change to the level and kind of support they may receive. It is intended that local authorities should continue to be able to support asylum-seekers under the interim arrangements in the same manner as they are doing now. This 'deeming' provision is contained in regulation 11.

7   The Government proposes to bring section 116 of the 1999 Act into force from 6 December 1999. This has the effect of preventing local authorities from supporting persons subject to immigration control under the provisions of section 21 of the National Assistance Act 1948, if they require such assistance solely by reason of their destitution; subsections (1) and (2) of section 117 of the 1999 Act will also be commenced at the same time. From that date asylum-seekers already supported by local authorities will be deemed onto the interim arrangements, and asylum-seekers requiring support for the first time will be able to apply for support under the interim arrangements. They will continue to be eligible for support under the interim arrangements until their claim for asylum has been determined; by virtue of section 94 of the 1999 Act and regulation 2(6) this is 14 days after a person is deemed to have received a decision from the Home Secretary on his asylum application, or if there has been an appeal, 14 days after the time for lodging any further appeal has expired.

8   However other persons subject to immigration control, for example, people who have limited leave to enter the country, people who have entered the country unlawfully or former asylum-seekers whose final

appeal has been determined, will also cease to be entitled to support from social services departments under the National Assistance Act 1948. The Home Office has already mounted an exercise to assist local authorities to identify these people, and inform them that they are no longer entitled to support. In the case of families with children, regulation 12 will prevent those families who are entitled to support under the interim scheme from claiming that form of support under section 17 of the Children Act (although they would be entitled to other forms of assistance connected with the welfare of a child). However other families of persons who have exhausted all rights of appeal against refusal of asylum, will continue to be entitled to claim assistance from local authorities under the Children Act until such time as they are removed from the country.

9   The interim arrangements will provide the basis for local authority support to in-country asylum-seekers whose application for asylum is made before 1 April 2000. The duty in respect of such people will continue after that date, although arrangements may be made by the Home Office to transfer case responsibility for certain classes of asylum-seeker, or all asylum-seekers supported by a particular authority, to the NASS support arrangements over succeeding months. The entitlement to continued support of the asylum-seeker transferred in this way would need to be reassessed. Further advice on these arrangements will be issued in due course.

10   The responsibility for supporting asylum-seekers under the interim arrangements will rest on the same classes of local authorities as are currently supporting them. These are, in England, London boroughs, the Corporation of London, metropolitan districts, county councils, and unitary authorities. In Wales the responsibility rests with county councils and county borough councils; regulation 2 refers. In the English shire counties, district councils (which are the housing authorities for that area) will, where requested, be under a duty to provide reasonable assistance to the shire county council who are providing support to asylum-seekers.

11   The interim arrangements provide for support to be given by local authorities to asylum-seekers who appear to be destitute. The definition of destitution is contained in section 95 of the 1999 Act; there are no plans to make supplementary regulations under the powers contained in section 95 to expand this definition for the purpose of the interim arrangements. It will be for local authorities to devise their own operational test of destitution, as they do under current social services legislation. In general local authorities will not need to reassess the destitution of people who are deemed from social services support onto the new interim arrangements. They should however be aware that the test of destitution is in effect a continuing test, so that they only have the duty to support any asylum-seeker for as long as he continues to be destitute; if he ceases to be destitute then the support under the interim arrangements must cease. By virtue of regulation 2(6) local authorities are also obliged to provide support to asylum-

seekers who appear to be likely to become destitute within a period of fourteen days. This ensures that authorities take action in advance of the destitution actually occurring.

12   Regulation 2 sets out the range of household members that are to be supported together under the interim arrangements. Essentially this is the asylum-seeker, his spouse or partner and any dependent children, any disabled adult who is dependent on that household plus anyone else who is treated as dependent on the asylum-seeker for the purposes of the asylum claim. Additionally the regulation makes provision for anyone else who is currently being supported as part of the family group under section 17 of the Children Act to be treated as eligible for support as part of that household group under the interim arrangements.

13   Regulation 7 sets out situations where support must be refused. Apart from excluding asylum-seekers who are eligible for social security benefits from support under the interim arrangements, the regulation also provides that support may not be given to a person who has made himself intentionally destitute. It is not expected that local authorities would need to rely on this provision routinely, but it does require them to refuse support to an asylum-seeker who has deliberately squandered his resources; in the case of families there would be a residual obliga- tion to provide assistance under section 17 of the Children Act. This regulation also provides that support must be refused where an appli- cation has already been made to another authority. This applies both to an application for support under these Regulations and to an appli- cation made within the previous twelve months for support under section 21 of the National Assistance Act or section 17 of the Children Act. This is to prevent asylum-seekers 'shopping around' different local authorities in search of a particular package of support that they prefer. Many local authorities currently stamp the reverse of the stand- ard acknowledgement letter ('SAL') or other official document issued to asylum-seekers by the Home Office, to indicate that an application has been made to that authority. It is recommended that this practice continues, so that where an authority is presented with a SAL showing such a stamp, it knows that the asylum-seeker has already made an application for support elsewhere.

14   Regulation 4 makes provision for authorities to provide temporary support pending the establishment of an applicant's entitlement. This is in line with current provisions, and ensures that immediate assist- ance can be given to an asylum-seeker and his dependants pending determination of his eligibility for support; this might turn on whether or not he really is an asylum-seeker, whether he is really destitute, or whether he falls within a category for whom support must be refused.

15   Regulation 5 governs the provision of support. It reflects the nature of present legislation in making differing provisions for the support of asylum-seekers whose households include a dependent child, and other asylum-seekers. In the case of single asylum-seekers and others without dependent children, support may only be provided as a com-

bined package of accommodation and assistance with essential living needs. It is open to local authorities to decide whether to provide this by way of accommodation in a full board hostel, or to provide the asylum-seeker with self-catering accommodation and separately with the resources to meet his essential living needs. In all cases the maximum amount of assistance that may be given by way of cash payments (rather than vouchers or support in kind) is £10 per week. In the case of families with dependent children support may be given either in respect of accommodation only or in respect of essential living needs only, or in respect of both. There is no limit on the proportion of support which may be given by way of cash payments for families, although under regulation 6 authorities are required to have regard to the cost of providing support.

16   The support may be made subject to conditions set out by the local authority. The conditions must be set out in writing and a copy of them given to the person who is provided with support. By virtue of regulation 8(2) failure to comply with these conditions without reasonable excuse could lead to the suspension or termination of support. It is envisaged that local authorities may wish to rely on this provision for setting conditions in relation to any tenancy or license granted to the asylum-seeker, on matters such as the maintenance of the property. Additionally Regulation 8 provides that where an asylum-seeker has left accommodation for more that seven days without reasonable excuse the support may be suspended or discontinued. It would be open to authorities to set a longer period, or not to operate this provision at all, if they choose. The provisions on offences contained in sections 105 to 109 of the 1999 Act took effect on Royal Assent, and it would be open to a local authority to institute proceedings under them were this necessary.

17   Paragraphs 73, 81 and 88 of Schedule 14 to the 1999 Act have the effect of removing asylum-seekers supported under Part VI of the Act from the security of tenure provisions in housing legislation. These provisions were commenced on Royal Assent, and since Schedule 9 falls within Part VI of the Act, have effect on tenancies granted under the interim arrangements. Their effect is that tenancies of local authority housing granted after the interim arrangements take effect are not secure tenancies, and tenancies of private landlords cannot be assured tenancies. The Department of the Environment, Transport and the Regions has made an order under section 9 of the Asylum and Immigration Act 1996 (The Housing Accommodation (Amendment) (England) Order 1999 SI No 3057) that has the effect of removing restrictions on the granting of tenancies of local authority housing to asylum-seekers supported under Part VI. DETR will be issuing guidance on this order shortly.

18   Regulation 6 sets out certain matters to which local authorities should have regard in providing support. They enable local authorities to take into account income, assets and other forms of support (for example, support in kind from friends or family) that are available, or might

reasonably be expected to be available, to the asylum-seeker and his dependants when deciding the level of support to be provided. In general, regulation 6 requires a local authority to strike a sensible balance between the needs of the individual asylum-seeker and the cost of providing support. They also absolve the local authority from being required to take account of the asylum-seeker's preferences as to the type of accommodation to be provided or the locality in which it is located.

19   Regulation 9 provides that a local authority may transfer a claim for support or the responsibility for providing support to another local authority by mutual agreement between the two authorities. The consent of the asylum-seeker is not required. Where a claim for support is transferred, it is the receiving authority that determines the person's eligibility for support (regulation 3(3)). This provision will allow for the voluntary dispersal of asylum-seekers away from pressure areas in London and the South East in accordance with arrangements that are being developed by the Local Government Association in consultation with the Home Office. In making such transfers local authorities are required, by virtue of paragraph 9 of Schedule 9 to the 1999 Act, to have regard to such guidance as the Secretary of State may issue on this subject. This guidance will be issued shortly.

20   Paragraphs 8 and 9 of Schedule 9 to the 1999 Act also contain provisions that would allow an upper limit to be set on the number of asylum-seekers that a local authority might be required to support, and would prevent asylum-seekers being placed in a particular locality by any local authority. Ministers took these powers in order to be able to mitigate the excessive burden of supporting asylum-seekers that certain authorities in London and the South East are currently facing. At the request of the Local Government Association they have not at this stage made any regulations under those powers. Like the Local Government Association they would prefer to see pressure on London and the South East mitigated by the voluntary dispersal arrangements that are currently being developed. However, if those voluntary arrangements fail to relieve pressure on London and the South East, Ministers will not hesitate to bring into force new regulations that rely on those powers, possibly at short notice. A draft of regulations that might be made under those powers is attached to this letter as Annex A, for information.

21   Local authorities will continue to be entitled to claim grant for the Home Office for supporting asylum-seekers, which will be paid under the new powers contained in section 110 of the 1999 Act. The grant will reimburse actual expenditure on the support and accommodation of asylum-seekers up to a maximum of £150 per week for single asylum-seekers and £220 per week for families. We shall be writing to you separately about claming this grant.

Yours sincerely,
Bob Eagle

Letter dated 1 December 1999 from National Asylum Support Service to all chief executives of local authorities in England and Wales

Dear Chief Executive

Support for asylum-seekers: guidance on the operation of the interim scheme

Introduction

1 This guidance should be read in conjunction with the Immigration and Asylum Act 1999 ('the 1999 Act'), the Asylum Support (Interim Provisions) Regulations (SI 1999 No 3056) (the Regulations), and the letter from Bob Eagle (NASS) dated 19 November on the regulations. The regulations apply to England and Wales and come into force on 6 December 1999.

2 Regulation 9 of the Asylum Support (Interim Provisions) Regulations 1999 provides that a local authority may transfer a claim for support or the responsibility for providing support to another local authority by mutual agreement between the two authorities. In making such transfers, local authorities are required, by virtue of paragraph 9 of Schedule 9 to the 1999 Act, to have regard to such guidance as the Secretary of State may issue on this subject. This letter constitutes such guidance.

Allocating accommodation to asylum-seekers

3 The Home Office, in consultation with voluntary and other agencies, has identified the following criteria for developing suitable cluster areas in which asylum-seekers' accommodation will be located when the main dispersal scheme comes into effect from 1 April 2000. Cluster areas will be where:
   – there is likely to be suitable accommodation available;
   – there is already a multi-ethnic population or infrastructure able to assist asylum-seekers; and
   – it would be possible to link in with existing communities and to develop the support of voluntary and community groups.

4 Ideally, the operation of the voluntary, interim dispersal scheme should lay the ground for cluster areas after 1 April, with those local authorities placing asylum-seekers in areas which in their judgement are able to meet the above criteria. However, it is recognised that many local authorities may not be in a position to place all the asylum-seekers they will receive during the viluntary scheme in such well-defined areas. They should, nevertheless, take into account all relevant details and information when making a decision on where to place an asylum-seeker transferred to their authority. These details include:

- the cultural background and language of the asylum-seeker;
- any particular needs regarding the type of accommodation required (for example, family accommodation, special needs or disabilities);
- the particular characteristics of the locality in which accommodation is situated;
- the accessibility of support structures – whether voluntary or statutory (in general, such support structures should be within reach of the accommodation by public transport).

5   The local authority receiving the transferred case should also ensure that it puts sufficient arrangements in place for aiding the asylum-seeker to travel to the accommodation allotted to him on arrival from the local authority where he presented for support.

6   The interim scheme is a voluntary one, which has been entered into by local authorities under the auspices of the Local Government Association and by the Association of London Government on the practical operation of the voluntary scheme.

Exceptional reasons to remain in the original local authority

7   Local authorities in London and Kent who refer asylum-seekers to another local authority should undertake an initial assessment to ensure that there are no exceptional reasons why the asylum-seeker should remain in the authority where he has presented. Best practice in this regard will be covered in the ALG guidance. Each case will need to be decided on its merits, but reasons for considering whether an asylum-seeker should remain in London or Kent might include:

- particular medical needs which can only be met locally (for example, access to the Medical Foundation for victims of torture);
- close family members already living in the areas.

Information provision to the Home Office

8   Local authorities should provide the National Asylum Support Service in the Home Office with the information it requires for the monitoring of the interim scheme. This is likely to be information concerning the asylum-seeker, where he first presented for support and where he has been offered accommodation. Forms for recording the required information will be distributed to local authorities shortly.

Dispersal and type of support which may be provided

9   Regulation 5 of the Statutory Instrument provides that in the case of single asylum-seekers and others without dependent children, support may only be provided as a combined package of accommodation and assistance with essential living needs, other than in exceptional circumstances. In the case of families with dependent children, support may be given either in respect of accommodation only or in respect of essential living needs only, or in respect of both. Clearly, should a family with dependent children present to a local authority for assistance with essential living needs only, they will not be transferred out of

that authority. (The interim scheme does not cover unaccompanied asylum-seeking children.)

10   If an asylum-seeker refuses to be dispersed without good reason, he will be refusing support offered to him under the interim arrangements. If he subsequently applies to any other local authority for support under the interim arrangments, that local authority will be bound by virtue of regulation 7(1)(b) to refuse him support. His only option will be to reapply to the authority where he first presented.

11   Any questions concerning this guidance should be directed to Judith Simpson, NASS on 0181 760 4819, or to Mike Canham, NASS on 0181 760 4931.

Yours sincerely
Judith Simpson

Letter from National Asylum Support Service: criteria for eligibility for 'hard cases' support

Rachael Reynolds
Head of Refugee Integration
National Asylum Support Service
4th Floor, Quest House, Cross Road,
Croydon, Surrey, CR9 6ER

Your Reference
Our Reference
Telephone: 020 8633 0516
Facsimile: 020 8633 0550
Website: www.homeoffice.gov.uk/ind/assd/assd.htm

Mr Dermot Boyle
Chief Executive
Refugee Arrivals Project
Room 1116, First Floor
Queen's Building
Heathrow Airport
MIDDX TW6 1DN

CRITERIA FOR ELIGIBILITY FOR NASS SUPPORT

1   I understand your office was enquiring recently about the way in which the 'hard cases' fund will operate post 3 April. Ministers have now considered the position and formed a view on what we should do. As you are aware we had hoped that the voluntary sector itself would be prepared to take on the administration of this task. Since that has not proved possible NASS will, for the time being at least, administer the scheme itself.

2   What we are clear about is that we cannot simply create a parallel if more basic support system to which there would be automatic recourse once NASS support has been terminated. Ministers remain of the view that those who have received a final negative decision should leave the country. We have therefore drawn up the criteria on this basis. A copy of the criteria we intend to use is at Annex A.

3   'Hard cases' support will mean basic full board accommodation outside of London. The ex-asylum seeker will have no access to other vouchers or cash. The ex-asylum seeker must also subject themselves to regular monthly reviews in which they will be expected to demonstrate the steps they have taken to enable themselves to leave the country. If there is not sufficient evidence that this has happened then hard cases support will be terminated.

4   Applications for 'hard cases' support should be made to NASS in writing setting out why the ex-asylum seeker believes himself/herself to be eligible. We expect those eligible to be very few in number but we will keep the situation under review.

5   If you have any questions about the operation of the scheme I would be happy to assist.

cc Nick Hardwick – Refugee Council
Sally Daghlian – Scottish Refugee Council
Mohammed Yusuf – Welsh Refugee Council
Sandy Buchan – Refugee Action
Annie Ledger – Migrant Helpline
Dave Wall – NIACRO

Eligibility for 'hard cases' support to those who:
– are no longer eligible for NASS support and have no access to any other support and
– can demonstrate that they are genuinely unable to leave the country due to a physical impediment, eg, through illness or late pregnancy or
– can demonstrate that their cases are genuinely exceptional and
– subject themselves to reviews of their cases monthly in which they can demonstrate the ways in which they have attempted to leave the country
– accept the basic accommodation provided by NASS on a full-board basis with no voucher or cash voucher access.
This support may be available to all ex-asylum seekers who have permission to apply for judicial review.

CRITERIA FOR ELIGIBILITY FOR 'HARD CASES' SUPPORT

A person is eligible for support (under section 4 of the Immigration and Asylum Act 1999) after 3 April 2000 if:
– his claim for asylum (within the meaning of Part VI of the Act) has been refused;
– he has been supported by the National Asylum Support Service or, after that date, by a local authority under Schedule 9 to the Act;

- he is no longer an asylum-seeker (within the meaning of Part VI of the Act);
- he appears to the Secretary of State to be destitute; and
- he has no other avenue of support [eg, friends, family, National Health Service and Community Care Act].
- Each case will be considered on its merits, but support will not normally be made available to an eligible person unless:
- it is not practicable for him to travel [to any other country], by reason of a physical impediment to travel, eg, illness or late pregnancy; or
- the circumstances of his case are exceptional.

Interim Arrangements for Asylum Seeker Support (Local Government Association Guidance Note to Local Authorities in England and Wales)

ANNEX 6: ASYLUM SEEKERS' TEMPORARY ACCOMMODATION
LGA/CIEH GOOD PRACTICE PRINCIPLES

1 Introduction

Regional consortia have a key role in ensuring and in monitoring the suitability of temporary accommodation for asylum seekers in the private rented sector in relation to:

- the provider;
- the location of the property;
- standards of management and maintenance at the property.

Placements of asylum seekers in such accommodation will take place under several different arrangements:

- placements made by local authorities 'out of borough';
- placements made by the regional consortia;
- contracts being negotiated by the Home Office to start after 1 April 2000.

Authorities should ensure that best use is made of the opportunity presented by contract negotiation with private sector providers to improve standards of accommodation.

(i) 'Out of Borough' Placement

'Out of borough' placements, mostly by authorities in London and the South East, are continuing under interim arrangements as there is insufficient accommodation being offered as yet to meet all the demand. Liaison between receiving and placing authorities should be established following the principles of the CIEH Code given below. However, these arrangements will cease after April 2000, after which date the Home Office will take lead responsibility for asylum seeker support.

(ii) Regional Consortia Placement

Where authorities are making placements within the area covered by a regional consortium, the key issue will be to ensure that effective liaison arrangements are established with all relevant agencies, particularly social services, environmental health and housing. In non-unitary areas, care should be taken to ensure that both county and district interests are contacted. As well as ensuring that standards of accommodation are met, housing authorities will have an overview of the effect that placement may have upon any strategic plans for the locality.

Local authorities are required to have regard to statutory guidance on the transfer of case responsibility under the interim arrangements (this was given in a letter from the Immigration and Nationality Directorate on 1 December 1999). Guidance sets out the following criteria for 'cluster areas' for the location of asylum seekers' accommodation:

– there is likely to be suitable accommodation available;
– there is already a multi-ethnic population or infrastructure able to assist asylum seekers;
– it would be possible to link in with existing communities and to develop the support of voluntary and community groups.

In recognition of the fact that it will not be possible to place all asylum seekers in well-defined cluster areas, the guidance requires authorities to take into account all relevant details and information when making a decision on where to place an asylum seeker transferred to their authority. These details include:

– the cultural background and language of the asylum seeker;
– any particular needs regarding the type of accommodation required (for example, family accommodation, special needs or disabilities);
– the particular characteristics of the locality in which accommodation is situated;
– the accessibility of support structures – whether voluntary or statutory (in general, such support structures should be within reach of the accommodation by public transport).

(iii) Home Office (National Asylum Support Service) Placement after 1 April 2000

Regional consortia are to be given a 'ring-holding' role, part of which is to ensure the suitability of placements made directly by the Home Office.

The Home Office is currently undertaking a competitive tendering exercise with private sector providers. Following selection of bidders offering value for money, they will then consult authorities in whose area accommodation is located seeking information on:

– whether any information is known about the accommodation provider which would be relevant for Home Office consideration;
– for confirmation that the current planning use class for each property offered allows that property to be used to house asylum seekers in this way, and advice on any outstanding enforcement activity;
– whether anything is known about the particular location of the proposed accommodation which would be inconsistent with declared objectives of

ensuring that asylum seekers are not placed in areas where they are likely to be isolated or particularly socially excluded.

It is expected that this consultation will take place in mid-February. Authorities will be expected to respond within very tight deadlines of around ten days.

2 Chartered Institute of Environmental Health Good Practice Principles on Asylum Seeker Accommodation

CIEH has compiled some good practice principles on the placement of asylum seekers, details of which are given below. (NB 'Environmental Health departments' include all those departments dealing with private sector housing enforcement. Depending on local arrangements 'placing authorities' Regional Consortia may themselves be responsible for placing asylum seekers in temporary accommodation. The principles are relevant to both existing and future placements.)

1   Liaison arrangements should be established between relevant Social Services, Housing and Environmental Health Departments. These arrangements should include contact arrangements and response times for liaison within and between authorities. Consideration should be given to formalising these arrangements in a Service Level Agreement. Each Local Authority should nominate officers within Environmental Health and Social Services/Housing as contact points.

Environmental health departments should undertake to confirm conditions within the accommodation and inform Social Services and Housing departments. Performance targets for a response should be agreed and monitored.

2   The placing authority should advise the receiving authority where asylum seekers are being housed and where they are moved out.

The receiving authority should report to the placing authority on the suitability of landlord, location and standards of management and maintenance at the accommodation.

3   The receiving authority should keep the placing authority informed of all relevant enforcement activity in respect of accommodation used for asylum seekers.

4   The HMO standards adopted by the receiving authority should be applied. If the placing authority wishes to visit a property this should be undertaken in consultation with the receiving authority. Such consultation arrangements might include joint visits.

Some authorities may have established a scheme for the registration of HMOs, the standards of which will be applicable to asylum seeker accommodation. Authorities should also be aware that the contract with private sector providers will contain specification of the standards with which accommodation is expected to comply. Details of this can be obtained from Joe Heatley at the Home Office (0208 760 4973).

5   Authorities and consortia involved in placing and receiving asylum seekers should ensure that information on irresponsible landlords is shared systematically. The CIEH will also be disseminating good

practice information via its network of local housing study groups. There will also be an opportunity to share information at the regular meetings of Regional Consortia lead officers convened by the LGA.

DETR Guidance on Homelessness (Asylum-seekers) (Interim period) (England) Order 1999 SI No 3126

Introduction

1   This guidance is issued by the Secretary of State for the Environment, Transport and the Regions under section 182 of the Housing Act 1996 and supplements the Code of Guidance on Parts VI and VII of the Housing Act 1996, issued on 20 December 1996. It explains the effect of the provisions of the Homelessness (Asylum Seekers) (Interim Period) (England) Order (SI 1999 No. 3126) ('the Order') which will come into force on 6 December 1999.

2   The Order, which is made under Paragraph 13 of Schedule 15 to the Immigration and Asylum Act 1999, modifies the provisions of Part VII of the Housing Act 1996 (the homelessness legislation) in respect of homeless applicants who are asylum seekers only. References to provisions are to provisions in the Housing Act 1996.

Article 3

3   Article 3 modifies s198 and provides that the conditions for referral of a case to another local housing authority are met if:
   - the authority to whom the application has been made has agreed with another local housing authority that the case will be referred to that other authority, and;
   - the other authority has provided written confirmation of the agreement to the referring authority, and;
   - neither the applicant nor any person who might reasonably be expected to reside with the applicant (ie.all other members of the applicant's household who are being accommodated with him or her) will run the risk of domestic violence in the area of the other authority.

4   When reaching agreement on the referral of a case, neither the authority to whom the application was made nor the other authority need have regard to:
   - any preference that the applicant (or any person who might reasonably be expected to reside with him or her) may have as to the location of the accommodation which is to be secured, or;
   - whether the applicant (or any person who might reasonably be expected to reside with him or her) has a local connection with the district of any local housing authority.

5 Authorities are reminded that, under s198, the option of referring a case to another local authority may be considered only where the authority would be subject to the duty under s193 to secure accommodation for a period of two years. Before proceeding with arrangements for referral, therefore, authorities will need to have completed their enquiries under s184(1) and notified the applicant of their decision as to the duty owed to him or her.

6 Where it is agreed between two authorities that a case will be referred, the referring authority will need to notify the applicant of this decision and the reasons for it, in accordance with s184(4). Applicants will have the right to request a review of a decision to notify another authority, and of the question whether the conditions for referral are met in their case, by virtue of s202(1)(c) and (d).

7 When considering making a referral under Article 3, although authorities must ignore personal preference they will still need to consider the individual circumstances of each case to determine whether it would be reasonable for the applicant (and all persons who might reasonably be expected to reside with him or her) to be referred to the other authority.

Article 4

8 Article 4 modifies s206 such that, when discharging their housing functions under Part VII in respect of applicants who are asylum seekers, authorities must have regard to the desirability in general of securing accommodation in areas in which there is a ready supply of accommodation. So far as possible, authorities should avoid placing applicants in areas where accommodation – particularly social accommodation – is in short supply.

Article 5

9 Article 5 modifies s208 by disapplying s208(1) in certain circumstances. The requirement in s208(1) that so far as practicable authorities must secure accommodation in their own district does not apply where an authority has the agreement of another authority that it may place an applicant who is an asylum seeker in accommodation in the district of the other authority. The other authority must have provided written confirmation of the agreement to the placing authority. Agreements may relate to the placing of all asylum seeker applicants in the other authority's area or an agreed number of such applicants.

10 In the absence of such an agreement it is open to an authority to place an asylum seeker in accommodation in the area of another authority, but s208(1) will apply and the placing authority will need to satisfy itself that it was not reasonably practicable to place the applicant within its own boundary.

Article 6

11   Article 6 modifies s210 such that, in considering whether accommodation is suitable for an applicant who is an asylum seeker, authorities
must have regard to the fact that the accommodation is to be temporary pending the determination of the applicant's claim for asylum and
must not have regard to any preference that the applicant (or any
person who might reasonably be expected to reside with him or her)
may have as to the locality of the accommodation secured.

Cessation of the Order

12   The Order will have effect for an interim period only. The interim
period will end when s186 is repealed. It is envisaged that this date will
be some time after 1 April 2000, when the new Home Office arrangements for providing support for asylum seekers under Part VI of the
Immigration and Asylum Act 1999 are planned to come into force.
Under the Part VI arrangements, the Home Office will assume
responsibility for providing accommodation and support for all asylum
seekers who need them. Broadly speaking, it is intended that asylum
seekers will no longer be eligible for assistance under Part VII of the
1996 Act after 1 April 2000, but those already being assisted prior to
this date will continue to be eligible, on the basis of accrued rights,
until such time as the duties owed to them are fully discharged or
cease.

Homelessness and Housing Management Policy Division
Department of the Environment Transport and the Regions
22 November 1999

Secretary of State's Approvals and Directions under section 21(1) and section 29(1) of the National Assistance Act 1948 (LAC(93)10)

APPENDIX 1

The Secretary of State for Health, in exercise of the powers conferred on her
by section 21(1) of the National Assistance Act 1948, hereby makes the
following Approvals and Directions –

Commencement, interpretation and extent

1   (1)   These Approvals and Directions shall come into force on 1st April 1993.
(2)   In these Approvals and Directions, unless the context otherwise requires,
'the Act' means the National Assistance Act 1948.
(3)   The Interpretation Act 1978 applies to these Approvals and Direction as it
applies to an Act of Parliament.
(4)   These Approvals and Directions shall apply only to England and Wales.

Arrangements to provide services for residents

4 The Secretary of State hereby directs local authorities to make arrangements in relation to persons provided with accommodation under section 21(1) of the Act for all or any of the following purposes –

(a) for the welfare of all persons for whom accommodation is provided;

(b) for the supervision of the hygiene of the accommodation so provided;

(c) to enable persons for whom accommodation is provided to obtain –

   (i)   medical attention,

   (ii) nursing attention during illnesses of a kind which are ordinarily nursed at home, and

   (iii) the benefit of any services provided by the National Health Service of which they may from time to time be in need, but nothing in this paragraph shall require a local authority to make any provision authorised or required to be provided under the National Health Service Act 1977;

(d) for the provision of board and such other services, amenities and requisites provided in connection with the accommodation, except where in the opinion of the authority managing the premises their provision is unnecessary;

(e) to review regularly the provision made under the arrangements and to make such improvements as the authority considers necessary.

APPENDIX 2

The Secretary of State for Health, in exercise of the powers conferred on her by section 29(1) of the National Assistance Act 1948, hereby makes the following Approvals and Directions –

Commencement, interpretation and extent

1 (1) These Approvals and Directions shall come into force on 1st April 1993.

   (2) In these Approvals and Directions, unless the context otherwise requires, 'the Act' means the National Assistance Act 1948.

   (3) The Interpretation Act 1978 applies to these Approvals and Directions as it applies to an Act of Parliament.

   (4) These Approvals and Directions shall apply only to England and Wales.

Welfare arrangements with voluntary organisations and otherwise

4 For the avoidance of doubt, these Approvals and Directions are without prejudice to the powers conferred on local authorities by section 30(1) of the Act (voluntary organisations for disabled persons' welfare).

International instruments

European Convention on Social and Medical Assistance and Protocol 1953

Section I: general provisions
Article 1

Each of the Contracting Parties undertakes to ensure that nationals of the other Contracting Parties who are lawfully present in any part of its territory to which this Convention applies, and who are without sufficient resources, shall be entitled equally with its own nationals and on the same conditions to social and medical assistance (hereinafter referred to as 'assistance') provided by the legislation in force from time to time in that part of its territory.

Section III: residence
Article 11

(a) Residence by an alien in the territory of any of the Contracting Parties shall be considered lawful within the meaning of this Convention so long as there is in force in his case a permit or such other permission as is required by the laws and regulations of the country concerned to reside therein. Failure to renew any such permit, if due solely to the inadvertence of the person concerned, shall not cause him to cease to be entitled to assistance.

(b) Lawful residence shall become unlawful from the date of any deportation order made out against the person concerned, unless a stay of execution is granted.

Article 12

The commencing date of the period of residence laid down in Article 7 shall in each country be established, in the absence of evidence to the contrary, on the basis of evidence supplied by official investigation or by the documents listed in Annex III or any documents recognised by the laws and regulations of the country as affording proof of residence.

Article 13

(a) Proof of continuity of residence may be shown by the production of any evidence acceptable in the country of residence, such as proof of occupational activity or the production of rent receipts.

(b) (i) Residence shall be regarded as continuous notwithstanding periods of absence of less than three months, provided that the absence is not caused by repatriation or deportation.

(ii) Periods of absence of six months or more shall be held to interrupt the continuity of residence.

(iii) In order to determine whether a period of absence of between three and six months shall interrupt the continuity of residence, regard shall be had to the intention or otherwise of the person concerned to return to the country of residence and to the extent to which he has preserved his connection therewith during the period of his absence.

(iv) Service in ships registered in the country of residence shall not be held to interrupt the continuity of residence. Service in other ships shall be treated in accordance with the provisions of sub-paragraphs (i) to (iii) above.

Article 14

There shall be excluded in the calculation of length of residence those periods during which the person concerned has been in receipt of assistance from public monies as laid down in the legislative measures mentioned in Annex I, except in the case of medical treatment for acute illness or short-term medical treatment.

Section IV: miscellaneous provisions
Article 18

The provisions of this Convention shall not limit the provisions of any national laws or regulations, international conventions or bilateral or multilateral agreements which are more favourable for the beneficiary.

Article 19

Annexes I, II and III shall constitute an integral part of this Convention.

Protocol *(signed but not yet ratified)*
Article 1

For the purposes of this Protocol the term 'refugee' shall have the meaning ascribed to it in Article 1 of the Geneva Convention, provided that each Contracting Party shall make a declaration at the time of signature or ratification hereof or accession hereto, specifying which of the meanings set out in paragraph B of Article 1 of that Convention it applies for the purpose of its obligations under this Protocol, unless such Party has already made such a declaration at the time of its signature or ratification of that Convention.

Article 2

The provisions of Section I of the Assistance Convention shall apply to refugees under the same conditions as they apply to the nationals of the Contracting Parties thereto.

Article 3

1 The provisions of Section II of the Assistance Convention shall not apply to refugees.

2   In the case of a person who has ceased to qualify for the benefits of the Geneva Convention in accordance with the provisions of paragraph C of Article 1 thereof, the period for repatriation laid down in Article 7(a)(i) of the Assistance Convention shall begin from the date when he has thus ceased to qualify.

Article 4
As between the Contracting Parties, the provisions of Articles 1, 2 and 3 of this Protocol shall be regarded as additional articles to the Assistance Convention, and the remaining provisions of that Convention shall apply accordingly.

1   This Protocol shall be open to the signature of the members of the Council of Europe who have signed the Assistance Convention. It shall be ratified.

2   Any State which has acceded to the Assistance Convention may accede to this Protocol.

3   This Protocol shall come into force on the first day of the month following the date of deposit of the second instrument of ratification.

4   As regards any signatory ratifying subsequently, or any acceding State, the Protocol shall come into force on the first day of the month following the date of the deposit of its instrument of ratification or accession.

5   Instruments of ratification and accession shall be deposited with the Secretary General of the Council of Europe, who shall notify the members of the Council and acceding States of the names of those who have ratified or acceded.

Annex I – Legislative measures regarding assistance referred to in Article 1 of the Convention
United Kingdom of Great Britain and Northern Ireland
Great Britain: The Social Security Act 1986 and regulations made thereunder so far as the Act and regulations relate to Income Support and Family Credit; and the Social Security Act 1986 and regulations made and directions given thereunder so far as the Act, regulations and directions relate to payments payable out of the Social Fund referred to in the directions as Crisis Loans.

Northern Ireland: The Social Security (Northern Ireland) Order 1986 and regulations made thereunder so far as the Order and regulations relate to the Income Support and Family Credit; and the Social Security (Northern Ireland) Order 1986 and regulations made and directions given thereunder so far as the Order, regulations and directions relate to payments payable out of the Social Fund referred to in the directions as Crisis Loans.

Laws and regulations concerning Great Britain, Northern Ireland and the Isle of Man establishing national health services.

Annex II – Reservations formulated by the Contracting Parties
The Government of the United Kingdom has formulated the following reservation:

Her Majesty's Government reserve the right to free themselves from their obligation under Article 1 in respect of any person who may be repatriated by virtue of the provisions of Article 7 but who fails to take advantage of the facilities offered for his repatriation (including free transport to the frontier of his country of origin).

Annex III – List of documents recognised as affording proof of residence, referred to in article 11 of the Convention
United Kingdom of Great Britain and Northern Ireland
An endorsement in the passport or other travel document; a residence permit issued to nationals of EEC member states; or a police certificate of registration.

Council of Europe Social Charter 1961

Part II
The Contracting Parties undertake, as provided for in Part III, to consider themselves bound by the obligations laid down in the following articles and paragraphs.

Article 1: The right to work
With a view to ensuring the effective exercise of the right to work, the Contracting Parties undertake:
1 To accept as one of their primary aims and responsibilities the achievement and maintenance of as high and stable a level of employment as possible, with a view to the attainment of full employment;
2 To protect effectively the right of the worker to earn his living in an occupation freely entered upon;
3 To establish or maintain free employment services for all workers;
4 To provide or promote appropriate vocational guidance, training and rehabilitation.

Article 12: The right to social security
With a view to ensuring the effective exercise of the right to social security, the Contracting Parties undertake:
1 To establish or maintain a system of social security;
2 To maintain the social security system at a satisfactory level at least equal to that required for ratification of the International Labour Convention (No 102) Concerning Minimum Standards of Social Security;
3 To endeavour to raise progressively the system of social security to a higher level;
4 To take steps, by the conclusion of appropriate bilateral and multilateral agreements or by other means, and subject to the conditions laid down in such agreements, in order to ensure:
   (a) Equal treatment with their own nationals of the nationals of other Contracting Parties in respect of social security rights, including the retention of benefits arising out of social security legislation, whatever

movements the persons protected may undertake between the territories of the Contracting Parties;

(b) The granting, maintenance and resumption of social security rights by such means as the accumulation of insurance or employment periods completed under the legislation of each of the Contracting Parties.

Article 13: The right to social and medical assistance

With a view to ensuring the effective exercise of the right to social and medical assistance, the Contracting Parties undertake:

1   To ensure that any person who is without adequate resources and who is unable to secure such resources either by his own efforts or from other sources, in particular by benefits under a social security scheme, be granted adequate assistance, and, in case of sickness, the care necessitated by his condition;

2   To ensure that persons receiving such assistance shall not, for that reason, suffer from a diminution of their political or social rights;

3   To provide that everyone may receive by appropriate public or private services such advice and personal help as may be required to prevent, to remove, or to alleviate personal or family want;

4   To apply the provisions referred to in paragraphs 1, 2 and 3 of this article on an equal footing with their nationals to nationals of other Contracting Parties lawfully within their territories, in accordance with their obligations under the European Convention on Social and Medical Assistance, signed at Paris on 11 December 1953.

Article 14: The right to benefit from social welfare services

With a view to ensuring the effective exercise of the right to benefit from social welfare services, the Contracting Parties undertake:

1   To promote or provide services which, by using methods of social work, would contribute to the welfare and development of both individuals and groups in the community, and to their adjustment to the social environment;

2   To encourage the participation of individuals and voluntary or other organisations in the establishment and maintenance of such services.

Article 15: The right of physically or mentally disabled persons to vocational training, rehabilitation and social resettlement

With a view to ensuring the effective exercise of the right of the physically or mentally disabled to vocational training, rehabilitation and resettlement, the Contracting Parties undertake:

1   To take adequate measures for the provision of training facilities, including, where necessary, specialised institutions, public or private;

2   To take adequate measures for the placing of disabled persons in employment, such as specialised placing services, facilities for sheltered employment and measures to encourage employers to admit disabled persons to employment.

Article 16: The right of the family to social, legal and economic protection

With a view to ensuring the necessary conditions for the full development of the family, which is a fundamental unit of society, the Contracting Parties undertake to promote the economic, legal and social protection of family life by such means as social and family benefits, fiscal arrangements, provision of family housing, benefits for the newly married and other appropriate means.

Article 17: The right of mothers and children to social and economic protection

With a view to ensuring the effective exercise of the right of mothers and children to social and economic protection, the Contracting Parties will take all appropriate and necessary measures to that end, including the establishment or maintenance of appropriate institutions or services.

Article 18: The right to engage in a gainful occupation in the territory of other Contracting Parties

With a view to ensuring the effective exercise of the right to engage in a gainful occupation in the territory of any other Contracting Party, the Contracting Parties undertake:

1 To apply existing regulations in a spirit of liberality;
2 T o simplify existing formalities and to reduce or abolish chancery dues and other charges payable by foreign workers or their employers;
3 To liberalise, individually or collectively, regulations governing the employment of foreign workers;
 and recognise:
4 The right of their nationals to leave the country to engage in a gainful occupation in the territories of the other Contracting Parties.

Article 19: The right of migrant workers and their families to protection and assistance

With a view to ensuring the effective exercise of the right of migrant workers and their families to protection and assistance in the territory of any other Contracting Party, the Contracting Parties undertake:

1 To maintain or to satisfy themselves that there are maintained adequate and free services to assist such workers, particularly in obtaining accurate information, and to take all appropriate steps, so far as national laws and regulations permit, against misleading propaganda relating to emigration and immigration;
2 To adopt appropriate measures within their own jurisdiction to facilitate the departure, journey and reception of such workers and their families, and to provide, within their own jurisdiction, appropriate services for health, medical attention and good hygienic conditions during the journey;
3 To promote co-operation, as appropriate, between social services, public and private, in emigration and immigration countries;
4 To secure for such workers lawfully within their territories, insofar as such

matters are regulated by law or regulations or are subject to the control of administrative authorities, treatment not less favourable than that of their own nationals in respect of the following matters:

(a) remuneration and other employment and working conditions;
(b) membership of trade unions and enjoyment of the benefits of collective bargaining;
(c) accommodation;

5   To secure for such workers lawfully within their territories treatment not less favourable than that of their own nationals with regard to employment taxes, dues or contributions payable in respect of employed persons;

6   To facilitate as far as possible the reunion of the family of a foreign worker permitted to establish himself in the territory;

7   To secure for such workers lawfully within their territories treatment not less favourable than that of their own nationals in respect of legal proceedings relating to matters referred to in this article;

8   To secure that such workers lawfully residing within their territories are not expelled unless they endanger national security or offend against public interest or morality;

9   To permit, within legal limits, the transfer of such parts of the earnings and savings of such workers as they may desire;

10   To extend the protection and assistance provided for in this article to self-employed migrants insofar as such measures apply.

Article 20: Undertakings

1   Each of the Parties undertakes:

(a) to consider Part I of this Charter as a declaration of the aims which it will pursue by all appropriate means, as stated in the introductory paragraph of that part;
(b) to consider itself bound by at least five of the following articles of Part II of this Charter:
     Articles 1, 5, 6, 12, 13, 16 and 19;
(c) in addition to the articles selected by it in accordance with the preceding sub-paragraph, to consider itself bound by such a number of articles or numbered paragraphs of Part II of the Charter as it may select, provided that the total number of articles or numbered paragraphs by which it is bound is not less than 10 articles or 45 numbered paragraphs.

2   The articles or paragraphs selected in accordance with sub-paragraphs b and c of paragraph 1 of this article shall be notified to the Secretary General of the Council of Europe at the time when the instrument of ratification or approval of the Contracting Party concerned is deposited.

3   Any Contracting Party may, at a later date, declare by notification addressed to the Secretary General that it considers itself bound by any articles or any numbered paragraphs of Part II of the Charter which it has not already accepted under the terms of paragraph 1 of this article. Such undertakings subsequently given shall be deemed to be an integral part of the ratification or approval and shall have the same effect as from the thirtieth day after the date of the notification.

4   The Secretary General shall communicate to all the signatory govern-

ments and to the Director General of the International Labour Office any notification which he shall have received pursuant to this part of the Charter.

5   Each Contracting Party shall maintain a system of labour inspection appropriate to national conditions.

United Nations Convention on the Rights of the Child 1989

Article 1

For the purposes of the present Convention, a child means every human being below the age of eighteen years unless under the law applicable to the child, majority is attained earlier.

Article 2

1   States Parties shall respect and ensure the rights set forth in the present Convention to each child within their jurisdiction without discrimination of any kind, irrespective of the child's or his or her parent's or legal guardian's race, colour, sex, language, religion, political or other opinion, national, ethnic or social origin, property, disability, birth or other status.

2   States Parties shall take all appropriate measures to ensure that the child is protected against all forms of discrimination or punishment on the basis of the status, activities, expressed opinions, or beliefs of the child's parents, legal guardians, or family members.

Article 3

1   In all actions concerning children, whether undertaken by public or private social welfare institutions, courts of law, administrative authorities or legislative bodies, the best interests of the child shall be a primary consideration.

2   States Parties undertake to ensure the child such protection and care as is necessary for his or her well-being, taking into account the rights and duties of his or her parents, legal guardians, or other individuals legally responsible for him or her, and, to this end, shall take all appropriate legislative and administrative measures.

3   States Parties shall ensure that the institutions, services and facilities responsible for the care or protection of children shall conform with the standards established by competent authorities, particularly in the areas of safety, health, in the number and suitability of their staff, as well as competent supervision.

Article 4

States Parties shall undertake all appropriate legislative, administrative, and other measures for the implementation of the rights recognized in the present Convention. With regard to economic, social and cultural rights, States Parties shall undertake such measures to the maximum extent of their available resources and, where needed, within the framework of international co-operation.

Article 5
States Parties shall respect the responsibilities, rights and duties of parents or, where applicable, the members of the extended family or community as provided for by local custom, legal guardians or other persons legally responsible for the child, to provide, in a manner consistent with the evolving capacities of the child, appropriate direction and guidance in the exercise by the child of the rights recognized in the present Convention.

Article 6
1   States Parties recognize that every child has the inherent right to life.
2   States Parties shall ensure to the maximum extent possible the survival and development of the child.

Article 13
1   The child shall have the right to freedom of expression; this right shall include freedom to seek, receive and impart information and ideas of all kinds, regardless of frontiers, either orally, in writing or in print, in the form of art, or through any other media of the child's choice.
2   The exercise of this right may be subject to certain restrictions, but these shall only be such as are provided by law and are necessary:
    (a) For respect of the rights or reputations of others; or
    (b) For the protection of national security or of public order, or of public health or morals.

Article 14
1   States Parties shall respect the right of the child to freedom of thought, conscience and religion.
2   States Parties shall respect the rights and duties of the parents and, when applicable, legal guardians, to provide direction to the child in the exercise of his or her right in a manner consistent with the evolving capacities of the child.
3   Freedom to manifest one's religion or beliefs may be subject only to such limitations as are prescribed by law and are necessary to protect public safety, order, health or morals, or the fundamental rights and freedoms of others.

Article 16
1   No child shall be subjected to arbitrary or unlawful interference with his or her privacy, family, home or correspondence, nor to unlawful attacks on his or her honour and reputation.
2   The child has the right to the protection of the law against such interference or attacks.

Article 22

1 States Parties shall take appropriate measures to ensure that a child who is seeking refugee status or who is considered a refugee in accordance with applicable international or domestic law and procedures shall, whether unaccompanied or accompanied by his or her parents or by any other person, receive appropriate protection and humanitarian assistance in the enjoyment of applicable rights set forth in the present Convention and in other international human rights or humanitarian instruments to which the said States are Parties.

2 For this purpose, States Parties shall provide, as they consider appropriate, co-operation in any efforts by the United Nations and other competent intergovernmental organizations or non-governmental organizations co-operating with the United Nations to protect and assist such a child and to trace the parents or other members of the family of any refugee child in order to obtain information necessary for reunification with his or her family. In cases where no parents or other members of the family can be found, the child shall be accorded the same protection as any other child permanently or temporarily deprived of his or her family environment for any reason, as set forth in the present Convention.

Article 26

1 States Parties shall recognize for every child the right to benefit from social security, including social insurance, and shall take the necessary measures to achieve the full realization of this right in accordance with their national law.

2 The benefits should, where appropriate, be granted, taking into account the resources and the circumstances of the child and persons having responsibility for the maintenance of the child, as well as any other consideration relevant to an application for benefits made by or on behalf of the child.

Article 27

1 States Parties recognize the right of every child to a standard of living adequate for the child's physical, mental, spiritual, moral and social development.

2 The parent(s) or others responsible for the child have the primary responsibility to secure, within their abilities and financial capacities, the conditions of living necessary for the child's development.

3 States Parties, in accordance with national conditions and within their means, shall take appropriate measures to assist parents and others responsible for the child to implement this right and shall in case of need provide material assistance and support programmes, particularly with regard to nutrition, clothing and housing.

Article 28

1 States Parties recognize the right of the child to education, and with a view to achieving this right progressively and on the basis of equal opportunity, they shall, in particular:

   (a) Make primary education compulsory and available free to all;

   (b) Encourage the development of different forms of secondary education, including general and vocational education, make them available and accessible to every child, and take appropriate measures such as the introduction of free education and offering financial assistance in case of need;

   (c) Make higher education accessible to all on the basis of capacity by every appropriate means;

   (d) Make educational and vocational information and guidance available and accessible to all children;

   (e) Take measures to encourage regular attendance at schools and the reduction of drop-out rates.

2   States Parties shall take all appropriate measures to ensure that school discipline is administered in a manner consistent with the child's human dignity and in conformity with the present Convention.

3   States Parties shall promote and encourage international cooperation in matters relating to education, in particular with a view to contributing to the elimination of ignorance and illiteracy throughout the world and facilitating access to scientific and technical knowledge and modern teaching methods. In this regard, particular account shall be taken of the needs of developing countries.

Article 29

1   States Parties agree that the education of the child shall be directed to:

   (a) The development of the child's personality, talents and mental and physical abilities to their fullest potential;

   (b) The development of respect for human rights and fundamental freedoms, and for the principles enshrined in the Charter of the United Nations;

   (c) The development of respect for the child's parents, his or her own cultural identity, language and values, for the national values of the country in which the child is living, the country from which he or she may originate, and for civilizations different from his or her own;

   (d) The preparation of the child for responsible life in a free society, in the spirit of understanding, peace, tolerance, equality of sexes, and friendship among all peoples, ethnic, national and religious groups and persons of indigenous origin;

   (e) The development of respect for the natural environment.

2   No part of the present article or article 28 shall be construed so as to interfere with the liberty of individuals and bodies to establish and direct educational institutions, subject always to the observance of the principle set forth in paragraph 1 of the present article and to the requirements that the education given in such institutions shall conform to such minimum standards as may be laid down by the State.

Article 30

In those States in which ethnic, religious or linguistic minorities or persons of indigenous origin exist, a child belonging to such a minority or who is indigenous shall not be denied the right, in community with other members of his or her group, to enjoy his or her own culture, to profess and practise his or her own religion, or to use his or her own language.

Article 31

1   States Parties recognize the right of the child to rest and leisure, to engage in play and recreational activities appropriate to the age of the child and to participate freely in cultural life and the arts.
2   States Parties shall respect and promote the right of the child to participate fully in cultural and artistic life and shall encourage the provision of appropriate and equal opportunities for cultural, artistic, recreational and leisure activity.

Article 39

States Parties shall take all appropriate measures to promote physical and psychological recovery and social reintegration of a child victim of: any form of neglect, exploitation, or abuse; torture or any other form of cruel, inhuman or degrading treatment or punishment; or armed conflicts. Such recovery and reintegration shall take place in an environment which fosters the health, self-respect and dignity of the child.

Declarations and Reservations
United Kingdom of Great Britain and Northern Ireland

Reservations

(c) The United Kingdom reserves the right to apply such legislation, in so far as it relates to the entry into, stay in and departure from the United Kingdom of those who do not have the right under the law of the United Kingdom to enter and remain in the United Kingdom, and to the acquisition and possession of citizenship, as it may deem necessary from time to time . . .

Table showing which countries are members of the European Union and European Economic Area and signatories/ratifications of the Council of Europe Social Charter and the European Convention on Social and Medical Assistance

Country	EU	EEA	ECSMA Date of signature†	CESC Date of signature	CESC Date of ratification
Austria	X	X	–	22/7/63	29/10/69
Belgium	X	X	11/12/53	18/10/61	16/10/90
Croatia			–	8/3/99	–
Cyprus			–	22/5/67	7/3/68
Czech Republic*			–	27/5/92	3/11/99
Denmark	X	X	11/12/53	18/10/61	3/3/65
Estonia			1/12/99	–	–
Finland	X	X	–	9/2/90	29/4/91
France	X	X	11/12/53	18/10/61	9/3/73
Germany	X	X	11/12/53	18/10/61	27/1/65
Greece	X	X	11/12/53	18/10/61	6/6/84
Hungary			–	13/12/91	8/7/99
Iceland		X	11/12/53	15/1/76	15/1/76
Ireland	X	X	11/12/53	18/10/61	7/10/64
Italy	X	X	11/12/53	18/10/61	22/10/65
Latvia			–	29/5/97	–
Liechtenstein		X	–	9/10/91	–
Luxembourg	X	X	11/12/53	18/10/61	10/10/91
Macedonia (Former Republic of Yugoslavia)			–	5/5/98	–
Malta			7/5/68	26/5/88	4/10/88
Netherlands	X	X	11/12/53	18/10/61	22/4/80
Norway		X	11/12/53	18/10/61	26/10/62
Poland			–	26/11/91	25/6/97
Portugal	X	X	27/4/77	1/6/82	30/9/91
Romania			–	4/10/94	–
Slovakia*			–	27/5/92	22/6/98
Slovenia			–	11/10/97	–
Spain	X	X	9/2/81	27/4/78	6/5/80
Sweden	X	X	11/12/53	18/10/61	17/12/62
Switzerland			–	6/5/76	–
Turkey			11/12/53	18/10/61	24/11/89
Ukraine			–	2/5/96	–
United Kingdom	X	X	11/12/53	18/10/61	11/7/62

Key: † All ratified except Estonia.
* CESC signature date is the date of signing by the former Czech and Slovak Federal Republic (Czechoslovakia).
EU: European Union
EEA: European Economic Area
ECSMA: European Convention on Social and Medical Assistance
CESC: Council of Europe Social Charter (also known as European Social Charter (ESC))
Up-to-date to 14 June 2001. Note that 10 countries have ratified the *revised* CESC: Bulgaria, Cyprus, Estonia, France, Ireland, Italy, Norway, Romania, Slovenia and Sweden (not the UK).

Home Office forms and decision letters

NASS letter issued on termination of support

ASD 35

Voyager House
30 Wellesley Road, Croydon, CR0 2AD
Tel: 0845 602 1739

Passport photo

Name: *Forename   Family Name*
dob   nationality   language
Address: *Address*

Dependants, if any
Dependants

Asylum application lodged on: *Asylum Lodged*
Support application received: *Application Date*
Support start date:

– Accommodation: *Accommodation Date*
– Subsistence: *Voucher Date*

Emergency vouchers issued:
Emergency Details

Change History

Accommodation:
Start Date   End Date   Address
Acc History

Vouchers:
Start Date   End Date   Value
Sub History

Date   Asylum Reason granted: *Leave Granted*

Support end date: *Termination Date*

483

Standard acknowledgement letter issued at port

THIS IS NOT A TRAVEL DOCUMENT   SAL 1.

198413

Immigration and Nationality Directorate

Block C
Whitgift
Centre
Croydon CR9 2AR   Home Office Reference:
Telephone 0870–606 7766
(GTN 3822)   Port Reference:

The person named below has applied for asylum in the United Kingdom and this is under consideration. The applicant may not take employment paid or unpaid unless already permitted to do so. Any application to take employment should be accompanied by this acknowledgement which will be endorsed accordingly. Persons without current permission to take employment may apply to the Home Office for such permission if their asylum application has not been resolved within six months.

Family name:..
Forename: ....
Date and place of birth:..
Nationality:..   DSS
Passport number: ....   Stamp
Date and place of arrival: ....
Date of application: ....
Address in UK: ....
....
....

CHANGES OF ADDRESS SHOULD BE NOTIFIED TO THE ISSUING OFFICE IMMEDIATELY.

NI number: (if applicable): ....
Accompanied by:...(If applicable: PTO for details)
Signature of applicant:..
Signature of issuing officer:..

This document is valid until a decision has been taken by the Secretary of State to grant/ refuse your asylum application

Receipt For Documents   Ind or IO stamp

Passport   ☐   Other (Please specify)   ☐
Travel Document   ☐
Identity Card   ☐
Birth Certificate   ☐

This document must be surrendered to the Immigration and Nationality Dept when a decision is taken by the Secretary of State on your asylum application, or your departure from the United Kingdom if sooner.

ANY UNOFFICIAL ALTERATION TO THIS DOCUMENT WILL RENDER IT INVALID

Standard acknowledgement letter issued 'in-country'

THIS IS NOT A TRAVEL DOCUMENT **SAL 2.**

ˈ30959

**Immigration and
Nationality Directorate**

Block C
Whitgift
Centre
Croydon CR9 2AR HO Reference:
Telephone 0870–606 7766
(GTN 3822)

The person named below has applied for asylum in the United Kingdom and this is under consideration. The applicant may not take employment paid or unpaid unless already permitted to do so. Any application to take employment should be accompanied by this acknowledgement which will be endorsed accordingly. Persons without current permission to take employment may apply to the Home Office for such permission if their asylum application has not been resolved within six months.

Family name: ....
Forename: ....
Date and place of birth: ....Nationality ....
Date of application:..Passport number:...........
Date and place of arrival: ....
Address in UK: ....
....
....
CHANGES OF ADDRESS SHOULD BE NOTIFIED TO THE ISSUING OFFICE IMMEDIATELY.

NI number: (if applicable): ....
Accompanied by:...(If applicable: PTO for details)
Signature of applicant:..
Signature of issuing officer:..

This document is valid until a decision has been taken by the Secretary of State to grant/ refuse your asylum application

Receipt For Documents Ind or IO stamp

Passport ☐ Other (Please specify) ☐
Travel Document ☐
Identity Card ☐
Birth Certificate ☐

This document must be surrendered to the Immigration and Nationality Dept when a decision is taken by the Secretary of State on your asylum application, or your departure from the United Kingdom if sooner.

ANY UNOFFICIAL ALTERATION TO THIS DOCUMENT WILL RENDER IT INVALID

Notice of temporary admission

Port Reference: TN2/9   IS 96
Home Office Reference:

UK IMMIGRATION SERVICE
TERMINAL 2 HEATHROW AIRPORT
HOUNSLOW
MIDDLESEX
TW6 1EN   Tel: **020 8745 6850**
                       Fax: **020 8745 6867**

To:
X:

                                              Tel:

IMMIGRATION ACT 1971	**NOTIFICATION OF TEMPORARY ADMISSION TO A PERSON WHO IS LIABLE TO BE DETAINED**

LIABILITY TO DETENTION

A   You are a person who is liable to be detained*

TEMPORARY ADMISSION RESTRICTIONS

B   I hereby authorise your (further) temporary admission to the United Kingdom subject to the following restrictions**:–

You must reside at the address shown at X above.

You may not enter employment, paid or unpaid, or engage in any business or profession.

You must report to an Immigration Officer (for further examination for the purpose of deciding whether you may be granted leave to enter) at:

   HEATHROW TERMINAL 2
   UK IMMIGRATION SERVICE
   TERMINAL 2 HEATHROW AIRPORT
   HOUNSLOW
   MIDDLESEX

at 10:00 on 17-MAR-01. Please telephone this office before setting out.

IF YOU DO NOT REPORT IN ACCORDANCE WITH THE RESTRICTIONS OF THIS NOTICE, ANY UNRESOLVED APPLICATION WHICH YOU HAVE MADE FOR LEAVE TO ENTER MAY BE REFUSED.

ANY CHANGE OF RESTRICION

If these restrictions are to be changed, an Immigration Officer will write to you.

* **Although you have been temporarily admitted, you remain liable to be detained**

* **You have NOT been given leave to enter the United Kingdom within the meaning of the Immigration Act 1971.**

Date **17-MAR-00**   Immigration Officer:

   * Paragraph 16 of Schedule 2 to the Act
   ** Paragraph 21 of Schedule 2 to the Act

Integrated Casework Directorate Letter ICD.0725 granting indefinite leave to remain as a refugee

Home Office
Immigration and Nationality Directorate
Integrated Casework Directorate
Block C
Whitgate Centre
Croydon
CR9 2AT
Telephone 0870 606 7766
Fax (020) 8760 3017

[*Address*]   Our Ref   [*Our Ref*]
                                               Your Ref   [*Your Ref*]
                                               Date   [*Date*]

Dear [*Salutation*]

Re: [*Title/Forenames/Surname/Nationality/Date of Birth*]

Vignette no. [*number*]

I am writing to tell you that you have been granted indefinite leave to remain in the United Kingdom as a refugee recognised under the 1951 United Nations Convention relating to the Status of Refugees and its 1967 Protocol. This means that you are free to stay in this country permanently. Passports of recognised refugees are not endorsed and you should keep this letter carefully as your authority to remain in the United Kingdom.

You should understand, however, that if during your stay in the United Kingdom you take part in activities involving, for example, the support or encouragement of violence, or conspiracy to cause violence, whether in the United Kingdom or abroad, so as to endanger national security or public order, the Secretary of State may deport you.

POLICE REGISTRATION
You no longer need to report changes of address or other details to the police. I return your police registration certificate which has been endorsed to show that you no longer need to be registered.

EMPLOYMENT
You do not need the permission of the Department for Education and Employment or the Home Office before taking a job. The Employment Service can help you find a job or train for work – any job centre or employment office will be able to help you and you can apply for a place on a government-sponsored training scheme if you meet the conditions for these schemes. You are free to set up in business or any professional activity within the regulations that apply to that business or profession.

If you want to live or work in the Isle of Man or one of the Channel Islands you must first ask the Island's immigration authorities.

NATIONAL ASYLUM SUPPORT SERVICE

Please read the following paragraphs carefully.
You have been granted indefinite leave to enter or remain in the United Kingdom as a refugee, or granted leave to enter or remain exceptionally because of the particular circumstances of your case.

The National Asylum Support Service may be providing you with accommodation, or subsistence in the form of vouchers, or both.

If you, and your dependents if you have any, are presently supported by the National Asylum Support Service you will no longer be entitled to that support 14 days after you were notified of this decision.

The 14-day period referred to above begins on the day on which you are notified of this decision. If this decision was sent by post then you are deemed to have been notified of it two days after it was sent. If an Immigration Officer handed you the decision then you were notified of it on that day.

As you will no longer be eligible for support 14 days after being notified of this decision, if you live in accommodation provided by the National Asylum Support Service, your accommodation provider will contact you about leaving the property, and you will not receive any vouchers after that date.

You may now be eligible to apply for assistance from organisations such as the Benefits Agency or Local Authority. You should contact them directly about this.

HEALTH, SOCIAL SERVICES AND EDUCATION

You are free to use the National Health Service and the social services and other help provided by local authorities as you need them. You will be able to get Social Security Benefit (including Income Support) if you meet the conditions. If you want to study for a degree or other approved course you can apply for a grant from your local education authority; you will be charged only home students' fees for any further or higher education courses you take.

If you need any of these services, take this letter with you and show it if there is any question about your entitlement to the service. Your local Social Security Office will give you more advice on Social Security Benefits. The Refugee Council, Bond Way House, 3–9 Bond Way, London, SW8 1SJ, (telephone 020 7582 6922), can advise on other welfare services. Your local Citizens Advice Bureau will help you with general questions.

TRAVEL ABROAD

Using your national passport to travel outside the United Kingdom could affect your status as a refugee. If you want to travel abroad you should apply for a Home Office Travel Document from the Travel Document Section (telephone 0870 241 0645), Immigration and Nationality Directorate, Integrated Casework Directorate, Block B, Whitgift Centre, Croydon, CR9 2AT. If you leave the United Kingdom with a Home Office Travel Document you will be allowed back into the country at any time while it is still valid.

Yours

Mr G E Baxter
Integrated Casework Directorate

Integrated Casework Directorate Letter ICD.0716 granting exceptional leave to remain

Home Office
Immigration and Nationality Directorate
Integrated Casework Directorate
Block C
Whitgate Centre
Croydon
CR9 2AT
Telephone 0870 606 7766
Fax (020) 8760 3017

[*Address*]

	Our Ref	[*Our Ref*]
	Your Ref	[*Your Ref*]
	Date	[*Date*]

Dear [*Salutation*]

Re: [*Title/Forenames/Surname/Nationality/Date of Birth*]

[*Other Applicants*]

Your application for asylum in the United Kingdom has been carefully considered by the Integrated Casework Directorate of the Home Office but I have to tell you that it has been refused for the reasons given in the enclosed **Reasons for Refusal** letter. It has been decided, however, that it would be right, because of the particular circumstances of your case, to grant you exceptional leave to [*enter/remain in*] the United Kingdom until [*date*]. You may appeal against the decision to refuse you asylum on the grounds that requiring you to leave the United Kingdom after that time would be contrary to the United Kingdom's obligations under the 1951 Convention Relating to the Status of Refugees.

You should understand that if during your stay in the United Kingdom you take part in activities involving, for example, the support or encouragement of violence, or conspiracy to cause violence, whether in the United Kingdom or abroad, the Secretary of State may curtail your stay or deport you.

You do not need the permission of the Department for Education and Employment or the Home Office before taking a job. The Employment Service can help you find a job or train for work – any job centre or employment office will be able to help you and you can apply for a place on a government-sponsored training scheme if you meet the conditions for these schemes. You are free to set up in business or any professional activity within the regulations that apply to that business or profession.

If you want to live or work in the Isle of Man or one of the Channel Islands you must first ask the Island's immigration authorities.

You are free to use the National Health Service and the social services and other help provided by local authorities as you need them. You will be able to get Social Security Benefit (including Income Support) if you meet the conditions.

If you need any of these services, take this letter with you and show it if there is any question about your entitlement to the service. Your local Social Security Office will give you more advice on Social Security Benefits. The Refugee Council, Bond Way House, 3–9 Bond Way, London, SW8 1SJ, (telephone 020 7582 6922), can advise on other welfare services. Your local Citizens Advice Bureau will help you with general questions.

NATIONAL ASYLUM SUPPORT SERVICE
Please read the following paragraphs carefully.
You have been granted indefinite leave to enter or remain in the United Kingdom as a refugee, or granted leave to enter or remain exceptionally because of the particular circumstances of your case.

The National Asylum Support Service may be providing you with accommodation, or subsistence in the form of vouchers, or both.

If you, and your dependants if you have any, are presently supported by the National Asylum Support Service you will no longer be entitled to that support 14 days after you were notified of this decision.

The 14-day period referred to above begins on the day on which you are notified of this decision. If this decision was sent by post then you are deemed to have been notified of it two days after it was sent. If an Immigration Officer handed you the decision then you were notified of it on that day.

As you will no longer be eligible for support 14 days after being notified of this decision, if you live in accommodation provided by the National Asylum Support Service, your accommodation provider will contact you about leaving the property, and you will not receive any vouchers after that date.

You may now be eligible to apply for assistance from organisations such as the Benefits Agency or Local Authority. You should contact them directly about this.

Your passport is enclosed, and endorsed with leave to [*enter/remain*] until [*date*]. Any application you make for further leave to remain will be carefully considered.

You no longer need to report changes of address or other details to the police. I return your police registration certificate which has been endorsed to show that you no longer need to be registered.

This grant of exceptional leave does not entitle your spouse or children under 18 to join you. An application for them to do so cannot normally be considered until 4 years from the date of this letter. The normal requirements of the Immigration Rules regarding support and accommodation of relatives would have to be satisfied. An application for family reunion may be granted at an earlier point if there are compelling compassionate circumstances.

You should be aware that if you travel abroad during the period of leave which you are now being granted, this leave will lapse. Any subsequent application you may make to return to this country will be considered as an application for fresh leave.

You should keep your present passport valid. If, however, your national authorities will not renew or replace your passport, or you can show that it would be unreasonable to expect you to approach your Embassy or Consulate here, you can apply for a Home Office Travel Document from the Travel Document Section (telephone on 0870 241 0645) at the Integrated Casework Directorate, Block C, Whitgift Centre, Croydon CR9 2AT.

Yours

Mr G E Baxter
Integrated Casework Directorate

Integrated Casework Directorate Letter ICD.0009 granting indefinite leave to remain after exceptional leave to remain

Home Office
Immigration and Nationality Directorate
Integrated Casework Directorate
Block C
Whitgate Centre
Croydon
CR9 2AT
Telephone 0870 606 7766
Fax (020) 8760 3017

[Address]

Our Ref	[Our Ref]
Your Ref	[Your Ref]
Date	[Date]

Dear [Salutation]

Re: [Title/Forenames/Surname/Nationality/Date of Birth]

I am writing to say that there are no longer any restrictions on the period for which you may remain in the United Kingdom. Your passport, which is enclosed, has been endorsed with vignette number [number].

You no longer need to report changes of address or other particulars to the police. Your police registration certificate, which is enclosed, has been stamped to show this.

You can now remain indefinitely in the United Kingdom.

You do not need permission from a Government Department to take or change employment and you may engage in business or a profession as long as you comply with any general regulations for the business or professional activity.

If you are thinking of going to live or work in the Isle of Man or one of the Channel Islands, you should first consult the Immigration authorities of the Island concerned.

If you leave the United Kingdom, you will normally be readmitted for settlement as a returning resident provided that:

– you did not receive assistance from public funds towards the cost of leaving this country;
– you had indefinite leave to enter or remain here when you last left;
– you have not been away for longer than 2 years; and
– you are returning for the purpose of settlement.

In order to be considered as settled here, you will have to be able to show that you are habitually and normally resident in this country, and that any absences have been of a temporary or occasional nature.

You will not be readmitted as a returning resident if you are resident overseas and only return here for short periods.

If your absence from the United Kingdom is for longer than 2 years but you can still demonstrate that you had indefinite leave to enter or remain here when you last left, and you are returning for the purpose of settlement, you may still qualify for admission as a returning resident if, for example, you have maintained strong connections with this country.

You do not require a visa to return to the United Kingdom provided you are returning for settlement after an absence of 2 years or less. However, if you are returning for settlement to the United Kingdom after an absence of over 2 years, you are advised to apply for an entry clearance at the nearest British Diplomatic Post in the country in which you are living. This should then facilitate your re-admission to the United Kingdom.

If you obtain a new passport or travel document, you may ask us to stamp it to show your immigration status before you travel. You should send it to this Directorate at the address at the top of this letter at least 2 months before you intend to travel.

If you do not have your passport stamped before you travel, when you return to the United Kingdom you will have to satisfy the immigration officer that you had indefinite leave to remain when you left. To do this, you will need to produce **either** the enclosed passport **or** other documentary evidence such as bank statements, notices of income tax coding, school or employment records, etc, relating to the earlier years of your residence in the United Kingdom. It may also be helpful to carry this letter with you.

A child born to you in the United Kingdom since 1 January 1983 who is not a British citizen may now be entitled to be registered as such a citizen and any child born to you while you remain settled here may be a British citizen automatically at birth. However, you should note that where the parents of a child have never been married to each other British Citizenship can only be derived from the mother.

More information about all aspects of British Citizenship (including by birth in the United Kingdom) and an application form for registration are available from the Integrated Casework Directorate, India Buildings, 3rd Floor, Water Street, Liverpool L2 0QN. Telephone 0151 237 5200.

Yours

Mr G E Baxter
Integrated Casework Directorate

Integrated Casework Directorate Letter ICD.0029 refusing refugee status without giving reasons ('pre-decision letter')

Home Office
Immigration and Nationality Directorate
Integrated Casework Directorate
Block C
Whitgate Centre
Croydon
CR9 2AT
Telephone 0870 606 7766
Fax (020) 8760 3017

[Address]
            Our Ref   [Our Ref]
            Your Ref   [Your Ref]
            Date   [Date]

Dear [Salutation]

Re: [Title/Forenames/Surname/Nationality/Date of Birth]

You have applied for asylum in the United Kingdom. Your application has been carefully considered, and a decision has now been taken that you do not qualify for asylum within the terms of the 1951 United Nations Convention relating to the Status of Refugees. The date on which your application is recorded as having been determined is [date].

The implications of this decision for your immigration status within the United Kingdom are being considered separately within the Immigration and Nationality Directorate. When that process is complete, you will receive a further letter from your port of entry.

You should be aware that this decision may affect your benefits. You should, therefore, contact your local benefits office.

Yours

Mr G E Baxter
Integrated Casework Directorate

Extract from *Hansard* debates

Hansard debates
9 November 1999 cols 983–985
Immigration and Asylum Bill

Mr Straw:
We recognise that, especially in the early stages, there may be cases in which support under the new system lasts longer than six months. Similarly, for in-country applicants, support through local authority vouchers may last longer than six months. For families, support through vouchers is the arrangement provided by many, but not all, local authorities, whereas for single asylum seekers it is the universal system of support provided by local authorities.

For that reason I agreed, earlier in the summer, following representations from colleagues, that families with children would not be brought into the new support system until the process targets for those cases could be achieved. We aim to achieve those by April 2000.

It may reassure my hon. Friends to know that since 1 October, all new applications from families with children have been identified for rapid processing. About 600 such applications were made in October, and most applicants have been given 14 days to prepare their case and return for interview. Of 78 families making personal applications in Croydon, decisions have been made in 50 cases, including two grants of refugee status and one of exceptional leave to remain. At the end of September, the average time for dealing with an asylum appeal to an adjudicator was 13 weeks, which is one month inside the four-month target.

Concerns were raised in the other place by the Bishop of Southwark and others who supported amendment No. 135. Those concerns have been raised in turn with me by my hon. Friend the Member for Wimbledon (Mr Casale), who passed on representations from the Council of Christians and Jews. I hope that what I have said about the interim arrangements and the bringing into force of new support arrangements for families will help to reassure my hon. Friend and those on whose behalf he made his points.

Mr David Lidington (Aylesbury): If the faster turnaround time for families with children is maintained, does the Home Secretary intend from 1 April next year to transfer families with children who are currently in the backlog of cases ahead of other applicants away from local authority support or social security benefits towards the new arrangements?

Mr Straw: The most practical way to proceed is that people whose cases exist before 1 April next year should remain the responsibility of the relevant local authority. That may not last forever, but from our negotiations with local authorities it seems to be the least disruptive arrangement. We may proceed differently in due course, but if someone has waited a year or two years in a particular area, it would be unacceptable to require that person to move in order to meet a national dispersal policy. Typically, such people will have made arrangements for schooling, health care and so on. Financial responsibility will move to the Home Office, but we will not move people who are settled, for the time being, and whose cases have frankly taken too long to be dealt with. I hope that that policy is acceptable across the House.

In discussing our targets for families and others, I am talking about meeting targets for most cases, not all. Some families will inevitably stay longer in the system. In relation to other cases, we have announced that we will make discretionary payments to asylum seekers – families or single people – who stay in the support system through no fault of their own for more than six months, another point on which concern was raised earlier in the year. There will be a single payment of £50 per person for an asylum seeker and his or her dependants. That would be additional to the normal support, and paid in the form of a cashable voucher. A further payment will be made in cases, hopefully small in number, where a person remains in the support system for more than 12 months.

The arrangements to be established under Part VI of the Bill will be fairer than the present system. They will be better than they are for some asylum seekers at the moment, and in all cases, they will certainly be no worse. They make more effective use of available resources, and they will be a disincentive to those who seek to exploit the asylum system for their own ends.

Mr Martin Linton (Battersea): Would my right hon. Friend tell me how confident he feels of his ability to meet the targets for single claimants by April 2001? In the Select Committee on Home Affairs, I asked the Lord Chancellor a similar question about the target for appointing adjudicators to enable the targets to be met, and he said that he would be a very brave man if he answered that.

Mr Straw: I am a brave man, so I shall answer the question. We aim to meet the target. The target for appeal cases has already been met, although we cannot guarantee that it will continue to be met as the number of asylum claimants increases.

It is well known – indeed, it has been a matter of considerable debate in the House – that the number of asylum seekers in this country has increased greatly in recent months and has created a huge burden, not least for local authorities in Kent. The number has not risen because we are a soft touch, as the Opposition claim – I reject that suggestion. The largest increase is in asylum seekers from countries in the former Republic of Yugoslavia, which has been subject to great violence and political disruption. Many of those people are genuine asylum seekers, others are chancers who masquerade as genuine asylum seekers. The second largest increase is in asylum seekers from Somalia, where there is no effective Government and great political violence. Although we also receive applications from countries where the risk of persecution is non-existent or tiny, the pressure on all European countries is related to the extent of political violence in other individual countries.

To put the matter in perspective, Ireland, which previously received no asylum claims, has received 1,000 applications in one month. Given the size of the Republic of Ireland, the proportion of claims is significantly higher per head of population there than in the United Kingdom.

The severe pressure on the Immigration and Nationality Directorate has increased. We are working hard to solve the problems that were caused earlier in the year by a combination of the computer system and a change of accommodation. I am happy to debate the terms for the computer system that the right hon. Member for Maidstone and The Weald signed in 1996. She almost signed blind a contract that contained no contingency arrangements. I shall debate the matter with her or her deputy at any time. I shall make the contract available to her so that she understands what she signed and why the combination of the contract and having to move to different accommodation created severe difficulties.

We have reversed the cuts in staff that the right hon. Member for Maidstone and The Weald planned. We have employed hundreds of new staff; hundreds more are being recruited. I hope that we shall meet the two-month plus four-month target for new applicants by April 2001, but I cannot guarantee that.

As I have already made clear, if asylum applicants remain in the system for more than six months through no fault of their own, we shall pay them periodic single payments of £50 a head every six months.

Mr Neil Gerrard (Walthamstow) rose –

Ms Abbott rose –

Mr Straw: I gave way earlier to my hon. Friend the Member for Hackney, North and Stoke Newington (Ms Abbott), but I shall do so again.

Ms Abbott: I am grateful to my right hon. Friend for giving way so gracefully. I am genuinely anxious to clarify the position of those whose cases form part of the black backlog. There are thousands of them in east London and other inner-city areas. My right hon. Friend said that such people would not be subject to dispersal. However, he also seemed to claim that the new support arrangements would apply to them – and they would thus lose their entitlement to benefits. Will my right hon. Friend clarify that point?

Mr Straw: On a phased basis, we intend to transfer formal responsibility for those people from local authorities. In many cases, we shall use the same local authorities as agents on behalf of the asylum support system. There is no argument between my hon. Friend and me. If people have waited for some time for the processing of a claim – whether it is genuine or unfounded; the circumstances of the transfer from their country are often traumatic – and have settled in an area, I, my hon. Friend the Under-Secretary and the officials in the Department have no interest in gratuitously disrupting reasonably settled lives. We shall transfer the responsibility for making payments to them, but that responsibility is essentially administrative. In almost every case, the asylum seeker will not notice the change.

'One-stop' services and reception services

One-stop services

Greater London (including Waterloo arrivals)
Refugee Council
240–250 Ferndale Road
London SW9 8BB
Tel: 020 7346 6770
Fax: 020 7346 6778

Eastern Region (Norfolk, Cambridgeshire, Suffolk, Essex)
Refugee Council
Unit 1
Observation Court
Princes Street
Ipswich IP1 1RR
Tel: 01473 221560

Reception and Advice Service
6 Cherry Orchard Road
Croydon CR0 6BA
Tel: 020 8603 0580

West Midlands (Shropshire, Staffordshire, Hereford & Worcester, Warwickshire, West Midlands)
Refugee Council
First Floor
Smithfield House
Digbeth
Birmingham
Tel: 0121 622 1515

Yorkshire (North Yorkshire, West Yorkshire
Refugee Council
1st Floor, Wade House
The Merrion Centre
Leeds, LS2 8NG
Tel: 0113 244 9404
Fax: 0113 246 5229

Yorkshire (South Yorkshire, Humberside)
Refugee Council
Northern Refugee Centre
Alpha House
10 Carver Street
Sheffield S1 4SS
Tel: 0114 281 5718

North East (Northumberland, Tyne & Wear, Durham, Cleveland)
North of England Refugee Service (NERS)
19 The Bigg Market
Newcastle upon Tyne NE1 1UN
Tel: 0191 222 0250
Fax: 0191 222 0239

Kent/Sussex (including Channel ports & Channel Tunnel terminals at Ashford & Cheriton)
Refugee Council
Room 210
Control Buildings
Eastern Docks
Dover CT16 1JD
Tel: 01304 203977
Fax: 01304 203995

Scotland
Scottish Refugee Council
94 Hope Street
5th Floor
The Standard Building
Glasgow G2 6QA
Tel: 0141 248 9797

Wales (Cardiff)
Welsh Refugee Council
Unit 8
Williams Court
Trade Street
Cardiff CF10 5DQ
Tel: 029 20666250
Fax: 029 20343731

Wales (Swansea)
Welsh Refugee Council
1Kingsway
Swansea SA1 5JQ
Tel: 01792 301729

East Midlands (Derbyshire, Nottinghamshire, Lincolnshire, Leicestershire)
Refugee Action
Melbourne Centre
Melbourne Road
Leicester LE2 0GU
Tel: 0116 261 4830

North West (Lancashire, Greater Manchester, Merseyside, Cheshire, Cumbria)
Refugee Action
24–26 Lever Street
Manchester M1 1DW
Tel: 0161 233 1200

South West (Cornwall, Devon, Somerset, Dorset, Avon, Wiltshire, Gloucestershire)
Refugee Action
Senate House
36 Stokescroft
Bristol BS1 3QD
Tel: 0117 989 2100

South Central (Buckinghamshire, Berkshire, Surrey, Hampshire, Oxfordshire, Hertfordshire)
Refugee Action
50 Oxford Street
Southampton SO14 3DL
Tel: 02380 248130

Reception services only

London Airports (Heathrow, Gatwick, Luton, Stansted, City)
Refugee Arrivals Project
Room 1116, 1st Floor
Queen's Building, Heathrow Airport
Hounslow
Middlesex TW6 1DN
Tel: 020 8759 5740
Fax: 020 8759 7058

Northern Ireland
NICEM (Northern Ireland Council on Ethnic Minorities)
3rd Floor
Ascot House
24–31 Shaftesbury Square
Belfast BT2 7BB
Tel: 02890 238645

For more information on the type of services available, contact the agency concerned. The Refugee Council has offices in London, Croydon, Leeds, Ipswich and Birmingham. For information on services in London and Croydon, please ring 020 7820 3085 or e-mail info@refugeecouncil.demon.co.uk. For services outside London, please contact the Leeds office: 0113 244 9404 or refugeecouncil.leeds@charity.vfree.com.

Main welfare entitlements and support

Main welfare entitlements and support for asylum seekers, refugees and people with ELR at 3 April 2000*

Services	Port Asylum-seeker pre-3 April 2000	In-country asylum-seeker/person awaiting appeal	New asylum-seeker from 3 April 2000	Person with exceptional leave to enter or remain (ELR)	Person with refugee status
National Health Service/GP services	Yes	Yes	Yes	Yes	Yes
Early years school provision	Yes	Yes	Yes	Yes	Yes
School provision 5–16	Yes	Yes	Yes	Yes	Yes
Further education (eg, college)	Overseas student rates in theory, but concessionary fees may be offered for part-time students on welfare benefits or vouchers			Same as home student – fees may apply	Same as home student – fees may apply
Higher education grants (eg, university)	No	No	No	After 3 years	Yes
Higher education fees	Overseas student rate – liable for full fees			Same as home student	Same as home student
Welfare benefits/NASS support[1]	90% of Income Support, 100% housing and council tax benefit	Vouchers and £10 cash for single people and couples; cash support for families	Vouchers and £10 cash per person per week[2]	Yes	Yes
Social housing	Temporary via homelessness legislation (if in priority need)	Temporary via statutory interim arrangements National Assistance or Children Act	NASS accommodation for destitute port applicants[2]	Yes	Yes
Social services (including community care)	Yes, but with exceptions[3]	Yes, but with exceptions[3]	Yes, but with exceptions[3]	Yes	Yes

* This table is a basic outline only. See chapters for qualifications and conditions.

1 There are some exceptions to the general rules listed in the table. Port applicants on appeal who have 'temporary admission' may retain entitlement to housing/council tax benefit. Other asylum-seekers (port/in-country) may have these entitlements, plus access to social housing on the basis of their nationality or country of origin.

2 From 3 April 2000, port applicants will be eligible for NASS support subject to certain criteria-testing for destitution. In-country applicants continued to be supported by local authorities until their phased entry into the NASS scheme.

3 Asylum-seekers will be excluded from the Children Act 1989 and some community care legislation, where need is based solely on destitution. Most other aspects of this legislation will apply to asylum-seekers and their dependants (eg, regarding child protection).

Resources

Asylum and immigration law resources (chapter 1)

Publications
- *Butterworths' Immigration Law Service*, Butterworths.
- *JCWI Immigration, Nationality and Refugee Law Handbook: a user's guide*, ed Chatwin, JCWI, forthcoming 2001.
- *MacDonald's Immigration Law and Practice*, MacDonald and Blake, Butterworths, 5th edn, forthcoming 2001.

Websites
- www.ein.org.uk

Electronic Immigration Network has extensive links to organisations and legal sources.

- www.unhcr.ch

UN Commission on Human Rights' website publishes country reports.

- www.homeoffice.gov.uk

Home Office website publishes law and policy including full text of the immigration rules and country assessments. Also has all the secondary legislation made under the Immigration and Asylum Act 1999 including commencement orders.

Government Offices and agencies

Home Office Immigration and Nationality Department (IND)
Asylum Group
Whitgift Centre
Wellesley Road
Croydon CR9 1AT

Immigration and Nationality
Enquiry Bureau (INEB)
Tel: 0870 606 7766
Enquiries about existing
applications: tel: 0870 608 1592
www.ind.homeoffice.gov.uk

Immigration Advisory Service (IAS)
County House
190 Great Dover Street
London SE1 4YB
Tel: 020 7357 7511
www.vois.org.uk/ias
Immigration advice and representation to asylum-seekers who have been refused asylum and have the right to appeal (government-funded).

*Office of the Immigration Services
Commissioner (OISC)*
6th Floor
Fleetbank House
2–6 Salisbury Square
London EC4 8JX
Tel: 020 7211 1500
Regulates provision of immigration
advice.

Parliamentary Ombudsman
Office of the Parliamentary
Commissioner
Millbank Tower
21–24 Millbank
London SW1P 4QP
Helpline: 0845 0154033
www.parliament.ombudsman.org.uk
Considers complaints about Home
Office maladministration.

Advice and information
Asylum Aid
28 Commercial Street
London E1 6LS
Tel: 020 7377 5123
www.asylumaid.org.uk
National organisation gives
immigration advice and campaigns.

*Greater Manchester Immigration Aid
Unit*
400 Cheetham Hill Road
Manchester M8 7EL
Tel: 0161 740 7722
www.ein.org.uk/gmiau
Immigration advice and
campaigning.

*Immigration Law Practitioners'
Association*
Lindsey House
40–42 Charterhouse Street
London EC1M 6JH
Tel: 020 7251 8363
www.ilpa.org.uk
Professional association of lawyers
and academics practising in or
concerned about immigration,
asylum and nationality law.

*Joint Council for the Welfare of
Immigrants (JCWI)*
Advice-line for general civic contract
holders: 0845 602 1020
Advice-line for public: 020 7251 8706
Legal advice about immigration and
nationality law.

Refugee Legal Centre (RLC)
39–45 Bermondsey Street
London SE13 3FX
Tel: 020 7827 9090
www.refugee-legal-centre.org.uk
Immigration advice and
representation including appeals
(government-funded).

Stonewall Immigration Group
c/o Central Station
37 Wharfdale Road
London N1 9SE
Tel: 020 7713 0620
www.stonewall-immigration.org.uk
Campaigns for immigration rights
for same-sex couples and asylum-
seekers.

Benefits resources (chapter 2)

Publications
- *Social Security Legislation 2000*, Sweet and Maxwell, 2000.
- *Welfare Benefits Handbook*, Child Poverty Action Group (CPAG) benefits guide published annually.

CPAG publish various other handbooks including:

- *Migration and Social Security*, 3rd edn, forthcoming (a useful handbook covering immigration and social security, including EC law)
- *Housing Benefit and Council Tax Benefit Legislation 2000/1*, 13th edn, Stagg & Poynter.

Websites
- www.cas.gov.uk
Commissioners' decisions and guidance.

- www.hywels.demon.co.uk
Commissioners' decisions.

- www.dss.gov.uk
DSS website with guidance, manuals and Commissioners' decisions.

- www.irssf.gov.uk
Independent review service publishes social fund directions.

Government offices and agencies

Benefits Agency
Chief Executive
Quarry House
Quarry Hill
Leeds LS2 7UA
Considers complaints against the Benefits Agency/claims for ex-gratia payments.
Freefone DSS tel: 0800 666555 for details of the local Benefits Agency office (or use the DSS website above).

Independent Review Service for the Social Fund
Centre City Podium
5 Hill St
Birmingham B5 4UB
Tel: 0121 606 2100

National Insurance Contributions Office
Inland Revenue
Longbenton
Newcastle upon Tyne NE 98 1ZZ
Tel: 0191 213 5000

Offices of the Social Security and Child Support Commissioners
Harp House
83 Farringdon St
London EC4A 4DH

Tax Credit Office Guidance Team
Room 312
Block 3
Norcross
Blackpool FY5 3TA

Advice and Information
London Advice Services Alliance (LASA)
Universal House
88–94 Wentworth Street
London E1 7SA
Tel: 020 7377 2738
Welfare benefits information and training.
www.rightsnet.org.uk – LASA's welfare rights website with discussion and current information about asylum support issues. Contains good links to other legal sites.

Child Poverty Action Group (CPAG)
1–5 Bath Street
London EC1V 9QA
Tel: 020 7253 3406
www.cpag.org.uk
Advisers' helpline tel: 020 7833 4627

National Association of Citizens'
Advice Bureaux (NACAB)
Middleton House
115–123 Pentonville Road
London N1 9LZ
Tel: 020 7833 2181
www.nacab.org.uk
For details of the local Citizens'
Advice Bureaux.

Asylum and interim support resources (chapters 3–5)

Publications
* *Another Country: Implementing Dispersal under the Asylum and Immigration Act 1999*, Audit Commission, June 2000, www.audit-commission.gov.uk. An Audit Commission report and recommendations on the dispersal arrangements.
* *Refugee Council Information Service: The Information Survivor Kit for Public and Voluntary Sector Employees*, Refugee Council, December 1999.

Government publications:
(some of these are available on the Home Office website or LGA website)

* *Asylum Seekers' Support, An information document setting out proposals for the new support scheme for asylum seekers in genuine need and inviting expressions of interest from potential service providers*, Home Office, March 1999.
* *Asylum-seeker Support: Proposed Interim Arrangements under Schedule 8 of the Immigration and Asylum Bill: a consultation paper*, Home Office, 20 August 1999.
* *Consultation document on the main regulations under Part VI of the Immigration and Asylum Act (1999)*, National Asylum Support Service, November 1999 (see NASS website).
* *Draft Memo of Understanding: the development of a commissioning strategy and creation of an enabling function by consortium. Financial Year 1999/2000*, National Asylum Support Service, November 1999.
* *NASS Policy Bulletins*, Home Office, IND. NASS's internal instructions, not currently published but available on request.
* *Fairer, Faster and Firmer: A Modern Approach to Immigration and Asylum*, Cm 4018, Chapter 11, HMSO, 27 July 1998.

Websites
* www.lga.gov.uk/lga/asylum
Local Government Association website, containing guidance on interim support scheme, information about legal and policy developments.

- www.publications.parliament.uk

Past and current Parliamentary debates on the support provisions are published on this site in *Hansard*.

Government offices and agencies

Asylum Support Adjudicators
Christopher Wren House
113 High Street
Croydon CR1 1GQ
Tel: 020 8688 3977
Fax: 020 8688 6075
ASAs hear asylum support appeals at the above address. Copies of their decisions are to be made available on the internet.

Local Government Ombudsman
21 Queen Anne's Gate
London SW1H 9BU
Tel: 020 7915 3210
www.open.gov.uk/lgo
Considers complaints about local authority maladministration.

National Asylum Support Service (NASS)
Quest House
Cross Road
Croydon CR9 6EL
Tel: 020 8633 0521
Helpline: 0845 602 1739
(Also based at Voyager House, 30–32 Wellesley Road, Croydon, CR02AD)
www.ind.homeoffice.gov.uk
Administers asylum support scheme.

Sodexho Pass Ltd
Old Cambridge Military Hospital
Hospital Road
Aldershot
Hampshire GU11 2AN
Tel: 01252 369 799
Private company which administers the NASS voucher scheme.
www.sodexho.co.uk

Treasury Solicitor
25 Queen Anne's Gate
London SW1 9BU
Tel: 0207 210 3039
Fax: 0207 210 3433
www.open.gov.uk/tsd
For service of legal proceedings on NASS (Secretary of State).

Advice and information (see also list of national one-stop services)
Refugee Council
3Bondway
London SW8 1SJ
Tel: 020 7820 3000
info@refugeecouncil.org.uk
www.refugeecouncil.org.uk
Information, advice, training and publications.

Housing resources (chapter 6)

Publications

- *Encyclopedia of Housing Law and Practice*, ed Arden, Sweet and Maxwell.
- *Far From Home: the housing of asylum-seekers in private rented accommodation*, Garvie, Shelter, February 2001.
- *Homelessness & Allocations*, Arden and Hunter, 6th edn, LAG, forthcoming 2001.
- *Repairs: tenants' rights*, Luba and Knafler, 3rd edn, LAG, 1999.

- *Guidelines for Registered Social Landlords on the provision of Housing and Support Services for Asylum-seekers*, Zetter and Pearl, Housing Corporation, November 1999, www.housingcorp.gov.uk

Websites
- www.housing.detr.gov.uk/information/provisions/index.htm
Department of the Environment, Transport and the Regions website – publishes housing regulations and guidance, eg, relating to the dispersal scheme.

Government offices and agencies
Independent Housing Ombudsman
Norman House
105–109 The Strand
London WC2R 0AA
Tel: 020 7836 3630
www.ihos.org.uk
e-mail: ombudsman@ihos.org.uk

Advice and information (see also general advice)
Shelter
88 Old Street
London EC1V 9HU
Tel: 020 7505 2000
www.shelter.org.uk
National housing organisation offering housing advice, information, training, and publications.

Community care/ health resources (chapter 7)

Publications
- *Community Care Assessments: a practical legal framework*, Gordon and Mackintosh, 2nd edn, Sweet and Maxwell, 1996.
- *Community Care and the Law*, Clements, 2nd edn, LAG, 2000.
- *Community Care Law Reports*, Legal Action Group, quarterly.

Advice and information
Public Law Project
Birkbeck College Room E608
University of London
Malet Street
London WC1E 7HX
Tel: 020 7467 9807
admin@plp.bbk.ac.uk
Specialist legal advice about public law and Human Rights Act issues.

Human Rights/ European/ international resources (chapter 8)

Publications
- *European Human Rights Law*, Starmer, LAG, 1999.
- *Housing and the Human Rights Act*, Luba, Jordan Publishing Ltd, 2000.
- *Housing and human rights law*, Baker, Carter and Hunter, LAG, 2001 forthcoming.

Websites
- www.europa.eu.int

Comprehensive European law site with legislation and case-law.

- www.conventions.coe.int

Council of Europe site with European treaties, conventions and list of signatories, eg, of Council of Europe Social Charter.

- www.echr.coe.int/

Judgments of European Court of Human Rights and other human rights materials.

- www.beagle.org.uk/hra/

Human rights materials.

Advice and Information

Advice on Individual Rights in Europe (AIRE Centre)
74 Eurolink Business Centre
49 Effra Road
London SW2 1BZ
Tel: 020 7924 0927
www.cec.org.uk/index.htm
Advice/information about EC law.

Interrights
Lancaster House
33 Islington High Street
London N1 9LH
Tel: 020 7278 3230
Advice and information about European and international human rights law.

Liberty (National Council for Civil Liberties)
21 Tabard Street
London SE1 4LA
Tel: 020 7403 3888
Advisers' helpline on human rights law.
www.liberty-records.demon.co.uk

General resources

Websites/legislation
- www.justask.org.uk

Community Legal Service (CLS) site for details of local CLS advisers.

- www.legislation.hmso.gov.uk

Acts of Parliament and statutory instruments.

- www.parliament.the-stationery-office.co.uk

Parliamentary debates (*Hansard*).

- www.opengov.uk

Statutes, statutory instruments and information about government departments can be found at the above sites.

- www.venables.co.uk/lawyers.htm

Legislation and case-law.

Advice and information

Advisory Centre for Education (ACE)
Unit 1C Aberdeen Studios
22 Highbury Grove
London N5 2DQ
Tel: 020 7354 8321
www.ace-ed.org.uk
Advice about education rights.

Commission for Racial Equality
Elliott House
10–12 Allington Street
London SW1E 5EH
Tel: 020 7828 7022
Advice and information about tackling race discrimination.
www.cre.gov.uk

Language Line
Tel: 020 7520 1400
info@language line.co.uk
Commercial telephone interpreting service.

Law Centres' Federation (LCF)
Duchess House
18–19 Warren Street
London W1P 5DB
Tel: 020 7387 8570
www.lawcentres.org.uk
Details of the local Law Centre.

Medical Foundation for the Care of Victims of Torture
96–98 Grafton Road
London NW5 3EJ
Tel: 020 7813 7777
www.torturecare.org.uk
Counselling and support for torture survivors.

Prisoners' Advice Service
Unit 305
Hatton Square
16–16A Baldwin Gardens
London EC1N 7RJ
Tel: 020 7405 8090
pas@tinyworld.co.uk

Terence Higgins Trust
52–54 Grays Inn Road
London WC1X 8JU
Tel: 020 7831 0330
www.tht.org.uk
Advice, support and campaigning for people affected by HIV/AIDS.

Index

Decision-making *continued*
care and attention 5.119
children 5.116–5.117
complaints 1.107
council tax benefit 2.17
date of determination 3.24–3.25,
5.118
detention 1.62
employment 1.114
favourable decisions 1.80–1.85,
2.93–2.106, 5.114–5.116
guidance 2.18
hard cases support 5.121–5.122
homelessness 6.1, 6.78,
6.109–6.112
housing 6.1
benefit 2.17, 2.91–2.92
Human Rights Act 1998, 5.119
jobseekers' allowance 2.19
letter of determination 1.84
notice 1.84–1.85
notification 5.114
procedure 1.80–1.85, 1.98–1.99,
1.112–1.120, 1.124
reasons 1.85
Refugee Convention 5.120
refugee status, on 1.87
refusal of claims 2.110–2.124
Secretary of State for Social Security
2.18
Social Fund 2.18
Social Security Appeal Tribunal
2.122–2.125
termination of support 5.114–5.122
time limits 5.118
transitional protection pending 2.13
unfavourable 1.80–1.85, 1.98–1.99,
2.106, 5.117–5.122
welfare benefits 2.17–2.18
withdrawal of support 3.126
writing in 5.114
Declarations of compatibility 8.4–8.5,
8.97
Delay
benefit claims 2.77–2.79, 2.126
community care assistance 2.79,
7.28
complaints 1.107–1.109

Delay *continued*
criminal offences 4.111–4.112
crisis loans 2.77
documents 1.128
effects of 2.66
interim payments 2.78
judicial review 1.109
lump sum, six-monthly 4.69
National Insurance numbers
2.71–2.76
urgent needs, where 2.77–2.79
Dependants. *See also* Children
accommodation 3.46, 3.80
appeals 3.45–3.46
categories of 3.31–3.42
definition 3.6, 3.28–3.46,
5.17–5.19
disabled family members over 18,
3.36–3.37
documents 3.42
eligibility for asylum support
scheme 3.6, 3.28–3.46
European Convention on Human
Rights 3.44, 3.46
extended families 3.46
family life, right to respect for 3.46
homelessness 6.22
Human Rights Act 1998, 8.36, 8.38,
8.40–8.41, 8.44–8.47
Immigration and Nationality
Directorate by, treated as 3.42
indefinite leave to remain 1.96
interim support 3.28, 5.17–5.19
problems arising from who can be
treated as 3.44–3.46
'relevant time' 3.43
same-sex couples 3.39
spouses 3.32–3.33
unmarried couples 3.38–3.40
urgent cases 2.83
Deportation
appeals 1.13, 1.100
entitlement to benefits 2.31
habitual residence 2.60
illegal entrants 1.36
inhuman or degrading treatment
1.48–1.49
overstayers 1.37

Discretion *continued*
  judicial review 3.166
  refusal of support 3.100
Discrimination. *See also* Racial
    discrimination
  accommodation 3.136, 4.32
  European Convention on Human
    Rights 1.129
  Human Rights Act 1998, 8.18, 8.25,
    8.34, 8.65
  identity 1.129
  voucher system 5.42, 5.55, 8.65
Dispersal
  accommodation 4.10, 4.26–4.40,
    5.41, 5.44–5.45, 5.61–5.90
  assessment of needs 5.77
  challenging 4.26–4.29, 4.33–4.40,
    5.76–7.86
  exceptional circumstances 4.30,
    5.78, 5.80, 5.85
  families 4.30, 5.83
  health 5.72
  HIV/AIDS 5.81–5.82
  homelessness 6.44
  Human Rights Act 1998, 8.55–8.60
    costs of 8.88–8.89
  immigration advice 5.73, 8.60
  impact of 5.71
  information 5.44–5.45
  inhuman or degrading treatment
    8.57
  interim support 5.44–5.45
  interpreters 5.73, 8.60
  local authorities 5.74, 5.79, 5.82,
    5.86
  London 5.44–5.45, 5.80, 5.84, 5.86
  medical treatment 5.81–5.82, 5.85,
    8.56
  peaceful enjoyment of possessions
    8.58
  religion 8.59
  self 5.74
  settlement in area 5.79
  subsistence only claims 5.41
  temporary support 4.10
  types of 5.74–5.76
  voluntary 5.74–5.76
  welfare 5.77, 5.82, 5.85

Documents. *See also* Visas
  asylum-seeker status 5.27–5.34
  ASU appointment letters 1.133,
    5.31
  community care services 7.114
  delay 1.128
  dependants 3.42
  emergencies 1.126
  exceptional leave to remain 1.95
  expiry of 1.95
  Home Office 1.33
  housing 6.130
  in-country applicants 5.29
  interviews 1.59
  misinterpretation of 2.100
  mistakes, in 1.128
  National Insurance numbers 2.76
  on-arrival applicants 5.29
  original 2.75
  passports 1.88
  photocopies 2.75
  port applicants 5.28
  problems with 5.32–5.34
  procedure 1.126–1.129, 1.133
  Refugee Convention 1.92
  screening interviews 1.59
  solicitors' letters 5.32
  standard acknowledgment letters
    5.28
  temporary admission 5.30
  travel 1.92
Domestic violence
  accommodation 3.85
  complaints 6.159–6.162
  homelessness 6.100
  housing 6.159–6.162

EC law
  co-operation agreements 2.41–2.42
  equal treatment 2.41
  'workers', definition of 2.40–2.43
Education
  age 1.117–1.118
  discretion 1.117
  free school meals 4.74, 5.58
  Further Education Funding Council
    1.118
  Human Rights Act 1998, 8.20

Eligibility for asylum support
  continued
  'support', meaning of 3.6
  suspension of 3.6, 3.99–3.139
  temporary support 3.14–3.15
  termination of 3.6, 3.99–3.139
  timetable 3.9
  voluntary sector 3.95
    reception assistants, help of
      3.93–3.94, 3.96
  withdrawal of support 3.124–3.133
Emergencies. *See also* Urgent cases
  accommodation 3.83, 3.95, 4.10
  appeals 2.121
  challenging decisions 2.121
  crisis loans 2.77
  destitution 3.56
  documentation 1.126
  eligibility for asylum support
    scheme 3.95, 3.98
  families in, support from 3.56
  Social Security Appeal Tribunal
    2.121
  temporary support 4.10
  urgent cases 2.77
Employment. *See also* Jobseekers'
    allowance
  actively seeking work 2.24
  appeals 1.114
  code of practice 1.115
  co-operation agreements 2.41–2.42
  criminal offences 1.115
  decision-making 1.114
  lawfully working, meaning of
    2.40–2.42
  National Insurance numbers 2.71
  permission to work 1.114
  principal asylum-seekers 1.114
  procedure 1.114–1.115
  racial discrimination 1.115–1.116
  subsistence only claims 5.43
  'workers', meaning of 2.40–2.43
Employment Service 2.19
Enter. *See* Leave to enter, Powers of
    entry
Entitlement to benefits 2.22–2.65
  actively seeking work test 2.24
  arrival, on 2.2

Entitlement to benefits *continued*
  child benefit 2.14
  contributory benefits 2.25, 2.65
  deported to UK, people 2.31
  eligibility criteria 2.24, 2.29, 2.65,
    3.13
  European Economic Area 2.29–2.30
  European nationals 2.29–2.30
  exclusions from 2.4, 2.26–2.31
  family members 2.30, 2.43
  habitual residence 2.57–2.64
  incapacity benefit 2.25
  lawfully present in UK 2.35–2.39
  lawfully working 2.40–2.42
  leave to enter 1.22, 2.28
  leave to remain 2.28
  maintenance 2.28
  maternity benefits 2.25
  means testing 2.24, 2.34
  non-contributory benefits 2.26
  non-means-tested benefits
    2.35–2.39
  ordinary residence 2.57–2.58
  persons subject to immigration
    control 2.22–2.23
    excluded 2.27–2.31
    not excluded, persons 2.32–2.43
  social fund 2.35–2.39
  steps for assessing 2.23
  temporary admission 2.36–2.39
  time for 2.66
  transitional protection 2.27,
    2.44–2.56
  unfavourable benefits 2.106
  urgent cases 2.82
Entry clearance
  asylum-seekers 1.32
  entry clearance officers 1.6
  leave to enter 1.6, 1.29
Entry powers. *See* Powers of entry
Equal treatment 2.41
Equality of arms 8.91
Errors. *See* Mistake
Essential living needs
  accommodation 4.52–4.52, 5.56
  asylum claims, expenses connected
    with 3.67
  children 3.68, 4.58

Community Care Law Reports

The only law reports devoted entirely to community care issues. Compiled by an expert team and published quarterly, each issue contains:

- editorial review
- community care law update
- law reports
- guidance
- cumulative index
- full tables

Training

Accredited with the Law Society, the Bar Council and the Institute of Legal Executives, LAG provides topical training courses for criminal practitioners at all levels of experience.

Conferences

LAG runs major conferences to examine issues at the cutting-edge of legal services policy and to inform practitioners of their implications.

For further information about any of Legal Action Group's activities please contact:

Legal Action Group
242 Pentonville Road
London N1 9UN

DX 130400 London (Pentonville Road)
Telephone: 020 7833 2931
Fax: 020 7837 6094
e-mail: lag@lag.org.uk
www.lag.org.uk